HATTER'S CASTLE

OTHER NOVELS BY
DR. CRONIN:

THE GREEN YEARS
THE KEYS OF THE KINGDOM
THE CITADEL
THE STARS LOOK DOWN
THREE LOVES
GRAND CANARY

HATTER'S CASTLE

by
A. J. CRONIN

LONDON
VICTOR GOLLANCZ LTD
14 Henrietta Street Covent Garden

First published May 1931
Second impression June 1931
Third impression July 1931
Fourth impression September 1931
Fifth impression (first cheap edition) April 1932
Sixth impression April 1932
Seventh impression July 1932
Eighth impression November 1932
Ninth impression January 1933
Tenth impression June 1933
Eleventh impression September 1933
Twelfth impression March 1934
Thirteenth impression January 1935
Fourteenth impression November 1935
Fifteenth impression November 1936
Sixteenth impression August 1937
Seventeenth impression December 1937
Eighteenth impression July 1938
Nineteenth impression April 1939
Twentieth impression January 1940
Twenty-first impression October 1940
Twenty-second impression February 1941
Twenty-third impression June 1941
Twenty-fourth impression July 1941
Twenty-fifth impression (re-set) October 1941
Twenty-sixth impression June 1942
Twenty-seventh impression July 1948
Twenty-eighth impression (re-set) March 1950

MADE AND PRINTED IN GREAT BRITAIN AT
THE STANHOPE PRESS LTD., ROCHESTER

CONTENTS

Book I   *page* 9

Book II   *page* 157

Book III   *page* 327

BOOK I

I

THE spring of 1879 was unusually forward and open. Over the Lowlands the green of early corn spread smoothly, the chestnut spears burst in April, and the hawthorn hedges flanking the white roads which laced the countryside, blossomed a month before time. In the inland villages farmers exulted cautiously and children ran bare-footed after watering-carts; in the towns which flanked the wide river the clangour of the ship-yards lost its insistence and, droning through the mild air, mounted to the foothills behind, where the hum of a precocious bee mingled with it and the exuberant bleating of lambs overcame it; in the city clerks shed their coats for coolness and lolled in offices execrating the sultry weather, the policy of Lord Beaconsfield, the news of the Zulu War, and the high cost of beer. Thus over the whole estuary of the Clyde, from Glasgow to Portdoran, upon Overton, Darroch, Ardfillan—those towns which, lying between the Winton and Doran hills, formed the three cardinal points of the fertile triangle upon the right bank of the firth—over the ancient Borough of Levenford, which stood bisecting exactly the base line of this triangle at the point where Leven entered Clyde, over all lay the radiance of a dazzling sun and, lapped in this strange benignant heat, the people worked, idled, gossiped, grumbled, cheated, prayed, loved, and lived.

Over Levenford, on this early day of May, thin wisps of cloud had hung languidly in the tired air, but now in the late afternoon these gossamer filaments moved slowly on to activity. A warm breeze sprang up and puffed them across the sky, when, having propelled them out of sight, it descended upon the town, touching first the high historic rock which marked the confluence of the tributary Leven with its parent stream, and which stood, a land-mark, outlined clearly against the opal sky like the inert body of a gigantic elephant. The mild wind circled the rock, then passed quickly through the hot, mean streets of the adjoining Newtown and wandered amongst the tall stocks, swinging cranes, and the ribbed framework of half-formed ships in the busy yards of Latta and Co. along the river's mouth. Next it wafted slowly along Church Street, as befitted the passage of a thoroughfare dignified by the Borough Hall, the Borough Academy, and the Parish Church, until, free of the sober street, it swirled jauntily in the advantageously open space of the Cross, moved speculatively between the rows of shops in the High Street, and entered the more elevated residential district of Knoxhill. But here it tired quickly of sporting along the weathered, red sandstone terraces and rustling the ivy on the old stone houses, and seeking the countryside beyond, passed inland once more, straying amongst the prim villas of the select quarter of Wellhall, and fanning the little round plots of crimson-faced geraniums in each front garden. Then, as it drifted carelessly along the decorous thoroughfare which led from this genteel region to the adjacent open country suddenly it chilled as it struck the last house in the road.

It was a singular dwelling. In size it was small, of such dimensions that it could not have contained more than seven rooms, in its construction solid, with the hard stability of new grey stone, in its architecture unique.

The base of the house had the shape of a narrow rectangle with the wider aspect directed towards the street, with walls which arose, not directly from the earth, but from a stone foundation a foot longer and wider than themselves, and upon which the whole structure seemed to sustain itself like an animal upon its deep-dug paws. The frontage arising from this supporting pedestal, reared itself with a cold severity to terminate in one half of its extent in a steeply pitched gable and in the other in a low parapet which ran horizontally to join another gable, similarly shaped to that in front, which formed the coping of the side wall of the house. These gables were peculiar, each converging in a series of steep right-angled steps to a chamfered apex which bore with pompous dignity a large round ball of polished grey granite and, each in turn, merging into and become continuous with the parapet which, ridged and serrated regularly and deeply after the fashion of a battlement, fettered them together, forming thus a heavy stone-linked chain which embraced the body of the house like a manacle.

At the angle of the side gable and the front wall, and shackled likewise by this encircling fillet of battlement, was a short round tower, ornamented in its middle by a deep-cut diamond-shaped recess, carved beneath into rounded, diminishing courses which fixed it to the angle of the wall, and rising upwards to crown itself in a turret which carried a thin, reedy flagstaff. The heaviness of its upper dimensions made the tower squat, deformed, gave to it the appearance of a broad frowning forehead, disfigured by a deep grooved stigma, while the two small embrasured windows which pierced it brooded from beneath the brow like secret, close-set eyes.

Immediately below this tower stood the narrow doorway of the house, the lesser proportion of its width giving it a meagre, inhospitable look, like a thin repellent mouth, its sides ascending above the horizontal lintel in a steep ogee curve encompassing a shaped and gloomy filling of darkly stained glass and ending in a sharp lancet point. The windows of the dwelling, like the doorway, were narrow and unbevelled, having the significance merely of apertures stabbed through the thickness of the walls, grudgingly admitting light, yet sealing the interior from observation.

The whole aspect of the house was veiled, forbidding, sinister, its purpose, likewise hidden and obscure. From its very size it failed pitifully to achieve the boldness and magnificence of a baronial dwelling, if this, indeed, were the object of its pinnacle, its ramparts and the repetition of its sharp-pitched angles. And yet, in its coldness, hardness, and strength, it could not be dismissed as seeking merely the smug attainment of pompous ostentation. Its battlements were formal but not ridiculous, its design extravagant but never ludicrous, its grandiose architecture containing some quality which restrained merriment, some deeper, lurking, more perverse motive, sensed upon intensive scrutiny, which lay about the house like a deformity, and stood within its very structure like a violation of truth in stone.

The people of Levenford never laughed at this house, at least never openly. Something, some intangible potency pervading the atmosphere around it, forbade them even to smile.

No garden fronted the habitation but instead a gravelled courtyard, bare, parched, but immaculate, and containing in its centre the singular decoration of a small brass cannon, which, originally part of a frigate's broadside, had long since joined in its last salvo, and after years in the junk yard, now stood prim and polished between two attendant symmetrical heaps of balls, adding the last touch of incongruity to this fantastic domicile.

At the back of the house was a square grassy patch furnished at its corners with four iron clothes poles and surrounded by a high stone wall, against which grew a few straggling currant bushes, sole vegetation of this travesty of a garden, except for a melancholy tree which never blossomed and which drooped against a window of the kitchen.

Through this kitchen window, screened though it was by the lilac tree, it was possible to discern something of the interior. The room was plainly visible as commodious, comfortably, though not agreeably furnished, with horse-hair chairs and sofa, an ample table, with a bow-fronted chest of drawers against one wall and a large mahogany dresser flanking another. Polished wax-cloth covered the floor, yellow varnished paper the walls, and a heavy marble timepiece adorned the mantelpiece, indicating by a subtle air of superiority that this was not merely a place for cooking, which was, indeed, chiefly carried on in the adjacent scullery, but the common room, the living room of the house where its inhabitants partook of meals, spent their leisure, and congregated in their family life.

At present the hands of the ornate clock showed twenty minutes past five, and old Grandma Brodie sat in her corner chair by the range making toast for tea. She was a large-boned, angular woman, shrunken but not withered by her seventy-two years, shrivelled and knotted like the bole of a sapless tree, dried but still hard and resilient, toughened by age and the seasons she had seen. Her hands, especially, were gnarled, the joints nodular with arthritis. Her face had the colour of a withered leaf and was seamed and cracked with wrinkles; the features were large, masculine, and firm; her hair, still black, was parted evenly in the middle, showing a straight white furrow of scalp, and drawn tight into a hard knob behind; some coarse short straggling hairs sprouted erratically like weeds from her chin and upper lip. She wore a black bodice and shawl, a small black mutch, a long trailing skirt of the same colour, and elastic-sided boots which, although large, plainly showed the protuberance of her bunions and the flatness of her well-trodden feet.

As she crouched over the fire, the mutch slightly askew from her exertions, supporting the toasting fork with both tremulous hands, she toasted two slices of bread with infinite care, thick pieces which she browned over gently, tenderly, leaving the inside soft, and when she had completed these to her satisfaction and placed them on that side of the plate where she might reach out quickly and remove them adroitly at once whenever the family sat down to tea, she consummated the rest of her toasting negligently, without interest. While she toasted she brooded. The sign of her brooding was the clicking of her false teeth as she sucked her cheeks in and out. It was simply an iniquity, she reflected, that Mary had forgotten to bring home the cheese. That girl was getting more careless than ever, and as undependable in such important matters as a half-witted ninny. What was tea to a woman without cheese? Fresh Dunlop cheese! The thought of it made her long upper lip twitch, sent a little river of saliva drooling from the corner of her mouth.

As she ruminated, she kept darting quick recriminative glances from under her bent brows at her grand-daughter, Mary, who sat in the opposite corner in the horse-hair armchair, hallowed to her father's use, and by that token a forbidden seat.

Mary, however, was not thinking of cheese, nor of the chair, nor of the crimes she committed by forgetting the one and reclining in the other. Her soft brown eyes gazed out of the window and were focused upon the far-off distance as if they saw something there, some scene which shaped itself enchantingly under her shining glance.

Occasionally her sensitive mouth would shape itself to smile, then she would shake her head faintly, unconsciously, activating thus her pendant ringlets and setting little lustrous waves of light rippling across her hair. Her small hands, of which the skin wore the smooth soft texture of petals of magnolia, lay palm upwards in her lap, passive symbols of her contemplation. She sat as straight as a wand, and she was beautiful with the dark serene beauty of a deep tranquil pool where waving wands might grow. Upon her was the unbroken bloom of youth, yet although she was only seventeen years of age there rested about her pale face and slender unformed figure a quality of repose and quiet fortitude.

At last the old woman's growing resentment jarred her into speech. Dignity forbade a direct attack, and instead she said, with an added bitterness from repression:

"You're sitting in your father's chair, Mary."

There was no answer.

"That chair you're sitting in is your father's chair, do you hear?"

Still no answer came; and, trembling now with suppressed rage, the crone shouted:

"Are you deaf and dumb as well as stupid, you careless hussy? What made you forget your messages this afternoon? Every day this week you've done something foolish. Has the heat turned your head?"

Like a sleeper suddenly aroused Mary looked up, recollected herself and smiled, so that the sun fell upon the sad still pool of her beauty.

"Were you speaking, Grandma?" she said.

"No!" cried the old woman coarsely, "I wasna speakin'. I was just openin' my mouth to catch flies. It's a graund way o' passin' the time if ye've nothing to do. I think ye must have been tryin' it when ye walked doun the toun this afternoon, but if ye shut your mouth and opened your een ye might mind things better."

At that moment Margaret Brodie entered from the scullery, carrying a large Britannia metal teapot, and walking quickly with a kind of shuffling gait, taking short flurried steps with her body inclined forward, so that, as this was indeed her habitual carriage, she appeared always to be in a hurry and fearful of being late. She had discarded the wrapper in which she did the house-work of the day for a black satin blouse and skirt, but there were stains on the skirt, and a loose tape hung untidily from her waist, whilst her hair, too, straggled untidily about her face. Her head she carried perpetually to one side. Years before, this inclination had been affected to exhibit resignation and true Christian submission in periods of trial or tribulation, but time and the continual need for the expression of abnegation had rendered it permanent. Her nose seemed to follow this deviation from the vertical, sympathetically perhaps, but more probably as the result of a nervous tic she had developed in recent years of stroking the nose from right to left with a movement of the back of her hand. Her face was worn, tired, and pathetic; her aspect bowed and drooping, yet with an air as if she continually flogged her jaded energies onwards. She looked ten years older than her forty-two years. This was Mary's mother, but now they seemed as alien and unrelated as an old sheep and a young fawn.

A mistress from necessity of every variety of domestic situations, Mamma, for so Mrs. Brodie was named by every member of the house, envisaged the old woman's rage and Mary's embarrassment at a glance.

"Get up at once, Mary," she cried. "It's nearly half-past five and the tea not infused yet. Go and call your sister. Have you finished the toast yet, Grandma? Gracious! you have burned a piece. Give it here to me. I'll eat it. We can't have waste in this house." She took the burned toast and laid it ostentatiously on her plate, then she began needlessly to move everything on the tea-table as if nothing had been done right and would, indeed, not be right until she had expiated the sin of the careless layer of the table by the resigned toil of her own exertions.

"Whatna way to set the table!" she murmured disparagingly, as her daughter rose and went into the hall.

"Nessie—Nessie," Mary called. "Tea—time—tea-time!"

A small treble voice answered from upstairs, singing the words:

"Coming down! Wait on me!"

A moment later the two sisters entered the room, providing instantly and independent of their disparity in years—for Nessie was twelve years old—a striking contrast in character and features. Nessie differed diametrically from Mary in type. Her hair was flaxen, almost colourless, braided into two neat pigtails, and she had inherited from her mother those light, inoffensive eyes, misty with the delicate white flecked blueness of speedwells and wearing always that soft placating expression which gave her the appearance of endeavouring continually to please. Her face was narrow with a high delicate white forehead, pink waxen doll's cheeks, a thin pointed chin and a small mouth, parted perpetually by the drooping of her lower lip, all expressive, as was her present soft, void smile, of the same immature and ingenuous, but none the less innate weakness.

"Are we not a bit early to-night, Mamma?" she asked idly as she presented herself before her mother for inspection.

Mrs. Brodie, busy with the last details of her adjustments, waved away the question.

"Have ye washed your hands?" she answered without looking at her. Then with a glance at the clock and without waiting for a reply she commanded with an appropriate gesture: "Sit in!"

The four people in the room seated themselves at table, Grandma Brodie being, as usual, first. They sat waiting, while Mrs. Brodie's hand poised itself nervously upon the tea-cosy; then into the silence of their expectation came the deep note of the grandfather's clock in the hall as it struck the half-hour and at the same moment the front door clicked open and was firmly shut. A stick rattled into the stand; heavy footfalls measured themselves along the passage; the kitchen door opened and James Brodie came into the room. He strode to his waiting chair, sat down, stretched forward his hand to receive his own special large cup, brimming with hot tea, received from the oven a large plateful of ham and eggs, accepted the white bread especially cut and buttered for him, had hardly seated himself before he had begun to eat. This, then, was the reason of their punctual attendance, the explanation of their bated expectancy, for the ritual of immediate service for the master of the house, at meal-times as in everything, was amongst the unwritten laws governing the conduct of this household.

Brodie ate hungrily and with obvious enjoyment. He was an enormous man, over six feet in height and with the shoulders and neck of a bull. His head was massive, his grey eyes small and deep set, his jaw hard and so resolutely muscular that as he chewed, large firm knobs rose up and subsided rhythmically under the smooth brown jowl. The face itself was broad and strong and would have been noble but for the insufficient depth of the forehead and the narrow spacing of the eyes. A heavy brown moustache covered his upper lip, partly hiding the mouth; but beneath this glossy mask his lower lip protruded with a full and sullen arrogance.

His hands were huge, and upon the backs of these and also of the thick spatulate fingers dark hairs grew profusely. The knife and fork gripped in that stupendous grasp seemed, in comparison, foolishly toyish and inept.

Now that Brodie had commenced to eat it was permissible for the others to begin, although for them, of course, there was only a plain tea; and Grandma Brodie led the way by fastening avidly upon her soft toast. Sometimes when her son was in a particularly amiable humour he would boisterously help her to small titbits from his plate, but to-night she knew from his demeanour that this rare treat would not come her way, and she resignedly abandoned herself to such limited savour as the food at her disposal provided. The others began to partake of the meal in their own fashion. Nessie ate the simple food heartily, Mary absent-mindedly, while Mrs. Brodie, who had privately consumed a small collation an hour before, trifled with the burnt bread upon her plate with the air of one who is too frail, too obsessed by the consideration of others, to eat.

An absolute silence maintained, broken only by the sucking sound which accompanied the application of the moustache cup to the paternal lips, the clanking of Grandma's antiquated dentures as she sought to extract the fullest enjoyment and nutriment from the meal, and an occasional sniff from Mamma's refractory nose. The members of this strange family tea-party manifested neither surprise, amusement, embarrassment, nor regret at the absence of conversation, but masticated, drank, swallowed without speech, whilst the minatory eye of Brodie dominated the board. When he chose to be silent then no word might be spoken, and to-night he was in a particularly sullen mood, lowering around the table and between mouthfuls casting a black glower upon his mother who, her eagerness rendering her unconscious of his displeasure, was sopping her crusts in her tea-cup.

15

At last he spoke, addressing her.

"Are ye a sow to eat like that, woman?"

Startled, she looked up, blinking at him. "Eh, wha' James? What for, what way?"

"What way a sow would eat, slushing and soaking its meat in the trough. Have ye not got the sense to know when you're eatin' like a greedy pig? Put your big feet in the trough as well, and then you'll be happy and comfortable. Go on! get down to it and make a beast o' yersel'. Have ye no pride or decency left in the dried-up marrow of your bones?"

"I forgot. I clean forgot. I'll no' do it again. Ay, ay, I'll remember." In her agitation she belched wind loudly.

"That's right," sneered Brodie. "Remember your pretty manners, you old faggot." His face darkened. "It's a fine thing that a man like me should have to put up with this in his own house." He thumped his chest with his huge fist, making it sound like a drum.

"Me," he shouted, "me!" Suddenly he stopped short, glared around from under his lowered bushy eyebrows and resumed his meal.

Although his words had been angry, nevertheless he had spoken, and by the code of unwritten laws the ban of silence was now lifted.

"Pass your father's cup, Nessie, and I'll give him some fresh tea. I think it's nearly out," inserted Mrs. Brodie propitiatingly.

"Very well, Mamma."

"Mary dear, sit up straight and don't worry your father. I'm sure he's had a hard day."

"Yes, Mamma," said Mary, who was sitting up straight and worrying nobody.

"Pass the preserves to your father then."

The smoothing down of the ruffled lion had commenced, and was to be continued, for after waiting a minute Mamma began again on what was usually a safe lead.

"Well, Nessie dear, and how did you get on at the school to-day?" Nessie started timidly.

"Quite well, Mamma."

Brodie arrested the cup he was raising to his lips.

"Quite well? You're still top of the class, aren't ye?"

Nessie's eyes fell. "Not to-day, father! only second!"

"What! you let somebody beat you! Who was it? Who went above ye?"

"John Grierson."

"Grierson! That sneakin' corn hawker's brat! That low-down bran masher! He'll crow about it for days. What in God's name came over you? Don't you realise what your education is going to mean to you?"

The small child burst into tears.

"She's been top for nearly six weeks, father," put in Mary bravely, "and the others are a bit older than her."

Brodie withered her with a look.

"You hold your tongue and speak when you're spoken to," he thundered. "I'll have something to say to you presently; then you'll have plenty of chance to wag your long tongue, my bonnie woman."

"It's that French," sobbed Nessie. "I can't get those genders into my head. I'm all right with my sums and history and geography but I can't do that other. I feel as if I'll never get it right."

"Not get it right! I should think you will get it right—you're going to be educated, my girl. Although you're young, they tell me you've got the brains—my brains that have come down to you, for your mother's but a half-witted kind of creature at the best o' times—and I'll see that you use them. You'll do double home-work to-night."

"Oh! yes, father, anything you like," sighed Nessie, choking convulsively over a final sob.

"That's right." A transient unexpected gleam of feeling, which was partly affection, but to a far greater extent pride, lit up Brodie's harsh features like a sudden quiver of light upon a bleak rock.

"We'll show Levenford what my clever lass can do. I'm looking ahead and I can see it. When we've made ye the head scholar of the Academy, then you'll see what your father means to do wi' you. But ye must stick in to your lessons, stick in hard." He raised his eyes from her to the distance, as though contemplating the future, and murmured, "We'll show them." Then he lowered his eyes, patted Nessie's bowed, straw-coloured head, and added: "You're my own lass, right enough! Ye'll be a credit to the name of Brodie."

Then as he turned his head, his gaze lit upon his other daughter, and immediately his face altered, his eye darkened.

"Mary!"

"Yes, father."

"A word with you that's so ready with your jabbering tongue!"

In his sardonic irony he became smooth, leaning back in his chair and weighing his words with a cold, judicial calm.

"It's a pleasant thing for a man to get news o' his family from outsiders. Ay, it's a roundabout way no doubt, and doesna reflect much credit on the head o' the house—but that's more or less a detail, and it was fair stimulatin' for me to get news o' ye the day that nearly made me spew." As he continued his tone chilled progressively. "But in conversation with a member of the Borough Council to-day I was informed that you had been seen in Church Street in conversation with a young gentleman, a very pretty young gentleman." He showed his teeth at her and continued cuttingly: "Who I believe is a low, suspicious character, a worthless scamp."

In a voice that was almost a wail, Mrs. Brodie feebly interposed:

"No! no! Mary! It wasn't you, a respectable girl like you. Tell your father it wasn't you."

Nessie, relieved to be removed from the centre of attention, exclaimed unthinkingly:

"Oh! Mary, was it Denis Foyle?"

Mary sat motionless, her glance fixed upon her plate, a curious pallor around her lips; then, as a lump rose in her throat, she swallowed hard, and an unconscious force drove her to say in a low, firm voice:

"He's not a worthless scamp."

"What!" roared Brodie. "You're speaking back to your own father next and for a low-down Irish blackguard! A blackthorn boy! No! let these paddies come over from their bogs to dig our potatoes for us but let it end at that. Don't let them get uppish. Old Foyle may be the smartest publican in Darroch, but that doesn't make his son a gentleman."

Mary felt her limbs shake even as she sat. Her lips were stiff and dry, nevertheless she felt compelled to say, although she had never before dared argue with her father:

"Denis has got his own business, father. He won't have anything to do with the spirit trade. He's with Findlay & Co. of Glasgow. They're big tea importers and have nothing at all to do with—with the other business."

"Indeed now," he sneered at her, leading her on. "That's grand news. Have ye anything more ye would like to say to testify to the noble character of the gentleman. He doesna sell whisky now. It's tea apparently. Whatna godly occupation for the son of a publican! Well, what next?"

She knew that he was taunting her, yet was constrained to say, appeasingly,

"He's not just an ordinary clerk, father. He's well thought of by the firm. He goes round the country on business for them every now and then. He—he hoped he might get on—might even buy a partnership later."

"Ye don't say," he snarled at her. "Is that the sort of nonsense he's been filling up your silly head wi'—not an ordinary clerk—just a common commercial traveller—is that it? Has he not told ye he'll be Lord Mayor o' London next? It's just about as likely? The young pup!"

With tears streaming down her cheeks Mary again interposed, despite a wail of protest from Mamma.

"He's well liked, father! Indeed he is! Mr. Findlay takes an interest in him. I know that."

"Pah! ye don't expect me to believe what he tells ye. It's a pack of lies, a pack of lies," he shouted again, raising his voice at her. "He's a low-down scum. What can ye expect from that kind of stock? Just rottenness. It's an outrage on me that ye ever spoke to him. But ye've spoken to him for the last time." He glared at her compellingly, as he repeated fiercely: "No! Ye'll never speak to him again. I forbid it."

"But, father," she sobbed, "oh! father, I—I——"

"Mary, Mary, don't dare answer your father back! It's dreadful to hear you speak up to him like that," came Mamma's voice from the other end of the table. But although its purpose was to propitiate, her interjection was on this occasion a tactical error, and served only to direct momentarily the tyranny of Brodie's wrath upon her own bowed head, and with a jerk of his eyes he flared at her:

"What are you yammerin' about? Are you talkin' or am I? If ye've something to say then we'll all stop and listen to the wonder o' it, but if ye've nothing to say then keep your mouth shut and don't interrupt. You're as bad as she is. It's your place to watch the company she keeps." He snorted and, after his habit, paused forcibly, making the stillness oppressive, until the old grandmother, who had not followed the trend of the talk or grasped the significance of the intermission, but who sensed that Mary was in disgrace, allowed the culmination of her own feelings to overcome her, and punctuated the silence by suddenly calling out, in a rancorous senile tone:

"She forgot her messages the day, James. Mary forgot my cheese, the heedless thing she is"; then, her ridiculous spleen vented, she immediately subsided, muttering, her head shaking as with a palsy.

He disregarded the interruption entirely and returning his eyes to Mary, slowly repeated:

"I have spoken. If you dare to disobey me, God help you! And one more point. This is the first night of Levenford Fair. I saw the start o' the stinking geggies on my way home. Remember! No child of mine goes within a hundred yards of that show ground. Let the rest of the town go; let the riff-raff of the countryside go; let all the Foyles and their friends go; but not one of James Brodie's family will so demean themselves. I forbid it."

His last words were heavy with menace as he pushed back his chair, heaved up his huge bulk and stood for an instant upright, dominating the small feeble group beneath him. Then he strode to his armchair in the corner and sat down, swept his adjacent pipe-rack with the automatic action of established habit, selected a pipe by sense of touch alone, withdrew it and, taking a square leather tobacco pouch from his deep side pocket, opened the clasp and slowly filled the charred bowl; then he lifted a paper spill from the heap below the rack, bent heavily forward, ignited the spill at the fire and lit his pipe. Having accomplished the sequence of actions without once having removed his threatening eyes from the silent group at table, he smoked slowly, with a wet, protruding underlip, still watching the others, but now more contemplatively, more with that air of calm, judicial supremacy. Although they were accustomed to it his family inevitably became depressed under the tyranny of this cold stare, and now they conversed in low tones; Mamma's colour was still high; Mary's lips still trembled as she spoke; Nessie fiddled with her teaspoon, dropped it, then blushed shamefully as though discovered in a wicked act; the old woman alone sat impassive, pervaded by the comfortable sense of her repletion.

At this moment there were sounds of someone entering the house, and presently a young man came into the room. He was a slender youth of twenty-four, pale-faced and with a regrettable tendency towards acne, his look slightly hangdog and indirect, his dress as foppish as his purse and his fear of his father would allow, his hands, particularly noticeable, being large, soft, dead white in colour, with the nails cut short to the quick, leaving smooth round pads of flesh at the finger ends. He sidled into a chair without appearing to regard anyone in the room, accepted silently a cup of tea which Mamma handed him, and began to eat. This, the last member of the household, was Matthew, sole son and, therefore, heir to James Brodie. He was permissibly late for this meal because, being employed as a clerk in the ship stores department in Latta's Shipyard, his hours of work did not cease until six o'clock.

"Is your tea right, Matt?" asked his mother solicitously, in a low voice.

Matthew permitted himself to nod silently.

"Have some of that apple-jelly, dear. It's real nice," begged Mamma in an undertone. "You're lookin' a bit tired the night. Have ye had a lot to do in the office to-day?"

He jerked his head non-committally whilst his pale, bloodless hands moved continuously, cutting his bread into small accurate squares, stirring the tea, drumming upon the table-cloth; he never allowed them to be still, moving them amongst the equipage of the table like an acolyte performing some hasty sacramental rite upon an altar. The downcast look, the bolted mouthfuls, this uneasy inquietude of his hands were the reactions upon his unstable nerves of that morose paternal eye brooding behind his back.

"More tea, son?" whispered his mother, stretching out her hand for his cup. "Try these water-biscuits too, they're new in to-day"; then adding, as a sudden thought struck her: "Has your indigestion bothered you to-day?"

"Not too bad," at last he murmured in reply, without looking up.

"Eat your tea slowly then, Matt," cautioned Mamma confidentially. "I sometimes think ye don't chew your food enough. Don't hurry!"

"Got to see Agnes to-night, though, Mamma," he whispered reprovingly, as though justifying his haste.

She moved her head in a slow, acquiescent comprehension.

Presently the old grandmother arose, sucking her teeth and brushing the crumbs from her lap, wondering, as she took her chair, if her son would talk to her to-night. When in the humour he would regale her with the choicer gossip of the town, shouting to her of how he had got the better of Waddel and taken him down a peg, how Provost Gordon had slapped him heartily upon the back at the Cross, how Paxton's business was going down the hill. No one was ever praised in these conversations, but they were delicious to her in their disparaging piquancy, toothsome in their sarcastic aspersion, and she enjoyed them immensely, fastening upon each morsel of personal information and devouring it greedily, savouring always the superiority of her son over the victim of the discussion.

But to-night Brodie kept silent, occupied by his reflections which, mellowed by the solace of his pipe, flowed into a less rancorous channel than that which they had followed at table. He would, he considered, have to tame Mary, who, somehow, did not seem like his child; who had never bowed down to him as lowly as he desired, from whom he had never received the full homage accorded him by the others. She was getting a handsome lassie though, despite her unsubdued nature— took the looks from him—but he felt he must, for his own satisfaction and her good, subdue that independent spirit. As for her acquaintance with that Denis Foyle, he was glad that the noise of it had reached his ears, that he had crushed the affair at the outset.

He had been astounded at her temerity in answering him as she had done to-night and could find no reason for it, but now that he had marked that tendency towards insubordination he would watch her more carefully in the future and eradicate it utterly should it again occur.

His gaze then rested upon his wife, but only for an instant; considering it her only worth that she saved him the expense of a servant in the house, he quickly looked away from her, with an involuntary, distasteful curl of his lips, and turned his mind to pleasanter things.

Yes, there was Matthew, his son! Not a bad lad; a bit sly and soft and sleek perhaps; wanted watching; and spoiled utterly by his mother. But going to India would, he hoped, make a man of him. It was getting near the time now and in only two or three weeks he would be off to that fine job Sir John Latta had got for him. Ah! folks would talk about that! His features relaxed, as he considered how everyone would recognise in this appointment a special mark of Sir John's favour to him, and a further tribute to his prominence in the town, how, through it, his son's character would benefit and his own importance increase.

His eye then fell upon his mother, less harshly, and with a more indulgent regard than that he had directed towards her at table. She was fond of her food, and even as she sat nodding over the fire he read her mind shrewdly, knew that she was already anticipating, thinking of her next meal, her supper of pease brose and buttermilk. She loved it, repeated like a wise saw: "There's naethin' like brose to sleep on! It's like a poultice to the stomach." Ay! her god was her belly, but losh! she was a tough old witch. The older she got, the tougher she grew; she must have good stuff in her to make her last like that, and even now she looked, to his mind, good for another ten years. If he wore as well as that, and he might wear better, he would be satisfied.

Finally he looked at Nessie and immediately his bearing became tinged, almost imperceptibly, with a faint indication of feeling, not manifest by any marked change of feature, but by his eye which became flecked with a softer and more considerate light. Yes! Let Mamma keep her Matt, ay, and Mary too—Nessie was his. He would make something of her, his ewe lamb. Although she was so young she had the look of a real smart wee thing about her and the Rector had said to him only the other night that she had the makings of a scholar if she stuck in hard to her work. That was the way to do it. Pick them out young and keep them at it. He was looking ahead, too, with something up his sleeve for the future. The Latta Bursary! The crowning success of a brilliant scholastic career. She had it in her to take it, if she was nursed the right way. Gad! what a triumph! A girl to win the Latta—the first girl to win it, ay, and a Brodie at that! He would see that she did it. Mamma had better keep her soft spoiling hands off his daughter. He would see to that.

He did not quite know what he would make of her, but education was education; there were degrees that could be taken later on at College, and triumphs to be won. They all knew in the Borough that he was a man of progress, of broad and liberal ideas, and he would bring this more emphatically before them, yes, ram it into their silly mouths. "Did ye hear the latest!" he could hear them chatter. "That clever lass o' Brodie's is awa' up to the College—ay, she's taken the Latta—fair scooped the pool at the Academy, and he's lettin' her travel up and down to the University. He's a liberal-minded man for sure. It's a feather in *his* bonnet right enough."

Yes! he would show them in the town. His chest expanded, his nostrils quivered, his eye became fixed and distant, as he gave rein to his fancy, while his unnoticed pipe went out and grew cold. He would make them recognise him, make them look up to him, would force them somehow, some day, to see him as he really was.

The thought of Nessie faded gradually from his mind, and he ceased to contemplate her future but, making himself the central figure of all his mental pictures, steeped himself delightfully in the glory she would bring to his name.

At length he bestirred himself. He knocked out the ashes of his pipe, replaced it in the rack and, with a last silent survey of his family, as though to say: "I am going, but remember what I've said, I'll still have my eye on ye!" he went into the hall, put on his square felt hat with the smooth well-brushed nap, took up his heavy ash stick, and was out of the house without a word. This was his usual method of departure. He never said good-bye. Let them guess where he was going in his spare time—to a meeting, to the council, or to the club; let them remain uncertain as to his return, as to its time and the nature of his mood; he liked to make them jump at his sudden step in the hall. That was the way to keep them in order, and it would do them a deal of good to wonder where he went, he thought, as the front door closed behind him with a slam.

Nevertheless, the removal of his actual presence seemed to bring some measure of relief to his family, and with his departure a cloud of constraint lifted from the room. Mrs. Brodie relaxed the muscles which for the last hour had been unconsciously rigid and, while her shoulders sagged more limply, the tension of her mind was released and her spirit revived feebly.

"You'll clear up, won't you, Mary?" she said mildly. "I feel kind of tired and far through to-night. It'll do me no harm to have a look at my book."

"Yes, Mamma," replied Mary, adding dutifully as was expected of her every evening. "You've earned a rest. I'll wash up the dishes myself."

Mrs. Brodie nodded her inclined head deprecatingly, but none the less in agreement, as she arose and, going to her own drawer in the dresser, took from its place of concealment a book, *Devenham's Vow*, by one Amelia B. Edwards, which, like every book she read, was on loan from the Levenford Borough Library. Holding the volume tenderly against her heart she sat down, and soon Margaret Brodie had sunk her own tragic, broken individuality in that of the heroine, comforting herself with the one of few solaces which life now held for her.

Mary quickly cleared the dishes from the table and spread upon it a drugget cover, then, retiring to the scullery, she rolled up her sleeves from her thin arms and began her task of washing up.

Nessie, confronted by the unencumbered table, which mutely reminded her of her father's incitement to work, glanced first at the engrossed figure of her mother, at her grandmother's unheeding back, at Matt now tilted back in his chair and picking his teeth with an air, then with a sigh began wearily to withdraw her books from her school satchel, laying them reluctantly one by one in front of her.

"Come and play draughts first, Mary," she called out.

"No, dear, father said home work. Perhaps we'll have a game after," came the reply from without.

"Will I not dry the dishes for you to-night?" she suggested, insidiously trying to procrastinate the commencement of her toil.

"I'll manage all right, dear," replied Mary.

Nessie sighed again and remarked to herself sympathetically, in a voice like her mother's:

"Oh! dear me!"

She thought of the other children she knew who would be fraternising to play skipping ropes, rounders, cat and bat, and other magical frolics of the evening, and her small spirit was heavy within her as she began to work.

Matthew, disturbed in his transitory reverie, by the reiterated murmurs close to his ear: je suis, tu es, il est, now restored his quill to his vest pocket and got up from his chair. Since his father had gone his manner had changed, and he now adopted the air of being slightly superior to his surroundings, as he shot his cuffs, looked at the clock significantly and went out of the room, with a slight but pronounced swagger.

The room was now silent but for the rustle of a turning page, the slight clink of china invading it from without, and the harrowing murmur: nous sommes, vous êtes, ils sont; but in a few moments the audible evidence of activity in the scullery ceased and shortly afterwards Mary slipped quietly through the room into the hall, mounted the stairs and tapped at her brother's room. This was a nightly pilgrimage, but had she now been suddenly bereft of every sense but that of smell, she could still have found this room by the rich, unctuous odour of cigar smoke which emanated from it.

"Can I come in, Matt?" she murmured.

"Enter," came a studied voice from within.

She entered. As she came in he who had spoken so dispassionately did not look up, but seated in his shirt-sleeves upon the bed in the exact position where, with the looking-glass upon his chest of drawers tilted to the correct angle, he could best see himself, continued placidly to admire himself and to puff great clouds of smoke appreciatively towards his image.

"What a lovely smell your cigar has, Matt," she remarked, with ingenuous approval.

Matthew removed the weed from his lips in a dashing manner, still regarding himself approvingly.

"Yes," he agreed, "and it should have at the money. This is a Supremo, meaning the best. Five for sixpence, but this single one cost me three halfpence. It was a sample, and if I like it I'll go in for a few. The smell is good, Mary, but the bouquet is what we smokers appreciate. No cigar is really first class unless it has bouquet. This has what is called a nutty bouquet." He removed his eyes unwillingly from the mirror and contemplating his cigar more closely, added: "Now I'll stop, I think I've smoked enough."

"Oh! go on," she encouraged. "It's lovely! Far nicer than a pipe!"

"No! I must keep the other half for this evening," he replied firmly, carefully extinguishing the glowing end against the cold china of his wash-basin and preserving the stub in his waistcoat pocket.

"Does Aggie Moir like you to smoke?" she murmured, drawing her conclusions from his actions.

"Agnes, if you please—not Aggie," he replied in a pained voice. "How often have I told you not to be familiar like that. It's vulgar. It's—it's a liberty on your part."

She lowered her eyes. "I'm sorry, Matt."

"I should hope so! Remember, Mary, that Miss Moir is a young lady, a very worthy young lady, and my intended as well. Yes! if you must know she does like me to smoke. She was against it at first but now she thinks it manly and romantic. But she objects to the odour of the breath afterwards and therefore gives me cachous. She prefers the variety called 'Sweet Lips.' They're very agreeable."

"Do you love Agnes very much, Matt?" she demanded earnestly.

"Yes! and she loves me a great deal," he asserted. "You shouldn't talk about things you know nothing about, but you've surely the sense to know that when people are walking out they must be fond of one another. Agnes worships me. You should see the things she gives me. It's a great thing for a young man to have an affinity like that. She's a most estimable girl."

Mary was silent for a moment, her eyes fixed upon him intently, then suddenly pressing her hand to her side, she asked involuntarily, wistfully:

"Does it hurt you when you think of Agnes—when you're away from her?"

"Certainly not," replied Matthew primly. "That's not a nice thing to ask. If I had that pain I should think I had indigestion. What a girl you are for asking questions, and what questions you do ask! We'll have no more of it, if you please. I'm going to practise now, so don't interrupt."

He rose up and stooping carefully to avoid creasing his best trousers, took a mandolin case from under the bed and extracted a mandolin decorated with a large bow of pink satin ribbon. Next he unrolled a thin yellow-covered music book entitled in large letters: *First Steps in the Mandolin*, and in smaller print below: *Aunt Nellie's Guide for Young Mandolin Players, after the method of the famous Señor Rosas*, opened it at page two, laid it flat upon the bed before him, and sitting down beside it, in an attitude of picturesque ease, drew the romantic instrument to him and began to play. He did not, alas, fulfil the expectation which his experienced posture aroused, or dash ravishingly into an enchanting serenade, but with a slow and laborious touch picked out two or three bars of "Nelly Bly," until his execution grew more and more halting and he finally broke down.

"Begin again," remarked Mary helpfully.

He rewarded her with an aggrieved look.

"I think I asked you to remain silent, Miss Chatterbox. Remember this is a most difficult and complicated instrument. I must perfect myself in it before I leave for India. Then I can play to the ladies on board during the tropical evenings. A man must practise! You know I'm getting on splendidly, but perhaps you would like to try as you're so clever."

He did, however, begin again and eventually tweaked his way through the piece. The succession of tuneless discords was excruciating to the ear, and, in common with the art of smoking, could only be indulged in during the absence of his father; but Mary, nevertheless, with her chin cupped in her hands, watched, rather than listened, admiringly.

At the conclusion Matthew ran his fingers through his hair with a careless, yet romantic gesture.

"I am perhaps not in my best form, to-night; I think I am a little 'triste,' pensive, Mary you know. Perhaps a little upset at the office to-day—these confounded figures—it disturbs an artistic temperament like mine. I'm not really understood down at the Yard." He sighed with a dreamy sadness befitting his unappreciated art, but soon looked up, anxious for encouragement, asking:

"But how did it really go? How did it seem?"

"Very like it," replied Mary reassuringly.

"Like what?" he demanded doubtfully.

"The Saucy Kate Galop, of course!"

"You little ninny," shouted Matthew. "It was 'Nelly Bly.'" He was completely upset, looked at her crushingly, then jumped off the bed and put the mandolin away in a huff, remarking, as he bent down: "I believe you only said it to spite me," and asserting disdainfully as he got up: "You've no ear for music, anyway." He did not seem to hear her profuse apologies, but turning his back took a very stiff high collar and a bright blue spotted tie from a drawer, and still occupied by his pique, continued:

"Miss Moir has! She says I'm very musical, that I've got the best voice in the choir. She sings delightfully herself. I wish you were more worthy to be her sister-in-law."

She was quite upset at her clumsy tongue and well aware of her unworthiness, but she pleaded:

"Let me tie your neck-tie anyway, Matt."

He turned sulkily and condescendingly permitted Mary to knot the cravat, a task she always undertook for him, and which she now performed neatly and dexterously, so that presenting himself again before the mirror, he regarded the result with satisfaction.

"Brilliantine," he demanded next, forgiving her by his command. She handed him the bottle from which he sprinkled copious libations of mellifluous liquid upon his hair and with a concentrated mien he then combed his locks into a picturesque wave.

"My hair is very thick, Mary," he remarked as he carefully worked the comb behind his ears. "I shall never go bald. That ass Couper said it was getting thin on the top the last time he cut it. The very idea! I'll stop going to him in future for his impertinence."

When he had achieved the requisite undulation amongst his curls, he extended his arms and allowed her to help him to assume his coat, then took a clean linen handkerchief, scented it freshly with Sweet Pea Perfume, draped it artistically from his pocket, and surveyed the finished result in the glass steadily.

"Smart cut," he murmured, "neat waist. Miller does wonderfully for a local tailor, don't you think?" he queried. "Of course I keep him up to it, and he's got a figure to work on! Well, if Agnes is not pleased with me to-night, she ought to be." Then, as he moved away, he added inconsequently, "And don't forget, Mary, half-past ten to-night, or perhaps a little shade later."

"I'll be awake, Matt," she murmured reassuringly.

"Sure now?"

"Sure!"

This last remark exposed the heel of Achilles, for this admirable, elegant young man, smoker, mandolinist, lover, the future intrepid voyager to India, had one amazing weakness—he was afraid of the dark. He admitted Mary to his confidence and companionship incontestably for the reason that she would meet him by arrangement on these nights when he was late and escort him up the obscure and gloomy stairs to his bedroom, without fail and with a loyalty which never betrayed him. She never considered the manner of her service to him, but accepted his patronising favour gratefully, with humility, and now as he went out, leaving behind him a mingled perfume of cigars, brilliantine, and sweet pea blossom and the memory of his bold and dashing presence, she followed his figure with fond and admiring eyes.

Presently, bereft of the tinsel of his personality, Mary's spirits drooped, and unoccupied, with time to think of herself, she became disturbed, restless, excited. Everyone in the house was busy: Nessie frowning over her lessons, Mamma deeply engaged in her novel, Grandma sunk in the torpor of digestion. She wandered about the kitchen, thinking of her father's command, uneasy, agitated, until Mamma looked up in annoyance.

"What's wrong with you—wanderin' about like a knotless thread? Take up your sewing, or if you've nothing to do, away to your bed and leave folks to read in peace!"

Should she go to bed? she considered perplexedly. No! it was too ridiculously early. She had been confined in the house all day and ought perhaps to get into the open for a little, where the freshness of air would restore her, ease her mind after the closeness of the warm day. Everyone would think she had gone to her room, she would never be missed. Somehow, without being aware of her movements, she was in the hall, had put on her old coarse straw bonnet with the weather-beaten little bunch of cherries and the faded pink ribbon, had slipped on her worn cashmere coat, quietly opened the front door and moved down the steps.

She was startled, almost, to find herself outside, but thought reassuringly that with such clothes it was impossible for her to go anywhere, and as she reflected that she had no really nice things to wear, she shook her head sadly so that the woebegone cherries which had hung from her hat through two long seasons, rattled in faint protest and almost dropped to the ground. Now that she was in the open her mind moved more freely and she wondered what Denis was doing. Getting ready to go to the fair, of course. Why was everyone else allowed to go and not she? It was unjust, for there was no harm in it. It was an institution recognised, and patronised tolerantly, by even the very best of the townspeople. She leant over the front gate swinging to and fro gently, drinking in the cool beauty of the dusk, fascinated by the seductive evening, so full of dew-drenched odours, so animate with the awakening life that had been still during the day. Swallows darted and circled around the three straight silver birches in the field opposite, whilst a little further off a yellow-hammer called to her, entreatingly: "Come out! Come out! Jingle, jingle, jingle the keys, jingle, jingle, jingle the keys!" It was a shame to be indoors on a night like this! She stepped into the roadway, telling herself that she would take a little walk, just to the end of the road before coming back for that game of draughts with Nessie. She sauntered on unobserved, noting unconsciously that in the whole extent of the quiet road no person was in sight. Denis was expecting her to-night at the fair. He had asked her to meet him, and she, like a mad woman, had promised to be there. The pity of it that she could not go! She was terrified of her father and he had absolutely forbidden it.

How quickly she reached the end of the road, and although she seemed to have been out only for a moment she knew that she had come far enough, that it was now time for her to go back; but as her will commanded her to turn, some stronger force forbade it, and she kept on, her heart thumping furiously, her steps quickening in pace with her heartbeats. Then, through the magic of the night, the sound of music met her ears, faint, enticing, compelling. She hastened her gait almost to a run, thought: "I must, oh! I must see him," and rushed onwards. Trembling, she entered the fair ground.

II

LEVENFORD FAIR was an annual festival, the nucleus of which was the congregation of a number of travelling troupes and side-shows, a small menagerie, which featured actually an elephant and a cage of two lions, an authentic shooting gallery where real bullets were used, and two fortune-tellers with unimpeachable and freely displayed credentials, which, together with a variety of other minor attractions, assembled at an agreed date upon that piece of public land known locally as the Common.

The ground was triangular in shape. On one side, at the town end, stood the solidly important components of the fair, the larger tents and marquees, on another the moving vehicles of pleasure, swings, round-abouts and merry-go-rounds, and on the third, bordering the meadows of the river Leven, were the galleries, coco-nut shies, lab-in-the-tub and molly-dolly stalls, the fruit, lemonade, hokey-pokey, and nougat vendors, and a multitude of small booths which engaged and fascinated the eye. The gathering was by far the largest of its kind in the district and, its popularity set by precedent and appreciation, it drew like a magnet upon the town and countryside during the evenings for the period of one scintillating week, embracing within its confines a jovial mass of humanity, which even now slowly surged around the trigon on a per-petually advancing wave of pleasure.

Mary plunged into the tide and was immediately engulfed. She ceased to become an entity and was absorbed by the sweep of pushing, laugh-ing, shouting, gesticulating beings, which bore her forward independent of her own volition, and as she was pushed this way and that, yet always borne onwards by this encompassing force, she became at once amazed at her own temerity. The press of the rough crowd was not what her idyllic fancy had pictured, the blatant shouts and flaring lights not the impressions of her imagination, and she had not been five minutes on the ground before she began to wish she had not come and to perceive that, after all, her father might be right in his assertion, wise to have forbidden her to come. Now she felt that, though the sole purpose of her coming was to see Denis, it would be impossible for him to discover her in such a throng, and as a sharp, jostling elbow knocked against her ribs, and a fat ploughboy trod upon her foot and grinned uncouthly in apology, she grew wretched and frightened. What manner of feeling had drawn her amongst these vulgar clowns! Why had she so impru-dently, rashly, dangerously disobeyed her father and come with such light and ardent unrestraint at the beck of a youth whom she had known for only one month?

As she swayed around she viewed that month in retrospect, recollect-ing with a melancholy simplicity that the swing doors of the Borough Public Library had been, in part, responsible. These doors bore on the inside the authoritative word "Pull," and, in obedience to that terse mandate, when coming out of the Library, one was supposed to pull strenuously upon them; but they were so stiff and heavy that, when one was cumbered with a book and unobserved by the compelling eye of the janitor of the Borough Buildings, it was much easier to disregard the law and push. Upon one memorable occasion she had, undoubtedly, pushed, and thrusting forward with no uncertain hand, had launched herself straight into the waist-coat of a young man in brown. The impetus of her exit allowed her to observe fully the colour of his neat suit. His hair, too, was brown, and his eyes, and his face which had tiny freckles of a deeper brown dusted upon it; and as she raised her startled eyes she had noticed immediately, despite her discomposure, that his teeth, when he smiled, as he did instantly, were white and perfect. Whilst she stared at him with wide eyes and parted lips, he had composed his features, had politely collected her fallen book, calmly opened it, and looked at her name on the borrower's ticket.

"I am sorry to have upset you, Miss Mary Brodie," he had said gravely, but smiling at her the while out of his hazel eyes. "These doors are exceedingly treacherous. They ought, of course, to have glass windows to them. It is entirely my fault, for hot having brought the matter before the Borough Council."

She had giggled insanely, immodestly, but alas, irrepressibly at his delicious raillery and had only ceased when he added, tentatively, as though it were of no importance: "My name is Foyle—I live in Darroch." They looked at each other for a long moment, while she, of course, had flushed like a fool (since then he had told her that it was an adorable blush) and had said timidly: "I'm afraid I must be going." What a weak remark, she now reflected! He had not attempted to detain her, and with perfect courtesy had stepped aside, lifted his hat and bowed; but all the way down the street she had felt those lively brown eyes upon her, respectful, attentive, admiring. That had been the beginning!

Presently she, who had never before seen him in Levenford, for the good reason that he had seldom come there, began to see him frequently in the streets. They were, in fact, always encountering each other, and although he had never had the opportunity to speak, he always smiled and saluted her, cheerfully yet deferentially. She began to love that gay spontaneous smile, to look for the jaunty set of his shoulders, to desire the eager radiance of his glance. Sometimes she discerned him with a group of the hardier and more intrepid spirits of Levenfold standing at the newly opened ice-cream saloon of Bertorelli's, and perceived with awe that these bold striplings accepted him as an equal, even as a superior, and this, together with the knowledge that he should frequent a place so wild and reckless as an Italian ice-cream shop, made her tremble. His slight acquaintance with her had, too, given her distinction, and, even in his absence, when she passed this group of the youthful elect a polite silence immediately ensued, and as one man the members of the band swept off their hats to honour her—thrilling, but disconcerting her.

A week later she had again visited the Library, and despite the fact that this time she carefully pulled the doors as a public gesture of self-reproach and censure, openly avowing her penitence, she again found Denis Foyle outside.

"What a coincidence, Miss Brodie!" he had said. "Imagine us meeting here again. Strange that I should be passing just at this moment." How could she know, poor thing, that he had been waiting for two hours on the opposite side of the street.

"May I see what book you are reading this week?"

"*Pomeroy Abbey*, by Mrs. Henry Wood," she had stammered.

"Ah! yes, volume two. I saw you had volume one last time you were here."

He had, she mused, given himself away there, and as she observed a slight, shy eagerness in his glance, realised that he was altogether less composed, less assured than upon their previous encounter, and a melting tenderness filled her as she heard him say fervidly:

"Will you permit me to carry your book for you please, Miss Brodie?" She blushed darkly now at her unladylike and unpardonable conduct, but the unalterable fact remained that she had given him the book, had surrendered the volume without a word, as though in effect she had meekly proffered him the modest volume in return for the sweet acceptance of his attentions. She sighed as she thought of that small, and apparently trivial beginning, for since that occurrence they had met on several, no, on many occasions, and she had become so enwrapped by a strange and incomprehensible regard for him that it left her hurt and lonely to be away from him.

With a start she came out of the past. By this time she had been once round the fair without seeing anything but a blur of gaudy colours, she became once more aware of her unpleasant predicament, of the hopelessness of ever distinguishing amongst this nightmare sea of faces that seethed around her the one she sought, and as she was now opposite an opening in the crowd which permitted access to the street she began with difficulty to squeeze her way out.

Suddenly a warm hand clasped her small, cold fingers. Hurriedly she looked up, and saw that it was Denis. A wave of security enveloped her and invaded her veins in a delicious sense of comfort, filling her with such relief that she pressed his hand in hers and in the open simplicity of her nature said hurriedly, ardently, before he could speak:

"Oh! Denis, I've been so miserable here without you! I felt as if I had lost you for ever."

He looked at her tenderly, as he replied:

"I was a fool to ask you to meet me here in all this crowd, Mary. I knew I would find you, but I quite forgot that you might get into the crush before then. My train was late, too. Have you been here long?"

"I don't know how long," she murmured. "It seemed like years, but I don't care now that you're here."

"I hope you didn't get pushed about in the crowd," he protested. "I blame myself for letting you come on by yourself. Indeed I do! I should have met you outside, but I hadn't an idea there would be so many here to-night. You're not annoyed?"

She shook her head negatively; and without concealing her delight in him, without upbraiding him for his tardiness or permitting him to see the risk she had taken in coming to meet him here, replied guilelessly, happily:

"It's all right, Denis. I don't mind the crowd—nothing matters now that you've found me."

"What a girl you are, Mary," he cried. "It's an angel you are to forgive me. But I'll not rest till I've made it up to you. Let's make up for lost time. I'll not be happy till I've given you the time of your life. What shall we do first? Say the word and it's as good as done."

Mary looked round. How changed everything was! how glad she was to have come! She saw that the people around were not rough but merely boisterous and happy, and had she now been confronted with the heavy-footed ploughboy she would have returned his rustic grin with an understanding smile. She saw everywhere colour, excitement, and movement; the shouts of the showmen animated her, the cracking of shots in the shooting-gallery thrilled without daunting her; the blare of music around intoxicated her, and as her sparkling eye was drawn by a ring of hobby horses leaping gaily round, circling, prancing, gambolling to the tune of the Kandahar Waltz, she laughed excitedly and pointed to them.

"These," she gasped.

"Sure!" cried Denis. "Your word is law, Mary! We'll kick off on the leppers. All aboard for the Donegal Hunt," He grasped her arm, leading her forward while magically the crowd, which had so oppressed her, seemed to melt before them.

"Here we are," he exclaimed gaily. "Two together, with tails like lions and teeth like dromedaries. Up you go, Mary! Yours will jump the side of a house by the wicked look in his eye."

They were seated on the horses, grasping the reins, waiting, circling at first slowly, then quickly, then whirling to the mad music, thrilled with the joy of movement, tearing round above the gaping, unmounted commoners who seemed far below the flying hoofs of their prancing chargers, chasing together through wide celestial spaces, soaring upwards in a spirited nobility of movement. When, at last, they slowly came to rest, he refused to allow her to dismount, but compelled her willing presence beside him for another, and another and still another turn, until, as her experience grew, and her confidence in the saddle increased, she relaxed the tenseness of her grip upon the reins and directing her mount by the light touch of one hand, relaxed her body to its curvetting movement and exhibited proudly to him the address and dexterity of her horsemanship. He praised her, encouraged her, revelling in her enjoyment, until at length Mary's conscience pricked her and, feeling that he would be ruined through her prodigal rashness, she implored him to come off. He laughed till his sides shook.

"We could stay on all night if you wanted to! It's nothing at all if you're happy."

"Oh! yes it is, Denis! It's an awful expense. Do let us get down," she begged. "I'm just as happy watching!"

"All right, then! We'll get off to please you, Mary; but we're only beginning. To-night it's a millionaire you're with. We're goin' through the whole bag of tricks."

"If you're sure you can afford it, Denis," replied Mary doubtfully. "It's simply wonderful here! But I don't want you to spend too much on me."

"Sure I couldn't spend enough on you, Mary!" he replied warmly, "if I spent every farthing I've got!"

That was the raising of the curtain; and now they plunged into the throng, feasting their eyes upon the panorama of gaiety and absorbing the merriment around them eagerly, joyously, and together.

An hour later, having experienced every variety of movement offered for their delectation, thrown balls at all conceivable objects from coconuts to sallies, seen the flea-bitten lions and the apathetic elephant, prodded the fat boy at the earnest request of the showman to ensure there being no deception, admired the smallest woman in the world, shuddered appreciatively at the living skeleton, and purchased every edible commodity from honey pears to cough candy, they stood, the most joyously animated couple in the whole show ground, before the biggest tent in the fair. It was the famous McInally's, which provided, as its posters indicated, a feast of refined and elegant entertainment. In front of the tent was a wooden platform now illuminated by four naphtha flares, and upon the centre of this stage stood the famous McInally himself, easily distinguishable by his glossy top hat and flowing frock coat, by his largely checked trousers and the enormous brass albert that stretched, yellow as gold and thick as a mayoral chain, across his whitish velvet waistcoat. On either side of him stood, to quote again from the red and blue lettered advance notices that plastered the walls and gateposts of the countryside, a coruscating galaxy of talent. On his right a tall, soulful gentleman in full but musty evening dress leant with a melancholy grace against a pole of the marquee, directing his romantic gaze upwards from the mob as though he sought upon an ethereal balcony some Juliet who might be worthy of him, and concealing as best he might the soiled condition of his linen by elongating his coat sleeves and folding his arms manfully across his shirt front. But this sombre Romeo did not constitute the sole attraction of the show, for at the other end of the stage on McInally's left, was poised a bewitching creature clad in pink tights and white ballet skirt, with a peaked yachting cap set at a rakish angle upon her head, executing from time to time a few mincing steps hinting at the promise of more ravishing movements to come and throwing kisses to the multitude below with an airy, graceful action of her arms that suggested she was drawing yards of streamers from her lips.

"Isn't she lovely?" whispered Mary, who by this time had drawn so close to her companion that she had taken his arm.

"If you saw her in daylight you would be surprised," replied the more sophisticated Denis. "I've been told something about her. As a matter of report," he continued slowly, as though liberating a baleful secret, "they say she squints."

"Oh! Denis, how can you say such a thing!" cried Mary indignantly. But she gazed doubtfully at the suggestive angle of the yachting cap. Was it merely saucy, or was its purpose more profoundly significant?

"Walk up, ladies and gentlemen, walk up!" shouted McInally, removing his hat with a flourish and holding it extended in a courtly gesture of invitation. "The Performance is going to begin. We are just about to commence. Positively the last Performance of the evening. An entertainment of the highest class, admission twopence and twopence only. Artistic, refined, and elegant—Gentlemen, you may bring your wives and sweethearts, an entertainment without a blush. The one and only McInally, positively of the highest class and one class only. Just about to begin! Gentlemen! on my left Madame Bolita in the most wonderful and artistic Terpsichorean exhibition of the century." At the mention of her name Madame pirouetted lightly, smiled coyly, extended her wrists coquettishly and drew out fresh streamers, which were, if anything, more tenacious than before.

"Ladies! on my right Signor Magini, the most renowned, accomplished vocalist, direct from the Opera Houses of Paris and Milan, in the illuminated song-scena of the age." Signor Magini, whose real name was Maginty, looked more romantically melancholy than ever and bowed dreamily as though ladies had mobbed him with bouquets in Paris and fought for his favour in Milan. "We are about to commence to begin. We are about to begin to commence! Walk up! Walk up! The last show to-night. We are closing down for the evening. Thanking you one and all for your kind attention. Walk up, walk up."

"It must be going to begin, said Denis. "He's told us so often. Shall we chance it?"

"Yes," thrilled Mary.

They went inside.

In the tent it smelt of paraffin, hot sawdust, and orange-peel and, feeling their way through the dim, redolent interior they found a vacant place, seated themselves, and after a moment of expectant waiting, were rewarded by the opening of the programme. This was divided into two

34

parts, the first given over to Madame Bolita, the second to the Signor from Paris and Milan; but whether the great McInally was drawn by the compelling odour of his supper of steak and onions issuing from his caravan at the rear, or whether he felt that there was time for yet another performance which should be positively the last, is impossible to say; certainly the entertainment was the essence of brevity.

Madame pirouetted, postured, and leaped heavily, accentuating the thuds of her descent upon the thin sounding board of the stage by short involuntary expirations which might in a less accomplished artiste have been mistaken for grunts, and accompanying her lighter movements by much snapping of her fingers and shrill cries of: "La! la! oh! la, la!" She would pirouette tremulously at the back of the platform, trip forward skittishly to the row of footlights, thrust back one substantial leg into the air with a disdainful kick, advance her chin languishingly upon one extended forefinger, and, swaying slightly upon her remaining support, survey the audience with an air of profound achievement. Then, mingling the faint, intermediate rattle of applause with a self-congratulatory "oh! la, la!" she would toss her head enticingly and bound off into a circular gambol which took her conveniently back to her original position. The climax of the first part of her act came with a noble effort when, her arms outstretched, her face contorted by endeavour, she subsided slowly and painfully into the splits, a position from which, however, she did not attempt to arise, but was rescued by the timely fall of the curtain.

"Not bad, considering her age," remarked Denis, confidentially, "but she'll go right through that stage one day, and never be heard of again."

"Oh! Denis," whispered Mary reproachfully. "You ,don't really mean that. Surely you liked her?"

"If you liked her, I liked her! But don't ask me to fall in love with her," he replied teasingly. "We'll see what she does next," he added, as, after an adequate pause, the curtain again rose to reveal a darker stage into which the adipose figure of the incomparable Bolita swung slowly. Shrouded in a long white gown, bereft of the yachting cap, but still discreetly veiled by long yellow tresses which hung luxuriantly about her, and wearing a large and incontestably angelic pair of wings, she floated through the obscure air and remained poised seraphically before their astonished gaze. Gone now were the fripperies of the dance, the tinsel of the ballet, as though, reformed and purged, she now disdained the creature who had cried: "Oh! la, la!" and performed the atrocity of the splits; thus she swam piously about the stage to the accompaniment of an audible creaking of the wire and pulley which supported her and the tinkling out of "The Rock of Ages," upon the piano in the wings. There was much applause chiefly in the shape of shrill whistles from the back benches and loud cries of "'core, 'core";

but encores were unheard of in the McInally régime and Madame, having taken her bow with fluttering wings, retired gracefully and turned into her caravan to see if little Katie Maginty, her grandchild, had gone to sleep.

Mary clapped her hands enthusiastically and turned to Denis.

"What's your opinion now?" she enquired earnestly, as though daring him to belittle such a heavenly creature. They sat very close together on the thin wooden form, their hands clasped, their fingers interlocked, and Denis, looking at her entranced upturned face, pressed her fingers as he replied, meaningly:

"I think you're wonderful!" It was the height of repartee! Mary laughed outright, but at the sound of her own laughter, so unusually gay and unrestrained, inversely there arose in her mind, as if by contrast, the picture of her home, and suddenly chilled, as though she had been plunged into icy water, she shivered and lowered her head. But with an effort she thrust away her despondency; comforted by Denis' nearness she looked up again to see that Magini was holding the stage. A white screen had been lowered and now the magic lantern at the back of the tent flashed upon it the title: "Tender and True" or "The Mariner's Maid." The jingling piano struck up the opening bars of the ballad and Magini began to sing, while as he sang the honeyed words, richly coloured slides were shown upon the screen, demonstrating the touching vicissitudes attending the progress of true love. The meeting of the sailor and the miller's daughter by the mill-stream, the parting, the lonely mariner in his hammock, the trials of the noble-hearted seaman on the deep, and the no less lachrymal tribulations of his beloved at home, the still horrors of the shipwreck, the stark heroism of the rescue, flashed in turn before the breathless gaze until the final reunion of the well-deserving lovers, with clasped hands by that same mill-stream—the first slide repeated—gave relief and satisfaction to the entire audience.

He next sang, by special request, "Juanita," dealing with the seductive charms of a lady, darker and more passionate than the sailor's dove-like affinity, and holding a wilder and more dangerous appeal. When he concluded, the cheering from the back benches was vociferous and prolonged and it was some time before he could be heard to announce his last number as "The Land of Love," a favourite song, he informed his audience, of Ciro Pinsuti's. In contrast to the others it was simple, melodious, and touching, and although the vocalist had never been further south than the limits of McInally's circuit at Dumfries, he sang with a pure and natural voice. As the soft waves of sound floated through the dark tent Mary felt herself swept towards Denis in a rush of throbbing tenderness and sympathy. The sublime elevation of her emotion filled her eyes with tears. No one had ever treated her like Denis. She loved him. Raised far above the level of her confined and monotonous existence by the glitter of the evening and the glamour of the music, she would, if he had demanded it, have died willingly for this young god-like creature whose side was pressed against her side in a bitter-sweet union: sweet because she adored him, and bitter because she must leave him.

The song was ended. With a start she realised that the performance was over, and linked by an understanding silence she passed with Denis out of the tent into the fresh night air. Now it was dark, the ground illuminated by flares, the crowd diminished but still gaily surging, yet for these two, filled by a deeper enchantment, the attraction of the fair had waned. They looked around undecidedly.

"Shall we do any more of this?" asked Denis slowly. Mary shook her head. The evening had been so wonderful she felt it should have lasted for ever; but it was over, finished, and the hardest task of all was to say good-bye to him. She would have to walk back, a weary way out of that land of love, and now, alas! it was time for the journey to begin.

"Come for a little stroll then," he urged. "It's not late yet, Mary. We'll not go far."

She could not leave him! With a premonitory sadness rising in her throat at the very thought of her departure, she felt blindly that she must be with him a little longer. She wished to delay the sad reaction from this excitement and enchantment; she wanted his presence always, to soothe her and comfort her. The poignancy of her present feeling for him hurt her like a wound in her side, and its potency drove from her mind the thought of her home, her father, every deterring thought that might have prevented her accompanying him.

"Come, Mary dear," he pleaded. "It's still early."

"For a little way then," she consented in a whispered tone.

The path they took followed the winding bank of the Leven with the rippling river on one side and on the other meadows of dewy pasture land. A full moon that shone like a burnished plate of beaten silver, hung high in the sky, amongst a silver dust of stars, and was bosomed in the mysterious depths of the dark water beneath. At times thin pencils of misty cloud streaked this white nimbus that lay so far above and yet so deeply within the river, like ghostly fingers shielding from the eyes a luminance too brilliant to endure. As they walked, silent in the beauty of the silvery radiance, the air, cool with the dew-drenched freshness of night and sweet with the scents of lush grass and wild mint, encompassed them softly and settled upon them like a caress.

Before them two large grey moths pursued each other along the pathway, fluttering fantastically among the tall sedges and rushes of the bank, silently circling and crossing, flitting, but always following each other, always together. Their wings shone in the white light like large sailing motes within a moonbeam and the whisper of their flight fell upon the quietude like the downward flutter of a falling leaf.

The river, too, was almost silent, gurgling and sucking softly at its banks, and the low purling song of the stream became part of the stillness of the night.

They had walked some distance and now the fair ground was marked only by a faint glare in the sky extinguished by the moon, and the brassy music by a weak whisper on the breeze obliterated by the stillness; yet Mary and Denis knew nothing of the music or the moon, and though unconsciously they absorbed the beauty around them they were aware only of each other. That she should be for the first time alone with Denis and isolated from the world, filled Mary with a tremulous happiness, set her heart beating in a wild and joyous sweetness.

Denis, too, the sophisticated young man of the town, was overwhelmed by an emotion that was strange and new. The easy currents of conversational small-talk which made him always the life and soul of a party, the blandishments that flowed naturally from his lips, were dried up at the source. He was silent as a mute at a funeral, and, he told himself, as dismal. He felt that his reputation was at stake, that he must make some remark, no matter how trivial. Yet while he cursed himself inwardly for a dolt, a blunderer, a simpleton, imagining that he was estranging Mary by his dumb stupidity, his tongue still remained dry and his quick brain so flooded by his emotions that he could not speak.

Outwardly they both walked placidly and sedately, but inwardly there surged in each a tide of pent-up feelings, and because they did not speak this feeling grew more intense.

In Mary's side there came an actual pain. They were so close together that the sense of intimacy filled her with inexpressible yearning, an unfathomable longing which found its only ease in the firm clasp upon her arm that linked her pulsating body to his and soothed her like a divine balm.

At length they stopped suddenly, involuntarily, turned, and faced each other. Mary lifted her face to Denis. The small oval of her features bore the pallor of the moonlight with a spiritual translucency. He bent and kissed her. Her lips were soft and warm and dry, and they offered themselves to his like an oblation. It was the first time she had kissed any man, and although she was perfectly innocent and entirely ignorant, yet the instincts of nature throbbed within her, and she pressed her lips close against his.

Denis was overwhelmed. His mild experience as a gallant had encompassed nothing like this, and, feeling as if he had received a rare and wonderful gift, without knowing what he did, he dropped spontaneously upon his knees beside Mary and, clasping his arms around her, pressed his face in homage against her dress. The smell of the rough worn serge of her skirt was fragrant to him; he felt her legs, so pathetically slender and immature, tremble slightly under his touch. Clasping her hand he drew her down beside him. Now he could see the little hollow in her neck and from it a tiny blue vein running down. As he took off her hat a ringlet of hair fell over her smoothly pale brow, and first he kissed that awkwardly, humbly, with a clumsiness which did him credit, before he laid his lips upon her eyes and closed them with his kisses.

Now they were in each other's arms, sheltered by rushes and bushes of broom, the soft grass plastic beneath them. The contact of their bodies gave them a delicious warmth so that there was no need of speech, and in silence they left the world, knowing and caring nothing but for each other. Her head lay back on his arm, and between her parted lips her teeth shone in the moonlight like small white seeds. Her breath was like new milk. Again he saw in the arch of her neck the small vein threaded under the smooth skin, like a tiny rivulet through virgin snow, and caressingly, he stroked it, gently tracing with his finger tips its lovely downward passage. How firm and round her breasts were, each like a smooth and perfect unplucked fruit enclosed within his palm for him to fondle! The pressure of his hand sent the hot colour into her face, and though her breath came faster, yet she suffered him. She felt these small virgin breasts, the consideration of which had never before invaded the realm of her consciousness, grow turgid, as if an ichor from her blood had filled them, and all her puny strength surged into them as though from her nipples drops might well forth to an invisible suckling. Then her mind was dazzled, and, as she lay with closed eyes in his embrace, she forgot everything, knew nothing, ceased to be herself, and was his. Her spirit rushed to meet his swifter than a swallow's flight and together uniting, leaving their bodies upon the earth, they soared into the rarer air. Together they floated upwards as lightly as the two moths and as soundlessly as the river. No dimension contained them, no tie of earth restrained the ecstasy of their flight.

The lights in the fair-ground went out one by one; an old frog, its large, sad eyes jewelled in the moonlight, broke through the grasses beside them, then noiselessly departed; a dim white mist sheathed the radiance of the river like breath upon a mirror; then, as the lace veils of vapour loomed over the land, crepuscular shadows filled the hollows of the meadows, and the earth grew faintly colder as though its heat had been chilled by the rimed air. With the falling mist all sound was blotted out and the stillness became absolute until after a long time a trout jumped upstream and splashed heavily in its pool.

At the sound, Mary stirred slowly, and consciousness of the world half returning, she whispered softly:

"Denis I love you. Dear, dear Denis! But it's late, very late! We must go."

She lifted her head heavily, moved her drugged limbs slowly, then, like a flash the recollection of her father, her home, her position here, invaded her mind. She started up, terrified, horrified with herself.

"Oh! what have I done? My father! What will become of us?" she cried. "I'm mad to be here like this."

Denis stood up.

"No harm will come to you, Mary," he said as he essayed to soothe her. "I love you! I will take care of you."

"Let me go then," she replied while tears ran down her pale cheeks. "Oh! I must be back before he gets in or I'll be shut out all night. I'd have no home!"

"Don't cry, dear Mary," he entreated, "it hurts me to see you cry. It's not so very late—not eleven o'clock yet! Besides I am responsible for everything, all the blame is mine."

"No! No!" she cried, "it's all my fault, Denis. I should never have come. I disobeyed my father. I'll be the one to suffer."

Denis placed his arm around her trembling form and, looking again into her eyes, said firmly:

"You will not suffer, Mary! Before we go I want you to understand one thing. I love you. I love you above everything. I am going to marry you."

"Yes, yes," she sobbed. "Only let me get home. I must. My father will kill me! If he's not late to-night something terrible will happen to me—to us both." She started off at a run up the path, slipping and stumbling in her anxiety to make haste, whilst he followed, trying to console and comfort her, uttering words of the most endearing tenderness. But, although at his words she ceased to weep, she still ran and did not speak again until they reached the edge of the town. There she stopped abruptly.

"Don't come any further, Denis," she panted. "This is enough! We might meet him—my father."

"But it's so dark on the road," he protested. "I'm afraid to leave you."

"You must go, Denis! He might come on us together."

"But the darkness?"

"I can't help that. I'll run all the way."

"It'll hurt you if you race home like that, Mary, and it's so black, the road seems so lonely now."

"Leave me! you must!" she cried. "I'll go myself! Good-bye!"

With a last touch of his hand she fled from him; her figure dissolved into the blackness, and was gone.

As he gazed into the impenetrable gloom, vainly trying to follow her rapid flight, wondering if he should call to her or follow her, he raised his arms in perplexity, as though beseeching her to return to him, then slowly he lowered them and, after a long passivity, turned heavily upon his heel, and took his dejected way towards his own home.

Meanwhile in a panic of urgency; Mary forced her tired body along the road, the same road that she had so lightly traversed earlier on this same evening, having lived, it seemed to her, a whole century in time and experience during the space of these few intervening hours. It was unthinkable that she, Mary Brodie, should be at this time of night alone in the open streets; the sound of her solitary footsteps frightened her, echoing aloud like a reiterated accusation for her father, for everyone to hear, shouting out the madness, the iniquity of her present situation. Denis wanted to marry her! He must be mad too— madly unaware of her father and of the circumstances of her life. The echoes of her steps mocked her, whispering that she had been bereft of her senses to plunge herself in this predicament, making the very contemplation of her love for Denis a painful and grotesque absurdity.

As she neared her home, suddenly she became aware of another figure in front of her, and the dread that it might be her father filled her with numb apprehension. Although he frequently did not return from the club until after eleven o'clock, sometimes he was earlier, and as she drew nearer, silently gaining upon the figure, she felt that it must be he. But, all at once, a gasp of relief escaped her, as she perceived that it was her brother, and, abandoning her caution, she ran up to him, panting:

"Matt! Oh! Matt! Wait!" and stumbling against him, she clutched his arm like a drowning woman.

"Mary!" he exclaimed, starting violently, hardly able to believe his eyes.

"Yes! It's me, Matt, and thank God it's you! I thought it was father at first."

"But—— But what on earth are you out for at this time of night?" he cried, in shocked amazement. "Where have you been?"

"Never mind just now, Matt," she gasped. "Let us get in quick before father. Please, Matt, dear! Don't ask me anything!"

"But what have you been up to? Where have you been?" he repeated. "What will Mamma think?"

"Mamma will think I've gone to bed, or that I'm reading in my room. She knows I often do that when I'm sitting up for you."

"Mary! This is a terrible escapade. I don't know what to do about it. It's shameful to find you out in the street at this time of night." He moved on a few steps then, as a thought struck him, stopped abruptly. "I wouldn't like Miss Moir to know about this. It's disgraceful! Such a going-on by my sister might prejudice me in her eyes."

"Don't tell her, Matt! Don't tell anybody! Only let us get in. Where is your key?" Mary urged.

Muttering under his breath, Matthew advanced to the front steps, and while Mary gasped with relief to see that the outer door was unbolted, which meant that her father had not returned, he opened the door.

The house was still, no one awaited her, no recriminations or accusations were hurled at her, and realising that she was miraculously undiscovered, in a transport of thanksgiving Mary took her brother's hand, and in the darkness they crept noiselessly up the stairs.

Inside her own room she drew a deep breath, and as she felt her way securely about its known confines, the very touch of familiar objects reassured her. Thank God she was safe! Nobody would know! She tore off her clothes in the dark and crept into bed, when instantly the cool sheets soothed her warm weariness and the soft pillow caressed her aching head. Her hot, tired body relaxed in an exquisite abandon, her trembling eyelids closed, her fingers uncurled from her palms, her head drooped towards her shoulder, and with her last waking thought of Denis, her breathing grew regular and tranquil. She slept.

III

JAMES BRODIE awoke next morning with the sun streaming in through his window. He had especially designated this room at the back of the house as his bedroom because, with an animal appreciation of sunshine, he loved the bright morning rays to strike in and waken him, to soak through the blankets into his receptive body, and saturate his being with a sense of power and radiance. "There's no sun like the morning sun," was one of his favourite sayings, one of his stock of apparently profound axioms which he drew upon largely in his conversation and repeated with a knowing and astute air. "The mornin' sun's the thing! We don't get enough o' it, but in MY room I've made sure o' all that's goin'."

He yawned largely and stretched his massive frame luxuriously, observed with half-opened yet appreciative eyes the golden swarm of motes that swam around him, then, after a moment, blinked questioningly towards the clock on the mantelpiece, the hands of which marked only eight o'clock; becoming aware that he had another quarter of an hour in bed, he put his head down, rolled over on his side, and dived beneath the blankets like a gigantic porpoise. But soon he came up again. Despite the beauty of the morning, despite the brosy odour of the boiling porridge which his wife was preparing downstairs and which, arising, gently titillated his nostrils, his present humour lacked the full complacency which he felt it should have held.

Moodily, as though seeking the cause of his discontent, he turned and surveyed the hollow on the other side of the big bed, which his wife had left a full hour ago when, according to custom, she had arisen in good time to have everything in order and his breakfast ready upon the table the moment he came down. What good, he reflected resentfully, was a woman like that to a man like him? She might cook, wash, scrub, darn his socks, brush his boots, aye, and lick his boots too; but what kind of armful was she now? Besides, since her last confinement, when she had borne him Nessie, she had been always ailing, in a weak, whining way, offending his robust vigour by her flaccid impotence, and provoking his distaste by her sickly habits. Out of the corner of his eye when she thought herself unobserved, as in the early hours of the morning when she left the bed before him, he would contemplate her almost stealthy dressing with disgust. Only last Sunday he had detected her in the act of concealing some soiled garment, and had roared at her like an angry ram: "Don't make a midden of my bedroom! It's bad enough for me to put up with you without havin' your dirty clothes flung in my face!" She had, he considered bitterly, long since been repugnant to him; the very smell of her was obnoxious to him, and had he not been a decent man, he might well have looked elsewhere. What had he dreamed last night? He thrust out his lower lip longingly and stretched his legs powerfully as he played with the vision of his sleep, thinking of the tantalising young jade he had chased through the woods who, though he had run like a stag, had been saved by the fleetness of her foot. She had run, faster than a deer, her long hair flying behind her, and with not a stitch on her back to cumber her, but still, despite her speed, had turned to smile at him enticingly, provokingly. If he had only gotten a grip of her, he thought, allowing his erotic fancy to riot delightfully as he lay back, basking his ponderous body in the sun, his parted lips twitching with a half lewd, half sardonic amusement, he would have made her pipe to a different tune.

Suddenly he observed that it was quarter past eight and, without warning, he jumped out of bed, put on his socks, trousers, and slippers, and pulled off his long nightgown. His naked torso gleamed sleekly and the muscles of his shoulders and back undulated like pliant knotted ropes under the white skin which shone like smooth satin, except where the thick brown hair was felted on the chest, dense and adherent as lichen upon a rock. For a moment he stood thus, placed before the small mirror above the washstand, admiring his clear eye, his strong white teeth, and running his fingers with a bristling sound over the stubble on his heavy jaw. Then, still stripped to the waist, he turned, took up a mahogany box of razors wherein lay seven special hollow-ground Sheffield blades with their ivory handles marked each with a day of the week, carefully picked out the one inlaid with the word Friday, tried the temper appreciatively against his thumb nail and began to strop it slowly upon the leather thong which hung near from its appointed hook. The strap was thick, and, as Matthew and Mary had testified in their younger days, of an enduring toughness, and as Brodie worked the razor slowly up and down upon its tan surface it set the true blade to an infinite keenness. When he had adjusted the edge to his satisfaction, he went to the door, picked up his hot shaving water which

43

was there, steaming, to the minute, returned to the mirror, lathered his face copiously, and began to shave with long, precise movements. He shaved meticulously, leaving his chin and cheeks as smooth as silk, cautiously avoiding the glossy curl of his moustache and sweeping the razor against his tense skin with such firm, measured strokes that it filled the silence of the room with a regularly intermittent rhythm of crisp, rustling sound. Shaved, he cleaned the razor upon a slip of paper taken from a specially cut pile, which it was Nessie's duty to prepare and replenish, re-stropped it and replaced it in its case; then, decanting the large ewer into its basin, he washed extravagantly in cold water, splashing it upon his face and sluicing lavish handfuls about his chest, head, and arms. This prodigal use of cold water even on the iciest mornings of winter was his inflexible habit, maintaining, he claimed, his perfect health, and saving him from the catarrhal colds which so frequently affected his spouse. "I slunge myself in cold water," he would often boast, "as cold as I can get it. Ay! I wad break the ice to dook myself, and the more frozen it is the warmer it makes me after. It doesna make me chatter or snivel wi' a red nose, like some folks I could mention. No! No! It makes me glow. Give me plenty cold, cold water—there's health in it"; and now, as he vigorously applied a coarse rough towel to his body, whilst he hissed between his teeth like an ostler, he felt a ruddy glow sweep through him and dispel in part the rankness of his early mood.

He finished his dressing by assuming, with scrupulous care, a shirt of fine, expensive linen, starched Gladstone collar and bird's-eye cravat fixed with a gold horseshoe pin, embroidered grey waistcoat, and long coat of superfine broadcloth. Then he went downstairs.

Breakfast he invariably ate alone. Matthew left the house at six, Nessie at half-past eight, his mother was never up before ten o'clock, Mrs. Brodie and Mary took their morning meal privately and when they chose in the dim regions where cooking was performed, and it fell therefore that Brodie sat down to his large bowl of porridge in solitary dignity. He enjoyed all his meals, but to breakfast in particular he brought, in the freshness of morning, a more lively appetite, and he now addressed himself eagerly to his porridge, and after, to the two fresh eggs lightly boiled to the requisite second and shelled into a large cup, to the large soft rolls and thick fresh butter, and to his coffee, a beverage of which he was inordinately fond and one permitted to no one else in the household.

As Mary passed soundlessly in and out of the room during the meal to serve him he noticed from beneath his lowered lids how pale she looked, but he made no remark, for it was his policy not to encourage his womenfolk to consider themselves ill; it gave him, nevertheless, an inward satisfaction as he attributed the subdued look and dark circles under her eyes to the shrewd attack he had launched on her on the previous night.

According to custom, when he had breakfasted, and that in silence, he left the house at nine-thirty precisely, and stood for a moment at his front gate looking back appreciatively at his property. His proud glance swept the small domain, observing that not a weed sprouted in the gravelled yard, not a spot disgraced the paintwork, not a blemish marked the grim grey stone, and approving with intense complacency the work of his own creation. It was his! Five years ago he had bought the land and approaching Urie the builder, had spoken to him at length, drawn rough diagrams, and described fully the nature of the house he desired. Urie, a blunt man and a man of substance, had looked at him in astonishment, saying:

"Man alive! you're not a stone-mason or you wouldna let your ideas run awa' wi' you like that. Your head must be in the clouds. Do ye realise what that sketch would look like in stone and mortar?"

"I'm going to live in it, Urie—not you," Brodie had replied steadily.

"But there's so much unnecessary work on it. Just take the expense o' piercin' this wee piece o' parapet! What good is it?" and Urie flicked the pencilled outline before him.

"I'm payin' for it, Urie—not you," again replied Brodie.

The builder had pushed his hat over his ears, scratched his head uncomprehendingly with his pencil, and expostulated: "You're not serious, Brodie! It would be all right if it were ten times as big, but you're only wantin' a six room and kitchen house. It's preposterous. You'll make yoursel' the laughin' stock o' the town."

"I'll attend to that," cried Brodie grimly. "God help the man that laughs at James Brodie to his face!"

"Come, come now, Brodie," the other had conciliated, "let me put you up a solid respectable bit villa, not this wee kind o' sham castle that you're haverin' about."

Brodie's eyes took on a strange expression, as though a dark fire flickered there, and he shouted out:

"Damn ye, Urie! Keep your tongue civil when ye speak to me. I want none o' your smug bandboxes. I want a house that befits me"; then in a flash he had recovered himself and in a normal, quiet tone added: "If you don't like it ye needna touch it. I'm givin' ye the chance, but if ye don't wish to take it there are other builders in Levenford."

Urie stared at him and whistled.

"Sits the wind in that quarter. Well! Well! If you're set on it I'll get a plan and an estimate out for you. A wilful man maun have his way. But don't forget I warned ye. Don't come and ask me to take the house down again once it's up."

"No! No! Urie," Brodie had sneered. "I'll only come back to ye if ye don't give me what I'm askin' for, and then it'll not be pleasant hearin' for ye. Get ahead wi' it now and don't blabber so much."

The plans had been prepared, passed by Brodie, and the building begun. From day to day he had seen it grow, going along in the cool evenings to the slowly mantling building, observing the exact adherence to his design, gloating over the smooth, white stone, testing the mortar between his fingers, caressing the shining lead pipes, weighing and fingering approvingly the heavy square slates. Everything had been of the best materials, and though this had taken heavy toll upon his purse, had in fact drained it—for he had always spent money freely upon himself, would indeed never have saved but for this one object— he was proud to have achieved it, proud to have left the rented house in Levengrove Place, proud in the possession of the inmost desire of his heart. He was right too. Nobody laughed openly. One night, shortly after the house had been completed, a loafer at the Cross stepped out from the toping gang that loitered there, and accosted Brodie.

"Good evening, Mr. Brodie," he hiccoughed, looking round at his fellows for approbation, then back at Brodie. "And how is the castle to-night?"

Brodie looked at him calmly. "Better than you," he replied, and smashed his fist with terrific violence into the rowdy's face, then, taking the clean linen handkerchief from his pocket, and wiping the blood from his knuckles, he threw it contemptuously on the ground beside the fallen man and walked quietly away.

Certainly Brodie's position in the town had altered sensibly in these last five years, and since the building of his house he was regarded with more significance, detachment, and misgiving; his social value increased at the price of singularity, and he became gradually a more notable figure with many acquaintances and no friends.

Now he took a final look at his property, squared his shoulders, and set off down the road. He had not proceeded far before he caught a glimpse of a peering face from behind the front-room curtains of one of the semi-detached houses further down, and he jeered inwardly to see that it was little Pettigrew, the grocer, who had recently moved into the select neighbourhood, and had at first sought to establish himself by walking ingratiatingly to the town with Brodie. The big man had tolerated this liberty for the first day, but when on the second morning he found the diminutive, unimportant grocer again waiting for him, he had stopped short. "Pettigrew," he had said calmly, "I'm afraid I'm not seein' so weel this mornin'. You're kind o' wee and shilpet to me the day and to-morrow I mightna see you ava'. Besides I'm a fast walker. Gang your own gait, man, but don't strain your bandy wee legs keepin' pace with me. Good morning to you." Now he smiled sardonically as he passed the house, reflecting that since then the nervous Pettigrew had avoided him like a plague and had formed the habit of watching him well out of sight before venturing into the street.

Soon he had traversed the quieter residential district and entered the town where, at the south end of Church Street, an artisan carrying his bag of tools touched his cap to him in passing. Brodie's chest expanded at this act of deference, accorded only to the most important figures in the town. "Good morning to you," he cried affably, setting his head further back in a proud geniality, marching round the corner into the High Street with his stick over his shoulder, and tramping up the incline like a soldier until he reached the crest of this main thoroughfare. There he stopped opposite an inconspicuous shop. The shop was old and quiet with a narrow, unostentatious front marked by a small single window that displayed no merchandise, but masked its face discreetly behind an interior screen of fine-meshed wire, which, though it veiled the window, revealed the hidden secret of the shop by bearing upon its drawn grey filigree, in faded gilt lettering, the one word—Hatter. It was, then, apparently a hat shop, but although it held the most commanding situation in the town, it not only disguised its character but seemed to remove itself from public observation, receding slightly from the common frontage of the street, and permitting the adjacent buildings to project beyond and above it, as though it wished to remain, despite the fixed solidity of its position, as unobserved and unobtrusive as it might, reserving its contents, and striving to conceal itself and all that lay within from vulgar, prying eyes. Above its doorway the sign, too, was bleached by age and weather, its paint finely cracked by sun, and smoothly washed by rain; but, still distinguishable upon it in thin sloped letters across its surface, was the name—James Brodie. This was Brodie's shop. Each morning, as he regarded it, the fact that he should possess it never failed to amuse him, and for twenty years he had inwardly regarded his business with a tolerant derision. It was of course the sole means of his livelihood, the unimpressive source of his stately and inspiring habitation, its solid, steady business the origin of his fine clothes and the money he rattled so easily in his pockets; yet his attitude towards it was that of a man who views with an indulgent yet contemptuous air some trifling and unbecoming foible within his own nature. He—Brodie—was a hatter! He was not ashamed of the fact, but gloried in its ridiculous incongruity, revelled in the contrast between himself and the profession of his adoption which he knew must continually present itself to the world at large. He turned and surveyed the street from his elevated position like a monarch offering himself freely to the public gaze. He was only a hatter! The richness of the absurdity of his position was always before him, inevitably appealed to him, and now an internal diversion shook him as he moved into his shop to start another day's work.

Inside, the shop was dark, neglected, and almost dingy, its dim interior bisected by a long counter which ran the length of the room, acting as a barrier between the public and the private divisions of the establishment and bearing upon its worn, indented surface at one end a graduated series of tarnished brass stands each supporting a hat or cap of different style and colour. At the other distant end, the counter joined the wall as a ledge capable of elevation, thus permitting ingress to a short row of steps leading to a door with a ground glass window on which was inscribed the word Office. Running backwards, beside and underneath this elevated compartment, was a small L-shaped cupboard of a back shop that, deprived of its original dimensions by the more recent imposition of the Office, contained with some difficulty in its limited extent an ironing-board and an iron stove which, with its perpetual blast, dried more thoroughly the already sapless and vitiated air. In the shop itself the walls were covered in a drab crimson paper upon which hung several old prints; although few hats were to be seen, and upon these no prices were displayed, behind the counter stood a series of wide mahogany drawers for caps, and a·long line of shelves upon which stacks of cardboard boxes ranged from floor to ceiling.

Behind the counter, and in front of this abundant but hidden stock, stood a young man whose appearance suggested that his stock of virtues must also be concealed. He was thin, with an etiolated countenance which palely protested against the lack of sunlight in the shop, and which was faintly pitted with honourable scars gained in his perpetual struggle against an addiction to boils, a disorder to which he was unhappily subject, attributed by his devoted mother to thin blood and against which she continually fortified him with Pepper's Quinine and Iron Tonic.

The general engaging aspect of his features was not, however, marred to any extent by these minor blemishes, nor by a small but obtrusive wart which had most inconsiderately chosen its location upon the extremity of his nose, and was well set off by a shock of dark hair, feathered, despite its careful oiling, and so frosted with dandruff that it shed its surplus flakes and formed a perpetual rime upon his coat collar.

The remainder of his person was pleasing, and his dress suited soberly to his position; but about him clung a peculiar, sour odour occasioned by a tendency towards free perspiration, particularly from his feet, a regrettable but unavoidable misfortune that occasionally induced Brodie to fling him out of the back door, which abutted upon the Leven, together with a cake of soap and a profane injunction to wash the offending members. This was Peter Perry, messenger, assistant, salesman, disciple of the stove and ironing-board, lackey of the master, and general factotum enrolled in one.

As Brodie entered he inclined his body forward, his hands pressed deeply on to the counter, fingers extended, elbows flexed, showing more of the top of his head than his face and, in a passion of obsequiousness, awaited his master's greeting.

"Mornin', Perry."

"Good morning, Mr. Brodie, sir," replied Perry with nervous haste, showing a little less of his hair and a little more of his face. "A very beautiful morning again, sir! Wonderful for the time of year. Delightful!" He paused appreciatively before continuing: "Mr. Dron has been in to see you this morning, on business he said, sir."

"Dron! what the devil does he want?"

"I'm sure I couldn't say, sir. He said he'd come back later."

"Humph!" grunted Brodie. He strode into his office, flung himself into a chair and, disregarding the several business letters that lay on the desk, lit his pipe. Then he tilted his hat well back on his head—it was a sign of personal superiority that he never removed it at his business —and took up the *Glasgow Herald*, that had been placed carefully to his hand.

He read the leading article slowly, moving his lips over the words; although occasionally he was obliged to go over an involved sentence twice in order to grasp its meaning, he persisted tenaciously. At times he would lower the paper and look blankly at the wall in front, using the full power of his sluggish mentality, striving to comprehend fully the sense of the context. It was a stern, matutinal task which Brodie set himself to assimilate the *Herald's* political editorial, but he considered it his duty as a man of standing to do so. Besides, it was thus that he provided himself with weighty argument for his more serious conversation, and to this purpose he never failed to accomplish the task, although by next morning he had completely forgotten the gist of what he had read.

Half a column had been battled with in this dogged fashion when a diffident tap upon the glass panel disturbed him.

"What is it?" shouted Brodie.

Perry, for only Perry could have knocked like that, replied through the closed door:

"Mr. Dron to see you, sir."

"What the devil does he want? Does he not know I'm at the *Herald's* leader and can't be disturbed?"

Dron, a dejected, insignificant individual, was standing close behind Perry and could hear every word, a fact of which Brodie was maliciously aware, and which induced him, with a satirical humour, to couch his replies in the most disagreeable terms and in the loudest tones he could. Now, with a faint grin upon his face, he listened over his lowered paper to the muffled consultation outside the door.

"He says, Mr. Brodie, he won't keep you a minute," insinuated Perry.

"A minute, does he say! Dearie me, now. He'll be lucky if he gets a second. I havena the least desire to see him," bawled Brodie. "Ask him what he wants, and if it's not important the little runt can save his breath to cool his porridge." Again there was a whispered colloquy, during which Perry, with vigorous pantomime more expressive than his words, indicated that he had done everything to further the other's interests compatible with his own safety and security.

"Speak to him yourself, then," he mumbled finally, in self-acquittal, seceding from the cause and backing away to his counter. Dron opened the door an inch and peered in with one eye.

"You're there, are you?" remarked Brodie, without removing his eyes from the paper, which he had again raised in a grand pretence of reading. Dron cleared his throat and opened the door a little further.

"Mr. Brodie, could I have a word wi' you just for a wee minute? I'll not keep ye more nor that," he exclaimed, working himself gradually into the office through the slight opening he had cautiously made for himself.

"What is it, then?" growled Brodie, looking up in annoyance. "I've no dealings wi' you that I'm aware of. You and me are birds that don't fly together."

"I ken that well, Mr. Brodie," replied the other humbly, "and that's the very reason I've come to see ye. I came more or less to ask your advice, and to put a small suggestion before ye."

"What is't, then? Don't stand there like a hen on a hot griddle."

Dron fumbled nervously with his cap. "Mr. Brodie, I havena been doin' too well lately at my trade, and I really came in regarding that little property o' mine next door."

Brodie looked up. "You mean the tumble-down shop that's been empty these three months past. Who could help seeing it? Man, it's an eyesore in the street."

"I ken it's been empty a long time," replied Dron meekly, "but it's an asset in a way—in fact it's about the only asset I've got now—and what wi' gettin' a bit desperate one way and another an idea struck me that I thocht might interest you."

"Indeed, now," sneered Brodie, "is not that interestin'! Ye have the lang head on ye, sure enough, to get all these inspirations—it'll be the Borough Council for ye next. Well! what is the great idea?"

"I was thinking," returned the other diffidently, "that with your grand business and perhaps a shop that was a little too small for ye, ye might consider extendin' by taking in my place and making one big premises with perhaps a plate-glass window or two."

Brodie looked at him cuttingly, for a long moment.

"Dear, dear! And it was to extend my business you worked out all this and came in twice in the one mornin'," he said at last.

"Indeed no, Mr. Brodie. I've just told ye things have been goin' rather ill with me lately, and what with one thing and another, and the wife expecting again soon, I must get a bend on to let my property."

"Now that's too bad," purred Brodie. "It's you small, snuffy men that will have the large families. I hope ye're not makin' me responsible for your latest addition though. Ay, ye're fond o' the big family, I know.

I've heard tell ye've that many weans ye can't count them. But," he continued in a changed voice, "don't make me responsible for them. My business is my own and I manage it my own way. I would as soon think of a cheap-lookin' plate-glass window as I would of giving away pokes o' sweeties with my hats. Demn you, man, don't you know I've the most distinguished people in the borough as my clients and my friends? Your empty shop's been a fester on my respectable office for months. Let it for God's sake. Let it by all means. Let it to auld Nick if ye like, but you'll never let it to me. Now get out and don't ever bother me like this again. I'm a busy man and I've no time for your stupid yammerin'!"

"Very well, Mr. Brodie," replied the other quietly, twisting his hat in his hands. "I'm sorry if I've offended ye, but I thought there was no harm in asking—but you're a hard man to speak to." He turned disconsolately to depart, but at that moment an agitated Perry shot himself into the room.

"Sir John's gig is at the door, Mr. Brodie," he stammered. "I saw it drive up this very minute!"

The assistant might deal with the less important, with, indeed, the bulk of the customers, to whom it was his duty to attend without disturbing Brodie, but when a personage came into the shop he knew his orders, and raced for his master like a startled greyhound.

Brodie lifted his eyebrows with a look at Dron which said: "You see!"; then, taking him firmly by the elbow, as he had no wish to be confronted by Sir John in the other's undistinguished company, he hurried him out of the office and through the shop, expediting his passage through the outer door with a final push. The indignity of this last, powerful, unexpected shove completely upset Dron, and, with a stagger, he slipped, his legs shot from under him, and he landed full upon his backside at the very moment that Sir John Latta stepped out of his gig.

Latta laughed vociferously, as he entered the shop and came close up to Brodie.

"It's the most amusing thing I've seen for ages, Brodie. The look on the poor man's face would have brought the house down at Drury's," he cried, slapping his thigh with his driving gloves. "But it's a blessing he wasn't hurt. Was he dunning you?" he asked slyly.

"Not at all, Sir John! He's just a bit blether of a man that's always making a public nuisance of himself."

"A little fellow like that?" He looked at the other appraisingly. "You know you can't realise your own strength, man! You're an uncommon powerful barbarian."

"I just flicked him with my pinkie," declared Brodie complacently, delighted to have so opportunely attracted the other's notice, and feeling it sweet incense for his pride to receive attention from the distinguished principal of the famous Latta Shipyard. "I could whip up a dozen like him with one hand," he added carelessly—"not that I would soil my fingers that way. It's beneath my consideration."

Sir John Latta was gazing at him quizzically along his finely chiselled nose. "You're a character, Brodie, you know! I suppose that's why we cherish you," he said. "The body of a Hercules and the mind of—well——" He smiled. "Shall we put a glove on it for you? You know the tag, 'odi profanum vulgus et arceo'?"

"Quite so! Quite so!" replied Brodie agreeably. "You've a neat way o' puttin' things, Sir John. There was something like that in the *Herald* this mornin'. I'm with you there!" He had not the least idea what the other was talking about.

"Don't let things run away with you though, Brodie," said Sir John, with a warning shake of his head. "A little of some things goes a long way. You're not to start knocking the borough about. And don't offer us too much baronial caviare. I hope you get my meaning. Well," he added, abruptly changing the subject and his manner, allowing the latter to become formal, more distant, "I mustn't dally, for I'm in really a hurry—I have a meeting—but I want a panama hat—the real thing, you know. I haven't felt sun like this since I was in Barbados. Get some down from Glasgow if needs be. You have my size."

"You shall have a selection to choose from at Levenford House this very afternoon," replied Brodie complacently. "I'll not leave it to my staff. I'll see to it myself."

"Good! And by the by, Brodie," he continued, arresting himself on his way to the door. "I almost forgot that my agents write me from Calcutta that they're ready for your boy. He can leave on the *Irrawaddy* on June the fourteenth. She's a Denny-built packet, nineteen hundred tons, you know. Fine boat! Our people will look after his berth for him."

"That is more than kind of you, Sir John," purred Brodie. "I'm deeply grateful. I'm most indebted for the way you've put yourself about for me over that matter."

"Nothing! Nothing!" replied the other absently. "We've got plenty young fellows at this end, but we want them at our docks out there—the right kind that's to say! The climate's really nothing to speak of, but he'll need to watch the life out there. It sometimes knocks a young fellow off his feet. I'll have a word with him if I've time. I hope he does well for your sake. By the way, how is that remarkably pretty daughter of yours?"

"Quite fair."

"And the clever little sprat?"

"Splendid, Sir John."

"And Mrs. Brodie?"

"Middling well, thank ye."

"Good! Well, I'm off now! Don't forget that hat of mine."

He was into his gig, a fine, spare, patrician figure of a man, had taken the reins from his groom and was off, spanking down the High Street, with the smooth, glossy flanks of the cob gleaming, and the high lights flashing on whirling spokes, gleaming metal, shining liveried cockade, and upon the rich lustre of varnished coachwork,.

Rubbing his hands together, his eye dilating with a suppressed exultation, Brodie returned from the doorway, and, to Perry, who had remained, a drooping, nebulous shadow in the background, he cried, with unwonted volubility:

"Did ye hear that conversation we had? Was it not grand? Was it not enough to make these long lugs o' yours stand out from your head? But I suppose the half of it was above ye. You'll not understand the Latin. No! but you heard what Sir John said to me—gettin' that post for my son and speirin' all about my family. Answer me, ye puir fool," he called out. "Did you hear what Sir John Latta said to James Brodie?"

"Yes, sir," stammered Perry, "I heard!"

"Did you see how he treated me?" whispered Brodie.

"Certainly I did, Mr. Brodie!" replied the other, with returning confidence, perceiving that he was not to be rebuked for eavesdropping. "I wasn't meaning to—to overhear or to spy on you, but I did observe you both, sir, and I agree with you. Sir John is a fine man. He was more than good to my mother when my father died so sudden. Oh! yes, indeed, Mr. Brodie, Sir John has a kind word and a kind action for everybody."

Brodie eyed him scornfully. "Faugh!" he said contemptuously. "What are you ravin' about, you witless creature! You don't know what I mean, you poor worm! You don't understand." Disregarding the other's crushed appearance as beneath his notice, he stepped upwards into his office once more, arrogantly, imperiously, and resumed his big chair, then, as he gathered together the sheets of his morning paper before his unseeing eyes, he muttered softly to himself, like one who dallies wantonly, yet seriously, with a profound and cherished secret: "They don't understand. They don't understand!"

For a full minute he remained staring blankly in front of him, while a dull glow lurked deeply in his eye, then, with a sudden toss of his head and a powerful effort of will, he seemed to thrust something violently from him as though he feared it might master him; shaking his body like a huge dog, he recollected himself, observed the paper in front of him, and, with a visage once more composed and tranquil, began again to read.

IV

"MARY, put the kettle on the fire. We'll be back in time for me to give Matt some tea before he goes off to see Agnes," said Mrs. Brodie, drawing on her black kid gloves with prim lips and a correct air, adding: "Mind and have it boiling, now, we'll not be that long." She was dressed for one of her rare sorties into the public street, strangely unlike herself in black, flowing paletot and a plumed helmet of a hat, and beside her stood Matthew, looking stiff and sheepish in a brand new suit, so new indeed that when he was not in motion his trouser legs stood to attention with edges sharp as parallel presenting swords. It was an unwonted sight on the afternoon of a day in midweek, but the occasion was sufficiently memorable to warrant the most unusual event, being the eve of Matthew's departure for Calcutta. Two days ago he had, for the last time, laid down his pen and picked up his hat in the office at the shipyard, and since then had lived in a state of perpetual movement and strange unreality, where life passed before him like a mazy dream, where, in his conscious moments, he became aware of himself in situations both unusual and alarming. Upstairs his case stood packed, his clothing protected by camphor balls, so numerous that they had invaded even the inside of the mandolin, and so powerful that the entire house smelled like the new Levenford Cottage Hospital, greeting him whenever he entered the house with an odious reminder of his departure. Everything that the most experienced globe trotter could desire lay in that trunk, from the finest obtainable solar topee given by his father and a morocco-bound Bible by his mother to the patent automatic opening water-bottle from Mary and the small pocket compass that Nessie had bought with the accumulation of her Saturday pennies.

Now that his leave-taking was at hand Matthew had experienced during the last few days a well-defined sinking feeling in the vicinity of his navel, and though of his own volition he would willingly and self-sacrificingly have abandoned the thrill of such a disturbing emotion, like a nervous recruit before an action, the pressure of circumstances forbade his retirement. The lions which had arisen in his imagination and leapt glibly from his tongue a short week ago to engage the fascinated attention of Mary and Mamma, now returned growling, to torment him in his dreams. Renewed assurances from people connected with the yard that Calcutta was at the least a larger community than Levenford failed to comfort him, and before retiring each night he cultivated the habit of searching for snakes which might be perfidiously concealed beneath his pillow.

For Mrs. Brodie the emotional influence of the occasion had provided a strong stimulus, as though she felt at last able to identify herself in a situation worthy of a leading character in one of her beloved novels.

Like a Roman matron renouncing her son to the State with spartan fortitude, or, more sensibly, a Christian mother sending out a second Livingstone on a mission of hope and glory, she forsook her meek despondency and, bearing up nobly, packed, repacked, devised, succoured, comforted, encouraged, and exhorted, and sprinkled her conversation with text and prayer.

Brodie had not missed the change in her, gauging with a sardonic eye the explanation of the transient phase. "You're makin' a bonny exhibition o' yourself, my woman," he had sneered at her, "wi' your posing and posturin', and your runnin' after that big gowk o' yours, and your cups o' tea and snashters at a' hours. Ye would think ye were Queen Victoria to look at ye. Is it a general ye're sendin' out to the war or what? that you're blowin' yerself out like a pig's bladder. I know well what will happen. Whenever he's away ye'll collapse, and we'll have ye back on our hands more o' a dreich empty bag than ever. Faugh! Let some sense in that silly skull o' yours, for God's sake."

She had felt him cold, unfeeling, even callous, as she feebly expostulated: "But, father, we maun give the boy his start. There's a great future in front o' him"; and though, thereafter, concealing her endeavours from her husband, she had redoubled, with an outraged, conscious rectitude, these spirited efforts on behalf of her young, potentially illustrious pioneer.

Now, having adjusted her gloves to a smooth, though nodose, perfection, she remarked: "Are you ready, Matt dear?" in a tone of such forced cheerfulness that it chilled Matthew's very blood. "We are going down, Mary, to the chemist's," she continued in a chatty manner. "The Rev. Mr. Scott told Agnes the other day that the best remedy for malaria was quinine—a wonderful cure he said, so we're off to get a few powders made up." Matthew said nothing, but visions of himself lying, fever-racked, in a crocodile-infested swamp rushed through his mind, and considering glumly that a few scanty powders seemed a paltry protection against such an evil, in his mind he sullenly repudiated the reverend gentleman's suggestion. "What does he know about it, anyway? He's never been there. It's all very fine for him to talk," he thought indignantly, as Mrs. Brodie took his arm and led him, an unwilling victim, from the room.

When they had gone Mary filled the kettle and put it on the hob. She seemed listless and melancholy, due, no doubt, to the thought of losing her brother, and for a week had moved in a spirit of extreme dejection which might reasonably have been entirely attributed to sisterly solicitude. Curiously, though, it was just one week since she had been with Denis at the fair, and though she longed for him, she had not seen him since. That had been an impossibility, as she knew him to be in the North travelling on business, from a letter posted in Perth which, startlingly, she had received from him. It was an event for her at any time to receive a letter (which, on such rare occasions, was inevitably perused by the entire household), but fortunately she had been first down that morning and so no other had seen it, or the sudden throbbing gladness of her face, and she had thus avoided detection, interrogation, and certain discovery.

What felicity it had been to hear from Denis! She realised with an inward thrill that he must have held this paper in his own hands, the hands which had touched her so caressingly, brushed the envelope with those lips which had sealed themselves upon hers, and, as she read the letter behind the locked door of her room, she flushed even in this privacy, at the impetuous, endearing words he wrote. It became evident to her that he desired to marry her and, without considering the obstacles which might be between them, took for granted apparently that she had accepted him.

Now, seated alone in the kitchen, she took the letter from her bodice and re-read it for the hundredth time. Yes! He wrote fervently that he was pining for her, that he could not exist without her, that life to him was now an endless waiting until he should see her, be near to her, be with her always. She sighed, ardently, yet sadly. She, too, was pining for him. Only ten days since that night by the river's brink, and each day more piteous, more dolorous than the one before!

On the first of the seven she had felt ill physically, while the realisation of her boldness, her disobedience of her father, the defiance of every canon of her upbringing struck her in one concentrated blow; but as time passed and the second day merged into the third and she still did not see Denis, the sense of iniquity was swamped by the sense of deprivation, and she forgot the enormity of her conduct in a straining feeling of his necessity to her. On the fourth day, in her sad bewilderment, when she had essayed so constantly to penetrate the unknown and unrealised depths of her experience that it began to appear to her like a strange, painful unreality, his letter had come, raising her at once to a pinnacle of ecstatic relief. He did, then, love her after all, and everything became obliterated in the joy of that one dazzling fact; but on the succeeding days she had gradually slipped from the heights, and now she sat realising the hopelessness of ever obtaining sanction to see Denis, asking herself how she could live without him, wondering what would become of her.

As she pondered, carelessly holding the letter in her hand, old Grandma Brodie entered unobserved.

"What's that you're reading?" she demanded suddenly, peering at Mary.

"Nothing, Grandma, nothing at all," Mary blurted out with a start, stuffing the crushed paper into her pocket.

"It looked to me gey like a letter, and ye seemed in a big hurry to hide it. You're always mopin' and moonin' over something now. I wish

I had my specs. I would soon get to the bottom o' it." She paused, marking the result of her observation malevolently on the tables of her memory. "Tell me," she resumed, "where's that glaikit brother o' yours?"

"Gone to get quinine at the chemist's with Mamma."

"Pah! what he needs is gumption—not quinine. He would need a bucket o' that to stiffen him up. Forbye, some strained castor oil and a drop of good spirits would be more useful to him outbye there. I've no time for sich a palaver that has been goin' on. Everything's upset in the house with the fiddle faddle of it a'. Tell me, is tea earlier to-night?" She clicked her teeth hopefully, scenting like a harpy the nearness of sustenance.

"I don't know, Grandma," replied Mary. Usually the old woman's unbashful eagerness for food left her indifferent, but to-night, in her own troubled perplexity, it nauseated her; without further speech she got up and, feeling that she must be alone and in a less congested atmosphere, went out into the back garden. As she paced back and forwards across the small green she felt it strangely cruel that life should continue to move heedlessly around her in the face of all her sadness and confusion, that Grandma Brodie should still crave greedily for her tea, and the progress of Matt's departure march indifferently along. The current of her thoughts had never flowed so despondently as, with restless movements, she seemed dimly to perceive that the circumstances of her life were conspiring to entrap her. Through the back window she saw Matthew and her mother return, saw Mamma bustle to prepare the table, observed Matthew sit down and begin to eat. What did they care that her brain throbbed with perplexity behind a burning forehead, that she wished one word of compassionate advice but knew not where to seek it? The barren drabness of this back garden, the ridiculous rear view of the outlines of her home, enraged her, and she desired with bitter vehemence to have been born into a family less isolated, less exacting, less inhuman, or, better, not to have been born at all. She envisaged the figure of her father, bestriding, like a formidable colossus, the destiny of the Brodies, and directing her life tyrannically—with an ever watchful, relentless eye. His word it was which had withdrawn her at the age of twelve from school, which she loved, to assist in the duties of the household; he had terminated her budding friendships with other girls because this one was beneath her, or that one lived in a mean house, or another's father had incensed him; his mandate had forbidden her to attend the delightful winter concerts in the Mechanics' Hall on the grounds that she demeaned herself by going; and now he would destroy the sole happiness that life now held for her.

A torrent of rebellion swirled through her; as she felt the injustice of such unnatural restraint, such unconditional limitation of her freedom, she stared defiantly at the meek currant shoots which grew half-heartedly in the hard soil around the garden walls. It was easier, alas, to put them out of countenance than Brodie, as though they, too, infected by the tyranny of their environment, had lost the courage to hold their slender tendrils erect.

A touch on her shoulder startled her, she who had just dared to show fight. It was, however, merely Matthew, who had come to speak to her for a moment before leaving to visit Miss Moir.

"I'll be home early to-night, Mary," he said, "so don't worry about —you know, staying up. And," he added hastily, "now that I'm going abroad I know you'll never mention it to a soul—I would never like it to be known—and thank you a lot for what you've done for me."

This unexpected gratitude from her brother, although its origin lay in a premature wave of nostalgia, and was fostered by the cautious instinct to safeguard his memory against his absence, touched Mary.

"That was nothing to do for you," she replied. "I was only too pleased, Matt. You'll forget all about that worry out there."

"I'll have other things to bother about, I suppose." She had never seen him so subdued, or less self-complacent, and a glow of affection for him warmed her, as she said, "You'll be off to see Agnes now. I'll walk to the gate with you."

As she accompanied him round the side of the house, taking his arm in hers, she sensed the change from the modish young man about town of a fortnight ago to this uncertain timorous youth now by her side. "You'll need to cheer up a bit, Matt," she remarked kindly.

"I don't feel like going now it's come to the bit," he ventured casually.

"You should be glad to get out of here," she replied. "I know I would gladly go. This house seems like a trap to me. I feel I'll never get away from it, as if I might wish to but could not." She paused a moment, then added, "But then you're leaving Agnes behind! That's bound to make all the difference. That's what's making you sad and upsetting you."

"Of course," agreed Matthew. The idea had not occurred to him before in this particular light, but as he turned it over in his mind it was distinctly comforting, and, to his vacillating self-esteem, profoundly reassuring.

"What does father think of Agnes and you?" Mary asked suddenly.

He gazed at her with astonished eyes before he replied, indignantly:

"What do you mean, Mary? Miss Moir is a most estimable girl. No one could think a word against her. She's a remarkably fine girl! What made you ask that?"

"Oh! nothing in particular, Matt," she replied vaguely, refusing to liberate the absurd conception which had arisen in her mind. Agnes Moir, worthy and admirable in every other way, was simply the daughter of a small and completely undistinguished confectioner in the town, and as Brodie himself, in theory at least, kept a shop, he could not repudiate Agnes on that score. But it was he who had obtained this position for Matthew, had insisted upon his going; and Matthew would be absent five years in India. She remembered like a flash the grim, sardonic humour in her father's eyes when he had first announced to his shrinking wife and his startled son, his intention of sending the latter abroad, and for the first time a faint glimmering dawned upon her of her father's mentality. She had always feared and respected him, but now, at the sudden turn of her thoughts, she began almost to hate him.

"I'm off, then, Mary," Matthew was saying. "Ta-ta just now."

Her lips opened to speak, but even as her mind grappled dimly with her suspicions, her eyes fell upon his weak, daunted countenance, striving ineffectually against discouragement, and she let him go without a word.

When he left Mary, Matthew tramped along more confidently, warming his enervated self-assurance at the glow she had unconsciously kindled within him. To be sure he was afraid of leaving Agnes! He felt that at last he had the reason fo his dejection, that stronger men than he would have wavered for a slighter cause, that his despondency did him credit as a noble-hearted lover. He began to feel more like Livingstone again and less like the raw recruit, whistled aloud a few bars of "Juanita," recollected his mandolin, thought, rather inconsistently, of the ladies on the *Irrawaddy*, or possibly in Calcutta, and felt altogether better. He had regained a faint shadow of his normal dash by the time he reached the Moir domicile and he positively leaped up the stairs to the door, for, as, unhappily, the Moirs were compelled to live above their shop, there were many stairs, and, worse, an entry by a close. He had, indeed, so far recovered that he used the knocker with considerable decision, and his manner had the appearance of repudiating the slightly inferior aspect of his surroundings as unworthy of a man whose name might one day shine in the annals of the Empire. He gazed, too, with a superior air, at the small girl who helped in the shop and who, now lightly disguised as a maid, admitted him and ushered him into the parlour where Agnes, released from the bondage of the counter—although business hours were not yet over—sat awaiting her Matt; to-morrow she could not be spared from her post of duty, and would be unable to accompany him to Glasgow, but to-night she had him for her own.

The parlour was cold, damp, unused, and formal, with large mahogany furniture whose intricate design lost itself in a voluptuous mystery of curves, with antimacassars veiling the sheen of horsehair, and waxcloth on the floor that glittered like a wet street. From the walls Highland cattle, ominous in oils, looked down dispiritedly upon the piano, that hall-mark of gentility, which bore upon its narrow, crowded surface three stuffed birds of an unknown species, perched mutely under a glass case amidst a forest of photographs. Agnes as an infant, as a baby, as a child, as a girl, as a young woman, Agnes in a group at the bakers' and confectioners' annual trip, at the Band of Hope social, at the church workers' outing—all were there!

Here, too, was Agnes in the flesh: literally, for although short in stature she was already inclined, like the furnishings of the room, to a redundancy of curves, which swelled particularly around her hips and bosom, that were full, with the promise of greater amplitude to come. She was dark, with sloe eyes under sable eyebrows, with olive cheeks and red almost thick lips, and upon her upper lip was a smooth umber shadow that lay softly, but with a dark, threatening menace of the future.

She kissed him with great warmth. She was five years older than Matthew, and she treasured him accordingly, and now, taking his hand, she led him forward and sat down with him upon the unsympathetic sofa which, like the parlour, was sanctified to their courtship.

"And this is the very last night," she mourned.

"Oh! don't say that, Agnes," he replied. "We can always think of each other! We'll be with each other in spirit."

Ardent church worker though she was, Agnes, from her appearance, had potentialities for a closer communion than this. She was, of course, unaware of it and would have repudiated it hotly, but her sigh was heavy as she said: "I wish you were nearer than India!" and came closer to him now.

"The time will fly, Agnes. In no time I'll be back with plenty of rupees." He was proud of his knowledge of the foreign currency and added: "A rupee is about one shilling and fourpence."

"Never mind the rupees just now, Matt; tell me you love me."

"I do love you, that's why I'm so upset at going away. I haven't been myself at all these last few days—quite off colour!" He felt truly noble to have laid the burden of his suffering at her feet.

"You won't even speak to any of these foreign ladies, will you, Matt? I wouldn't trust them as far as I could see them—a pretty face may cover a wicked heart. You'll remember that, won't you, dear?"

"Certainly, Agnes."

"You see, dear, there must be great temptations for a handsome young man out in these hot countries. Women will go to such lengths to get hold of a man once they get their eye on him, especially if he's a good young man—that excites them all the more, and your little Agnes won't be there to watch over you, Matt. I want you to promise to be careful for my sake."

It was delightful for him to feel that he was so ardently desired, that already she was jealous of him to desperation, and, with one eye fixed already upon his future conquests abroad, he murmured solemnly: "Yes, Agnes, I see the truth of what you say. The way may be hard for me, but I'll let no one spoil me for you. It'll not be my fault if anything comes between us."

"Oh! Matt, dear," she whispered, "don't even speak of that. I'll hardly be able to sleep for thinking of all the hussies that might be after you. Of course I am not unreasonable, dear. I would like you to meet good, earnest women, perhaps lady missionaries or workers in the Christian field out there. A few motherly women out there would be nice for you to know. They would take good care of you, perhaps darn your socks for you. If you were to let me know I could write to them."

"Of course, Agnes," he replied, unattracted by her suggestion and with a strong conviction that such elderly ladies as she had just described would not constitute the society of his election. "Of course, I can't say I'll meet anyone like that. I'll have to see how things are first."

"You'll fall on your feet all right, Matt," she assured him fondly. "You couldn't help it the way you get round people. Then your music will be a great help to you socially. Have you got all your songs packed?" He nodded his head complacently, saying: "And the mandolin. I put a new pink ribbon on it yesterday!"

Her sable brows contracted at the thought of those who might receive the benefit of this decoration, knotted on such a romantic instrument, but she did not wish to press him too far so, with an effort, she controlled her apprehensions and, forcing a smile, deflected the conversation into a nobler channel.

"The church choir will miss you, too, Matt. The choir practice won't be the same place without you." He protested modestly, but she would not permit his humility. "No!" she cried, "don't deny it, dear. Your voice will be missed in that church. Do you remember that night after the practice when you first walked home with me, dear? I'll never forget the way you spoke to me. Don't you remember what you said?"

"I can't think the now, Aggie," he answered inattentively. "Did you not speak to me first?"

"Oh! Matt," she gasped, widening her eyes at him reproachfully, "how can you? You know you smiled at me over your hymn book all that night, and you did speak first. I only asked if you were going my way." He nodded his head apologetically, as he replied: "I remember now, Agnes! We ate all that big bag of liquorice all sorts you had with you. They were real nice, too."

"I'm going to send you out a big tin box of sweets every month," she promised eagerly. "I wasn't going to mention it, but as you speak of it I might as well tell you, dear. I know you're fond of a good sweet and you'll never get good confectionery out in those parts. They'll carry perfectly well if I send them in a tin." He thanked her with a satisfied smile, but, before he could speak, she hurried on, striking on the heat of his gratitude.

"There's nothing your Agnes will not do for you, Matt, if you just

61

don't forget her," she continued fervently. "You've never to forget me for a minute. You've got all my photographs with you! Put one in your cabin straight away, won't you, dear?" She laid her head more heavily on his shoulder and gazed up at him entrancingly. "Kiss me, Matt! That was nice. It's so delightful to feel that we are engaged. It's almost as binding as matrimony. No good girl could feel like I do without being affianced to her young man."

The couch being apparently without springs, Matt began to feel uncomfortable under the considerable weight he was supporting. His calf-love for Miss Moir, developed under the insidious flattery of her attentions, was not strong enough to stand the strain of this powerful amatory embrace.

"Would you permit me to smoke?" he suggested tactfully. Agnes looked up, her liquid eyes swimming beneath the inky tangle of her hair.

"On the last night?" she asked reproachfully.

"I thought it might pull me together," he murmured. "The last few days have been very heavy for me—all that packing has been such a strain on a man."

She sighed and raised herself reluctantly, saying:

"All right then, dear! I can refuse you nothing. Have just a few puffs if you feel it will so you good. But you're not to over-smoke yourself in India, Matt. Remember your chest is not strong." Then, graciously, she added: "Let me light this one for you as it's the last time." She timidly ignited the slightly bent weed he withdrew from his waistcoat pocket and watched him fearfully as he blew out thick clouds in manful taciturnity. Now she could only love and admire him from a distance, but at arm's length she still fondled his watch chain.

"You'll miss your little Aggie, won't you, Matt?" she asked soulfully, but coughing slightly as she inhaled the noxious odour from his cigar.

"Most dreadfully," he replied solemnly. This was what he really enjoyed, himself smoking heroically, she at his feet in fond womanly admiration. "It will be—unbearable." He would have liked to say, dashingly: "Hell," but out of respect he used the less manly expression, and he shook his head as if he doubted his ability to stand the strain of it all.

"We must suffer for each other's sake," said Agnes, with a sigh. "I feel it will make you do great and good work out there, Matt. You'll write and tell me all your doings."

"I'll write to you and Mamma every mail," promised Matthew.

"I'll be in close touch with Mamma, of course," responded Agnes, as if she were already a daughter of the house.

He felt that the prayers of two loyal adoring women would ascend in unison for him as he faced his stern task abroad, but the cigar, despite his efforts to prolong it, was burning his lips, and at length he regretfully discarded it. Immediately Agnes nestled her head upon his chest: "Kiss me again, dear!" she said. Then after a pause she whispered, suggesting alluringly, "You'll come back to me a big, strong, fierce man, won't you, Matt? I like to be crushed hard in your arms, as hard as ever you like." As he placed a limp arm around her shoulders he felt somehow that too much was being demanded of a man who had to face the perils of an arduous and unknown journey in the morning.

"I'm really ashamed to show my feelings like this," she continued bashfully, "but there's no harm in it, Matt, is there? We'll be married whenever you come back. Indeed it breaks my heart to think we couldn't have got married before ye left. I would willingly have gone out with you!"

"But, Agnes," he protested, "it's not the country for a white woman, at all."

"There's plenty go out there, Matt, plenty! Officers' wives, and what not! I'll go back with you if you've got to go out again when your time's up," she said firmly. "It's just the fact that you've got to make your way that has hindered us, dear."

He was silent, startled at the decision in her words, never having viewed himself as being so near the altar, nor having quite suspected the extent of her ascendancy over him, thinking too, that the embrace, was being protracted indefinitely. At length he said:

"I'm afraid I must be going now, Aggie."

"But it's so early yet, Matt," she asserted petulantly. "You never leave before ten o'clock as a rule."

"I know, Agnes, but I've got a big day ahead of me to-morrow," he replied importantly. "Got to get on the packet by noon."

"This separation is going to kill me," said Agnes dramatically, unwillingly releasing him.

As he stood up, straightening his tie, shaking down his trousers, and inspecting the damage to his creases, he felt that it was worth while, that it was good to know that women would die for him.

"Good-bye, then, Agnes," he exclaimed gallantly, straddling his legs and throwing out both hands towards her. "We shall meet again." She flung herself again into his proffered arms and buried her head against him, whilst the force of her sobs rocked them both.

"I feel I should never let you go," she cried, brokenly, as he separated from her, "I should never give you up like this. You're going too far away. I'll pray for you, though, Matt! May God take care of you for me," she wept as she saw him down the stairs.

Out again in the street he felt consoled, uplifted, strengthened by her grief, as though the devastation he had wrought within her virgin heart ennobled him, added inches to his stature. But as he retired early to bed in preparation for the fatigues of the next day he reflected in his more mature and worldly vein that perhaps Miss Moir had been lately a little pressing in her attentions upon him, and as he fell asleep he realised that a man might as well think twice before tying himself up in a hurry, especially if that man were such a knowing blade as Matthew Brodie.

Next morning, although he awoke early, it was nine o'clock before Mamma let him get up.

"Don't rush! we'll take it easy. Conserve your strength, my boy," she said, as she brought him his morning tea. "We've plenty of time, and you've a long journey ahead of you."

She apparently visualised him journeying to Calcutta without repose, and in consequence of his deterred rising he was only half-dressed when his father called to him from the foot of the stairs. Brodie would not depart an inch from his habit; he would, indeed, have considered it a weakness to wait to see his son away, and at half-past nine he was off to business in the usual fashion. As Matthew came scuttering down the stairs in his braces, a towel in his hand, his wet hair over his pallid brow, and came up to his father in the hall, Brodie fixed a magnetic eye upon his son and held for a moment the other's wavering glance. "Well, Matthew Brodie," he said, looking down at his son, "you're off to-day, and that means good-bye to your home for five years. I hope to God you are goin' to prove yourself in these years. You're a sleekit, namby-pamby fellow and your mother has a' but spoiled ye, but there must be good in ye. There must be good," he cried, "because you're my son! I want that brought out in ye. Look a man between the eyes and don't hang your head like a dog. I'm sending you out there to make a man of ye. Don't forget that you're the son, ay, and the heir of James Brodie.

"I've got you everything you want," he continued. "A position of trust and of great possibilities. I've given you the best outfit money can buy and best of all I've given you a name. Be a man, sir, but above all be a Brodie. Behave like a Brodie wherever you are, or God help you." He shook hands firmly, turned, and was gone.

Matthew finished dressing in a maze, aided by Mamma—who continually darted in and out of his room—ate his breakfast without tasting it, and was startled by the cab at the door before he could collect himself. Other farewells were showered upon him. Old Grandma Brodie, cross at being disturbed so early, called out from the head of the stairs as she clutched her long nightgown above her bare, bony feet: "Good-bye to ye, then, and watch you don't get drouned on the way over." Nessie, in tears long before the time, from the very solemnity of the occasion, could only sob incoherently: "I'll write to you, Matt! I hope the compass will be useful to you." Mary was deeply affected. She clasped her arms round Matthew's neck and kissed him fondly. "Keep a stiff upper lip, Matt dear. Be brave, and nothing can hurt you, and don't forget your own loving sister."

He was in the cab with Mamma, sitting in hunched apathy, being bumped unmercifully, on the way to the station, while Mrs. Brodie looked proudly out of the window. In her mind's eye she saw people nudging each other as they watched the sweep of her spanking equipage, and saying: "That's Mrs. Brodie seein' her laddie off to Calcutta. She's been a good mother to that boy, ay and a fine fellow he is, too, an' all, an' all." Indeed it was not every day that a mother in Levenford took her son to the boat for India, she reflected complacently, drawing her paletot more becomingly around her, and sitting up grandly in the decrepit vehicle as though it were her private carriage.

At the station she paid the cabman with a conscious air, glancing sideways from under her hat at the few chance loungers under the archway, and to the man who carried the luggage she could not forbear to remark, casually: "This young gentleman is for India." The porter, staggering under the heavy case and stupefied by the reek of camphor which emanated from it, twisted his red neck round the angle of the box and gaped at her obtusely, too overcome to speak.

Although they were now on the platform the train of destiny was late, for the schedule of the Darroch and Levenford joint railway, never the object of public approbation, did not to-day belie its reputation and was apparently not working to any degree of accuracy. Mamma tapped her foot restlessly, pursed her lips impatiently, looked repeatedly at the silver watch that hung around her neck by its chain of plaited hair; Matthew, filled with a despairing hope that there might have been a breakdown on the line, looked vaguely, disconsolately, at the porter who, in turn, gazed with open mouth at Mrs. Brodie. He had never seen her before and, as his oafish look engulfed her brisk, nonchalant demeanour, so outwith the compass of his local experience, he took her for a prodigy—a traveller at least of European experience.

At last a clanking noise was heard in the distance, sounding the knell of Matt's last hope. The train smoked its way into the station, and in a few minutes puffed out again with Mrs. Brodie and Matthew inside, facing each other on the hard wooden seats, and leaving the porter looking incredulously at the penny piece which the lady had magnificently pressed into his palm. He scratched his head, spat disgustedly, dismissed the whole episode as a mystery beyond the powers of his comprehension.

In the train Mrs. Brodie utilised every lull in the din, when her voice might be audible, to utter some lively remark to Matthew, and between these parentheses she contemplated him vivaciously. Matthew squirmed in his seat; he knew he was the object of a cheering-up process and he loathed it. It's all right for her, he thought moodily, she hasn't got to go.

At length they reached Glasgow, after a journey that was, for Matthew, mournfully short. They made their way out of the station down Jamaica

Street and along the Broomielaw to where the S.S. *Irrawaddy* was lying at Stobcross dock with steam up, and two tugs in attendance. She seemed to them an enormous ship with paddles wide as the spread of a bat's wings, and a funnel which dwarfed the masts of all the other shipping, and Mamma remarked, admiringly: "My word! that's a great big boat, Matt! I'll not be so feared for ye when I think on ye aboard o' that. That lum is as high as the Town steeple. Look at a' these folks on deck too. I suppose we maun go on board." Together they advanced up the gangway and gained the deck, where the flurry of embarkation had begun and an exaggerated bustle and confusion prevailed. Sailors leaped about the deck performing miracles with ropes; officers in gold braid shouted importantly and blew whistles loudly; stewards pursued passengers and passengers ran after stewards; Anglo-Indians returning to the country of their selection glared passionately at all who got in their way; relatives on the verge of bereavement stubbed their toes over iron stanchions and piles of luggage.

In the face of this hustling activity Mrs. Brodie's spirit quailed. The superior look of the purser as he directed them below intimidated her, and though she had intended at least to approach the captain of the vessel and turn over Matthew, in the appropriate manner, to his especial care, now she wilted; as she sat in the stuffy confines of the den which was to serve Matt as cabin for the next eight weeks, and felt the gentle lift and fall of the boat against the fenders of the quay, she realised that the sooner she went ashore the better.

Now that the actual farewell was at hand the spurious exaltation derived from her romantic imagination collapsed, as her husband had sardonically foreseen, like a pricked bladder. She was herself again, the weak woman who had given birth to this child, suckled him at her breast, seen him grow to manhood, and now was about to see him leave her. A tear crept slowly down her cheek.

"Oh! Matt," she cried, "I've tried to bear up well for ye, son—for your own dear sake, but I'm sorry to lose you. I doubt if you're the man for these foreign parts. I would rather you stayed at home."

"I don't want to go either, Mamma," he implored eagerly, as though at the last moment she might stretch out her hand and pluck him from his awful predicament.

"You'll need to go now, my son. It's gane too far to be altered now," she replied sadly, shaking her head. "Your father has it wished all along. And what he says must be done. There's just no other way about it. But you'll do your best to be a good boy, won't you, Matt?"

"Yes, Mamma."

"You'll send home something of your pay for me to put in the Building Society for you?"

"Yes, Mamma."

"You'll read a chapter of your Bible every day?"

"Yes, I will, Mamma."

"And don't forget me, Matt."

Matthew burst into broken, uncouth sobs.

"I don't want to go," he blubbered, catching at her dress. "You're all sending me away and I'll never come back. It's my death I'm goin' out to. Don't let me go, Mamma."

"Ye maun go, Matt," she whispered. "He would kill us if we came back thegither."

"I'll be sick on the boat," he whined. "I feel it comin' on already. I'll get the fever out there. You know I'm not strong. I tell ye, Mamma, it'll finish me."

"Wheesht, son!" she murmured, "ye maun calm yoursel'. I'll pray to the Lord to protect ye."

"Oh! well, Mamma, if I'm to go, leave me now," he wailed. "I can't stand any more. Don't sit there and mock me. Leave me and be finished with it!" His mother stood up and drew him into her arms; at last she was a woman. "Good-bye, son, and God bless you," she said quietly. As she left the cabin with streaming eyes and shaking head, he flung himself impotently upon his bunk.

Mrs. Brodie stepped off the gangway and set out for Queen Street station. As she retraced her steps through the docks her feet dragged along the very pavements over which she had advanced so airily; gradually her body drooped forward, her dress trailed behind heedlessly; her head inclined itself pathetically; a mantle of resignation descended upon her; she had emerged completely from her dreams, and was again the hapless and handless wife of James Brodie.

In the train homewards she felt tired, exhausted by the rapid flight of emotions that had traversed her being. A drowsiness crept over her and she slept. In the shadows of her sleeping brain spectres sprang from their lurking places and tormented her. Someone was thrusting her downwards, crushing her with stones; square grey stones were all around, compressing her. Upon the earth beside her lay her children, their cadaverous limbs relaxed in the inanition of extreme debility, and, as the walls slowly drew in nearer upon them, she awoke with a loud shriek which mingled the blast of the engine's whistle. The train was entering the outskirts of Levenford. She was home.

V

On the following morning about ten o'clock, Mrs. Brodie and Mary were together in the kitchen, according to their custom of consulting together to discuss the household plans for the day when the master of the house had departed after breakfast. This morning, however, they sat without reviewing the possibilities of their cleaning or mending, without debating whether it should be stew or mince for the day's dinner, or considering whether father's grey suit required pressing, and instead remained silent, somewhat subdued, with Mrs. Brodie mournfully sipping a cup of strong tea and Mary gazing quietly out of the window.

"I feel good for nothing, to-day," said Mamma at length.

"No wonder, Mamma, after yesterday," Mary sighed. "I wonder how he's getting on? Not homesick already, I hope."

Mrs. Brodie shook her head. "The seasickness will be the worst, I'm gey afeared, for Matt was never a sailor, poor boy! I remember only too well when he was just twelve, on the steamer to Port Doran, he was very ill—and it wasna that rough either. He would eat greengages after his dinner, and I didna like to stop him and spoil the day's pleasure for the wee man, but he brought them up and the good dinner too, that had cost his father a salt half crown. Oh! but your father was angry with him, and with me too, as if it was my fault that the boat turned the boy's stomach."

She paused reminiscently, and added: "I'm glad *I* never gave Matt a hard word, anyway, now that he's away far, far. No! I never gave him a word in anger, let alone lifted my hand to him in punishment."

"You always liked Matt best," Mary agreed, mildly. "I'm afraid you'll miss him sorely, Mamma!"

"Miss him?" Mrs. Brodie replied. "I should just think I would. I feel as weak as if—as if something inside of me had gane away on that boat and would never come back. But he'll miss me too, I hope." Her eye glistened, as she continued: "Ay, grown man though he is, he broke down in his cabin like a bairn when he had to say good-bye to his mother. It's a comfort to me, that, Mary, and will be, until I get the consolation of his own dear letters. My! but I'm lookin' forward to these. The only letter he's ever written me was when he was nine years old and was away for a holiday at Cousin Jim's farm, after he had been poorly with his chest. It was that interestin' too—all about the horse he had sat on, and the wee trout he had caught in the river. I've got it in my drawer to this very day. I maun redd it out for mysel'. Ay!" she concluded, with a melancholy pleasure, "I'll go through all my drawers and sort out a' the things of Matt's, that I've got. It'll be a wee crumb o' comfort till I hear from him."

"Will we do out his room to-day, then, Mamma?" asked Mary.

"No, Mary—that's not to be touched. It's Matt's room, and we'll keep it as it is until he wants it again—if ever he does." She drank a mouthful of tea appreciatively. "It was good of you to make me this, Mary, it's drawing me together. He ought to get good tea in India, anyway, that's the place for tea and spices. Cold tea should be refreshin' to him in the heat," she added. Then, after a pause, "Why didn't you take a cup yourself?"

"I feel upset a bit myself this morning, Mamma."

"You've been looking real poorly these last few days. You're as pale as paper, too."

Mary was the least beloved by Mrs. Brodie of all her children, but in the deprivation of the favourite, Matthew, she drew closer to her.

"We'll not do a bit of cleaning in the house to-day, either of us; we both deserve a rest after all the rush we've had lately," she continued. "I might try and ease my mind in a book for a wee, and you'll go out this morning for your messages to get a breath of air. It'll do ye good to get a walk while it's dry and sunny. What do we need now?"

They conned the deficiencies of the larder, whilst Mary wrote them down on a slip of paper against that treacherous memory of hers. Purchases at various shops were involved, for the housekeeping allowance was not lavish, and it was necessary to buy every article in the cheapest possible market.

"We maun stop our order o' the wee Abernethies at the baker's, now that Matt's away. Your father never looks at them. Tell them we'll not be requirin' any more," said Mamma. "My! but it's an awfu' emptiness in the house to think on the boy bein' away; it was such a pleasure for me to give him a nice, tasty dish."

"We'll not need so much butter either, Mamma! He was fond of that too," suggested Mary, with her pencil reflectively tapping her white front teeth.

"We don't need that anyway this morning," retorted Mamma, a trifle coldly, "but I want you to get this week's *Good Thoughts* when you're out. It's the very thing for Matt, and I'm going to send it to him every week. It'll cheer him up to get it regularly, and do his mind a world o' good."

When they had examined and weighed up all the requirements of the household, and carefully estimated the total cost, Mary took the money counted out from her mother's thin purse, slipped on her bonnet, picked up her fine net reticule, and set out upon her errands. She was happy to be in the open, feeling, when she was out of doors, freer in her body and in her mind, less confined, less circumscribed by the rooted conformity of her environment. Additionally, each visit to the town now held for her a high and pulsating adventure, and at every turn and corner she drew a deep, expectant breath, could scarcely raise her eyes for the hope and fear that she might see Denis. Although she had not had another letter, mercifully, perhaps, for she would then surely have been detected, an inward impression told her that he was now home from his business circuit; if he in reality loved her he must surely come to Levenford to seek her. An instinctive longing quickened her steps and made her heart quicken in sympathy. She passed the

Common with a sense of embarrassment, observing, with one quick, diffident glance, that nothing remained of the merry-making of last week but the beaten track of the passage of many feet, blanched squares and circles where the booths and tents had stood, and heaps of debris and smoking ashes upon the worn, burned-out grass; but the littered desolation of the scene gave her no pang, the departure of its flashing cohorts no regret, for in her heart a memory remained which was not blanched, or trampled, or burned out, but which flamed each day more brightly than before.

Her desire to see Denis intensified, filled her slender figure with a rare æther, setting a mist upon her eyes and a freshness upon her cheeks like the new bloom upon a wild rose; her aspiration rose into her throat, and stifled her with a feeling like bitter grief.

Once in the town she lingered over her shopping, delaying a little by the windows, hopeful that a light touch upon her arm might suddenly arouse her, taking the longest possible routes and traversing as many streets as she dared, in the hope of encountering Denis. But still she did not see him, and now, instead of veiling her glance, she began to gaze anxiously about her, as though she entreated him to come to her to end the unhappiness of her suspense. Slowly the list of her commissions dwindled and, by the time she had made her last purchase, a small furrow of anxiety perplexed her smooth brow, while her mouth drooped plaintively at its corners as the latent antithesis of her longing now took possession of her. Denis did not love her, and for that reason he would not come to her! She had been mad to consider that he could continue to care for her, a creature so little befitted to his charm and graceful beauty; and, with the bitter certainty of despair, she became aware that he would never see her again, and she would be left like a wounded bird, fluttering feebly and alone.

Now it was impossible to procrastinate her return, for, with a sudden pathetic dignity, she felt she could not be seen loitering about the streets, as though she lowered herself commonly to look for a man who had disdained her; and she turned quickly, with the reticule of parcels dragging upon her arm like a heavy weight as she moved off towards home. She now chose the quiet streets, to hide herself as much as possible, feeling miserably that if Denis did not wish her, she would not thrust herself upon him; and in a paroxysm of sad renunciation, she kept her head lowered and occupied the most inconsiderable space possible upon the pavement which she traversed.

She had so utterly resigned herself to not seeing Denis that, when he suddenly appeared before her from the passage leading out of the new station, it was as if a phantom had issued from the unsubstantial air. She raised her downcast eyes as though, startled and unbelieving, they refused to allow the sudden transport of the vision to pass beyond into her being, to flood it with a joy which might be unreal, merely the delusive mirage of her hopes. But no phantom could hurry forward so eagerly, or smile so captivatingly, or take her hand so warmly, so closely, that she felt the pulse of the hot blood in the ardent, animate hand. It was Denis. Yet he had no right to be so gay and elated, so carefree and dashing, his rapture untouched by any memory of their separation. Did he not understand that she had been forced to wait through weary days of melancholy, had only a moment ago been plunged in sad despondency, even to the consideration of her abandonment?

"Mary, it's like heaven to see you again, and you've the look of one of the angels up above! I only got back home late last night and I came the first moment I could get away. How lucky to catch you like this!" he exclaimed, fervently fixing his eye upon hers.

Immediately she forgave him. Her despondency melted under the warmth of his flow of high spirits; her sadness perished in the gay infection of his smile; instead, a sudden, disturbing realisation of the sweetly intimate circumstances of their last meeting seized her, and a mood of profound shyness overtook her.

She blushed to see in the open day this young gallant who, cloaked by the benign darkness, had pressed her so closely in his arms, who had been the first to kiss her, to touch caressingly her virgin body. Did he know all that she had thought of him since then? all the throbbing recollections of the past and the mad, dancing visions of the future that had obsessed her? She dared not look at him.

"I'm so delighted to see you again, Mary, I could jump for joy! Are you glad to see me again?" he continued.

"Yes," she said, in a low, embarrassed voice.

"I've so much to tell you that I couldn't put in my letter. I didn't want to say too much for fear it would be intercepted. Did you get it?"

"I got it safely, but you mustn't write again," she whispered. "I would be afraid for you to do that."

What he had said was so indiscreet that the thought of what he had left unsaid made a still higher colour mantle in her cheeks.

"I won't need to write for a long time, again," he laughed meaningly. "Sure, I'll be seeing you ever so often now. I'll be at the office for a month or two until my autumn trip; and speaking of business, Mary dear, you've brought me the luck of a charm—I've twice as many orders this time. If ye keep inspirin' me like that you'll make a fortune for me in no time. Bedad! you'll have to meet me if only to share the profits!"

Mary looked around uneasily, feeling already in the quiet street a horde of betraying eyes upon her, sensing in his impetuosity how little he understood her position.

"Denis, I'm afraid I can't wait any longer. We might be seen here."

"Is it a crime to talk to a young man, then—in the morning anyway?" he replied softly, meaningly. "Sure there's no disgrace in that. And if ye'd rather walk I could tramp to John o' Groats with you! Let me carry your parcels for a bit of the way, ma'am."

Mary shook her head. "People would notice us more than ever," she replied timidly, already conscious of the eyes of the town upon her, during that reckless promenade.

He looked at her tenderly, protectively, then allowed his resourceful glance to travel up and down the street with what, to her devoted eyes, seemed like the intrepid gaze of an adventurer in a hostile land.

"Mary, my dear," he said presently, in a jocular tone, "you don't know the man you're with yet. 'Foyle never knows defeat,' that's my motto. Come along in here!" He took her arm firmly and led her a few doors down the street, then, before she realised it and could think even to resist, he had drawn her inside the cream-coloured doors of Bertorelli's café. She paled with apprehension, feeling that she had finally passed the limits of respectability, that the depth of her dissipation had now been reached, and looking reproachfully into Denis' smiling face, in a shocked tone she gasped:

"Oh, Denis, how could you?"

Yet, as she looked round the clean, empty shop, with its rows of marble-topped tables, its small scintillating mirrors, and brightly papered walls, while she allowed herself to be guided to one of the plush stalls that appeared exactly like her pew in church, she felt curiously surprised, as if she had expected to find a sordid den suited appropriately to the debauched revels that must, if tradition were to be believed, inevitably be connected with a place like this.

Her bewilderment was increased by the appearance of a fat, fatherly man with a succession of chins, each more amiable than the preceding honest one, who came up to them, smilingly, bowed with a quick bend of the region which had once been his waist, and said:

"Good-day, Meester Doyle. Glad to see you back."

"Morning, Louis!"

This, then, was the monster himself.

"Had a nice treep, Meester Doyle? Plenty business, I hope."

"Plenty! you old lump of blubber! Don't you know by this time I can sell anything. I could sell a ton of macaroni in the streets of Aberdeen."

Bertorelli laughed and extended his hands expressively, while his chuckle wreathed more chins around his full, beaming face.

"That woulda be easy, Meester Doyle. Macaroni is good, just the same as porreedge; makes a man beeg like me."

"That's right, Louis! You're a living example against the use of macaroni. Never mind your figure, though. How's all the family?"

"Oh! just asplendeed! The bambino weel soon be as beeg as me. Already he has two chins."

As he rolled with laughter, Mary again gazed aghast at the tragic spectacle of a villain, who concealed his rascality under the guise of a fictitious mirth and a false assumption of humanity. But her conflicting thoughts were interrupted by Denis, as he tactfully enquired:

"What would you like, Mary—a macallum?"

She had sufficient hardihood to nod her head; for although she would not have known a macallum from a macaroon, to have confessed her ignorance before this archangel of iniquity was beyond her.

"Very good, very nice," agreed Bertorelli, as he ambled away.

"Nice chap, that," said Denis, "straight as a die; and as kind as you make them!"

"But," quavered Mary, "they say such things about him."

"Bah! He eats babies, I suppose! Pure, unlovely bigotry, Mary dear. We'll have to progress beyond that some day, if we're not to stick in the dark ages. Although he's Italian he's a human being. Comes from a place near Pisa, where the famous tower is, the one that leans but never falls. We'll go and see it some day—we'll do Paris and Rome too," he added casually.

Mary looked reverently at this young man who called foreigners by their Christian names and who toyed with the capitals of Europe, not boastingly like poor Matt, but with a cool, calm confidence, and she reflected how pulsating life might be with a man like this, so loving, and yet so strong, so gentle, and yet so undaunted. She felt she was on the way to worshipping him.

Now she was eating her macallum, a delicious concoction of ice-cream and raspberry juice, which, cunningly blending the subtly acid essence of the fruit with the cold mellow sweetness of the ice-cream, melted upon her tongue in an exquisite and unexpected delight. Under the table Denis pressed her foot gently with his, whilst his eyes followed her naïve enjoyment with a lively satisfaction.

Why, she asked herself, did she enjoy herself always so exquisitely with him? Why did he seem, in his kindness, generosity, and tolerance, so different from anyone she had known? Why should the upward curl of his mouth and the lights in his hair, the poise of his head, make her heart turn with happiness in her breast?

"Are you enjoying this?" he asked.

"It really is nice here," she conceded, with a submissive murmur.

"It's all right," he agreed. "I wouldn't have taken you, otherwise. But anywhere is nice so long as we are together. That's the secret, Mary!"

Her eyes sparkled back at him, her being drew in the exudation of his courageous vitality, and, for the first time since their meeting, she laughed spontaneously, happily, outright.

"That's better," encouraged Denis. "I was beginning to worry about you." He leant impulsively across the table, and took her thin, small fingers in his.

"You know, Mary dear, I want you so much to be happy. When I first saw you I loved you for your loveliness—but it was a sad loveliness.

73

You looked to me as if you were afraid to smile, as if someone had crushed all the laughter out of you. Ever since our wonderful time together, dear, I've been thinking of you. I love you and I hope that you love me, for I feel we are just made for each other. I couldn't live without you now, and I want to be with you, to watch you unfold out of your sadness and see you laugh at any silly, stupid joke I make to you. Let me pay my court to you openly."

She was silent, moved immeasurably by his words, then at last she spoke:

"How I wish we could be together," she said sadly. "I—I've missed you so much, Denis. But you don't know my father. He is terrible. There is something about him you don't understand. I'm afraid of him and he—he had forbidden me to speak to you."

Denis' eyes narrowed.

"Am I not good enough for him?"

Mary gripped her fingers, tightly, involuntarily, as though he had wounded her.

"Oh! don't say that, dear Denis. You're wonderful and I love you, I'd die for you; but my father is the most domineering man you could ever imagine, oh!—and the proudest man too."

"Why is he like that?—He has nothing against me? I've nothing to be ashamed of, Mary. Why do you say he is proud?"

Mary did not reply for a moment. Then she said slowly: "I don't know! When I was little I never thought about it, my father was like a god to me, so big, so strong, every word that he uttered was like a command. As I grew older I seemed to feel there was some mystery, something which makes him different from ordinary people, which makes him try to mould us into his own fashion, and now I almost fear that he thinks——" She paused and looked up at Denis nervously.

"What?" he urged.

"I'm not sure, oh! I can hardly say it." She blushed uncomfortably as she haltingly continued: "He seems to think we are related in some way to the Winton family."

"To the Wintons," he exclaimed incredulously. "To the Earl himself! How on earth does he make that out?"

She shook her head sadly, miserably. "I don't know. He never lets himself speak of it, but I know it's in the back of his mind all the time. The Winton family name is Brodie, you see—oh! but it's all so ridiculous."

"Ridiculous!" he echoed. "It does seem ridiculous! What does he expect to get out of it?"

"Nothing," she exclaimed bitterly. "Only the satisfaction to his pride. He makes life miserable for us at times. He compels us, makes us live differently from other people. We're apart in that house of ours that he built himself, and like him it oppresses us all." Carried away by

74

the expression of her fears, she cried out finally: "Oh! Denis, I know it's not right for me to talk like this about my own father, but I'm afraid of him. He would never—never allow our engagement."

Denis set his teeth. "I'll go and see him myself. I'll convince him in spite of himself, and I'll make him let me see you. I'm not afraid of him. I'm not afraid of any man living."

She jumped up in a panic. "No! No, Denis! Don't do that. He would punish us both dreadfully." The vision of her father, with his fearful, brute strength, mauling the beauty of this young gladiator, terrified her. "Promise me you won't," she cried.

"But we must see each other, Mary. I can't give you up."

"We could meet sometimes," said Mary.

"That leads nowhere, dear; we must have some definite understanding. You know I want to marry you." He looked at her closely; he knew her ignorance to be such, he was afraid to say any more. Instead, he took up her hand, kissed the palm softly, and laid his cheek against it.

"Will you meet me soon?" he asked inconsequently. "I would like to be in the moonlight with you again to see it shining in your eyes, to see the moonbeams dancing in your hair." He lifted his head and looked lovingly at her hand, which he still held in his. "Your hands are like snow-drops, Mary, so soft and white and drooping. They are cool like snow itself against my hot face. I love them, and I love you."

A passionate longing seized him to have her always with him. If necessary he would fight; he would be stronger than the circumstances that separated them, stronger than fate itself; in a different voice he said firmly:

"Surely you will marry me even if we've got to wait, won't you, Mary?"

While he sat silent, against the garish background of the empty shop, his hand lightly touching hers, awaiting her answer, she saw in his eyes the leaping of his kindred soul towards her, in his question only the request that she be happy with him always, and, forgetting instantly the difficulty, danger, and total impossibility of the achievement, knowing nothing of marriage but only loving him, losing her fear in his strength and sinking herself utterly in him, her eyes looked deeply into his, as she answered:

"Yes."

He did not move, did not cast himself upon his knee in a passion of protesting gratitude, but in his stillness a current of unutterable love and fervour flowed from his body into hers through the medium of their touching hands and into his eyes there welled up such a look of tenderness and devotion that, meeting hers, it fused about them like an arch of radiance.

"You'll not regret it, dear," he whispered, as he leaned across the table and softly kissed her lips. "I'll do my utmost to make you happy,

Mary! I've been selfish, but now you will always come first. I'll work hard for you. I'm making my way fast and I'm going to make it faster. I've got something in the bank now, and in a short time, if you'll wait, Mary, we'll just walk off and get married."

The dazzling simplicity of the solution blinded her, as, thinking how easy it would be for them to run away suddenly, secretly, without her father knowing, to loose themselves utterly from him, she clasped her hands together and whispered:

"Oh! Denis, could we? I never thought of that!"

"We can and we will, dear Mary. I'll work hard so that we can manage soon. Remember my motto! we'll make that our family crest. Never mind the Wintons! Now, not another word or another worry for that little head of yours. Leave everything to me, and remember only that I'm thinking of you and striving for you all the time. We may have to be careful how we meet, but surely I can see you occasionally— even if it's only to admire the elegant little figure of you from a distance."

"I'll have to see you sometimes; it would be too hard to do without that," she murmured, and added ingenuously: "Every Tuesday I go to the Library to change Mamma's book, and sometimes my own."

"Didn't I find that out for myself, you spalpeen!" smiled Denis. "Sure enough I'll know all about your mother's taste in literature before I'm finished. And don't I know the Library! I'll be there, you may be sure. But can you not give me a photo of your own dear self to keep me going, in between times?"

She hung her head a little, conscious of her own deficiencies and the oddity of her up-bringing, as she replied: "I haven't got one. Father didn't approve of it."

"What! Your parents are behind the times, my girl. We'll have to waken them up. To think that you've never been taken is a shame; but never mind, I'll have your sweet face before the camera the moment we're married. How do you like this?" he enquired, as he produced a misty brown photograph of a jaunty young man standing with cheerful fortitude, mingled with an inappropriate air of hilarity, amongst what appeared to be an accumulation of miniature tombstones.

"Denis Foyle at the Giants' Causeway last year," he explained. "That old woman that sells shells there, you know the big curly ones that sing in your ear, told my fortune that day. She said I was going to be the lucky, lucky gossoon, and indeed she must have known I was going to meet you."

"Can I have this, Denis?" she asked shyly. "I think it's lovely."

"It's for you, and no other, provided you wear it next your heart."

"I must wear it where nobody sees it," she answered innocently.

"That'll suit me," he replied, and smiled teasingly at the sudden rush of colour and understanding which flooded her modest brow. But immediately he amended, honourably:

"Don't mind me, Mary. As the Irishman said, 'I'm always puttin' me foot in it with me clumsy tongue.'"

They both laughed, but as she dissolved in gaiety, feeling that she could have listened to his banter for ever, she saw the purpose behind it, and loved him for the attempt to hearten her against their separation. His courage made her valiant, his frank but audacious attitude towards life stimulated her as a clear cold wind might arouse a prisoner after a long incarceration in stagnant air. All this rushed upon her as she said involuntarily, simply:

"You make me glad and free, Denis. I can breathe when I'm with you. I did not know the meaning of love until I met you. I had never thought of it—did not understand—but now I know that, always, for me, love is to be with you, to breathe with the same breath as you———"

She broke off abruptly, covered with confusion at her boldness in speaking to him like this. A faint recollection of her previous existence, of her life apart from him, dawned upon her, and, as her eye fell upon the heap of parcels beside her, she remembered Mamma, who would be wondering what had become of her; she thought of her already appalling lateness, of the necessity for prudence and caution, and starting up abruptly, she said, with a short sigh:

"I'll really need to go now, Denis."

Her words burdened him suddenly with the imminence of her departure, but he did not plead with her to stay, and he stood up, like a man, at once, saying:

"I don't want you to go, dear, and I know you don't want to go either, but we've got the future straightened out better now. We've only got to love each other and wait."

They were still alone. Bertorelli, in vanishing irrevocably, had, monster though he might be, betrayed none the less a human understanding and a tactful appreciation of their situation which might weigh in the balance—however lightly—against the atrocities that had been imputed to him. They kissed quickly, when her lips swept his like the brush of a butterfly's wing. At the door they shared one last look, a silent communion of all their secret understanding, confidence, and love, which passed between them like a sacred talisman before she turned and left him.

Her reticule now a featherweight, her steps rapid, fluent to her dancing heart, her head in the air, her curls straying and sailing buoyantly behind her, she was home before the rapture of her thoughts had abated. As she swept into the kitchen Mrs. Brodie looked at her questioningly from around the inclination of her nose.

"What kept you, girl? You took a long time to get that pickle of messages. Did you meet anyone you knew? Was anybody speirin' about Matt?"

Mary almost giggled in Mamma's face. For a ridiculous instant she considered the effect upon her mother were she to tell her she had just eaten an ambrosial sweetmeat, served by an outrageous ruffian, who tortured bambinos with macaroni, in a forbidden haunt of iniquity, and in company with a young man who had virtually proposed a honeymoon in Paris. It was well that she refrained, for had she yielded to this absurdity in the exhilaration of her spirits Mrs. Brodie, if she had not doubted her daughter's sanity, would certainly have swooned immediately.

"The air must have done you good, anyway," continued Mamma, somewhat suspiciously. "You've got quite a colour."

Credulous as she was, the maternal instinct that was in her doubted such immediate efficacy in the usually impotent Levenford air.

"Yes! I feel much better now," replied Mary truthfully, with twitching lips and sparkling eyes.

"Grandma was saying something when you were out about a letter she had seen you reading," persisted Mrs. Brodie, trailing after her nebulous idea. "I hope you're not up to any mischief your father would disapprove of. Don't set yourself up against him, Mary. Them that has tried it have aye regretted it. There's only one finish to that!" She sighed reminiscently, and added: "He finds out eventually, and he'll be at you in the end, ay, and make it a bitter, bitter end."

Mary shook off her mantle with a shrug of her shoulders. In the space of the last hour her slim figure had regained its youthful and imperious vitality. She stood erect, filled with a fierce and confident joy.

"Mamma," she said gaily, "don't worry about me. My motto is now, 'Mary never knows defeat!'"

Mrs. Brodie shook her pathetically inclined head sadly, and, filled with a vague, uncomprehending foreboding, gathered up the messages; with a more melancholy inclination of her head, like an incarnate presage of misfortune and ill-omen, she passed slowly out of the room.

VI

"Nessie! Mary!" shrilled Mrs. Brodie, in a fine frenzy of service, as she skittled about helping Brodie to dress, "come and put on your father's gaiters."

It was the morning of Saturday the twenty-first of August, and one of the red-letter days in James Brodie's calendar. In a large-patterned, black and white check knickerbocker suit he sat, his face like a full red sun, trying to struggle into his gaiters, which had not been used since a year that day, when, though he now chose to forget the fact, he had experienced the same difficulty in assuming them.

"What kind of witless trick was it to put a man's gaiters away damp?" he girned at his wife. "They'll not meet on me now. Desh it all, can't a man keep a thing decent in this house? These have shrunk."

Inevitably, when anything went wrong, the onus was thrust upon his wife's narrow shoulders.

"A man can't leave a thing about, but some senseless creature wastes it for him. How am I to go to the Show without gaiters? Ye'll be askin' me to go without my collar and tie next."

"But, father," meekly replied Mrs. Brodie, "I think you must be wearing a shade larger boot this year. This new pair I ordered for you myself were something broader than the others."

"Nonsense!" he grunted. "You'll be saying that my feet have got bigger next."

Here Nessie burst into the room like a young foal, followed more slowly by Mary.

"Quick, girls," urged Mamma, "do up your father's gaiters for him. Look sharp now, he's behind time!" The young handmaidens launched themselves upon their knees, applying their nimble fingers with dexterity and strength to the task before them, whilst Brodie lay back, simmering, darting black glances at the apologetic figure of his wife. The catastrophe was the more unfortunate for Mrs. Brodie as, upon this day in particular, he might reasonably be relied upon to be in a good temper, and the thought of spoiling for herself the rare chance of a day without a rage, of having activated the passive volcano, was more humiliating to her than the actual insults of the moment.

It was the day of the Levenford Cattle Show, an outstanding agricultural event, which drew the pedigree of the county as regards both its stock and its human inhabitants. Brodie loved the show and made his attendance of it an unfailing annual institution. He loved the sleek cattle with their swollen udders, the full-muscled Clydesdale stallions, the high-stepping cobs in the ring, the fat-flanked porkers and thick, close-knit sheep, and he prided himself on his judgment of a beast.

"I, a hatter!" he seemed to say, as he stood close to the judges, one hand gripping his famous ash plant, the other deep in his front pocket, "I'm more fitted for the job than them."

He was in his element, in the forefront of the judging, prominent amongst the best of them. Then, sauntering round the marquees with his hat well back on his head, he would slice with his penknife a sliver from this cheese and a sliver from that, tasting them critically; savour the different butters, the cream, the buttermilk; rakishly chaff the sonsiest of the dairymaids, who stood behind their exhibits.

That part of him which lay close to the soil flourished on days like these. From his mother's family, the Lumsdens, who had for generations farmed in the Barony of Winton, he drew that deeply rooted inheritance of the love of the land, its produce and beasts. His body craved the hardy exercise of the farm, for in his youth he had driven his team through the loam of Winton, and had known also the thrill of the feel of the gun butt against his cheek. From his father, James Brodie, that bitter, morose, implacable man, of whom he was the sole child, he had derived a pride which nourished itself upon a desire to possess the land. Only the vicissitudes following his impoverished father's death, when the latter had killed himself by falling from his horse, had driven him, as a young man, into the abomination of trade.

But another, and a stronger reason, existed which impelled him to the Show, namely, the craving to associate on equal terms with the gentry of the county and the borough. Conducting himself there not obsequiously, but rather with a trace of arrogance, nevertheless a nod of recognition, a word of greeting, or a few moments conversation with a notability of rank or distinction gratified him inwardly, and intoxicated him with an aberrant delight.

"I've done it, father. I've finished first!" cried Nessie triumphantly. With her small fingers she had succeeded in buttoning up one of the refractory spats.

"Come along, Mary," implored Mrs. Brodie. "You're such a slow-coach. Your father hasn't got all day to wait."

"Let her take her time," said Brodie sardonically. "I might as well be late now I'm about it. In fact, you might like to keep me here all day between you."

"She is never as quick at a thing as Nessie," sighed Mamma.

"That's it," at last said Mary, standing up with benumbed fingers. Her father eyed her critically.

"You know you're getting lazy, that's what's wrong with you, my girl. Good sakes, now I look at you you're getting as big as the side of a house. You should eat less and work more."

He stood up, contemplating himself in the mirror, whilst Mamma led the girls from the room, and, as his reflection gazed back at him from the glass with gradually increasing approval, his self-complacency was eventually restored. His thick muscular legs were set off to perfection by the rough knickerbockers, and under the fleecy homespun stockings his calves swelled nobly; his shoulders were as broad and straight as a wrestler's; not an ounce of fat marred his body; his skin was as unblemished as a child's. He was the perfect figure of a country gentleman, and, as the fact which he already knew was borne in upon him more forcibly by the glamour of his image, he twirled his moustache and smoothed his chin with satisfied vanity.

At this point the door of his room slowly opened and Grandma Brodie put her head round the door jamb, insinuatingly, espying how his mood lay before she spoke.

"Can I have a look at you before you go, James?" she wheedled, after a cautious pause. This day produced upon her decaying sensibility an emotion akin to excitement, sponsored by the forgotten memories of her youth which rushed incoherently in upon her. "You look real grand. Ye're the fine figure o' a man," she told her son. "Losh! but I wish I was going with ye."

"You're too old in the tooth for me to show you, mother," jibed Brodie, "although ye might get a ribbon for toughness."

Her dull ears prevented her from hearing properly, her distant thoughts from understanding the full import of his remark. "Ay, I'm gettin' a trifle old to go," she lamented, "but I've seen the day I would have been among the foremost there at the milkin', and the showin', and the jiggin' after, and then the tig-taggin' on the lang drive hame in the cool o' the night air. It a' comes back to me." Her dull eyes glistened. "What grand scones and bannocks we used to have there, though I paid but little heed to them in they days." She sighed regretfully, at her lost opportunities.

"Tuts, woman, can ye not keep your mind off your meat? You would think you were starved to hear you," Brodie chided her.

"No! No! James. I'm very grateful for all that you give me, and that's plenty. But maybe to-day if you were to see a nice, wee bit Cheddar cheese, no' too dear—there's a wheen o' bargains to be had at the end o' the day—perhaps you might pick it up for me." She leered at him ingratiatingly.

Brodie burst into loud laughter. "Gad! you'll be the death of me, woman. Your god's in your belly. I expect to be seeing Sir John Latta to-day. Do you want me to be carrying pokes and parcels when I meet him," he shouted at her as he strode uproariously out of the room.

His mother hastened to the window of her room to see him swagger out of the house. She would sit there most of the day, straining her vision upon any passing stock, feasting her eyes upon the coloured cards—the red firsts, the blue seconds, the green thirds, and the indifferent yellows, which meant only highly commended—revelling in the press and bustle of the country throng, trying, but always unsuccessfully, to catch a glimpse of some old, familiar face amongst the passing crowd. There was always the chance too, ever present in her mind—its very improbability whetting her fancy provokingly—that her son might bring her back some small gift. She had asked for this, at any rate, and could do no more, she reflected complacently, as she settled herself eagerly in her chair to begin her pleasant vigil.

Downstairs on his way out, Brodie turned to Mary: "You better go down to the business and remind that ass Perry I'll not be in all day." The shop was known in the Brodie household only under the term of "the business"; the former term would have been considered paltry, even degrading. "He mightna remember that there's no holiday for him to-day. He's quite capable of forgetting his head, that one is. And run all the way, my lassie, it'll take some of the beef off you."

To Mamma he said, "I'll be back when you see me!" This was his valediction on such rare occasions as he chose to bid his wife farewell, but it was, in reality, a mark of unusual magnanimity, and Mamma accepted it with an appropriate gratitude.

"I hope you'll enjoy yourself, James," she said timidly, suiting her reply to his mood and the memorable nature of the event. Only on such infrequent and remarkable occasions did she dare use his baptismal name, but when they arose she ventured it in her reply, feeling that it consolidated what small and unsubstantial position she held in his esteem.

She did not dare to consider the attraction which the Show might offer to her; it was deemed sufficient gratification for her to admire the retreating, well set-up figure of her husband, as he went off by himself upon any excursion of pleasure, and the preposterous idea that she might accompany him never entered her head. She had no clothes, she was required at home, her strength was insufficient to support the hardships of a day in the fresh air—any one of these, or of a dozen further reasons, was, by her timid logic, sufficient to debar her from going. "I hope it'll keep fine for him," she murmured as, well pleased, she went back to wash the breakfast dishes, whilst Nessie waved good-bye to her father's back from the parlour window.

When the door had closed behind the master of the house Mary went slowly upstairs to her room, sat down on the edge of her bed and looked out of the window. She did not, in the clear brightness of the morning, see the three tall birch trees, their smooth boles shining with a lustrous sheen, standing upright like silver masts; she did not hear the whispered rustle of the leaves, flickering dark and light as they turned in the faint breeze. Engrossed within herself, she sat thinking of that remark which her father had made, turning it over in her mind uneasily, unhappily. "Mary, you're getting as big as a house," he had sneered, meaning, she fully realised, that she was developing, filling out, as befitted her age and rapid growth. Nevertheless, that single utterance, like a sudden shaft of light darting in, then out, of the darkness of her ignorance, had suddenly originated in her mind a profound disquiet.

Her mother, like a human ostrich, burying her head nervously at the slightest suggestion of the subject when it appeared on the domestic horizon, had not enlightened her on even the most elementary aspects of sex, and to any direct, ingenuous question which her daughter might address to her in this connection, Mamma would reply, in horror: "Hush at once, Mary! It's not a nice thing to talk about. Good girls don't think of such things. That was a shameful thing to ask." Her acquaintance with other girls had been always so slight that she had never achieved information on this matter through the light, tittering remarks in which even the most simpering, pink and white maidens of the town occasionally indulged. Stray fragments of such conversations which she might have overheard fell upon uncomprehending ears, or were repudiated by the natural delicacy of her feeling, and she had lived in an unconscious simplicity, discrediting perhaps, if she ever considered this, the fable that babies were achieved through the assistance of the stork, but being sublimely unaware of the most rudimentary realities of procreation.

Even now the fact that for three months the normal functions of her body had been disturbed had not ruffled the limpid pool of her virgin mind, but this morning her father's coarse remark, twisted by some hidden convolution of her mind into a different sense, distorted into a different interpretation, had struck her with a crushing violence.

Was she different now? Agitatedly she ran her hands over her limbs and body. It was her body, her own, belonging entirely to herself; how could it have altered? In a panic she jumped up, locked her bedroom door, and tore off her cashmere bodice and skirt, her petticoat, her clinging slip, undressed completely until she stood, bewildered, in a chaste nudity, touching her body with confused hands. Never before had she studied her figure with anything but a passing interest. She gazed stupidly at her creamy white skin, raised her arms above her head, lengthened her lithe, lovely figure into a taut, flawless beauty. The small mirror upon her table revealed in its inadequate depths no blemish or imperfection to confirm or allay her unformed fears, and, though she twisted her head this way and that, her frightened eyes could detect no branding disfigurement crying aloud of an inward ugliness. She could not tell whether she was different, whether her bosom was fuller, the shell pink of her nipples less delicate, the soft curve of her lips more profound.

A fearful indecision took possession of her. Three months ago, when she had lain in Denis' arms in a state of unconscious surrender, her instincts had blindly guided her, and with closed eyes she had abandoned herself utterly to the powerful currents which permeated her being. Neither reason, had she wished it, nor knowledge, had she possessed it, intervened; in effect, while experiencing the rending emotions of a pain intolerably sweet, and a pleasure unbearably intoxicating, she had been so moved out of her own being that she had known nothing of what was actually taking place. Her feelings then had lifted her above consideration, but now she dimly wondered what mysterious chemistry had been inaugurated by the power of their embrace, if, perhaps, her lips against his, in some strange combination, had altered her irrevocably in some profound, incomprehensible manner.

She felt powerless, lost in a perplexity of indecision, feeling that she must act to dispel immediately this sudden ferment in her mind, but unaware of how she should accomplish this. As she sombrely resumed the garments that lay scattered around her feet, she abandoned immediately the idea of approaching her mother, knowing well that Mamma's timid soul would leap in terror at the very mention of the topic. Involuntarily she turned towards the thought of Denis, her perpetual consolation, but instantly, and adding to her dismay, she was aware that she would not see him for at least a week, reflected, further, that she might see him on this next occasion for a moment only. Since that wonderful talk with him in Bertorelli's their meetings had been short— although so sweet—and by agreement carefully guarded, and while such fleeting glimpses of Denis as she thus obtained constituted the only felicity of her life, she felt now conclusively that, in these hasty exchanges of encouragement and love, she would never muster courage to invoke, even indirectly, his advice; at the mere idea a shameful blush pervaded her.

She was again dressed, and, unlocking the door, went downstairs, where Mamma, having finished what she called putting a face on things, had settled down luxuriously to an uninterrupted hour with her book. There were no problems like hers in such books, sadly reflected Mary, no indication in the vows, kissed finger tips, sweet speeches, and happy endings, of the elucidation of her difficulty.

"I'll go down to the business with father's message. He asked me to go in the forenoon," she said, after a moment's indecision, addressing her mother's bowed, rapt figure.

Mrs. Brodie, sitting in the drawing-room of a Sussex manor, surrounded by the society of her election, and in earnest conversation with the evangelical vicar of the parish, did not reply, did not even hear her daughter's voice. When immersed in a book she was, as her husband had put it, its slave.

"You're a perfect slave to that trash," he had once sneered at her when she had failed to respond to his question. "To see ye slaverin' ower it is like a drunkard wi' a bottle. Ye wad sit readin' there if the house was burnin' about our ears."

Observing, therefore, with a clouded eye that it was useless to disturb her mother, that under the present circumstances she could not obtain from her a coherent, still less a comforting word, Mary departed silently, and unnoticed, to execute her errand.

On the way to the town she remained immersed in her sad, questioning thoughts, walking limply, her head drooping, with slow steps; but although her journey was thus protracted, she reached her destination before she had even glimpsed the solution of her enigma.

In the shop Peter Perry was alone, lively, expanded, important, in the magnificence of sole responsibility, and he welcomed her with nervous effusion, his face lighting up with delight and his white cheeks becoming even more pale from the joyous shock of seeing her.

"This is an unexpected pleasure indeed, Miss Mary. Not often we have the pleasure of seeing you down at the business! Dear me! A great pleasure! A great pleasure!" he repeated agitatedly, rubbing his thin, transparent, tapering fingers together with quick, rustling movements; then he paused, completely at a loss. He was actually unnerved by the stroke of circumstances which had delivered Mary at the shop on the very day when, her father being absent, he might be permitted to talk to her, and, in his confusion, the scintillating conversations he had so frequently conducted in his imagination between himself and a bevy of queenly young ladies of the highest society, and which he regarded as a form of rehearsal for an occasion such as that which now presented itself, fled from him on the four winds. He was silent, he who had longed for this opportune moment, saying: "If a fellow could get the chance he might cut a pretty good dash with Miss Mary," and tongue-tied, he who addressed his ironing-board, through the steam in the back shop, with fluent, contemptuous ease. A paralysing dumbness lay upon the man who, in his romantic leisure moments in bed on Sunday mornings, his eye fixed on his brass bed-knob as on a coronet, had charmed a duchess with his courtly speech. He felt his flesh wilt, his skin tingle damply, the perspiration exude clammily from his pores; he lost his head completely and, his professional manner taking the bit between its teeth, he blurted out: "Pray be seated, madam, what can I do for you to-day?"

He was horrified, and what blood lay in his veins rushed painfully to his head, making her image swim before him through a haze of embarrassment. He did not colour—that was an impossibility for him—but his head swam with giddiness; yet to his amazement and relief, Mary manifested neither indignation nor surprise. In plain truth her thoughts were still sadly distant, she had not quite recollected herself from the march of her dreary reverie, had not heard him, and instead of showing astonishment, she took quite gratefully the chair he had automatically proffered, and sank down upon it with a tired sigh.

Then in a moment she looked up, as though seeing him for the first time.

"Oh! Mr. Perry," she exclaimed, "I—I must have been thinking. I had no idea you were there."

He was slightly dismayed. Looking at his emasculate figure, it seemed the last possibility in the world that he should cherish, in the traditional manner, a secret passion for his employer's daughter, but such was indeed the case, and, in his highest, wildest, and most furtive flights, he visualised even a partnership for an exceedingly worthy young man, to be achieved through an alliance to the house of Brodie more binding than that of sordid trade. Mary, completely unaware of such optimistic visions, but vaguely pitying in her heart the timorous youth who lived in such manifest apprehension of her father, gazed at him mildly.

"I have a message for you, Mr. Perry," she said. "Mr. Brodie will not be in to-day and asks that you will attend to the business in his absence."

85

"Oh! quite, Miss Brodie! I quite understood that your father would be at the Show to-day. In fact I have made all arrangements to be here all day! I shall lunch here. I know well that the chief is extremely fond of such functions." Had Brodie heard himself referred to in such terms he would have annihilated his assistant with a single glance, but Perry had now recovered himself, was prepared to do himself justice, and privately considered his last florid remark rather good. "But even in the chief's absence the work will go on, Miss Brodie—and I hope—go on well," he continued euphoniously. "You, personally, may rest assured I shall do my best, my very utmost to make things go smoothly." He was so earnest in his manner, his moist eye glistened so eloquently that, despite her apathy, Mary found herself thanking him, though for what reason she scarcely knew.

Just then a customer came in, a shipwright who demanded a new cap and, though Mary would have gone at his entry, a languor of mind held her passive and relaxed, a lassitude of body bound her to the soothing comfort of the chair. She felt disinclined to begin her return home, and under her eye, although it followed his movements indifferently, Perry, seizing a delightful chance to exhibit his ability, served his client magniloquently, accomplishing feats of extreme nimbleness and dexterity with boxes and the short step ladder, and eventually with paper and string. When the purchaser had gone he returned with a conscious air and, leaning across the counter, remarked confidentially: "Your father has a wonderful business here, Miss Brodie—practically a monopoly." He was proud of that too, and although it came out of a book on Economics he was wrestling with at nights, he gave the term the flavour of his own deep and original deduction. "Not that—if I might venture to suggest it—it might not be increased by a few new ideas, a little novelty, perhaps, some new developments, even an extension of the business—it could be done," he added insinuatingly.

She did not reply, which oppressed him with the feeling that somehow he did not seem to be holding her attention; the conversation appeared to him rather one-sided.

"I hope you are well?" he enquired, after a considerable pause.

"Quite well," she echoed mechanically.

"You look to me, if I may say so, somewhat thinner in the face."

She raised her eyes.

"You think I'm thinner."

"Decidedly!" He seized the opportunity to regard her impassive, shadowed face with an expression of respectful solicitude and, as he leaned upon the counter, supported his small chin in his long fingers and posed his figure generally with an air of studied admiration.

"In fact," he continued boldly, "although as beautiful as ever, if you will permit me to say so, you look slightly indisposed. I am afraid the heat of the day is trying you. Could I get you a glass of water?"

Before she could refuse he had raised himself in a passion of service, was off like a shot, returned instantly with a brimming tumbler of sparkling water and had pressed the cold, clouded glass into her unresistant hand. "Drink it, Miss Mary," he insisted, "it will do you good." As she took a few sips so as not to hurt his feelings, a sudden anxious thought filled him with concern.

"I trust you have not been ill. You are so pale. Have you seen your physician?" he enquired in his best manner.

At his affected words Mary stopped with the glass half raised to her lips as though a light had broken upon her with a sudden effulgence, showing her a pathway she must follow. She looked at Perry with the full force of her attention, then turned her gaze through the open doorway and beyond, whilst her mind filled with a sudden resolution that made her lips firm and straight.

For a moment she remained still, then, with a quick impulse, she got up and murmured: "I must go now, Mr. Perry. Thank you for your kindness"; and before he could collect himself, she moved quietly away and went out of the shop, leaving him gazing blankly at the tumbler, the vacant chair, the empty air. What a strange girl, he thought, to go like that when he was behaving so admirably to her; but then, to be sure, women were strange creatures, and on the whole he had, he considered, acquitted himself very creditably. Mr. Perry began to whistle.

When Mary walked into the street she turned, not to the right, which was the direction for home, but to the left which would take her, if she pursued the road to its termination, to the far, Knoxhill end of the Borough. Peter Perry's chance remark had given her the solution she had been blindly seeking, and it was that which now impelled her in this contrary direction. She would go and see a doctor. Doctors were wise, trustworthy, kind; they healed, advised, comforted, yet respected one's confidence. Immediately she thought of the only practitioner she knew, Dr. Lawrie who, although he had not been in her home once in ten years, was nominally the family doctor, and she now remembered vividly the last time he had spoken to her, when he had placed his hand upon her small head and remarked with a pompous benignity: "Penny for a curl, young lady! Come along! Is it a bargain? You'll never miss it." She had been ten then, and while he had not secured the ringlet she had received the penny. Although she had not met him since, she saw him frequently, driving in his dogcart, everywhere and at every hour, always in a hurry and, in her eyes, maintaining always the look her childish mind had memorised, of one learned, august, and apart. He lived at Knoxhill, in a large residence, old, mottled by lichen, but still imposing, breasting the ascent half-way up the hill, and as she made her way resolutely along the street she recollected having heard that his hour of consultation began at noon.

It was a considerable distance to the doctor's house, and soon she was forced to ease the impulsive rapidity of her pace, she who a few months ago could have run the whole way without once losing breath. As her steps flagged her resolution faltered slightly, and she began to wonder how she would approach him. The thought of seeking his advice had dawned upon her so happily that the difficulties of achieving this object had not occurred to her; but now they obtruded themselves upon her notice painfully, obviously, and with every step became more insurmountable. Should she begin by consulting him about her health? He would, she realised, instantly marvel that she should have come alone, without the escort and protection of her mother. Such a thing was unheard of and she conceived that he might even refuse to see her in her unaccompanied state; if he consented to see her and she advanced, in her inexperience, some insufficient reason for her visit, she felt certain that with a few searching questions he would riddle any flimsy tissue which she might fabricate, and leave her helpless and ashamed. At this she reflected sadly that the only way would be to tell the truth absolutely, and to throw herself upon his mercy. Suppose, then, he were to disclose the visit to her parents, did the purpose she sought to achieve justify such a frightful hazard? Her thoughts wandered in on a maze of unreasoning perplexity as she began to ascend the incline of Knoxhill.

At length she reached the gate of the doctor's residence, where his big, brass plate, dented in its early, uneasy days by an occasional stone from some mischievous urchin, and now polished into a smooth, undecipherable, respected serenity, shone like the eye of an oracle, compelling thither the weary and the sick.

Outside the gate, as she stood for a moment quelling her misgivings and mustering her courage, she saw approaching in the distance an elderly man whom she recognised as an acquaintance of her father's, and realising with a sudden start that she could not risk going in whilst he was in sight, she turned her back upon him and walked slowly past the house. From out of the corner of her eye she observed the big, solid house with its severe Georgian porch, its windows swathed in mysterious saffron curtains, felt it, with a growing uneasiness, looming more largely upon her, felt her doubts rush back upon her with a greater and more disquieting force. It was a mistake to visit a doctor who knew her so well. Denis might not like her taking a step like this without first consulting him; another time would be more propitious for her visit; she was not ill, but well and as normal as ever; she was making herself the victim of her own imagination, obviously, unnecessarily, dangerously.

Now the street was clear and she perceived that she must enter at once or not at all; telling herself that she would go in first and face her difficulties afterwards, she had placed her hand upon the gate-handle when she recollected that she had no money with her to pay the fee which, even if he did not demand it, she must at once discharge to avoid a complication leading to discovery. She withdrew her hand, and was

88

again beginning to resume her indecisive pacing upon the pavement, when, abruptly, she saw a maid looking from behind the curtains of a front window. Actually the maid observed nothing, but to Mary's excited fancy the servant's eye appeared to be regarding her suspiciously, and in the accusation of this apparent scrutiny the last shreds of her resolution dissolved. She felt she could endure the suspense of her indecision no longer, and with a guilty countenance she moved off hastily down the street, as though detected in some atrocious action.

As she fled down the street, retracing the whole of the weary way she had come, the repression of her unrelieved desire almost stifled her. She felt herself a blunderer and a coward; her face burned with shame and confusion; she felt she must at all costs avoid the public gaze. To keep away from anyone who might know her, and to return home as quickly as possible, she did not follow the High Street but took instead the alternative route—a narrow, shabby alley named College Street, but referred to always as the Vennel—which branched off the circuitous sweep of the main thoroughfare and drove, under the railway, directly towards the Common. With lowered head she plunged into the murk of the Vennel as if to hide herself there, and hurried along the mean, disreputable street with its ill-paved causeway and gutters filled with broken bottles, empty tins, and the foul litter of a low quarter. Only the desire to rush from recognition drove her through this lane which, tacitly forbidden to her, she never entered; but even in her precipitate flight its misery laid a sordid hand upon her.

Women stared at her from open courts as they stood idle, slatternly, bare armed, talking in groups; a mongrel dog chased her, barking, snapping at her heels; a cripple, dirty and deformed, taking his ease upon the pavement, shouted after her for alms, pursuing her with his voice whiningly, importunately, insultingly.

She hurried with a greater speed to escape from the depressing confines of the lane, and had almost made her way through, when she discerned a large crowd of people bearing down upon her. For one tragic, transient instant she stood still, conceiving this to be a mob rushing to assault her. Immediately, however, the sound of a band fell upon her ears, and she observed that the host, surrounded by an attendant rabble of dirty children and racing, mangy curs, descending upon her like a regiment marching to battle, was the local branch of the Salvation Army, newly formed in Levenford. In the rush of its youthful enthusiasm its devoted members were utilising the holiday by parading the low quarters of the town—even at this early hour of the day—to combat and offset any vice or debauchery that might be liberated on the occasion of the Cattle Show.

Onwards they came, banners flying, dogs barking, cymbals crashing, the band blaring out the hymn: "Throw out the Life-line," whilst the soldiers of both sexes joined their voices loudly with harmonious fervour.

As they advanced she pressed herself against the wall, wishing the pavement to open beneath her feet and engulf her, and while they swept past, she shrank into herself as she felt the buffet and sway of the surging bodies coarsely against her own. Suddenly, as they rolled past, a female private of the army, flushed with righteousness and the joy of her new uniform, seeing Mary there so frightened and humiliated, dropped for a moment her piercing soprano and, thrusting her face close to Mary's, whispered in one hot, penetrating breath:

"Sister, are you a sinner? Then come and be saved; come and be washed in the Blood of the Lamb!"

Then, merging her whisper into the burden of the hymn, she sang loudly: "Someone is sinking to-day," swung again into the fervent strains and was gone, tramping victoriously down the street.

A sense of unutterable degradation possessed Mary as she supported herself against the wall, feeling with her sensitive nature that this last disgrace represented the crowning manifestation of an angry Providence. In the course of a few hours the sudden, chance direction of her thoughts into an obscure and foreign channel had altered the whole complexion of her life. She could not define the feeling which possessed her, she could not coherently express or even understand the dread which filled her, but as she stumbled off upon her way home she felt, in a nausea of self-reproach, that she was unworthy to live.

VII

On the Monday after the Cattle Show a considerable commotion occurred in the Brodie household. The ra-ta-tat of the postman on that morning was louder than usual and his mien fraught with a more important significance, as he handed to Mrs. Brodie a letter embellished by a row of strange stamps, a thin, flimsy oblong which crackled mysteriously between her agitated fingers. Mamma, with a palpitating heart, looked at this letter which she had been anticipating for days. There was no need for her to consider who had sent it, for she recognised immediately the thin, "foreign" envelopes which she had herself solicitously chosen and carefully packed for Matt. She was alone, and, in a transport of gratitude and expectation, she pressed the envelope to her lips, then close against her bosom, until, after a moment, as though she had by contact absorbed its hidden message directly into her heart, she withdrew it and turned it over in her red, work-wrinkled hands.

Although she felt that the letter was exclusively hers she saw that it was addressed to Mr. and Mrs. James Brodie, and she dared not open it; she dared not run upstairs and cry joyfully to her husband: "A letter from Matt!"; instead she took this first, precious, unsubstantial bulletin from abroad and placed it carefully upon her husband's plate. She waited. She waited submissively, yet with an eager, throbbing impatience, for the news from her son, returning from time to time into the kitchen from the scullery to reassure herself that the letter was still there, that this phenomenal missive, which had miraculously traversed three thousand leagues of strange seas and exotic lands to reach her safely, had not now suddenly vanished into the empty air.

At last, after what seemed to her an eternity, Brodie came down, still showing in his disposition, she observed thankfully, remnants of the previous day's pleasure. Immediately she brought him his porridge and, having placed this gently before him, stood expectantly a short distance off. Brodie took up the letter, weighed it silently on the palm of his huge hand, seemed to consider it dispassionately, weighed it ostentatiously again, then put it down unopened before him and commenced to eat his porridge. As he supped one spoonful after another, bent forward in a crouching attitude with both elbows upon the table, he kept his eyes fixed upon the envelope and maliciously affected not to see her.

Under the refinement of his malice she remained in the background, her hands pressed tightly together, her body tense with a fever of anticipation, until she could no longer endure the suspense.

"Open it, father," she whispered.

He affected a violent, exaggerated start.

"Bless my soul, woman, you near scared the life out me. What are ye hangin' about there for? Oh! I see! I see! It's this bit o' a thing that's drawin' ye." He jerked his spoon towards the letter and lay back negligently in his chair, contemplating her. He was, he told himself in the full flush of his amiability, having a rare game with her. "Ye've the look o' a wasp ower the jam pot," he drawled. "The same kind o' sickly hunger about ye. I was thinkin' mysel' it looked pretty thin; pretty poor stuff, I've no doubt."

"It's the thin note-paper I bought for him to save postage," Mamma pleaded. "Ye can get a dozen sheets o' it into the one envelope."

"There's not a dozen sheets here. No, I question if there's more nor two or three at the outside. I hope that doesna mean bad news," he said sadly, cocking one small, spiteful eye at her.

"Oh! will ye not open it and put my mind at rest, father?" she implored. "I'm fair eaten up with anxiety, ye must surely see."

He lifted his head arrestingly.

"There's plenty time—plenty o' time," he drawled, spinning out the words. "If ye've waited ten weeks another ten minutes 'll not burst ye. Away and bring me the rest o' my breakfast."

Sighing with uncertainty, she was obliged to drag herself away from the letter, and go back to the scullery to dish up his bacon and eggs whilst she trembled continually in the fear that he might read the epistle and suddenly destroy it in her absence.

"That's the spirit," he cried broadly, as she hastily returned. "I havena seen ye run like that since the day ye ate the green grosets. I know how to make ye souple. I'll have ye dancin' in a minute."

But she did not reply; he had baited her into dumbness. Accordingly when he had finished breakfast he again picked up the letter.

"Well, I suppose we better see what is inside it," he drawled casually, taking as long as he could to slit the envelope and extract the largely written sheets. Silence reigned whilst he protracted his reading of the epistle intolerably, but all the time Mamma's anxious eyes never left his face, seeking there some expression which might transmit to her a verification of her hopes and a negation of her fears. At length he threw it down, declaring:

"Nothing in it! A pack o' nonsense!"

The moment he relinquished them, Mrs. Brodie threw herself upon the sheets and, seizing them with longing, brought them close to her myopic eyes and drank the closely written lines thirstily. She observed at once from the superscription that the letter had been written on board the *Irrawaddy*, and that it had been posted almost immediately the ship berthed.

"Dear Parents," she read on, "I take up my pen to write you after a most fearful and unending attack of mal de mer, or more plainly, sea-sickness. This dreadful affliction settled upon me first in the Irish Sea, but in the Bay of Biscay I was so ill I wished to die, and would have prayed to be thrown to the fishes but for the thought of you at home. My cabin being close and unendurable, and my berth companion turning out to be a vulgar fellow—addicted to a heavy indulgence in drink—I at first attempted to remain on deck, but the waves were so gigantic and the sailors so uncharitable that I was forced to descend again to my hot, disagreeable quarters. In this confined space, as I lay in my bunk I was rattled about in a most awful and distressing manner, sometimes being lifted up to the ceiling and sticking there for a minute before falling heavily. When I had fallen back on my berth my stomach seemed to have remained above, for so much did I experience a feeling of emptiness and exhaustion that it seemed as if my middle was devoid of its contents. To make matters worse I could in addition eat nothing, but vomited all the time, night as well as day. My cabin-mate, as the term goes here, who occupied the lower bunk, used the most frightful language on the first night when I was sick and made me get up in my nightshirt in the cold, heaving cabin to change places with him. The only thing which kept down and indeed which kept my poor body and soul together was a nourishing drink which one of the stewards kindly brought me. He called it stingo, and I must confess that I found it agreeable and that it was truly the means of saving my life for you. Altogether it was a frightful time I can well assure you.

"Well, to continue, by the time we had passed Gibraltar, which is nothing but a bare one-sided rock, much bigger than our own Levenford Rock but not so pretty, and were well into the Mediterranean, I managed to get my sea legs. The sea here was more blue than anything I have seen—tell Nessie it was more blue even than her eyes—and I was the more able to enjoy this and also the lovely colours of the sunsets as it was so mercifully calm. I could still hardly swallow a bite, but at Port Said we took in supplies of fruit and I was able to eat some fresh dates and some very delicious oranges, which were very sweet, and skinned easily like tangerines, but much larger. I had also a fruit called a papaia which is juicy like a small melon but with a green skin and a pinkish colour of flesh. Very refreshing! I think they did me good, in fact I am sure they did me great good.

"I did not go ashore here as I had been warned that Port Said was a very wicked place and dangerous for Europeans unless armed. A gentleman on board here told me a long story about an adventure he had in a heathen temple and in other places there, but I will not repeat it from motives of modesty and also as I am not sure that he was speaking the truth. But it seems that there are astonishing things out here. In this connection tell Agnes I am true to her memory. I forgot to say that they come off to the ship in boats at Port Said and sell very good rahat-lakoum which is an excellent sweet although you would never judge so from the name.

"We passed very slowly through the Suez Canal, a narrow ditch bounded on either side by miles of sandy desert with purple mountains in the distance. This canal is not much to look at and passes through some dull-looking sheets of water called the Bitter Lakes, but it is, they say, very important. Sometimes we saw men with white cloaks, mounted —not on camels as you at home might have expected—but on fast horses on which they galloped away whenever they caught sight of the ship. I must tell you that I also saw palm trees for the first time—just like the one in the church hall, only very much larger and thicker. In the Red Sea the heat was very great but after we had well passed Aden and some curious islands called the Twelve Apostles, when I was just hoping to have a nice time by joining the ladies in deck games, conversation, and music, the heat again suddenly became frightful. Mamma, those drill suits you got me are no use they are so thick and heavy. The correct thing to do is to have them made in India by a native. They say they are very clever at it and have the right material which is tussore silk and certainly not that drill you got me. Also while on this subject please tell Mary that the glass piece of the flask she gave me smashed in the first storm, and Nessie's compass is points different from the one on the ship.

"Anyway I went down with the heat, and although eating better—I like the curries very much—I lost pounds. I am sure I got very thin and this caused me much embarrassment which, together with my lack of energy, debarred me from joining in social life and I could only sit alone, thinking of my unused mandolin, and looking unhappily at the ladies and at the sharks which followed the ship in great numbers.

"After the heat came the rain, what is referred to here as a monsoon—a chota (small) monsoon, but it was wet enough for me—just like a never-ending Scotch mist which drenched everything all day long. We went through the mist until we reached Ceylon, putting in at Colombo. This has a wonderful harbour. I could see miles and miles of calm water. Very comforting! We had had it rough in the Indian Ocean. Some people went ashore to buy precious stones, moonstones, opals, and turquoises, but I did not go as they say you are simply robbed and that the moonstones are full of flaws, that is cracks. Instead my friend the steward gave me a choice Colombo pineapple. Although it was large I was surprised to find that I could finish the whole of it. Very palatable! My bowels were a trifle loose on the following day and I thought I had dysentery but mercifully have been spared this, also malaria, so far. It must have been the pineapple.

"However, the worst thing of all was yet to come. In the Indian Ocean we had a typhoon, which is the worst kind of horrible storm you could ever imagine. It all began by the sky going quite purple, then dark yellow like brass. I thought it very pretty at first but suddenly all we passengers were ordered below and I took this rightly as a bad omen, for all at once the wind hit the ship like a blow. A man who was standing at his cabin had his hand caught by the sudden slam of the door and his thumb was torn right off. A seaman had his leg broken also. It was terrible.

"I was not sick, but must now confess I was almost apprehensive. The sea came up, not like the waves in the Bay of Biscay, but with a fearful high swell—like round hills. I was obliged soon to give over looking through the porthole. The ship groaned so much in her timbers I thought she would surely burst asunder. The rolling was most awful; and on two occasions we went over so far and remained there so long I feared we should never come back. But Providence was kind and finally we reached the delta of the Ganges, great banks of sand and very muddy water. We had a pilot to take us up from the mouth of the Hooghly—and we went up the river so slowly that we took days. On the banks are a multitude of little patches of cultivation all irrigated by ditches. I have seen coco-nut palms, also bananas growing on the trees. The natives here are, of course, black and seem to work in nothing but loin cloths, although some have turbans. They squat on their haunches as they work on their patches, but some also cast nets in the yellow river water and catch fish which are said to be good. The whites have sun helmets—father, your topee is the very thing.

"Now I must close. I have written this letter at intervals, and now we have docked. I am much impressed with the size of the place and the docks. The sky here seems full of house tops and minarets.

"I read a bit of my Bible every day. I am not indisposed. I think I shall do well here.

"With love to all at home, I remain,

"Your dutiful son,

"MATT."

Mamma drew in her breath ecstatically, as she wiped away the tears which seemed to have escaped from her overflowing heart. The frail instrument of her being swelled in a pæan of joy and gratitude, singing within her: "What a letter! What a son!" The news seemed too potent for her, alone, to contain, and a wild impulse seized her to run into the open street, to traverse the town waving aloft the letter, crying out the brave chronicle of this epoch-making voyage.

Brodie read her mood distinctly, with a derisive penetrating eye. "Call out the bellman," he said, "and shout the news through the Borough. Go on. Have it blurted out to everybody. Pah! wait till ye get, no' his first, but his twenty-first, letter. He's done nothing yet but eat fruit and be namby-pamby."

Mamma's bosom heaved indignantly.

"The poor boy's had a dreadful time," she quivered. "Such sickness! Ye mustna begrudge him the fruit. He was aye fond o' it." Only this aspersion upon her son made her answer him back. He looked at her sardonically: "It seems ye made a fine mess of the outfit! My topee was the only fit article he had," he said, as he rose from the table.

"I'll take it up with that manager at Lennie's this very day," cried Mamma in a choking voice. "He told me with his own lips that drill was being worn out there. The idea of such deceit! It might have sent my son to his death o' sunstroke."

"Trust you to make a mess o' anything, auld wife," he launched at her pleasantly, as a parting shot. But now his arrows did not penetrate or wound; they did not reach her as she stood in that far-off land, where tall palms waved majestic fronds against an opal sky, and soft bells pealed from temples in the scented dusk.

At last she started from her reverie.

"Mary!" she called out to the scullery. "Here's Matt's letter! Read it and take it to Grandma when you've finished with it"—adding presently in an absent voice, "then bring it back to me." Immediately she returned to her sweet meditation, considering that in the afternoon she would send the precious missive to Agnes Moir. Mary should take it down, together with a jar of home-made jam and a cake. Agnes might have had a letter herself, although that, Mrs. Brodie complacently reflected, was doubtful; but at any rate she would be overjoyed to hear, in any manner, of the heroic tidings of his journey and the splendid news of his arrival. To send down the letter at once was also, Mamma was well aware, the correct thing to do, and the added libations of cake and jam would embellish the tit-bit delightfully for Agnes, a good, worthy girl of whom she consistently approved.

When Mary returned, Mamma demanded: "What did Matt's grandma say about his letter?"

"Something about wishing she could have tasted that pineapple," remarked Mary indifferently.

Mamma bridled as she carefully took the sacred letter from her daughter. "The like of that," she said, "and the poor boy nearly drowned and consumed by sharks. You might show a little more interest yourself with your brother in such danger. Ye've been trailing about like a dead thing all morning. Now, are ye listening to me? I want you to run over to Agnes with it this afternoon. And you're to take a parcel over to her as well."

"Very well," said Mary. "When am I to be back?"

"Stay and have a chat with Agnes if you like. And if she asks you to wait for tea, I'll allow you to do so. You can come to no harm in the company of a Christian girl like that."

Mary said nothing, but her lifeless manner quickened. A frantic plan, which had hung indefinitely in her mind during the previous sleepless night, began already to take substantial form under this unexpected offering of chance.

She had resolved to go to Darroch. To venture there alone would be for her, at any time, a difficult and hazardous proceeding, fraught with grave possibilities of discovery and disaster. But if she were to undertake such an unheard of excursion at all, the timely message of Mamma's was clearly her opportunity. She knew that a train left Levenford for Darroch at two o'clock, covering the four miles between the two towns in fifteen minutes, and that the same train made the return journey, leaving Darroch at four o'clock. If, incredibly, she ventured upon the expedition, she saw that she would have more than one hour and a half to accomplish her purpose, and this she deemed to be adequate. The sole question which concerned her was her ability to deliver her message successfully before two o'clock, and, more vitally, whether she could disentangle herself from the embarrassing and effusive hospitality of Agnes in time for her train.

With the object of speed in her mind she worked hard all morning, and had finished her household duties before one o'clock when, snatching a few mouthfuls of food, she hurried upstairs to change. But, as she reached her room at the head of the stairs, a remarkable sensation overtook her. She felt suddenly light, ethereal, and giddy; before her startled eyes the floor of her bedroom moved gently upwards and downwards, with a slow see-sawing instability; the walls, too, tottered in upon her like the falling sides of a house of cards; across her vision a parabola of lights danced, followed instantly by darkness. Her legs doubled under her and she sank silently down upon the floor in a faint. For a long time she lay recumbent upon her back, unconscious. Then gradually her prone position restored her feeble circulation, tiny currents of blood seemed to course again under the dead pallor of her skin, and with a sigh she opened her eyes, which fell immediately upon the hands of the clock that indicated the time to be half-past one. Agitatedly she raised herself upon her elbow, and, after several fruitless attempts, at last forced herself to stand upright again. She felt unsteady and languid, but her head was light and clear, and with soft, limp fingers, that felt to her useless for the purpose, she compelled herself to dress hastily. Then hurriedly she went downstairs.

Mamma met her with the letter and the package and a host of messages, greeting, and injunctions for Agnes. So engrossed was she in her benevolent generosity that she failed to notice her daughter's distress.

"And don't forget to tell her it's the new season's jam," she called out, as Mary went out of the gate, "and that the cake has two eggs in it," she added. "And don't leave the letter. Say I want it back!" she shouted, finally.

Mary had twenty minutes to get to the station, which was enough time and no more. The heavy parcel, containing two pounds of cake and two pounds of jam, dragged upon her arm; in her weak state the thought of the rich cake sickened her, and the sweet jam smeared itself cloyingly over her imagination. She had no time to deliver it to Agnes, and manifestly it was impossible for her to carry it about all afternoon. Already in her purpose she stood committed to a desperate act, and now an incitement to further rashness goaded her. Something urged her to dispose of Mamma's sumptuous present, to drop it silently in the gutter or cast it from her into an adjacent garden. Its weight oppressed her, and her recoil from the contemplation of its contents thrust her into sudden recklessness. Beside the pathway stood a small boy, ragged, barefooted, and dirty, who chalked lines disconsolately upon a brick wall. As she passed, with one sudden, unregenerate impulse, Mary thrust the bundle upon the astounded urchin. She felt her lips move, heard herself saying: "Take it! Quick! Something to eat!"

The small boy looked up at her with astonished, distrustful eyes which indicated, more clearly than articulate speech, his profound suspicion of all strangers who might present him with heavy packages under the pretext of philanthropy. With one eye still mistrustfully upon her, he tore open the paper cover to ensure he was not being deceived, when, the richness of the contents having been thus revealed to his startled eyes, he tucked the parcel under his arm, exploded into activity before this peculiar lady might regain her sanity, and vanished like a puff of

D

smoke down the street.

Mary felt shocked at her own temerity. A sudden pang struck her as to how she would conceal from Mamma her inexcusable action, or failing this, how she might ever explain away the dissipation into thin air of the fruits of her mother's honest labour. Vainly she tried to obtain comfort by telling herself she would deliver the letter to Agnes when she returned after four, but her face was perturbed as she hastened onwards to the station.

In the train for Darroch she made a powerful effort to concentrate her fatigued attention upon the conduct of her scheme, tracing mentally in advance the steps she would take; she was determined that there should be no repetition of the weakness and indecision of the day before. Darroch she knew sufficiently well, having visited it several times before it had become vested for her with a halo of glamour and romance as the place in which Denis lived. Since she had known that he resided there, the drab town, consisting in the main of chemical and dye works, the effluent of which frequently polluted the clear Leven in its lower reaches, had undergone a manifest and magical metamorphosis. The ill-cobbled, narrow streets assumed a wider aspect because Denis moved along them, and the smoke-splashed buildings became more splendid because amongst them he had his being.

As she drew slowly nearer to this enchanted place Mary, in spite of her crushing anxiety, felt actually a breathless anticipation. Although it was not her intention to see Denis, she could not suppress a throb of excitement at drawing near to him in his own environment.

When the train steamed into Darroch station she quickly left her compartment, surrendered her ticket, and was amongst the first of the small handful of passengers to leave the platform. Walking without hesitation, and as rapidly as her strength permitted, she passed along the main street, inclined sharply to the left, and entered a quieter residential locality. None of the persons she encountered knew her; her appearance caused neither stir nor interest. Darroch, though lacking the county atmosphere, was as large a township as Levenford, was, indeed, the only other large town within a radius of twelve miles, and it was easy for Mary to slip unnoticed through the busy streets, and to submerge her identity beneath that of the crowd which thronged them. It was for these very reasons that she had chosen Darroch for her present purpose.

When she had proceeded half-way along the secondary street she observed, to her relief, that her memory had served her correctly, and, confronted by a crescent of terrace-houses she advanced resolutely to the end house, and at once rang the bell loudly. A diminutive maid in a blue cotton overall opened the door.

"Is the doctor at home?" asked Mary.

"Will you please to come in," replied the small domestic, with the indifferent air of one who is tired of repeating the formula endlessly.

Mary was shown into the waiting-room. It was a poor room with dull walls and a thin, worn carpet upon the floor, furnished by an array of chairs, in varying degrees of decrepitude, and a large oak table bearing several tattered, dog-eared, out-of-date periodicals and a pink china pot containing a languishing aspidistra.

"What is the name?" apathetically enquired the slave of the door.

"Miss Winifred Brown," replied Mary distinctly.

Clearly she was, she now saw, a liar! Whilst she should have been in Levenford, sitting in amiable conference with her brother's legitimately engaged fiancée, here she was, having cast her mother's parcel from her, four miles away, giving a false name, and waiting in the house of a strange doctor, whose name and domicile she had recollected only by fortunate chance. The faint colour, which had entered her face as she enunciated the fictitious name, now violently flushed it at these thoughts, and it was with difficulty that she essayed to thrust the feeling of guilt from her as she was ushered into the consulting-room.

The doctor was a middle-aged man, bald, untidy, disillusioned, and the possessor of an indifferent, cheap practice. It was not his usual consulting hour, which caused him a justifiable annoyance, but his economic position was such as to compel him to see patients at any hour. He was a bachelor and his housekeeper had just served him up a midday meal of fat boiled beef with suet puddings, which he had eaten hurriedly, and, as a result, the chronic indigestion, due to badly cooked food, irregular hours, and septic teeth, to which he was a martyr, was beginning to gnaw at him painfully. He looked surprisedly at Mary.

"Is it a call?" he enquired.

"No! I have come to consult you," she replied, in a voice which seemed far away and unrecognisable as her own.

"Be seated, then," he said abruptly. Immediately he sensed the unusual and his irritation deepened. He had long ceased to derive interest from the clinical aspect of his cases, and any deviation from the humdrum routine of ordinary practice associated with the rapid issuing of bottles, containing dilute solutions of cheap drugs and colouring agents, always dismayed him; he was, in addition, anxious to get back to his couch and lie down; a spasm of pain gripped his middle as he remembered that his evening surgery would be heavy this night.

"What is it?" he continued, shortly.

Haltingly she began to tell him, blushed, faltered, went on again, speaking in a daze. How she expressed herself she did not know, but apparently his aroused suspicions were confirmed.

"We must examine you," he told her coldly. "Will it be now, or shall you return with—your mother?" Hardly understanding what he meant, she did not know how to reply. His impersonal manner discouraged her, his callous air chilled her, and his general slovenly appearance, with ragged, untrimmed moustache, uncared for finger nails, and grease spots on his waistcoat, affected her equally with a sense of strong antipathy. She told herself, however, that she must go through with her ordeal, and in a low voice she said: "I cannot come back again, doctor."

"Take your things off, then, and prepare yourself," he told her bluntly, indicating the couch as he went out of the room.

In her awkward timidity she had barely time to loosen her clothing and lie down upon the shabby, torn settee before he returned. Then with eyes shut and clenched teeth she submitted herself to his laboured and inexpert examination. It was agony for her, mentally and physically. She shrank in her fastidious mind from his coarse and uncouth presence, and the touch of his unskilful fingers made her wince with pain. At last it was over and, with a few short words, he again left the room.

Inside the space of five minutes she was back again in her chair, dressed, and gazing dumbly at him as he lumbered back to his desk.

The doctor was for once slightly at a loss. He had met this calamity frequently in women of a different class, but he was, despite his obtuse, case-hardened intellect, aware that this girl, who was nothing more than a frightened child, was uninstructed and innocent. He felt that her unconscious defloration had undoubtedly coincided with her conception. He realised why she had so self-consciously given him an assumed name, and in his dry, empty heart a vague pity stirred. At first, with all the anxiety of the unsuccessful practitioner jealous of his meagre reputation, he had suspected that she desired him to apply some means of terminating her condition, but now he realised fully the extent of her sublime ignorance. He moved uncomfortably in his chair, not knowing how to begin.

"You are not married?" he said at length, in a flat voice.

She shook her head with swimming, terrified eyes.

"Then I advise you to get married. You are going to have a baby."

At first she hardly understood. Then her lips contorted with a quivering spasm, her eyes overflowed and tears ran soundlessly down her face. She felt paralysed, as though his words had bludgeoned her. He was talking to her, trying to tell her what she must do, what she must expect, but she scarcely heard him. He receded from her; her surroundings vanished; she was plunged into a grey mist of utter and incomparable dejection, alone with the obsessing horror of certain and inevitable calamity. From time to time fragments of his meaning came to her, like haggard shafts of daylight glancing suddenly through the swirling wreaths of fog which encircled her.

"Try not to worry," she heard him say; then again through the enveloping pall came the words, "You are young, your life is not wasted."

What did he know or care? His well-meant platitudes left her untouched and cold. Instinctively she realised that to him she represented merely a transient and unwelcome incident in his monotonous day, and, as she rose and asked to know his charge, she detected instantly in his eye a half-veiled flicker of relief. Her intuition had not deceived her, for, having taken his fee and shown her to the door, he fled immediately to his bismuth bottle, took a large dose, settled himself down, with a sigh of relief, to rest and straight away completely forgot her.

As she passed out of the house into the street it was just three o'clock. She had an hour to wait for her train—if ever she would take it. In a torture of mind she walked down the street whispering to herself: "God! O God! why have You done this to me? I've never done You any harm. Stop this from happening. Stop it!" A blind unreason possessed her as to why, and how, her body had been singled out by the Almighty for this obscene experiment. It struck her as a supremely unjust manifestation of the Divine omnipotence. Strangely, she did not blame Denis; she felt herself simply the victim of some tremendous, incomprehensible fraud.

No! she did not blame Denis; she felt, instead, that she must fly to him. Caution was now abandoned to the winds in the extremity of her anguish and, with a strained face, she walked along Main Street, at the far end of which stood the Lomond Wine and Spirit Vaults—Owen Foyle, proprietor. Around the corner was a wide, double gate leading into a yard, from which an open, winding stair ascended to the Foyle house.

She crept up this stairway and knocked faintly at the door. From inside came the tinkle of a piano. The tinkle continued, but no one came in answer; then she heard a voice cry, "Rosie, me chick, is that somebody at the door? See if anybody's there." Someone replied, in childish tones: "I'm at my scales, mother; you go, or wait and let them knock again." And the sound of the piano was resumed with redoubled energy and a loudness expressive of intense application.

After a moment's irresolute pause Mary was about to knock upon the door more loudly, when suddenly, as she advanced her hand, a sharp whistle shrilled from outside the yard, and drew gradually nearer to her.

She turned and, at the same moment, Denis appeared at the foot of the stairs, his head tilted back enquiringly, his eyes widening with surprise as he perceived her. Observing immediately that Mary was in acute distress, he ran up the steps.

"Mary!" he exclaimed hurriedly, "what is it?"

She could not reply, could not utter his name.

"What is the matter, dearest Mary?" murmured Denis, coming close to her, taking her cold hand and smoothing it gently in his. "Is it your father?"

She shook her head without gazing at him, knowing that if she did so, she must break down abjectly.

"Come away," she whispered. "Come away before anyone comes."

Oppressed, he followed her slowly down the steps.

In the street, he asked fiercely: "Have they been bad to you at home? Tell me quickly what the trouble is, dear? If anybody has touched you I'll kill him."

There was a pause, then she said slowly, indistinctly, painfully, dropping each word from her lips like a leaden weight:

"I am going to have a baby."

His face whitened as if he had received a frightful wound and became gradually more pale, as though his strength and vigour flowed out from him. He dropped her hand and looked at her with dilated, starting eyes.

"Are you sure?" he jerked out at last.

"I'm sure."

"How do you know?"

"Something seemed wrong with me. I went to a doctor. He told me."

"A—a doctor? It's certain, then?"

"Certain," she echoed, dully.

It was irrevocable, then. With one sentence she had thrust upon his shoulders a load of misery and responsibility, which turned him from a gay, whistling boy into a mature and harassed man. Their love-making had been a trap, the playful dalliance and the secret meetings of the past merely snares to lure and entangle him in this draggled predicament. The pleasant, sanguine expectations of marrying her, all the alluring preparations which he had contemplated, now felt like chains binding and drawing him towards an obligation he must inevitably fulfil. A heavy sigh burst from him. In the masculine society in which he moved nothing was considered more derogatory to the male, or more ridiculous, than to be victimised into a marriage of necessity. His prestige would be lost, he would be lampooned at the street corners, his name would become an obloquy. He felt the position so intolerably for himself that he was moved by a desire to escape and in a flash he thought of Canada, Australia, America. He had often thought of emigrating, and the prospects that existed in these new countries for an unattached young man never appealed to him more entrancingly than at this moment. Another thought struck him.

"When did the doctor say that you would——" He paused, unable to complete the sentence. Nevertheless she was now able to understand his meaning.

"He said February," she replied, with an averted face.

Only five more months and he would be the father of her child! That exquisite night they had spent together by the Leven was to produce a child, a child that would be nameless unless he married her immediately. The pressing necessity for marriage again obtruded itself distastefully upon him. He did not know how long she might remain undiscovered before the condition of her pregnancy became obvious.

Although he had at times heard stories bandied amongst his companions, of how peasant girls working on the land had remained in this state of pregnancy, undetected until the actual birth occurred, he doubted if Mary had the strength or fortitude to continue the concealment for any length of time. And yet she must do so. He was not in a position to provide a home for her immediately. She must wait. There was, of course, nothing visible yet. He looked at her closely, and as he observed her pendent figure, weighted with an infinitely heavier despondency than his, for the first time he began to think of her rather than himself.

Now that she had told him she waited helplessly, as if, attending in submission for him to direct her movements, her attitude invoked him dumbly as to what she should do. With a powerful effort he pulled himself together, yet, as he spoke, his words sounded harsh and unconvincing in his ears.

"This is a bit of a mess we're in, Mary, but we'll straighten it out all right. We must go and talk it over."

"Have I got to go back home to Levenford?" she asked in a low tone.

He pondered a minute before replying: "I'm afraid it's best for you to do that. Did you come in by train?"

"Yes, and if I'm going back I must leave here at four." He took out his watch, which indicated half-past three. Although they had exchanged only a few sentences they had been standing there, in the street, for half an hour.

"You can't wait till the next," he agreed. "It's too late."

An idea struck him. The waiting-room at the station was usually empty at this time; they could go there until her train departed. He took her arm and drew it into his. At this, the first sign of tenderness he had manifested towards her since she had told him the dreadful news, she looked at him piteously and her drawn features were transcended by a pale smile.

"I've only got you, Denis," she whispered, as they moved off together. At the station, however, the waiting-room was unfortunately full; an old woman, some farm servants, and two dye-workers from the print works sat staring at each other and at the plain board walls. It was impossible to talk there, so Denis took Mary to the far end of the platform, where, as the short walk had given him time to collect himself and the soft feel of her arm reminded him of her charm and beauty, of the delightful attractions of her fresh body, he mustered a smile.

"It's not so bad, Mary, after all, so long as we stick together."

"If you left me now, Denis, I should drown myself in the Leven. I'd kill myself somehow."

As her eyes met his, he could see that she meant absolutely every grim word she uttered, and he pressed her arm again, tenderly. How could he, even for an instant, have considered leaving this lovely, defenceless creature who, but for him, would still have been a virgin and who now, because of him, was soon to be a mother. And how passionately attached to him she was! It thrilled him with a fierce joy to see her complete dependence upon him and her submission to his will. His spirit was recovering from the cutting injury which it had received, and he began to think coherently, as his normal self.

"You'll leave everything to me!" he said.

"Everything," she echoed.

"Then you must go home, dear, and try to behave as if nothing had happened. I know how difficult it will be, but you must give me as long as possible to make our arrangements."

"When can we be married?" It cost her a powerful effort to utter the words, but in her new-found knowledge she felt dimly that her body would remain unchaste until she knew when he would marry her.

He reflected.

"I have a big business trip towards the end of the year—it means a lot. Could you wait until after then?" he asked doubtfully. "I could fix up everything by then—and we could be married and go straight into a little cottage somewhere—not in Darroch or Levenford—but perhaps in Garshake."

His idea of a cottage in Garshake cheered them both, and each immediately visioned the quiet, old village that clustered so snugly around an arm of the estuary.

"I could wait for that," Mary replied wistfully, viewing in her mind's eye one of the small, whitewashed cottages of which the village was composed—one smothered in red rambler roses, with a doorway festooned by creeping nasturtiums—in which her baby would mysteriously come into her arms. She looked at Denis and almost smiled.

"I'll not fail you, dear," he was saying. "If you will be brave—and hold out as long as ever you can."

The train was now in the station, and the old woman, the farm servants, and the two workmen were scrambling to their places. She had time only to take a hurried farewell of him as he helped her into a seat, but, as the train began to move, he ran along beside her until the last moment, holding her hand, and before he was forced to let go, she called to him, courageously:

"I'm remembering your motto, Denis, dear!" He smiled and waved his cap bravely, encouragingly, in reply, until the train circled the bend and they were torn from each other's sight.

She was certainly valiant, and now that she knew the worst she was prepared to exercise all her hardihood to achieve her only hope of happiness. Seeing Denis had saved her. He was, and would be, her salvation, and strengthened by the thought that he shared her secret, she now felt fortified to endure anything until he would take her away with him for good. She shuddered at the recollection of her visit to the doctor, but firmly she blotted out from her mind the odious experiences of the last two hours. She would be brave for Denis!

Back again in Levenford she hastened to deliver the letter to Agnes Moir, and discovered to her relief that Agnes had gone upstairs for tea. She therefore left the letter for her at the shop with all Mrs. Brodie's messages of attachment and affection, and escaped, mercifully, without questioning.

As she took the way home she reflected that her mother was sure to discover at a later date her defection in the matter of the parcel, but, involved in a deeper and more serious trouble, she did not care. Let Mamma scold, weep, or bewail, she felt that she had only a few months more until she would be out of a house which she now detested. Every sense within her turned towards the suggestion Denis had tentatively advanced, and in her imagination she consolidated it into actuality; thrusting the thought of her present condition from her, she concentrated her sanguine hopes eagerly upon the cottage she would share with him in Garshake.

VIII

BRODIE sat in his office reading the *Levenford Advertiser*, with the door slightly open so that he could, at infrequent intervals, raise a vigilant eye towards the shop without interfering with the comfortable perusal of his paper. Perry was ill, confined to bed, as his agitated mother had announced to Brodie that morning, from a severe boil which partially prevented his walking and debarred him entirely from sitting down. Brodie had muttered disagreeably that he required his assistant to stand up, not to sit down, but on being assured that the sufferer would certainly be relieved through constant poulticing and be fit for duty in the morning, he had consented with a bad grace to allow him the day off. Now, enthroned on his chair at the top of the row of steps leading to his sanctum, Brodie devoted an almost exclusive attention to the report of the Cattle Show. He was glad that business was quiet this morning and that he was not constrained to lower himself to the menial work of the shop, which he detested, and which was now entirely Perry's obligation. A few moments ago he had been obliged to leave his seat to serve a labouring man who had rolled uncouthly in, and, in his indignation, he had hustled the man out with the first hat he could lay hands on. What did he care, he asked himself, whether or not the thing suited? He couldn't be bothered over these infernal trifles; a thing like that was Perry's job; he wanted to read his paper in peace, like any other gentleman.

With an outraged air he had come back and began again at the opening lines of the report.

"The Levenford and District Annual Cattle Show," he read, "took place on Saturday the 21st inst. and was attended by a large and distinguished gathering." He perused the whole report slowly, carefully, sedulously, until at the finish of the article he came upon the paragraph beginning: "Amongst those present." His eye glimmered anxiously then flared into triumph, as he saw that his name was there! Amongst the distinguished names of the borough and county, towards the end of the list no doubt, but not absolutely at the end, stood the name of James Brodie. He banged his fist triumphantly upon his desk. By Gad! that would show them! Everyone read the *Levenford Advertiser*—which was published once a week, on Friday—and everyone would see his name flourishing there, near to no less a personage than the Lord Lieutenant of the County. Brodie glowed with vanity. He liked the look of himself in print. The capital "J" of the James had a peculiar, arresting curl, and as for his surname—nay his family name—spelt in the correct manner, not with a "y," but with the terminal "ie," he was prouder of this than of all his other possessions together. He cocked his head to one side, never removing his eyes from this arresting name of his. Actually he had read through the wordy report, tantalising himself in its verbosity, simply to find himself living in the public eye through the medium of these two printed words. He gloated over them.

James Brodie! His lips unconsciously formed the words as he rolled them silently over upon his tongue. "You're a proud man, Brodie," he whispered to himself. "Eh! you're proud; and by God! you have reason to be." His eyes blurred with the intensity of his feeling, and the entire list of dazzling personages, with their titles, honours, and distinctions, fell out of focus into one solitary name which seemed indelibly to have stamped its image upon his retina. James Brodie! Nothing seemed to surpass these simple yet suggestive words.

A slight deviation of the current of his ideas caused his nostrils to dilate with resentment at the thought of having been called upon to lower himself in his own eyes, by serving a common workman this very morning. That had been well enough twenty years ago when he was a struggling man forced into business by necessities over which he had no control. But now he had his hired servant to do this work for him. He felt the encounter of this morning a slur upon his name, and a choleric indignation swelled within him at the unfortunate Perry for having failed him.

"I'll boil him," he cried, "the pimply little snipe." He had never been meant for business, that he had always known, but, as he had been compelled to adopt it, he had transmuted its substance into something more appropriate to his name and bearing. He had never considered himself a man of commerce but had, from the first, adopted the part of the impoverished gentleman obliged to live by an unfitting and unbecoming occupation. Yet his very personality had, he felt, strangely dignified that occupation into something worthy of him. It had ceased to be paltry and had become unique. From the outset he had never run after people; they had, indeed, been obliged to whistle to his tune and to meet him in all his foibles and vagaries.

In his early days he had once thrown a man out of his shop for an impolite word; he had startled the town into recognising him; he did not curry favour, but stood bluntly as if to say: "Take me as I am or leave me"; and his anomalous policy had been singularly successful. He had achieved a reputation for rude honesty and downright dealing; the more arbitrary of his maxims were repeated like epigrams in the gossip of the town; amongst the gentry he had been recognised—in the local term—as a "character," and his original individuality had acquired for him their patronage. Yet, the more his personality had unfolded, the more he had disdained the vehicle of its expansion.

He felt himself now a personage, superior to the claims of trade. A vast satisfaction possessed him that he should have attained eminence despite the unworthy nature of his profession. His vast pride could not differentiate between the notoriety he had achieved and the more notable distinction which he desired. He was spurred onward by his success. He wished to make his name resound. "I'll show them," he muttered arrogantly. "I'll show them what I can do."

At that moment someone came into the shop. Brodie looked up in irritation, his lordly glance daring the intruder to demand attention from the compeer of the county's nobility; but curiously, he was not asked to descend. A young man leapt lightly over the counter, mounted the steps, and came into the office, shutting the door behind him. It was Denis Foyle.

Three days ago, when Denis had seen the train take Mary away from him, an avalanche of remorse had fallen upon him and had immediately swept over and engulfed him. He considered that he had acted towards Mary with a cold and cowardly selfishness. The sudden blow to his self-esteem had taken him so completely unawares, that he had, for the moment, forgotten how much he really cared for her. But he did love her; indeed, he realised more maturely, and in her absence, that he craved for her. The burden of her condition lent her, in his more complete consideration, a pathetic appeal which he had previously resisted. If his situation was unpleasant, hers was unbearable, and he had offered nothing in alleviation but a few weak and mawkish condolences. He had writhed inwardly to contemplate what she must now think of his abject and unresourceful timidity, and the realisation that he had no certain access to her to tell her all that he now experienced, to express his contrition and adoration with the utmost fervency, filled him with despair.

For two days he endured these steadily growing feelings, when, suddenly, a definite and extraordinary line of action presented itself to him.

He thought it bold, strong, and daring. In reality it was the reflex of the battery of self-reproaches upon his taut nerves, and although it was merely rash, presumptuous, and foolish, it represented an outlet for his constrained feelings, and he saw in it the opportunity to vindicate himself in his own and in Mary's eyes.

Essentially, it was this urge to justify himself which now moved him, as he stood before Brodie, saying:

"I came in like this, Mr. Brodie, because I thought you mightn't agree to see me otherwise—I'm Denis Foyle of Darroch."

Brodie was astounded at the unexpectedness of this entry and at the audacity it betokened, but he made no sign. Instead he settled himself more deeply in his chair; his head seemed to sink right into the magnitude of his shoulders, like a rock sunk on the summit of a hill.

"Son of the pub keeper?" he sneered.

"Exactly," replied Denis politely.

"Well, Mister Denis Foyle"—he emphasised the mister ironically—"what do you want here?" He began to hope to goad Foyle into an assault, so that he might have the pleasure of thrashing him.

Denis looked straight at Brodie and, disregarding the other's manner, proceeded according to his plan.

"You may be surprised at my visit, but I felt I must come to you, Mr. Brodie. I have not seen your daughter, Miss Mary Brodie, for over three months. She has consistently avoided me. I wish to tell you frankly that I have an attachment for your daughter, and have come to ask your permission to allow me to see her."

Brodie gazed upwards at the young man with a heavy mask-like face which permitted nothing to penetrate of the tide of rising amazed anger he felt at the other's demand. After a moment's lowering stare at Foyle, he said, slowly: "I am glad to hear from your own lips I have been obeyed! My daughter has refused to see you because I forbade her to look at ye! Do ye hear me. I forbade her, and now that I've seen what ye are I still forbid her."

"Why, Mr. Brodie, may I ask?"

"Must I explain my actions to you? The fact that I order it is enough for my daughter. I do not explain to her, I command."

"Mr. Brodie, I should be glad to know your objection to me. I should do my best to meet you in any way you desired." With all his power Foyle tried to propitiate the other. "I'm very anxious to please you! Let me know what to do and I'll do it."

Brodie fleered at him:

"I want ye to take your smooth face out o' my office and never show it in Levenford again; and the quicker ye do't the better ye'll please me."

With a deprecating smile Foyle replied:

"Then it's only my face you object to, Mr. Brodie." He felt he must win the other round somehow!

Brodie was beginning to become enraged; the fact that he could not beat down this young sprig's eyes, nor yet provoke him to temper, annoyed him. With an effort he controlled himself and said, sneeringly:

"I'm not in the habit of exchanging confidences with your kind, but as I have a moment to spare, I will tell you what I object to. Mary Brodie is a lady, she has blood in her veins of which a duchess might be proud, and she is my daughter. You are a low-down Irish scum, a nothing out of nothing. Your father sells cheap drink, and I've no doubt your forebears ate potato peelings out o' the pot."

Denis still met his eyes unflinchingly, although the insults quivered inside him. Desperately he forced himself to be calm. "The fact that I am Irish surely does not condemn me," he replied in a level voice. "I don't drink—not a drop. In fact I'm in a totally different line of business, one which I feel will one day bring a great return."

"I've heard about your business, my pretty tatie-picker. Long trips over the countryside, then back to loaf about for days. I know your kind. If ye think that you can make money by hawkin' tea round Scotland then you're stupid, and if ye think ye can make up for your rotten family by takin' up a trashy job like that, then you're mad."

"I wish you would let me explain to you, Mr. Brodie."

Brodie contemplated him savagely.

"Explain to me! You talk like that to me, you damned commercial traveller. Do you know who you're speakin' to? Look!" he roared, flourishing the paper and thrusting it in front of the other. "See this, if you can read! These are the people I associate with——" He inflated his chest and shouted: "I would as soon think of letting my daughter consort with you as I would let her mix with swine."

With a considerable effort Foyle controlled his temper.

"Mr. Brodie," he pleaded. "I wish you would listen to me. Surely you must admit that a man is what he makes himself—that he himself controls his own destiny irrespective of what his parents may be. I am not ashamed of my ancestry, but if that is what you object to, surely it does not damn me."

Brodie looked at the other frowningly.

"Ye dare to talk that damned new-fangled socialism to me!" he roared angrily. "One man is as good as another, I suppose! What are we comin' to next. You fool! I'll have none of ye. Get out!"

Denis did not move. He saw clearly that this man was not amenable to reason; that he might batter his head against a stone wall with more avail; he saw that, with such a father, Mary's life must be a procession of terrifying catastrophes. But, because of her, he determined to maintain his control, and, quite quietly, he said: "I am sorry for you, Mr. Brodie. You belong to an age that is passing; you do not understand progress. And you don't understand what it is to make friends; you must only make enemies. It is not I who am mad!"

Brodie got up, lowering, his rage like that of an angry bull. "Will you get out, you young swine?" he said thickly, "or will I smash you?" He advanced towards the other, heavily. In a second Denis could have been out of the office, but a hidden antagonism had been roused in him by Brodie's insults and, although he knew he ought to go for Mary's sake, nevertheless he remained. Confident that he could take care of himself, he was not afraid of the other's lumbering strength and he realised, too, that if he went now, Brodie would think he had driven him out like a beaten dog. In a voice suffused by resentment he exclaimed:

"Don't touch me! I've suffered your insults, but don't go any further!"

At these words Brodie's anger swelled within him until it almost choked him.

"Will I not, though," he cried, his breath coming in quick noisy gusts. "I've got ye like a rat in a trap, and I'll smash ye like a rat."

With a heavy ferocious stealth he advanced slowly towards the other, carefully manœuvred his towering bulk near to him; then, when he was within a yard of Denis, so near that he knew it was impossible for him to escape, his lips drew back balefully upon his gums, and suddenly he raised his mammoth fist and hurled it with crushing force full at young Foyle's head. A sharp, hard, brittle crack split the air. There had been no head for him to hit; quicker than a lightning flash, Foyle had slipped to one side, and Brodie's hand struck the stone wall with all the power of a sledge-hammer. His right arm dropped inertly to his side; his wrist was broken. Denis, looking at him with his hand on the door knob, said quietly:

"I'm sorry, Mr. Brodie. You see that after all there are some things you do not understand. I warned you not to try anything like that." Then he was gone, and not a moment too soon. The heavy, mahogany, revolving chair, thrown across the room by Brodie's left arm, like a shot from a catapult, crashed against the light door and shivered the glass and framework to atoms.

Brodie stood, with heaving nostrils and dangling arm, staring stupidly at the wreckage. He felt conscious of no pain in his injured arm, only an inability to move it, but his swelling breast was like to burst with defeated fury. The fact that this young pup above everyone had bearded him, and gotten away with it, made him writhe with wounded pride; the physical hurt was nothing, but the damage to his pride was deadly.

The fingers of his left hand clenched convulsively. Another minute, he was certain, he would have cornered him and broken him. But to have been outdone without so much as a blow having been struck against him! Only a faint remnant of self-control and a glimmering of sense prevented him from running blindly into the street after Foyle, in an effort to overtake and crush him. It was the first time in his life that anyone had dared to take the upper hand of him, and he ground his teeth to think that he had been outfaced and outwitted by the effrontery of such a low-born upstart.

"By God!" he shouted to the empty room, "I'll make him pay for it."

Then he looked down at his useless hand and forearm which had already become blue, swollen, and œdematous. He realised that he must have the condition seen to and also that he must invent some story to explain it—some balderdash about having slipped on the stairs, he thought. Sullenly he went out of the shop, banged shut the front door, locked it, and went off.

Meanwhile it had dawned upon Denis, since his departure, that by his rash action he had done incalculable harm to Mary and himself. Before the interview he had imagined that he might ingratiate himself with her father, and so obtain his consent to see her. This, he had assumed, would make it easy for them to arrange the events towards a definite plan of escape. Indeed, he had fondly estimated that Brodie might view him with less disapproval, might even conceive some slight regard for him. To have succeeded in this project would undoubtedly have expedited the course of such sudden steps as they might later be obliged to take, would also have tempered the shock of the subsequent and inevitable disclosure.

He had not then known Brodie. He had frequently considered Mary's delineation of him, but had imagined that her account was perhaps tinged with filial awe, or that her sensitive nature magnified the stature of his odious propensities. Now he fully understood her terror of Brodie, felt her remarks to have erred on the side of leniency towards him. He had a few moments ago seen him in a condition of such unbalanced animosity that he began to fear for Mary's safety; he cursed himself repeatedly for his recent imprudent action.

He was completely at a loss as to what step to take next, when, suddenly, as he passed a stationer's shop in the High Street, it occurred to him that he might write her a letter, asking her to meet him on the following day. He entered the shop and bought a sheet of notepaper and an envelope. Despite his anxiety his power of blandishment remained, and he wheedled the old lady behind the counter to sell him a stamp, and to lend him pen and ink. This she did willingly, with a maternal smile, and whilst he wrote a short note to Mary, she watched him solicitously, out of the corner of her eye. When he had finished he thanked her gracefully and, outside, was about to drop the letter in the pillar-box when a thought struck him, and he withdrew his hand, as if it had been stung. He turned slowly round to the kerb and then, after a moment, at the confirmation of his thought, he tore the letter into small pieces and scattered them in the gutter. He had suddenly realised that if, by chance, this communication were intercepted, Brodie would immediately apprehend that he had wilfully deceived him, that Mary had been meeting him continually and clandestinely. He had made one serious mistake that day and he was determined not to commit another. Buttoning up his jacket tightly, he plunged his hands in his pockets and, with his chin thrust pugnaciously forwards, he walked quickly away. He had decided to reconnoitre the neighbourhood of the Brodie's house.

Unfamiliar with the locality, he became slightly out of his reckoning in the outskirts of the town, but, by means of his general sense of direction, he made a series of detours and at length arrived within sight of Mary's home. Actually he had never seen this house before, and now, as he surveyed it, a feeling of consternation invaded him. It seemed to him more fitted for a prison than a home, and as inappropriate for the housing of Mary's soft gentleness as a dark, confined vault might be for a dove. The squat, grey walls seemed to enclose her with an irrevocable clasp, the steep-angled ramparts implied her subjection, the deep, embrasured windows proclaimed her detention under a constrained duress.

As he surveyed the house, he murmured to himself: "I'll be glad to take her away from there, and she'll be glad to come. That man's not right! His mind is twisted somewhere. That house is like him, somehow!"

With his mind still clouded by apprehension, he wormed himself into a hollow in the hedgerow behind him, sat down on the bank, lit a cigarette, and began to turn over certain projects in his mind. Faced with the imperative necessity of seeing Mary, he began to review mentally a series of impossible plans and incautious designs of achieving the object. He was afraid of making another imprudent blunder, and yet he felt that he must see her at once, or the opportunity would be for ever lost. His cigarette was almost burned out when, suddenly, the stern look vanished from his face, and he smiled audaciously at the obvious simplicity of the excellent expedient which had struck him. Nothing was to prevent him, now, in open daylight, from advancing boldly, and knocking upon the front door. Mary would almost assuredly open the door herself, whereupon he would signify immediately for silence and, after delivering a note into her own hands, leave as urbanely and openly as he had come. He knew enough of the household to understand that, with Brodie at business and little Nessie at school, the only other person who might answer the door would be Mrs. Brodie. If this latter contingency occurred, she did not know him, Brodie would not yet have warned her against him, and he would merely enquire for some fictitious name, and make a speedy and apologetic departure.

Rapidly he tore a leaf out of his pocket-book and scribbled on it, in pencil, a short message, telling her that he loved her and asking her to meet him outside the Public Library on the following evening. He would, for preference, have selected a more secluded meeting-place, but he feared that the only pretext she might advance for leaving the house would be to visit the Library. When he had finished he rolled the paper into a small, neat square, pressed it tight in his palm, and, flicking the dust from his clothing, sprang up. He turned his head briskly towards his objective and had assumed all the ingenuous artlessness of a simple visitor, when all at once his face fell, his brow darkened, and he flung himself violently back into his hiding-place. Coming along the pavement, and approaching the house from the lower end of the road, was Brodie himself, his wrist bandaged, his arm supported by a sling.

Denis bit his lip. Nothing, apparently, went right with him! It was impossible for him to approach the house now, and he realised bitterly that Brodie, in his resentment, would almost certainly caution the household against him, and so jeopardise the chances of utilising his scheme successfully upon another occasion. With a heavy heart he considered, also, that Brodie's anger might react upon Mary, although he had so carefully protected her during his unhappy interview at the shop. He watched Brodie draw nearer, detected with concern that the injured wrist was encased in plaster, observed the thunder blackness of his face. saw him crash open the gate and finally let himself into the house. Denis experienced a strong sense of misgiving. So long as Mary lived beside that monstrous man, and in that monstrous house, he realised that he would never be at rest. Straining his ears for some sound, some cry, some call for help, he waited outside interminably. But there was only silence—silence from behind the cold, grey walls of that eccentric dwelling. Then, finally, he got up and walked dejectedly away.

IX

MARY BRODIE sat knitting a sock for her father. She leaned slightly forward, her face pale and shadowed, her eyes directed towards the long steel needles which flashed automatically under her moving fingers. Click-click went the needles! Nowadays she seemed to hear nothing but that sound, for in every moment of her leisure she knitted. Mamma had decreed sententiously that, as the devil found work more readily for idle hands, Mary must keep hers employed, even in her spare moments, and she had been set the task of completing one pair of socks each week. She was now finishing her sixth pair!

Old Grandma Brodie sat watching, with her lips pursed up as if they had been stitched together. She sat with her withered legs crossed, the pendent foot beating time to the clinking music, saying nothing, but keeping her eyes perpetually fixed upon Mary, inscrutable, seeming to think all manner of things that no one, least of all Mary, could know of. Sometimes, Mary imagined that those bleared, opaque eyes were penetrating her with a knowing, vindictive suspicion, and when her own eyes met them, a spark of antagonism was struck from the stony pupils. She had, of late, felt as if the eyes of the old sibyl were binding some spell upon her which would compel her to move her tired fingers ceaselessly, unwillingly, in the effort to utilise an unending skein of wool.

It was an agreeable diversion for the crone to watch the young girl, but, in addition, it was her duty, the task assigned to her six weeks ago. Her head shook slightly as she recollected that incredible afternoon when her son had come in, with his arm bandaged and his face black as night, remembered the solemn conclave between Brodie and his wife behind the locked door of the parlour. There had been none of the usual bluster, no roaring through the house, only a dour grinding silence! What it had been about she had been unable to guess, but certainly some grave disaster had been in the air. Her daughter-in-law's face had been drawn with fright for days afterwards; her lips had twitched while she had enrolled her as an auxiliary in the watching of Mary, saying only: "Mary's not allowed out of the house. Not a step beyond the front gate. It's an order." Mary was a prisoner, that was all, and she, in effect, the gaoler. Behind the mask of her face she revelled in the thought of it, of this disgrace for Mary. She had never liked the girl, and her occupation now afforded her the deepest gratification and delight.

Her present meditations were interrupted by the entry of Mrs. Brodie. Mamma's eyes sought out Mary.

"Have you turned the heel yet?" she enquired, with a forced assumption of interest.

"Nearly," replied Mary, her pale face unchanging from its set, indifferent apathy.

"You're getting on finely! You'll set your father up in socks for the winter before you've finished."

"May I go out in the garden a minute?"

Mamma looked out of the window ostentatiously. "It's smirring of rain, Mary. I think you better not go just now. When Nessie comes in maybe it'll be off, and you can take her out for a stroll round the back."

Mamma's feeble diplomacy! The will of Brodie, wrapped up in too plausible suggestions, or delivered obviously in the guise of uplifting quotations from Scripture, had pressed round Mary like a net for six weeks, each week of which had seemed like a year—a year with long, long days. So oppressed and weakened in her resistance was she now, that she felt obliged to ask permission for her every action.

"May I go up to my room for a little, then?" she said dully.

"Certainly, Mary! If you would like to read, dear, take this"; and, as her daughter went slowly out of the room, Mrs. Brodie thrust upon her a bound copy of Spurgeon's sermons that lay conveniently ready upon the dresser. But immediately Mary had gone, a glance passed between the two women left in the room, and Mamma nodded her head slightly. Grandma at once got up, willingly forsaking her warm corner by the fire, and hobbled into the parlour, where she sat down at the front window, commanding from this vantage a complete view of anyone who might attempt to leave the house. The constant observation ordained by Brodie was in operation. Yet Mamma had hardly been alone a moment before another thought crossed her mind. She pondered, then nodded to herself, realising this to be a favourable opportunity to execute her husband's mandate, and, holding her skirts, she mounted the stairs, and entered her daughter's room, determined to say a "good word" to Mary.

"I thought I would come up for a little chat," she said brightly. "I havena had a word with you for a day or two."

"Yes, Mamma!"

Mrs. Brodie considered her daughter critically. "Have you seen the light yet, Mary?" she asked slowly.

Mary knew instinctively what was coming, knew that she was to receive one of Mamma's recently instituted pious talks which had made her at first either tearful or rebellious, which had never at any time made her feel better spiritually, and which now merely fell senselessly upon her stoic ears. These elevating discourses had become intolerable during her incarceration and, together with every other form of high-minded exhortation, had been thrust upon her, heaped upon her head like reproaches, at all available opportunities. The reason was not far to seek. At the conclusion of that awful session in the parlour Brodie had snarled at his wife: "She's your daughter! It's your job to get some sense of obedience into her. If you don't, by God! I'll take the strap across her back again—and over yours too."

"Do you feel yourself firm on the rock yet, Mary?" continued Mamma earnestly.

"I don't know," replied Mary, in a stricken voice.

"I can see you haven't reached it yet," Mamma sighed gently. "What a comfort it would be to your father and me if we saw you more abounding in faith, and goodness, and obedience to your parents." She took Mary's passive hand. "You know, my dear, life is short. Suppose we were called suddenly before the Throne in a state of unworthiness—what then? Eternity is long. There is no chance to repent then. Oh! I wish you would see the error of your ways. It makes it so hard for me, for your own mother that has done everything for you. It's hard that your father should blame me for that stiff, stubborn look that's still about ye—just as if ye were frozen up. Why, I would do anything. I would even get the Rev. Mr. Scott himself to speak to you, some afternoon when your father wasna in! I read such a comforting book the other day of how a wayward woman was made to see the light by one of God's own ministers." Mamma sighed mournfully, and after a long impressive pause, enquired:

"Tell me, Mary, what is in your heart now?"

"I wish, Mamma, you'd leave me a little," said Mary, in a low tone. "I don't feel well."

"Then you've no need of your mother, or the Almighty either," said Mamma with a sniff. Mary looked at her mother tragically. She realised to the full the other's feebleness, ineptitude, and impotence. From the very beginning she had longed for a mother to whom she could unbosom her inmost soul, on whom she might have leaned clingingly, to whom she might have cried passionately: "Mother, you are the refuge of my torn and afflicted heart! Comfort me and take my suffering from me! Wrap me in the mantle of your protection and shield me from the arrows of misfortune!"

But Mamma was, alas, not like that. Unstable as water, and as shallow, she reflected merely the omnipresent shadow of another stronger than herself. Upon her lay the heavy shade of a mountain whose ominous presence overcast her limpid nature with a perpetual and compelling gloom. The very tone of this godly conversation was merely the echo of Brodie's irresistible demand. How could she speak of the fear of Eternity when her fear of Brodie dwarfed this into insignificance, into nothingness? For her there was only one rock, and that the adamantine hardness of her husband's furious will. Woe! Woe! to her if she did not cling submissively to that! She was, of course, a Christian woman, with all the respectable convictions which this implied. To attend church regularly on Sundays, even to frequent, when she could escape from her duties, an occasional fervent, week-night meeting, to condemn the use of the grosser words of the vocabulary, such as "Hell" or "Damn," fully justified her claim to godliness; and when, for her relaxation, she read a work of fiction, she perused only such good books as afforded the virtuous and saintly heroine a charming and godly husband in the last chapter, and as afforded herself a feeling of pure and elevated refinement. But she could no more have supported her daughter in this crisis of her life than she could have confronted Brodie in his wrath.

All this Mary comprehended fully.

"Will you not tell me, Mary?" Mamma persisted. "I wish I knew what was goin' on inside that stubborn head of yours!" She was continually in fear that her daughter might be secretly contemplating some discreditable step, which would again arouse Brodie's ungovernable fury. Often in her shuddering anticipation she felt, not only the lash of his tongue, but the actual chastisement with which he had threatened her.

"There's nothing to tell you, Mamma," replied Mary sadly. "Nothing to say to you."

She was aware that, if she had attempted to unburden herself, her mother would have stopped her with one shrill, protesting cry and, with deaf ears, have fled from the room. "No! No! I don't tell me! Not a word more. I won't hear it. It's not decent," Mary could almost hear her crying as she ran. Bitterly she repeated:

"No! I've nothing at all to tell you!"

"But you must think of something. I know you're thinking by the look of you," persisted Mrs. Brodie. Mary looked full at her mother.

"Sometimes I think I would be happy if I could get out of this house and never come back," she said bitterly. Mrs. Brodie held up her hands, aghast.

"Mary!" she cried, "what a thing to say! Ye should be thankful to have such a good home. It's a good thing your father doesna hear ye— he would never forgive such black ingratitude!"

"How can you talk like that," cried Mary wildly. "You must feel as I do about it. This has never been a home to us. Can't you feel it crushing us? It's like part of father's terrible will. Remember I haven't been out of it for six weeks and I feel—oh! I feel broken to pieces," she sobbed.

Mrs. Brodie eyed these tears gratefully, as a sign of submission. "Don't cry, Mary," she admonished; "although ye should be sorry for talking such improper nonsense about the grand place you're privileged to live in. When your father built it 'twas the talk o' Levenford."

"Yes," sobbed Mary, "and so are we. Father makes that so, too. We don't seem like other people. We're not looked on like ordinary people."

"I should think not!" bridled Mrs. Brodie. "We're far and above them."

"Oh, mother," cried Mary, "you would never understand what I mean. Father has frightened you into his own notions. He's driving us, driving us all into some disaster. He keeps us apart from people. We've got no friends. I never had a chance like anybody else; I've been so shut off from everything."

"And a good job, too," interposed Mamma. "It's the way a decent girl should be brought up. You should have been shut off a bit more, by the way you've been goin' on."

Mary did not seem to hear her, but, gazing blindly in front of her, pursued that last thought to its bitter end. "I was shut up in a prison— in darkness," she whispered; "and when I did escape I was dazzled and lost my way." An expression of utter hopelessness spread slowly over her face.

"Don't mumble like that," cried Mamma sharply. "If ye can't speak up honestly to your mother, don't speak at all. The idea! Ye should be thankful to have folks to take care of ye, and keep ye in here out of harm."

"Harm! I haven't done much harm in the last few weeks," echoed Mary, in a flat voice.

"Mary! Mary!" cried Mamma reprovingly, "you should be showing a better spirit. Don't answer so sulkily. Be bright and active, and show more respect and deference to your parents. To think of the low young men of the district running after you should bring the blush of shame to your face. You ought to be glad to stay in to escape from them, and not be always hanging about looking so gloomy. Why! when I think what you're being protected from——" Mamma stopped for very modesty, and shuddered virtuously as she pushed Spurgeon's sermons nearer Mary. Concluding on the highest and most elevated note, she arose and, as she retreated to the door, said significantly: "Have a look at that, my girl. It'll do ye more good than any light talk ye might hear outside." Then she went out, closing the door behind her with a soft restraint which harmonised with the godly thoughts which filled her mind. But Mary did not touch the book that had been so persistently thrust upon her; instead, she looked hopelessly out of the window. Heavy masses of cloud shut out the sky, turning the short October afternoon more quickly towards the night. A soft, insistent rain blurred the window panes; no wind stirred; her three silver birches, bereft of leaves, were silent in a misty, melancholy reverie. She had of late gazed at them so often, that she knew them in every mood, and thought of them as her own. She had seen them shed their leaves. Each leaf had come fluttering down sadly, slowly, like a lost hope, and with each fall Mary had cast away a fragment of her faith. They had been like symbols to her, these three trees, and so long as they had breathed through their living foliage, she had not despaired. But the last leaflet had gone and this evening, like her, they were denuded, enwrapped in cold mist, lost in profound despondency.

Her child was living in her womb. She had felt it throb with an ever increasing surge of life; this throbbing, living child that no one knew of but Denis and herself. She was undiscovered. Concealment, which had at first so much worried her, had not been easy, but now it did not trouble her at all; for, at this moment, her mind was occupied by a deeper and more awful contemplation.

Yet, as she sat so passive by her window, she recollected how the first movement within her had caused her a pang, not of fear, but of sublime yearning. She had been transcended by a swift illumination which lit up the dark spaces of her mind, and a fierce desire for her child had seized her. This desire had, through many dark hours, sustained her fortitude, had filled her with a brave endurance of her present misery. She had felt that she now suffered for the child, that, the more she endured, the more she would be recompensed by its love.

But that seemed a long time ago, before hope had finally left her. She had then still believed in Denis.

Since that afternoon when she had gone to Darroch she had not seen him. Imprisoned in the house by the will of her father, she had lived through these six, unendurable weeks without a glimpse of Denis.

Sometimes she had imagined she had seen his figure lurking outside the house; often, at night, she had felt that he was near; once she had wakened with a shriek to a faint tapping on her window; but now she realised that these had merely been illusions of her disordered fancy, and she was finally convinced that he had deserted her. He had abandoned her. She would never see him again.

She longed for night to come to bring sleep to her. In the beginning of her sorrow she had been unable to rest, then, strangely, she had slept profoundly, with a slumber often pervaded by exquisite dreams, dreams that were filled with an extraordinary felicity. Then she was always with Denis amongst enchanting surroundings, exploring with him a sunlit land of gay, old cities, and mingling with laughing people, living upon strange and exotic foods. These pleasant phantasies, by their happy augury for the future, had at one time cheered and comforted her; but that was past; she sought now no visions of unreality. The sleep which she desired was a dreamless one. She had resolved to kill herself. Vividly she remembered her words to him on Darroch Station, when she had, with an unconscious, dreadful foreboding, told what she would do if he deserted her. Her only refuge lay in death. Unknown to anyone she had concealed in her room a packet of salts of lemon which she had removed from the high shelf above the wash-tubs in the scullery. To-night she would go to bed in the usual way and, in the morning, they would find her dead. The living child that had never breathed would be dead too, she realised, but that was the best thing that could happen. Then they would bury her with her unborn child in the wet earth and she would be finished and at peace. She got up and opened a drawer. Yes! it was there safely. With calm fingers she opened slightly one end of the white packet and gazed at the harmless appearance of the contents within. Unconsciously, she reflected how strange it was that these inert, innocent crystals should be so full of deadly potentiality; yet she was aware that they held no menace for her, but only a benign succour. They would enable her with a single, quick motion to escape from the hopeless, cumulative bondage of her existence and, when she swallowed them, she would drain in one final, convulsive gulp the last bitter dregs of life itself. Tranquilly, she reflected that at bed-time she must bring up water in a cup to dissolve the crystals.

She replaced the packet, closed the drawer, and, returning to the window, sat down and began again to knit. She would finish the sock to-night for her father. As she thought of him she had no active emotion towards him—everything within her was passive, as though her feelings had already died. He never spoke to her. His arm was healed. His life went on unchanged and, even after she was dead, would go on unchanged, with the same unfailing regularity, in the same proud indifference, smoothed by the same adulation and cringing subservience from Mamma.

She stopped knitting for a moment and glanced out of the window. Nessie was coming in from school. Compassion invaded her for her small, susceptible sister who had been at first infected with her misery. She would be sorry to leave Nessie. Poor Nessie! She would be all alone! Strangely, however, the diminutive figure did not enter the gate, but instead, stood in the gathering dusk making a peculiar, determinate sign. It was not Nessie, but another small girl who, posted indomitably in the rain, waved her arm upwards with a significant, yet hidden intention. Mary looked at her fixedly, but as she did so the movements ceased, and the little puppet moved away. Two people then came into view and passed out of sight down the road, leaving it void and black as before. A sigh burst from Mary, expressive of the dispersion of a dim, unborn hope; she rubbed her eyes vaguely and covered them dumbly with her hands.

She removed her hands, and immediately again viewed the child waving more emphatically, more appealingly than before. She stared uncomprehendingly, then, feeling that she must be the victim of some strange hallucination of her disordered senses, expecting the phenomenon to vanish as instantaneously and magically as it had appeared, slowly, unbelievingly, she opened her window and looked out. Immediately, out of the dim obscurity, a round object, thrown with unerring accuracy, struck her upon the shoulder and dropped with a soft thud at her feet, whilst at the same instant the street became vacant and empty. Mechanically, Mary closed the window and sat down again. She would have dismissed the whole episode as a delusion of her tired brain but for the fact that upon the floor lay the missile which had impinged upon her out of the gathering darkness, like a small innocuous meteor falling from the invisible sky. She looked at the round object more closely. It was an apple.

She stooped and retrieved the apple, which felt smooth and polished and warm, as if for a long time it had been harboured in hot, human hands, and as she held it in her small palm, she scarcely knew why she should have abandoned her knitting for the contemplation of so absurd an object. It was, she recognised—of the pippin variety—a King Pippin—and immediately there flashed across her memory a remark once made to her by Denis: "We're fond of apples at home," he had said; "we always have a barrel of King Pippins standing in the pantry." At this sudden thought, from merely looking perplexedly at the apple, she began to inspect it closely, and discovered, to her surprise and growing agitation, a faint circular cut made necessarily by a fine blade, encircling the entire core. Her wan cheeks flooded with a high, nervous colour as she plucked at the short dried stem which was still adherent to the apple, but they paled instantly, and the blood drained from her face, as a neat round plug of the firm, white fruit came away easily in her grasp, revealing a hollowed-out centre which was packed tightly with a roll of thin paper. With frantic haste and a pitiful agitation her nervous fingers fumblingly extracted and unrolled the cylinder, then, suddenly, the action of her fluttering heart almost ceased. It was a letter from Denis! He had written to her. He had not abandoned her. Her wild, incredulous eyes fastened themselves avidly upon this letter which had reached her with all the timely mercy of a reprieve. Feverishly she read on, saw that it had been written almost a fortnight previously, that it addressed her in most fervent terms. A great joy came upon her like a full, dazzling light suddenly turned upon her, blinding her by its unexpectedness, warming her with its radiance. The words of the letter shone before her eyes, their meaning flooded her like a glow of heat penetrating a chilled and icy body. She had been mad to doubt him. He was Denis—her Denis—and he loved her!

He loved her, had tried with all his power to reach her, had attempted, even, to place a message through her window by night. She saw now that she had been right in feeling that he was near to her, but her foolish cry of fear had driven him away. Still, nothing mattered in the face of his wonderful news. Her heart beat as she read that he had taken their house—the cottage in Garshake. They could move into it upon the first of January. It was called Rosebank—in summer a bower of roses, in winter a warm, safe haven to enclose them both. He was doing all that lay within his power, and he was not afraid! She was touched beyond measure at his endeavours, at what he had done for her. How he had worked for her! He would have come to her openly, but for the fact that their plans were not mature. They must have a roof to cover them, a house to shelter them, before they could take any drastic step; until then, he must be wary for her sake. Yes! she must wait—wait a little longer; wait until his last summer trip of the year was over, until he could devote himself to her. Then he would take her away with him for ever, care for her, and look to her safety and comfort. Her eyes grew dim with tears of happiness as she read his promises to cherish her. Could she wait? She must wait. She could endure anything, so long as he took her to him in the end.

When she had finished the letter, for a moment she remained quite still, as though the shock of unexpected happiness had petrified her into stone and she sat like a marble effigy, rigid and motionless. Then, slowly, a pulsating essence flowed through her veins; mysterious currents, set in motion by the moving words of his letter, circulated in her being; after what had been an eternity of death-like inanition she lived and, as in an awakening Galatea, a tinge of life pervaded her, colour rushed into her face, her body, her limbs. Her eyes sparkled eagerly with the joy of living, her constrained lips parted softly, fervidly, and the sad immobility of her face was transfigured by a rush of sanguine joy. Like a watcher forgotten upon some solitary isle, who, worn with an endless, fruitless vigil, has long abandoned hope, the sudden sight of the means of her rescue filled her with an unbelievable, almost unbelieving ecstasy. The loud beating of her reawakened heart sang in her ears with a rapturous refrain; the pale hands holding the letter became animate, vitalised, and active; eagerly the fingers seized a pencil that lay near and wrote urgently on the reverse side of the paper.

It was a short note, saying that she was well and, now that she had heard from him, happy. She said nothing of the tortures of mind she had suffered, or of the abyss into which she had been sinking. She told him she would abide gladly in her present home if only he came for her in December, and she blessed him repeatedly for his letter. She had not time to write more, for, outside the house, in the rapidly fading light, she discerned that the patient, tenacious figure of the child had again reappeared, and was gazing expectantly towards the window. It was Rose—it must be Rose—that small devoted sister he had spoken of. She blessed Rose! And now, replacing the message in the hollow apple, she raised the window sash and, throwing with all her strength, watched the sphere go sailing through the air and bound twice upon the road before coming to rest. Dimly she glimpsed Rose running to recover it, saw her extract the letter and place it in her coat pocket, observed her wave her hand significantly, triumphantly, and, as if to symbolise the sweetness of her triumph, go off down the road, exultantly munching the bruised and battered pippin. A quiver of grateful admiration ran through Mary as the small figure passed out of sight, marching indomitably with the same invincible air, the same jaunty courage as Denis. A slight smile of recollection moved her as she remembered Rose's careless touch upon the piano. The folly of judging the intrepid messenger by the execution of those scales!

And now Mary arose and stretched her limbs luxuriously. She raised her arms above her head in an attitude of unconscious aspiration and whilst her figure seemed to draw itself upwards, her head fell back, her throat grew taut. As she gazed towards heaven, her face filled with a supreme thanksgiving, which seemed insensibly to pass into an invocation for the future. She was alive again, brave, filled with new hope, new courage. Little pricking streams ran through her skin. Suddenly, as she lowered her arms and again relaxed her body, she felt hungry. For weeks she had eaten nothing but the insipid, choking mouthfuls thrust down at meal times under the eye of her father, and the delicious return of the zest to live now made her voracious.

Within her body the unformed child leapt and throbbed, as if in sympathy and gratitude for the reprieve which had been granted to it.

And Mary, feeling the weak impotence of that thankful impulse, was moved with a sudden pity. In the revulsion of her feeling she turned quickly, in a passion of self-reproach, to the drawer where she had concealed the salts of lemon, and lifting the packet in a frenzy of disgust, concealed it in her hand and hastened downstairs. As she hurried past the half-open door of the parlour, she saw old Grandma Brodie nodding drowsily, and she realised happily that Rose had not been observed, that for once the sentinel slept at her post. Quickly she went through the kitchen and entered the scullery where, with a feeling of aversion, she thrust the contents of the packet, not back upon its shelf, but into the sink, where a rapid stream from the tap washed it away from her for ever. Then, with a new freedom, she went to a cupboard, poured out a glass of milk and cut herself a thick wedge of cold steamed pudding left over from dinner. The pudding was luscious and full of soft, sweet currants; her teeth bit into it with a sapid relish. The milk tasted like a draught of some rich nectar, cool as the froth from melting snow-flakes. She was prolonging her meal as long as possible, by sipping slowly and nibbling the last crust of pudding, when her mother entered the scullery. Mamma looked at Mary curiously.

"You're hungry?" she remarked. "I wish I could eat like that. The sermons have improved your appetite."

"Let me cut you a piece of this, Mamma."

"No! we're to have it heated up to-morrow. It doesn't matter about me."

By her attitude Mrs. Brodie conveyed that Mary was selfish to consume the pudding, that she herself would have desired it, but that she was deliberately sacrificing her personal gratification in the interests of the common good. Mary looked apologetic. With the first mouthful she had enjoyed for weeks she had been made to feel greedy.

"I'm glad to see you in a better frame of mind, anyway," said Mamma, noting the look. "Keep it up for your father to-night. I want him to see I've been speaking to you."

Here a light step sounded in the hall. This time it was, in reality, Nessie, who came in gaily, glistening like a young seal from the rain.

"It's awfully wet now," she cried; "and I want a piece and jelly."

Her mother looked at her fondly. "Ye've a braw colour on your cheeks, dear. That's the way I like my bairns to look; not white and miserable." This was a veiled hint to Mary, and as a further reproof to her elder daughter, Mamma gave Nessie, as a treat, not bread and jelly, but white bread with butter and carraway seeds spread upon it.

"Carvie! Lovely!" cried Nessie; "and I deserve it. Oh! Mary, you do look better to-night yourself. I'm glad! You'll soon be bonny like me," she added with a giggle, inconsequently twirling about.

"Why do you deserve it, pettie?" queried Mamma.

"Well!" replied Nessie importantly, "we had the school inspector this afternoon, and the whole junior school had what he called a memory test, and who do you think was first?"

"Who?" demanded Mamma, with bated breath.

"Me!" shrieked Nessie, waving her bread and carvie.

"My word!" said Mamma, "your father will be pleased." She looked at Mary, as if to say: "That's the kind of daughter I prefer." Actually she was not in the least exultant at the scholastic success. What delighted her was that she had, in this achievement, a tangible asset to put the lord and master of the house in a complacent frame of mind.

Mary looked at Nessie tenderly, feeling how near she had been to leaving her for ever.

"That was just splendid!" she said, and placed her cheek lovingly against her sister's cold, wet face.

X

A STILLNESS lay over Levenford. Sunday afternoon was always quiet; the morning bells had then rung themselves out; the bustle of the shops and the noise of shipyards were hushed; no step echoed in the empty street; the people, sunk in the lethargy produced by a heavy dinner following a long sermon, sat indoors, stiffly trying to read, or slept uncomfortably in their chairs.

But this afternoon was unusually still. A dull, yellow sky pressed down upon the town and imprisoned it in a vault of heavy silence. Within this vault the stagnant air was difficult to breathe and filled the lungs with a sense of vitiation. The streets seemed narrowed, the houses nearer to each other, and the Winton and Doran Hills, usually so majestic and remote, were low and close at hand as if, cowering from the encroaching sky, they crept in upon the town for protection. The trees stood petrified in the sultry air, their stripped branches dropping like stalactites in a cave. No birds were to be seen. Desolate and depopulated, the landscape lay in such an oppressive silence as might precede a battle, and the deserted town, empty of life and movement, stood like a beleaguered city fearfully awaiting the onset of an attack.

Mary sat upstairs at her bedroom window. Now, at every opportunity, she stole away to her room, finding in that retreat alone, a sanctuary in which she obtained solitude and refuge. She felt ill. In church that morning an intolerable sickness had seized her, and during dinner she had been compelled to remain quiescent and uncomplaining while her head and body ached incessantly. Now, as she sat with her chin cupped in both hands, looking out upon the strange immobility of the land, she wondered if it lay within her power to last out the next two days.

With a faint shudder, she reviewed in her mind her struggles of the past eight weeks. In his first note Denis had asked her to wait only until the middle of December, but it was now the twenty-eighth day of that month, and she had still to endure the torture of her life at home for another two days. It was, she realised, not his fault. He had been obliged to extend the scope of his business activities in the North and was now acting for his firm in Edinburgh and Dundee. They were pleased with his work; the delay was in actuality advantageous; but at present she found it hard to bear.

Only two more days! Then with Denis beside her in their snug, strong cottage by the Garshake shore—a fastness to enclose them both—she could face anything. She had visioned their cottage so continuously that it stood always firm, white, and steadfast in her mind, like a beacon, a shining emblem of protection, drawing her towards its safety. But she was losing faith in her ability to continue the struggle against the growing lassitude of her body and the ever-present dread of discovery.

She was, in effect, seven and a half months pregnant, but her fine, firm body had, until lately, retained its shape adequately. She had grown more mature, and paler in her face, but no gross distortion in her form had taken place, and any alteration in her appearance had been attributed to the effects of the more rigid discipline to which she had been subjected. But recently, she had been obliged to lace herself more tightly, and to strain to hold her back and shoulders erect in order to maintain, in the face of greater difficulty, and with unceasing effort, the semblance of her natural figure. The cramping grip of her corset almost stifled her, but she was now compelled to suffer this continually, to sit passively under the cold eye of Brodie whilst she felt her child turn protestingly under the unnatural restraint, and to preserve in the face of everything an aspect of unconcern and tranquillity.

She imagined, too, that of late, in spite of her every precaution, Mamma had entertained a vague uneasiness regarding her. Frequently she had looked up to intercept a doubting, questioning glance levelled acidly at her. Faint unformed suspicions, she realised, moved like latent shadows in her mother's mind, and only the preposterous nature of their purport had hitherto prevented them from assuming a more definite shape.

The last three months had dragged past more slowly and more fearfully than all the years of her life which had preceded them, and now, with the climax imminent and relief at hand, her strength seemed to be leaving her. To-day, a numb pain in her back added to her distress, and at intervals small, sweeping waves of suffering traversed her. As the memory of all that she had endured rose poignantly before her, a tear splashed down her cheek.

This quiet movement, the coursing of a tear-drop upon her face which disturbed her sad, statuesque passivity, had its counterpart in nature. Whilst she gazed, the front gate, which had all day hung half-open upon its listless hinges, was impelled into sluggish motion, and swung slowly shut with a loud clang, as though an invisible hand had negligently pushed it. A moment later, a heap of dead leaves which lay in the far corner of the courtyard, stirred, and a handful eddied, raised themselves spirally upwards on the air with a sighing susurrus, then subsided and were still.

Mary viewed both of these movements with a sensation of disturbance; perhaps her state induced such disquiet, for they had been in themselves insignificant, but the contrast of the sudden, unwarranted movements against the close, imperturbable quiet of the day was starkly arresting. The hush outside deepened, whilst the brassy sky grew more sombre and crept lower to the earth. As she sat, quiescent, awaiting another surge of pain, the front gate again swung gently open, hesitated, and recoiled with a more resounding concussion than before; the long, drawn-out noisy creak of the opening gate came to her like an interrogation and the quick-following clang like an abrupt and decisive reply. A faint ripple undulated across the field which lay opposite and the long grasses ruffled like smoke; under her staring eyes, a wisp of straw lying in the roadway was suddenly whisked high into the air and flung far out of sight by an unseen and inexplicable force. Then the silent air was filled with a soft, quick pattering, and a mongrel dog came racing down the street, its sides panting, its ears laid back flat, its eyes cowering. With a startled curiosity Mary marked its stricken aspect, and asked herself the reason for its haste and terror.

The answer to her unspoken question came like a sigh from a long way off, a low-pitched hum which swept in from beyond the Winton Hills, and echoed around the house. It encircled the grey walls, twisted sinuously through the embrasures of the parapet, whirled amongst the chimneys, spun around the solemn, granite balls, dwelt an instant at Mary's window, then receded in a gradual diminuendo, like the roar of a defeated wave upon a shingle shore. A long silence ensued, then the sound returned, swelling in from the distant hills more loudly, remaining longer than before, and retreating more slowly to a vantage point less remote.

At the end of this last, shivering drone the door of the bedroom opened, and Nessie came precipitately in. "Mary, I'm frightened," she cried. "What's that noise? It's like a great, big, humming-top."

"It's nothing but the wind."

"But there's no wind at all. Everything's as quiet as the grave—and what a colour the sky is! Oh! I'm feared of it, Mary."

"There's going to be a storm, I think, but don't worry, you'll be all right, Nessie."

"Oh! dearie me," cried Nessie, with a shiver, "I hope there'll be no lightning. I'm that scared of it. If it hits you they say it burns you up, and if you sit near steel that attracts it more than anything."

"There's not a steel thing in the room," Mary reassured her.

Nessie came closer.

"Let me stay with you a little," she entreated; "you seem to have been far away from me lately. If ye let me bide with you that sound will not seem so fearsome." She sat down and placed her thin arm around her sister; but instinctively Mary drew away.

"There you are again! You won't even let me touch you. You don't love me like you used to," Nessie grieved, and, for a moment, it looked as though she would rise and go out in childish pique. Mary sat silent; she could not justify her action, but she took Nessie's hand and pressed it gently. Partly reassured by this gesture, Nessie's hurt expression faded and she pressed Mary's hand in return. Thus, hand in hand the two sisters looked out silently upon the panting earth.

The atmosphere had now become dry and rare, and infused with an acrid, saline character which irritated the nostrils like brine. The dun sky had darkened to a blackish purple, meeting the near horizon like smoke, blotting out distant objects and throwing into strange relief those that were near. The sense of increasing isolation from the outer world thus produced was terrifying to Nessie. She gripped Mary's hand more tightly as she cried: "These clouds are coming on top of us. It's like a big black wall. Oh! I'm feared of it. Will it fall on us?"

"No, dear," whispered Mary, "it can't hurt us." But the dark, enclosing barrier still advanced, and upon its summit streaks of lighter saffron lay, like spume upon the crest of a breaking comber. Against this background the three birch trees had lost their soft, silvery mobility; stiff and livid, they gripped the soil more tenaciously with their sinewy roots, their stems standing straight, with closely furled branches, like masts awaiting oppressively the batter of a hurricane.

From amongst the now hidden hills came a secret mutter like the tattoo of muffled drums. It seemed as if it rolled along the crests of the hill-tops, bounding down the ravines, across the streams and up the gulleys, the close following notes chasing each other with a frantic revelry.

"That's thunder," shivered Nessie. "It's like guns firing."

"It's a long way off," Mary comforted her. "It may pass over us without breaking here."

"I feel it's going to be a terrible storm. Will we both go to Mamma, Mary?"

"You go if you like," replied Mary, "but you're just as safe here, dear."

The thunder drew nearer. It ceased to rattle continuously, and instead pealed brokenly; but now each peal was loud as an explosion, and each succeeding explosion more violent than the one before. This ominous quality of approach conveyed to Nessie the impression that she was the focus of some blind, celestial fury, which was surely converging upon her, and would ultimately destroy her.

"I'm sure it'll get us," she gasped. "Oh! there's the lightning."

An ear-splitting crash accompanied the first flash of lightning, a thin, blue streak which darted raggedly across the dead sky, as if the detonation of the thunder had suddenly cracked the bowl of the firmament, allowing, for one quivering instant, a dazzling and unearthly light to penetrate.

"It's forked!" cried Nessie. "That's more dangerous than sheet. Come away from the window!"; she tugged at Mary's arm.

"You're as safe here as anywhere," Mary repeated.

"Oh! it's no good saying that. This room of yours gets the worst of it! I'm going away to Mamma. I'll put my head below the blankets in her room till that awful lightning stops. Come away or you'll be struck"; and she rushed out of the room in a panic.

Mary did not follow her but continued to watch the growing storm alone. She felt like a lonely watcher in a tower, obsessed by pain and danger, for whose diversion a gigantic tourney was waged by nature's forces. The discord which raged outside was a drastic anodyne, which served to distract her from her increasing pain, the pangs of which seemed to her to be slowly intensifying. She was glad to be alone once more, glad that Nessie had left her. It was easier for her to suffer in solitude. The thunder fulminated wildly, and the lightning cascaded like fluid across the sky with a blinding intensity. Often, the onset of her pain would synchronise with a flash, and then she felt that she, a speck within the universe, was linked by the chain of light to this titanic upheaval of the heavens.

As the distracting influence of the storm upon her failed, the disturbance ceased to be palliative; she began, involuntarily, to interpret it in terms of her bodily suffering, and became herself involved in the tumult around her. The rolling waves of thunder lifted her in their upward sweep, and carried her off upon their undulating echoes, until, suddenly, a violet lightning flash would stab her with pain, and cast her down again upon the ground. When the thunder failed, the wind, which had been rapidly increasing in volume, swept her back again into the midst of the chaos. This wind especially frightened Mary, began, indeed, to terrify her. The first soughing onset and retreat which had whirled the leaves then left them motionless, had been but the prelude to a series of deeper and more powerful attacks. Now there was no retreat, and with crushing vigour the full force of the blast struck the land. Mary felt the strong, stout house tremble to its foundations, as though an infinity of tearing fingers were rending each stone from its bed of mortar. She saw her own trees whipped downwards, like drawn bows bent double under some prodigious strain; with each gust they bent, then, liberated, again sprang upwards with a twanging sound. The arrows they released were invisible, but they penetrated Mary's room as shafts of pain. The long grasses in the field were no longer gently ruffled, but were flattened as though a gigantic scythe had decimated them. Each fierce blast of the gale battered at the windows, rattling them in their frames, then rushed howling around the house, with all the uncouth demons of sound loosed and rampant upon its wings.

Then the rain began. It fell at first in heavy, solitary gouts which stained the wind-swept pavements with spots each as large as a crown piece. Faster and faster came the drops, until a solid sheet of water deluged the earth. Water splashed upon the open roadways, hissed and dripped from the roofs and gutters of houses, spattered against trees, flattened shrubs and bushes by its very density and weight. Water flooded everything. The gutters were at once filled to overflowing and ran like torrents; the streets became watercourses, and running streams, filled with floating debris, sluiced along the main thoroughfares.

With the commencement of the rain the lightning gradually ceased, the thunder passed over, and the air chilled perceptibly; but the storm, instead of abating, grew more violent with every moment. The wind gained velocity. Mary heard it drive the rain in waves, like sea surf, upon the roof of the house, then she faintly heard a snap and saw the flag-staff, riven from the turret, fall clattering to the ground.

At this she got up, and began to pace up and down the room, hardly able to endure the racking ache which now seemed continually an element of her being. She had felt nothing of the kind before, nothing to equal this in all her life. She wondered, uncertainly, if she should ask her mother for some remedy, thinking that a hot application might perhaps do good, but, reluctantly, she abandoned the idea as dangerous. She did not know that such an antidote would have been ineffectual, for, although she had no apprehension of her condition, she was already advanced in the throes of a premature labour. Like the untimely dark-ness of the premature night which now began to fall upon the outraged earth, this precipitate travail had already, and too soon, begun to lay its mantle of suffering upon her. The mental hardships she had undergone were demanding an undreamed of toll, which she could not escape, and she had now, in all her unpreparedness, unconsciously begun to solve the dreadful mystery of the nativity of her child.

By this time she felt that it was impossible for her to go downstairs for tea, and, in despair, she loosened her corset, and began again to pace up and down the narrow confines of her room. Between these pacings she stopped, supporting her body between her open palms. She dis-covered that it was easier for her to meet the paroxysms in a stooping posture and, from time to time, she stood crouching against the end of her bed, her forehead pressed downwards against the cold metal of the rails.

As she remained heedlessly like this, in one of these spasms, suddenly the door opened, and her mother entered the room. Mrs. Brodie had come to satisfy herself that Mary had suffered no ill effects from the storm, and to reprimand her for not taking greater precautions, for Nessie had run to her with the story that lightning was striking into the room. She was herself terrified by the tempest, and her overstrung nerves were quiveringly set for an outburst of recrimination. But now, as she stood, unobserved, regarding her daughter, the rebuke that lay half-formed upon her lips remained unuttered. Her jaw dropped slowly, she gasped, whilst the room, rocked by the fury of the wind, seemed to oscillate about her. Mary's abandonment, her relaxed attitude, the profile of her unrestrained figure, plucked at the instrument of the mother's memory and touched a hidden chord in her mind, bringing back suddenly the unforgettable remembrance of her own travail. An illuminating flash, more terrible than any lightning stroke, pierced her understanding. All the latent, the unthought of and unthinkable misgivings, which had been dormant within her, bounded before her in one devastating conviction. The pupils of her eyes dilated into pools of horror and, clutching her shrunken bosom with her left hand, she raised her right drunkenly, and pointed her finger at Mary.

"Look—look at me!" she stammered.

With a start Mary turned and, her brow dewed with perspiration, looked at her mother dumbly. Immediately the mother knew, knew inexorably, and Mary saw that she was discovered. Instantly a shriek burst from Mrs. Brodie like the cry of an outraged animal. Higher and more piercing than the wind it shrilled inside the room, and echoed screechingly through the house. Again, and again, she shrieked, lost in the grasp of hysteria. Blindly, Mary clutched at her mother's dress.

"I didn't know, Mamma," she sobbed. "Forgive me. I didn't know what I was doing."

With short, stabbing blows Mrs. Brodie thrust Mary from her. She could not speak; her breath came stertorously from her in panting spasms.

"Mamma! dear Mamma! I understood nothing! I didn't know I was wicked. Something's hurting me now. Help me!" she begged her.

The mother found her tongue with difficulty.

"The disgrace! Your father!" she moaned. "Oh! it's a nightmare. I'm not awake."

She screeched again, madly. Mary was terrified; this outcry imprisoned her in a cell of iniquity; she heard in each scream the wide broadcast of her disgrace.

"Oh! please, Mamma, don't call out like that," implored Mary, her head hanging abjectly; "only stop, and I'll tell you everything."

"No! No!" shrieked Mamma. "I'll hear nothing! Ye'll have to face your father. I'll be party to nothing. I'm not responsible. It's only yourself to blame."

Mary's limbs trembled violently. "Dear Mamma! is there no excuse for me?" she whispered. "I was no ignorant."

"Your father will kill ye for this," screamed Mrs. Brodie. "It's your fault."

"I implore you, Mamma," pleaded Mary feverishly, "not to tell father. Help me for two days more—only two days"—she cried desperately, trying to bury her head on her mother's breast—"dear, kind Mamma. Keep it between us till then. Only two days more! Please—Oh! please!"

But again her mother, terrified beyond reason, thrust her off and cried out wildly:

"You must tell him at once. I'm no' to blame. Oh! the wickedness of ye to get us into such trouble. Oh! the wickedness, the wickedness!"

Then, with a bitter finality, Mary realised that it was hopeless to entreat her mother further. A great fear descended on her and, with it, the rushing desire to escape. She felt that if she left her, Mamma might recover her control. She desired urgently to get out of the room, and pushing past her mother, she began hastily to descend the stairs. But when she was half-way down, suddenly she raised her head and saw at the foot of the staircase, standing in the hall, the heavy figure of her father.

Brodie had the custom, every Sunday afternoon after dinner, of resting. He went with the regularity of clockwork into the parlour, closed the door, drew the curtains, removed his frock coat, and laid his ponderous bulk down upon the sofa, where he slept heavily for two or three hours. But to-day he had been disturbed by the storm, and he had slept only in snatches, which was worse than not sleeping at all. The loss of his sleep had aggravated him, rendering his temper sour, and, in addition, he took it as a matter of great annoyance to his sense of order that his time-honoured ritual should have been deranged in such an outrageous fashion. The culmination of his vexation had been achieved when he had been aroused from a snatch of sleep by the fall of the flagstaff from his house. He was in a flaming rage and, as he stood in his shirt-sleeves, looking at Mary, his upturned face reflected the bitter resentment of his mood.

"Have we not enough noise outside that you must start that infernal din upstairs?" he shouted. "How can a man sleep with such a fiendish blattering in his ears? Who was making that noise? Was it you?" He glared at her.

Mamma had followed Mary, and now stood swaying upon the top landing, rocking herself to and fro, with her arms clasped upon her breast. Brodie turned his inflamed eye upon her.

"This is a braw house for a man to rest in," he flared. "Do I not work hard enough for ye through the week? What is this day made for, will ye tell me? What's the use of all that godly snivellin' talk of yours if ye must go and ring our ears like this. Can I not lay down for a minute without this damned wind howlin', and you howlin' like a hyena too?"

Mrs. Brodie did not reply but still swayed hysterically at the top of the stairs.

"What are you going on about? Are you gone silly?" bawled Brodie. "Has the thunder turned your reason to make ye stand like a drunken fish wife?"

Still she was silent, and it then dawned upon him, from her manner, that some disaster had occurred.

"What is it?" he shouted roughly. "Is it Nessie? Has the lightning hit her? Is she hurt?"

Mamma shook her whole body in a frantic negation—the catastrophe was worse than that!

"No! No!" she gasped. "It's her—her!" She raised her hand accusingly against Mary. Not even the most shadowy instinct of protection was in her. Her terror of Brodie in this awful calamity was so unbounded that her only impulse was to disclaim all responsibility, all knowledge of the crime. She must at all costs defend herself from any charge of liability in the matter.

"For the last time," raged Brodie, "I ask ye what it is. Tell me, or by God I'll come up to ye both."

"It wasn't my fault," cringed Mrs. Brodie, still shielding herself from the undelivered charge, "I've brought her up always like a Christian girl. It's her own natural badness." Then, realising that she must tell or be beaten, she strained her body to the utmost, threw her head back and, as if each word cost her an unbearable effort of ejaculation, sobbed: "If you must know. She's going—she's going to have a child."

Mary stiffened, whilst the blood drained from her face. Her mother, like Judas, had betrayed her. She was lost—trapped—her father below, her mother above.

Brodie's great frame seemed to shrink imperceptibly; his bellicose eyes became faintly bemused, and, in a muddled fashion, he looked at Mary.

"What wha'——" he muttered. He raised his eyes uncomprehendingly to Mamma, saw her frantic plight, and again lowered his gaze upon Mary. He paused, whilst his mind grappled with the inconceivable, unfathomable news. Suddenly he shouted: "Come here!"

Mary obeyed. Each step she took seemed to lower her into her own tomb. Brodie seized her roughly by the arm and looked her up and down. A sickening feeling went through him. "My God!" he repeated to himself, in a low tone. "My God! I believe it's true. Is it?" he cried thickly. Her tongue lay mutely in her mouth from shame. Still holding her arm he shook her unmercifully, then, releasing her suddenly, allowed her to recoil heavily upon the floor.

"Are you with child? Tell me quickly or I'll brain you," he shouted.

As she told him, she thought he would surely kill her. He stood there looking at her as if she were a viper that had stung him. He raised his arm as if to strike her, to crush her skull with one blow of his hammer fist, to wipe out with one blow her obliquity and his dishonour. He wanted to strike her, to trample on her, grind her under the heels of his boots into a mangled, bloody pulp. A vast brutal passion seethed in him. She had dragged his name into the mire. The name of Brodie! She had lowered his heritage into the slime of ill-fame. The whole place would reek of it. He would see the smirks, the sneers, the significant nods as he strode down the High Street; at the Cross he would hear the stray word of mockery and the half-muffled laugh of derision. The niche he had cut and was still carving for himself would be shattered, the name, the reputation he had made for himself would be ruined, and he himself cast downwards in contumely through this thing that lay weeping at his feet. But he did not strike her. The intensity of his feeling burned suddenly into a heat which turned his gross rage into a subtle and more dangerous channel. In a different manner he would show her! He saw sharply a means of vindicating his honour. Yes! by God, he would show them in the Borough how he dealt with this sort of thing .They would see the stand that he was taking. She was now no daughter of his. He would cast her from him as unclean.

Then, suddenly, a second, loathsome suspicion came into his mind, a suspicion which gathered in aversion, becoming more certain the longer he contemplated it. He roused Mary with his huge, heavy boot. "Who was the man?" he hissed at her. "Was it Foyle?" He saw from her look that he was right. For the second time that hateful young upstart had dealt him a crushing blow, this time more deadly than before. He would rather it had been anyone, the basest and most beggarly scoundrel in the town, anyone but Foyle! But it was he, the smooth-faced, blarneying, young corner boy who had possessed the body of Mary Brodie; and she, his child, had suffered him to do so. A lucid mental picture, revolting in its libidinous detail, rose up and tortured him. His face worked, the skin around his nostrils twitched, a thick, throbbing vessel corded itself intumescently upon his temple. His features, which had at first been suffused with a high angry flush, now became white and hard as chiselled granite. His jaw set ruthlessly like a trap, his narrow forehead lowered with an inhuman barbarity. A cold ferocity, more terrifying than the loud-mouthed abuse which he usually displayed, tempered his rage like an axe blade. He kicked Mary viciously. The hard sole of his boot sank into her soft side.

"Get up, you bitch!" he hissed, as he again spurned her brutally with his foot. "Do you hear me? Get up."

From the staircase the broken voice of Mamma senselessly repeated: "I'm not to blame! I'm not to blame!" Over and over came the words: "I'm not to blame. Don't blame me." She stood there abjectly, cringingly, protesting ceaselessly in a muttering voice her inculpability, whilst behind her the terrified figures of Nessie and the old woman were dimly outlined. Brodie gave no heed to the interruption. He had not heard it.

"Get up," he repeated, "or I'll help ye up"; and, as she rose, he lifted her to her feet with a final jerk of his foot.

Mary staggered up. Why, she thought, did he not kill her and be done with it? Her side, where he had kicked her, stabbed with a lancinating hurt. She was too terrified to look at him. She felt that he was torturing her only to destroy her in the end.

"Now," he ground out slowly from between his clenched teeth, with words that bit into her like vitriol, "you'll listen to me."

As she stood there, bent and drooping, he moved his head slightly and thrust forward his hard, relentless face into hers. His eyes gleamed closely, with a concentrated, icy glitter that seared her with its chill.

"You'll listen to me, I say. You'll listen to me for the last time. You are not my daughter any longer. I am going to cast you out like a leper! Like a leper—you filthy slut! That's what I'm going to do to you and your unborn bastard. I'm going to settle with your fancy man in my own time, but you—you're going out to-night."

He repeated the last words slowly, whilst he pierced her with his cold eyes. Then, as though reluctant to abandon the satisfaction of her abasement under his glare, he turned slowly, walked heavily to the door and flung it open. Immediately a terrific inrush of wind and rain filled the hall, clattering the pictures on the walls, billowing the hanging coats on the stand, and rushing upwards with the force of a battering-ram towards the clinging group upon the stairs.

"It's a beautiful night for a stroll," snarled Brodie, with drawn lips. "It's dark enough for you to-night! You can walk the streets to your heart's content to-night, you strumpet!"

With a sudden thrust of his arm he caught her by the neck and compressed it within his huge, prehensile grasp. No sound but the howling of the wind filled the hall. Of the three terrorised onlookers, the uncomprehending child, the mother, and the half-fearful, half-gloating old woman, not one spoke. They stood paralysed to silence. The feel of her soft yet resistant throat fascinated him; he wanted to squeeze it like a pipe-stem until it snapped, and, for an instant, he stood thus, fighting the impulse; but he started violently and, with a sudden tug, dragged her to the door. "Now," he shouted, "you're going out and you'll never come back—not until you crawl back and grovel down to lick these boots that have kicked you."

At that, something within Mary spoke. "I will never do that," she whispered from her pale lips.

"No!" yelled Brodie. "You will never come back, you harlot!"

He pushed her, with a violent, final thrust, from him. She disappeared into the raging blackness beyond. As she vanished completely to sight and sound, as though she had stepped over a precipice, he stood there in an ecstasy of passion, his fists clenched, filling his lungs with the wet, saline air, shouting at the pitch of his voice: "Don't come back, you whore! you whore!" He shouted the last word again, and again, as if its repetition afforded him, in its coarse vituperation, a satisfaction, an alleviation of his fury. Then he turned upon his heel and shut her out into the night.

XI

MARY rested where she had fallen. She felt stunned, for Brodie's final, brutal thrust had thrown her, heavily, flat upon her face, into the rough, gravel courtyard. The rain, driven in straight, parallel spears, impinged painfully upon her lightly covered body and spattered the surface of the puddle in which she lay. Already she was soaked to the skin, but the wetness of her rain-saturated clothing brought, at that moment, only a refreshing coolness to the fever that burned within her. She had felt under her father's terrible eyes that he would surely murder her and now, although her bruised and aching body still burned, a sense of escape filled her mind and transfigured its terror to lightness and relief. She had been cast out shamefully, but she was alive, she had left for ever a home which had become lately a hated prison; and now she plucked together her shattered forces and bravely fixed her mind upon the future.

Denis, she became aware amongst the fearful confusion of her thoughts, was perhaps sixty miles away; she was enveloped in a storm of unprecedented magnitude; she had no coat, no hat, insufficient clothing and no money; but now she had courage. Firmly, she compressed her wet lips as she desperately endeavoured to examine her position. Two courses lay open to her: the one to attempt to reach the cottage at Garshake, the other to go to Denis' mother at Darroch.

It was twelve miles to Garshake and, beyond the fact that she knew that it was named Rosebank, she had no knowledge of where the cottage stood; besides, even if she succeeded in getting inside, she would be alone, penniless, and without food; and now she realised that she needed succour of some kind. She therefore abandoned all thought of reaching Rosebank and turned, inevitably, to the alternative idea. She must go to Denis' mother! At least she would receive shelter from her, shelter until Denis returned. His mother would not refuse her that; and she hearteningly recollected that once Denis had said to her: "If the worst happened, you could come to my mother." She would do that! She must do that.

To get to Darroch she would be obliged to walk. She was not aware of any train which left Levenford for Darroch on Sunday night; and if one did, indeed, run she did not know its time of departure, nor had she the cost of her ticket. Two routes therefore offered themselves for her choice. The first was the main artery of communication between the two places, a broad main thoroughfare nearly five miles long, the other, a narrow, unfrequented road running directly across the open countryside, narrowing here to a lane and there to a mere track, but avoiding the circuitous windings of the outskirts of both towns, and shorter than the former by almost two miles. Her strength was now so insufficient, and her sufferings so great, that she decided to take the latter route because it was the lesser distance. She thought she could walk three miles.

Prostrate upon the ground and protected by the high wall of the courtyard she had not appreciated the full power of the storm, which was, indeed, the worst which had ravaged the Scottish Lowlands for over a century. The wind, springing from the south-west, tore past at the unprecedented velocity of sixty miles an hour. In the town only those driven by necessity were abroad, and, of these, only the hardiest remained for more than a few moments in the open. Slates torn from the roofs of houses sailed downwards through the air, each with the force and cutting violence of a falling guillotine; whole chimney-pots were wrenched off, flung through the air entire, and dashed upon the cobble-stones below; the large, thick, plate-glass window of the Building Society's office was blown into pieces, like dry parchment, by the force of the wind alone. Amongst the roar of the hurricane the reports of falling objects as they struck upon the streets came continuously, like a bombardment. In the Newtown the gable of a newly erected house was caved in by the blast and the wind, entering the aperture like a wedge, prised off the roof and seized it. Off flew the entire roof, its sides extended like the planing wings of a bird, soaring through the air, until finally the wind ceased to support it and it dived like a plummet into the black water of the estuary a full three hundred yards away.

In the low-lying parts of the town the ceaseless rain caused such flooding that entire areas lay under water; houses stood apart like isolated dwellings rising from a strange lagoon, and the deluge, rushing around them, percolated the walls, entered through doors and windows, and completely inundated the lower floors.

The lightning which ran riot over the surrounding countryside produced a less diffuse but more deadly havoc. A shepherd, herding on the Doran hills, was struck instantly dead by a fulgent stroke; two farm servants sheltering under a tree were struck down and their charred bodies crushed by the fall of the riven tree; livestock suffered severely; countless sheep and cattle were killed as they lay in the open or sought a more precarious shelter under trees, and a full score of cattle crouching against a wire fence were electrocuted by the conduit of the fluid current.

A thunderbolt fell, and, crashing into a sailing barque at anchor in Port Doran Bay, sank it instantly. Other ships, in the river mouth and in the Firth, dragged their anchors and broke their moorings and were battered by the waves as they ran aground on the Doran shore.

Unaware of all this, Mary slowly raised herself to her feet. The wind took hold of her and almost cast her down again, but she bore against it, and, inclining her body sharply into the teeth of the gale, set out through the pitch of the night. Her sodden garments flapped about her like drenched sails and hampered her movements, clinging bindingly to her legs at each step she took. As she left the front of her home a leaden gutter, stripped from the coping by a single gust, came hurtling viciously towards her, like a last malevolent gesture from the house; but, though it passed dangerously near her head, it missed her and buried itself deeply into the wet ground.

She had not proceeded a hundred yards before she was compelled to rest. Though this point marked the situation of the last lamp-post of the road, now the darkness was unrelieved and, for a moment, she imagined the light had been blown out, but as she resumed her way, she tripped upon the prone column of the disrupted lamp. With head downwards she stumbled on, feeling her way like a blind woman and keeping the road only through her sense of direction and by her familiarity with it. The noise about her was frightful, so deafening that if she had shouted aloud she would not have heard her own voice. The wind, like some gigantic orchestra, traversed madly the gamut of its compass. The deep diapason of the pipe-organ mingled with the reedy treble of clarionets; bugles shrilled against the bass of oboes; the wailing of violins, the clash of cymbals, the booming of drums were blended together into an unearthly cacophony of dissonance.

Every now and then, out of the blackness, unseen objects struck her. Flying twigs of trees stung her face, torn-up branches and shrubs flung themselves against her. Once a soft, sessile tentacle entwined itself about her neck and arms. She shrieked with terror, lifting her soundless voice against the hurricane, thinking that living arms had corded themselves about her, but, as she raised her hands in panic, she discovered that she was enveloped by a sheaf of hay blown from some obliterated stack.

With the utmost difficulty she had now traversed about a mile of her journey, and, though she was not yet half-way towards her objective, the most fearful part lay immediately ahead. Here the road closed in almost to a pathway and wandered, unflanked by any guiding fence or boundary, without line of demarcation from the adjacent woodland, through a thick grove of firs. This wood was always tenebrous, with gloomy trees that whispered elegies, but now, in this fearsome night, which itself lay around her like a dense forest, the wood became frightful and repulsive, like the central darkness, the very heart of the forest of the night. She shuddered to think of entering it. Once, when a child, upon an expedition with some others, she had lost herself amongst these stern, austere trees, had run amongst them, forlornly seeking her companions, and she now recalled with painful vividness her youthful terror, a terror which returned upon darker wings as, mustering all her courage and her strength, she plunged into the coppice.

It was almost impossible to trace the pathway. Gropingly she crept along, keeping both arms extended, with flat palms outstretched in front of her. This extension of her arms gave her an excruciating hurt in that side of her chest where her father had kicked her, but she was obliged to hold them so in order to protect her head and face from the contact of the trees, and to ascertain more exactly the direction of her laborious progress.

The wind which, in the open land, had maintained a constant direction, now whirled around the tree trunks with a hundred currents and eddies, in a manner which rendered direct forward movement impossible. Mary was tossed this way and that way, like a ship beating its course amongst a swirl of treacherous tides, without moon or stars to guide her in the perilous pitch of the night. She had begun to wander from the path when, suddenly, an erratic vortex caught her, swept away her balance, and flung her violently to the left. She fell with all her weight, and the palm of her left hand impaled itself upon the dagger-sharp point of a low, broken fir branch which projected horizontally from the main trunk. For one agonising moment her hand remained nailed to the wood, then she plucked it free, and staggered to her feet.

Onwards she went. She was now utterly lost. She wanted to get out of the wood but she could not. Dizzily she felt her way from tree to tree, the blood streaming from her wounded hand, permeated by terror, by the throbbing of her injured side and the recurrent pains within her body. Chilled to the bone, her wet hair streaming dankly, her skin infiltrated with rain water, she mazed about the wood in the darkness. She stumbled, and got up, swayed backwards and staggered onwards, to the insane music of the tornado as it bellowed through the trees. The pandemonium of sound dinning upon her ears seemed of itself to swing her about, controlling her movements by its stupendous rhythm. Light-headedly she gyrated, amongst the rending avulsion of uprooting trees, lost to everything but pain and her desire to escape from the horror of this besetting forest.

Her head became light and giddy, and now it seemed to her that the blackness was peopled with wild, living creatures that dashed about her, touching her, plucking at her with their fingers, pressing against and hurrying past her in an orgy of stampeding movement. She felt the cold, gusty breathing of the wet things as they slid their way and buffeted through the forest. They whispered into her ears strange, sad tidings of Denis and of her child; they bellowed loudly in her father's tones, and wailed like her mother. Every sound about her she construed into the weird and incoherent speech of these visionary beings. At intervals she knew she was going mad, that no forms surrounded her, that she was alone, deserted, forgotten in the wood, but, as she staggered on, her mind again became obscured, clouded by the visions of her terror.

Suddenly, when it seemed as though she must completely lose her reason, she paused in a kind of numb wonder. She raised her tortured eyes upwards to the sky and beheld the moon, a thin crescent, pale and without radiance, which lay flat upon its back amongst the banked clouds, as though the gale had blown it over. She saw it only for a moment, then it was obscured by the racing clouds, but she observed that the wind now came upon her in one direct, tearing line of motion that she no longer felt the hard trunks of the firs. She was out of the wood! She sobbed with relief, and immediately ran blindly to escape from it, and from the gibbering creatures it contained. She had lost the road, together with all sense of her bearings, and the instinct of flight alone impelled her as, with a crouching, stumbling motion, she hastened anywhere. The wind was now assisting her, lifting her from her feet and lengthening her shambling steps. She was in some kind of field, and long, dank grasses whipped her legs as she slid forward upon the soft turf. It was not cultivated land, for she passed amongst clumps of bracken, slipped and stumbled against half-buried, moss-grown boulders, and ripped through clusters of bramble bush; but she was now beyond logical thought and did not pause to deduce her whereabouts from the nature of the country she traversed.

Then, all at once, amongst the tumult, she became aware of a deep, sonorous cadence, which, as she went on, grew louder, and swelled to the roar of rushing water. It was the sound of a broad river, swollen to overflowing, and so engorged by turbid waters that its rushing turbulence sounded in her ears like the resonance of a cataract. With every step she took this sound grew louder till it seemed as though the river, glutted with the debris of the uplands, advanced menacingly upon her, bearing, unseen amongst the seething waters, palings and fencing, the debris of a dozen bridges, whole tree trunks, and the bodies of dead sheep and cattle.

She was now upon its brink before she understood that it was the Leven; the same Leven which had sung to her so softly with its lilting purl, which had added to the rapture of Denis and herself as, meandering past, it had serenaded them to love. Now, like herself, it was altered beyond recognition. The moon was still obscured, and nothing was visible to her, but as she stood terrified, listening upon the high, exposed bank, for an instant, in her fearful extremity, she was tempted to let herself slide into these invisible, booming waters below, to forget and be forgotten. A shudder ran through her bruised body as she repulsed the thought. Like a command to live came the thought that, no matter what happened, she still had Denis. She must live for Denis, and now she felt him beckoning to her. She turned abruptly from the sound as though to cut off its appeal but, as she moved, in the careless hurry of her recoil, her wet shoe slipped, she stumbled, her foot again slithered on the surface of a greasy clod and she shot feet first down the steep slope. Her hands clutched desperately at the short grass and rushes of the bank, but the weeds that she grasped broke immediately in her clasp, or uprooted easily from the wet soil. Her feet tore two furrows in the yielding clay as she dug them fiercely into it in a fruitless effort to save herself. With her arms she clung to the wet bank, but she found nothing to retard her descent.

The smooth surface of the declivity was as steep and treacherous as that of a glacier and, instead of arresting her fall, these frantic movements only served to increase her speed. She was precipitated with irresistible momentum into the unseen river below. She entered the water with a soundless splash and immediately sank down amongst the long water weeds which grew from the bottom, whilst water rushed into her lungs as she gasped from shock and terror. The force of the current drove her body rapidly along the river bed, amongst the entangling grasses, and swept her down stream for thirty yards before she came at last to the surface.

She could not swim but, instinctively, with the effort of preservation, she made a few, feeble, despairing strokes, trying to keep her head above the surface of the water. It was impossible. The intense spate of the torrent had raised a series of high, undulating waves which swept repeatedly over her, and finally, a swirling undertow caught her legs and sucked her down. This time she remained under so long that her senses almost left her. Bells rang in her ears, her lungs were ballooned, her eyeballs bursting; red stabs of light danced before her; she was suffocating. But she came once more to the surface and, as she emerged, inert and half insensible, the end of a floating log of wood was flung by a wave into her right armpit. Unconsciously, she seized it and feebly clasped it against her. She floated. Her body was submerged, her hair streaming behind her in the current, but her face lay above water and, with great, gasping breaths, she filled and refilled her chest with air. With all feeling suspended but the necessity of respiration she clung to the log, amidst the strange flotsam that dashed every now and then against her, and was borne rapidly down the river. Her rate of movement was so great that, as consciousness returned to her more fully, she realised that, if she did not quickly reach the bank, she would soon be swept amongst the sharp rocks which spiked the rapids that lay immediately above Levenford. With the remains of her strength, and still clinging to the log, she kicked out with her legs. The cold of the river water was infinitely more cutting than of the rain, cutting from the frigidity of an ice-crusted, snow-capped mountain source, and from the added chill of tributary hill streams fed by melted snow. This cold pierced to the marrow of Mary's bones; her limbs lost all sensation and, although her legs moved feebly at the command of her will, she did not feel them stir. The air, too, had become so frigid that hailstones began to fall. They were large pellets, hard as stone, sharp as icicles, that churned the water like shot and bounced off the log like bullets. They rained mercilessly upon Mary's face and head, bruising her eyes, whipping her cheeks, and cutting her lower lip. Because she must hold the log so grimly with both her hands she could not shield herself and she was compelled to suffer this pitiless, pelting shower, unprotected. Her teeth chattered; her wounded hand was seared and freezing; dreadful cramps seized her middle; she felt she was perishing from the cold. The immersion in the glacial water was killing her. At that moment, as she struggled towards the bank, a single thought obsessed her—not of herself or of Denis, but of the child within her. A compelling instinct suddenly flowered within her as though a message, passing by some strange communication between the child and her own being, had suddenly told her that, if she did not quickly get out of the water, it must die.

Never before had she thought so lovingly of the child. At times she had hated it as part of her own despicable body, but now an overpowering desire for it overtook her. If she died it must die. She thought of the living infant, entombed in her drowned body, floating out to sea, moving more and more feebly in the prison of her lifeless flesh. Without speech she prayed that she might live, live to give it birth.

She had now reached a point where the engorged river had burst its banks and overflowed into the neighbouring fields. She could feel this quieter water to the left of her and, with her puny force, she essayed to direct herself to it. Again and again, she tried to draw away from the main stream only to be sucked back again. She had almost abandoned hope when, at a sharp bend of the river, her log was suddenly deflected from its course by a powerful eddy, and she floated into an area where she could feel no waves, no swirl, no wild onrush. She let the log drift on until it came to rest, then, trembling, she lowered her legs. They touched bottom and she stood up, thigh deep in the water. The weight of the water and her frozen state almost prevented her moving, but, though gaining only inches at a time, she moved slowly away from the sound of the river. At length she was clear of the flood. She looked round. To her intense joy she saw, amidst the impenetrable darkness around her, a light. The sight of this light was like a divine balm laid suddenly upon each of her wounds. For what seemed to her like years she had been moving in a world of tenebrous shadows, where each step was fraught with obscure suspense and an unseen danger that might annihilate her. The faint, unflickering ray gleamed serenely, and in the dim illumination she saw comfort and serenity. Hereabouts she recollected was situated a small and isolated croft, but whosoever dwelt here could never refuse to shelter her in her terrible condition on so terrible a night. Cowering, she advanced towards the light.

Now she could hardly walk. Low in her body a heavy weight seemed to bear her down and lancinating pains tore her with every movement. Bent almost double, she persisted on her way. The light had been so near and yet, the further she advanced, the more it seemed to recede from her! Her feet squelched deep into the inundated ground so that it was an effort to withdraw them, and with each step she seemed to sink deeper into the marshland which she was now obliged to cross. Still, she progressed, going deeper and deeper into the swamp, sinking to her knees as she plodded through a foul admixture of mud and water. One of her shoes was plucked from her foot by the adhesion of the quagmire and she was unable to retrieve it; her skin, blenched white by her prolonged immersion, now became smeared and splashed with mire; the remnants of her clothing trailed behind in draggled tatters.

At length, it appeared to her that she was slowly gaining ground and approaching nearer to the light of the croft, when abruptly, following a forward step, she failed to find bottom with her feet. She began to sink into the bog. She shrieked. The warm, quaggy mud sucked at her legs with a soft insistence, drawing her downwards into its embrace. She was unable to withdraw either foot and, at her struggles, gaseous bubbles erupted from the slough and stifled her with their miasma. Downwards she sank. It seemed to her that she had been saved from the clean, cold death of the river in order to be destroyed more fittingly here. This sludge was a more suitable winding sheet than the pure water of the mountain streams. In such corruption as this her violated body had been destined to disintegrate and, dissolving, become finally part of its substance. To have surmounted such peril as she had that night endured, and to be robbed of succour when within sight of it, infuriated her. In a passion of endeavour she struggled to support herself; with a shriek she flung herself forward, clawing wildly at the wet moss which covered the surface of the morass. The glutinous stuff offered little hold, but with such frenzy did she tear at it with her extended fingers that she succeeded, with a last superhuman effort, in drawing herself clear by the power of her arms alone. Then, pantingly, she dragged her body to a firmer part of the marsh, where she lay completely exhausted. She could now no longer walk, and therefore, after a few moments rest, she began to crawl slowly forward on all fours like a stricken animal. But in escaping from the bog she had utilised the last dregs of her strength; although she was on solid ground and no more than fifty yards from the house, she realised that she would never attain it. She gave up, and, sobbing weakly, lay on the ground, hopeless, with powerless limbs relaxed, whilst a fresh downpour of rain deluged her. Yet, as she lay there, the faint lowing of cattle came to her through the storm. After a moment she again heard the sound and, looking to the right, she perceived, dimly outlined in the obscurity, the darker outlines of a low building. She became aware through the drifting vapours in her brain that here was shelter of some kind. Raising herself, she staggered with a last, delirious effort, into the shed, and collapsed unconscious upon the floor.

The sanctuary she had attained was a poor outbuilding, the mean byre of the small farm. Being built of thick stones with the crevices closely stuffed with moss, it was warm inside, and, having so insignificant a height, the chilling blast rushed over it, so that it had, in addition, escaped the fury of the wind. The air was filled with the blended odours of straw, dung, and the sweet smell of the animals themselves. The three milch cows standing in their stalls moved with gentle, resigned movements, their bodies almost invisible, but their pale udders faintly luminous amongst the shadows. The cows, their large, sad eyes inured to the darkness, looked with a docile timidity at the strange human creature which rested, scarcely breathing, upon the floor of the byre. Then, having identified it as passive and harmless, they turned their heads disinterestedly, and again began calmly ruminating with silent moving jaws.

For only a few moments Mary remained in happy insensibility. She was restored to consciousness by the powerful spur of pain. Waves of pain swept over her. The pain began in her back, travelled round her body and down the inside of her thighs with a slow, fulminating grip which gradually crept to an intolerable crisis. Then suddenly it left her, limp, drained, and helpless.

During the whole of her tragic journey she had endured these pangs. Now they became insupportable, and, lying amongst the ordure of the shed, she suffered with closed eyes. Her arms and legs were extended flaccidly; her body, which Denis had named his shrine, was pressed into the steaming dung and plastered with drying mud. Moans of pain broke from between her clenched teeth; a damp sweat beaded her forehead and trickled slowly over her shut eyelids; her features, disfigured by filth and distorted by her insupportable experiences, were rigidly set, but around her head the emanation of her sufferings seemed to have condensed in a faint, translucent radiance which encircled her dying face like a nimbus.

The inactive intervals of her pains grew shorter whilst the paroxysms lengthened. When a pain abated the passive anticipation of the next was torture. Then it would begin, graspingly envelop her, permeate her with agony, and squander itself through her every nerve. Her cries were combined with the shriek of the ever-present wind. Everything she had undergone was as nothing compared to her present torture. Her body writhed about the stone floor feebly; blood mingled with the sweat and dirt about her. She prayed for death. Dementedly she called upon God, on Denis, on her mother. She besought the clemency of her Saviour in gasps, which broke in anguish from between her clenched teeth. In answer to her cries only the wind responded. Rising up, it shrieked and mocked at her as it rushed about the shed. She lay abandoned until, at last, when she could not have lived through one further exacerbation, the gale rose to its loudest, highest pitch and, amidst the culmination of the storm, she was delivered of a son. Till the last torture abated she was conscious. Then, when there was no more pain for her to endure, she relapsed into the deep well of forgetfulness.

The child was small, puny, premature. Bound still to its insensible mother it clawed feebly at her, and at the empty air, with its diminutive fingers. Its head sagged upon its frail neck. It rested there, scarcely breathing, while the mother lay slowly blanching from a slow, seeping hæmorrhage. Then it cried with a weak and fitful cry.

As if in answer to that call the door of the shed opened slowly, and the rays of a lantern dimly penetrated the darkness. An old woman came into the byre. A thick, plaid shawl was wrapped round her head and shoulders; her wooden, solid clogs clattered as she walked. She had come to reassure herself as to the safety and comfort of her beasts and now she went to them, smoothing their necks, patting their sides, talking encouragingly to them. "Eh, Pansy lady," she muttered. "Come up, Daisy! Come awa', Belle; come up, leddy, leddy! Come, leddy, leddy! But what a night! What a storm! But dinna steer, dinna fash, ye're a' richt, my hinnies! You've a good, stout roof abin ye, ye maunna be frichted! I'm near enough tae ye. You'll be——" Abruptly she broke off, and raised her head into a listening attitude. She imagined she had heard within the byre a faint, puling cry. But she was old and deaf and her ears rang with the echo of the hurricane, and, mistrusting her own perception of the sound, she was about to turn away and resume her task when she distinctly heard the slight, plaintive call repeated.

"Guidsakes! what—is't—at a', at a'," she murmured. "I'm shair I heard something—— Something unco' like a wean greetin'." With an unsteady hand she lowered her lantern, peering about in the darkness; then suddenly she paused, with incredulous, awestruck eyes. "The Lord save us!" she cried, "it's a bairn and—and its mother. God in Heaven, she's deid! Oh! the nicht that this has been! What a thing for ma auld een to see!" In a second she had placed her lantern on the stone floor and was down upon her aged knees. She had no fastidious delicacy as she plied her coarse hands with the adept, experienced movements of a woman of the soil to whom nature was an open book. Quickly, but without flurry, she disengaged the child and wrapped it warmly in a corner of her plaid. Then she turned to the mother and, with an expert pressure, at once evacuated the womb, and controlled the bleeding. All the time she spoke to herself, while she worked: "Did ye see the like! She's nearly gane! the puir thing! and her so young and so bonnie. I maun dae ma best for her. That's better though. What in God's name did she no' come to the house, though. I would have letten her in. Ah, well, 'twas the will o' the Almighty I cam' out to the beasts." She slapped Mary's hands, rubbed her cheeks, covered her with the remainder of the plaid, and hastened off.

Back in her comfortable kitchen she shouted to her son, who sat before the huge crackling log fire: "Quick man! I want ye to run like fury to Levenford for a doctor. Ye maun get yin at a' costs. There's an ill woman in the byre. Go, in God's name, and no' a word frae ye. It's life or death."

He stared at her dully. "What," he cried stupidly, "in our byre?"

"Ay," she shouted, "she's been driven in by the storm. If ye dinna hurry she'll be gane. Haste ye! Haste ye awa' for help."

He got up mazedly and began to struggle into his coat.

"It's the maist unheard o' thing," he muttered; "in our byre. What's wrang wi' her, ava', ava'?"

"Never mind," she flared; "gang awa' this meenute. Never mind the horse. Ye maun rin like fury."

She hustled him out of the door, and when she had assured herself that he had gone, took a pan, poured into it some milk from a jug on the dresser, and hurriedly heated it upon the fire. Then she took a blanket from the kitchen bed, her own bed, and rushed again to the cowshed, with the blanket on her arm and the hot milk in her hand. She wrapped Mary tightly in the blanket and, raising her head gently, poured with difficulty a few drops of hot milk between her blue lips. She shook her head doubtfully. "I'm afraid to move her," she whispered, "she's gae far through."

Taking the infant in the crook of her arm, she removed it to the warm kitchen, and returned with a clean, damp cloth and another blanket for Mary.

"There, ma bonnie, that'll hap ye up warm," she whispered, as she encompassed the limp form in this second covering. Then, tenderly, with the cloth, she wiped the inspissated mud from the white cold face. She had done all that was possible, and now she waited patiently, crouching down, without once removing her eyes from Mary, from time to time chafing the lifeless hands, stroking the cold brow beside her. For almost an hour she remained thus.

At last the door was flung open, and a man entered the byre in a bluster of wind and rain.

"Thank God ye've come, doctor," cried the old woman. "I was feared ye wouldna."

"What is the trouble?" he demanded abruptly, as he advanced towards her.

In a few words she told him. He shook his head dispassionately and bent his tall, spare form down beside the figure on the floor. He was a young man, this Dr. Renwick, skilful in his work, but new to Levenford and anxious to build up a practice, and this had drawn him out on foot on such a night when two other doctors approached before him had refused to go. He looked at Mary's pale, sunken face, then felt her soft, fluttering pulse; whilst he contemplated the second hand of his watch with a serene tranquillity the old woman gazed at him anxiously.

"Will she die, think ye, doctor?"

"Who is she?" he said.

The old wife shook her head negatively.

"I dinna ken, ava', ava'. But what a bonnie, wee thing to suffer so much, doctor." She seemed to entreat him to do all he could.

"The baby?" he enquired.

"In the kitchen! 'Tis alive the now, but 'tis a puir, feeble bit bairn."

The physician in him looked coldly, critically at the inert figure before him, but the man in him was touched. He seemed to trace, with his experienced eye, the record of all her sufferings, as though the history of these was indelibly delineated upon her features. He saw the pinched nostrils of the thin straight nose, the sunken rings of her dark eyes, and the piteous droop of the pale, soft lips. A feeling of compassion awoke in him, tinctured by a strange, flowing tenderness.

He took up again the frail, relaxed hand and held it in his as though to transfuse a current of life from his vital body into hers, then, as he turned the hand, and saw the gash which transfixed the palm, he cried, in spite of himself: "Poor child! She's so young and helpless." Then, ashamed of his weakness, he continued roughly: "She's in a bad way. Hæmorrhage, bad hæmorrhage, and shock. Shock from God knows what misery. It's a case for the Cottage Hospital," he added finally.

At these words the young farmer, who had been silent in the background, spoke from the door:

"I'll have the horse in the shafts of the cart in a minute if ye like, doctor."

Renwick looked at the old woman for confirmation. She nodded eagerly, her hands supplicating him.

"Very well, then!" He braced his shoulders. In this case he saw no chance of fee, only its difficulties and danger, and a hazard to his unformed reputation. But he was moved to take it. He felt he must take it. His dark eyes lit with a flashing desire to save her. "It's not only the shock," he said aloud; "I don't like her breathing. Might be pneumonia there, and if so——" He shook his head significantly, turned and bent over his bag, and, extracting from it some temporary restoratives, applied these as best the circumstances permitted. When he had finished, the cart, a rough farm waggon as deep and heavy as a tumbrel, stood ready at the door. The infant was swaddled in blankets and placed carefully in one corner, then they lifted Mary up and placed her beside her child. Finally, Renwick clambered in and, while he supported Mary in his arms, the crofter jumped into his seat and whipped up the horse. Thus they set out into the night for the Cottage Hospital, the strange ambulance bumping and jolting slowly along, the doctor protecting the limp figure in his arms, as best he could, from the shocks of the rough road.

The old woman saw them disappear, then she sighed, turned, shut the byre door, and with bowed back went slowly into her house. As she entered the kitchen the grandfather's clock in the corner chimed eight, solemn strokes. She went quietly to the chest of drawers, picked up her Bible and, slowly assuming her old, steel spectacles, opened the book at random and began soberly to read.

XII

THE wind, which blew fiercely in the west, blew still more furiously in the east. On the Sunday afternoon, when havoc ranged in Levenford and amongst the surrounding townships, still greater devastation roamed amongst the counties of the Eastern sea-board.

In Edinburgh, as Denis buffeted his way along Princes Street, the wind, tearing along the grey, weather-beaten thoroughfare, ballooned his coat about his ears and lifted him off his feet. He loved that wind; it made him feel strong to fight a passage against it. Hat in hand, his hair disordered, his lips parted, he cleaved his way along. The wind sang against his teeth like the song of a gigantic humming-top, and he sang too, or uttered spontaneous, inarticulate sounds, expressive of the virile exuberance that seethed within him. Of the few people in the street, most turned involuntarily to look at him, and muttered enviously, from blue, shivering lips: "My certies, he's a hardy chiel, that one!"

It was quarter to four. Denis had made an early tea at McKinleys' "Family and Commercial Temperance Hotel." They did things well there, no show, indeed, but a lavish abundance of good food, and he had eaten his way through a large trencher of sausages and white-pudding, cleared a plateful of oatcakes, and emptied the tea-pot in Ma McKinley's own, private parlour. Old Mother McKinley would do anything for Denis—just the way he had with her, and with most people —and he always went there when in Edinburgh. She had, in parting, given him a thick packet of sandwiches to sustain his body until his late arrival in Dundee, and a large, smacking embrace to support his spirit until she saw him again. It was good to have friends like that, he thought warmly, as he felt the comforting wad of sandwiches buttoned against his side, whilst he strode out on his way to Granton, to take the ferry-boat across the Firth of Forth for Burntisland. His only grievance against the weather was his fear that it might prevent them running the ferry, but if there was no boat, he was, he told himself facetiously, feeling vigorous enough to swim across the firth.

Although it blew so hard, there was as yet no rain and, as it was only three miles to Granton, he disdained the usual conveyance to the ferry and decided to walk. It was fine to be alive! This wind intoxicated him; the feel of it upon his cheek made him want to live for ever. As he drove his feet hard upon the pavement he knew he would cover the distance easily under the hour at his disposal.

His reflections, as he strode along, were pleasant. Business was opening out beyond his expectations and to-morrow, in Dundee, he hoped to consolidate his position with Blain & Co. Young Mr. Blain was the force in the firm; he liked him immensely, and he felt that if he could convince him, persuade him to deal with Findlay's, the day would be won. He began to think out a smart, little speech to open his conversation on the morrow. He declaimed the address magnificently to the wind and to the empty streets as he walked along, enjoying himself immensely, emphasising his points by telling gesticulations, so that by the time Granton was reached he had riddled young Mr. Blain with epigrams, bombarded him with technicalities, and reduced him to impotence by solid argument. Now, to his relief, he observed that the ferry bumped at her small pier with every indication of departure, and hastening his steps, he went on board the vessel. From the low deck of the boat the firth looked darker and more threatening than from the jetty, with white spume slapping over the crests of the slate-grey waves. The small boat rocked heavily, and the rope hawsers attached from the vessel to the squat bollards on the quay creaked and thumped, as the combined strain of wind and tide pulled upon them. Denis, however, was an excellent sailor and, unperturbed, he joined three other passengers who were gathered in the bow of the boat, looking gloomily across the firth, a disconsolate sense of danger binding them closer together.

"I don't like the look o' it," said one.

"Ay, it's gey and threatenin' like," said another.

"I'm beginning to wish I had taken the wife's advice and stayed at home," said the third, with a feeble attempt at jocularity.

Denis rallied them.

"Do you think the captain would put out the boat if he wasn't sure of getting over?" he cried, heartily. "It's only five miles across—a mere nothing. Why, in twenty years we'll be jumping across a ditch like this, or walking over on stilts."

They looked at him doubtfully, but he laughed, joked, bantered them until they surrendered, and, in the space of five minutes, he had them enrolled under his banner. They accepted him as a leader; their fearful anticipation vanished; indeed, one of the group produced a small, flat bottle.

"Will we have a wee drappie before we start?" he asked, with a wink. It was the height of conviviality! The host partook first, then the two others sipped with the moderation of guests, but Denis refused.

"I'm so full of sausage, I'm afraid to chance it," he replied, with a gesture of broad pantomime towards the unruly water, indicating that his sole desire in life was to retain the excellent meal he had just paid for. They laughed delightedly; the fact that this reckless, intrepid youth might be as ridiculously ill as he suggested, filled them with a returning sense of their own worth. And Denis encouraged them, adapting himself to the level of their society with verve, and telling stories with such spirit that they did not fully observe the departure, or the tossing in the firth. One grew greenish, and another swallowed queasily, but they would have died rather than disgrace themselves in the eyes of this young Hector now relating to them, in the climax of his fifth story, the brilliant repartee which the Irishman had made to the Englishman and the

Scotsman, under circumstances of a particularly ludicrous and embarrassing character.

The few other passengers were less assured, and remained huddled together as the boat pitched about like a cockleshell in the stormy water. They clung to the stanchions, lay upon the deck, or were openly sick, whilst the spray-laden wind howled through the rigging, and the fierce, snapping waves burst over the low bulwarks, covering the deck with a sheet of water which flooded from side to side with each roll of the ship.

But at length they drew near Burntisland, passed out of the stormy water and, after considerable manœuvring, made fast. The skipper of the little vessel came off the bridge, dripping in his oilskins.

"I'm not sorry to be in," Denis heard him say. "I didna like it. It's the worst crossing we've ever made."

The passengers disembarked hastily, although some had suffered so acutely that they were obliged to be carried off the ship on to the jetty, and here the small band of heroes bade Denis farewell.

"You're not going any further, then?" said Denis.

"Na! Na!" said the spokesman, looking up at the clouds, "we're all Burntisland lads, praise be, and it'll be a long time before we have another jaunt o' this nature to Edinburgh. Hame looks guid enough to me after that blatter o' sea."

They shook hands with him solemnly, feeling that they would never forget him. "Man, he was a cure, yon fellow that cam' ower the Forth i' the storm," they would repeat to each other long afterwards. "He didna give a hang about anything."

When they had left him, Denis made his way to the station. The train for Dundee, being run in conjunction with the Granton ferry, and due to depart at 5.27 p.m., was already waiting, and as it was now twenty minutes past five, he walked along the platform looking through the windows to secure an empty third-class compartment. A larger number of people than might have been expected from the nature of the weather, were travelling, and he traversed the length of the train up to the engine without seeing a vacant carriage. At the engine, the guard stood talking to the driver and Denis, recognising in the former an acquaintance that he had made—with his usual facility—upon a previous journey, went up and accosted him.

"And how's Davie McBeath?" he cried. The guard turned his head, and, after a moment's hesitating scrutiny, his eye cleared.

"It's yourself, then, Mr. Foyle," he replied cordially. "I couldna place ye for a minute.

"Sure there's not another like me out of Donegal," grinned Denis.

"Do you get weather like this over there?" asked McBeath. "Mitchell," he indicated the driver, "and me are just discussing the gale; we're no' so sure of the wind. It's in a bad quarter."

"Will it push the old, puffing billy backwards?" laughed Denis. Mitchell shook his head doubtfully.

"It's no' just exactly that," he exclaimed, and his look spoke more than his words; then, turning to his mate in the cab he asked:

"How is the gauge, John?"

The black face of the stoker looked up, his teeth showing whitely as he smiled.

"You've enough steam to take ye to Aberdeen!" he said. "Ay, and urther than that if ye like."

"Dundee'll be good enough for me, and for you, too, Johnnie Marshall," replied the other, dryly.

"Will she stand it, think ye?" enquired McBeath seriously, for the moment ignoring Denis.

"I canna say," replied Mitchell cryptically, "but we're shair tae find out, ay, and soon enough."

"What's all the mystery?" asked Denis, looking from one to the other.

The grinning face of the stoker looked up from the open door of the furnace, whilst the reflection of the flames played across his dusky, shining face.

"They're a' feared o' a wee bittie o' a brig," he guffawed, as he shovelled; "they dinna ken what steel and cement mean yet."

"Get awa' wi' ye, man," growled Mitchell angrily. "Ye've twa mile o' it and that wind is blowin' richt at it—ay and hammerin' like the picks o' ten thousand devils." At his words a hush seemed to fall on the group, then with a start McBeath looked at his watch. "Well," he said, "whatever we think, the schedule says go, and go we must. Come away, Mr. Foyle."

"What exactly is the trouble?" asked Denis, as he walked up the platform with the guard. Davie McBeath glanced at him out of the corner of his eye, but he did not reply; instead, he changed the subject significantly, saying:

"That's a grand new ulster you've got."

"You like it."

"Ah! I do that! It's a real cosy thing for a night like this, and real smart too."

"Is it smart enough for a wedding, Davie?" asked Denis, nudging the other confidentially.

"It is that!" replied the guard unthinkingly; then he looked up, interestedly.

"What! what! ye're not thinkin' o'——" Denis nodded his head.

"I'm not thinking, man. I'm certain. Tuesday's the day, and like enough I'll wear this coat. Sure, it's part of my trousseau!"

McBeath gazed at the other quizzically, then his dry features relaxed, and they both laughed heartily.

"Weel! weel! you don't say!" cried Davie. "Man! you're a caution! Ye're moving ahead fast. I'm sure I wish ye the best o' everything —to you and the wee lass, whoever she may be. She'll be braw, if I ken ye richtly. Come along, now. We canna put a bridegroom in with all these people in the thirds." He looked along his nose at Denis as he opened an empty first-class compartment. "It wouldn't be safe."

"Thanks, Davie," said Foyle, appreciatively. "You're a good sort. I'll send you a bit of the cake to sleep on." Then he added, more seriously: "See you later, at Dundee." The guard gave him a smile and a nod as he walked off, and a moment later the whistle blew, the flag waved, and the train moved out of the station.

Alone in his magnificence, Denis looked about him with satisfaction, and, reclining back upon the cushions, he raised his feet upon the opposite seat and fixed his eyes meditatively upon the ceiling. But slowly his gaze grew distant, and, piercing the low roof, reached far away. He was thinking of Mary.

He would, he reflected soberly, be married on Tuesday, not exactly in the manner he had hoped, nor in the fashion he had sometimes planned, but married none the less. The manner of the marriage did not matter, the fact remained that he would be no longer a bachelor, and already he began to feel older and more responsible. A comforting glow pervaded him as he considered the nobility of his action in accepting, so willingly, this responsibility. He repulsed the thought that he had ever wished to repudiate the consequences of his love. "No," he cried aloud, "I'm not the sort of skunk to let down a girl like Mary." He became aware vividly of her trust, her loveliness, her faith in him, thought of her at first tenderly, then with a faint anxiety; thinking of the storm, he hoped, for her sake, that it had not touched Levenford. Here, despite the happy tenor of his mind, he began to feel unaccountably depressed; the subdued happiness, which had succeeded his exuberance at the commencement of his journey, now turned slowly to an unaccountable melancholy. He tried to shake this off, fixing his mind on the roseate future that awaited Mary and himself in their cottage at Garshake, envisaging the wonderful career he would carve for himself, thinking of the holidays, the trips abroad they would later enjoy—but he could not dispel the shadow that had clouded his bright optimism. He began to be afraid for her, and to ask himself if he had been wise to postpone taking her from her home until so late.

It began now to rain, and the windows of his compartment became blurred with a dismal covering of wet and slush. The pounding wind flung great gobs of sleet against the sides of the train with a sound like the slash of a wet cloth, whilst the rain hissed upon the roof of the carriage like fierce streams from the nozzle of a gigantic hose. His depression deepened, and his mind filled with a more mournful misgiving, as, with a sad regret, he visioned the sweet, mysterious beauty of her body and thought how he had deflowered that beauty. At his violating touch a child had become a woman, who must have suffered bitterly by his act; her slender virginity had become bloated through him, and, in the effort of concealment alone, she must have endured misery; the intimate symmetry of her form appeared to him as something which he had destroyed, which she would never again regain. A sigh broke from him as, slowly, the train drew to a standstill at a wayside station. The train, which was not express, had already made several halts at intermediate stations without his having particularly observed them, but here, to his annoyance, the door of his compartment opened and an old countryman entered. He seated himself blandly in the opposite corner, steaming from the rain, whilst puddles of water ran off him on to the cushions and floor; emanating from him, and mingling with the steam, came the spirituous odour of a liquid more potent than rain-water. Denis stared at him, then remarked coldly: "This is a first-class compartment."

The old fellow took a large red and white spotted handkerchief from his pocket and blew his nose like a trumpet.

"'Deed it is," he said solemnly, affecting to look round the carriage. "I'm glad you told me. It's a rale pleasure for me to travel in style; but the first-class that ye speak o' doesna make muckle difference to me, for I havena got a ticket at all"; and he laughed uproariously, in a tipsy fashion.

Denis was so far below his normal humour that he failed to appreciate the situation. In the ordinary way he would have amused himself intensely with this unexpected travelling-companion, but now he could only gaze at him glumly.

"Are you going far?" he finally asked.

"To Dundee—bonnie Dundee. The town ye ken—not the man. Na! Na! I'm not thinkin' o' the bonnets o' bonnie Dundee—I mean the bonnie town o' Dundee," the other replied, and having thus explained himself with a grave and scrupulous exactitude, he added, meaningly: "I hadna time to get my ticket, though."

Denis sat up. He would, he realised, have to endure this for the rest of the journey, and he resigned himself to it.

"What's the weather like now?" he asked. "You look wet!"

"Wet! I'm wet outside and inside. But the one counteracts the other ye ken, and to a hardy shepherd like me wet clothes just means lettin' them dry on ye. But mind ye, it is a most awful, soughin' night all the same, I'm glad I'm not out on the hills."

He nodded his head several times, took a small, foul stump of clay pipe from his pocket, lit it, covered it with its metal cap, and, inverting it from the corner of his mouth, sucked noisily; when he had filled the carriage with smoke, he spat copiously upon the floor without removing the pipe from his mouth.

Denis looked at the other with compassionate disgust, and as he tried to picture this gross, bibulous old yokel as a young man, then wondered moodily if he himself might ever degenerate to such a crapulous old age, his melancholy grew more profound. Unconscious of the effect he had produced, the old shepherd continued: "Ah! It's good-bye to the hills for me. That sounds kind o' well, think ye no'? Ay! Good-bye to the hills. Man!"—he laughed, slapping his thigh—"It's like the name o' a sang. Good-bye to the Hills. Weel, onyway, I'm going back to my native town, and you'll never guess what for." He tittered vehemently, choking himself with smoke.

"You've come into some money, perhaps?" hazarded Denis.

"'Deed, no! The bit of money I've got is what I've saved by hard and honest work. Try again." As Denis remained silent he went on, garrulously.

"Ay! you'd never think it, but the plain truth is that I'm going——" He paused to wink prodigiously, then blurted out, "I'm goin' to Dundee to get married." Observing with manifest enjoyment the effect he had produced, he meandered on——

"I'm a hardy blade, although I'm not so souple as I was, and there's a fine, sonsie woman waiting for me. She was a great friend of my first wife. Ay! I'm to wed early the morn's mornin'. That's the way I'm takin' this train and breakin' the Sabbath. I maun be in time, ye ken."

As the other wandered on, Denis gazed at him with a curious repulsion, due, in the main, to the strange coincidence of his own circumstances. Here, then, was another bridegroom, linked to him in this narrow compartment by a bond of corresponding position. Did this disreputable veteran mirror the image of his contumely, or reflect to him a dolorous premonition of his future?

In dismay Denis asked himself if he were not as contemptible in the eyes of his own kind as this grey-beard was in his. A tide of self-depreciation and condemnation rushed over him as he began to review the manner of his life. An unusual humility startled him by the rapidity and force of its onset, and in this despair he remained, subdued and silent, until the train clattered into the station of St. Fort. Here his companion rose and got out of the compartment, remarking, as he did so: "We've a good way to go yet. I'll just get out and see if I canna get haud o' something to keep out the cauld. Just a wee dram to warm the inside o' the stammack." In a moment, however, he came back, to say reassuringly: "I'll be back! I'm not away, mind ye. I wouldna leave ye like that. I'll be back to keep ye company till we get to Dundee." Then he tramped off.

Denis looked at his watch and saw that it was five minutes past seven. The train was up to time, yet, as he put his head out of the window, he found that the strength of the wind had increased beyond endurance.

Passengers getting out of the open doors were bowled along the platform, and the heavy train, as it stood stationary, seemed to rock upon its wheels. Surrounding McBeath he saw a wind-beaten group clamouring:

"Is it safe for us to gang on, guard?"

"What a wind it is! Will the train stand it?"

"Will it keep on the line?"

"Lord, save us, what a night this is! What about the bridge? Oh! I wish we were a' hame!"

He thought his friend the guard looked perturbed and irritable, but although McBeath did indeed feel anxious, with the charge of a hundred people upon his mind, he maintained in his replies the even and imperturbable calm of officialdom.

"Safe as the Bank of Scotland, Ma'am."

"Wind forsooth! Tuts, it's only a bit breezie, man. Think shame o' yourself."

"Ay, it'll haud the line and ye'll be hame wi' your lassock in an hour, ma fine wumman!" Denis heard him repeat placidly, composedly, impenetrably. His calmness seemed to reassure them completely, and at his comforting words the people broke up and entered their compartments.

At length the all clear was given and the train again began to move. As it did so Denis observed the figure of his travelling companion staggering against the wind in an effort to attain the rearmost carriage, but in his anxiety and haste, the old shepherd slipped and fell prostrate upon the platform. The train drew away from him, he was irrevocably left behind and, as they moved out of the station Denis caught a last glimpse, under the gusty flicker of the station lamp, of the perplexed, discomfited face, filled with almost ludicrous desolation. As he sat in his corner, while the train approached the southern edge of the Tay Bridge, Denis reflected with a sombre humour that the other would assuredly be late for his nuptials in the morning. Perhaps it was a lesson meant for him. Yes, he must profit by this strange, unpleasant coincidence. He would not fail Mary on Tuesday!

The train moved on and, at thirteen minutes past seven, it reached the beginning of the bridge. At this point, before entering upon the single line of rails over the bridge, it slowed down opposite the signal cabin, to allow the baton to be passed. Without this exchange it was not permitted to proceed, and, still filled by a sense of misgiving, Denis again lowered his window and looked out, to observe that everything was correct. The force of the gale almost decapitated him but, in the red glare cast by the engine, he discerned, stretching dimly into the distance, the massive girders of the bridge, like the colossal skeleton of an enormous reptile, but of steel, strong and adamantine. Then, all at once, he saw the signalman descend the steps from his box with consummate care, clutching the rail tightly with one hand. He surrendered the baton to the stoker, and, when he had accomplished this, he climbed back into his cabin with the utmost difficulty, fighting the wind and being assisted up the last few steps by the hand of a friend held out to him from within.

And now the train moved off again, and entered the bridge. Denis raised his window and sank back in his seat composedly, but, as he was carried past the signal-box, he received the fleeting impression of two pale, terrified faces looking at him from out of it, like ghostly countenances brushing past him in the blackness.

The violence of the gale was now unbounded. The wind hurled the rain against the sides of the train with the noise of a thousand anvils, and the wet snow again came slobbering upon the window panes, blotting out all vision. The train rocked upon the rails with a drunken, swaying oscillation, and although it proceeded slowly, cautiously, it seemed, from the fury and rush of the storm, to dash headlong upon its course. Thus, as it advanced, with the blackness, the noise of the wheels, the tearing rush of the wind, and the crashing of the waves upon the pier of the bridge below, there was developed the sensation of reckless, headlong acceleration.

As Denis sat alone, in the silent, cabined space of his compartment, tossed this way and that by the jactation, he felt suddenly that the grinding wheels of the train spoke to him. As they raced upon the line he heard them rasp out, with a heavy, despairing refrain: "God help us! God help us! God help us!"

Amidst the blare of the storm this slow, melancholy dirge beat itself into Denis' brain. The certain sense of some terrible disaster began to oppress him. Strangely, he feared not for himself, but for Mary. Frightful visions flashed through the dark field of his imagination. He saw her, in a white shroud, with sad, imploring eyes, with dank, streaming hair, with bleeding feet and hands. Fantastic shapes oppressed her which made her shrink into the obliterating darkness. Again he saw her grimacing, simpering palely like a sorry statue of the Madonna and holding by the hand the weazened figure of a child. He shouted in horror. In a panic of distress he jumped to his feet. He desired to get to her. He wanted to open the door, to jump out of this confining box which enclosed him like a sepulchre. He would have given, instantly, everything he possessed to get out of the train. But he could not.

He was imprisoned in the train, which advanced inexorably, winding in its own glare like a dark, red serpent twisting sinuously forward. It had traversed one mile of the bridge and had now reached the middle span, where a mesh of steel girders formed a hollow tube through which it must pass. The train entered this tunnel. It entered slowly, fearfully, reluctantly, juddering in every bolt and rivet of its frame as the hurricane assaulted, and sought to destroy, the greater resistance now offered to it. The wheels clanked with the ceaseless insistence of the tolling of a passing-bell, still protesting, endlessly: "God help us! God help us! God help us!"

Then, abruptly, when the whole train lay enwrapped within the iron lamellæ of the middle link of the bridge, the wind elevated itself with a culminating, exultant roar to the orgasm of its power and passion.

The bridge broke. Steel girders snapped like twigs, cement crumbled like sand, iron pillars bent like willow wands. The middle span melted like wax. Its wreckage clung around the tortured train, which gyrated madly for an instant in space. Immediately, a shattering rush of broken glass and wood descended upon Denis, cutting and bruising him with mangling violence. He felt the wrenching torsion of metal, and the grating of falling masonry. The inexpressible desolation of a hundred human voices, united in a sudden, short anguished cry of mingled agony and terror, fell upon his ears hideously, with the deathly fatality of a coronach. The walls of his compartment whirled about him and upon him, like a winding-sheet, the floor rushed over his head. As he spun round, with a loud cry he, too, shouted: "God help us!" then, faintly, the name: "Mary!"

Then the train with incredible speed, curving like a rocket, arched the darkness in a glittering parabola of light, and plunged soundlessly into the black hell of water below, where, like a rocket, it was instantly extinguished—for ever obliterated! For the infinity of a second, as he hurtled through the air, Denis knew what had happened. He knew everything, then instantly he ceased to know. At the same instant as the first, faint cry of his child ascended feebly in the byre at Levenford, his mutilated body hit the dark, raging water and lay dead, deep down upon the bed of the firth.

BOOK II

I

THE cutting cold of a March morning lay upon the High Street of Levenford. Large, dry snowflakes, floating as gently and softly as butterflies, insistently filled the air and lay deeply upon the frosted ground. The hard, delayed winter had been late of coming and was now tardy of passing, thought Brodie, as he stood in the doorway of his shop, looking up and down the quiet, empty street. Strangely, the quietness of the street consoled him, its emptiness gave him freer space to breathe. During the last three months it had been hard for him to face his fellow townsmen, and the lack of stir about him came as a respite to his suffering but unbroken pride. He could, for a moment, relax his inflexible front and admire his own indomitable will. Yes, his task had been difficult for the last three months but, by God, he had done it! The arrows they had launched at him had been many and had sunk deeply, but never by a word, never by a gesture, had he betrayed the quivering of his wounded and outraged pride. He had conquered. He pushed the square hat further back upon his head, thrust his thumbs into the armholes of his waistcoat, and, with his blunt nostrils doggedly sniffing the keen air, gazed aggressively down the silent thoroughfare. In spite of the biting cold he wore no overcoat or scarf; his intense satisfaction in the hardihood of his physique was such that he disdained this sign of weakness. What would I do with a coat, with MY constitution? was his contemptuous attitude, despite the fact that this morning he had been obliged to break a thin skin of ice upon the cold water in his ewer before he could sluice himself. The algid weather suited his disposition. He revelled in the iron frost, filled his chest invigoratingly with the chilled air, whilst the suction of his breath drew the white, sailing snowflakes on to his tongue, where they lay like melting hosts, filling him with a new refreshing force.

Suddenly, he saw a man approaching. Only Brodie's stimulated pride kept him at his door, for he recognised the figure as that of the glibbest, smoothest gossip in the Borough. "Damn his sleekit tongue," he muttered, as he heard the slow, muffled steps approach and saw the other deliberately cross the roadway. "I would like to rive it from his mouth. Ay! he's comin' over. I thought he would."

Up came Grierson, wrapped to his blue ears. As Brodie had anticipated, he stopped.

"Good morning to you, Mr. Brodie," he began, stressing the "you" with a nicety of accent that might have been interpreted as deferential, or merely as ironic.

"Morning," said Brodie shortly. He had suffered acutely from the hidden venom of that tongue in the past, and he distrusted it profoundly.

"The frost still holds firm, I fear," continued the other. "It's been a hard, hard winter, but, man, it doesna seem to affect you a bit. I believe you're made o' steel, you can thole anything."

"The weather suits me weel enough," growled Brodie, eyeing the other's blue nose contemptuously.

"The trouble is, though," replied Grierson smoothly, "that a' these hard frosts maun break some time. The ice has got to crack one day. There maun be a thaw, and the harder the frost the softer the thaw. There'll be a big change in the conditions here some day." He raised a guileless glance towards the other.

Brodie fully understood the double significance of the words, but he was not clever enough to reply in kind. "Is that so?" he said heavily, with a sneer. "Man, you're clever, clever."

"Na, na, Mr. Brodie. It's juist fair intuition! What the Romans ca'ed takin' the omens frae the weather."

"Indeed! ye're the scholar as weel, I see."

"Man!" went on Grierson, unperturbed, "this morning a wee robin-redbreast flew into my house—it was so perished like." He shook his head. "It must be awfu' weather for the birds—and onybody that hasna got a home to go to." Then, before Brodie could speak he added: "How are all the family?"

Brodie forced himself to reply calmly: "Quite well, thank ye. Nessie's gettin' on grandly at school, as no doubt ye've heard. She'll be runnin' awa' with all the prizes again this year." That's one for you, thought Brodie, with your big, stupid son that's always done out of first place by my clever lass.

"I hadna heard! But it's fine all the same." Grierson paused, then in a soft voice, remarked: "Have ye had ony word from the other daughter lately—Mary, I mean?"

Brodie gritted his teeth, but he controlled himself and said slowly: "I'll thank you not to mention that name again in my hearing."

Grierson manifested a great show of concern.

"'Deed, I'm sorry if I've upset you, Mr. Brodie, but I had aye a bit regard for that lass o' yours. I was gey upset at her lang illness, but I had heard tell the other day that she had gotten a post away in London, and I was wonderin' if it was through these folks in Darroch—the Foyles, I mean. Still I've nae doubt ye ken as little as me." He screwed up his eyes and glanced sideways at the other, as he continued: "Ay, I took great notice o' the affair. In a human sort o' way, ye ken. I was real touched when the wee, bit bairn died in the hospital."

Brodie eyed him stonily, but the torture continued.

"They say it was a real bonny wean, and the doctor was much upset when it slipped through his fingers. He took a great interest in the mother's case. I'm no' surprised either, it was so unusual, with the complications o' pneumonia and all." He shook his head, mournfully. "Man! what a calamity though, that the father wasna' spared to make an honest woman o'—ahem, ahem! Forgive me, Mr. Brodie! I clean forgot! I was just lettin' my silly tongue run away wi' me." Grierson was abjectly apologetic. He had rubbed Brodie on the raw, made him wince, and was clever enough to know when to withdraw.

Brodie looked right through the other. Inwardly he writhed, but in a low, strained voice he said: "Let your mealy-mouthed tongue run on like the Wellhall burn, it makes no odds to me."

It was a mistaken attitude, for it immediately offered an opportunity to renew the baiting which Grierson was not slow to seize. He laughed, with a soft, unctuous titter.

"That's richt, that's richt! That's the spirit that never flinches! I can't but admire ye, Mr. Brodie," he went on, "at the firm stand ye've taken amongst the disgrace o' it all. A man that had such an important standin' in the Borough might easily have been broken richt to bits by such a come-down, for there's no doubt that for months the whole town has been ringin' wi' it."

"The gabble of the Cross is of no moment to me," retorted Brodie, with a heaving breast. He could have killed the other with his glance, but he could, with dignity, use no other weapons, and his pride forbade him to retreat.

"Ay, ay," replied Grierson speculatively, "but it might shake up *another* man to be the butt o' a' these dirty divots, and the laughin' stock o' the place. Man!" he added, in a low tone, almost as an afterthought, "it would be enough to drive an ordinary man to the drink for consolation."

Brodie lowered at him from beneath his bushy eyebrows. Had they been calumniating him on that score, too? "Nothing like a wee droppie to cheer up a man, especially in this weather," drawled Grierson, in an insinuating tone.

"Well, I maun be off. It's cold work standin' bletherin'. Good day to you, Mr. Brodie." Grierson passed quickly out of range with meek, bowed head, without giving the other time to reply. Although he shivered from his stand in the freezing air, inwardly he warmed himself at a fire of delicious self-appreciation. He glowed at the thought of the quiver in Brodie's fierce eye as his delicately pointed barbs had sunk home, and feasted his recollection on the great, heaving sigh that the cumulation of their poison had finally produced. He chuckled at the richness of the jest to relate at the club this evening; they would laugh till they burst at the story, as he would tell it. He tee-heed to himself in anticipation. And why shouldn't he have lowered the stuck-up runt? What did he think he was, with his insolent, haughty airs? Besides, what man would have turned his own child out, like a dog, on such a night? It had been the death of the bairn. Ay, he had nearly killed Mary by it too, if reports were to be believed! Pneumonia, and child-birth fever, and God only knows what she had suffered. It was scandalous, yes, even if she was a precious ——. He went on, and out of sight, still hugging his reflection closely.

Brodie watched him down the road, his lips drawn into a thin, crooked line. That was the way of them, he thought. They would try to stone him, to kick him, to batter him to bits now that he was down. But, at the very idea, he drew himself up proudly. He was not down! Let them that suggested it wait and see. The whole, damnable business would have blown over, would be only dimly remembered, in another month or two. His real friends, the gentry, the big people of the district, must feel for him only sympathy and regret. But, at the memory of what he had endured, his tense lips quivered slightly. All those weeks, whilst Mary had lain between life and death at the Cottage Hospital, he had stood with the hard, craggy indifference of a rock, immovable in his determination to outcast his daughter. By her own act she had outlawed herself, and he had proclaimed openly that he would let her rot beyond the bounds of decent society. Under the wordless wilting of his wife, under the loud-tongued gossip and hotly fluctuating opinion of the town, under the pressure of a biting, private interview with Dr. Renwick, under the contumely of public affronts and reproaches, he had remained immutable and unyielding. He had not looked near her, and the consideration of his inflexible resolution now soothed his ruffled spirit. But they did not know what he had suffered; the blow to his pride had been almost mortal. With a grim relief he diverted his thoughts to the solace which had comforted him through these bitter months, and he allowed his mind to dwell gloatingly upon the Tay Bridge disaster! He did not consider with any satisfaction the death of the bastard infant—he had from the first disowned it—but the thought of Foyle's broken body— the pitiful remains of which had been recovered, and now lay putrefying in Darroch soil—had rarely been out of his thoughts. It was the salve for his wounded arrogance. His imagination had riotously indulged itself amongst a host of vivid, morbid details. He did not care that a hundred others had perished; the loss of the entire train was but the instrument of a just vengenace. This one man had wronged him, had dared to oppose him, and now he was dead. It was a sweet consolation!

He was turning to go into his shop when he was again accosted. A little man, with all the restless timidity of a rabbit, had bolted out from next door to speak with him. It was Dron. Contempt marked Brodie's drawn features as he gazed at the jerky agitation of the other, and his self-assurance, restored always by an appreciation of the terror he could inspire in others, returned, whilst he surmised disdainfully the object of the little man's visit. Would he be going to tell him about the arrival of his brat? he wondered, as he noted the peculiar, suppressed look that marked him.

Dron's aspect was certainly remarkable, as, trembling with a repressed excitement, rubbing his hands rapidly together with a rustling sound, his pale eyelashes blinking ceaselessly, his legs shaking as though with tetanus, he essayed, stammeringly, to speak.

"Out with it, then," sneered Brodie. "and don't keep me on my own door-step any longer. What species o' animal is it ye've been blessed wi' this time?"

"It's no exactly that," said Dron hurriedly, with a fresh spasm of fidgets. Then he added slowly, like one who has rehearsed it carefully: "I was just wonderin' if you were quite sure you didna want these premises o' mine I offered you last back end." He jerked his head in the direction of the empty shop. "You may have forgotten that you threw me out on the pavement that day, but I havena! I havena forgotten that ye flung me out on the broad o' my back." His voice rose in a shrill crescendo at the last words.

"Ye fell down, my little mannie, that was all. If ye chose to sit on your backside outside my place o' business I canna blame ye; but if it's no' as pleasant a position as ye might find, then talk to your wife about it. It's no affair o' mine," said Brodie, calmly. Yet the other's eye fascinated him, pervaded as it was by two antagonistic emotions warring for supremacy, filled by such a look as might occupy the half-terrified, half-exultant eye of a rabbit that views an enemy caught in its own snare.

"I was askin' ye if ye were sure," Dron palpitated, without heeding the interruption; then he hurried on:

"I say are ye quite sure ye dinna want these premises o' mine? Because if ye did want the shop, ye canna have it. I havena let it! I havena let it! I've sold it! I've sold it to the Mungo Hat & Hosiery Company." He shouted out the last words in triumph, then he rushed on. "I've gotten more than my price—for they have unlimited capital. They're going to fit up a grand, big emporium with everything, and a special window and a special department for hats and caps. I knew ye would like to hear the news, so I couldna wait. The minute I had signed the contract I came round." His voice rose gloatingly, almost to hysteria. "Put that in your pipe and smoke it, you gurly, big bully!" he yelled. "Smoke it till it sickens ye. That'll learn ye to mishandle folks weaker than yoursel'." Then, as if in fear that Brodie would attack him, he whirled round and scuttled off to his burrow.

Brodie stood perfectly still. Dron's pusillanimous ebullition disturbed him not at all, but his news was catastrophic. Would misfortune never desert him? The Mungo company, originating in, and at first confined solely to, Glasgow, had for some time past been reaching out tentacles

F   161 into the adjacent countryside; like pioneers, realising the advantage of the principle of multiple shops, they had invaded most of the townships in Lanarkshire and now they were stretching slowly down the Clyde. This incursion, Brodie knew, had meant disaster for many a local shop-keeper; for, not only did the Company indulge in such flashing pyro-technics as bargain sales and glittering window displays, wherein their articles were marked, not in plain honest shillings, but in deceptive figures ending cunningly in $11\frac{3}{4}d.$, and were actually adorned by trumpery cards which tempted the fancy seductively under such terms as: "The Thing for the Bairns," or "Real Value," or even "Exquisite," but they cut prices ruthlessly in the face of competition. They were in Darroch and Ardfillan, that he knew, but, although they were not exclusively hatters, he had often flattered himself into thinking that they would leave Levenford alone because of his old-established, deeply rooted business. He had told himself disdainfully that they wouldn't sell a hat in a year. And now they were coming! He was aware that it would be a fight, and he would make it a bitter fight, in which he would let them try what they could do to James Brodie, then take the con-sequences. A sudden realisation took him of the proximity they would occupy to him, and bitter a surge of black resentment made him shake a menacing fist at the empty shop as he turned and went into his own.

To Perry, meekly ubiquitous as always, he threw out: "What are ye glumping at there, you dough-faced sheep? Do some work for a change. That empty look of yours fair scunners me."

"What would you like me to do, sir? I'm not serving."

"I can see you're not serving. Do you mean to infer that I have no customers, me that's got the best and most solid business in the town. It's the snow that's keeping folks away, you fool. Clear up the place a bit, or take a bar of soap and go out and wash your feet," shouted Brodie as he banged into his office.

He sat down. Now that he was alone, and his bold front to the world slightly lowered, the almost imperceptible change in him became faintly discernible in the tincture of hollowness which touched the smooth, firm line of his cheek, in the tenuous line of bitterness that ran downwards from the angle of his mouth. On his desk the *Herald* lay unopened—he had not looked at a paper for months, an omission supremely significant—and now, with a gesture of negligent distaste, he slashed it off his desk and on to the floor with a fierce swap of his open palm. Immediately his hand sought his pocket, and he drew out, with familiar unconsciousness, his pipe and tobacco pouch, looked at them suddenly as if he wondered how they had come into his hands, then laid them on the desk before him, with a grimace of aversion. He did not wish to smoke on this morning which had been so consistently miserable for him. Although there was a bright coal fire in the room and, despite his vaunted indiffer-ence to the inclemency of the weather, he suddenly felt chilly: whilst a shiver ran through him he reflected on what Grierson had said. "There's nothing to keep out the cold, or cheer a man up, like a wee droppie." A wee droppie! what an expression for a grown man to use, thought Brodie; but it was like Grierson to talk like that, with his soft, pussy voice and his creeping, sneaking ways. The obvious construction of the remark which rose to his mind was that, at the Cross, they had him a drunkard already, he who hadn't touched drink for months.

He jerked out of his seat impatiently, and looked through the frosted window at the snow which was everywhere, on the ground, on the frozen Leven, on the house tops, in the air, falling relentlessly, as though it would never cease to fall. The drifting flakes appeared to Brodie each like an oppression in itself supportable, but becoming insufferable by weight of numbers. As he cogitated, a dormant molecule of thought began to swell within his mind. He felt in his dull brain the blind injustice of the veiled accusation that he had been consoling himself with drink. "That's it," he muttered. "I'm gettin' the blame, and none of the comfort." The desolation of the scene again struck frigidly upon him. He shivered once more and continued to talk to himself. This propensity of articulate self-communion was entirely new, but now, as he spoke thus, the process of his ideas became more lucid and less entangled. "They say I'm takin' a dram do they; it's the sort of thing the measly swine would say, without rhyme nor reason; but by God! I will take them at their word. It's what I'm needin' anyway, to take the taste o' that braxy out o' my mouth—the poor, knock-kneed cratur' that he is, wi' his 'wee droppies.' Him and his sleekit 'beg your pardons' and 'by your leaves,' and his scrapin' and bowin' down in the dirt. Some day I'll kick him and keep him down in it. Ay, I maun have something to clean my mouth after this mornin's wark." His face grimaced dourly as he added ironically, still addressing the empty room: "but thank you all the same, Mister Grierson—thank you for your verra acceptable suggestion."

Then his features changed; suddenly he experienced a wild and reckless desire to drink. His body felt strong, so brutally powerful that he wanted to crush iron bars; so eagerly alive, with such vast potentiality for enjoyment, that he felt he could empty huge reservoirs of liquor. "What good does it do me to live like a blasted stickit minister—they talk about me just the same. I'll give them something to babble about, blast them!" he cried, as he pulled his hat down over his eyes and strode darkly out of the shop.

A few doors off stood a small, quiet inn, "The Winton Arms," owned by an elderly, respectable matron named Phemie Douglas, famed for her liquor, her virtue, and her snug sitting-room—known as "Phemie's wee back parlour" to the choicer spirits amongst the better class of the townspeople, for whom it was a favourite howff. Brodie, however, on entering the tavern, avoided this social centre, as he now had no time for words; he wanted to drink, and the longer he waited the more he desired it. He entered the public bar, which was empty, and demanded from the barmaid a large whisky toddy. "Hurry up and bring it," he said, in a voice dry from the violence of his craving. Now that he had ordained that he would drink, nothing could stop him, nothing arrest the swelling urge which made his throat dry, caused his hands to clench and unclench restlessly, made his feet stamp chafingly upon the sawdust floor of the bar whilst he awaited the hot whisky. When she brought it he drank the scalding liquid in one, long breath.

"Another," he said impatiently.

Altogether he had four, large whiskies, hot and potent as flame, which he consumed as rapidly as he obtained them, and which now worked within him like the activation of some fiery ferment. As he glowed, he began to feel lighter; the shadows of the last three months were lifting; they still swirled like smoke clouds about his brain, but nevertheless they lifted. A sardonic leer played about his mouth as a sense of his superiority, and of his invulnerable personality, impressed him, but this was the sole expression of the thoughts which rushed within him. His body remained quiet, his actions grew cautious, more restrained; he remained absolutely within himself, whilst his bruised pride healed itself in the roseate thoughts which coursed swiftly through his mind. The barmaid was young, attractive, and quite desirous of being talked to by this strange, huge man, but Brodie ignored her, did not even observe her, as, wrapped in the splendid emancipation from his hateful despondency, and engrossed in the incoherent but dazzling consideration of his future plans and triumphs, he remained silent, staring blankly in front of him. Finally he asked for a bottle of whisky, paid for it, and went out.

Back in his office he continued to drink. His brain clarified with each glass, grew more dominant, more compelling; his body responded more quickly and more perfectly to his movements; he now sanctioned with an intense approval all his recent actions.

The empty bottle stood on the table before him, bearing on the label the words: "Mountain Dew," which struck his bemused fancy as notably appropriate; for now he felt as powerful as a mountain and as sparkling as dew.

"Yes," he muttered, addressing himself to the bottle, "you mark my words; they can't down me. I'm more than a match for them. I can master them. Everything I did was right. I wouldna draw back a step o' the road I took wi' her. Just you wait and see how I'll go ahead now. Everything will be forgotten and nothing will stop me! I'll get the whip hand o' them."

Actually he did not know whom he was indicting, but he included largely and indeterminately in that category, all who he imagined had opposed him, slighted him, or failed to recognise him as the man he was.

He did not now think of the threatened opposition to his business, which became, in the swollen magnitude of his disdainful pride, too petty, too ridiculously ineffectual to affect him adversely. The opposition which he recognised was universal, intangible, yet crystallised in the feeling that any man's hand might be raised against his sacrosanct dignity: and now this obsession, always latent within him, strengthened and became more corrosive in his mind. And yet conversely, whilst the danger to his position loomed the more largely before him, his faith in his ability to conquer such a menace was augmented and exalted in such a manner as to render him almost omnipotent.

At last he started, took out his watch and looked at it. The hands, which appeared larger and blacker than usual, showed ten minutes to one.

"Time for dinner," he told himself agreeably. "Time to see that braw, tidy wife o' mine. It's a grand thing for a man to have such a bonnie wife to draw him hame." He got up impressively, but with a slight, almost imperceptible sway, and walked solidly out of his office, disregarding the awestruck, cringing Perry absolutely. He stalked through the shop and into the street, gained the middle of the street, and held it like a lord. Along the crown of the causeway he swaggered, head erect, shoulders thrown back, planting his feet in front of him with a magnificent sense of his own importance. The few people who were abroad gazed at him in amazement, and as, from the corner of his eye, he saw them glance, their astonishment fed his vanity, his intoxicated assurance battened on their wonder. "Take a good look," his attitude seemed to say. "It's Brodie you're lookin' at—James Brodie, and, by God, he's a man!" He walked through the snow the whole way home as though he headed a triumphal procession, keeping so exactly in the centre of the road, and holding so undeviatingly to his course, that such traffic as traversed the streets had perforce to go round him, leaving him the undisputed king of the causeway.

Outside his house he paused. The white envelope of snow vested it with an unreal and delusive dignity, softening the harsh lines, relieving the squat and rigid contours, blending the incongruous elements with its clinging touch so that, before his fuddled eyes, it reared itself in massive grandeur, looming against the opaque, slate-coloured sky with an illusion of infinite dimensions. He had never liked it so well or admired it so much, and a sense of elation that he should possess it held him as he marched to the front door and entered his home.

In the hall he removed his hat and, with wide extravagant gestures, scattered in all directions the thick snow that had caked upon it, amusedly watching the mushy gobbets go slushing against the roof, the walls, the pictures, the chandelier; then, wildly, he stamped his heavy boots upon the floor, dislodging hard, pressed lumps of ice and snow. It would give that handless slut of his something to do to clean up his mess, he thought, as he walked into the kitchen with the air of a conqueror.

Immediately, he sat down and delved into the huge, steaming bowl of broth, sweet with the essence of beef and bones, and stiff with the agglutination of barley, that stood on the table anticipating his arrival, the ignored reminder of his wife's devotion and forethought. Just the thing for a cold day, he thought, as he supped greedily with the zest of a ravenous animal, lifting huge, heaped spoonfuls rapidly to his mouth and working his jaws incessantly. The meat and small fragments of bone that floated through the pottage he rent and crushed between his hard teeth, revelling in the fact that for weeks his appetite had not been so keen or the taste of food so satisfying upon his tongue.

"That was grand," he admitted to Mrs. Brodie, smacked his lips coarsely at her, "and a good thing for you. If ye had singed my broth on a day like this I would have flung it about your lugs." Then, as she paused at the unusual praise, he bellowed at her: "What are ye gawkin' at; is this all I've to get for my dinner?"

At once she retreated, but, as she hastily brought in the boiled beef and an ashet of potatoes and cabbage, she wondered fearfully what had drawn him from out his perpetual, grim taciturnity to this roaring, devilish humour. He hacked off a lump of the fat beef and thrust it upon his plate, which he then loaded with potatoes and cabbage, began to eat, and with his mouth full, regarded her derisively.

"My, but you are the fine figure of a woman, my dear," he sneered, between champing mouthfuls. "You're about as straight as that lovely nose o' yours. No, don't run away." He raised his knife, with a broad, minatory gesture, to arrest her movement, whilst he finished masticating a chunk of beef. Then he went on, with a fine show of concern: "I must admit ye havena got bonnier lately; all this worry has raddled ye; in fact, you're more like an old cab-horse than ever now. I see you are still wearin' that dish clout of a wrapper." He picked his teeth reflectively with a prong of his fork. "It suits you right well."

Mamma stood there like a wilted reed, unable to sustain his derisive stare, keeping her eyes directed out of the window, as though this abstracted gaze enabled her better to endure his taunts. Her face was grey with an ill, vitreous translucency, her eyelids retracted with a dull, fixed despondency; her thin, work-ugly hands played nervously with a loose tape at her waist.

Suddenly a thought struck Brodie. He looked at the clock. "Where's Nessie?" he shouted.

"I gave her some lunch to school, to save her coming back in the snow."

He grunted. "And my mother," he demanded.

"She wouldna get up to-day for fear of the cold," she whispered.

A guffaw shook him. "That's the spirit you should have had, you fushionless creature. If ye'd had that kind o' gumption ye would have stood up better, and no' run done so quick." Then, after a pause, he continued: "So it's just you and me together. That's very touchin', is't not? Well! I've grand news for ye! A rich surprise!"

Immediately her look left the window; she gazed at him with a numb expectation.

"Don't excite yourself, though," he scoffed. "it's not about your fine, bawdy daughter. You'll never know where she is! It's business this time. You're always such a help and encouragement to a man that I must tell ye this." He paused importantly. "The Mungo Clothing Company have taken the shop next door to your husband—ay—next door to Brodie—the Hatter." He laughed uproariously, "So maybe ye'll find yourself in the poor-house soon!" He howled at his own humour.

Mrs. Brodie restored her gaze into space. She suddenly felt weak and sat down; but as she did so his mocking eye darkened, his face, already flushed with hot food, flamed sullenly.

"Did I tell ye to sit down, ye limmer! Stand up till I've done with ye." Like an obedient child, she rose.

"Maybe the fact that these blasted swine are goin' to have the audacity to settle on my door-step doesna mean much to you. You get your meat and drink too easy perhaps, while I've got to work for it. Does your weak mind not see it's going to be a fight to a finish—to their finish?" He banged his fist on the table. His ranting gaiety was wearing off and giving place, instead, to a morose reactionary temper. "If ye canna think—ye can serve. Go and get my pudding."

She brought him some steamed apple dumpling, and he began to attack it wolfishly, whilst she stood like some bedraggled flunkey at the other end of the table. The news he had given her caused her little concern. In the shadow of Brodie's dominant personality she did not fear pecuniary disaster; although he kept her household allowance parsimoniously tight, she understood, always, that money was free with him, and often she had seen him draw out from his pocket a shining handful of golden sovereigns. Her dejected spirit was grappling with another care. She had not received a letter from Matthew for six weeks, and, before that, his communications to her had been growing increasingly brief, and so irregular as to cause her the deepest vexation and misgiving. Mary she had now abandoned as irrevocably lost to her; she did not even know her whereabouts, except that it had been rumoured that the Foyles had found her a situation of some sort in London, but of what nature she did not know; now it was Matthew upon whom she built her entire hopes and affection. Nessie was so absolutely Brodie's exclusive favourite that only Matt was now left to Mamma. But, apart from this, she had, indeed, always loved him best and, now that he was neglecting to write to her, she imagined that ill-health or misfortune had surely befallen him. Suddenly she started.

"Give me some sugar. What are you moping and moonin' about?" Brodie was shouting at her. "This dumplin' tastes like sourocks. You've got as much hand for a dumplin' as my foot." The more the effect of the liquor left him the more surly he became. He snatched the sugar basin from her, sweetened the pudding to his liking, then consumed it with every indication of dissatisfaction.

Finally, he rose, shaking himself in an effort to dispel the heavy lethargy which was beginning to affect him. Going to the door he turned to his wife and said cuttingly: "Ye'll get sitting down now! I've no doubt the moment my back's turned you'll be crouching at the fire wi' your trashy books, while I'm away working for you. Don't tell me you're not lazy; don't tell me you're not a slut. If I say so, then ye are—and that's the end o't. I know ye for what you are—you lazy besom." In his own increasing ill-temper he sought sullenly for some new means of wounding her, and, as an idea of a parting shot of extreme subtlety struck him, his eyes gleamed, maliciously, with the humour of using Dron's news of this morning, speciously, as a pretext for her discomfiture.

"Now that we've got opposition in the business," he continued slowly, pausing at the door, "we must economise. There'll have to be less wastin' and throwin' out in this house, and for a start I've made up my mind to cut down your allowance for the house. Ye'll get ten shillings a week less from now on, and don't forget I want no savin' on my food. Ye maun just cut out what ye waste and give me the same as usual. Do ye hear me. Ten shillings a week less for ye! Think over that when ye're at your novelettes." Then he turned, and left the room.

II

WHEN her husband had gone Mrs. Brodie did, indeed, sit down, feeling that if, by his departure, she had not been permitted to rest her tired body, she would have fallen at his feet upon the floor from sheer weariness and from a gnawing pain within her side. This pain was peculiar, like a slow, harassing stitch which, though she was so inured to it as almost to ignore it, continually dragged upon her strength and rendered her, when she remained standing for any length of time, unduly and incomprehensibly fatigued. But, as she sat there, it was apparent from her features, which had aged considerably in the last three months, and which now bore the look of remote concentration, that she was not selfishly occupied by the consideration of her own physical disabilities, but was influenced by a deeper and more moving cause for sorrow.

Brodie's last threat had not yet greatly affected her, she was, at the moment, too crushed to realise its portent, and, although she vaguely understood that his conduct had been unusual and his manner exceptional, she had no suspicion of the cause. Nor was she greatly perturbed at his abuse. On this especial side of her nature she was so calloused to the lash of his tongue that she now hardly noticed a variation in the mode of her chastisement, and against any of his sneering charges it never occurred to her to attempt to defend herself; she could not have uttered the mildest or most logical assertion in her favour contrary to his will. Long ago she had realised, with a crushing finality, that she was chained to a man of domineering injustice, that her sole defence would be to develop a supine indifference to every irrational imputation with which he vilified her. She had not entirely succeeded, and he had broken her, but she had at least evolved the faculty of inhibiting him from her meditation in his absence from the home. Therefore, the moment he went out, she directed her thoughts away from him, and automatically they returned to the object of her recent solicitude—her son.

At first, Matt's letters had reached her with a satisfying and affectionate regularity, and with these initial letters he had every month sent her the sum of five pounds to invest for him in the Levenford Building Society. She had loved the tone of these early letters; they had been to her so engrossingly interesting, of such an elevated sentiment, and so filled with strongly expressed moral rectitude. Then, gradually, a slow transition had occurred, and his letters, though still appearing regularly with each mail, had dwindled in volume, and altered in principle, so that, though she had devoured the few husks of scanty and frequently disturbing news within them, her maternal craving had not been satisfied; nor had the half-hearted, stereotyped expression of regard, with which they had invariably concluded, stifled her vague misgivings. When he had thus cut down his epistles to the shortest and most meagre limits, she had begun to write to him reprovingly, but alas, ineffectually, and his acknowledgment of her first letter in this spirit had been to ignore it completely, and to miss the mail for the first time since he had left her. His omissions subsequently had grown more frequent, more disturbing, and now she had not heard from him for nearly six weeks.

Agnes Moir had suffered in the same respect, and his later letters to her had been indifferent in sentiment to the point of actual coldness, filled with veiled, then direct allusions, to the unsuitability of the Indian climate for a wife, and interpolated by intimations as to his unworthiness, or unwillingness, to accept her chastely proffered matrimonial relationship. Miss Moir's soft, amorous nature had received a rude and painful check, by these chilling and infrequent effusions. Now, as she thought of Agnes, Mamma, with the irrational yet inherent notion of seeking consolation in a despondency equal to her own, decided despite her own lassitude and the inclemency of the weather, to visit her future daughter-in-law. A glance at the clock told her that she had two free hours which she could utilise for this purpose without being missed by any of the household—an important point as, since Mary's banishment, Brodie expected her to account to him for her every absence from the house.

Accordingly, she got up and, ascending to her room, discarded her wrapper by allowing it to slide from her to the floor; without once regarding herself in the glass she made her toilet by giving her face a quick wipe with the wetted end of a towel. She next withdrew from the wardrobe what was revealed to be, after removing several pinned, protecting sheets of paper, an old sealskin jacket. The jacket, a relic of the days before her marriage, was now worn, frayed, shiny, and in places of a drab, brownish tinge. It had been kept and worn intermittently for a period of over twenty years, and this decayed and dilapidated coat, which had once enclosed her young, virgin figure, held as much tragedy as Margaret Brodie herself. She did not, however, view it in this sombre light, regarding it as sealskin, real sealskin, no longer perhaps elegant in cut, but still genuine sealskin, and treasuring it accordingly as the most splendid garment she possessed. For a moment she forgot her sorrow as, holding up the jacket, denuded of its wrappings, to the satisfaction of her appraising eyes, she shook it gently, touched the faded fur with caressing fingers, then, with a sigh, as though she had shaken out from its musty texture faded recollections of her forgotten youth, slowly she assumed it, when at least it had the merit of covering her rusty gown and sheathing warmly her decrepit figure. Her next action was to cram upon her untidy hair, and to stab carelessly into position, a black hat plumed with a withered pinion which trailed, with a frightful travesty of coquetry, behind her left ear; having thus accomplished completely her vesture for the outer air, she hastened downstairs and left the house with a mien which was almost stealthy.

In the street, unlike her husband, she did not swagger her way down the middle of the road, but instead, crept along the inside of the pavement with short, shuffling steps, her head inclined, her face blue with cold, her figure shirking observation, her entire aspect a graphic exposition of resigned martyrdom. The snow turned her dull sealskin to glittering ermine, blew into her eyes and mouth and made her cough, penetrated her thin, inadequate boots and soaked her feet so profusely that, long before she reached the Moirs' shop, they squelched at every step.

Despite the unexpectedness of this visitation, Agnes was delighted to see her, and welcomed her warmly, whilst a quick look passed between the two women, each searching the other's eyes for some recorded sign of better tidings. Immediately they knew their eager hope to be unfulfilled, deferred, and their eyes fell dejectedly; but they still voiced the question which each had, silently, already answered.

"Have you had anything this week, Aggie?"

"Not yet, Mamma." She fondly addressed Mrs. Brodie by that term in the sanguine anticipation of her future relationship. "Have you?"

"No, dear, not yet, but maybe the mail is delayed by the bad weather," said Mrs. Brodie, in a despondent tone.

"I shouldn't be surprised," replied Agnes, forlornly.

Actually each attempted to delude the other, for they knew by heart the incidence of the posts from India, and the mystery of the passage of mail ships was now to them an open book; but to-day, under the intolerable burden of their growing uncertainty, this feeble effort of deception was useless and they now gazed at each other blankly, for a moment, as if they had already exhausted their entire range of conversation. Agnes, by virtue of her position as hostess, recovered first, and collecting her forces said, considerately:

"You'll have a cup of tea with me, Mamma. You're all wet and cold from the snow."

Mrs. Brodie assented dumbly and followed her into the little back shop where, amidst a profusion of empty biscuit tins, sweet bottles, and wooden chocolate boxes, a small iron stove threw out a meagre heat.

"Sit down there, Mamma," continued Agnes, opening the metal window of the stove and placing a chair before this small glowing mouth. "The weather's keeping us as quiet as can be, so I'll have time for a crack with you."

By mutual consent an armistice was tacitly proclaimed for the cessation of their unhappy exchanges, and, whilst Agnes boiled the kettle, Mamma steamed her damp boots at the fire and agreed, meditatively:

"Ay! 'Twas snowin' heavy again as I came along. It's good to see a blink of heat on a day like this."

At these words Agnes threw a small shovelful of coke on to the red embers, and enquired:

"Will you have tea or cocoa, Mamma? I've got some fresh Epps' in this week."

"I think I would prefer the cocoa. It's more sustaining, and nourishing like, than tea on a cold day. That's one thing about you, Agnes, you always offer a body something tasty."

"I can surely do that for you, Mamma," replied Miss Moir, pursing her lips significantly. "It would be a pity if I couldn't put myself about a bit for you. Will ye not take your coat off?" and she made an advance to assist in the removal of the sealskin.

"No! No! thanks," cried Mamma hastily, with a drearful consciousness of her deficiencies underneath. "I'll not be biding that long." But her eyes watered gratefully as she took the cup of hot cocoa and sipped it appreciatively; she even accepted and nibbled a sweet biscuit; then, as comfort stole through her, she sighed:

"It's been a hard winter for me. I don't know how I've come through it."

"I well know that, Mamma! You have suffered."

"Ay, I've suffered! I never thought I could have endured such disgrace, Agnes, I didn't merit it. And I think her father blames me for not having watched Mary better." She could hardly bring herself to articulate her daughter's name, it had been so firmly proscribed from her lips.

"Nobody could be blamed for her fall but herself, Mamma. Your influence could only have been for good—wickedness is in the person that sins. You'll just need to let me take her place."

"That's good o' ye, Agnes, but there's times at night I can't get her out of my head. I never thought I should miss her so much—she was always that quiet and douce about the house—and I don't even know where she is."

"You must forget her now," insisted Agnes gently.

"Her father wouldna let me speir a word about her. Not even when she was near dyin' in the hospital. Not even when the puir bairn died."

Agnes drew her mouth together.

"I'm not sure if I should tell you, Mamma," she began, slowly, "and it's not a pleasant subject for me—it's not the thing for a nice girl to be connected with even indirectly—but I heard the other day that she was in London." She gave to the name of the city an accent of imputation and opprobrium which seemed to summarise her opinion of its manifold potentialities for wickedness.

"Do ye know what she's doing?" cried Mamma.

Agnes veiled her eyes and shook her head.

"I can't be sure," she replied, lowering her voice, "but I've been told—only been told mind you—that it's service."

"A servant!" gasped Mamma. "Oh dearie me! what a thing to come to! It's terrible! What would her father say if he knew! A Brodie a servant!"

"What else is she fitted for," replied Agnes, with a faint toss of her head. "We should be thankful it's an honest occupation, if indeed it is so."

Despite the bond between Mrs. Brodie and herself it gave her a pleasurable sense of moral and social superiority to impart this news, which she had avidly sought amongst the tittle-tattle of the town.

"A servant in London!" repeated Mamma, faintly, "It's awfu'. Could these folks in Darroch no' have done something for her?"

"Indeed that's the very point," cried Agnes. "These Foyles wanted the child for the sake of the son's memory, so as to take it back to Ireland with them—they've gone back there ye know. Ye can't believe all ye hear; of course there's all sorts of stories about, but I believe the truth is that, when it died, they took a spite at her and got rid of her the quickest they could!"

Mrs. Brodie shook her head negatively.

"That wouldna be difficult," she retorted. "Mary was always an independent girl; she would take charity from nobody—no, she would work for her living first."

"Well, anyway, Mamma, I didn't like telling you, but I thought it best you should know. Anyway, your responsibility for her is ended. Mind you, although she has lowered the name of my intended, I bear no grudge against her. I hope she may in time repent; but you have got others to think of."

"Ay, that's true, Agnes! I maun swallow the bitter pill; but I will say this—I never thought much of Mary, never valued her until I lost her. Still I maun forget if I can, and think of them that's left to us." She sighed heavily. "What's come over our poor Matt at all, at all? It fair breaks my heart not to have news o' him. Can he be ill, think ye?" They were now embarked upon the consideration of the subject vital to them both, and, after a moment's thought, Miss Moir shook her head, dubiously.

"He's said nothing about his health," she replied. "He's been off his work once or twice I know, but I don't think it was from sickness."

"Maybe he wouldn't like to frighten us," said Mrs. Brodie, diffidently. "There's agues and fevers and jaundice and all kinds of awfu' troubles out in these foreign parts. He might even have got sunstroke, although it's strange to think of such a thing with all this snow about us here. Matt was never a strong boy." Then she added, inconsequently: "He aye had a weak chest in the winter, and bronchitis, that needed thick garments."

"But, Mamma," cried Agnes impatiently, "he would never get bronchitis in a hot country. They would never get snow like this in Calcutta."

"I ken that, Agnes," replied Mrs. Brodie firmly, "but a weakness like that might work inwardly in a hot country, and forbye if he opened his pores he might sit doun and get a chill, as easy as look at ye."

Agnes did not seem to take kindly to this train of thought and she arrested it by a pause, after which she said, slowly:

"I've been wondering, Mamma, if some of these black persons have not been exerting an evil influence over Matt. There's people called Rajahs—rich heathen princes—that I've read awful things about, and Matt might be led away. He might be easily led," she added solemnly—recollecting, perhaps, her own enticement of the receptive youth.

Mrs. Brodie instantly had visions of all the potentates of India luring her son from grace with jewels, but indignantly she repudiated the sudden, baleful thought.

"How can ye say that, Agnes?" she cried. "He kept the best of company in Levenford. You should know that! He was never the one for bad companions or low company."

But Agnes who, for a Christian woman, had an intensive knowledge of her subject, which must necessarily have come to her through the marvellous intuition of love, continued relentlessly:

"Then, Mamma, I hardly like to let the words cross my lips, but they have wicked, wicked attractions out there—like dancing girls that—that charm snakes and dance without——" Miss Moir, with downcast eyes, broke off significantly and blushed, whilst the down on her upper lip quivered modestly.

Mrs. Brodie gazed at her with eyes as horrified as if they beheld a nest of those snakes which Agnes so glibly described; demoralised by the appalling suddenness of a suggestion which had never before entered her mind, she wildly visualised one of these shameless houris abandoning the charming of reptiles to charm away the virtue of her son.

"Mat's no' a boy like that!" she gasped.

Miss Moir compressed her lips delicately and bridled, then raised her heavy eyebrows with an air of one who could have revealed to Mrs. Brodie secrets regarding the profundities of Matthew's passionate nature which had hitherto been undreamed of. As she sipped her cocoa her attitude seemed to say: "You ought to know by now the propensities of your children. Only my inviolate and virtuous maidenhood has kept your son pure."

"Ye've no proof, have ye, Agnes?" wailed Mrs. Brodie, her apprehension strengthened by the other's strange air.

"I have no definite proof, of course, but I can put two and two together," replied Miss Moir coldly. "If you can read between the lines of these last letters of his he's always at that club of his, and playing billiard matches, and out at night with other men, and smoking like a furnace." Then, after a moment's silence she added, petulantly: "He should never been allowed to smoke. It was a step in the wrong direction. I never liked the idea of these cigars; it was downright fast!"

Mrs. Brodie wilted visibly at the obvious insinuation that she had countenanced her son's first step on the road to ruin.

"But, Aggie," she blurted out, "you let him smoke an' all, for I mind well he persuaded me by saying ye thought it manly."

"You're his mother. I only said to please the boy. You know I would do anything for him," retorted Agnes with a sniff which verged almost into a sob.

"And I would do everything for him, too," replied Mrs. Brodie hopelessly; "but I don't know what's going to come of it at all."

"I've been seriously wondering," pursued Agnes, "if you ought not to get Mr. Brodie to write a strong letter to Matt, sort of, well, reminding him of his duties and obligations to those at home. I think it's high time something was done about it."

"Oh! that wouldna do at all," cried Mamma hastily. "It would never do. I could never approach him. It's not in me, and besides it's not the kind of thing his father would do." She trembled at an idea so antagonistic to her invariable line of conduct towards Brodie, so contrary to her usual concealment of everything that might provoke that imperial wrath, and she shook her head sadly, as she added: "We maun do what we can ourselves, for his father wouldna stir his finger to help him. It may be unnatural, but it's his style. He thinks he's done a' he should do."

Agnes looked grieved. "I know Matt was always afraid—always respected his father's word," she said, "and I'm sure you don't want any more discredit on the family."

"No, Agnes, I don't like to contradict you to your face, but I'm certain you're not on the right track. I would never believe wrong of my boy. You're anxious, like me, and it's put you on the wrong idea. Wait a bit and you'll have a grand, big budget of good news next week."

"It can't come quick enough for me," replied Miss Moir, in a frigid tone which coldly indicated her grievance against Mrs. Brodie in particular, and her growing resentment, fed by the recollection of Mary's recent disgrace, against the name of Brodie in general. Her breast heaved and she was about to utter a bitter, contumacious reproach when suddenly the shop door bell went "ping," and she was obliged, with heightening colour, to rise servilely to answer the call, and to serve a small boy with an inconsiderable quantity of confectionery. This supremely undignified interruption did nothing towards restoring her equanimity but, instead, activated her to a lively irritation and, as the penetrating voice of her client demanding a halfpennyworth of black-striped balls clearly penetrated the air, the obstinate perversity of her temper deepened.

Unconscious of the working of this angry ferment in Miss Moir's exuberant bosom Mrs. Brodie, in her absence, sat huddled in her chair before the stove, her thin chin sunk in the scraggy wetness of the sealskin coat. Surrounded externally by struggling currents of steamy vapour, there struggled also, within her mind, a dreadful uncertainty as to whether she might not be responsible for some vague and undetermined weakness in Matt, through a fault in his upbringing. A frequent expression of Brodie's a decade ago flashed into her mind, and she now saw vividly, in her anguish, her husband's contemptuous face as, discovering her in some fresh indulgence towards Matthew, he snapped at her: "You're spoiling that namby-pamby brat of yours. You'll make a braw man o' him!" She had, indeed, always attempted to shield Matt from his father, to protect him from the harshness of life, to give him extra luxuries and privileges not accorded to her other children. He had never had the courage to play truant from the Academy, but when he had desired, as he frequently did, a day off or had been for some reason afraid to attend school, it was to her that he had come, limping and whining: "Mamma, I'm sick. I've got a pain in ma belly." Whenever he had feigned illness, of whatever kind, he had affected always that limping, hobbling, lame-dog gait, as though the agony arising in any organ of his body flew immediately to one leg, paralysing it and rendering him incapable of locomotion. She had seen through him, of course, but though undeceived by his pretences, a wave of her foolish maternal love would rush over her and she would compliantly answer: "Away up to your room then, son, and I'll fetch ye up something nice. Ye've got a friend in yer mother, anyway, Matt." Her stultified affections were obliged to find an outlet, and she had lavished them upon her son, feeling the imperative need, in that harsh household, of binding him to her by bonds of love. Had she spoiled his manhood by her indulgence? softened her son into a weakling by lax, tolerant fondness? Immediately her mind formulated the idea, her heart indignantly repudiated it, telling her that she had shown him nothing but kindness, gentleness, and lenience, had wished for him nothing but what was good; she had slaved for him, too, washed, darned, knitted for him, brushed his boots, made his bed, cooked the most appetising meals for him.

"Ay," she muttered to herself, "I've served that laddie hand and foot. Surely he can never forget me? I've taken the very bite out my mouth for him."

All the toil she had expended upon her son, from the washing of his first napkins to the final packing of his trunk for India, rose up before her, and she was confronted with a sense of the bewildering futility of all her love and service in the face of his present treatment of her. She blindly asked herself if it were her incompetence alone which had rendered her enormous and unremitting efforts useless, so that he now used her so indifferently and left her in such harassing suspense.

Here, a sudden sound startled her, and she looked up wanly, to observe that Agnes had returned and was addressing her in an uneven tone of ill-repressed vindictiveness.

"Mamma," she cried, "I'm going to marry Matt. I'm going to be his wife and I want to know what's going to be done about this. You've got to do something at once."

Mamma regarded her humbly, with the mild, moist blue eyes that shone meekly from under the grotesque, bedraggled black hat.

"Don't start on me, Agnes, dear," she said submissively. "I've had enough to stand in my time without having a hard word from you. I'm not fit to answer ye back, ye can surely see," and she added feebly, "I'm just a done woman."

"That's all very well," cried Agnes in a huff, "but I'm not going to have Matt taken away like this. He belongs to me as much as anyone. I'm not going to give him up."

"Aggie," replied Mamma, in a dead voice, "we don't know anything; we can't tell what's happening; but we can pray. Yes! that's what we can do. I think I would like us to put up a prayer in this very room. Maybe the Almighty, the same Lord God that looks down on Matt in

India, will look down on us two anxious women here and show us a light to comfort us."

Agnes, touched on her weakest side, was mollified, and the stiffness of her figure relaxed, the glitter faded from her eye as she said: "Maybe you're right, Mamma. It would be a comfort." Then, more as a polite formality than anything else, she asked: "Will you speak, then, or will I?"

"You do it better than me," said Mrs. Brodie, unassumingly. "You put up a word for us both."

"Very well, Mamma," replied Agnes complacently.

They knelt down in the small, stuffy room, amongst the jumbled clutter on the floor of bottles, boxes, tins, surrounded by the untidy litter of straw packing and sawdust, their altar a packing-case, their ikon a framed advertisement upon the wall. Still, they prayed.

Agnes, kneeling straight and upright, her thick, short body tense with an almost masculine vitality, and potent with the pressure of her restraint, began to pray in a loud, firm voice. Amongst the godly people in the church movements with which she was identified Miss Moir was noted for the power and richness of her spontaneous prayer, and now the words flowed from her lips in an eloquent stream, like the outpourings of a young and fervent priest supplicating for the sins of mankind. Yet she did not petition, she seemed indeed to demand, and her dark eyes glowed, her full bosom heaved with the intensity of her appeal. All the fire of her nature entered that passionate prayer. Her words were proper, modest, stereotyped, but in essence it was as though she throbbingly implored the Almighty not to cheat her of the man she had captivated and subdued by the meagre charms with which He had endowed her. No one had ever looked at her but Matt, she knew her attractions to be limited, and, if he failed her, she might never marry. All the suppressed feeling dammed within her had been restrained within bounds only by visions of the joyous promise of the future, and she now tacitly implored the Almighty not to defraud her of the fulsome fruition of these desires in the state of holy matrimony.

Mamma, on the contrary, seemed to sink down in a supine mass, like a heap of discarded, draggled clothing; her head sagged with a pleading humility; the faint, speedwell blue of her pathetic eyes was washed with tears; her nose flowed with lacrymation. As the loud, fervent words fell upon her ears, the image of her son rose before her and, while at first she applied her handkerchief furtively, soon she used it profusely, and at length she wept openly. All the time, her heart seemed to beat out the words: "O God! If I did wrong over Mary, don't punish me too much. Don't take Matt away from me. Leave me, still, my son to love me." When the prayer was ended there was a long pause, then Agnes rose, extended her hand to Mamma and helped her to her feet; facing each other closely, amicably, the two women now regarded each other with a glow of understanding and sympathy. Mamma nodded her head gently, as if to say: "That'll do it, Agnes. It was wonderful." New life seemed to have possessed them both. This outpoured confession of all their hopes, fears, and desires to the unknown heavens towards a Supreme, Omniscient, and Omnipotent Being left them assured, comforted, and fortified. Now they were positive that all would be well with Matthew and, as Mamma at length turned to go, invigorated and refreshed, a look passed between them expressive of their sweet, secret co-operation and they kissed each other a sanguine, affectionate good-bye.

III

Towards the middle of March, the empty shop next door to Brodie's became the nucleus of a seething activity. Previously, when, in its unoccupied wretchedness, it had been to him a perpetual eyesore against the refinement of his establishment, he had viewed it with contemptuous disgust; but, immediately after Dron's communication that it had been sold, he began to see it with a different, a peculiar, and more intense disfavour. Every time he passed in or out of his own business he darted a furtive, antagonistic glance at the vacant, dilapidated premises, quickly, as if he feared to have that glance intercepted, yet vindictively, as though he vented his spleen upon the inanimate building. Its two empty windows were no longer vacuous, but became to him hateful, and each morning as he came along, fearing, yet hoping, that signs of the incoming of the new company would be evident, and still the same shabby, void aspect met his gaze, he experienced a compelling desire to hurl a heavy stone with all his force, to shiver the blank and glass panes. As day followed day for an entire week, and still nothing happened, this deferred action angered him—he had been so strung up for battle and he began to ponder, obtusely, if the whole idea was simply a spiteful invention of Dron's, concocted in order to irritate him. For the space of one full day he felt convinced that the shop had not been sold and, during that time, he scoffed openly, with a flaunting triumph, but immediately, a short announcement in the *Levenford Advertiser*, stating briefly that the Mungo Company would open a new branch at 62 High Street at the beginning of the month of April, and that the fullest details would be given in the following week's issue, destroyed this transitory illusion; the conflict, occurring solely in Brodie's own perverted mind, between himself and the inert building, reopened more bitterly than before.

Shortly after this pretentious announcement in the *Advertiser*, a dapper, urbane visitor had come into Brodie's shop and, with an agreeable, yet deprecatory, smile, presented his card in introduction.

"Mr. Brodie, I am, as you see, the district manager of the Mungo Hat & Hosiery Company. I want us to be friends," he said, holding out his hand affably.

Brodie was dumbfounded, but beyond ignoring the proffered hand, he gave no indication of his feelings and made no departure from his usual manner. "Is that all ye want?" he asked abruptly.

"I understand your very natural feelings," the other began again. "You already consider us your enemies. That is really not strictly so. Although we are, in a sense, business opponents, we have found by experience that it is often mutually advantageous for two establishments of the same nature—such as yours and ours—to be together."

"Do ye tell me, now," said Brodie ironically, as the other paused impressively, and, not knowing his man or the symptoms of his gathering wrath, expansively continued.

"Yes, that *is* so, Mr. Brodie. We find that such a combination attracts more people to that particular centre, more shopping is done there, and this, of course, is advantageous to both shops. We multiply the trade and divide the profits! That's our arithmetic," he concluded, as he imagined, rather neatly.

Brodie looked at him icily.

"You're talkin' a lot of damned lies," he said roughly. "Don't think ye can pull the wool over my eyes like that, and don't refer to my business in the same breath as your own gimcrack huckster's trade. You've come here to try and poach on my preserves and I'm goin' to treat you like a low poacher."

The other smiled. "You surely can't mean that! I represent a reputable firm; we have branches everywhere, we are not poachers. I am going to open the new branch myself, and I want to be with you. And you," he added flatteringly, "well—you certainly don't look like a man who could fail to understand the value of co-operation."

"Don't talk to me about your blasted co-operation," cried Brodie, "if that's the name ye give to stealing other folks' custom."

"I hope you don't mean us to infer that you have the exclusive rights to monopolise the hat trade here," said the other, with some indignation.

"I don't care about the right, I have the might, and I tell ye I'll smash you!" He flexed up his great biceps with a significant gesture. "I'll smash you to bits."

"That surely is a childish attitude, Mr. Brodie! Co-operation is better than competition every time. Of course, if you choose to fight," he waved his hand deprecatingly, "we have large resources. We have had to cut our prices before, in similar circumstances, and we can easily do it again."

Brodie threw a glance contemptuously at the pasteboard of the visiting-card which lay crushed in his hand. "Man! Mr.—whatever your name is—you talk like a penny novelette. I don't intend to reduce my prices one farthing," he drawled, pityingly. "I have the connection here, that's all, and I'm just man enough to keep it."

"I see," the other had replied succinctly; "you are definitely going out of your way to demand open hostility."

"By God!" Brodie thundered at him, "that's the only true word you've spoken yet, an' I hope it's the last thing ye will say."

At these final and unmistakable words the other had turned and walked quietly out of the shop, then, upon the following day—the fifteenth of March—a small corps of workmen had descended upon the place next door.

They were working now, irritating him intensely by the sound of their labour, by each tap of their hammers which beat with exasperating monotony into his brain. Even in the intervals of silence he was harassed by their presence, kept anticipating the onset of the staccato tattoo, and, when it recommenced, a pulse within him throbbed dangerously in the same tapping rhythm. When the rending of saws on wood came through the dividing wall he winced, as if the saw had rasped his own bones, and at the cold steely sound of the chisels upon stone he frowned, as if they carved upon his brow, above and between his eyes, a deep, vertical furrow of hatred.

They were gutting the shop. The men worked quickly and in the rush to complete their operations as rapidly as possible, worked also overtime; double wages apparently meant nothing to the Mungo Company! At the end of a week they had cleared out the old window frames, the doorway, the dilapidated shelves and counter, the whole worn wreckage of a bygone age, and now the denuded frontage leered at Brodie like a mask, its window spaces the sightless sockets of eyes and its empty doorway the gaping, toothless mouth. Then the plasterers and decorators added their efforts to those of the joiners and masons, altering visibly, from day to day, by their combined exertions and skill, the entire aspect of the structure. Brodie hated every phase of its change, and he encompassed within his growing aversion for the transformed building these workmen who, through their labours, were reconstructing it so admirably, and making it the finest and most modern shop in the Borough. On an occasion when one of these had entered Brodie's establishment and, touching his cap, asked civilly if he might be obliged with a bucket of water to make tea for himself and his mates next door, as their own supply had been temporarily suspended at the main, Brodie had shot the astonished man out of his shop. "Water!" he had snarled. "Ye want water, and ye have the impertinence to come here for your favours. Ye'll get none of it. If the whole gang o' ye were fryin' in hell I wouldna so much as put a drop on one o' your tongues. Get out!"

But his animadversion had no effect upon their activities, serving only, or so it seemed to him, to stimulate these, and moodily he observed thick, scintillating plate-glass windows of a green actinic translucency come into place, rich show-cases appear like mushrooms in the space of a night, an ornately lettered sign-board emerge—glittering! Finally, under his eyes, in broad daylight—the crowning anathema—a model of a huge top-hat, sumptuously and opulently gilt, was erected above the doorway, where it swung jauntily from its supporting pole with every breath of air.

Brodie's demeanour to the town during this period gave, in general, no marked indication of the emotions which he repressed. He manifested outwardly only calm indifference, for his very pride forbade him to speak; and to his acquaintances who rallied him on the matter of the encroachment he exhibited an air of profound contempt towards the new company, met Grierson's gall-dipped witticisms at the Philosophical Club with the assumption of a careless and superior unconcern.

The general opinion was that Brodie would undoubtedly carry the day against the invaders.

"I give them six months," remarked Provost Gordon judiciously, to the select junto of the club one evening, in Brodie's absence, "before Brodie drives them out. He's an unco' deevilish man that, for an enemy. Dod, he's quite capable o' layin' a charge o' gunpowder under their braw new shop."

" 'Twould be a risky job wi' that sparky temper o' his," inserted Grierson.

"He'll spark them out," replied the Provost. "He fair beats me, does James Brodie. I know of no man alive who would have come through a' that awfu' pother and disgrace about his daughter without turnin' a hair, or once hangin' his heid. He's a black deevil when his purpose is set."

"I'm not so sure, Provost; na, na, I'm not just so sure," drawled the other, "that the very deliberateness o' him michtna thwart its aim purpose, for he's that obstinate he would try to outface a mule. Forbye, Provost, he's gotten so big for his shoes now that folks—aye, even the county folks who liket it at first—are beginnin' to get a wheen sick o' it. That grand style o' his is juist like the lordly salmon; a wee bittie is all right, but if ye get it served up a' the time, man, ye get awfu' scunnered by it."

Seeing himself thus the object of their speculation, and sensing its slightly favourable tone, Brodie began to feel that the public eye was turned encouragingly towards him as a defender of the old, solid order of the Borough against the invasion of the trumpery new, and he became, in his appearance, even more of the dandy, ordered two new suits of the finest and most expensive cloth, bought himself in the jeweller's at the Cross a smart, opal tiepin which he now wore in place of his plain gold horseshoe. This pin was immediately the object of criticism amongst the cronies, and was passed from hand to hand in admiration.

"'Tis a bonnie stone—although I'm no judge," tittered Grierson. "I hope it hasna ruined you to buy it."

"Don't judge my savings by yours. I know weel enough what I can afford," retorted Brodie roughly.

"Na! Na! I wouldna dream o' doin' that. Ye're so lavish wi' your money ye maun be worth a mint o' it. I'll warrant ye'll have a wheen o' siller stowed away for a rainy day," lisped Grierson ambiguously, as his eye flicked Brodie's with ironic insight.

"They say an opal's gey unlucky. The wife's sister had an opal ring that brought her a heap o' misfortune. She had an unco' bad slip the very month she got it," demurred Paxton.

"That'll no' happen to me," replied Brodie coarsely.

"But are ye not feared to wear it?" persisted Paxton.

Brodie looked at him fixedly.

"Man," he said slowly, "you ought to know I'm feared of nothing on this God's earth."

Curiously, although he directed the most scrupulous attention towards his own attire and personal appearance, he would not for an instant entertain the idea of sprucing up his business premises by renewing the drab aspect of his shop, but seemed actually to glory in its unalterable, but recently accentuated, dinginess. When Perry, who had cast a persistently envious eye upon the growth of the dazzling magnificence next door, remarked upon the contrast and timidly suggested that perhaps a touch of paint might benefit the exterior, he said, impressively: "Not a finger do we lay on it. Them that wants to buy their hats in a painted panopticon can do so, but this is a gentlemen's business and I'm going to keep it so." In this attitude he waited the first attack of the enemy.

With the final steps of restoration and reconstruction completed, at last the opening day of the rival establishment arrived. Astonishing progress had been made during the last week of March and a full blaring column in the *Advertiser* had announced that the first of April would mark the inauguration of the new establishment. Behind the thick green blinds and shuttered entrance, a feeling of occult mysticism had prevailed during the whole of the previous day, and through this veil the district manager of the company, who had been deputed to take charge of the local branch for the initial months, had been observed flitting restlessly, like a shadow, symbolic of secrecy. Obviously the policy of the Mungo Company was to dazzle Levenford by their display in one sudden, blinding revelation; they would rend the cover from the windows and the Borough as a whole would be staggered by the vision of what it saw. Such, at least, were Brodie's ironic thoughts as, on the first of April, he left his house at 9.30 to the second, no sooner no later, and began the usual walk to his business in exactly his usual manner. As he came down the High Street in perfect composure he looked, although his manner was perhaps a trifle over-emphasised, the least perturbed man in Levenford. The satirical nature of his reflections fed his vanity and consolidated his rooted belief in himself, stifling the vague misgiving that had for days fluttered at the back of his brain. Now that the moody period of waiting was at an end and the fight actually begun, he became once more the master of his fate and his bearing now seemed to say: "Let me get at it. I've been waitin' on this. And now you're ready for me, by God, I'm ready for you." He loved a fight. Furthermore, he felt spurred in this incentive to contest, by his additional anticipation that the heat of the battle would remove his mind from the dull depression into which the blow to his intimate family pride had recently plunged him. Already his heart lifted to the joy of the fight as he told himself that he would show them the stuff that James Brodie was made of, would demonstrate again to the town the spirit that was in him, would, by a crushing defeat to these Mungo upstarts, restore his prestige in the eyes of the Borough to even a higher level than before. With a stiff back and expanded chest, with his stick cocked over his shoulder—an exultant mannerism he had not indulged in for months—he strode confidently along the street.

He reached the new shop, saw instantly that, at last, it was open. Whilst a lesser man might have, more circumspectly, completed his inspection by peering from the corner of his eye as he walked past, this prying was not in Brodie's nature, and he arrested himself openly, ostentatiously, in the middle of the pavement, and with his stick still upon his shoulder, his feet planted firmly apart, his massive head thrown back, he gazed sardonically at the double-fronted spectacle before him. A deliberate smile spread over his features. A ponderous guffaw shook him. His whole attitude became expressive of his delightful realisation that the display before him was more trashy and new-fangled than he had dared to hope, more ludicrous than he had preconceived even in his wildest expectations. One window was crammed from floor to ceiling with hats, hats of every conceivable form, variety, and style, mounting upwards in graduated tiers amongst festoons of ties and sprouting bouquets of coloured handkerchiefs, ornamented at tasteful intervals by garlands of socks and stockings, and embellished by an array of gloves arranged like fern fronds, with limp yet politely extended fingers. The indication that the purpose of this strikingly artistic exhibition was not purely decorative was clearly, yet tactfully, conveyed by the fact that each article bore a small ticket stamped M.H.H., with the price in plain red figures below. But although he perceived this composite tableau, it was, however, the other window which riveted Brodie's quizzical attention, where his contemptuous eyes observed the unthought-of novelty of two wax figures. Wax figures—incredible! Still, there they were, a gentleman of perfect complexion and address gazing with fixed, ambiguous fondness upon the form of a small boy who, from his clear skin, wide blue eyes, and bland innocuous simper was undoubtedly the model son of this model father. They stood, the right hand of the father and the left hand of the son extended with the same delicate gesture, as if to say: "Here we are. Gaze upon us. We are here for your admiration."

Their clothing was immaculate, and Brodie's eye travelled from the creases of their trousers to the brilliance of their ties, over the glaze of their collars, the snowy whiteness of their prominent handkerchiefs, the sheen of sock and stocking, to the curly brimmed Derby on the parental brow and the natty pill-box upon the juvenile head, until finally it rested upon the neat card on which was printed: "Dressed by the M.H.H. Co. Let us do the same for you."

"Dummies," muttered Brodie. "Demned dummies. It's not a hat shop; it's a demned waxworks." They represented to him the joke of a lifetime, for these figures had never been seen in Levenford—although it had been recently rumoured that such innovations were appearing in the larger Glasgow warehouses—and he considered that they would soon be the laughing-stock of the Borough.

As he remained in arrogant contemplation, suddenly a man came out of the shop, carrying a brown paper parcel. Instantly Brodie's sneer was transfixed by a sudden mortifying apprehension, and a pang shot through him like a knife stab. Had they, then, begun to do business already? He had never seen the man before, and he tried to reassure himself that, in all probability, this was merely a belated workman performing some omitted task or collecting his forgotten gear; nevertheless, a neat parcel aroused his suspicion, disturbed him deeply, and in a less arrogant manner, he moved his firmly rooted limbs and went slowly through his own doorway.

Perry, inevitably, was there to greet him, moved this morning, by the progress of current events, to a more obsequious deference, and bearing in his mind perhaps the faint aspiration that he might, in the face of this new opposition, have the opportunity to show to his patron something of his real value, to achieve in some measure a realisation of his blighted hopes.

"Good morning to you, Mr. Brodie, sir." For this especial occasion Perry had concocted a mild witticism which he considered in his own mind both clever and amusing, and, plucking up all his courage, he now had the temerity to liberate it upon Brodie. "This is the first of April, sir," he said nervously. "Do you observe the inference, since they"—he always referred to his new neighbours in this ambiguous manner—"since they have opened on All Fools' Day."

"No," growled Brodie, looking from under his brows, "but tell me, you that's so clever."

"Well, it's all through the town, Mr. Brodie, that you'll make April gowks of them," gushed Perry, and, as he saw the effect of his remark, he tittered sympathetically, then writhed in the exuberance of his satisfaction, for Brodie had laughed shortly, pleased by the notion of the general adulation of the town implied in Perry's flattering, but, though he knew it not, fabricated remark. His huge fingers flexed in slowly on his palm.

"Ay, I'll mak' a gowk o' them, right enough! I'll take some o' the conceit out o' them, take some o' the gilt off their gingerbread. They don't know who they're up against yet, but, by gad, I'll learn them." How, exactly, he did not quite know, but at this moment, although he had no vestige of a settled policy in his brain, his confidence in his own ability to crush the opposition was supreme.

"Did ye notice the stookies in the window?" he queried, absently.

"Yes! oh yes! Mr. Brodie. A new idea from the larger houses. Rather original, of course, and up to date." In the first flush of his conversational success he had almost the optimism to hope that "the guv'nor" might perhaps order a brace of these intriguing models on the spot. His eyes glowed enthusiastically, but he had perforce to lower them under Brodie's glower, realising that he had this time said, apparently, the wrong thing.

"Up to date, ye say. It's a deshed museum! They'll have a crowd round that bluter of a window o' theirs."

"But, sir," ventured Perry timidly, "is that not desirable. If you would attract people and draw their attention outside, they're more likely to come inside. It's a sort of advertisement."

Brodie looked at him obtusely for a moment, then growled, angrily: "Has the same bug been bitin' you, that you're itchin' for the common herd to batter at our doors. If it has, get the poison out your system quick, or it'll be as much as your job is worth."

Perry looked at him humbly, and observed, meekly: "It's all grist to your mill though, sir." Then, removing himself to safer ground, he hastened to observe: "I see they're going in for a sort of general outfitting as well, Mr. Brodie, sir."

Brodie nodded sullenly.

"You wouldn't care to branch out with a few extra lines yourself, sir, a novelty or two perhaps. Say a brace or a smart glove! Very refined indeed, a nice glove, sir." Perry almost pleaded at the bubbling urge of all the ideas repressed within him.

But his bright, insinuating suggestions fell on deaf ears. Brodie paid no heed to him, but stood, moved by an unusual impulse of self-analysis, absorbed in the contemplation of his strange departure from his invariable routine. Why, he asked himself, was he hanging about the shop instead of entering his office with his usual imperial negligence? He was going to smash them next door, of course, but would he do it by sitting calmly at his desk, attempting to read the *Glasgow Herald*? He felt he must do something, take some definite line of conduct, but as he moved about, chafing at his desuetude, his sluggish mentality offered him no tangible suggestions towards the powerful action which he craved. If only he could have used the terrific strength of his body in this present cause, then he would have toiled till the sweat poured from him, till his joints cracked with the strain of his effort; he would willingly have embraced the supporting pillars of the opposing shop and, uprooting them, have dragged down the entire edifice about him; but some dim perception of the uselessness of his brute force dawned upon him and stung him bitterly.

At this point a woman, holding by the hand a small child of about six years of age, entered the shop. She was obviously of a poor class, and advanced to Perry who greeted her deferentially.

"I wanted a bonnet for ma wee boy. He's goin' to the school next week!" she said, confidentially.

Perry beamed upon her.

"Certainly, madam! What can I show you for the little man?"

Suddenly a strange impulse, a fierce inclination against his hated opposition, seized Brodie, and, although these customers were obviously of an inferior class, and clearly of that type whom he invariably left to his assistant, he was impelled to go forward.

"Let me do it," he said, in a harsh, unreal tone.

The woman gazed at him timidly and, instinctively in awe of him, her lightly worn assurance fell from her; she became, not a lady who was selecting, yes and paying for, a hat to set her son bravely out upon the adventure of school, that first step upon the mysterious highway of life, but merely a mean, shabby, workman's wife.

"This young gentleman served me the last time," she whispered irresolutely, indicating Perry. "I was in last year and he suited me nicely."

The little boy instantly sensed his mother's discomfiture, felt also the lowering oppression of the huge, dark figure above him, and, burying his face in his mother's dress, he began to whine plaintively.

"Mammie! Mammie, I want to go hame," he sobbed. "I don't want to stay here. I want hame."

"Stop greetin' now. Stop your greetin' at once, will ye." The poor woman, utterly humiliated, stood discomposed and faltering whilst the wailing child burrowed his head dourly into the sanctuary of her person; she shook him, and the more fiercely she shook him the louder he howled; her face coloured with shame and annoyance; she herself was near enough to tears. "Can that black-browed Brodie not keep out o' the place? it's the bairn's hat I wanted—not him," she thought, angrily, as she lifted the yelling child in her arms and said with great embarrassment: "I better come back another time. He's a bad boy. I'll come again when he can behave himself." While she cast, for appearance sake, this specious aspersion against her own child, her outraged maternal instinct assured her that she would never return. She had turned to go, and would have vanished irrevocably, when Perry in a low, tactful voice suggested tentatively from the background:

"Perhaps a sweetie——?" and from an unsuspected recess in a drawer he adroitly produced a large peppermint drop and poised it prominently, alluringly, between his finger and thumb. Instantly the child stopped crying and, exposing one large, brimming, doubtful eye from out the folds of its mother's bodice, lifted it calculatingly towards the sweet. The mother, at this indication of trust, halted, questioningly regarding the child.

"Would you?" she queried.

With a final, convulsive sob the boy nodded his head trustingly towards Perry, and stretched forward a small, avid claw. They returned. The sweet quickly bulged the wet, shining, young cheek, and, peace now being restored, Perry continued to soothe the child, to propitiate the mother, to minister to them both until finally, the notable purchase, for such he now made them feel it to be, was satisfactorily effected. As they departed, he showed them to the door with the same ubiquitous courtesy, receiving the mother's last grateful glance upon the top of his lowered unassuming head, whilst Brodie, who had moved sullenly, ponderously to the background, looked on gloomily.

Perry returned, rubbing his hands with satisfaction. Strange young man that he was, he built his conceit only upon his imaginary powers and took no credit for the undoubted attributes of quickness and intuition which were actually his; though he had just achieved a triumph of diplomacy and tact, yet his sole feeling was a humble satisfaction that he had saved the customer for Brodie before the eyes of the august master himself. He glanced up deferentially as the other spoke.

"I didna know we gave away sweeties wi' our hats," was all that Brodie said, as he turned sombrely into his office.

The day had begun; and it wore steadily on, with Brodie remaining still shut up in his room, immersed in his own, intimate thoughts. Across his stern face shadows drifted like clouds across the face of a dark mountain. He suffered. Despite the iron hardness of his will he could not prevent his responsive ears from quickening to every sound, from anticipating the gradual halting of footsteps as they drew near his shop, from analysing the lightest noise without his office, as if to differentiate the entry of a customer from Perry's restless pacings; yet, to-day, he felt that, though he had never before consciously noted them, the sounds were few and unsuggestive. The sun poured through the window upon him, the slush of the thaw which had succeeded the long frost was now completely gone, and the day was crisply dry, yet warm, so that in this dawning hint of spring the streets would, he knew, fill with people, happy, eager, thronging the shops; yet no chatter of enquiring voices broke the outer silence.

The blank, dividing wall which stood before him seemed to dissolve, under his piercing gaze and reveal, in the premises next door, a bustling and successful activity. A reaction from his sneering confidence of the morning took him, and he now morbidly visioned crowds of people jostling each other there in a passionate eagerness to buy. Savagely, he bit his lip and again picked up his discarded paper in an effort to read; but in a few moments, to his annoyance, he returned to himself to find that he gazed stupidly at the wall in front: as though it hypnotised him.

Moodily, he reflected how delightful it had been in the past to lie back in his chair—for what else had he done—with an eye through the half-open door, lording it over Perry and those who entered his domain. The menial duties of the business were entirely Perry's, who fetched and carried to his royal word, and he himself had not mounted the steps or lifted his hand to the shelves, or bound up a parcel for longer than he could remember. Most customers he ignored; with some he would stroll in whilst they were being served, nod casually, pick up the hat under review, pass his hand over its nap or bend the brim in haughty approval of his own merchandise, saying with his air: "Take it or leave it, but ye'll not get a better hat anywhere." Towards only a few, a handful from the best families of the county, did he actually direct his personal service and attention.

It had then been so delightful to feel assured that people must come to him, for, in his blind autocratic way, he had scarcely realised, had not paused to consider, that the absence of competition and lack of choice might drive many people to him, that necessity might be the mainstay of his business; but now, as he sat alone, he became unhappily aware that, for the time being at least, his monopoly was at an end. Nevertheless he would not, he firmly determined, alter his conduct; if he had not been obliged to run after people to solicit their paltry custom, he would not now be coerced into so doing; he had run after no man in his life and he now swore a solemn oath that he would never do so.

The dim, early days of his beginning in Levenford, so long since that he had almost forgotten, returned mistily to him; but through these mists he saw himself as a man who had never curried favour, nor fawned, nor acted the subservient toady. Though there had been no Perry then, he had been upright and honest and determined, had worked hard and asked no favour. And he had succeeded. He glowed as he thought of his slow rise in importance and consequence, of his recognition by the Council, his election to the Philosophical Club, of the gradual conception of his house, of its building, and, since that date, of the growing and subtle change in his situation to that unique, isolated, notable position which he now held in the town. It was, he told himself, the good blood that ran in his veins which had done that for him, which had brought him to the top, where he belonged, despite the handicaps which had beset him in his youth, that blood of his ancestors which—as in a noble horse—would always tell, and which would not fail him now.

Waves of anger at the injustice of his present position swept in on him, and he jumped to his feet. "Let them try to take it from me," he cried aloud, raising up his fist; "let them all come! I'll wipe them out like I destroy all who offend me. There was a rotten branch on the tree of my name," he shouted loudly, "and I cut it off. I'll smash everybody that interferes with me. I am James Brodie, and be damned to everybody and everything. Let them try to hinder me, to thieve my trade from me, try to take all I've got; let them do it! Whatever comes, I am still *myself*."

He subsided in his chair, unconscious of the fact that he had arisen, unaware that he had shouted to the empty room but hugging only, with a gloating satisfaction, that last precious thought. He was himself—James Brodie—no one but he understood, could ever comprehend, the full comfort, the delicious pride which that possession gave him. His thoughts rioted away from his present vicissitudes into a land of exalted dreams and longings, and, with his head sunk in his chest, he lost himself in the sublime contemplation of some future day when, unchecked, he would unleash the uncontrolled desires of his pride, when he would appease to satiation his craving for eminence and homage.

At last he sighed and, like a man awakening from the dreams of a drugged sleep, he blinked and shook himself. He looked at his watch, realised with a start that the end of this day, and of his self-ordained seclusion, was approaching. He arose slowly, yawned prodigiously, stretched himself, and, banishing from his features all traces of his recent, indulgent reverie, hardened his face again into a mask of hard indifference and went into the shop to review, as was his custom, the business of the day. This was invariably a pleasant duty, into which he infused a lordly dignity, giving himself the air of a feudal ruler receiving tribute from his vassal. Always Perry had a heap of gleaming silver, often a few gleaming sovereigns, and sometimes a rustling bank note to be transferred to the master's deep, hip pocket; and, when this had been effected, Brodie would run a casual eye over the lists of sales—casual, inasmuch as he recognised that Perry would never cheat him—it would, in his own words, "have been a pity for the little runt had he tried"—would slap his bulging pocket, assume his hat and, with a last curt command, be off, leaving Perry to close up and shutter the shop.

But, to-night, an unusual air seemed to cling to Perry, giving him an aspect at once blurred and disconsolate. Usually he opened the cash drawer with a proud and subservient flourish, as though to say: "We may not be much, but this is what we've done for you to-day, Mr.

Brodie, sir"; now, however, he pulled the drawer timidly open, with a faint deprecating twitch.

"A very quiet day, sir," he said meekly.

"The weather's been good," remonstrated Brodie testily. "What have you been playin' at? There's been plenty folks about."

"Oh! there's been a stir on the streets," replied Perry, "but quite a number—that's to say, a few have gone in——" He faltered. "They had an attractive window," he concluded lamely.

Brodie looked down at the drawer. Only six, miserable, silver shillings lay in the till.

IV

THE Levenford Philosophical Club was in convocation. Although to-night the session was by no means a plenary one, the room was comfortably filled by smoke and by a gathering of six members who, now ranged in comfortable chairs around the cordial fire which blazed upon the hearth, philosophised in this congenial atmosphere at their ease. Of those present two were engaged upon a silent game of draughts, easy, harmonious, relaxed, whilst the others lay back, smoked, talked, and wooed the inspiration of worthy thoughts by frequent, comforting sips of their grog.

The conversation was sporadic, the pauses, despite the choice richness of the language employed, sometimes more pregnant than the actual spoken words, the wave of a pipe more pungent than a pithy adjective, the glances of the members abstract, cogitative, and intellectually remote. Wearing modestly the distinction of their higher cerebration, they sat within the hallowed precincts of the club—the rallying-point of all these honest burghers in Levenford who might claim to be more notable than their fellow men—and, in the consciousness of their distinction, were at least content. To have achieved this club was, in itself, a feat which immediately conferred a cachet upon these happy individuals and rendered each the envy of less fortunate beings. To these the member would remark, of an evening, with, perchance, a nonchalant yawn: "Well! I think I'll away down to the club. There's a bit discussion on the night," and saunter off, whilst jealous eyes followed him down the street. To outsiders, those not of the elect, the social prestige of the club loomed largely, but so, also did the suggestion of its profound intellectual significance, for the sonorous name—Philosophical—breathed of the rarer and more refined realms of pure reason. True, a classical master who had come to the Levenford Academy, bearing the letters of a degree of Oxford University after his name, had remarked to a colleague: "I was keen to join when I heard the name but, to my disgust, I discovered it was nothing more than a smoking and drinking clique." What did he know, the ignorant English clown? Was he unaware of the six lectures, followed by lengthy debates, which took place at regular intervals during the winter? Had he not seen the neatly printed syllabus, which, like an amulet, reposed invariably in each member's top, right-hand, waistcoat pocket, containing the titles of this year's subjects of information and discussion? Had he but chosen he might have cast his grudging eyes upon such profound themes as:

"Our Immortal Bard—with Readings,"
"The Homing Pigeon in Health and Sickness,"
"The Growth of Shipbuilding in the Royal Borough on the Clyde,"
"Scottish Wit and Humour—with Local Anecdotes," or even,
"From Rivet-boy to Provost—the Life Story of the Late Respected Mathias Gloag of Levenford."

Such, indeed, were the weighty lectures to be delivered, but if, on these evenings when the associates' brains were not taxed by these deep matters, and their minds disengaged from solving the problems of race and nation, some trifling relaxation occurred—what disgrace lay in a gossip or a smoke, a game of the dambrod or even whist? And, as Phemie's tidy house was convenient to the back door, what harm was it to send round occasionally for a bit glass or even to adjourn at times to the "wee back parlour"?

Such arguments were, of course, unanswerable! It was, in addition, the function and practice of this unofficial town council to discuss in detail, and sit in deliberation upon, the people of the Borough, and their affairs. The ramifications of this subsidiary branch of their philosophising ranged from such diverse matters as the shrewish temper of Gibson's wife to the appropriate remonstration to be made to Blair of the Main's Farm, regarding the insanitary propensities of his cows upon the public highway; and a singularly reassuring feature, speaking volumes for Levenford equity, was the fact that the very members themselves had no prerogative or privilege immunising them from discussion by their fellow commentators. To-night, James Brodie was the subject of the discussion initiated by a chance glance at the empty chair in the corner, a contemplative pause, and the remark:

"Brodie's late to-night. I wonder will he be comin'."

"He'll be here, right enough," remarked Provost Gordon. "I've never known him so regular. He maun keep up his morale, ye ken." He looked round for approval at the use of this appropriate and noble-sounding word. "What I mean to infer," he explained, "is that he's got to put a face on things now, or else go under a' thegether."

The others sucked at their pipes and nodded silently. One of the draughts players moved a man, then looked up reflectively into the warm aromatic air, and said:

"Dod! time passes like a flash! It must be nearly a year now since he flung out that daughter o' his, on the night o' the big storm."

Paxton, who had the reputation of a head for figures, remarked:

"It'll be a year exactly in a fortnight's time; but it might be a single day for all that Levenford's seen o' Mary Brodie since then. I aye maintained, and I still maintain, that it was a bitter cruel thing that James Brodie did that night."

"Where is the lassock now?" queried someone.

"Weel," responded Paxton, "the story was that the Foyles of Darroch got her a position; but that's a' nonsense. She went off all by herself. The doctor wished to help her but she just up and away. It's said now that she's got a post in a big house in London—nothin' more nor less than a servant she would be—puir thing. The Foyles didn't do a thing for her afore they went back to Ireland."

"That's right," said the second draughts player; "old Foyle was fair broken up by the loss o' that boy o' his. 'Twas an awfu' thing, and no mistake, that Tay Bridge disaster. I'll never forget that night. I had been out at the guid sister's and had to get back hame in the teeth o' the wind, when a flyin' slate skiffed my ear by an inch. It nearly took ma heid off."

"That wad have been a worse calamity to the town than the loss o' the Bridge, John," sniggered Grierson from his corner. "We would need to ha' put ye up a braw monument at the Cross, like the braw new Livingstone statue in George Square up in the city. Think what ye've missed. If it had struck ye, man, ye would have been another o' Scotland's heroes."

"Weel, the new bridge maun be a bit stronger before they get me to gang across it. 'Twas a perfect scandal that a' they good lives were flung awa'. I contend there should have been a punishment for them that was to blame," said the first draughts player, covering the discomfiture of his companion.

"Man! Ye canna punish the Almighty," drawled Grierson; "'twas an act of God, and ye canna claim damages off Him—at least not successfully."

"Wheesht, man, Grierson," admonished the Provost—by virtue of his position. "Watch that tongue o' yours; that's downright blasphemy ye're talkin'."

"Na! Na! Provost," soothed Grierson. "It's just the law—a wee bit o' the law ye ken. No offence to the company, or the Almighty, or yourself," he added, with a leer.

There was an uncomfortable pause, when it looked as if the harmony of the discussion might be destroyed, but eventually the Provost continued:

192

"Brodie maun be losing trade hand over fist these days. I never see a soul in his shop."

"The prices the Mungo Company's sellin' at wad empty anybody's shop that tried to compete wi' them," said Paxton, with some show of sympathy. "They've made up their minds to feenish him first and make their profits after. He's got on the wrang side o' the fence a' thegether. It looks to me gey like ruin."

"Ruin is the richt word," drawled Grierson, who from his corner looked knowingly as if he could, if he chose, disclose a large, ripe plum of information on the subject.

"But he maun be a warm man though, Brodie. He's aye free o' his money—splashin' it about like water, spendin' it on anything that might take his fancy. He has the best o' everything, and then ye wad think that wasna good enough for him. Look at his dress, look at his braw new tiepin and signet ring, and besides," the speaker looked round cautiously before he uttered the next words, "look at his graund country-castle." A slight smirk seemed to traverse the entire party, and covert glances of well-subdued amusement were exchanged.

"Look at his auld wife's boots, her elegant clothes, and braw appearance," replied Grierson. "Look at his bank balance—his wee Nessie was a fortnight late wi' her fees at the Academy this quarter. Look at the flicker in his proud eye when he thinks ye're not watchin' him. I tell you that the big, big man—that he thinks he is—is beginnin' to feel a wee bittie vexed about things." An intense undercurrent of innuendo lay behind the words as he continued: "I may be wrong but, in my humble opinion, I consider that James Brodie is goin' through the worst time o' his life. And if he's not careful he'll be down where he's flung many another man—right down in the gutter!"

"Ay, he's an awfu' man to make enemies. Speakin' o' the gutter, though, I maun tell you this one." Paxton took a few reflective draws at his pipe. "I was passin' Brodie's shop the other Saturday night when a kind o' commotion stopped me." He puffed again twice. "There was a big, drucken street-worker in the shop, fu' as a whelk, and fu' o' his week's wages—in the mood to fling out the pound notes like a harrier's trail—I saw the roll o' notes in his hand—and he stood there swayin' afore Brodie, ordering a couple o' hats and a couple o' bonnets, and this and that and goodness knows a' what. He was in the mood to buy up the whole shop, ay and pay for't too. Brodie, and God knows he must have needed the money sorely, stood glarin' at him out o' his starin' red eye." Reaching the climax of his story he sucked interminably at this pipe, before removing it, pointing it emphatically, and proceeding: " 'If ye can't say "please" when ye address me,' Brodie was snarlin', 'then ye'll get nothing here. Other places,' he sneered, 'might stand that style o' thing. Go there if ye choose, but if ye come to me ye'll behave yourself or get out.' I didna hear what the other said in reply, but it must have outraged Brodie frightful, for he louped the counter and gripped the other's neck, and before ye could say knife had flung him out o' the shop right into the dirty gutter, where he lay, knocked stupid, at my feet."

A pregnant pause succeeded the anecdote.

"Ay," sighed the first draughts player at last, "he has an unco' temper. His pride is fair terrifyin' now. It's his worst enemy. He used no' to be so conspicuous in that respect, but of late years it's fair run awa' wi' him. He's as proud as Lucifer."

"And 'tis my belief he'll have the same fall," inserted Grierson. "He's bloated with his own vanity! It's worked on him till it's like a very mania."

"And the rideeclous cause o't too!" said Paxton, in a low cautious tone; "that claimin' kinship wi' the Wintons! I'll swear he thinks he should be the Earl himself. 'Tis strange, too, the way he hides it, yet feasts on it."

"They wouldna own him. Brodie may have the name. He may look like the Wintons. But what's in a name and what's in a likeness?" said the first draughts player. "He hasna a shadow o' proof."

"I'm afeared what proof there was had a big, black bar through it," remarked Grierson judicially; "for I'm gey and certain that onything that might have happened lang back took place the wrang side o' the blanket. That's why our friend willna blatter it out. That's maybe the bonnie kinship."

" 'Tis not only kinship that he claims," said Provost Gordon slowly. "Na! Na! the disease has swelled beyond that. I hardly like to come over it to ye and deed I'm hardly sure myself, but I'll mention no names and ye mustna repeat it. I had it from a man who saw James Brodie when he was the worse o' liquor, mad ravin' drunk. There's no' many has seen that," he continued, "for he's a close man in they things. But this night his dour tongue was loosed and he talked and——"

"Another time, Provost," cried Paxton suddenly.

"Wheesht, man, wheesht."

"Talk o' the deevil."

"About that new trap o' yours now, Provost, will ye——"

Brodie had entered the room. He came in heavily, blinking at the sudden transition from the darkness to the lighted room, and frowning from the bitter suspicion that he had been at the moment of his entry the object of their backbiting tongues. His dour, hard face had to-night a pale grimness, as he looked round the company, nodding his head silently several times in salutation, more in the manner of a challenge than a greeting.

"Come away in, come away in," remarked Grierson smoothly, "we were just wonderin' if the rain that was threatenin' had come on yet."

194

"It's still dry," said Brodie gruffly. His voice was flat, had lost its old resonant timbre, was, like the brooding mask of his face, inexpressive of anything but stoic endurance. He took out his pipe and began to fill it. An old man, the messenger and factotum of the club, dignified as such by a green baize apron, put his head round the door in speechless enquiry, and to him Brodie shortly remarked: "The usual."

A momentary silence descended upon the group whilst the old man retreated, was absent, returned shamblingly with a large whisky for Brodie, then finally departed. The Provost felt it his duty to break the awkward stillness which had descended upon the group and, looking at Brodie, he said, in a kindly tone, moved in spite of himself by the other's ghastly look:

"Well, Brodie man, how are things with ye? How's the world waggin' now?"

"Oh! fair, Provost! very fair," replied Brodie slowly. "Nothing to complain about." The grim assumption of indifference in his tone was almost tragic, and deceived none of the assembly, but Gordon, with an assumption of heartiness, retorted:

"That's fine! That's the ticket! We're expectin' every day to see the Mungo Company wi' the shutters up."

Brodie accepted this polite fiction and the spurious murmur of assent from the group which followed it, not with the blatant satisfaction which it would have provoked six months ago but, in the face of his present position, with a blank indifference which the others did not fail to observe. They might discuss him freely in his absence, criticise, condemn, or even vilify him, but when he was in their midst their strongly expressed feelings weakened sensibly under the shadow of his actual presence, and they were impelled, often against their wish, to make some flattering remark which they did not mean, and which they had not intended to utter.

He was a man whom they thought wiser to humour, better to keep on the right side of, safer to propitiate than to enrage, but now, as they noted his moody humour, and slyly watched his oppressed demeanour, they wondered if his iron control might be at last beginning to fail him.

A gentle, insinuating voice from the corner, addressing the company at large, broke into their general air of meditation.

"If you're thinkin' o' the Company's shutters goin' up you'll have a' to bide a wee—na, na, they'll not be shuttin' up shop—for a bit any way—not for a bittie," drawled Grierson.

"How's that?" queried someone.

"Oh! just a little private information," answered Grierson complacently, pursing his lips, placing his finger tips together and beaming on the company, especially upon Brodie, with an aspect of secret yet benevolent comprehension. Brodie looked up quickly from beneath his tufted eyebrows, not fearing the man but dreading, from his past experience, the sly, meek attitude which betokened in the other a deep and calculating venom.

"What is it then, man?" asked Paxton. "Out with it!"

But now that he had thoroughly aroused their curiosity, Grierson was in no haste to divulge his secret information and still smiled sleekly, keeping them on tenterhooks, tantalising them with the plum which would not drop from his lips until it was juicy with ripeness.

"Odd! you wouldna be interested," he purred. "'Tis just a leetle piece o' local news I happened to get wind o' privately."

"Do you know yourself, Brodie?" asked Paxton, in an effort to terminate the irritating procrastination.

Brodie shook his head mutely, thinking bitterly how Grierson got his finger first into every pie, how he was always the last to remove it.

"It's just a wee, insignificant bit of information," Grierson said, with increased satisfaction.

"Then out with it, ye sly deevil!"

"Well, if you must know, the district manager o' Mungo's is goin' away, now that they're so firmly established. I'm told they're doin' uncommon weel." He smiled blandly at Brodie and continued: "Ay! they've made a clever move, too, in offering the vacant post—and a real fine post it is an' all—to a Levenford man. He's been offered it and he's accepted it."

"Who is't then?" cried several voices.

"Oh, he's a real deservin' chap, is the new local manager o' the Mungo Company."

"What's his name then?"

"It's our friend's assistant, none other than young Peter Perry," drawled Grierson, with a triumphant wave of his hand towards Brodie.

Immediately a babble of comment broke out.

"Man, ye don't say so!"

"The auld, weedowed mother will be unco' pleased about that."

"What a step up for the young fellow!"

"He would jump at it like a cock at a groset."

Then, as the first flush of excitement at the unexpected tit-bit of local gossip subsided, and the real realisation of its meaning to Brodie dawned upon them, a silence fell, and all eyes were turned upon him. He sat perfectly still, stunned at the news, every muscle in his huge body rigid, his jaw set, his teeth gripping the stem of his pipe with the increasing pressure of a slowly closing vice. So Perry was leaving him, Perry upon whom of late he had come to depend utterly, realising at last that he had himself got out of the way of serving, that he was above it now, and was unable to lower himself to such lackey's work had he even desired it. A sharp crack split the attentive silence, as, with the onset of a pang of sudden bitterness, his teeth compressed themselves with such a vicious, final force upon his pipe that the stem snapped through.

As though in a trance, he looked at the riven pipe in his hand for a long second, then spat out the broken end coarsely upon the floor, looked again stupidly at the ruined meerschaum, and muttered to himself, unconscious that they heard him:

"I liked that pipe—liked it weel. It was my favourite."

Then he became aware of the ring of faces regarding him as though he sat in an arena for their contemplation, became aware that he must show them how he met the bitter shock of the blow, or better, show them that it held no bitterness for him. He stretched out towards his glass, raised it to his lips with a hand as steady as a rock, looked steadily back at Grierson, whose gaze immediately slipped off that unwavering stare. He would at that moment have given his right hand for the power to utter some cutting, withering retort which would shrivel the other by its very potency, but, despite a fury of endeavour, his brain was not sufficiently agile, his slow, ponderous wit refused to function, and all that he could do was to say, with an attempt at his habitual, sneering grimace:

"It's of no concern, not the slightest! Not the slightest concern to me!"

"I hope he'll not take any o' your trade with him," said Paxton solicitously.

"Now I come to think on't 'tis a downright dirty trick, Mr. Brodie," came in a toadying tone from one of the draughts players. "He kens a' your customers."

"Trust these Mungo bodies to move smartly. They're a deevelish clever lot in my opeenion," said another voice.

"Myself, I think it's raither a poor spirit," drawled Grierson consideringly. "Somehow it gives me the impression that he's just like a rat leavin' the sinkin' ship."

There was a sudden hush whilst everyone sat aghast at the audacity of this remark, the most direct affront that had ever been offered to Brodie in that club room. They expected him to arise and rend the puny form of Grierson, tear him apart by the sudden exertion of his brute strength, but instead he remained inert, unheeding, as if he had not heard or understood the other's remark. With his thoughts sunk in a gloomy abyss, he reflected that this was the most deadly blow he had suffered of any, although already they had smote him hip and thigh.

They had lavished their abundant capital in the struggle against him. In a dozen ways had exercised their ingenious cunning, but now in taking Perry they had snapped his last mainstay. Appropriately, he recollected his assistant's strange suppressed manner that night, his half-intimated, half-exultant look, as if he had been glad yet regretful, as if he had wished to speak and yet could not summon courage to do so. Strangely, he did not blame Perry, realising in justice that the other had merely accepted a better offer than he could have made, and instead any animosity that stirred within him turned against the Mungo Company itself. His feeling, however, was at this moment, not truly one of hatred, but rather of curious compassion for himself, a sad consideration that he, so noble, so worthy, should suffer at such treacherous hands, should in consequence be compelled continually to assume this false front of indifference, when hitherto his careless arrogance had, unwittingly, protected him like armour. Then, amongst his meditations, he became again aware of the circle of watching eyes and the imperative need for speech, and hardly knowing what he said, yet whipping himself to anger, he began:

"I've always fought fair! I've always fought wi' clean hands. I wouldna lower myself to the level o' bribery and corruption, and if they've bribed that pimply, little snipe to leave me then they're gey and welcome to him. It'll save me the bother o' sackin' him—ay, they can keep him while they last. I don't give a tinker's curse about the whole affair." Reassured by his own speech, carried away by the expression of a sentiment he had not felt, his words grew louder, more confident, his glance more defiant and assured. "No! not a tinker's damn do I give," he cried. "But I'll not have him back again. Oh, dear, no! Let him draw his bribes while he can—and when he's able—for when they're burst and a' to hell, and he comes whinin' back for his auld job, then I'll see him in hell as weel, before I lift a hand to help him. He's unco' quick to run away. I've no doubt he thinks his fortune's made—the poor fool—but when he's back in the sheuch I took him out o', he'll regret the day he ever left the house o' James Brodie."

He was transfigured, exalted by his speech, now believing utterly in this declamation which contrasted so absolutely with his sombre, sensible perception of a moment before, and, his spirit asserting itself more powerfully in the very recognition of its power he glared back at them with wide, excited pupils. He hugged within himself the reflection that he could still control, dominate, overawe them, and as at last an idea, delightful and appropriate, struck him he drew himself up and cried:

"No! it'll take more than that to upset James Brodie in spite o' what our wee friend in the corner has had the nerve to suggest. When ye hear me complainin' it'll be enough to get out your crape, and it'll be a lang, lang time before ye need mournin' on that account. It's a joke though"—his eye flickered round them with a rampant facetiousness —"by gad! it's a joke that's worth a dram to us a'. Gentlemen," he cried, in a lordly voice, "shall we adjourn so that you may join me in a glass?"

They at once applauded him, delighted with his generous spirit, delighted at the thought of free refreshment, scenting ahead the chance of a carousal.

"Good for you, Brodie!"

"Scotland for ever! A man's a man for a' that."

"I'm wi' ye, juist a wee deoch-an-dorris to keep out the cauld."

"There's life in the auld horse yet!"

The Provost himself slapped him on the back. "Man, Brodie! you're a caution. Ye've the pluck o' a lion, the strength o' a bull, ay and the pride o' the deevil—there's no beatin' of ye. I believe ye wad dee before ye took a lickin'." At these words they stood up, concurring, and all but Grierson swarmed round him so that he stood amongst them, his fierce glance encompassing them, encouraging yet rebuking, sanctioning yet subduing, approving yet admonishing, like an emperor surrounded by his court. His blood, the blood that was noble like an emperor's, coursed more imperially in his veins than did the thin, serous fluid that was in theirs. In his heavy brain he felt he had achieved a great and noble action, that his gesture, in the teeth of disaster, had been sublime.

"Lay on, MacDuff," they cried, stirred by the unwonted laxity and magnanimity of his usually unapproachable nature, impatient to savour the rich, golden liquor he would provide for them. As he led them through the back door of the club into the outer air and they filed, eventually, into Phemie's wee back parlour, he felt the danger was over, that he was again the master of them.

Soon the drinks were flowing as they toasted him jubilantly, in McDonald's finest Chieftain whisky, for his generosity, his discrimination, his strength. As he flung out a golden sovereign, birling it grandly on to the round, mahogany table, a faint glimmering of sense at the back of his mind whispered to him how little he could afford it now, but he thrust the thought back again, stamped it out fiercely with a loud: "Here's to us—wha's like us?"

"It's a be-autiful dram, this," purred Grierson, smacking his lips appreciatively as he held his glass up to the light. "A beautiful dram, mild as mother's milk and smooth as—weel smooth as the nap on one o' our friend's braw hats. The only pity is that it's so dreshed more expensive than orner stuff." He tittered spitefully, knowingly towards Brodie.

"Drink it up then, man!" replied Brodie loudly. "Lap it up when ye get the chance. You're no' payin' for't. By God, if we were a' as mean as you, the world would stop goin' round."

"That's one to put in your pipe, Grierson," laughed Paxton, hoarsely.

"Speakin' o' stinginess—did ye hear the latest one about our wee friend here?" cried the Provost, with a nod towards Grierson, and a wink at Brodie.

"No! what was it?" they chorused. "Tell us, Provost."

"Weel," replied Gordon, with a knowing look, "it's short and sweet. The other day a wheen bairns were playin' about outside our friend's grain store, beside a big sack o' beans at the door, when up comes the son o' the house. 'Get away, boys,' young Grierson cries, 'and don't touch these beans or my feyther'll find out. He's got every one o' them counted!' "

A roar of appreciation arose from the assembly, through which Grierson murmured easily, blinking through the smoke:

"I'll no deny I ken how many beans make five, Provost, but it's a handy thing these days wi' so much hardship and poverty about."

But Brodie, upon his throne, the already warmed pith of him flaming under the potent whisky, neither heard nor heeded the innuendo as, filled with a wild elation, the desire to act, to liberate his strength, to smash something, seized him, and, raising his empty glass high above his head, he suddenly shouted, without point in the conversation: "To hell with them! To hell with these measly Mungo swine!" and shattered the heavy tumbler violently against the wall.

The others, now mellow for his mood, responded gleefully.

"That's the spirit!"

"Another round, gentlemen."

"No heeltaps."

"Gie us a song, Wullie."

"Speech! Speech!" came their shouts.

At this point a discreet knock upon the door, followed by the noiseless entry, felt-slippered yet formidable, of the landlady interrupted the fluid current of their hilarity.

"Ye're merry the night, gentlemen," she said with a thin, tight-lipped smile which inferred that their gaiety was not entirely becoming to them or wholly pleasing to her. "I hope ye'll no' forget the good name o' the house." Much as she valued their connection she was too remote, too virtuous, altogether too much of an institution to be imposed upon by them. "I dinna like to hear the smash o' glass," she added, acidly.

"Tits, Phemie, woman, it'll be payed for," cried Brodie. She nodded slightly, as though to convey to him that she had already taken that for granted, but in a slightly mollified tone she remarked:

"What's the occasion?"

"Just a little celebration given by our esteemed member at the head o' the table," murmured Grierson. "I dinna ken what it's to celebrate exactly, but ye micht ca' it a beanfeast without any beans."

"Never mind him, Phemie, send us in another hauf mutchkin," cried a voice.

"Will ye have a wee hauf yersel', Phemie?" remarked the Provost, breezily.

"Come awa' and sit on my knee, Phemie," cried one of the erstwhile draughts players—now, alas, incapable of differentiating a crowned man from a peppermint oddfellow.

"Send in the whisky, Phemie," demanded Brodie. "I'll make them a' behave themselves."

She reproved them individually and collectively with her glance, raised a warning forefinger, and padded out as silently as she had come, murmuring as she went:

"Dinna forget the name o' the house. I'll send ye in the speerits, but ye maun keep quiet, ye maun mind the good name o' the house."

When she had gone the ball of their gaiety rolled off again, quickly gathered speed, and bounded more exuberantly than before.

"Never mind Phemie," cried a voice, "her bark is waur than her bite, but her face is waur than the two o' them thegither."

"Ye wad think this public o' hers was a tabernacle o' righteousness," cried another, "she's that uncommon godly about it. She wad have ye drink like ye were in the kirk."

"There's a braw, wee tittie in the front pews, onyway," replied the more bibulous draughts player. "They say Nancy, the barmaid, is as obleegin' as she's bonnie." He winked round the assembly knowingly.

"Tits, man, tits!" cried the Provost reprovingly. "Don't file the nest that you're sittin' in."

"That's the cuckoo ye wad be meanin'," replied the other agreeably; "but I'm no' that."

"Would ye like me to give ye a verse o' Burns?" called out Paxton. "I'm just ripe to let ye have 'The Devil amang the Tailors.' "

"Our chairman promised us a bit speech, did he not?" remarked Grierson, insinuatingly.

"Ay! Come awa' wi' that speech ye were goin' to give us," cried the Provost.

"Speech!" they insisted again. "Speech from the chairman."

Brodie's soaring pride, wafted higher by their tipsy cries, reached upward to a sublimated region where his limitations ceased, in the refined air of which his tongue seemed fluent, his incapacity for the articulate utterance of his inner thoughts forgotten.

"Very well," he called out, "I'll give ye a speech." He rose, inflating his chest, widening his eyes at them, swinging slightly from side to side on the fulcrum of his feet, wondering, now that he had risen, what he should say.

"Gentlemen," he began at length, slowly, but amidst ready applause, "ye all know who I am. I'm Brodie, James Brodie, and what that name means, maybe ye can guess." He paused, surveying each member of the group in turn. "Ay, I'm James Brodie, and in the Royal Borough of Levenford, and beyond it, too, it is a name that is respected and esteemed. Show me the man that says a word against it and I'll show you what these two hands will do to him." He shot out his huge hands wildly and let them throttle the vacant air before him, missing in his emotion the general apathy, the gloating relish in Grierson's satirical eyes, and seeing only reverence. "If I but chose I could tell you something that would startle ye to the very core." Then, as his eyes swept round the table, he lowered his voice to a hoarse, confidential whisper, shook his head cunningly. "But no! I'm not goin' to do it! Guess if ye like, but I'm not goin' to tell ye now—ye may never know. Never!" He shouted the word. "But it's there; and so long as I breathe breath into this body o' mine I will uphold my name. I've had an unco' trouble lately that would have bent a strong man and broken a weaker one, but what has it done to me? I'm still here, still the same James Brodie, but stronger, more determined than before. 'If your hand offend ye cut it off' says the Scriptures—I've had to cut my own flesh and blood, ay but it was without flinchin' that I used the axe. I've had trouble within and trouble without, sneakin' rogues and thievin' swine at my very ain' door, false friends and dirty enemies round about me, ay and sly, sleekit backbiters as weel." He looked grimly at Grierson. "But through it all and above it all James Brodie will stand hard and fast like the Castle Rock, ay and wi' his head as high above the air," he shouted, thumping his chest with his big fist and concluding in a loud full voice: "I tell ye I'll show ye all! I'll show every one o' ye." Then, having reached the climax of his feelings, for the spontaneous words had rushed from him unknowingly at the urge of his emotions, he sat down heavily, saying in a natural undertone: "And now we'll have another dram all round."

The last part of his speech was appreciated, loudly cheered, applauded by a rattle of glasses upon the hard table, echoed by Grierson's suave drawl:

"Good! I havena enjoyed a speech like that since Drunken Tam harangued the Baillies through the windae o' the jail."

They drank to him, to his oration, to his future; someone sang in a broken falsetto; Paxton protested, unheeded, that he, too, wanted to make a speech; the second draughts player attempted to tell a long, involved, and unseemly story; there were several songs with shouted choruses. Then, abruptly, Brodie, who had, with altered mood, remained cold, impassive, and disdainful amongst their mirth, jerked back his chair and got up to go. He knew the value of these sudden departures, felt the restrained dignity of his leaving the sodden dogs to sing and rant in the fashion that fitted them, whilst he departed at the moment when he could so retire with majesty and honour.

"What's the matter, man? Ye're not awa' hame yet," cried the Provost. "It's not near struck the twal' yet!"

"Bide a wee and we'll punish another haulf mutchkin atween us a'."

"Is the wee wifie waitin' on ye, then?" whispered Grierson blandly.

"I'm away," he cried roughly, buttoning up his jacket and stamping his feet, and, ignoring their profuse protests, he looked at them solemnly, saying:

"Gentlemen! Good night."

Their shouts followed him out of the room into the cool night wind, and filled him with a thrilling elation which increased inversely as the sounds of their homage weakened; the cries were like hosannahs, diminishing, yet pursuing, on the cold, sweet air that rose like frosted incense from the rimed streets. It had been a night, he told himself, as he made his way homewards amongst the white-limned houses that stood like silent temples in a deserted city, and, as he swelled with self-esteem, he felt he had justified himself in his own and in their eyes. The whisky in him made his step elastic, springy, and youthful; he wanted to walk over mountains in this crisping exaltation that sparked equally within him and in the delicious atmosphere around him; his body tingled and he thought in terms of wild, erotic, incoherent desires, peopling the dark rooms of every house he passed with concealed yet intimate activity, feeling, with a galling sense of injustice, that he must in future find some outlet for the surge of his suppressed and unattracted flesh. The short distance which he traversed to his home whetted his appetite for some fitting termination to the glorious evening and, almost in expectation, he let himself into his house and shot home the lock of the outer door with a flourish of the heavy key.

A light, he observed, still burned in the kitchen, a manifestation at once unusual and disturbing, as, when he came in late, all lights had been extinguished save that which burned faithfully in the hall, waiting to illuminate his return. He looked at his watch, saw the time to be half-past eleven, then viewed again the light which winked at him in the dim hall as it shone from beneath the closed door. With a frown he replaced his watch, stalked along the lobby, and seizing the door-handle firmly, with one push burst into the kitchen; there he stood erect, surveying the room and the figure of his wife as she sat crouching over the dull embers of the fire. At his entry she started, oppressed, although she awaited him, by the sudden intrusion into her dejected reverie of his frowning, unspoken disapproval. As she looked round in trepidation, showing red, inflamed eyes, he glared at her more angrily. "What's the matter with you?" he said, emphasising the last word like a gibe. "What are ye doin' up at this hour wi' your bleary, baggy een like saucers?"

"Father," she whispered, "ye'll not be angry, will ye?"

"What in God's name are ye snivelling for?" Was this the kind of homecoming that he merited, and on such a night as this had been? "Can ye not be in bed before I come in," he gnashed at her. "I don't have to look at ye there, ye auld trollop. You're a beautiful specimen o' a thing to come hame to, right enough. Did ye expect me to tak' ye out courtin' on this braw, moonlight night? You that's got as much draw in ye as an auld, cracked pipe."

As she looked upwards into his dark, disgusted face she seemed to shrink more into herself, her substance became less than a shadow, coherent speech failed her, but tremblingly, indistinctly, she articulated one word: "Matt!"

"Matt! Your dear, wee Matt! What's wrong wi' him next?" he fleered at her. "Has he swallowed another plum stane?"

"This letter," she faltered. "It—it came for me this mornin'. I've been feared to show you it all day," and, with a shaking hand, she handed him the crushed sheet of paper which she had all day hidden against her terrified, palpitating breast. With a derisive growl he rudely snatched the letter from her fingers and slowly read it, whilst she rocked herself to and fro distractedly, wailing with a tongue which was now loosed in the defence of her son: "I couldna keep it to mysel' a minute longer. I had to sit up for ye. Don't be angry wi' him, father. He doesna mean to vex you, I'm sure. We don't know the facts and it must be a terrible country out there. I knew something must be wrong wi' the boy when he stopped writin' regular. He'll be better at hame."

He had finished reading the few scrawled lines.

"So your big, braw, successful son is comin' hame to ye," he snarled. "Hame to his loving mother, and all her loving care."

"Maybe it's for the best," she whispered. "I'll be glad to have him back and to nurse him back to strength if he needs it."

"I ken you'll be glad to have him back, ye auld fool—but I don't give a damn for that." He again considered the crushed sheet with aversion before compressing it into a ball within his shut fist and jerking it furiously into the fireplace.

"What's the reason o' him throwin' up his good job like this?"

"I know no more nor yourself, father, but I think he must be poorly in himself. His constitution was aye delicate. He wasna really fitted for the tropics."

He showed his teeth at her.

"Fitted, your silly, empty head. 'Twas you made him a milk and water softie with all your sapsy treatment o' him. 'Matt dear,' he mimicked, 'come to your mother and she'll gie ye a penny. Never mind your father, lambie dear, come and Mamma will pet ye, dearie.' Is't that what brings him fleein' back to your dirty apron strings? If it is I'll string them round his neck. 'P.S. Please tell father,' " he sneered, quoting the burnt letter. "He hasna even the gumption to write to me himself, the washy, pithless pup. He's got to get his sweet, gentle mother to break the guid news. Oh! he's a right manly whelp."

"Oh! James, would ye no' comfort me a little?" she implored. "I'm that downright wretched. I dinna ken what has happened and the uncertainty is fair killin' me. I'm feared for my bairn."

"Comfort ye, auld wife!" he sang at her. "I would look well, would I not, puttin' my arm round a bag like you?" Then, in a harsh tone of repugnance, he continued: "I canna thole ye! Ye know that! Ye're as much good to me as an empty jeely jar. Ye're just about as much a success o' a wife as ye are o' a mother. One o' your litter has made a bonnie disgrace o' ye, and this one seems to be on his way. Ay, he seems well on his way. He's a credit to your upbringing o' him." Then his eyes darkened suddenly. "Take care though ye don't interfere wi' my Nessie. She belongs to me. Don't lay a finger on her. Keep your soft fiddle faddle away from her or I'll brain ye."

"Ye'll give him a home, father," she moaned. "Ye'll not show him the door?"

He laughed hatefully at her.

"It would kill me if ye turned him out like—like——" She broke down completely.

"I'll have to think about it," he replied, in an odious tone, revelling in the thought of keeping her in suspense, diverting against her all his indignant displeasure at Matthew's sudden defection and thrusting the entire blame upon her of this failure of her son. Hating her already in his defeated desire for the pleasure she could not give him, he loathed her the more inordinately because of this failure of her son, and he would, he told himself, let her pay for it dearly, make her the chopping block for the keen blade of his wrath. The fact that Matthew should have given notice and be sailing for home was entirely her offence; invariably the faults of the children made them hers, their virtues his.

"You're too just a man not to hear what he's to say, or what he wants, father," she persisted, in a ridiculous, wheedling voice. "A fine, big man like you wouldna do onything like that. Ye would give him a hearin', let him explain—there's bound to be a reason."

"There'll be a reason right enough," he sneered at her. "He'll want to come and live off his father, I've no doubt, as if we hadna enough to do without feedin' his big, blabby mouth. That'll be the reason o' the grand home comin'. I've no doubt he thinks he's in for a grand soft time here, wi' me to work for him and you to lick the mud off his boots. Damn it all—— It's too much for a man to put up wi'." A gust of passion mixed with a cold sleet of antipathy caught him. "It's too much," he yelled at her again. "Too blasted much." Raising up his hand as though to menace her with its power, he held it there for one tense moment, then with a sudden gesture he directed it towards the gas, turned out the light and, throwing the effacing darkness around her, went heavily out of the room.

Mrs. Brodie, left in the obliterating blackness, the last dying spark of the cinders of the fire barely silhouetting the amorphous outlines of her contracted figure, sat cowed and still. For a long time she waited, silent and reflective, while her sad thoughts flowed from her like dark waves, oppressing and filling the room with a deeper and more melancholy obscurity. She waited whilst the embers grew cold, until he would be undressed, in bed, and perhaps asleep, then she moved her set, unwilling frame, crept out of the kitchen, like a hunted animal from its cave, and crawled warily upstairs. The boards which had groaned and creaked when Brodie ascended were noiseless under her frail weight, but, though her movements were soundless, a faint sigh of relief emanated from her into the darkness as, at the door of the bedroom, the heavy sound of her husband's breathing met her. He slept, and, feeling her way into and about the room she shed her shabby, spotted garments; laying them in a heap on her chair ready for the morning, she crept cautiously into bed, fearfully keeping her wilted body away from his, like a poor weak sheep couching itself beside a sleeping lion.

<h1 style="text-align:center">V</h1>

"MAMMA," said Nessie, on the following Saturday, "what is Matt coming back for?"

She was playing about the house and dragging after her mother in the desultory, querulous manner of a child to whom a wet Saturday morning is the worst evil of the week.

"The climate wasna suitable to him," replied Mrs. Brodie shortly. It was deeply rooted in the mind of Mamma as an essential tenet of the Brodie doctrine that from the young must be kept all knowledge of the inner workings of the affairs, relationships, and actions of the house, the more so if they were disagreeable. To questions concerning the deeper and more abstract aspects of Brodie conduct and, indeed, of life in general the consoling answer was: "You'll know some day, dear. All in good time!" and, to divert interrogations, the issue of which could not be avoided, Mamma considered it no sin to lie whitely and speciously to maintain inviolate the pride and dignity of the family.

"There's dreadful fevers out there," she continued; and a vague idea of improving Nessie's natural history made her add, "and lions, tigers, elephants, and giraffes, and all manner o' curious beasts and insects."

"But, Mamma!" persisted Nessie, "Jenny Paxton said it was all through the Yard that our Matt had got the sack for not attendin' to his work."

"She told a wicked untruth then. Your brother resigned his position like a gentleman."

"When will he be back, Mamma? Will he bring me anything, do you think? Will he bring me a monkey and a parrot? I would like a parrot better than a monkey. A monkey would scratch me but a parrot would talk to me and say, 'Pretty Polly,' and that's more than a canary can do, isn't it?" She paused meditatively, then resumed, "No; I'll not have that, I would have to clean its cage. I think I would like a pair of honky-tonky, morocco slippers or—or a bonnie, wee string o' coral beads. Will ye tell him, Mamma?"

"Be quiet, girl! How can I write to him when he's on his way home? Besides, Matt has more to think of than beads for you. You'll see him soon enough."

"Will he be here soon, then?"

"You'll know all in good time, Nessie." Then, voicing her own hopes, she added: "It might be in about ten days, if he left soon after his letter."

"Ten days! that's fine," Nessie chanted, and began to skip about with a more lively air. "I'll maybe have some fun when Matt comes back, forbye the wee string o' beads. It's been terrible since——" She stopped abruptly against the blank, forbidding wall of a subject absolutely interdicted, looked timidly at her mother, paused for a moment in confusion, then, as she saw that she was not to be reprimanded, began again, by a childish association of ideas: "What does it mean to be in deep water, Mamma?"

"What are ye talkin' about now, Nessie. Ye run on like a spoutin' waterfall. Can ye not let me get my work done."

"One of the girls in the class asked if my father could swim, because she heard her father sayin' that James Brodie was gettin' into deep water."

"Will you stop tormentin' me with your silly nonsense, Nessie," cried Mamma. "Your father can look after himself without your help. It's an impertinence for his name to be lifted like that." Nevertheless, the childish question touched her with a sharp, sudden misgiving, and, as she picked up a duster and went out of the kitchen, she wondered vaguely if there was any intrinsic reason for the exacerbation of Brodie's meanness with her, for the whittling and paring of her housekeeping allowance which had for months past made it impossible for her to make ends meet.

"Oh! it's not me, Mamma," replied Nessie, narrowing her small mouth virtuously, and following her mother into the parlour. "It's what the other girls in the class say. You would think there was something funny about us the way they go on. I'm better than them amn't I, Mamma? My father could beat all theirs tied together."

"Your father's a man in a million." It cost Mrs. Brodie an effort to say these words, but she uttered them heroically, unconscious of the ambiguous nature of her phrase, striving only to maintain the best traditions of the house. "Ye must never listen to a thing against him. Folks say bitter things when they're jealous o' a man."

"They're just a lot of cheeky, big things. I'm going to tell the teacher if they say another word about us," concluded Nessie, pressing her nose against the window like a small blob of putty. "It's still raining, coming down heavy as heavy—hang it!"

"Nessie! Don't say hang it. It's not right. You're not to use bad words," reprimanded Mamma, interrupting her polishing of the brass candlesticks on the burr walnut front of the piano. She would take no chances with Nessie! The first sign of error must be corrected! "Remember, now, or I'll tell your father," she threatened, addressing her heated face again towards the piano which, open for the nonce, smiled at her in fatuous agreement, its exposed keys grinning towards her like an enormous set of false teeth.

"I wanted to go and play—that was all," came the plaint from the window, "but there's puddles everywhere, even if it does go off. I've got to work so hard at these old lessons through the week, it's a shame if a girl can't get a little bit of playtime on a Saturday." Disconsolately, she continued to view the dismal prospect of the wet December landscape, the wet roadway, the rain-drenched fields, the still, dripping branches of the birches opposite, the melancholy lack of movement save for the steady downward fall of water. But her facile prattle did not cease for long and, despite the depressing scene, in a moment she had recommenced: "There's a sparrow sittin' on our cannon. Oh! there's another—there's two wee sparrows cowriein' down in the rain on our brass cannon. What do we keep a cannon like that for? It doesn't shoot and it always needs cleanin'. I've never noticed how funny it looked till the now, Mamma!" she pestered, insistently, "what is it there for? Tell me."

"A kind of ornament to set off the house, I suppose that was your father's idea," came the harassed voice from the back of the piano.

"It would have been better to have had a plot of pansies, or a wee monkey-puzzle tree like Jenny Paxton has in front o' her house," replied Nessie; then, continuing slowly, voicing her facile thoughts aloud, she chattered on: "There's not a breath in these trees across the fields. They're standin' like statues in the rain. 'Rain rain go to Spain! Never more come back again!' That'll not put it away though. That's only a story like Santa Claus. He's got a white beard. What is a Spaniard like I wonder. Has he a black face? The capital of Spain is Madrid. Correct. Up to the top of the class, Nessie Brodie. Good for you! That'll please father. What a day for a Saturday holiday. Here am I doin' geography on it. Not a body on the street. No! I'm wrong, I believe there's a man. He's comin' up the road. It's not a man, it's a telegraph boy!" It was a rich and unusual discovery in the dull, uninteresting prospect, and she fastened upon it delightedly. "Mamma! Mamma! somebody's going to get a telegram. I see the boy in the road. He's comin' right up here. Oh! look, look," she called out in a rapturous effervescence of expectation and excitement, "he's comin' into our house!"

Mrs. Brodie dropped her duster and flew to the window, through which she saw the boy coming up the steps, and immediately she heard the door-bell peal with such violence that it sounded in her startled ears like a sound of alarm. She stood quite still. She feared telegrams with a dreadful intensity as the harbingers of swift, unexpected calamity; they spoke not to her of happy births or joyous weddings but of the sudden, unconceived disaster of death. As she stood motionless a second, ominous ring of the bell fell upon her ears, and, as though the powerful pull tugged at the cords of her memory, reminded her of that previous solitary occasion in her life when she had received a telegram, the message which had announced the death of her mother. Without looking at Nessie she said, hoarsely: "Go to the door and see what it is."

Yet when Nessie, bubbling with anticipation, had run out of the room, she sought to calm herself; she reflected that perhaps the messenger had come only to collect information regarding an unknown name or an undecipherable address, as, living in the last house in the road, such inquiries were not infrequently addressed to them. She strained her hearing to the utmost, essaying to catch some hopeful sounds that might indicate a colloquy at the door, but vainly, for immediately Nessie was back, waving an orange slip with all the triumph of her own personal discovery.

"It's for you, Mamma," she announced breathlessly; "and is there an answer?"

Mamma took the telegram into her hand as though she touched a poisonous viper and, turning it over fearfully, inspected it with the profound horror with which she might have viewed this dangerous reptile. "I can't see without my glasses," she murmured, afraid to open the telegram, and trying feebly to gain time.

In a flash Nessie had gone in and in a flash returned, bearing the steel-rimmed spectacles. "Here you are, Mamma! Now you'll manage to read it. Open it."

Mrs. Brodie slowly put on her glasses, again looked timorously at the dreadful thing in her hand and, turning to Nessie in a panic of indecision and fear, faltered:

"Perhaps I better leave it to your father. It mightna be my place to open a thing like this. It's a job for your father, is't not, dear?"

"Oh, come on, Mamma, open it," urged Nessie impatiently. "It's addressed to you and the boy's waiting for the answer."

Mrs. Brodie opened the envelope with stiff, ungainly fingers, tremblingly extracted the inner slip, unfolded it, and looked at it. For a long time she looked at it, as though it had contained, not nine words, but a message so lengthy and complicated that it passed her comprehension. As she gazed, gradually her face became dead, like grey ashes, and seemed to shrink into a smaller and more scanty compass; her features became pinched and drawn, as though some sudden icy blast had extinguished the feeble glow which animated them and frozen them into a strange, unnatural immobility.

"What is it, Mamma?" asked Nessie, on her tiptoes with curiosity.

"Nothing," repeated Mrs. Brodie in a dull, mechanical voice. She sat down limply upon the sofa with the rustling slip of paper fluttering between her shaking fingers.

Outside in the porch, the waiting boy, who had for some moments been moving impatiently, now began to whistle restlessly and to kick his toes noisily against the step, thus informing them in his own fashion, that it was no part of his duty to wait upon this doorstep for the duration of an entire day.

"Do you want the boy to wait for an answer?" continued Nessie curiously, observing, but not fully comprehending, her mother's strained immobility.

"No answer," automatically replied Mamma.

At Nessie's injunction the telegraph boy departed, still whistling loudly and unconcernedly, recognising his importance as the instrument of destiny, yet totally unmoved by the ravages of his missive of destruction.

Nessie came back to the parlour and, regarding her mother, thought her appearance ever more strange, seemed with a more prolonged scrutiny hardly to recognise her.

"What's the matter with you, Mamma? You look so white." She touched her mother's cheek lightly, felt it, under her warm fingers, to be be cold and stiff as clay; then, with an uncanny intuition, she continued: "Was it something about Matt in the telegram?"

At the name of her son Mrs. Brodie returned from her frigid rigidity into the conscious world. Had she been alone she would have melted into an abandoned flood of tears, but in Nessie's presence her weak spirit made a powerful effort to check the sobs rising in her throat and, struggling for control, she endeavoured to think with all the forces of her benumbed intellect. Urged by the strongest motive in nature to an effort of mind and will which would nominally have been far beyond her, she turned with a sudden movement to the child.

"Nessie," she breathed, "go up and see what Grandma's doing. Don't mention this wire, but try and find out if she heard the bell. You'll do that for Mamma, won't you, dear?"

With the quick perception that was the basis of her smartness Nessie understood exactly what her mother required of her, and embracing gleefully the task, which was that kind of confidential mission she adored to perform, she nodded her head twice, slowly, understandingly, and strolled casually out of the room.

When her daughter had gone, Mrs. Brodie unrolled the ball into which the telegram had been crumpled within her contracted fingers, and although the message had seared itself upon her memory, unconsciously she gazed at it again, whilst her quivering lips slowly framed each individual word—"Wire my forty pounds Post Restante Marseilles immediately. Matt."

He wanted his money! He wanted the savings that he had sent home to her, the forty pounds that she had invested for him in the Building Society! She saw immediately that he was exiled in Marseilles, in trouble, in some desperate strait, and that the money was a vital and immediate necessity to remove him from the meshes of a dreadful and dangerous entanglement. Someone had stolen his purse, he had been sandbagged and robbed, the vessel had sailed and left him stranded, without any of his belongings, in Marseilles. Marseilles—the very name—unknown, foreign, sinister, chilled her blood and suggested to her every possible evil that might befall her beloved son, for, on the sole evidence of this cryptic and appalling demand, she conceived him to be, definitely, the innocent victim of deplorable and harrowing circumstances. Sifting the available facts to the uttermost she observed that the wire had been handed in at Marseilles that morning—how soon had travelled the unhappy tidings!—which indicated to her that he had been in a fit state to dispatch the message, that he should be, at least, in no immediate physical danger. He had recovered, perhaps, from the effects of the vicious assault upon him, and now merely awaited patiently and anxiously the arrival of his own money. As her thoughts ran through these innumerable winding channels of her supposition they converged inevitably, despite a dozen deviations in their courses, to the one, common, relentless termination, to the conclusion that she must send his money. A pitiful shudder shook her at the very thought. She could not send it; she could send nothing. She had spent every penny of his forty pounds.

During the past nine months her financial struggles had been desperate. Brodie had progressively cut her allowance until he had at length reduced it by half, yet he expected the same excellent food supplied, where he was concerned, in the same excessive quantities; and did she manifest the slightest indication of economy upon the table she became the object of a fierce sarcastic tirade, in which he vituperated her as an incompetent bungler who lacked the ability even to manage adequately the petty exchequer of the home. He taunted her with the superior ability of his old mother, producing specious evidence of the old woman's housewifely efficiency, relating in detail the delicious, inexpensive meals she had prepared for him before his marriage, threatening, despite his mother's age, to transfer the management of the house into her more competent hands. It had been useless for Mamma to protest weakly that he gave her insufficient money, that food prices were rising, that the growing Nessie required more clothes, new boots, more expensive school books, that Grandma Brodie would not relinquish one single item of the comforts and luxuries to which custom had habituated her. It would have been equally ineffective, had she attempted it, to convince him that she spent not one farthing upon her own personal expenses, that she had not bought herself a new garment for three years, that in consequence she was the epitome of bedraggled inelegance, exposing herself, by the very unselfishness of this economy, to his gibes and sneers. Seeing her thus, despite a few feeble, ineffective initial protests, accept the reduced amount and apparently manage with it, he concluded that he had been too lavish in the past and, as money was so tight with him that he exulted in the opportunity to economise at her expense, he had tightened his purse strings to the limit and ground her further under the pressure of his heel.

Although she struggled to make one shilling do the work of two by buying in the cheapest markets, by bargaining and wheedling until she had achieved a reputation for mean shrewishness, it could not continue. Bills had become overdue, tradesmen had become impatient and finally, in despair, she had chosen the path of least resistance and drawn upon Matthew's money. Immediately, matters became easier. Brodie's growls about the food became less frequent, the old woman's whining, senile recriminations abated, Nessie had a new coat, the school fees were paid, and the long-suffering butcher and grocer were appeased. She herself obtained nothing, no clothing, no trivial trinket, no indulgence of her fancy, nothing but a transient immunity from the reproaches of her husband and the worries of her debts. She had consoled herself for her action by telling herself that Matt had really meant the money for her, that he loved her so that he would desire her to take it; again, she had reasoned that she had not spent it upon herself, that she would undoubtedly save and collect it for him in better times and fairer financial weather.

Forty pounds! It was a ruinous sum! Although she had expended it so easily the thought of obtaining it again was incredible. Under her former circumstances, and by the most penurious thrift, she might achieve this amount in, perhaps, the long term of a year; but the sum was required immediately. Her lips quivered as her heart quailed within her, but immediately she rallied herself, bracing herself to be brave for Matt's sake. She set her mouth firmly and looked up as Nessie returned to the room.

"Grandma was tidying up her drawer," whispered Nessie to her mother, with the air of a conspirator. "She didn't hear the bell and she doesn't know a thing about it. I found out ever so carefully!"

"That's a good, clever girl," said Mamma. "Nobody's to know about that telegram, Nessie. You're not to open your mouth yourself, about it. That was for me and nobody else. I trust you now! And I'll give ye something nice if ye don't tell." Then she concluded vaguely, feeling that some form of explanation was expected of her: "It was just from an old friend in the country—an old friend of Mamma's who is in some slight distress."

Nessie placed her left forefinger on her closed lips, delighted to share in a confidence of her mother's, implying by this precocious gesture

hat she was worthy to be trusted with the most private and mysterious
secrets of the universe.

"That's right, now. Don't forget that you've given your word. Your
father need know nothing about it," said Mrs. Brodie, as she got up.
She desired to remain passively considering the situation, but it was
nearly noon, and she had the dinner to prepare. No matter what anxiety
affected her, the work of the house must go on, meals must appear upon
the table with an inexorable punctuality, the master must be propitiated,
fed adequately and succulently. As she began to peel a large potful of
potatoes she tried to reach some decision as to what she should do.

At the outset she realised that she would obtain no help from her
husband. She would have steeled herself to anything for Matt's sake,
but it was an impossibility for her to face her husband and demand a sum
of the absurd magnitude of forty pounds, realising with certainty, as she
did, beforehand, that he would infallibly refuse to send the money.
To bring the matter uselessly, in this manner, to his knowledge would be
to reveal to him her own culpability, arouse his prodigious wrath, and
yet obtain no tangible result. Even as she reasoned thus she could visual-
ise him sneering: "He's in Marseilles, is he? Well! let him walk or swim
back. It'll do the poor dear a heap o' good."

She next considered the possibilities associated with Agnes Moir.
There was no doubt but that Agnes, who, like Mamma, could refuse
him nothing, would be instantly willing to send money to Matthew,
despite the shameful coldness and neglect she had suffered from him
during the last few months, but it was, unhappily, an equal certainty
that she did not possess forty pounds. The Moirs, although respectable,
were poor, privation lay very near to their door, and it was unthinkable,
even if they wished Agnes to have the money, that they could suddenly
produce a large sum like this. Additionally, there had been a strong hint
of reproach in Miss Moir's attitude to her lately which contained a
justifiable suggestion of suffering and injured innocence. How could she
then, in the face of such wounded purity of conscience, confess herself
the thief of her own idolised son's money. The impeccable Miss Moir
would condemn her immediately, would perhaps repudiate her before
the eyes of the entire town.

She therefore abandoned Agnes, but, whilst she mechanically performed the actions of cooking the dinner, her mind continued to work
furiously, racing against time. When Brodie came in she served the meal
without once removing her fierce concentration from the problem that
obsessed her, and with such unusual abstraction that she placed before
Brodie, in mistake, Nessie's small plate.

"Are ye drunk, woman?" he roared at her, gazing at the diminutive
portion, "or am I expected to repeat the miracle o' the loaves and
fishes?"

As she hastily changed the plates Mamma blushed guiltily at this outward manifestation of her secret cogitations; but how could she have said, in extenuation: "I was thinking of how I could raise forty pound for Matt?"

"She'll have been takin' a wee sook at the bottle to keep her strength up," tittered Grandma Brodie maliciously. "That's how she'll have been passin' the time this mornin'."

"So that's where the money for the house goes," sneered Brodie taking up his mother's lead; "in tipple! well, we maun see what's to be done about that."

"Maybe that's what's gie'n her that red neb and watery een, I'm thinkin'," replied the old woman.

Nessie said nothing, but her too obvious side-glances of fealty and co operation towards Mamma were so pregnant with meaning that they almost defeated their object. Still, the crisis was not precipitated and, after dinner, when Brodie had departed and the old woman retreated upstairs, Mamma breathed more freely, and turning to Nessie said:

"Will you clear up, dear? I've got to go out for a few messages. You're a great help to Mamma to-day, and if you've got the dishes washed when I come back, I'll bring you a pennyworth of sweeties." In her awful dilemma she was capable even of subtle strategy in a small matter like this and, although the rain had ceased, Nessie consented willingly, lured by the bait of sweetmeats, charmed to be recognised by her mother as so supremely grown up.

Mrs. Brodie put on a hat and coat, the latter the very paletot she had worn when she escorted Matt to Glasgow on his departure, and hurried out of the house. She quickly crossed the Common and took the road which ran behind the station, then, at the junction of Railway Road and College Street, she paused outside a small, low-browed shop which bore above the crooked lintel of its doorway the disreputable insignia of three brass balls. Upon the window was a notice which stated in dirty white letters, and, through the defection of certain letters and the broken condition of others, with some uncertainty: Gold, Silver, Old False Teeth Bought, Money Lent; whilst behind this, chalked on a small un prosperous looking slate, was the terser and less prepossessing phrase: Rags Bought. With a fearful misgiving Mrs. Brodie contemplated this the only pawnshop in the respectable Borough of Levenford. To enter these precincts was, she knew, the most abysmal humiliation to which a respectable person could descend; and the greater crime of being detected entering therein meant disgrace, dishonour, and social annihilation. She realised all this, realised further her inability to cope with the hidden horrors within, yet she compressed her lips and glided bravely into the shop as quickly and unsubstantially as a shadow. Only the loud revealing tinkle of the bell attached to the door marked her entry, and surrounded by its mellifluous reiterations, she found herself facing a counter in a small box-like compartment which appeared to be one of three. Here the number three had apparently a cabalistic significance both without and within, yet in the compartment she was more private than she could have hoped. Even in this debased society there were apparently instincts of delicacy! When the tinkle of the bell had ceased, her nostrils became gradually and oppressively aware of an odour, emerging permeatingly from some unseen point, of boiling fat tinctured with the aroma of onions. With a sudden faintness at the greasy, nauseating odour, she closed her eyes, and when she opened them a moment later, a short, squat man magically confronted her, having issued unseen, like a genie, from behind the heavy opaque cloud of vapour that infiltrated the inner shop. He had a long, square beard, iron grey and slightly curling, bushy eyebrows of the same colour and texture beneath which bright, beady eyes twinkled like a bird's; his hands and shoulders moved deferentially, but these black pellets of eyes never left Mrs. Brodie's face. He was a Polish Jew whose settlement in Levenford could be adduced only to his racial proclivity for courting adversity and who, failing to eke out an existence by usury in the hard soil of the Borough, was reduced to merely subsisting—or so it seemed—by the buying and selling of rags. Being mild and inoffensive he did not resent the abusive epithets which greeted him as, shouting: "Anyrag anybone! anybottle to-day!", he drove his donkey-cart upon his rounds, and he made no complaints except to bewail, to such as would hear him, the absence of a synagogue in the town.

"Yeth?" he now lisped to Mrs. Brodie.

"You lend money," she gasped.

"Vot you vont to pawn?" he thrust at her. Although his voice was gentle, she was startled at such crudity of expression.

"I've nothing here now. I wanted to borrow forty pounds."

He glanced sideways at her, regarding her rusty, unfashionable clothing, her rough hands and broken nails, the tarnish on the thin, worn, gold band of her solitary ring, her ludicrous battered hat—missing, with his glittering eyes, no item of her sad and worthless attire. He thought she must be mad. Caressing his fleshy, curved nose between his finger and thumb he said, thoughtfully:

"Zat es a lot of monesh. Ve must ave security. You must bring gold or jewels if you vish to raise zat amount."

She should, of course, have had jewels! In her novels these were the touchstone of a lady's security, but, apart from her wedding ring, she had only her mother's silver watch—which she might, with good fortune, have pledged for fifteen shillings—and, realising something of the insufficiency of her position she faltered:

"You would not lend it on my furniture or—or on note of hand. I saw—in the papers—some people do that, do they not?"

He continued to rub his nose, considering, beneath his benignly tallowed brow, that these Gentile women were all alike—scraggy and worn and stupid. Did she not realise that his business was conducted on the basis of shillings, not of pounds? and that, though he could produce the sum she required, he would require security and interest which he had realised at his initial survey to be utterly beyond her? He shook his head, gently but finally, and said, without ceasing to be conciliatory, using indeed, to that end his deprecating hands:

"Ve don't do zat beesness. Try a bigger firm—say en ze ceety. Oh yes! Zey might do et. Zey have more monesh zan a poor man like me."

She regarded him with a palpitating heart in stunned, humiliated silence, having braved the danger and suffered the indignity of entering his wretched hovel without achieving her purpose. Yet she was obliged to accept his decision—she had no appeal—and she was out once more in the dirty street amongst the puddles, the littered tin cans and the garbage in the gutter, without having procured even one of the forty pounds she required. She was utterly abased and humiliated yet, as she walked quickly away, she appreciated with a growing anxiety that, though she had achieved nothing, Matt would at this very moment be waiting in immediate anticipation of the arrival of the money. Lowering her umbrella over her face to avoid detection she hastened her steps feverishly towards home.

Nessie awaited her in a small imitation apron, triumphantly playing the housewife over her neat pile of clean crockery, preparing herself for her just reward of sweetmeats, but Mamma thrust her roughly aside.

"Another time, Nessie," she cried. "Don't bother me! I'll get you them another time." She entered the scullery and plunged her hand into the box where old copies of newspapers and periodicals, brought home by Brodie, were kept for household purposes, chiefly the kindling of fires. Removing a pile of these she spread them out upon the stone floor and flung herself before them, on her knees, as though she grovelled before some false god. She hurriedly ran her eye over several of these sheets until, with an inarticulate cry of relief, she found what she sought. What had that wretched Jew said? "Try a bigger firm," he had told her, in his indecently garbled English, and, accordingly, she chose the largest advertisement in the column, which informed her with many glowing embellishments that Adam McSevitch—a genuine Scotsman— lent £5 to £500, without security, on note of hand alone, that country clients would be attended promptly at their own homes, and, memorable feature, that the strictest and most inviolable secrecy would be preserved —nay, insisted upon—between the principal and his client.

Mrs. Brodie breathed more calmly as, without removing her hat or coat, she rose to her feet, hurried to the kitchen and sat down and composed a short, but carefully worded letter, asking Adam McSevitch to attend her at her home on Monday forenoon at eleven o'clock. She sealed the letter with the utmost precaution, then dragged her tired limbs out of the house and into the town once more. In her haste the constant pain in her side throbbed more intensely, but she did not allow it to interfere with her rate of motion and, by half-past three, she succeeded in reaching the general post office where she bought a stamp and carefully posted her letter. She then composed and dispatched a wire to "Brodie: Poste Restante: Marseilles," saying, "Money arrives Monday sure. Love. Mamma." The cost of the message left her stricken, but though she might have reduced the cost by omitting the last two words, she could not force herself to do so. Matt must be made to understand, above everything, that it was she who, with her own hands, had sent the wire, and that she, his mother, loved him.

A sense of comfort assuaged her on her way home; the feeling that she had accomplished something, and that on Monday she would assuredly obtain the money, reassured her, yet nevertheless, as the day dragged slowly to its end, she began to grow restless and impatient. The consolation obtained from her definite action gradually wore off and left her sad, inert, and helpless, obsessed by distressing doubts. She fluctuated between extremes of indecision and terror; felt that she would not obtain the money, then that she would be surely discovered; questioned her ability to carry through the undertaking; fled in her mind from the fact, as from an unreal and horrid nightmare, that she of all people should be attempting to deal with money-lenders.

Sunday dragged past her in an endless succession of interminable minutes, during the passage of which she glanced at the clock a hundred times, as if she might thus hasten the laboured transit of time and so terminate her own anxiety and the painful expectancy of her son. During the slow hours of the tardily passing day, she formed and reformed the simple plan she had made, trembled to think how she would address Mr. McSevitch, was convinced that he would treat her as a lady, then felt certain that he would not, re-read his advertisement secretly, was cheered by his comforting offer to lend £500, then shocked by the amazing effrontery of it. When she retired eventually to rest, her head whirled with confusion, and she dreamed she was overwhelmed by an avalanche of golden pieces.

On Monday morning she could hardly maintain her normal demeanour, she shook so palpably with apprehension, but, mercifully, her anxiety was not detected and she sighed with relief when first Nessie, and then Brodie, disappeared through the front door. She now had only Grandma Brodie to dispose of, for, from the moment she had written her letter, she had fully appreciated the obvious danger of having the inquisitive, garrulous, and hostile old woman about the house at the time fixed for the interview. The danger that she might stumble upon the entire situation was too great to be risked, and Mamma, with unthought of cunning, prepared to attack her upon her weakest point. At half-past nine therefore, when she took up to the old woman, upon a tray, her usual breakfast of porridge and milk, she did not, as was her usual custom, immediately leave the room, but instead sat down upon the bed, and regarded its aged occupant with an assumed and exaggerated expression of concern.

"Grandma," she began, "you never seem to get out of the house these days at all. You look real peaky to me the now. Why don't you take a bit stroll this morning?" The old dame poised the porridge spoon in her yellow claw, and cast a suspicious eye upon Mamma from under her white, frilled nightcap.

"And where would I stroll to on a winter's day?" she asked, distrustfully. "Do ye want me to get inflammation of the lungs so as you can get rid o' me?"

Mamma forced a bright laugh, an exhibition of gaiety which it tortured her heart to perform.

"It's a lovely day!" she cried, "and do ye know what I'm going to do with ye? I'm just going to give you a florin, to go and get yourself some Deesides and some oddfellows."

Grandma looked at the other with a dubious misgiving, sensing immediately a hidden motive, but tempted by the extreme richness of the enticement. In her senile greediness she loved particularly the crisp biscuits known as "Deeside," she doted upon those large, flat, round sweets so inappropriately named oddfellows; in her own room she endeavoured, always, to maintain a stock of each of these delicacies in two separate tins inside her top drawer; but now, as Mamma was well aware, her supplies were exhausted. It was a tempting offer!

"Where's the money?" she demanded, craftily. Without speaking, Mamma revealed the shining florin in the middle of her palm.

The crone blinked her bleared eyes at it, thinking with rapid, calculating glances, that there would be enough for the Deesides, the oddfellows, and maybe a wee dram over and above.

"I micht as weel take a dauner, then," she muttered slowly, with the semblance of a yawn to indicate indifference.

"That's right, Grandma—I'll help ye," encouraged Mamma as, trembling with an exultation she feared to display, realising that so far victory was hers, she assisted the other out of bed. Before the old woman could have time to change her mind, she happed her in her voluminous clothing, tied a multitude of tapes, drew on the elastic-sided boots, brought her the jet-spangled bonnet, held out and enveloped her in the black, beaded cape. Then she presented her with her false teeth upon the charger of a cracked saucer, handed her the two-shilling piece and, having thus finally supplied her with the weapons and the sinews of the war about to be waged on the Deesides, she led the old woman down the stairs, and saw her go tottering out along the road, before the clock showed half-past ten. Exercising the utmost dispatch, she now made all the beds, washed the dishes, tidied the house, made herself, in her own phrase, decent, and sat down breathlessly at the parlour window to await her visitor.

As the hands of the marble timepiece on the parlour mantelpiece drew near to eleven, Mamma shook with trepidation, as though she expected a cab to dash up to the house and the front bell to ring, simultaneously with the first stroke of the hour. As the clock eventually struck eleven strokes, and was silent, she wondered if Mr. McSevitch would bring the money in golden sovereigns in a bag, or present it to her in immaculate notes; then, as the hands indicated five minutes, ten minutes, then fifteen minutes past the appointed time and still no one came, she grew restless. If her visitor did not come at the hour she had specially indicated, all her carefully thought out arrangements would go for nothing, and she shuddered to think what would happen if he arrived during the dinner hour, when her husband would be in the house.

At twenty minutes to twelve she had almost abandoned hope when, suddenly, she observed two strange gentlemen appear opposite the house. They arrived on foot and carried no bag, but were dressed exactly alike, in a manner which Mrs. Brodie felt might represent the peak of elegance, the most dashing summit of contemporary male fashion. Their Derby hats, that curled till brim met crown, were tilted rakishly above glossy side whiskers; their very short jackets were tight to the waist, with long rolling lapels, so that the chest of each had the appearance of swelling forward like that of a pouter pigeon, whilst the curve of the lower part of the back swept protrudingly, but equally enticingly, in an obverse direction; their check trousers, maintaining an agreeable looseness in the upper portions, clung more sympathetically to the figure as they descended, and terminated finally with the tightness of spats around small, inconspicuous, but none the less shining, shoes. Each wore a large, heavy watch chain high up across his spotted, fancy waistcoat whilst, even at such a distance as that from which she viewed them, she noted upon their fingers a coruscation of jewelled rings which sparkled and flashed with every fluent movement. No strangers of such composed address or brilliant plumage had, in the memory of Mrs. Brodie, ever flitted down upon the town of Levenford and, with a beating heart and a fascinated eye, she realised instinctively—although her antici-ipation had visualised a patriarchal gentleman in an Inverness cloak with a bluff manner and a benevolent shaggy beard—that these men of the world were the emissaries of McSevitch—genuine Scotsman.

From the middle of the roadway they looked knowingly at the house, as though their eyes, having embraced and criticised every archi-tectural feature of its outer aspect, bored like gimlets through the hard stone walls, examining the inadequacies of its inner structure, and con-temptuously discovering a host of deficiencies hitherto concealed even from its occupants.

At length, after a prolonged, impassive stare, one of the two turned his head slowly and, out of the corner of his mouth, said something to his companion, who on his part pushed his hat further back upon his head, veiled his protuberant eyeballs, and laughed with an experienced air.

Like a sudden, startled victim of diplopia, Mrs. Brodie now saw them advance simultaneously, proceed through the gateway abreast, saw them glance in unison at every stone on the courtyard, and, as they paused before the cannon in front the porch, she shrank back behind the concealment of her curtain.

"Bit o' junk that, but solid stuff—brass by the look on it," she heard one say as he fingered his large, pearly tiepin. The other flicked the gun barrel with his finger nail, as though he wished to see if it might ring true, but immediately he withdrew the finger and thrust it hastily into his mouth. "Ow! it's bloody hard, anyway," floated in through the half-open window towards Mamma's astounded ears. The bell rang. Mechanically she went to answer it and, as she threw open the door, she was confronted by two identically competent smiles which met and returned her shrinking gaze with a dazzling exhibition of gold and ivory.

"Mrs. Brodie?" said one, extinguishing his smile.

"You wrote?" said the other, doing likewise.

"Are you from Mr. McSevitch?" she stammered.

"Sons," said the first, easily.

"Partners," said the second, gracefully.

Overcome by the ease of their manners, but none the less shaken by a faint misgiving, she hesitatingly took them into the parlour. Immediately their sharp eyes, which had been glued upon her, detached themselves, and darted round every object in the room, in abstracted yet eager estimation until, finally, as the orbits of their inspection intersected, their glances met significantly and one addressed the other in a tongue unknown to Mrs. Brodie. The language was strange, but the tone familiar, and, even as she winced at its disparaging note, her cheeks coloured with a faint indignation as she thought that such words as these were, at least, not genuine Scottish. Then, alternately, they began to bombard her.

"You want forty pounds, lady?"

"On the quiet—without anyone knowin'—not even the old man, lady."

"Been havin' a little flutter, perhaps?"

"What do you want it for, lady?"

Their well-informed glances devastated her as they moved their fingers, sparkling their rings affluently, demonstrating agreeably that they had the money, that she it was who desired it. She was at their mercy.

When they had drawn everything from her regarding the house, her husband, herself, and her family, they exchanged a nod and, as one man, arose. They toured the parlour, then tramped loudly and indifferently through the house, fingering, handling, stroking, twiddling, and weighing everything in it, peering, poking, and prying into every room with Mamma at their heels like a debased and submissive dog. When they had reviewed the most intimate details of the life of the household as manifested to them in the interior of cupboards, the inside of wardrobes, the contents of drawers, and made her blush painfully as, penetrating even to her bedroom, they regarded with a knowing air the space beneath her bed, they at last descended the stairs, looking everywhere but at her. She could see refusal in their faces.

"I'm afraid it's no good, lady. Your furniture's poor stuff, heavy, old-fashioned, won't sell!" said one, at last, with an odious show of candour. "We might lend you two tens on it—or say even twenty-four pounds. Yes, say twenty-five at the outside limit and on our own terms of interest," he continued, as he produced a quill toothpick from his waistcoat pocket and assisted his calculations by its assiduous application. "What say?"

"Yes, lady," said the other, "times is bad these days, and you're not what you might call a good loan. We're always polite to a lady—funny the number of ladies we does business with—but you haven't got the security."

"But my things are all good," quavered Mamma in a faint voice; "they've been handed down in the family."

"You couldn't given them away now, ma'am," the gentleman with the toothpick assured her, shaking his head sadly. "No, not even in a downright gift. We've reached the limit, the fair limit. How about that twenty-five pounds of good money?"

"I must have forty pounds," said Mamma, weakly, "anything else is no good." She had set the fixed sum in her mind and nothing short of its complete achievement would satisfy her.

"You've nothing else to show, lady?" said one insinuatingly. "Funny what you ladies will shake out when you're put to it. You've nothing up your sleeve for the last?"

"Only the kitchen," replied Mrs. Brodie humbly, as she threw open the door, loath to allow them to depart, desiring despairingly to entice them into the plain apartment for a last consideration of her appeal. They went in, following her reluctantly, disdainfully, but immediately their attention was riveted by a picture which hung conspicuously upon the wall, framed in a wood of mottled, light yellow walnut. It was an engraving entitled "The Harvesters," was marked First Proof, and signed J. Bell.

"Is that yours, lady?" said one, after a significant pause.

"Yes," said Mrs. Brodie, "it's mine. It was my mother's before me. That small pencil sketch in the corner of the margin has been much admired."

They talked in low tones before the picture, peered at it through a glass, rubbed it, pawed it possessively.

"Would you like to sell this, lady? Of course it's nothing to make a noise on—oh dear, no!—but we would offer you—yes—five pounds for it," said the second eventually, in an altered, ingratiating tone.

"I can sell nothing," whispered Mamma. "Mr. Brodie would notice it at once."

"Say ten pounds then, lady," exclaimed the first, with a great show of magnanimity.

"No! No!" returned Mamma, "but if it's worth something will ye not lend me the rest of the money on it? If it's worth something to buy it's surely worth something to lend on." She waited in a fever of anxiety, hanging upon the inflections of their voices, upon their quick, expressive gestures, upon the very lift of their eyebrows while they held colloquy together upon her picture. At last, after prolonged argument, they agreed.

"You win, then, lady," said one. "We'll lend you the forty pounds, but you'll have to give us your bond on the picture and the rest of the furniture as well."

"We're giving the money away, lady," said the other, "but we'll do it for your sake. We see you need the money bad; but you must understand that if you don't pay up, that picture and your furniture belongs to us."

She nodded dumbly, feverishly, filled with a choking, unendurable sense of a hard-bought victory. They went back into the parlour and sat down at the table, where she signed the endless papers that they produced for her, appending her signature where they indicated with a blind, reckless indifference. She understood that she would have to repay three pounds a month for two years, but she cared nothing for that and, as they counted out the money in crisp pound notes, she took it like a woman in a dream, and, like a sleepwalker, she showed them to the door. In spite of everything she had got the money for Matt.

Early that afternoon she wired off the money. In the overwrought state of her imagination she seemed to see the clean bank notes actually rushing through the blue to the salvation of her son and, when they had gone, for the first time in three days she breathed peacefully, and a mantle of tranquillity descended upon her.

VI

On the following morning Brodie sat at breakfast, cold, moody, detached, the two, sharp, vertical furrows—lately become more intensely grooved

—marking the centre of his forehead between his sunk eyes like cicatriced wounds, and giving to his gloomy visage a perpetual air of brooding perplexity. Caught in the unrelieved severity of the pale morning light his unwary countenance, relieved of observation, seemed to justify the idle remark uttered in the Paxton home that now he was beyond his depth, and, from behind that low wall of his harassed forehead, the confusion of his mind seemed to obtrude itself so forcibly that, even as he sat still and quiet at table, he appeared to flounder helplessly with all the impotent brute strength of a harpooned whale. His diminutive intellect, so disproportionate to his gigantic body, could not direct him towards safety and, while he lashed out in the most mistaken directions in his efforts to avoid a final catastrophe, he still saw that disaster steadily closing in upon him.

He, of course, knew nothing of the wire or of Mamma's action on the previous day. Mercifully, he was not aware of the unauthorised feet that had so boorishly tramped through his domain, yet his own worries and misfortunes were more than sufficient to render his temper like tinder, ready to ignite and flame furiously at the first spark of provocation, and now, having finished his porridge, he awaited with ill-concealed impatience his special cup of coffee which Mrs. Brodie was pouring out for him at the scullery stove.

This morning cup of coffee was one of the minor tribulations of Mamma's harassed existence, for, although she made tea admirably, she rarely succeeded in making coffee to Brodie's exacting taste, which demanded that it must be freshly brewed, freshly poured, and steaming hot. This innocent beverage had become a convenient peg upon which to hang any matutinal grievance, and most mornings he complained bitterly about it, on any or every pretext. It was too sweet, not strong enough, had too many grounds in it; it burned his tongue or was full of the straggling skin of boiled milk. No matter how she made it the result was declared unsatisfactory. The very action of carrying his cup to the table became to her a penance as, knowing the tremor of her hand, he insisted further that the cup must be brimming full and that not a single drop must be spilled upon the saucer. This last transgression was the most deadly that she could commit, and when it occurred he would wilfully allow the drop from the bottom of the cup to fall upon his coat, and would then roar:

"Ye careless besom, look what you've done! I can't keep a suit of clothes for your feckless, dirty ways."

Now, as she entered with the cup, he flung at her an irascible look for having kept him waiting exactly nine seconds, a look which developed into a sneering stare as, maintaining the brimming cup erect and the saucer inviolate by a tense effort of her slightly trembling hand, she walked slowly from the scullery door to the table. She had almost achieved her objective when suddenly with a frantic cry she dropped everything upon the floor and clutched her left side with both hands. Brodie gazed with stupefied rage at the broken crockery, the spilled coffee, and, last of all, at her distorted figure writhing before him amongst the wreckage on the floor. He shouted. She did not hear his bellow, she was so pierced by the sudden spasm of pain which transfixed her side like a white-hot skewer from which burning ripples of agony emanated and thrilled through her flesh. For a moment she suffered intensely, then gradually as though this awful cautery cooled, the waves of pain grew less and with a bloodless face she rose to her feet and stood before her husband, heedless at that instant of her enormity in upsetting his coffee. Relief at her emancipation from pain gave her tongue an unusual liberty.

"Oh! James," she gasped, "that was far the worst I've ever had. It nearly finished me. I really think I should see the doctor about it. I get the pain so much now and I sometimes feel a wee, hard lump in my list." Then she broke off, becoming aware suddenly of his high, affronted dignity.

"Is that a fact now?" he sneered; "we're goin' to run to the doctor for every touch o' the belly ache that grips us, we can so well afford it! And we can afford to scale the good drink on the floor and smash the china! Never mind the waste! Never mind my breakfast; just smash, smash a' the time." His voice rose with each word, then changed suddenly to a sneering tone—"Maybe ye would like a consultation of a' the doctors in the town? They might be able to find something wrang wi' ye if they brought round a' their learned books and put their empty heads together about ye! Who was it ye would be speirin' to see now?"

"They say that Renwick is clever," she muttered, unthinkingly.

"What!" he shouted, "ye talk o' goin' to that snipe that fell foul o' me last year. Let me see you try it!"

"I don't want to see anybody, father," cringed Mamma; "it was just the awfu' pain that's been grippin' me off and on for so long; but it's away now and I'll just not bother."

He was thoroughly infuriated.

"Not bother! I've seen you botherin'! Don't think I havena seen you with a' your dirty messin'. It's been enough to scunner a man and I'll put up wi' it no longer. Ye can take yersel' off to another room. From to-night onwards ye'll get out of my bed. Ye can move out o' my road, ye fusty old faggot!"

She understood that he was casting her out of their marriage bed, the bed in which she had at first lain beside him in love, where she had borne for him her children. For nearly thirty years of her life it had been her resting place; in sorrow and in sickness her weary limbs had stretched themselves upon that bed. She did not think of the relief it would afford her to have her own, quiet seclusion at nights away from his sulky oppression, to retire to Mary's old room and be alone in peace; she felt only the cutting disgrace of being thrown aside like a used and worn-out vessel. Her face burned with shame as though he had made some gross, obscene remark to her, but, as she looked deeply into his eyes, all that she said was:

"It's as you say, James! Will I make ye some more coffee?"

"No! keep your demned coffee. I'll do without any breakfast," he bawled. Although he had already eaten a large bowl of porridge and milk, he felt that she had wilfully defrauded him out of his breakfast, that he was again suffering because of her incompetence, her malingering assumption of illness. "I wouldna be surprised if ye tried to starve us next, with your blasted scrimpin'," he shouted finally, as he pranced out of the house.

His black resentment continued all the way to the shop, and although his mind left the incident, the sense of injustice still rankled while the thought of the day before him did nothing to restore his serenity. Perry had now left him, amidst a storm of contumely and reproaches no doubt, but he had nevertheless gone, and Brodie had been able to substitute for his rare and willing assistant only a small message boy who merely opened the shop and ran the errands. Apart from the loss of trade through the defection of the competent Perry, the onus of supporting the entire work of the shop now lay upon his broad but unaccustomed shoulders, and, even to his dull comprehension, it became painfully evident that he had entirely lost the knack of attending to such people as now drifted into his shop. He hated and despised the work, he never knew where to find things, he was too irritable, too impatient, altogether too big for this occupation.

He had, also, begun to find that his better-class customers, upon whose social value he had so prided himself, were insufficient to keep his business going; he realised with growing dismay that they patronised him only upon odd occasions and were invariably neglectful, in quite a gentlemanly fashion of course, of the settlement of their indebtedness to him. In the old days he had allowed these accounts to run on for two, three, or even four years, secure in the knowledge that he would eventually be paid; they would see, he had told himself in a lordly fashion, that James Brodie was not a petty tradesman grasping for his money, but a gentleman like themselves who could afford to wait another gentleman's convenience. Now, however, with the acute drop in the cash income of the business, he was in such need of ready money that these large, outstanding amounts by the various county families became a source of great anxiety, and although he had sent out, with much laborious auditing and unaccustomed reckoning, a complete issue of them, apart from a few, including the Latta account, which were paid to him immediately, the entire bundle might have been posted into the middle of the Leven for all the result that immediately accrued to him. He fully realised that it was useless to send them out again, that these people would pay in their time and not in his; the mere fact that he had already requested settlement with an unusual urgency might possibly estrange them from him altogether.

His own debts to the few, conservative, wholesale houses whom he favoured had grown far beyond their usual limits. Never a good business man, his usual method had been to order goods when, and as, he pleased, and to pay no heed to amounts, invoices, or accounts until the dignified representative of each house visited him at recognised intervals, in the accepted and friendly manner consonant between two firms of standing and reputation. Then, after a polite and cordial conversation upon the topics of the moment, Brodie would go to the small, green safe sunk in the wall of his office, unlock it grandly, and produce a certain canvas bag.

"Well," he would remark, imposingly, "what is our obligation to-day?"

The other would murmur deprecatingly, and, as if urged against his will to present the bill, would produce his handsome pocket book, rustle importantly amongst its papers, and reply suavely:

"Well, Mr. Brodie, since you wish it, here is your esteemed account"; whereupon Brodie, with one glance at the total, would count out a heap of sovereigns and silver from the bag in settlement. While he might more easily have paid by cheque, he disdained this as a mean, pettifogging instrument and preferred the magnanimous action of disbursing the clean, bright coins as the worthier manner of the settlement of a gentleman's debts. "That's money," he had once said in answer to a question, "and value for value. What's the point o' writin' on a small slip of printed paper. Let them use it that likes it—but the braw, bright siller was good enough for my forebears, and it'll be good enough for me." Then, when it was stamped and signed, he would negligently stuff the other's receipt in his waistcoat pocket and the two gentlemen would shake hands warmly, and part with mutual expressions of regard. That, considered Brodie, was how a man of breeding conducted such affairs.

To-day, however, although he expected a visit of this nature, he took no proud satisfaction from the thought but, instead, dreaded it. Mr. Soper, himself, of Bilsland & Soper Ltd., the largest and most conservative firm with whom he dealt, was coming to see him and, contrary to the usual procedure, he had actually been advised of this call by letter, an unexpected and unwonted injury to his pride. He well knew the reason of such a step, but nevertheless he felt the full bitterness of the blow to his self-esteem, anticipated, too, with sombre dismay the interview which was in prospect.

When he reached the shop he sought to lose his unhappy forebodings in the work of the day, but there was little to occupy him; business was at a standstill. Yet, attempting some show of activity, he walked cumbersomely about the shop with the ponderous movements of a restless leviathan. This spurious display did not deceive even the small errand boy who, peering fearfully through the door of the back shop, saw Brodie stop every few moments whilst in the midst of some unnecessary operation and gaze blankly in front of him, heard him mutter to himself in a vague yet intense abstraction. With the street urchin's cunning he guessed that his employer was on the verge of disaster and he felt, with a strong measure of relief, that it would not be long before he was obliged to set about finding for himself another, and a more congenial, situation.

After an interminable, dragging hiatus, during which it seemed as if the entire hours of the forenoon would pass without a customer appearing, a man entered whom Brodie recognised as an old customer. Thinking that here was someone who, if not important, was at least loyal, he advanced with a great show of heartiness and greeted him.

"Well, my man," he said, "what can we do for you?" The other, somewhat taken aback by such cordiality, asserted laconically that he only required a cloth cap, a plain ordinary cap like the one he had purchased some time before, a grey check, size six and seven eighths.

"Like the one you're wearing?" asked Brodie, encouragingly.

The other looked uncomfortable.

"Naw," he replied, "this is a different yin; this is ma Sunday bonnet."

"Let me see," said Brodie, and struck by a dim idea he put out his hand, suddenly removed the cap from the other's head, and looked at it. Inside, on the shiny sateen lining, was stamped M. H. & H., the hated symbol of his rival next door. Immediately his face flooded with angry resentment and he flung the cap back at its owner. "So!" he cried, "ye've been goin' next door for your braw and fancy stuff, have ye? To wear on Sundays forsooth! And then ye've the impertinence to come in to me for a plain, ordinary bonnet after ye've given them the best o' your trade. Do ye think I'm goin' to take their leavin's? Go back and buy a' the trashy rubbish in their waxworks museum. I'll not serve ye for a pound note."

The other looked exceedingly discomfited. "Aw! Mr. Brodie. I didna mean it like that. I juist gie'n them a trial for a kind o' novelty. It was really the wife's doin'. She egged me on to see what the new place was like. That's like the women ye ken—but I've come back to ye."

"And I'm not goin' to have ye," roared Brodie. "Do ye think ye can treat me like that? I'll not stand it. It's a man that's before ye, not a demned monkey on a stick like they've got next door," and he banged his fist on the counter.

It was a ridiculous position. It was as though he expected the man to fawn at his feet and implore to be reinstated as a customer; as though, in his absurd rage, he expected the other to beg to be allowed the honour of buying from him. Something of this amazement dawned in the workman's face; he shook his head, uncomprehendingly.

"I can get what I want elsewhere. I've nae doubt you're a grand gentleman, but you're cuttin' off your nose to spite your face."

When he had gone, Brodie's passion suddenly subsided, and his face took on a mortified expression as he realised that he had done a foolish thing which would react injuriously upon his business. This man that he had refused to serve would talk, talk exaggeratedly in his resentment, and probably a garbled version of his action would be circulating freely in Levenford in the course of a few hours' time. People would make unfavourable comments about him and his high-handed ways, and although in the past he would have revelled in their adverse gossip, exulted uncompromisingly in their cackle, now he felt, in the light of his past experience, that people who heard the story would determine that they would not be subject to a similar indignity, that they would give his business a wide berth in the future. He wrinkled up his eyes at these disturbing thoughts and he damned the man, the people, and the town.

When one o'clock arrived he threw out to the boy that he would be gone for half an hour. Since Perry's departure had deprived him of a responsible person to leave in charge, it was only on rare occasions that he went home for his mid-day meal and, on such occasions, although his business had diminished so considerably, he was impatient to the point of irritability when he undertook the longer journey home for dinner; he felt, with a strange and unwarranted optimism, that he might be missing something which might vitally affect the business for the better. To-day, therefore, he took only a few paces down the street and went into the Winton Arms. Previous to the last twelve months it was unthought of for him to enter these doors except in the late evening, and by the special, private door allotted to himself and his fellow Philosophers; but now these visits had become usual and to-day, Nancy, the pretty barmaid, had a cold pie and some pickled red cabbage for his lunch.

"What will ye drink to-day, Mr. Brodie—a glass of beer?" she asked him, from under her dark curling lashes.

He looked at her heavily, noticing, despite his despondency, how a few, tiny, yellow freckles set off her creamy white skin like the delicate, golden specks upon a robin's egg.

"You ought to know I never drink beer, Nancy. I can't abide it. Bring me some whisky and cold water."

Nancy opened her lips to speak, but, although she wished to say that she thought it a pity to see a fine man like himself taking so much drink through the day, she was afraid, and she uttered no words. She thought Mr. Brodie a grand upstanding gentleman with, if her information was accurate, a perfect scarecrow of a wife, and, mingled with her interest, was compassion, an especial sorrow for him now that he bore this air of deep yet melancholy abstraction. He was, for her, invested with the essential elements of romance.

When she brought him his whisky he thanked her with an upward look of his dark, moody face, which seemed not to dismiss but to encourage her, and as she hovered about the table whilst he ate his lunch, waiting for an opportunity to anticipate his needs, he observed her carefully out of the corner of his eyes. She was a fine little jade, he thought, his gaze travelling upwards from her small foot in its neat shoe, over her well-turned ankle under the close black stocking, sweeping her tight firm hips and breasts, neat yet full, rising to her lips, which were red like the outer petals of fuchsia flowers against the whiteness of her skin. And, as he surveyed her, he was suddenly moved. A sudden, terrific desire for all the lustful pleasures that he had been denied rushed over him; he wished to rise immediately from the table and crush Nancy in his huge embrace, to feel a young, hard, resistant body in his arms instead of the torpid, slavish lump that he had for so long been obliged to accept. For the moment he would scarcely swallow, and his throat went dry with the urge of another appetite. He had heard stray, little whispers and veiled allusions about Nancy that whetted his hunger fiercely, told him it was a hunger which would be easy to appease; but with a tremendous effort of will he controlled himself and went on eating mechanically, his glowing eyes fixed upon his plate.

"Some other time," he kept telling himself, realising that this important engagement of the afternoon must be faced, that he must restrain himself, curb himself against the time of the interview with Soper, which might be filled with a critical significance for the future of his business. He did not look at her again during his short meal, although now her presence fascinated him, and the brush of her body against his arm as she removed his plate made him clench his teeth. "Some other time! Some other time!"

Silently he accepted the biscuits and cheese she brought him and quickly consumed them, but when he had finished he got up and, standing close to her, significantly pressed a coin into her warm hand.

"You've looked after me real well these last weeks," he said, looking at her strangely. "I'll not forget ye."

"Oh! Mr. Brodie, I hope this doesna mean you'll not be back," she cried in concern. "I would miss ye if ye didna come in again."

"Would ye miss me, then?" he replied slowly. "That's good! You and me would suit not bad thegither I'm thinkin'. So don't worry. I'll be back all right." He paused and added in a low voice: "Yes! and maybe ye ken what for."

She mustered a blush and affected to hang her head, feeling, despite her fear to the contrary, that he had noticed her and was disposed to favour her with his regard. She was interested in him, obsessed by his strength; because she was not a virgin her nature responded more ardently to the suggestion of vital force which emanated from him. He was such a free man with his money, too, was Mr. Brodie!

229

"A big man like you couldna see much in such a wee thing as me," she murmured, provokingly; "ye wouldna want to try!"

"I'll be back," he repeated and looked at her intently, penetratingly, then turned on his heel and was gone.

For an instant she stood quite still, her eyes sparkling with satisfaction, her affectation of meekness abandoned, then she ran to the window and stood on tiptoes to watch him go down the street.

Back again in his shop Brodie made a powerful effort to dismiss the warm images which so pleasantly permeated his mind and tried to prepare his ideas for the forthcoming visit of Mr. Soper. But his thoughts lacked continuity or coherence, he was unable, now as always, to formulate any definite, original plan of campaign; the instant he started to consider the possibilities of an idea his mind wandered off at a tangent and he began to think again of Nancy, of the warm look in her eyes, of the chances of arranging a meeting with her. In disgust he gave up the struggle, and feeling that he must blindly await the developments of the interview before he could attempt to cope with them, he got up and went into his shop to await the arrival of his visitor.

As he had said so exactly in his letter, at three o'clock precisely Mr. Soper arrived at the shop, and Brodie, who stood ready, immediately came forward and greeted him; but as they shook hands, Brodie seemed to sense more firmness and less effusiveness in the other's grasp, though he ignored this suspicion and said, with a great assumption of cordiality:

"Come away into my office, Mr. Soper. Moderate weather for the time of year. Yes! very mild indeed."

Somehow his visitor was not inclined to discuss the weather. As they sat down on opposite sides of the desk he looked at Brodie with a politely formal mien, then looked away. He was well aware of Brodie's position and for the sake of old association had intended to be kind; but now, the rank odour of spirits which clung to the other and the loose, easy manner of his greeting prejudiced him intensely. Soper himself was a man of well-defined ideas on moral grounds, being a strong adherent of the sect of Plymouth Brethren, and, in addition, a handsome contributor to the Scottish Temperance Association; as he sat there in his rich, well-fitting clothes, contemplating his admirably kept finger nails, he drew in his lips in a manner totally adverse to Brodie's interest.

"If this open weather continues they'll be gettin' on well with the ploughin'. I saw they had made a bend at the Main's Farm the other day I was out," Brodie persevered, his sluggish wit failing to attune itself to the other's inimical attitude, his obtuse mind compelling him to continue to force remarks in the usual strain set by the precedent of such interviews in the past. "I often take a bit run into the country when I have the opportunity—ay! I'm real fond o' seein' a good pair o' horses turnin' up the fine, rich land up by there."

Soper let him run on, then suddenly, in a cold, incisive voice he cut in.

"Mr. Brodie, your total indebtedness to my firm is exactly one hundred and twenty-four pounds ten shillings and sixpence. I am here at the request of my co-partners to request payment."

Brodie stopped as if he had been shot.

"Wha'—what?" he stammered, "what's come on ye?"

"I appreciate that it is a large sum, but you have postponed payment of our bills on the last three visits of our representative, and in consequence of the large amount involved and the fact that you are an old client I have, as you may have surmised, made this personal visit to request settlement."

In Brodie's mind two opposing forces, rage at the other's manner and consternation at the amount of his debt, dragged against each other violently. Although he had no records for verification, he knew at once that Soper's figure must, although it appalled him, be correct; these people never made mistakes. But the other's chilling attitude left him aghast, and the fact that he was powerless to deal with it as he would have wished infuriated him. If he had possessed the money he would have paid Soper instantly and closed his account with the firm on the spot; but he was well aware of his inability to do this and, with an effort, stifled his fury.

"You'll surely give an old client like myself time to settle?" he managed to articulate, as a negative confession of his inability to find the money.

"You have paid us nothing for over twelve months, Mr. Brodie, and we are naturally becoming anxious. I'm afraid I must ask you to meet this bill now."

Brodie looked at him, then at his safe set in the wall which contained, he knew, less than five pounds, thought futilely of his banking account which had dwindled to an inconsiderable trifle.

"If you don't," Soper was continuing, "I'm afraid we must press. We don't like it, but we shall have to press."

Brodie's eye grew sullen like that of a baited bull.

"I cannot pay," he said. "I cannot pay to-day. But there will be no need for ye to press, as ye call it; ye should well know that James Brodie is an honest man. I'll pay ye—but you must give me time to raise the money."

"How do you propose to do that, might I ask, Mr. Brodie?"

"Ye can ask till you're blue in the face, man, but it's no duty of mine to enlighten you. All that ye need to know is that you'll have your precious money by the end o' the week. I have said it and my word is my bond."

Looking at him, Soper's face softened slightly.

"Yes," he said after a pause, "I know that. I know you've had your difficulties, Mr. Brodie. These undercutting companies with their modern shops," he shrugged his shoulders expressively. "But we have our troubles as well, and we have our own obligations to meet. There's little room for sentiment in business, nowadays. But still—how exactly are things with you?"

As Brodie tried to think of a devastating reply, suddenly it seemed to him with a grim humour what nothing would shock the other more than the plain truth.

"Less than three pounds has come into the business in two weeks," he shot out abruptly. "How do ye like that?"

The other raised his well-kept hands in horror.

"Mr. Brodie, you shock me! I had been told, but I did not know it was as bad as that." He looked at Brodie's harsh face for a moment then said, in a more kindly tone: "There's a saying on 'change, man, which you might well consider. It's sometimes better to cut your losses. Cut your losses rather than go under. Don't batter your head against a brick wall. You'll forgive me—but you understand what I mean." He rose to go.

"I don't understand! What the devil do you mean?" asked Brodie. "I'm here, I've always been here, and, by God, I'll stay here."

Soper paused on his way to the door.

"I mean this kindly to you, Mr. Brodie," he exclaimed, "and what I say is offered to you in a helpful spirit of advice. You can take it or leave it, but experience tells me that you are in an impossible position here. You've had a grand thing here in your day but now, these folks next door have got you beat a hundred ways. Man alive, remember this is the year 1881. We're all moving with new ideas and up-to-date methods but you, and the wheels of progress have run ye down. It's a wise man who knows when he's beat, and if I were you I would shut up my shop and get out with what I could. Why don't you get out of here and try something else? A big man like you could stock a farm and work it with the best." He held out his hand frankly, and said in parting: "You'll not forget us at the end of the week!"

Brodie gazed after him with a flat expressionless face, gripping the edge of the desk until the sinews on the back of his hands showed white under the dark, hairy skin, and the veins rose up like twisted cords.

"Stock a farm!" he muttered. "He surely doesna know what little I have left"; and, as his thoughts rushed outwards into open spaces in a wild regret, he whispered to himself: "He's right though! That would have been the life for me if I could have managed it. I could have settled down close to the land I love so weel, the land that should be mine. But I canna do't now. I maun battle on here."

He was now aware that he would have to bond his house, his sole remaining asset, in order to find the money to settle his account with Soper and to discharge the remainder of these obligations which had gradually accumulated upon him. No one would know, he would go secretly to a lawyer in Glasgow, who would arrange everything, but already, he felt dully as if his own house did not belong to him. It was as if, with his own hand, he was compelled to begin the destruction and disintegration of the solid structure he had seen arise stone by stone, like the gradual erection of an edifice of his own hopes. He loved his house, yet he would have to pledge it to maintain the honour of his name. Above everything he must keep untarnished his reputation for equity and honesty, must demonstrate at once that he—James Brodie— could owe no man a penny. There were some things that he could not do! Then, with a sudden turn of his mind, he seemed by contrast to remember something; his eye glistened, his lower lip protruded slowly, and his mouth twisted into a warped smile. Amongst the desert of his troubles he suddenly espied a green oasis of pleasure. There were some things that he could do! Darkly, a hidden purpose concealed within him like the secret of a crime, he went out of the shop, heedlessly leaving it untenanted, and slowly directed his course towards the Winton Arms.

VII

Mrs. Brodie was resting on the parlour sofa, an unwonted indolence on her part, more especially at this early hour of the afternoon when she should have been industriously occupied in washing the dinner dishes. To-day, however, her forces had spent themselves sooner than usual and she had felt that she must rest before nightfall.

"I'm so knocked up," she mentioned to Grandma Brodie, "I feel ready to drop. I think I'll lie down a wee."

The old woman had eyed her reprovingly and, moving hastily out of the room for fear she herself might be asked to wash up, had replied:

"It surely doesna take much to upset you, you're always moanin' and groanin' about your health they days. When I was your age I did twice your work and never blinked an eye ower it."

Nevertheless, on her departure, Mamma had gone quietly into the parlour and lain down, and now, feeling better, refreshed and restored, she reflected idly that if only she had made a habit of this short afternoon repose earlier in her life she might have worn better; still, she felt thankful that, for the past ten days she had suffered no recurrence of her excruciating pain but merely that dragging ache which, through long familiarity, she now almost ignored.

Nearly three weeks had elapsed since the dispatch of the money to Matt, and for all the acknowledgment which she had received, the forty pounds might still have rested securely in the coffers of McSevitch.

To think, even of that ridiculous, hateful name made her shiver slightly, it was costing her so dear to scrape together the first instalment of her debt, to stint and save parsimoniously so that, from time to time, she might thankfully place some coins in the tin box specially put aside, hidden in her own drawer for this not to be forgotten purpose. It seemed to her, from the painful difficulty of her accumulation, as if this debt would hang threatening above her head for the next two years, like a perpetually suspended sword.

Here, of course, she made no allowance for Matt, and now, amidst the harassing thoughts of her present position, the mere consideration of his return caused a pallid smile to enliven her features. She was firmly assured in her inmost heart that the moment he came back he would stretch out his hand lovingly, compassionately, and with one word relieve her of this racking responsibility. The corners of her drawn lips relaxed as she reflected that it would not be long before her son was once more in her arms, comforting her, rewarding her a hundred-fold for the superhuman effort she had made on his behalf. She pictured the last stages of his journey, saw him, an impatient manly figure, pacing the deck of the ship, disembarking impetuously, now driving hurriedly through crowded, thronging streets, sitting restlessly in the corner of his railway compartment, and finally flinging himself eagerly into the cab which would restore him to her.

The vision of his return hung before her, dazzled her with its imminence, yet as she looked idly out of the window and gradually observed that a cab, loaded with luggage, had driven up at the gate, her brow became furrowed incredulously, as if she failed to believe what she saw. It could not be Matt—her boy—her own son—and yet, miraculously, it was he, home to her at last, stepping out of the cab nonchalantly, as though he had not traversed three thousand miles of sea and land to come to her. With an incoherent cry she raised herself, stumbled to her feet, ran precipitately out of the house, and had enveloped him in her arms almost before he was out of the cab.

"Matt!" she panted, overcome by the excess of her feelings. "Oh! Matt!"

He started back a little, protesting,

"Half a chance, Mamma. Take it easy. You'll smother me if you go on like that."

"Oh! Matt! my dear boy!" she whispered, "you're back to me at last."

"Whoa up, Mamma!" he cried. "Don't weep all over me. I'm used to a dry climate. There now! Don't make a handkerchief of my new tie."

At his protests she at last relinquished her embrace, but would not altogether let him go, and clutching his sleeve fondly, as though fearful that she might again lose him, exclaimed fervently:

"I can hardly believe I've got you back again, son. It's a sight for my tired eyes to see you, for I was thinking about you the minute you drove up. I've missed you wearily, wearily!"

"Well, we're certainly here again, old girl," he quizzed her; "back to the same old Levenford, same old ancestral home, and same old Mamma!"

Mrs. Brodie looked at him dotingly. Everything here might be the same, but he had altered, was profoundly different from the raw youth who had left her only two years ago.

"My! Matt!" she cried, "you've got a real smart look about you. There's an air about you that fair takes my breath away. You're a man now, my son!"

"That's right," he agreed, surveying his surroundings rather than her. "I've learned a thing or two since I saw you last. I'll show them some style in this old Borough before very long. Gad! but everything here seems poky compared with what I've been used to." Then, turning commandingly to the cabby he shouted:

"Bring in my luggage you! *jilde!*"

She observed proudly that he, who had departed with one small, brass-bound chest, now returned with a galaxy of bags and trunks; and could he, on that memorable day when she had let him go fluttering from under her wings, have addressed a cabman in terms of such autocratic disdain? She could not forbear from expressing her fond admiration at the change as she followed his swaggering figure into the hall.

"Oh! that's nothing," he exclaimed carelessly; "I've been used to a retinue of servants out there—blacks you know—and a man gets so accustomed to ordering them about, 'tis no trouble to make this old *gharry wallah* jump to it. Pay him, though, will you, Mamma! I happen to have run out of change at the moment." His look conveyed a sense of superiority to the task of paying a mere cabman, and with a final condescending survey, he moved off and entered the house. Mamma ran for her purse and at once settled with the man, and as she returned, closing the front door securely lest her son might suddenly be taken from her again, the pile of boxes in the hall gladdened her, her heart sang joyously the words: "He's back! Matt's back for good!"

She rejoined him in the kitchen where he was reclining in the armchair, his legs extended, his arms drooping over the sides of the chair, his whole pose indicative of fashionable ennui.

"Rather fatiguing journey!" he murmured, without moving his head. "I find the trains in this country very noisy. Give a man a confounded headache."

"Rest ye—rest ye then, my boy," she exclaimed. "You're home now, that's the main thing." She paused, having so many things to say that she did not know where to begin, yet realising that, before she could permit herself to indulge her selfish curiosity, she must restore his strength with some honest food prepared by her own loving hands.

"I'm dying to hear all about it, Matt," she said, "but let me get you a bite of something first."

He waved the suggestion of food aside.

"Yes! dear—a little cold ham or a cup of lentil soup. You could surely take that. You mind that nice nourishing soup I used to make for you. You were always fond of it."

Matt shook his head definitely, saying: "I don't want to eat just now. I'm used to a late dinner at night now—besides I had a snack in Glasgow."

She was slightly disheartened, but still insisted: "You'll be thirsty after your journey, son. Have a cup of tea. There's nobody can make it like me."

"All right, then," he assented. "Go ahead if that's the best you can do!"

She did not quite grasp his meaning, but rushed in a passion of love to get him the tea and, when she brought him the large steaming cup, she seated herself upon a low stool before him, watching with hungry eyes his every gesture. He was not discomposed by her eager stare but, as he sipped his tea, he casually drew a bright leather case from his pocket and, extracting a thick cheroot, withdrew the straw from it and lit up, demonstrating more plainly than words could tell that he was master of himself, a finished man of the world.

Whilst she studied his easy gestures and admired the fashionable negligence of his suit of smooth, light cloth, she became aware with some concern that his face had altered, grown older than she had expected. His eyes, particularly, had aged and seemed darker than before, with a fine network of wrinkles besetting the corners of the lids; his features had sharpened, his complexion turned to a more sallow, even yellowish tinge, whilst his cheeks seemed to be tightly stretched upon the framework of his jaws. She felt convinced now that some harsh and bitter experience had marred his separation from her and, deeming him to have recovered somewhat, her tone was gentle as she said:

"Tell me, Matt, all about it."

He regarded her from beneath his half-closed eyes, and replied abruptly:

"About what?"

"Oh! just everything, son! Ye can't deceive your mother's eyes. Somebody's been hard on you—unjust too. But I know so little. Tell me how you left India and what—what happened on the way back?"

His eyes opened more fully and, waving his cigar, he immediately grew voluble.

"Oh! that!" he said, "that's soon explained. There's nothing to tell there. I simply threw up my job because it got on my nerves! To be quite honest, Mamma, I couldn't stand the damned dock *wallah* who ran the office. Everything was a fault with him. If a man were a bit late in the morning, after an evening at the club, or if there happened to be a day taken off work—just for a little social engagement you know— he was simply unbearable." He contemplated her with an injured air as he drew at his cigar, and added indignantly: "You know how I could never abide being put upon. I was never the one to endure being bossed about by anyone. It's not my nature. So I told him in plain language what I thought and walked out on him."

"Did ye not speak to Mr. Waldie about it Matt?" she queried sharing his resentment. "He's a Levenford man and a good man. He has a great name for fairness."

"It's him I mean, the *soor*!" retorted Matthew bitterly. "He's the very one that tried to drive me like a coolie. Not a gentleman!" he added. "Nothing but a damned, psalm-singing slave driver."

Mamma's expression grew vaguely troubled and confused.

"Was that the reason of it, son? It wasna right if he did that to you." She paused, then ventured timidly: "We thought it might be your health?"

"Health's as sound as a bell," said Matthew sulkily. "It was the blasted job. I liked everything else out there. It was a fine life if I had been left alone. But he won't cook me, the old swine. I'll go abroad again—Burma! or Malay this time. I'll never stay in this rotten place after what I've seen."

Mrs. Brodie's heart sank. Here was her son barely home, restored only this moment to her arms, and in the next breath he talked of leaving her, of returning, like Alexander, to attempt fresh conquests in these wild foreign lands which terrified her.

"Ye'll not be thinkin' of that for a bit, dear," she quavered. "Maybe you'll get a post at home that would suit you better. Then you wouldna need to leave me again."

He laughed shortly.

"Do you believe I could live in a hole like this after the kind of life I've had out there. What can you offer me here to make up for it? Think of it," he cried. "I had the club, dinners at the mess, dances, the races, polo matches, servants to wait on me hand and foot—every single thing I could want."

He dazzled her with his romantic mendacity so that she saw him mixing in exclusive Society, at regimental dinners, rubbing shoulders with officers in their red mess jackets, with ladies in gleaming satin, and, overcome by the inadequacy of anything that she could offer in return, she could only say weakly:

"I know there's not much of that at home, son. But I'll—I'll do my best to attend to you, to make you comfortable here." He made no reply and, at his eloquent silence, she hesitated, dismayed that the conversation should languish in this fashion, as though after two years he had nothing to tell her, no eagerness to discover how she had fared in his absence. "Did ye have a good voyage home?" she ventured at last.

"Tolerable! Quite tolerable," he admitted. "Weather was good but I got bored towards the end. I left the ship at Marseilles."

"That was where I sent ye the—your money," she remarked haltingly. "Ye got it safe?"

"Yes, I got it all right," he replied, negligently. "Took a devilish age to come through though. Long to come and quick to go."

"I suppose ye had some grave need of a' that siller, Matt?"

"That's right," he replied. "*I* needed it—that was enough, wasn't it?"

"True enough, Matt," she answered. "I knew from your wire you had sore need of it. But it was such a sum of money!"

"Sum of fiddlesticks," he retorted angrily. "You would think it wasn't my own the way you talk. I worked for it, didn't I? I didn't rob ye for it. It was mine to spend as I liked."

"Spend," she echoed; "ye needed it for something more than just the spendin' of it."

He burst into a high laugh.

"Mamma! you'll be the death of me! You know I came back overland. How could a man get along without a little pocket money?" He broke off and regarded her with mock solemnity. "I tell you what I did, Mamma. I went around all the blind beggars in Paris and shared out the cash amongst them. That was the last little fling I had in gay Paree before getting home to this excitin' spot."

She was totally submerged, and the vision of Paris rose before her, indicating clearly that she had demeaned herself, thrust herself into the clutches of unchristian moneylenders for the sole purpose of sending him with a full purse into the unchaste delights of a wicked city. For what wild and reckless extravagances on his part would she be compelled to pay tribute over the next two years? Despite her burning love she said reproachfully, and at the grave risk of offending him:

"Oh! Matt, I would rather ye hadna visited such a like place. I'm not saying you did wrong with the money, dear, but that—that city must be full of temptations for a young man. I'm afraid it was a mistaken thing to do, and I'm sure Agnes would think the same."

Again he laughed rudely.

"What Agnes thinks or says means as much to me now as the squeak of an old boot. I know what she would think all right, and as for her talk there's too much hymn book about that for my taste. I'll never sit on her sofa again. No! She's not the woman for me, Mamma! I'm finished with her."

"Matt! Matt!" burst out Mamma. "Don't talk like that. Ye can't mean what you say. Agnes is devoted to you."

"Devoted!" he retorted. "Let her keep that for them that wants it. What else has she got? Nothing! Why," he continued expansively, I've met women with more in their little finger than she has in her whole body. Charm! Vivacity! Life!"

Mrs. Brodie was horrified and, as she gazed at her son appealingly, a sudden thought struck her.

"Ye havena broken the pledge, have ye, son," she quavered anxiously.

He looked at her queerly, asking himself if the old girl thought he was still at her apron strings. Perhaps he had been too unguarded with her.

"Just a spot of Hollands occasionally," he replied smoothly. "We have to take it out there, you know, for the good of the liver."

She immediately visioned his liver as a dry, absorbent sponge driving him to imbibe spirits to saturate it, and feeling the mercy of his return to what was, in a double sense, a more temperate climate, she returned bravely to the charge.

"Agnes is a good girl, Matt! She would be the salvation of any man. She's waited on you faithfully. It would break her heart if ye gave her up now."

"All right, Mamma," he replied sauvely. "Don't worry! Don't get excited! I'll see her if you like." It suddenly occurred to him that, imbued with his more potent worldly experience, it might be amusing to see Miss Moir again.

"That's good of you, son. You go and see her. I knew you would do that for me." She was at once relieved, feeling the power of her love over him, knowing that when the young people came together everything would be right again. If he had strayed, Agnes would bring him back to the narrow pathway, and now, hastily, for fear he might suddenly take back his promise, she passed on, reclaiming him further.

"I'm afraid you have had a very gay life out there, Matt. I don't blame ye, my boy, but it would be difficult to keep your mind fixed on the more godly matters of life." His vague allusions had shocked her; she must know more, be at all costs reassured. And she continued interrogatively: "Still you did read your chapter every day, didn't you, son?"

He moved restlessly in his chair, glanced at her resentfully.

"That sounds just like old Waldie, Mamma," he replied impatiently. "You'll be asking me if I walked down Chowringee Road with a text slung round my neck, or thumped a bible out on the maidan in the evenings."

"Don't, Matt! Don't! I don't like to hear you talk so lightly," trembled Mamma. Far from allaying her suspicions he was increasing them. "Maybe you'll go to the meeting again with Agnes now you're back. You mean so much to me now. I want ye to be happy, and there's never any happiness apart from goodness in this life, dear."

"What do you know about happiness?" he retorted. "You always looked miserable enough before."

"You'll go to the meeting with Agnes, won't ye, Matt?" she persisted. "Try just the once to please me."

"I'll see," he replied evasively. "I'll go if I want to go, but don't sermonise me any more. I don't like it, I'm not used to it and I won't have it."

"I know that you'll go for my sake," she whispered, placing her worn hand on his knee. "Ye ken that Mary's away now and that I've nobody but you. You were aye my own boy!"

"I knew Mary was away all right," he snickered. "Where is she since her little accident?"

"Hush! Hush! Don't speak like that," she returned hastily. "That's shameful talk!" She paused, shocked, then added: "She's in London we think, but her name's forbidden in the house. For goodness' sake don't talk that way before your father."

He threw off her caressing hand.

"What do I care for father," he blustered. "I'm a man now. I can do what I like. I'm not afraid of him any longer."

"I know that, Matt! You're a fine big man," she wheedled, "but your father's had an awfu' time since ye left. I'll rely on ye not to try his temper too much. I'll just get the brunt of it if ye do. Don't tell him any of these things you've told me. He's that touchy nowadays he mightna like it. He's worried—business is not what it used to be."

"It serves him right," he said, sulkily, as he rose, feeling that she had, as usual, rubbed him the wrong way. "You would think I cared an anna piece what happened to him. Let him try any tricks on me and it'll be the worse for him." He made his way to the door, adding: "I'm going up for a wash now."

"That's right, Matt! Your own room's prepared. I've kept it ready for you since the day ye left. Not a soul has been in it, and not a hand has touched it but my own. The bed has been well aired for you, too. You go and freshen yourself up and I'll lay the tea while you're upstairs." She watched him eagerly, awaiting some expression of appreciation for her forethought, but he was still offended at her and went into the hall without a word. She heard him pick up a bag and march upstairs and, straining her ears, listening to every movement he made above; she heard him go into Grandma's room, heard this new, swaggering laugh of his as he greeted the old woman with a boisterous flourish. Despite her confused disquiet the sounds which he made above comforted her and she became filled with a glowing sense of gratitude at the feeling of his proximity; she had her own son actually in the house beside her after all these weary months of separation. She breathed a prayer of gratitude as she quickly began to make preparations for the evening meal.

Soon Nessie came bounding in. She had seen the trunks in the hall and rushed up to Mamma in a flutter, crying:

"Is he home, Mamma? What great big boxes! Where is he? I wonder if he's brought me a present from India. Oh! I want to see Matt! Where is he?" At Mrs. Brodie's word she dashed upstairs, calling out expectantly to Matt, all eagerness to see him. In a few moments, however, she came down slowly, stood again before Mamma, this time dejectedly, frowning her little petulant frown, her swelling excitement entirely collapsed. "I hardly knew him," she remarked, in her old-fashioned way. "He's not like our Matt a bit. He didn't seem in the least glad to see me."

"Tuts, Nessie!" exclaimed Mamma. "You're haverin'. He's had a long journey. Give him time to settle down."

"When I went in he was drinkin' something out a wee leather bottle. He said not to bother him."

"He would be doing his unpackin', child. Don't be so impatient. He's got other things to think of just now, forbye you."

"When I asked him about my compass he said he had thrown it away—he said something I didna understand—something about it bein' like your nose."

Mrs. Brodie coloured deeply, but made no reply. She felt sure that Nessie must be making some mistake, must have misconstrued the remark, yet her heart was heavy at the thought of what might have been implied.

"I thought he might have brought me a wee string o' coral beads or something like that," persisted Nessie. "Grandma's real upset too, she thought he might have minded her with a keepsake. He seems to have brought nothing for anybody."

"Don't be selfish, Nessie!" cried Mamma sharply, venting all her pent-up feeling in this rebuke. "Your brother has enough to do with his money without squandering it on you. Not another word out of your head! Away and call Grandma down to make the toast," and, pursing her lips closely together, Mrs. Brodie inclined her head more rigidly to its angle of endurance, set herself resignedly to arrange the tea things upon the table.

When tea time drew near Matthew came down to the kitchen. A faint flush tinged the yellow of the skin around his prominent cheek bones, his speech was more profuse than when he had arrived, and, detecting a faint but suggestive odour upon his breath, instantly Mamma knew that he had been fortifying himself for the meeting with his father. Observing him covertly she perceived that, despite his vaunting talk, he dreaded this coming encounter; at once her recent humiliation was forgotten and all her instincts rose again to his protection.

"Sit down by the table, on your chair, son! Don't tire yourself out any more."

" 'S all right, Mamma," he replied. "I'll keep on my pins. Been cramped up travelling these last few days. I like to stretch myself a bit." He moved restlessly about the room, nervously fingering everything within reach, looking repeatedly at the clock, and getting in her way as she passed to and from the table.

Grandma Brodie, who had entered behind him and now sat by the fireside, called out:

"Man! you're like a knotless thread. Is that a habit you've picked up off these black men to wander about like that? It fair makes my head giddy to look at ye." She was still bitter about not having received a present from him.

Eventually he sat down, joining the others at the table. In spite of all his resistance the approach of half-past five was cowing him; all the firm resolutions which he had formed for days past to stand up to his father and assert himself as a man of the world began to ooze from him, and his especial determination to maintain a nonchalant assurance at this first interview gradually wilted. Coming home, it had been easy for him to tell himself that he cared nothing for his father—now, as he sat in his old chair at the same table and within the same unaltered room, waiting, his ears anxiously alert for that firm heavy footstep, the over-whelming sweep of old associations deluged him, and, losing all his acquired dash and hardihood, he became the nervously expectant youth once more. Instinctively he turned to his mother, and to his annoyance found her limpid eye regarding him with a sympathetic understanding. He saw that she appreciated his emotions, that his apprehension was apparent to her, and a furious resentment against her stirred him as he exclaimed:

"What are you looking at now? It's enough to make a man jump when you look at him like that." He stared at her angrily until she lowered her eyes.

At half-past five the well-remembered click of the door startled him; the sound was exactly to the second, for Brodie, after a prolonged period of irregularity in his meals, had now resumed, with an utter disregard for business, his habits of scrupulous punctuality. Now, as his father came into the room, Matthew gathered himself together, controlled the movements of his hands, prepared himself for a bitter onslaught of words. But Brodie did not speak, did not once look at his son. He sat down and began to partake comfortably of his tea, which he seemed to enjoy immensely. Matthew was abashed. In all his visualisations of the meeting nothing like this had ever occurred, and now he had an almost irresistible impulse to cry out, like a schoolboy in disgrace: "Look, father, I'm here! Take notice of me!"

Brodie, however, took no notice of him, but went quietly on with his meal, staring straight ahead of him, and saying no word until it seemed as though he had no intention of recognising his son. But at last, after a long time, when the tension in the room had grown almost unbearable, he turned and looked at Matthew. It was a penetrating gaze which saw everything and expressed everything, pierced the outside shell of hard bravado into the soft, shrinking flesh beneath, permeated and illuminated the deep recesses of Matthew's mind, and which said:

"You've returned at last, then. I know you! Still a weakling and now a failure!"

Under that glance Matthew seemed to diminish visibly in stature and, although he fought with all the strength in him to meet his father's eyes, he could not. His own gaze wavered, quailed, and, to the intense humiliation of his swaggering vanity, fell downwards to the ground.

Brodie smiled grimly, then having, without uttering one word, brow-beaten the other to subjection, he spoke, saying only, with a cutting inflection:

"You've arrived!" Yet, expressed within the short compass of these simple words were a dozen sarcastic, objectionable meanings. Mamma trembled. The baiting of her son had begun and, though she saw that it was going to be worse than she had feared, she dared not say a word for fear of aggravating her husband's mood. Her eyes fell upon her Matt with a terrified, compassionate sympathy as Brodie continued: "It's a real pleasure to see your braw, handsome face again, although it has turned as yellow as a guinea. Ye were aye a bit pasty faced now I think o't, but all the gold ye've been savin' out by there has fair jaundiced ye." He surveyed Matthew critically, warming to his work, finding an outlet in this sardonic onslaught for all his bitter sufferings of the past months.

"It's worth it, though, no doubt it's worth it," he continued. "You'll have brought us a hantle o' gold from these foreign parts ye've been slavin' in. Ye'll be a rich man now? Are ye rich?" he shot out again.

Matthew shook his head dismally, and at this silent negation, Brodie's eyebrows lifted in a stupendous sneer.

"What!" he cried, "ye havena brought back a fortune? That beats a'! I thought from the way you've been jauntin' about Europe and from those grand big boxes in the hall that ye must be worth a mint o' money at least. Then, if ye're not as rich as all that, why did ye get yoursel' thrown out o' your position?"

"I didn't like it," muttered Matthew.

"Dear! dear!" remarked Brodie, appearing to address the company at large. "He didna like his position. He maun be a big man to be so hard to please as all that; and the downright honesty of the man to admit that he didna like it." Then, turning to Matthew, and hardening his tone, he exclaimed: "Do ye not mean that it didna like you? I've been told here in Levenford that you were soundly kicked out o' it— that they got as sick of the sight o' ye out there as I am already." He paused, then continued suavely: "Still, I may be wronging you. I've

243

no doubt ye've got something splendid in view—some marvellous new position. Have ye not?"

His tone demanded a reply and Matthew muttered: "No," sulkily hating his father now with a violence which shook him, feeling it an unbearable humiliation that he, the travelled, the experienced, the sophisticated buck, should be spoken to like this; he swore inwardly that, though at present he made no resistance, when he was stronger, more recovered from his journey, he would be revenged for every insult.

"No new post to go to!" Brodie continued, with assumed affability. "No post and no money! You've just come back to live off your father. Come back like a beaten dog. Ye think it's easier to sponge on me than to work, I suppose."

A tremor ran through Matthew's frame.

"What!" cried Brodie, "are ye cold? It's the sudden change from the great heat ye've been called upon to endure when you were workin' yourself into the jaundice outbye. Your dear mother will have to get ye some warm clothes out o' these grand, big cases o' yours. I mind weel she was aye plaisterin' ye with flannels when ye were a boy. And now that you're a braw, full-grown man she mustna let ye get a chill. Na! Na! you're too precious and valuable for that." He passed up his cup for more tea, remarking: "I havena made such a good tea for a long time! It fair gives me an appetite to see your pokey face back again."

Matthew could endure these taunts no longer, and giving up the pretence of eating, he got up, mumbling to Mamma in a broken voice: "I can't stand this any longer. I don't want any tea. I'll away out!"

"Sit down!" thundered Brodie, pushing the other back with his closed fist. "Sit down, sir. Ye can go when I tell ye to and not before. I'm not done with ye yet." Then, as Matthew subsided into his seat, he continued, cuttingly: "Are we not to have the privilege of your society next? Ye've been away two years and yet you canna bide in the house two minutes. Can ye not see that we're all waiting to hear about these wonderful adventures you've had out there? We're just hanging on the words that are ready to drop from your lips. Come on! tell us all about them."

"Tell you about what?" answered Matthew sullenly.

"About the grand, excitin' time ye've had outbye. About the rajahs and princes you've been hob-nobbin' with—about the elephants and the tigers ye've shot—tell us quick before ye've time to mak' it up. Ye'll be a perfect daredevil now, I suppose? There'll be no end to what ye can do?"

"I can maybe do more than you think," muttered Matthew under his breath.

"Indeed, now!" sneered Brodie, catching at the other's words. "You're going to surprise us, are ye? It's the same story as before, always what you're goin' to do. Never what ye've done, mind ye, ut always what's comin' off next! Gad! when I look at ye there with hat cringin' look about ye, and all these fine, flashy clothes on ye, it nakes me wonder what ye will do." His anger rose until it almost hoked him, but with an effort he controlled it and continued in his mooth, ironic voice: "Never mind though! It's such a treat to have ye ack that we mustna be too hard on ye. The main thing is that you've ome back safe and sound from all the terrible dangers that ye're too nodest to speak about. We must have the notice o' your return put in he *Advertiser*. Then all your braw friends—especially your lady friends —will ken that you're home. They'll be swarmin' round ye like flies ound a honey pot. That's what ye like, isn't it—to have the women ettin' ye and runnin' after ye?"

Matthew made no reply and after a moment's pause Brodie con- inued, drawing back his lips sardonically:

"I suppose next Sunday that mother o' yours will have ye all toshed p and have ye out at the kirk for the general admiration o' her braw ongregation. Ye might even squeeze your way into the choir again if e were sleekit enough, to let them all hear your bonnie voice lifted up praise o' the Lord. It would be a real manly thing to sing in the choir gain—would it not? Answer me, ye dummy. Do ye hear what I'm ayin' to ye?"

"I'll not sing in any choir," retorted Matthew, thinking sullenly that : was like his father to bring up this memory of the past and use it, erisively, to force him into a ridiculous position.

"The prodigal son refuses to sing," sneered Brodie. "Did ye ever ear the like o't—and him that had the lovely, lovely voice. Well my ne man," he continued with a snarl, "if ye'll not sing for your mother ou'll sing for me. You'll sing to the tune I pipe. Don't think that I an't see through ye. I do! ye've disgraced yourself and me. Ye hadna ie grace to stick to your job like a man—ye must come running back ome to your soft mother like a beaten cur. But don't think ye can try iat with me. Keep yourself in order when I'm about or, by God! it'll e the waur o' ye. Do ye understand what I mean?" He rose from the ible abruptly, and stood glaring down at his son. "I'm not finished ith ye yet. I'll knock the fancy notions out o' your head before I'm one with ye. I warn ye—keep out of my path, sir, or I'll smash ye own as ye stand. Do ye hear me?"

Matthew, emboldened by seeing that his father was about to go and oaded by the very humiliation of his position, raised his head and ooked sideways at the other, muttering:

"I'll keep out of your way, all right."

Brodie's eye flamed fiercely in return. He grasped Matthew's noulder.

"You dog!" he shouted, "don't look at me like that. Don't dare o do it or I'll break you. You thing that calls yourself by the name o'

Brodie. You're a disgrace to me, sir, yes! a bigger disgrace than you bitch of a sister." Then as Matthew's eye again fell, he continued, disgus mingling with his anger: "It scunners me to think a man of noble bloo could beget a whelp like you. You're the first Brodie to be called coward, but by God you are one none the less. You're a hangdog cowar and I'm ashamed o' ye!" He shook his son like a sack of bones, the suddenly released his hold and allowed him to collapse inertly back int the chair.

"Watch what you're about, my man. I'll have my eye on ye," h cried, forbiddingly, as he walked out of the room.

When he had gone Nessie and Grandma continued silently to loo at Matthew, but Mamma dropped on her knees beside him and place her arm around his shoulder.

"Never mind, Matt! never mind, my own son! I love ye, onyway! she wept.

He thrust down her arm whilst the muscles of his face twitched unde the pale skin.

"I'll pay him out yet," he whispered, as he rose up. "I'll get eve with him. If he's not done with me I'm not done with him."

"You're not going out now, son," cried Mrs. Brodie fearfully. "Ye bide in with me to-night, won't you? I want ye to be beside me."

He shook his head.

"No!" he said, controlling his voice with an effort, "I must go out. He licked his dry lips. "I've got some—some old friends to look up I'm goin' out now. Give me a key."

"Don't go, son," she implored. "Don't let what your father sai upset ye. He doesna mean it. He's worried himself. Stay in with you mother now, there's a good lad. Ye've had no tea at all. Stay in an I'll make ye something nice. I love ye, Matt. I love ye so much I woul do anything for ye!"

"Give me the key, then," he replied. "That's what I want."

Silently she gave him her own key. He thrust it into his pocket, saying "I'll be late! Don't sit up for me."

She followed him, wavering in fear, to the door. "Ye'll be careful Matt, won't ye. Keep out o' mischief for my sake, son. Don't let him drive ye to anything rash. I couldna bear it now that you're safely bac to me."

He made no reply but was gone, disappearing rapidly into the dark ness beyond. Her ears followed his steps until they died into the quie of the night, then, with a short, dry sob she turned and went back t the kitchen. She did not know what was going to happen, but she feare exceedingly.

VIII

NEXT morning Mrs. Brodie woke early, while it was still almost dark, but, as she stirred, she heard in the distance the first, faint, challenging cock crow, betokening, despite the obscurity, the imminent dawn of another day. Although she had waited up late on the night before, she had not seen Matthew come in, and now, after a troubled sleep, her first thought was to assure herself that he was well. As she dressed there was no need for her to be timorously silent for fear of disturbing her husband, since she was now alone in the small room that had been Mary's, yet, from long habit, her actions were as stealthy and inaudible as the movements of a shadow. The dim light entered the window of the bedroom and vaguely revealed her ghostly, drooping figure as she shivered into her clothes. Her underclothing was so patched, darned, and repaired as to become at any time a puzzle to assume and now, in the cold obscurity of the chill February air, her insensitive, roughened fingers fumbled confusedly with the coarse, worn garments. As she dressed thus, by sense of touch, her teeth chattered slightly, giving the sole audible indication of her presence and activity.

When she had covered her body by solving the intricate riddle of her enigmatical vestments, she rubbed her hands soundlessly together to induce some sign of circulation and slid out of the room in her stockinged feet.

Matthew's bedroom, being at the back of the house and facing east, was better illuminated; as she silently entered it she saw amongst the disordered confusion of bedclothes, the outlines of his regularly breathing form, and she too again breathed regularly with relief. His face looked leaden in the bluish pallor of the morning light, as the corners of his mouth dry sordes had formed, and sleaves of dark hair lay tangled upon his brow. Between his lips his tongue seemed to protrude slightly as though it had become too swollen and bulky for its normal confines, and with each respiration it acted as a dull sounding-board for the hoarse passage of his breath.

Mamma gently restored the blankets and coverlet to a more orderly comfort, ventured even to stroke the tumbled locks of hair from his eyes, but as, at her touch, he stirred uneasily and muttered, she drew back, quickly removing her hand, yet leaving it poised in mid air above his head as though unconsciously she blessed him in his sleep. Her gaze, too, was like a benediction, maintained for a many moments. At length, reluctantly, she slowly withdrew her eyes from his face and turned to go. On her way out of the room she observed that his coat, vest, and trousers were strewn in disarray on the floor, that his shirt had been flung into one corner, his collar and tie into another and, as though glad to render him service, she stooped, picked up the scattered garments, folded them neatly upon a chair, looked again at his sleeping face, and went quietly away.

Downstairs, everything lay exposed in the stale, repugnant ebb of the low tide of early daybreak; the night, receding like an ocean, had left the furniture disordered, the dead fire dirty with grey, powdered ashes, the pile of unwashed dishes cluttering the scullery sink obscenely, like wreckage upon a desolate shore.

In the usual way, before she stirred herself into jerky activity to lay and light the fire, blacklead the grate, wash the dishes, sweep the floor, boil the porridge, and perform the endless necessities of the morning, she would first indulge herself with a cup of strong tea, feeling, in her own words, that it drew her together. The hot, fragrant liquid was like a healing draught, comforting her, warming her, clearing away the mists in her brain, and resigning her to the hardships of another day.

This morning, however, although she hurriedly infused and poured out a cup of tea, she did not herself drink it but, having carefully cut and delicately buttered two thin slices of bread, she placed these, together with the tea, appetisingly upon a tray, which she then carried up to Matthew's room.

"Matt," she whispered, touching him lightly upon the shoulder, "here's some tea for ye, son. It'll freshen ye up." Although she bent over him he still snored on, exuding with each breath the reeking halitus of stale liquor, which disturbed her deeply, made her, in her agitation, speak more loudly. "Matt! Here's something nice for ye!" That was what she used to say to him, coaxingly, when he was a boy, and at her words he stirred, half awake, twisted impatiently, and with eyes still closed, muttered:

"Let me sleep, boy. Go to hell. Don't want any chota hazri."

Unhappily, she shook him.

"Matt, dear, this tea will do you good. It's nice for ye in the morning."

At this he opened his eyes and surveyed her from under listless, stuporous lids; within his dark pupils she could see the dull, unhappy comprehension of his position slowly reawaken.

"It's you, is it," he slurred; "what you want wakenin' me like this. Let me sleep."

"But the nice tea, dear! so refreshing. I went straight down and made it myself."

"You're always flinging tea at me! Let me sleep, damn it all!" He hunched round his back at her and was at once asleep again.

Mamma looked miserably from his prone figure to the tray still in her hands, as though unable to comprehend his refusal or the full force of his abuse, then, moved by the thought that he might later reconsider his decision, she laid the tray down on a chair by the bedside, covered the cup warmly with the saucer, inverted the plate protectingly over the fresh bread, and turned disconsolately away.

He was on her mind all morning. The fire kindled, the dishes became clean, the boots were brushed, the porridge bubbled, she took up her husband's shaving water, then began to lay the table whilst she thought of him, lamenting the words he had used to her, mourning the revealing odour of his breath, yet all the time excusing him in her mind. The shock of coming home, of his father's treatment, had upset him; as for his language, he had, poor boy, been in a rough land, and had not been fully awakened when he spoke to her. Whilst she forgave him, the still house began to stir, light and heavy sounds vibrated through the ceiling, doors were opened and shut upstairs, and now, confronted by the fear that some further disturbance might arise between Brodie and her son, she listened anxiously for the noise of some sudden outburst, the clash of angry voices, even for the sound of a blow. To her intense relief none came, and after Nessie had come downstairs and been hurriedly fed, and packed off with her satchel of books, Brodie descended and began to breakfast in sombre, solitary silence. She had taken the utmost care that everything should be perfect for him this morning in order to lull him into a more amiable mood, was prepared, even, to lie blatantly about Matt's coming in late; but although his mood seemed to her unpropitious, her fear proved to be unfounded and he departed without a single reference to his son.

When he had gone she breathed more easily and, her tranquillity further restored by a belated cup of tea, she prepared Grandma's breakfast and took it upstairs shortly before ten o'clock. When she had visited the old woman she tiptoed across the landing and listened with her ear to the door of Matt's room; hearing only the rise and fall of his breathing she softly opened the door. She saw at once that nothing had been touched and, to her wounded feelings, it seemed as though the undisturbed tray mutely rebuked her, that the plate still investing the untouched bread and butter, and the saucer still uselessly covering the long since cold tea, were like tokens of her folly and presumption. He still slept. Confusedly she wondered if his removal from what she considered to be an antipodean hemisphere might not have inverted the hours of his repose, and, in rendering him active at night and drowsy by day, have thus made it a necessity for him to sleep through certain hours of the forenoon. Unconvinced in mind but none the less eased a little in heart, feeling that if not this, perhaps some kindred reason existed for his behaviour, she did not disturb him, and again passed quietly out of the room.

Hesitatingly she addressed herself to her household duties in an effort to divert her attention, but as the forenoon drew on, uneasiness gradually possessed her; she comprehended that if their son was still in bed when Brodie returned for dinner a disastrous scene might take place. Anxiously she pricked her ears for the first evidence of his retarded activity and, towards noon, was rewarded by hearing the faint creak of his bed as it surrendered his body, the sound of his step upon the boards above. Hastily decanting water into a jug from the kettle which stood ready boiling, she rushed upstairs to leave it outside his door.

He was a long time dressing, but about quarter to one he came slowly downstairs and entered the kitchen. She greeted him fondly.

"I'm glad that you've had a nice long sleep, dear, but you've had no breakfast. Will you have a bite before your dinner? Just say the word, it'll not be the least bother for me to get ye a——" It had been on her tongue to offer him the universal panacea—a cup of tea—but mercifully she recollected his remark of the morning in time and added: "anything that's in the house."

"I never eat much in the morning." He was smartly dressed in a different suit from the day before, in a smooth, fawn hopsack with a puce shirt and natty brown tie to match; as he fingered the bow of his tie with white plastic fingers that trembled slightly, he eyed her doubtfully, judging erroneously from her adulatory manner that she could not fully have realised his discomfiture of the night before. "I miss the fresh fruit my servants used to bring me," he asserted, feeling that some further explanatory remark might be required of him.

"You'll have some nice apples to-morrow, Matt," she replied eagerly. "I'll put in the order sure. If ye just tell me what you'd like or the kind of food you've been used to outbye, I'll do my best to get it for ye."

His attitude repudiated the idea of such sour wizened apples as she might obtain for him in this unproductive land; he waved his hand eloquently, and retorted shortly:

"I meant mangoes, fairy bananas, pineapple. Nothing but the best is any use to me."

"Well, son, we'll do our utmost, anyway," she replied bravely although somewhat out of countenance at the grandiloquence of his remark. "I've got a nice dinner for ye anyway. Then, if ye feel like it afterwards, I was thinking maybe we might have a bit stroll together."

"I'm going out for *tiffin*," he inserted coldly, as though her suggestion was ridiculous and to be seen walking with her decrepit, outlandish figure the last thought his superior mind would entertain.

Her face fell, and she stammered:

"I—I had such nice nourishin' broth for ye, boy, as sweet as anything."

"Give it to the old man," he retorted bitterly. "Give him a bucketful. He can stand it." He paused for a moment, then continued in a more ingratiating tone: "I wonder though, Mamma, if you would lend me a pound or two for to-day. It's such a confounded nuisance but my bank drafts have not come through from Calcutta yet." He frowned at the annoyance of it all. "It's causing me no end of inconvenience. Here am I stuck up for a little ready cash all through their beastly delay. Lend me a fiver and you shall have it next week."

A fiver! She almost burst into hysterical tears at the word, at the painful absurdity of his request that she should lend him at a moment's notice five pounds—she who was bleeding herself white to scrape together the monthly toll that would soon be levied on her, who had, apart from the three pounds she had laboriously collected for the purpose, only a few paltry copper and silver coins in her purse!

"Oh! Matt," she cried. "Ye don't know what you're askin'. There isna such a sum in the house!"

"Come on now," he replied rudely, "you can do it fine. Toll out. Where's your bag?"

"Don't speak to me like that, dear," she whispered. "I canna bear it. I would do anything for ye, but what you're askin' is impossible."

"Lend me one pound then, seeing you're so stingy," he said, with a hard look at her. "Come on! give me a miserable pound."

"Ye can't understand, son," she pleaded. "I'm so poor now I can hardly make ends meet. Your father doesna give me enough for us to live on." A yearning desire took hold of her to tell him of the manner in which she had been obliged to raise the money to send to him at Marseilles, but she stifled it, realising with a sudden pause that this moment, above all, was not propitious.

"What does he think he's doing? He's got his business and this precious wonderful house of his," Matthew sneered. "What is it he's spending the money on now?"

"Oh! Matt, I hardly like to tell ye," she sobbed, "but things seem to be in a bad way with your father in the business. I'm—I'm feared the house is bonded. He hasna said a word to me but I saw some papers lyin' in his room. It's terrible. It's the opposition that's started against him in the town. I've no doubt he'll win through, but in the meantime I've got to make one shillin' do the work of two."

He looked at her in sullen amazement, but refused, none the less, to be diverted from the issue.

"That's all very well, Mamma!" he grumbled. "I know you. You always had something tucked away for a rainy day. I want a pound. I tell you I've got to have it. I need it."

"Oh, my dear, have I not told ye how ill-off we are," she wept.

"For the last time, will ye lend me it?" he threatened.

As she again sobbingly refused him she thought, in her agitation, for the space of a horrified instant, that he was going to strike her, but abruptly he turned upon his heel and left the room. As she stood there, her hand clutching her side, she heard him banging about through the rooms upstairs and finally come down, pass through the hall without speaking, and slam out of the house.

When the reverberating echoes of the bang of the door had died upon the air they still resounded in her brain like an ominous portent of the future, and involuntarily she raised her hands to her ears to blot them out as she sat down at the kitchen table, an abject, disillusioned figure. She felt, as she rested there, her head supported in her hands, that the story of the bank draft must be a specious lie, that he, having spent the forty pounds, was now penniless. Had he almost threatened her? She did not know, but he had wanted the money badly, and she, alas, had been unable to give it to him. Before she could analyse her emotions further, and realising now that she should have been in a position to accede to his later demand, that in a fashion the fault had been hers, on top of her misery came a great rush of tenderness. Poor boy, he had been used to mixing with gentlemen who spent money freely, and it was only fair that he should have money in his pocket like the rest. It was, in fact, a necessity after the high society life he had been leading. It was not just to expect a young man as well put on as Matt to go out without the means of backing up his smart appearance. He had really not been to blame and, in some degree, she regretted not having given him at least a few shillings, if he would have accepted them from her. As the affair became thus presented to her in a more satisfactory light and she was filled by a sense of her own inadequacy she rose and, drawn by an irresistible attraction she went up to his room and with loving care began to tidy the litter of wearing apparel which encumbered it. She now discovered that his clothing was not so plentiful as might have been expected from first appearances, finding one trunk to be completely empty, two of his cases to be filled with thin drill suits and another stuffed untidily with soiled linen. Eagerly, she seized upon socks to darn, shirts to mend, collars to starch, feeling it a joy to serve him by attending to these needs, beatitude even to touch his garments.

Eventually, having restored order amongst his things and arranged, for her attention, a large bundle which she bore away in triumph, she entered her own room, made her bed, and began in a more cheerful spirit to dust the furniture. As she came to the shallow china toilet tray that rested on the small table by the window an undetermined sense of perplexity affected her; a familiar impression to which she had long been accustomed in her subconscious mind was now lacking. She pondered absently for a moment, then suddenly realised that she did not hear the intimate, friendly tick of her watch which, except on those state occasions when she wore it, lay always upon this small tray of hers which now confronted her, denuded of all but a few stray hairpins. When she had been compelled to change her room she had of course brought this tray with her and the watch had still remained upon it; indeed, for twenty years the touch of this tray had been consonant with her audition of the watch, and at once she appreciated the variation.

Although she knew that she was not wearing the watch she clutched at her bodice, but it was not there, and immediately she began to look for it in a flurry, searching everywhere in her own room, in Brodie's room, downstairs in the parlour and in the kitchen. As her unsuccessful search was prolonged, a worried look appeared on her face. It was her mother's watch, a fine scrolled silver shell with a gilt face, delicate spidery hands, and a Swiss mechanism which never failed to register the exact minute, and although it was not valuable she had for it, and for the small faded daguerreotype of her mother clipped inside the case, a rare and sentimental affection. It was her only trinket and for this fact alone she treasured it deeply. As she stooped to survey the floor she knew that she had not mislaid it and she asked herself if someone had not accidentally interfered with it. Suddenly she straightened up. Her face lost its annoyance, and instead became stricken. She realised in an illuminating flash that Matt had taken her watch. She had heard him in her room, after she had refused to give him the money, and he had rushed out without speaking to her. She knew irrevocably that he had stolen her watch for any paltry sum he might obtain for it. She would gladly have given him it as she had given him everything in life that was hers to give, but he had thieved it from her with a sly, sneaking baseness. With a hopeless gesture she pushed back a wisp of grey hair that had been disarranged in her futile search. "Matt! my son," she cried out aloud, "you know I would have given you it! What way did ye steal it?"

On this, the day following her son's return, when she had glowingly anticipated content and the mitigation of her worries, she found herself sunk more deeply into the well of her dejection. Dinner passed and the afternoon proceeded eventlessly towards evening. Amidst the trouble of her thoughts the fall of dusk and the fading of the short grey twilight made her wish poignantly to see him. Only let them be alone together, the mother and the son, and she felt she would soften any hardness in his heart. He could not, she was convinced, withstand the entreaty of her affection; he would be at her feet in penitence and remorse if only she could express to him in words the love that was in her heart. But still he did not appear and, when the clock struck the half hour after five and he did not come in for tea, she was immeasurably distressed.

"I suppose that braw mannie o' yours is ower feared to come in," Brodie sneered at her as she handed him his tea. "He's deliberately avoidin' me—skulkin' outside there until I've gane out again. Then he'll come sneakin' in for your sympathy and consolation. Don't think I don't see through it all, although it's behind my back."

"No, indeed father," she quavered, "I assure ye there's nothing to keep from ye. Matt has just gone out to look up some o' his friends."

"Is that so, now?" he answered. "I didna ken he had any friends, but from what you make out he must be the popular hero right enough! Well, tell your model son, when ye see him, that I'm savin' up a' that I've got to say until I meet him next. I'll keep it hot for him."

She made no reply, but served him with his meal, and when he went out set herself again to wait.

At seven o'clock, about an hour after Brodie had left the house, Matthew did, indeed, return. He came in quietly with a slight indication upon his face of the old downcast expression of his youth, sidled into the room and, looking at Mamma ingratiatingly, said in a soft voice:

"I'm sorry I'm late, Mamma dear. I hope I haven't put you about?"

She looked at him eagerly.

"I *have* worried about you, Matt! I didn't know where you had gone!"

"I know," he replied in a subdued voice. "It was downright thoughtless of me. I don't think I have quite got used to being here. I may have got a little careless since I've been away, Mamma, but I'll make up for it to you."

"It's not like you to be careless," she cried, "except to yourself, going without your food like this. Have you had your tea?"

"No," he replied, "I haven't, but I'm real hungry now, though. Have you something for me to eat?"

She was touched, convinced, despite her day of despondency, that this was her own son again who had sloughed off the skin of his wicked Indian experiences.

"Matt!" she said earnestly, "you ought to know better than ask. Your supper is in the oven this very minute." She ran to the oven and produced, impressively, for his inspection a thick cut of findon haddock cooked in milk, a dish of which he had been particularly fond in the past. "Wait just half a minute," she cried, "and I'll be ready for you."

Grandma Brodie had gone up to her room but Nessie was occupying the table with her homework. Nevertheless, in a few moments, Mamma had spread a white cloth upon half of the table and had covered it with every requisite of an appetising meal.

"There, now," she said, "I told ye I wouldn't be long. There's no one can do a thing for ye like your own mother. Sit in, Matt, and let us see what *you* can do."

He rolled his eyes up at her gratefully and bowed his head.

"Oh! Mamma, you're too kind to me! I don't deserve it. It's like heaping coals of fire on my head after the way I've gone on. It does look good though, doesn't it?"

She nodded her head happily, watching him eagerly as he drew in his chair, sat down, and began to eat with large, quick mouthfuls. "Poor boy, he must have been starving," she thought, as the succulent white flakes of the fish melted magically under the soft, relentless attack of his knife and fork. Nessie, sucking the stump of a pencil at the other end of the table, watched him over the edge of her book with a different emotion.

"Some folks are luckier than others," she remarked enviously. "We didn't get finnan haddie to-night."

254

Matt looked at her with a wounded expression, then placed the last large piece of fish carefully in his mouth.

"If I had known, Nessie," he expostulated, "I would have offered you some. Why did you not speak before?"

"Don't be so selfish, girl," cried Mamma sharply. "You've had enough and plenty, and you know it. Your brother needs some decent food now. He's had a hard time lately. You get on with your lessons. Here, Matt—try some of these oatcakes."

Matt thanked her with a warm, upward look and continued to eat. At his attitude Mamma was overjoyed and, the loss of her watch now completely forgotten, she regarded him benevolently, happily, every mouthful he took causing her an intense enjoyment, as if the food which he consumed was savoured by her own palate with infinite relish. She observed with sympathy that his face was marked by smuts; amazed at her own shrewdness, she surmised that he had brushed into a dusty hedge, that he had been hiding outside from his father. She was concerned, so that benevolence gave way to protection; he was her own boy once more and she would shelter and defend him against the world.

"Did ye enjoy that, son?" she asked finally, hungering for his praise. "I took special pains with it. I knew ye always liked it."

He smacked his lips.

"It was lovely, Mamma! Better than all the curries I had to put up with out in India. I tell you I've missed your cooking. I've never had a decent dish like that since I left."

"Is that the case, son," she exclaimed. "It gladdens me to hear it. Now! is there anything else you would like?"

Out of the corner of his eye he saw on the dresser a dish of small apples which he imagined she must have procured for him. He looked at her for a moment reflectively.

"I think, Mamma, I would like an apple," he said with the simplicity of one who has pure desires. She was overjoyed to have anticipated his wish and at once brought over the dish.

"Just what I thought. I gave the boy the order this morning," she said delightedly, proving her thoughtfulness of his every wish. "You said you wanted fruit and I said that you should have it."

"Thank you, Mamma! I don't wish to smoke," he explained, as he bit with difficulty into the hard fruit, "and I'm told an apple destroys the craving. What need have I to smoke, anyway? It doesn't do me any good."

Mrs. Brodie laid her hand caressingly on his shoulder as she murmured:

"Matt, it does my heart good to hear you say that. It's worth more to me than anything on this earth. I'm happy. I feel we're going to understand each other better. now. It must have been the long separation that upset us both, but these misunderstandings are sent from above to try us. I prayed for understanding to come to the both of us, and the prayer of an unworthy woman has been answered."

He lowered his eyes, for a moment, in remorse while he persisted in his efforts with the apple, then, looking up and choosing his words with extreme care, he said slowly, unveiling another rapturous surprise for her:

"You know, Mamma, I saw Agnes this afternoon."

She started with surprise and pleasure.

"Of course," he hurried on, before she could speak, "I can't say much just now. You mustn't ask me anything. My lips must be sealed on what passed between us, but it was very satisfactory." He smiled at her deprecatingly. "I thought you would be pleased to hear, though."

She clasped her hands in ecstasy, her bliss only tempered by the thought that it was not she herself, but another woman in the person of Miss Moir, who had, perchance, turned her son's steps back to righteousness. Still, she was overjoyed and, stifling the unworthy thought, she ejaculated:

"That's good! that's grand! Agnes will be as happy as I am about it." Her bowed back straightened slightly as she raised her moist eyes to heaven in a pæan of unspoken gratitude; when she looked down again to earth Matthew was addressing Nessie.

"Nessie, dear! I was selfish a minute ago but I'll make up for it now. I'm going to give you this half of my apple if you leave Mamma and me together a little. I want to talk to her privately."

"Nonsense, Nessie!" exclaimed Mamma, as Nessie stretched out her hand agreeably. "If you're to have a bit apple don't take the bite out your brother's mouth."

"Yes, Mamma. I'm going to give this to Nessie!" insisted Matt, in a kindly voice, "but she must let you and me have a little chat now I've got something to say that's for your ears alone!"

"Well, Nessie," said Mrs. Brodie, "take it, and thank Matt for it and don't let us have any more of your ungrateful remarks in the future. You can leave your homework in the meantime and go into the parlour and do your practising for half an hour. Away with you, now. Take the matches, and be careful how you light the gas."

Glad to be relieved from her hated books, Nessie skipped out of the room and soon the halting tinkle of the piano came faintly into the kitchen, interpolated at first by pauses barren of melody, co-related to the lifting of the apple from the bass end of the keyboard.

"Now, Matt," said Mrs. Brodie warmly, drawing her chair close to his, feeling that her improbable dream of the morning was about to be fulfilled, and hugging herself with a trembling satisfaction.

"Mamma," began Matthew smoothly, inspecting his hands carefully, "I want you to forgive me for being so—well—so off-hand since I came back; but you know I've been worried. I've had a lot on my mind."

256

"I could see that, son!" she agreed, compassionately. "My heart has gone out to you to see how you've been upset. It's not everybody that understands your sensitive nature the way I do."

"Thank you, Mamma," he exclaimed; "you're kind as ever you were, and if you forget any hard words I've said I'll be grateful. I'll try and be a better man."

"Don't belittle yourself in that fashion, Matt," she cried. "I don't like to hear it. You were aye a good boy. Ye were always my own son— I never knew ye do a really wrong action."

He lifted his eyes for an instant and shot a quick furtive glance at her, then immediately veiled them, murmuring:

"It's nice to be in with you again, Mamma."

She smiled devotedly at his words, recollecting that as a boy it had been a manifestation of his childish pique to be "out with her," and, when she was eventually restored to favour to be "in with her."

"We'll never be out with each other again, will we, dear?" she countered, fondly.

"That's so, Mamma," he agreed, and allowed an impressive pause to elapse before remarking casually: "Agnes and I are going to the prayer meeting to-night."

"That's splendid, Matt," she whispered. He was definitely reclaimed! "I'm that pleased about it. Oh, but I would like to come with you both!" She halted timidly. "Still—I—I suppose ye would rather be your two selves. It's not for me to interfere."

"It might be as well, perhaps, Mamma," he admitted deprecatingly. "You know how it is!"

She looked at the clock, observing that it was quarter to eight. She regretted exceedingly having to break up this heart to heart talk, but with true unselfishness, she said, with a not unhappy sigh:

"It's nearly eight as it is, I'm afraid. You'll have to be stirring now or you'll be late," and she made as though to move.

"Just a minute, though, Mamma!"

"Yes, dear!"

"I wanted to ask you another thing!" He hesitated and looked at her soulfully, having, from his point of view, reached the critical point of the interview. "Mamma," he murmured irresolutely.

"What is it, Matt, my dear?"

"It's just like this, Mamma! I may as well be honest with you! I've been an awful spendthrift," he confessed. "People have taken advantage of my generosity. I have no money just now. How can I go about with Agnes with nothing in my pocket?" He had the air of one, the victim of his own open-handedness, from whom the words fell shamefully. "I'm used to having some cash always with me. It makes me feel so small to be without it, specially when I'm with a lady, back in my own town. Could you not help me, Mamma, until I get started again?"

She saw at once that it was a supremely reasonable request. She had been right in assuming that her boy, accustomed to high and lavish society, could not confront Levenford penniless; still less could he encounter Miss Moir in such a penurious predicament. In the flush of her reunion to him she threw caution to the winds and, with a magnificent sacrifice, she arose silently, unlocked her drawer and withdrew from it the square box which contained her accumulated savings for the initial repayment of her heavy debt. She looked adoringly at Matthew, heedless of the future, remembering only that she was the mother of this loving and devoted son.

"This is my all, Matt," she said soberly, "and I've saved it dearly for a most important and necessary cause. But I am going to give ye some of it."

His eyes gleamed as she opened the box and took out a pound.

"Take this for your pocket, son," she said simply, holding out the note to him in her outstretched hand, her worn face softened by love, her bent figure drooping a little towards him. "I give it to you gladly. It's yours!" It was a sacrifice of supreme and touching beauty.

"How much have ye altogether?" asked Matthew ingenuously, rising up and going close to her. "You've got a lot in there, right enough."

"There's nearly three pounds here," she replied, "and it's been a weary job for me to save it. Times are hard with us now, Matt—harder than ye might think. I'll need every penny of this by the end of the month."

"Mamma! Let me keep it for you," he said wheedlingly. "I'll keep it till the end of the month. I'll not spend it. I might as well keep it in my pocket as let you lock it in that old tin box. What a funny place to keep your money!" He made the idea of her little box as a receptacle for money appear almost ludicrous. "I'll be your banker, Mamma! It's nice for me to feel I have something to fall back on, even if I never have the need for it. Just the feel of it beside me would make me comfortable. Come on, Mamma! a pound is nothing, really, to a fellow like me." He held out his hand coaxingly.

She looked at him with a vague, frightened doubt in her eyes.

"It's most important for me to have this money by the end o' the month," she stammered. "I don't know what'll happen if I haven't got it."

"You shall have it then," he assured her. "What a worrier you are! Leave it to me. I'm as safe as the Bank of England!" He took the money out of the open box as he continued talking volubly, reassuringly. "You're not going to let your Matt go about like a pauper, are you, Mamma?" He laughed at the very idea. "A gentleman needs a little ready brass to give him assurance. You'll be right as rain, Mamma," he continued, edging into the hall. "I'll see to that! Don't sit up for me now, I'll like as not be late."

He was out and away with a last, gay wave, and she was left with the open, empty box in her hands, staring at the panels of the front door that had closed behind him. She sighed convulsively whilst the piano chattered in her ears with a false sprightliness. Blindly she suppressed the recurrent thought of her missing watch and an inchoate doubt as to the wisdom of so weakly allowing him to take the money. Matt was a good boy! He was hers again and their mutual love would surmount any obstacle and conquer all difficulties. He was on his way to worship God with a good Christian girl. Happiness flowed into her heart once more, and she returned to the kitchen, well content with what she had done.

She sat down, gazing into the fire, a faint reminiscent smile upon her face at the memory of his tenderness to her. "He did relish that fish, the boy," she murmured to herself. "I maun make him some more nice dishes." Then, suddenly, as she was about to recall Nessie to her lessons the door bell rang with a short, trenchant peal. Mamma felt startled as she got up, it was so far beyond the time of an ordinary visitor. Matthew had his key, he could not have returned like this; the least thing upset her nowadays, she reflected, as she cautiously opened the door. Miss Moir, palely outlined in the glimmer of the lobby lamp, stood before her.

"Oh! Aggie dear, it's you," she exclaimed in some relief, pressing her hand to her side. "I got quite a fright. You've just missed Matthew by a few minutes."

"Can I come in, Mrs. Brodie?" Again Mamma was startled. Not once in the space of three years had Agnes addressed her in such terms, and never in such a strange, unnatural voice.

"Come in—of course ye can come in, but—but I'm telling you Matthew has gone out to meet ye."

"I would like to speak to you, please."

In amazement Mamma admitted a frozen-faced Agnes. They went into the kitchen.

"What's it a' about, dear?" she faltered. "I don't understand this in the least. Matt's away to meet you. Are ye not well?"

"Quite well, thank you," came from Miss Moir's stiff lips. "Did you know that—that Matthew came to see me this afternoon?" She had the utmost difficulty in uttering his name.

"Yes! he's just told me. He's gone to take you to the meeting; Matt has gone to get you," repeated Mrs. Brodie stupidly, mechanically, as a fearful spasm gripped her heart.

"It's a lie!" exclaimed Agnes. "He's not gone to see me or to look near any meeting."

"What!" faltered Mamma.

"Did he tell you what happened to-day?" said Agnes, sitting up

259

straight and gazing in front of her with hard eyes.

"No! No!" halted Mamma. "He said he couldna speak about it yet."

"I can well believe that," cried Agnes bitterly.

"What was it, then?" whimpered Mrs. Brodie; "tell us for God's sake."

Agnes paused for a moment, then, with a quick indrawing of her breath, she steeled herself to her humiliation. "He came in smelling of drink, in fact he was nearly the worse of it. In spite of that I was glad to see him. We went into the back shop. He talked a lot of nonsense— and then he tried to borrow—to borrow money off me." She sobbed dryly. "I would have given him it, but I saw he would just spend it on spirits. When I refused he called me awful names. He swore at me. He said I was a ——" She broke down completely. Her big eyes gushed tears. Her full bosom panted with hard sobs; her large mouth drew into bibbering grimaces. In a frenzy of lamentation she flung herself at Mrs. Brodie's feet. "But that wasna everything," she cried. "I had to go into the shop a minute. When I came back he tried to—he tried to insult me, Mamma. I had to struggle with him. Oh! if only he had been kind to me I would have given him what he wanted. I don't care whether I'm wicked or not. I would! I would!" she shrieked. Her sobs strangled her. "I love him, but he doesn't love me. He called me an ugly bitch. He tried to take—to take advantage of me. Oh! Oh! Mamma, it's killing me. I wanted him to do it, if only he had loved me. I wanted it!" she repeated in a high hysteria. "I had to tell ye. I'm worse than Mary was. I wish I was dead and finished."

She flung back her head and gazed wildly at Mrs. Brodie. The eyes of the two women met and fused in a dull horror of despair, then Mamma's lips twisted grotesquely, her mouth drew to one side, she made as though to speak but could not, and with an incoherent cry she fell back helplessly in her chair. As Agnes gazed at the limp figure her eyes slowly grew startled, her thoughts withdrew gradually from her own sorrow.

"Are ye ill?" she gasped. "Oh! I didn't think it would take you like that. I'm so upset myself I never thought it might make you feel as bad as that. Can I not get you anything?"

Mamma's eyes sought the other's face, but still she did not speak.

"What can I do for you?" cried Agnes again. "You look so bad I'm frightened. Will I get you some water—will I get the doctor? Speak to me."

At last Mamma spoke.

"I thought my boy was going out with ye to worship the Lord," she whispered in a strange voice. "I prayed that it should be so."

"Oh! don't talk like that," exclaimed Agnes. "You'll need to come and lie down a wee. Come and lie down till you're better!"

"My side hurts me," said Mamma dully. "It must be that my heart is broken. Let me go to my bed. I want to be quiet and by my lone in the darkness."

"Let me help you, then," cried Agnes, and taking the other's passive arm she drew her to her feet, supported her, and led her unresistingly up the stairs to her bedroom. There she undressed her, and assisted her to bed. "What else can I do for you?" she said, finally. "Would you like the hot bottle?"

"Just leave me," replied Mamma, lying on her back and looking directly upwards. "Ye've been kind to help me, but I want to be by myself now."

"Let me sit with you for a bit! I don't like to go away yet awhile."

"No! Agnes. I want ye to go!" said Mrs. Brodie, in a dull flat voice. "I want to shut myself in the darkness. Turn out the gas and leave me. Just leave me be."

"Will I not leave the gas in a peep?" persisted Agnes. "No matter what's happened I can't think to go away like this."

"I wish the darkness," commanded Mrs. Brodie, "and I wish to be alone."

Agnes made as though to speak but, feeling the futility of further protest, she took a last look at the inert figure upon the bed, then, as she had been bidden, turned out the gas. Leaving the room in blackness she passed silently from the house.

IX

As Matthew shut the front door upon Mamma, and ran lightly down the steps, he was filled with a lively humour and as he smiled knowingly, the sham meekness fell from his face like a mask. "That's the way to work the old woman. Smart! Done like an artist too," he chuckled to himself, "and not bad for a first touch." He was proud of his achievement, and felt in agreeable anticipation that he would do even better next time, that Mamma must have a tidy sum tucked away in a safe place. It would be his for the asking! The few shillings which he had received by pawning her watch had disgusted him, for he had expected it to be worth considerably more, but now that he had a few pounds in his pocket, his prestige and cheerfulness were restored. Just let him have the cash, he told himself gleefully, and he was all right. He knew how to disport himself with it!

The lights of the town twinkled invitingly. After Calcutta, Paris, London, he would find Levenford contemptibly small, yet this very disdain filled him with a delightful self-esteem. He, the man of the world, would show them a few things in the town to-night; yes, by gad! he would paint it a bright, vermilion red! At his thoughts a throaty laugh broke from him exultantly and he looked about him eagerly. As he swung along he saw dimly on the other side of the street the moving figure of a woman and, looking after the indistinct figure, he leered to himself: "That one's not much good to a man, she's in too much of a hurry. What does she want to run like that for?" He did not know that it was Agnes Moir on her way to see his mother.

He quickened his steps through the darkness that wrapped him like a cloak, revelling in this obscurity which made him feel now more dashing, more alive than the broad light of day. What manner of youth had he once been, to be afraid of this stimulating opacity? It was the time when a man woke up, when he could have some fun! Memories of lotus-eating nights he had spent in India recurred vivaciously to him and, as they rose before him, whetting his anticipation, he muttered: "These were the nights. These were the splurges. I'll go back all right. Trust me!" Gaily he plunged into the first public-house in the street.

"Gin and angostura," he cried in an experienced tone, banging a pound note down on the bar. When the drink came he drained it in a gulp and nodded his head affirmatively, sophisticatedly. With the second glass in his hand he gathered up his change, slipped it into his pocket, tilted his hat to a rakish angle, and looked round the saloon.

It was a poor sort of place he noted indifferently, with drab red walls, poor lights, dirty spittoons and sawdust on the floor. Heavens! sawdust on the floor, after the rich, thick piled carpet into which his feet had sunk so seductively in that little place in Paris. Despite his demand there had been no bitters in his gin. Still, he did not care, this was only the opener! His first and invariable proceeding on these jovial excursions was to get a few drinks into himself quickly. "When I've got a bead in me," he would say, "I'm as right as the mail. Man! I'm a spunky devil then." Until he felt the airy spinning of wheels within his brain he lacked drive, daring, and nerve; for, despite his bluster, he was at heart the same soft, irresolute weakling as before and he required this blurring of his impressionable senses before he could enjoy himself in perfect self-confidence. His susceptible nature reacted quickly to the suggestive urge of alcohol and his bold dreams and pretentious longings were solidified thereby into actualities, so that he assumed with every glass a more superior aspect, a more mettled air of defiance.

"Anything happening in this hole to-night?" he enquired largely of the barman—it was the class of tavern which, of necessity, had a large, powerful male behind the bar. The barman shook his close-cropped bullet head, looking curiously at the other, wondering who the young swell might be.

"No!" he replied cautiously, "I don't think so. There was a mechanics' concert in the Borough Hall on Thursday!"

"Gad!" replied Matthew, with a guffaw. "You don't call that sort of thing amusement. You're not civilised here. Don't you know anything about a neat little place to dance in, with a smart wench or two about. Something in the high-stepping line."

"You'll no' get that here," replied the tapman shortly, wiping the bar dry with a cloth, and adding sourly: "this is a decent town you're in."

"Don't I know it," cried Matt expansively, embracing with his glance the only other occupant of the room—a labouring man who sat on a settle against the wall watching him with a fascinated eye from behind a pint pot of beer. "Don't I know it. It's the deadest, most sanctimonious blot on the map of Europe. Aha! but you should see what I've seen. I could tell you stories that would make your hair stand on end. But what's the odds. You don't know the difference here between a bottle of Pommeroy and a pair of French corsets." He laughed loudly at his own humour, viewing their incredulous faces with an increasing merriment, then suddenly, although gratified at the impression he had created, he perceived that no further amusement, no further adventure was to be had there, and, moving to the door with a nod of his head and a tilt of his hat, he lounged out through the swing doors into the night.

He sauntered slowly along Church Street. That delicious woolly numbness was already beginning to creep round the back of his ears and infiltrate his brain. An easy sensation of well-being affected him; he wanted lights, company, music. Disgustedly he looked at the blank, shuttered shop windows and the few, quickly moving pedestrians, and parodying contemptuously the last remark of the barman, he muttered to himself: "This is a decent graveyard you're in." He was seized by a vast and contemptuous loathing for Levenford. What good was a town of this kind to a seasoned man like him whose worldly knowledge stretched from the flash houses in Barrackpore to the Odeon bar in Paris?

Moodily, at the corner of Church Street and High Street, he turned into another saloon. Here, however, his glance immediately brightened. This place was warm, well lit, and filled with the animated chatter of voices; a glitter of mirrors and cut glass threw back myriads of coruscating lights; stacks of bottles with vivid labels were banked behind the bar, and through half-drawn curtains he saw, in another room, the smooth, green cloth of a billiard table.

"Give me a Mackay's special," he ordered impressively. "John Mackay's and no other for me."

A plump, pink woman with jet drop ear-rings served him delicately. He admired the crook of her little finger as she decanted the spirits, considering it the essence of refinement, and although she was matronly he smiled at her blandly. He was such a lion with the ladies! A reputation like his must be sustained at all costs!

"Nice snug little place you've got here," he remarked loudly. "Reminds me of Spinosa's bar in Calcutta. Not so large but pretty well as comfortable!" There was a hush in the conversation, and feeling with satisfaction that he was being stared at, he sipped his whisky appreciatively, with the air of a connoisseur and went on: "They don't give you the right stuff out there, though! Not unless you watch them! Too much blue vitriol in it. Like the knock-out gin at Port Said. Nothing like the real John Mackay." To his satisfaction a few people began to collect round him; an English sailor in the crowd nudged him familiarly and said, thickly:

"You been out there too, cocky?"

"Just back!" said Matt affably, draining his glass. "Back across the briny from India."

"And so have I," replied the other, staring at Matthew with a fixed solemnity, then gravely shaking hands with him, as though the fact that they had both returned from India made them brothers now and for all time. "Bloody awful heat out there, isn't it, cocky? Gives me a thirst that lasts till I get back."

"Have a wet, then?"

"Naow! You have one along o' me!"

Agreeably they argued the point until they finally decided by tossing.

"Lovely lady," cried Matthew with a killing glance at the fat barmaid. He won, and the sailor ordered drinks for everyone in the small coterie. "Right with the ladies every time," sniggered Matthew. He was glad that he had won and the sailor, in the exuberance of his drunken hospitality, glad to have lost. Whilst they drank they compared their amazing experiences and the mob gaped whilst they discussed mosquitoes, monsoons, bars, bazaars, ship biscuits, pagodas, sacred and profane cows, and the contours and anatomical intimacies of Armenian women. Stories circulated as freely as the drinks until the sailor, far ahead in the matter of inebriation, began to grow incoherent, maudlin, and Matt, at the outset of his night's enjoyment and swollen with an exuberant dignity, set himself to look for an excuse to shake him off.

"What can a man do in this half-dead town?" he cried. "Can't you squeeze out some excitement here." This was not the society he had moved in before leaving for India and no one recognised him; as, indeed, they did not know him to be a son of the ancient Borough he preferred them to regard him as a stranger, a dashing cosmopolitan. They could think of nothing worthy of him and were silent until finally someone suggested:

"What about billiards?"

"Ah! a game of pills," said Matt thoughtfully, "that's something in my line."

"Billiards!" roared the seaman. "I'm true blue I am! I'll play anybody alive for—for anything you like to—what—I——" his voice deteriorated into a drunken dribble of sound. Matthew considered him dispassionately.

"You're the champion are you? Good enough. I'll play you fifty up for a pound a side," he challenged.

"Right," shouted the other. He surveyed Matthew with lowered lids and an oscillating head, indicating, in incoherent yet unmistakable picturesque language, that he would be soused for a son of a sea cook if he would go back on his word. "Where's your money?" he asked solemnly, in conclusion.

Each produced his stake, which the onlooker who had first suggested the game had the honour of holding, and, as no one had ever played in the place for such an unheard of sum, the crowd, simmering with excitement, surged into the billiard-room behind them amidst considerable commotion, and the game commenced.

Matthew, looking dashingly proficient in his shirt sleeves, began. He was, he fully understood, a good player, having practised assiduously in Calcutta, often indeed during the daytime when he should have been perched upon his office stool, and he realised with an inward complacency that the other, in his present condition, could be no match for him. Professionally, he ran his eye along his cue, chalked it and, feeling that he was the focus of the combined admiration of the gathering, broke the balls, but failed to leave the red in baulk. His opponent, swaying slightly upon his feet, slapped his ball on the table, took a rapid sight at it and slammed hard with his cue. His ball struck the red with terrific violence and, pursuing it eagerly all round the table through a baffling intricacy of acute and obtuse angles, finally bolted after it into the bottom right-hand pocket. The crowd voiced its appreciation of the prodigious fluke. He turned and, supporting himself against the table, bowed gravely, then exclaimed triumphantly to Matthew:

"Whadeye think of that, cocky? Who's topsy-boozy, now? Didn't I say I was true blue? Wasn't that a shot? I'll play you with cannon balls next time." He wanted to stop the game for a profound dissertation upon the merits of his marvellous stroke and a lengthy explanation of how he had performed it, but, after some persuasion, he was prevailed upon to continue. Though he readdressed himself to the game with the air of a conqueror his next shot was hardly so successful, for his ball, struck hard on the bottom, bounced skittishly across the cloth, hurdled the edge of the table in its stride, and landed with a thud on the wooden floor amidst even louder and more prolonged applause than had greeted his previous effort.

"Wha' do I get for that?" he enquired, owlishly, of the assembly at large.

"A kick on the arse!" shouted somebody at the back. The seaman shook his head sadly, but they all laughed, even the fat barmaid who was craning her neck to see the fun and who tittered involuntarily, but recovering herself with a start, quickly merged her merriment into a more modest cough.

It was now Matthew's turn to play, and though the balls were favourably placed, he began with great caution, making three easy cannons and then going in off the red. Next, he began to play a series of red losing hazards into the right middle pocket, so accurately that at every stroke the object ball returned with slow, unerring exactitude to the required position below the middle of the table. The crowd held its breath with profound and respectful attention whilst he continued his break. Under the bright lights his white, fleshy hands swam over the smooth baize like pale amœbæ in a green pool; his touch upon the cue was as delicate and as gentle as a woman's; the spirits in him steadied him like a rock. This was the greatest joy that life could offer him, not merely to show off his perfect poise and masterly ability before this throng, but to draw upon himself this combined admiration and envy. His empty vanity fed itself upon their adulation greedily.

When he had made thirty-nine he paused significantly, rechalked his cue, and neglecting, obviously, an easy ball which lay over the pocket, he addressed himself ostentatiously to a long and difficult cushion cannon. He achieved it, and with three, further, quick shots ran out with his unfinished break of fifty. A storm of cheering filled the room.

"Go on sir! Don't stop! Show us what you can do!"

"Who is he? The man's a marvel!"

"Stand us a pint, mister. It's worth that, anyway!"

But with a lordly assumption of indolence he refused to continue, pocketed his winnings, and flung his cue into the rack; now that he had made his reputation he was afraid to mar it. They surrounded him, clapping him on the back, pushing and shoving each other, trying to shake hands with him, whilst he gloried in his popularity, laughing, talking, gesticulating with the rest. His opponent, having been with difficulty convinced that the game was over, manifested no regrets, but flung his arm tipsily round Matthew's shoulder.

"Did you see that shot of mine, cocky?" he kept repeating, "it was worth a pound—worth five pounds. It was a—a regular nor'easter— a pickled ripsnorter. I'm true blue I am," and he glared defiantly round, seeking for anyone who might dispute it.

They all went back to the bar where the whole assembly had beer at Matthew's expense. He was their hero; they toasted him, then dispersed into small groups throughout the room discussing, stroke by stroke, the memorable achievement of the victor.

Matt swaggered about the room, lording it over them. He had no false reticence, no mock modesty, but visited each group, saying to this one: "Did you see that cannon of mine off the cushion? Pretty neat, wasn't it? Judged to a hair's breadth!" to another: "Dash it all, I've made a break of two hundred on my day—more than two hundred!"

and to a third: "The poor barnacle, what chance had he against the likes of me? I could have beat him with my walking-stick." He lauded himself to the skies and the more he drank the more his silly vanity ballooned itself, until the room seemed to him to become filled with a babble of voices all lifted up to him in honeyed, fulsome flattery. His own tongue joined in the pæan, the light gleamed about him like a thousand candles lighted in his honour, his heart swelled with gratification and delight. He had never had a triumph like this before; he considered himself the finest billiards player in Levenford, in Scotland, in the Kingdom; it was something to be able to make a break of fifty like that; why did they want to degrade him by shoving him into an office when he could play billiards in such a marvellous fashion?

Suddenly, at the height of his jubilation, the fickle favour of the crowd waned; a heated argument had developed between two new-comers—an Irish navvy and a bricklayer—and the general attention left him and fixed itself upon the protagonists, whilst the mob goaded on each in turn in the hopes of provoking a fight. After all, he had only bought them beer—the price of popularity was higher than that—and almost at once he found himself alone, in a corner, friendless and forgotten. He almost blubbered with dismay at the sudden change in his condition, reflecting that it was always the same, that he could never maintain the centre of the stage for a sufficient length of time but was shoved, before he wished it, into the background. He wanted to run after them and recapture their errant favour, to shout: "Look! I'm the man that made the break of fifty! Don't forget about me. I'm the great billiards player. Gather round me again! You'll not see a player like me every day!" His vexation deepened, merged insensibly into resentment, and in his disgust he swallowed two large whiskies, then, with a last indignant look which swept scowlingly over them all, he went out of the bar. No one noticed him go.

Outside, the pavements tilted slightly as he walked, moving like the deck of a liner in a mild swell; yet, cunningly, he adapted his balance to this gentle regular roll so that his body swayed slightly from side to side—but nevertheless maintained its upright poise. The exhilaration of the movement charmed him and soothed his wounded conceit. As he traversed the High Street he became aware that, in manœuvring so skilfully amongst the intricate difficulties of this perpetually alternating plane, he was accomplishing a noted feat, one ranking equally, perhaps, with his remarkable achievement at billiards.

He felt that it was not late, and with great difficulty he attempted to make out the time from the lighted dial of the Town clock; with his legs wide apart and his head thrown back he struggled with the abstruse dimensions of time and space. The steeple oscillated gently and wavered in harmony with the earth, the hands were indistinct, but he thought that it was just ten o'clock and his satisfaction at his cleverness was unbounded when, a moment later, the clock struck ten. He counted the chiming notes with sage, explanatory beats of his arm as though he himself were tolling the bell.

Even for a dead and alive town like Levenford it was too early for him to go home. A man like Matthew Brodie to return home at the childish hour of ten o'clock? Impossible! He rammed his hand into his trousers pocket and feeling the reassuring crackle of a pound note and the clinking touch of silver coins, he thrust his hat more firmly on his head and once more set off down the street. Disappointingly few people were about. In a real city he would have known what to do; it was the easiest thing in the world to fling himself into a cab and, with a knowing wink, tell the driver to take him to the *bona robas*; he had only to lie back, luxuriously, and smoke his cigar whilst the spavined horseflesh dragged him happily to his destination. But here there were no cabs, no excitement, no women. The one girl whom he discovered and addressed gallantly ran from him panic-stricken, as though he had struck her, and he damned the town for its blatant, bourgeois piety, cursed the female population in its entirety for the reputable habit of retiring early, for the unhappy integrity of its virtue. He was like a hunter after game who, the more it evaded him, became the more desperate in his pursuit and he swayed up the High Street and down again, fruitlessly essaying to find some means of combating the melancholy of drunken despondency which began slowly to settle upon him. At last, when he felt that he must enter another tavern to drown the sorrow of his failure all at once he remembered! He paused abruptly, slapped his thigh extravagantly at his unaccountable lapse of memory, and allowed a slow smile to expand his features as he recollected that house in College Street which, in his youth, he had always hurried past with averted eyes and bated breath. Rumours regarding this tall, dark, narrow house, sandwiched between the Clyde Dress Agency and the mean pawnshop at the foot of the Vennel, had spread from time to time like tiny ripples on the flat, impeccable surface of Levenford's respectability, giving the house a mysterious but tacitly acknowledged reputation amongst the knowing youth of the town. Its curtains were always drawn and no one entered by day, but at night lights discreetly appeared, footsteps came and went, sometimes music was heard. Such an iniquity, however veiled, must long ago have been expunged from so ancient and reputable a Borough, but a controlling hand of protection seemed to lie over the house, not perhaps sanctioning but rather concealing its inoffensively, immoral existence; it was even hinted by malicious individuals that certain baillies and prominent citizens found a not infrequent occasion upon which to make use of this rendezvous, in, of course, an eminently sedate and genteel manner.

"That's the hidey-hole for you, Matt. You'll see if ye were right or wrong. You've often wondered what's inside and now you're going to find out," he muttered to himself, delightedly, as he lurched towards College Street, bent upon investigating the horrors at which his immature experience had shuddered. It struck him suddenly as the most ludicrous jest imaginable that he should be on his way to a bawdy house in Levenford, and he burst into peals of laughter so that he was obliged to stop, and roll helplessly against the side of a wall, whilst inane guffaws shook him and tears of mirth coursed down his face. When he was able to proceed, his despondency of a few short moments ago was gone, and he felt with a delicious, inward appreciation that he was enjoying himself infinitely more than he had expected. The alcohol he had absorbed had not yet reached the zenith of its stimulation and, with every floundering step he took, he became more stupidly heedless and more sublimely hilarious.

He entered the Vennel. The narrow street seemed more full of life than all the wide main streets of the town together; it teemed with an unseen activity. From the pens and closes and from behind even the thin walls of the houses came an endless variety of sounds—voices, laughter, the howl of a dog, the music of a melodeon, singing. He perceived that they did not retire early here, felt that he was in his element, and outside a lighted window, from which emerged a roistering chorus, he stood rooted, then suddenly, like a provoked dog, he threw back his head and lifted his loud, inebriate voice in unison with the harmony within. The music ceased immediately and, after a pause, the window was thrown up and a stream of slops descended in a curving arch towards him. It missed him, however, by a foot, merely splashing slightly about his legs, and he retired down the street gaily, with the full honours of the encounter.

Half-way down, his nostrils dilated to the succulent odour of frying ham arising from the cooking of some belated supper in a house which he was passing, and reaching him through the night in a spicy, savoury vapour. Immediately he felt hungry and, looking around, discerned over the way a small shop still open, a nondescript eating house devoted to the sale of such delicacies as pies, puddings, potted head, and tripe and onions. Moved by a sudden impulse, he strode across the street and muttering to himself drunkenly: "Ladies can wait. Matt needs little nourishment. Must keep strength up, m'boy " he entered the place magnificently. Inside, however, his whisky-hunger overcame his style and he shouted: "Throw us a meat pie quick, and swill in plenty of gravy."

"Penny or twopenny?" queried the greasy youth behind the counter.

"Sixpenny! you *soor*," replied Matthew, amiably. "Do you think I want any of your small trash? you *bobachee*. Pick me the biggest in the bunch and push it over here, *jilde*!" He slapped the coin down, took up the newspaper-wrapped package offered in return and, disdaining to consume the pie upon the premises, walked out. Down the street he went, tearing off the paper wrapping and stuffing handfuls of the delicacy into his mouth, eating voraciously, leaving behind him a track which became at once the joy and contention of all the starveling cats of the alley.

When he had finished, he breathed a sigh of content and, recollecting his manners, sucked his fingers and wiped them fastidiously upon his handkerchief. Then he hurried more urgently forward, full of meat and drink, ready now for the subtler and more piquant enchantments of the dessert. He came eventually to the house, found it, indeed, without difficulty, for it was not easy to forget one's way in Levenford, and for a moment he stood outside, contemplating the narrow veiled illumination of the windows. As he remained there, momentarily a faint return of his adolescent awe touched him strangely, made him hesitate, but urged by the wild thought of the pleasure that lay therein for him, he seized the knocker and hammered loudly at the door. The clangour thundered up and down the street with a rude insistence, and, when he desisted, echoed to and fro across the narrow canyon of the lane, leaving, after the final reverberation had ceased, a startled silence which seemed to fall upon the outside, to grip even the inside of the house. There was a long pause during which he stood swaying upon the door-step and, when he had almost made up his mind to knock again, the door was opened slowly, and for a small way only. Still, he was not dismayed by the inhospitable meagreness of this narrow aperture but, wise in his experience, immediately thrust his foot into the opening.

"Good evening, dear lady," he simpered. "Are you at home?"

"What do you want?" said a hard, low-toned, female voice from the interior darkness.

"The sight of your pretty face, my deah," he replied, in his best manner. "Come along now. Don't be so cruel and heartless. Give me a look at your bright eyes or your neat ankles."

"Who are you?" repeated the other harshly. "Who told you to come here?"

"I'm an old inhabitant, sweet creature, lately returned from abroad and not without the wherewithal." He jingled the money in his pocket enticingly, and laughed with a short, empty laugh.

There was a pause, then the voice said firmly:

"Go away! You've made a mistake. This is a respectable house. We'll have nothing to do with you whatever," and she made as though to close the door in his face. In the ordinary way he would have been deterred by this rebuff and would undoubtedly have slunk off, but now his foot prevented the door from closing and he replied, with some show of bluster:

"Not so fast, ma'am. Don't be so high and mighty! You're dealing with a tough customer here. Let me in or I'll make such a hullabaloo you'll have the whole street at your door. Yes, I'll bring the town down about your ears."

"Go away at once or I'll get the police on you," said the other in a less firm tone, after a momentary silence that seemed fraught with indecision.

He winked triumphantly at the darkness, feeling that he was winning, realising proudly that he could always bluff the women.

"No you won't," he replied craftily, "you don't want any police down here. I know that better than you do. I'm the gentleman you want to-night—just wait till you see."

She made no answer and, her silence encouraging him, her reticence serving to excite his lust, he muttered:

"I'll come and take a peep at you, Dolly," and, pressing his shoulder into the slight open space of the doorway, he forcibly insinuated himself into the hall. There he blinked for a moment in the light of the lamp which she held in her hand and which was now thrust forward into his face, then his jaw dropped and he stared boorishly, incredulously at her. Across the thrawn, forbidding face of the woman a gross purple nævus lay like a livid weal, stretching like a living pappy fungus which had eaten into and destroyed her cheek and neck. It fascinated him morbidly with the attraction of a repulsive curiosity.

"What do you want?" she repeated in a rasping voice. He was disconcerted; with an effort, he removed his eyes from her face, but as he gazed round the wide, high-vaulted hall his confidence returned at the thought that there were other rooms in the house, rooms sealed with an alluring mystery. She herself was only the bawd; there must be plenty of fun waiting for him behind one of these doors in the house. He looked at her again and immediately her disfigurement obtruded itself upon him, so forcibly that he could not release his attention from it and, despite himself, muttered stupidly:

"Woman, that's an awful mark on your face. How did ye come to get it?"

"Who are you?" she repeated, harshly. "For the last time I ask you, before I have you thrown out."

He was off his guard.

"My name's Brodie—Matthew Brodie," he mumbled in an absent, sottish voice. "Where are the young wenches? It's them I want to see! You'll not do!"

As he spoke she, in her turn, stared at him and, in the flickering light of the lamp, it seemed as if amazement and agitation in turn swept across her grim features. At length, she said, slowly:

"I told you that you had mistaken the kind of house that this is! You'll not find much to amuse you here. Nobody lives in this house but me. That's the plain truth. I advise you to leave at once."

"I don't believe you," he cried sullenly, and, his anger growing, he set up a great hubbub, shouting: "You're a liar, I tell you. Do you think I'm a fool to be put off with a yarn like that? I'll see you further before I go away. Do you think I'll let myself be put off by a thing like you?—me that's travelled to the other end of the world. No! I'll break into every room in this damned house sooner than be beat."

At the uproar which he created a voice called out from upstairs and immediately she thrust her hand over his face.

"Shut your mouth, will you," she cried fiercely. "You'll have the whole place about my ears. What the devil are you to come in and disturb an honest woman like this? Here! wait in this room till you're sober. Then I'll have it out with you. Wait until I come back or it'll be the worse for you." She seized him by the arm and, opening a door in the lobby, pushed him roughly into a small sitting-room. "Wait here, I tell you, or you'll regret it all your born days," she shot at him, with a forbidding look, as she shut the door and enclosed him within the cold, uninviting chamber. She was gone before his fuddled brain had realised it and now he looked round the small cold parlour into which he had been thrust with a mixture of disgust and annoyance. Luscious memories recurred to him of other houses where he had moved in a whirl of mad music and wild, gay laughter, where bright lights had danced above the rich warmth of red plush and eager, undressed women had vied with each other for the richness of his favours. He had not been three minutes in the room before his drunken senses collected themselves and, as his mind realised the absurdity of having permitted himself—a man of such experience—to be shut up out of the way in this small cupboard, his will shaped itself towards a fiery resolution. They would not close him up in this box of a place with fine sport going on under his very nose! He moved forward and, with a crass affection of caution, opened the door and tiptoed once more into the wide lobby, where a faint murmur of voices came to him from upstairs. Surreptitiously he looked round. There were three other doors opening out of the hall and he surveyed them with a mixture of expectation and indecision, until, choosing the one immediately opposite, and advancing carefully, he turned the handle and looked in. He was rewarded only by the cold darkness of a musty, unoccupied room. Closing this door, he turned to the one which adjoined it, but again he was disappointed for he discovered here only the empty kitchen of the house; and swinging round with a snort of disgust, he plunged heedlessly into the last room.

Immediately he stood stock still, whilst the thrill of a delicious discovery ran through him. Before his eyes, seated reading a newspaper beside the comfortable fire, was a girl. Like a frantic searcher who has at last discovered treasure he uttered deep in his throat a low exultant cry and remained motionless, filling himself with her beauty, fascinated by the warm reflection of the firelight upon the soft curve of her pale cheek, noting her slender body, the shapely curve of her ankles, as, still unconscious of him, she held her feet to the fire. She was attractive and, seen through the haze of his distorted, craving senses, she became to him at once supremely beautiful and desirable. Slowly he advanced towards her. At the sound of his step she looked up, her face at once became disturbed, and she dropped her paper, saying quickly: "This room is private, reserved."

He nodded his head wisely, as he replied:

"That's right. It's reserved for me and you. Don't be afraid; nobody will disturb us." He sat down heavily on a chair close to her, and tried to take her hand in his.

"But you can't come in here!" she protested in a panic. "You've no right to do such a thing. I'll—I'll call the landlady."

She was as timid as a partridge, and, he told himself greedily, as smooth and plump. He longed to bite the round contour of her shoulder.

"No! my dear," he said thickly, "I've seen her already. We had a nice long talk outside. She's not bonny, but she's honest. Yes! she's got my money, and I've got you."

"It's impossible! You're insulting me," she cried out. "There's been a mistake. I never set eyes on you before. I'm expecting someone here any minute."

"He can wait till I've gone, dearie," he replied coarsely. "I like the look of you so well I would never let you go now!"

She jumped to her feet indignantly.

"I'll scream," she cried. "You don't know what you're about. He'll kill you if he comes in."

"He can go to hell, whoever he is. I've got you now," shouted Matt, gripping her suddenly before she could shriek.

At that moment, when he hugged her close to his rampant body, whilst he bent down to her face, the door opened and, as he raised his head furiously to vituperate the intruder, he gazed straight into the eyes of his father. For what seemed an eternity of time the three figures remained motionless as though the three emotions of surprise, anger, and fear had petrified them into stone; then gradually, as Matt's arm relaxed, the limp figure of the girl slipped silently out of his embrace. Then as if this movement induced him to speak, yet without for an instant removing his eyes from his son's face, and in words as cold and penetrating as steel, Brodie said:

"Has he hurt ye, Nancy?"

The pretty barmaid of the Winton Arms came slowly up to him and tremblingly sobbed:

"Not much. It was nothing at all. He didna hurt me. Ye just came in time."

His lips compressed themselves firmly, and his gaze became more fixed as he replied:

"Don't weep then, lassie! Run awa' out."

"Am I to wait in the house for ye, dear?" she whispered. "I will, if ye wish it."

"No!" he exclaimed, without an instant's hesitation.

"Ye've had enough to thole. Run awa' hame." His eyes dilated and his hands opened and shut as he continued slowly: "I want to have this —this gentleman to myself—entirely to myself."

As she brushed past him he stroked her cheek, without looking at her, without relaxing a muscle of his face.

"Dinna hurt him," she whispered fearfully. "He didna mean anything. Ye can see he's not himself."

He did not reply, but when she had gone he shut the door quietly and came close up to his son. The two men looked at each other. This time Matt's eyes were not beaten down for he immediately lowered them and gazed deliberately at the floor. Through his inebriated mind a wild succession of thoughts whirled. The immediate sinking fear he had experienced was replaced by a contrary emotion which rushed upwards in a fierce and bitter resentment. Was his father inevitably doomed to thwart him? The memory of each humiliation, every taunt, all the beatings he had endured from the other throughout his life seethed through his pot-valiant brain like white fire. Was he to submit patiently to another thrashing because he had unwittingly obtruded upon his father's low woman? Mad with drink and frustrated lust, inflamed by the hot tide of his hate, he stood still, feeling blindly that now, at least he was beyond fear.

Brodie gazed at the lowered head of his son with a burning passion which at last burst the bonds of his iron control.

"You dog!" he hissed from between his clenched teeth. "You dared to do that! You dared to interfere with me and with what is mine. I warned ye to keep out of my way and now I'll—I'll strangle you." He put out his great hands to clutch the other's neck but with a jerk Matt broke away from him, staggering to the other side of the table, from where he glared insanely at his father. His pale face was bedewed with sweat, his mouth worked convulsively, his whole body shook.

"You're as bad as me, you swine!" he yelled. "Don't think you can come it over me any longer. You wanted that bitch for yourself. That was all. But if I can't get her I'll see that you don't. I've suffered enough from you. I'm going to suffer no more. Don't look at me like that!"

"Look at ye!" roared Brodie. "I'll do more than look at ye! I'll choke ye till I squeeze the breath out of your worthless body."

"Let me see you try," shouted the other, with a heaving breast. "You'll choke me none—you'll grind me down no longer. You think I'm feared of you, but by God! I'm not. I'll show you something you don't expect."

A more brutal rage surged in Brodie at this unexpected defiance and his eye glared but, without speaking, he began slowly to advance round the table towards his son. Yet, strangely, Matthew did not move. Instead, with a wild shout of delirious exultation he plunged his hand into his hip pocket and withdrew a small derringer which he clutched fiercely in his grasp and pointed directly at his father.

"You didn't know I had this, you swine," he shrieked. "You didn't know I had brought this from India. There's a bullet in it that's a keepsake for you. Take it now, damn ye. Take it now, you sneering bully!" And shutting his teeth behind his pale lips, he jerked back his forefinger and pulled the trigger. There was a bright yellow flash and a sharp explosion which sounded loudly within the confines of the room. The bullet, fired at close range, furrowed Brodie's temple and buried itself in the mirror of the overmantel, amidst a crashing of glass which tinkled upon the floor amongst the dying echoes of the shot.

For a second, Brodie stood aghast, then, with a loud cry, he rushed forward and struck his son a fearful blow with his mallet fist full between the eyes. Matthew dropped like a pole-axed animal, striking his head against the table leg as he fell. He lay senseless upon the floor, bleeding from his nose and ears.

"You murderer!" panted Brodie, staring with glittering eyes at the insensate form beneath him. "You tried to murder your own father." Then, as he stood thus, a furious knocking came upon the door, and the woman of the house burst into the room, trembling, her gruesome face becoming more ghastly as she gazed at the pistol and the inanimate figure on the floor.

"My God!" she gasped. "Ye havena—ye havena shot your own son?"

Brodie pressed his handkerchief to his raw, scorched temple, his face rigid, his chest still heaving painfully.

"Leave us," he commanded, still keeping his gaze upon Matthew. "It was him tried to kill me."

" 'Twas him fired at you, then," she cried, wringing her hands. "I knew no good would come o' him bustin' in like he did. Whatna noise that pistol made, too!"

"Get out o' here then," he ordered roughly. "Get out or there'll be more noise—if that's all that concerns you."

"Dinna do anything rash," she implored him. "Remember the name o' the house."

"Damn you and your house! The only name it has is a bad one," he shouted, forcing his fierce gaze on her. "Don't ye know I was nearly deid," and seizing her by the shoulder, he thrust her out of the room. When he had closed the door behind her he turned and again grimly contemplated the prone figure, then advancing, he stood over it and stirred it with his foot.

"You would have murdered your father," he muttered. "By God I'll pay you for it." Then he moved slowly to the table, sat down and,

275

folding his arms across his chest, patiently awaited the other's recovery.

For five minutes there was absolute silence in the room, except for the slow tick-tock of a clock that hung against the wall and the occasional fall of a cinder in the grate; then, suddenly, Matt groaned and moved. Holding his head in both hands, whilst blood still streamed from his nose, he tried to sit up but failed, and subsided again upon the floor with a low moan of pain. The blow which he had received had almost fractured his skull and now he felt sick with concussion. He had yet no consciousness of his father's presence as the room swam around him and a violent nausea affected him. He felt deathly sick, hiccoughed and then vomited. The disgusting accumulation of his stomach contents gushed from his mouth and mixed revoltingly with the pool of blood upon the floor. It appeared as if he would never stop retching, as though the reflex straining of his body would kill him, but at last he ceased, and after lying weakly upon his side, he rose, and staggered dizzily to a chair by the table. His face was pale and streaked with blood, his eyes puffed and swollen, but with such vision as was left to him he now saw, and gazed dumbly at, his father.

"You're still here you see," whispered Brodie softly, "and so am I." He uttered the last words with a slow intensity as he drew his chair nearer to that of his son. "Just the two of us alone in this room. Isna' that grand? It's a rare delight for me to be with ye like this, and to see ye so close to me." He paused for a moment, then snarled: "Your dear mother would love ye if she could only see you now. The sight o' your face would fair fill her heart with joy! The look o' these smart clothes that you've spewed such a braw new pattern ower would fair chairm her! Her big braw son!" Matthew was incapable of speaking, but speech was not required of him; Brodie picked up the pistol and, turning it over ostentatiously before his son's shrinking gaze, continued, in a more restrained and contemplative tone: "Man, when I see you there, I'm surprised that a thing like you had the courage to try to murder me. Ye're such a poor bit o' dirt. But although I'm not anxious to have a bullet in my brain it's a pity, in a way, that ye didna succeed. Ye would have danced so brawly at the end of a halter, swingin' from side to side with the rope round your yellow neck."

Matthew, now quite sober, turned a dead, piteous face towards his father, and, impelled by the instinct of flight, weakly tried to get up, in an endeavour to escape from the room.

"Stay where you are, you dog!" flared Brodie. "Do you think I'm done with ye yet? Ye'll leave here at my pleasure, and there's just the chance ye might never leave at all."

"I was out of my head, father," Matt whispered. "I didn't know what I was doin'—I was drunk."

"So ye take a dram, do ye?" sneered his father. "The very idea, now! That's another gentlemanly habit ye brought back from abroad.

No wonder ye have such a bonny aim wi' a gun."

"I didna mean to fire," whispered the other. "I only bought the pistol for show. Oh! I'll never, never do it again."

"Tuts! man," jibed Brodie, "dinna make such rash promises. Ye might want to murder somebody in real earnest to-morrow—to blow their brains out so that they lay scattered on the floor."

"Father, father, let me go," whined Matthew. "Ye can see fine I didn't mean it."

"Come! come!" jeered Brodie, "this'll never do. That's no' like the big man you are—that's not like your mother's dashin' son. Ye must have spewed a' the courage out o' ye by the look o' things. We maun gie you another drink to pull ye together." He seized the bell that lay on the table and rang it loudly. "Just consider," he continued with a dreadful laugh, "a dead man couldna have rung that bell. Na! I couldna have given ye a dram if ye had murdered me."

"Don't say that word again, father," Matt sobbed. "It makes me feared. I tell ye I didn't know what I was doing."

Here the landlady of the house came in and, with tight lips, silently regarded them.

"We're still a' alive, ye see," Brodie sang out to her gaily, "in spite of all the pistols and gunpowder and keepsakes from India; and since we're alive we're goin' to drink. Bring us a bottle o' whisky and two glasses."

"I don't want to drink," Matt quailed. "I'm too sick." His head was splitting in agony and the very thought of liquor nauseated him.

"What?" drawled Brodie. "Ye don't say! and you the seasoned vessel that carries revolvers about wi' ye. Man, ye better tak' what's offered, for ye'll need a good stiffener before I hand ye over to the police!"

"The police!" gasped Matt, in terror. "No! No! you wouldna do that, father." His fear was abject. He was now, through the blow, the reaction of his feelings, and the close proximity of his father, reduced to the level of an invertebrate creature who would have willingly crawled at the other's feet if he could thereby have propitiated him.

Brodie eyed his son repugnantly; he read his mind and saw the arrant cowardice staring from his bloodshot eyes. He was silent whilst the woman entered with the bottle and glasses, then, when she had withdrawn, he muttered slowly to himself:

"God help me! Whatna' thing is this to bear my name?" Then bitterly he took up the bottle and poured out two glasses of neat spirit.

"Here" he shouted, "we'll drink to my big, braw son. The fine man from India! The lady's man! The man that tried to kill his father!" Fiercely he thrust the glass at his son. "Drink it, you dog, or I'll throw it in your teeth." He drained his glass at a gulp, then fixed a minatory eye upon the other whilst Matthew painfully forced himself to swallow his portion of the spirit.

"Now," he sneered, "we'll make a fine comfortable night o' it, just you and me. Fill up your glass! Fill it up, I say!"

"Oh! father, let me go home," cried Matt—the sight and taste of the whisky now loathsome to him—"I want to go home. My head is bursting."

"Dear! dear!" replied Brodie, in a broad mimicry of his wife's voice. "Our Matt has a wee bit headache. That must have been where I struck you, son. That's terrible! What shall we do about it?" He affected to think deeply whilst he again emptied his glass. "Man, I can't think of anything better than a leetle speerits. That's the remedy for an honest man like you—some good honest whisky." He filled out another full glass of the raw liquor and bending forward, seized his son's jaw with vice-like fingers, prised open the weak mouth, then quickly tilted the contents of the glass down Matt's gullet; whilst Matthew gasped and choked he continued, with a frightful assumption of conviviality: "That's better! That's much better! And now tell me—don't hesitate, mind ye, but be quite frank about it—tell me what ye thought of Nancy. She's maybe no so weel born as your mother, ye ken, but she doesna stink in her person. Na! she's a clean wee body in some respects. A man canna have it both ways, apparently." Then dropping his assumed smoothness he suddenly snarled, in a devilish voice: "Was she to your taste, I'm askin' you?"

"I don't know. I can't tell," whined Matthew, realising that whatever answer he gave would be the wrong one.

Brodie nodded his big head reflectively.

"Man, that's true enough! I didn't give ye enough time to sample her. What a pity I came in so soon. I might have given ye another ten minutes thegither." Deliberately he whipped his own imagination on the raw with a dark unconscious sadism, knowing only that the more he tortured himself the more torment he gave his son. The more he saw his son's painful thoughts revolt from the consideration of his recent excesses, the more thickly he thrust these repugnant ideas upon him.

"Man," he continued, "I couldna help but admire the bold, strong way you handled her, although she couldna have refused anything to a braw callant like you. Ye would have thocht ye were fetchin' wi' a man the way ye gripped her."

Matthew could endure it no longer. He had reached the limit of his endurance and laying his head, which throbbed with the beat of a hundred hammers, upon the table, and bursting outright into weak, blubbering tears, he cried:

"Father, kill me if ye like. I don't care. Kill me and be done with it but, for God's sake, let me be."

Brodie looked at him with baffled, embittered fury; the hope he had entertained of taunting his son into another wild assault so that he might experience the delight of again battering him senseless to the floor, died within him. He saw that the other was too weak, too broken, too pitifully distressed to be provoked into another outburst and a sudden, rankling resentment made him bend over and catch him a tremendous buffet on the head, with his open hand.

"Take that, then, you slabbering lump," he shouted loudly; "you haven't even got the guts of a sheep." All the refinement of his anger, the sneering, the sarcasm, the irony, vanished, and instead, his rage flamed over like a raging sea whilst his face grew black with rabid fury like the dark clouding of an angry sky. "You would lay your fingers on my woman! You would lift your hand against me! Against me!" he roared.

Matt raised his eyes weakly, imploringly. "Don't look at me," bellowed Brodie, as though a sacrilege had been committed by the other. "Ye're not fit to lift your eyes above the level o' my boots. I canna look at ye but what I want to spit on ye. Take that, and that, and that." With every word he cuffed the other's head like an empty cask, sending it juddering against the table. "God!" he cried in disgust, "what are ye! Your head sounds like an empty drum. Have ye got to be drunk before ye can stand up for yourself? Have ye no sense of pride in the blood that's in ye? Have ye no pride to be heir to the name I gave ye?" Then, in the height of his fury, he suddenly seized Matt by the arm and, lifting him like a huddled marionette, dragged him to his feet. "For what am I wasting my time on ye here? We'll go home!" he cried. "I'll take ye home. Now we must deliver ye safely to your mother, out o' this wicked house. It's not the place at all for the son of such a godly woman." He linked his arm through Matt's and propped the staggering, half insensible figure against his own, then, flinging some money on the table, he rammed his hat on his head. "Can ye sing?" he shouted, as he trailed Matt out into the drab, empty street. "We maun have a bit chorus on the way home. Just you and me—to show folks what good friends we are. Sing, you dog!" he threatened, twisting the other's arm agonisingly. "Sing, or I'll kill ye!"

"What will—what will I sing?" came the panting, tormented voice of his son.

"Sing anything. Sing a hymn. Ay!" he gloated over the idea, "that's terra appropriate. Ye've juist missed murdering yer faither—ye maun sing a hymn o' praise and thanksgiving. Give us the Old Hundred, my young, braw man. Begin!" he ordered.

"All people that on earth do dwell," quavered Matt.

"Louder! Quicker!" shouted Brodie. "Give it pith! Put your heart into it. Pretend ye're just out o' the prayer meetin'." He marched the other off, supporting him, dragging him, bolstering him up when he

staggered on the uneven street, beating time to the tune, and fro
time to time joining his voice in the refrain with a blasphemous satir

Down the narrow Vennel they went, towards their home, the wor
ringing sonorously through the stillness of the imprisoned air. Faint
grew their steps and more faintly came the sound until, finally, the la
fading whisper was lost in the peaceful darkness of the night.

X

MRS. BRODIE lay on the thin, straw mattress of her narrow bed, enco
passed by the darkness of her room and the silence of the house. Nes
and Grandma were sleeping, but since Agnes had left her, she ha
remained strainingly awake for the sounds of Matt's return. Her min
since the shock she had received earlier in the evening, was blank a
dully incapable of thought, but, whilst she waited, she suffered phy
cally. Her acute pain had returned to her! Restlessly she twisted fr
side to side, trying one position and then another in an effort to allevi
the boring volleys of pain which enfiladed the entire length of her bo
Her feet were cold and her hot hands moved constantly on the frett
surface of the patchwork quilt that covered the bed. Automatically,
the darkness, her fingers moved over each pattern as though s
unconsciously retraced the labour of her needle. Dimly, she long
for a hot bottle to draw the blood from her congested head into t
icy numbness of her legs and feet, but she was too languid to stir a
she feared, too, in a vague way, to move from the safe harbour of h
room, dreading that some new misfortune might beset her, that s
might perhaps encounter some fresh and terrifying experience on t
stairs.

Slowly the seconds ticked into minutes, sluggishly the minutes dragg
into hours and, through the peace of the night, she heard actually t
faint distant note of the Town clock as it struck twelve whisperi
notes. In effect, another day had begun when she must soon face t
melancholy round of the daylight hours and all that the new da
would bring to her. But her introspection did not follow this cour
As the significance of the hour broke upon her she murmured onl
"He's late! They're both awfu' late!" With the characteristic pessimis
of a defeated spirit, she now sounded the abyss of melancholy possibil
to its deepest extent, and wondered, miserably, if Matt had encounter
his father in the town. Intangible contingencies following upon t
chance of this meeting made her tremble, even as she lay passive up
the bed.

At length, when her anxiety had reached an intolerable pitch, s heard steps outside in the road. Desperately she wished to rush to the window to try to penetrate the gloom outside, but she could not make the effort, and was compelled to lie still, waiting with anxious fears for the click of the front door latch. Soon, indeed, she heard this sound but with the opening of the door her perturbation increased, for, immediately, she distinguished the loud bawling voice of her husband, derisive, compelling, dominant, and in reply the cowed, submissive tones of her son. She heard the ponderous movement of a heavy body noisily ascending the stairs and the slurred footsteps of a lighter, less vital, and more exhausted frame following behind. On the landing outside her room her husband said, in a loud, hectoring voice:

"Go to your kennel now, you dog! I'll be ready for you again in the morning." There was no answer but the quick scuffle of feet and the loud bang of a door. Comparative quiet again descended upon the house, penetrated only by an occasional sound from Brodie's bedroom, the creaking of a board, the scrape of a chair, the clatter of his boots as he discarded them upon the floor, the creak of the springs as he flung his huge bulk upon the bed. With this final sound, unbroken silence did, again, completely envelop the house.

The helplessness of her position seemed to intensify her perception and give her intuition an added force. She realised that the possibility she had dreaded had actually taken place and, in addition, that some crushing misadventure had befallen her son. She had at once sensed this latter fact from the shambling irregularity of his step and the hopeless impotence of his voice, but now her imagination ran riot, and she began to fill the torpid hush of the night with distressing sounds. She thought she heard someone weeping. Was it, she asked herself, a faint movement of air around the house or, in truth, the subdued sobbing of her son? If it were he, what rash act might not such misery induce? She pictured him, the errant but still beloved child, contemplating some desperate means of self-destruction. Immediately the sobbing turned to soft sad music which swelled with the funereal insistence of a dirge. She tried, with all her power, to compose herself to sleep but could not. In the suspended state of her mind, swinging between reality and dreams, the lament broke over her like grey waves upon a forgotten shore, mingling with the lost, desolate cries of sea-birds. She saw, amidst pouring rain and the raw, wet clods of fresh-turned clay, a rough, plank bier upon which lay a yellow coffin, saw this lowered, and the heavy clotted lumps of earth begin to fall upon it. With a low cry she twisted upon her back. Her half-conscious visions suddenly became dissipated by a fierce onset of bodily suffering. The excruciating pang, that had stricken her occasionally before, now flung itself upon her with a fierce and prolonged activity. It was unbearable. Hitherto this particular spasm had been, though of deadly intensity, only of short duration, but now her agony was continual. It was, to her, worse by far than the pangs of childbirth, and it flashed upon her that she suffered so fearfully because she had betrayed her daughter and allowed her to be cast headlong in her labour into the storm. She felt her enfeebled heart fibrillate with the stunning violence of the pain. "O God!" she whispered, "take it from me. I canna thole it longer." Yet it did not leave her but increased in strength until it was impossible for her to endure it; wildly, she struggled up, clutching her long night-gown about her. She swayed as she walked, but her anguish forced her on; she tottered in her bare feet into her son's room, and almost fell across his bed.

"Matt," she panted, "my pain is on me. It willna leave me—run—run for the doctor. Run quick, son!"

He had been hardly asleep and now he sat up, startled to be confronted by this new, terrifying apparition; she frightened him horribly, for he could discern only a long white shape that lay supinely across his bed.

"What is it?" he cried. "What do you want with me?" Then, as he perceived dimly that she was ill, he exclaimed: "What's wrong with you, Mamma?"

She could hardly breathe. "I'm dyin'. For the Lord's sake, Matt—a doctor! I canna live wi' this pain. It'll finish me if ye dinna hurry."

He leapt out of bed, his head swimming with the residue of his own recent experience, and, as a passion of remorse gripped his already prostrate spirit, he became again a frightened, remorseful boy.

"Is it my fault, Mamma?" he whined; "is it because I took your money? I'll not do it again. I'll get the watch for you too. I'll be a good boy!"

She scarcely heard him, was far beyond understanding his words.

"Run quick!" she moaned. "I canna thole this longer."

"I'll go! I'll go!" he ejaculated, in a passion of abasement. Frantically, he struggled into his trousers, flung on his jacket, and pulled on his shoes, then ran downstairs and out of the house. With long, lurching steps he raced down the middle of the road whilst the wind of his passage lifted the matted hair from off his bruised and swollen forehead. "O God!" he whispered as he ran, "am I going to kill my mother next? It's all my fault. It's me that's to blame. I haven't done right with her." In the dejection following his debauch he felt himself responsible, in every way, for his mother's sudden illness and a gross, lachrymal contortion shook him as he shouted out to the Deity wild, incoherent promises of reformation and amendment if only Mamma might be spared to him. As he careered along, with head thrown back, bent elbows pressed against his sides, his shirt widely open over his panting chest, his loose garments fluttering about him, he ran like a criminal escaping from justice, with no apparent motive but that of flight. Though his broad purpose was to reach the town, he had at first, in the misery and conflict of his thoughts, no definite objective, but now, when his breath came in short, flagging puffs and a stitch penetrated his side, making him feel that he could run no further, he bethought himself more urgently of finding a doctor. In the distress of his exhausted condition he perceived that he could not continue the whole way to Knoxhill for Dr. Lawrie.—It was too far! Suddenly he remembered that Mamma, in one of her voluminous letters, had mentioned a Dr. Renwick of Wellhall Road in a sense which he imagined to be favourable. With this in mind he swerved to the left at the railway bridge, and, after spurring on his jaded body to a further effort, he saw, to his relief, a red light outside one of the shadowy houses in the road.

Panting, he drew up at the door, searched in a flurry for the night-bell, found it, and tugged at the handle with all his pent-up fear. So violent had been his pull that, as he stood there, he heard a long-continued pealing inside the silent house; then, after a few moments, a window above him was thrown up and the head and shoulders of a man protruded.

"What is it?" called out an incisive voice from overhead.

"You're wanted at once, doctor!" cried Matthew, his anxious upturned face gleaming palely towards the other. "My mother's ill. She's been taken very bad."

"What's the nature of her trouble?" returned Renwick.

"I couldn't tell you, doctor," exclaimed Matthew brokenly. "I knew nothing about it till she just collapsed. Oh! But she's in awful pain. Come quickly."

"Where is it, then?" said Renwick, resignedly. He did not view the matter from the same unique and profoundly disturbing aspect as Matthew; it was, to him, merely a night call which might or might not be serious, the repetition of a frequent and vexatious experience—the loss of a good night's rest.

"Brodie's the name, doctor. You surely know the house at the end of Darroch Road."

"Brodie!" exclaimed the doctor; then, after a short pause, he said in an altered, interrogative tone: "Why do you come to me? Your mother is not a patient of mine."

"Oh! I don't know anything about that," cried Matthew feverishly. "She must have a doctor. Ye must come—she's suffering so much. I beg of ye to come. It's a matter of life or death."

It was a different Renwick from two years ago, one to whom success had given the power of differentiating, of refusing work he did not wish, but now he could not resist this appeal.

"I'll come, then," he said shortly. "Go on ahead of me. I'll be after you in a few moments."

Matthew sighed with relief, poured forth a babble of effusive gratitude towards the now closed window, then turning, hurriedly made his way home. Yet, when he arrived at the house, he was afraid to go in alone and stood shivering outside, in his insufficient garments, feeling that he must wait for the doctor's support before he could enter. Although he buttoned his jacket to the neck and held it close about him, the chilly night air pierced him like a knife, yet the fear that he might make some terrible discovery, that he might perhaps find Mamma lying lifeless upon his bed, kept him standing indecisively at the gate, trembling with cold and fear. He had not long to wait, however, for soon the yellow blurs of two gig lamps came into sight round the bend of the road and approached towards him with a more diffuse brilliancy. Finally they drew into the side of the road and stopped with their full glare upon him and, from the darkness behind, Renwick's voice came crisply:

"Why haven't you gone in? It's folly to stand like that after running. You'll catch your death of cold hanging about there with every pore of you open." He jumped out of his gig and, from the contrasting obscurity beyond, advanced towards the other into the circle of light. "Man alive!" he said suddenly, "what's happened to your head? Have you had a blow?"

"No!" stammered Matthew awkwardly, "I—I fell down."

"It's an ugly bruise," returned Renwick slowly, looking at the other questioningly; yet he said no more but swung his bag forward in his hand and with it motioned the other towards the house.

They went in. Stillness and blackness immediately surrounded them.

"Get a light, man, for heaven's sake," said Renwick irritably. The longer he was with Matthew the more his quick judgment estimated and condemned the other's weakness and indecision. "Couldn't you have seen to all this before I arrived? You'll need to pull yourself together if you want to help your mother."

"It's all right," whispered Matthew, "I have a box in my pocket." With a shaking hand he struck a match and lit the small gas jet in the hall, and, in this dim, wavering gleam together they moved forward, following their own flickering shadows as they mounted the stairs. The door of Mrs. Brodie's room stood half open and, from within, came the sound of quick breathing, at which Matthew broke down and sobbed: "Thank God, she's alive!"

By a miracle of heroic endeavour she had made her way back to her own room and now lay helpless, like a wounded animal that, by a last supreme effort, has reached its lair. The doctor took the matches from Matthew's useless fingers and, having lit the gas in the bedroom, guided him quietly out of the room, then closing the door, he turned and seated himself beside the figure upon the bed. His dark, sombre eyes fixed themselves upon the outlines of her ravaged figure, and as he gently felt the quick, compressible pulse and noted the sunken hollows where emaciation had already touched her, his face shadowed slightly

t the suspicion already forming in his mind. Then he laid his palm
upon her body softly, with a sensitive touch which registered immediately
the abnormal resistance of her rigid muscles, and simultaneously the
concern of his face deepened. At this moment she opened her eyes and
fastened them appealingly upon his, then whispered, slowly:

"You've come!" Her words and her regard recognised him as her
deliverer. He altered his expression, adapting his features, the instant
he looked at him, to an air of kind and reassuring confidence.

"It hurts you here," he indicated gently, by a pressure of his hand,
"This is the place."

She nodded her head. It was wonderful to her that he should immediately divine the seat of her pain; it invested him with a miraculous
and awe-inspiring power; his touch at once seemed healing and his
gently moving hand became a talisman which would discover and
infallibly reveal the morbid secret of her distress. Willingly she submitted her racked body to his examination, feeling that here was one
in whom lay an almost divine power to make her well.

"That's better," he encouraged, as he felt her relax. "Can you let
me go a little deeper—just once?" he queried. Again she nodded her
head and, following his whispered injunction, tried to breathe quietly,
whilst his long, firm fingers sent shivers of pain pulsating through her.
"That was splendid!" He thanked her with a calm consideration.
"You are very brave." Not by so much as the flicker of his eyelids could
he have discerned that, deep in the tissues of her body, he had discovered nodules of a wide-rooted growth which he knew to have progressed far beyond the aid of any human skill. "How long have you
had trouble?" he asked casually. "Surely this is not the first attack
you've had?"

With difficulty she spoke.

"No! I've had it for a long time, off and on, doctor, but never for
such a spell as this. The pain used to go away at once, but this one is
a long time in easin'. It's better, mind you, but it hasna gone."

"You've had other symptoms—surely, Mrs. Brodie," he exclaimed,
his speaking eye conveying a meaning beyond his simple words. "You
must have known you were not right. Why did you not see about it
sooner?"

"I knew well enough," she answered, "but I seemed never to have
the time to bother about myself." She made no mention of her husband's
intolerance as she added: "I just let it gang on. I thought that in time
it would go away."

He shook his head slowly in a faint reproof, saying:

"You've neglected yourself sadly I'm afraid, Mrs. Brodie. It may
mean that you'll be laid up in bed for a little. You must make up your
mind for a rest—that's what you've needed for a long time. Rest and
no worry!"

"What's wrong with me, then," she whispered. "It's—it's nothin, serious?"

He raised himself from the bed and surveyed her kindly.

"What did I say about worrying," he replied. "I'm coming agai to-morrow for a fuller examination, when you have no pain. Just now you are going to have a good sleep. I've something here to give yo relief."

"Can you ease me?" she murmured weakly. "I couldna bear yo again."

"You'll have no more of that," he comforted her. "I'll see to it. She watched him silently as he picked up his bag, opened it and pr duced a small phial from which he measured some drops carefull into a glass; then, as he added some water and turned to her agai she placed her worn hand on his and said, movingly: "You're so kin to me. It's no wonder your name's on a' bodies' tongues. I canna b thank you for your goodness in coming to me to-night, and thank yo I do with all my heart."

"You drink this, then," he murmured, gently pressing her dr calloused fingers. "It's the very thing for you."

She took the glass with all the sublime trust of a young child an drained it to the dark dregs, forced even a faint, tragic smile to h pale lips as she whispered:

"That was bitter, doctor. It maun be good medicine."

He smiled back at her reassuringly.

"Now rest," he ordained. "You need a good long sleep"; and, wi her hand still in his, he sat down again beside her, waiting whilst th opiate took effect. His presence reassured her by its benign, magnet power; the talisman that she clasped as though she feared to relinquis it, comforted her; occasionally her eyes would open to regard hi gratefully. Then her pupils contracted slowly, the drawn lines of h features became erased, drowsily she murmured:

"God bless you, doctor. 'Twas you saved my Mary's life, and ye make me better too. Come to me again—please." Then she slept.

Slowly he disengaged his hand from her now flaccid grasp, repacke his bag, and stood gazing at her dormant form. His face, wiped clea of its protecting film of sanguine assurance, was heavy with a sad knov ledge, mingled with a pensive, human sympathy. He remained motio less for a moment, then he covered her more warmly with the be clothes, lowered the gas, and went out of the room.

At the foot of the stairs Matt was awaiting him, his pale, apprehensi countenance shiny with the blanched pallor of a sickly moon.

"How is she?" he asked in a low tone. "Is she better?"

"She is out of pain now, and sleeping," answered Renwick. "Th was the immediate necessity for your mother." He looked directly the other, wondering how much he could tell him.

"Where is your father?" he asked, finally. "I feel I ought to see him."

Matthew's glance wilted, his bruised eyes fell downwards, his body moved uneasily as he whispered:

"He's asleep in bed. I don't want to disturb him. No! we better not wake him. It wouldn't do any good."

Renwick's face became stern at the other's abject look. What manner of house was this? he asked himself, and what manner of people? The mother, the son, yes, even that poor child Mary, all were terrified of the one omnipotent being, the master of the house, this outrageous Brodie.

"I do not know," he said at length, enunciating his words with cold distinctness, "whether it will be desirable for me to continue the conduct of this case, but you may tell your father that I shall call to see him to-morrow."

"Is she going to be bad for long, then?" mumbled Matthew.

"For about six months at the outside."

"What a long time!" said Matt, slowly. "She does all the work. How will we manage in the house without her?"

"You will have to manage," said the doctor, severely. "And high time it is that you started to learn."

"What way?" asked Matthew stupidly.

"Your mother is dying of an incurable, internal cancer. She will never get out of that bed again. In six months she will be in her grave."

Matt collapsed as if the other had struck him; weakly, he sat down upon the stairs, Mamma dying! Only five hours ago she had been running after him, had served him with a delicate meal cooked by her own hands, but now she lay stricken upon a bed from which she would never arise. With his head bowed upon his hands he did not see the doctor go out or hear the sound of the closing door. Prostrated by grief and remorse he looked, not forward, but backward; his mind, swayed by memory, roamed through the whole period of his life; his vivid recollection strayed through all the pathways of the past. He felt the tender petting of her hands, the caress of her cheek, the touch of her lips upon his brow. He saw her coming to his room as he lay petulantly on his bed, heard her say soothingly: "Here's something nice for you, son." Her features appeared before him in every expression, coaxing, pleading, wheedling, but all bearing the same indefinable stamp of love for him. Then he saw her face finally composed in the calm, complacent rigidity of death, and in its serenity he still observed upon the pale lips the smiling tenderness which she had always shown to him.

Alone on the stairs he broke down, and whispered to himself, again and again:

"Mamma! Mamma! ye were aye so good to me!"

XI

"Where's my hot water?" shouted Brodie. "Hot water! My shaving water!" He stood upon the landing outside his room, dressed in his shirt and trousers, bawling to the regions below. For the first time since he could remember, his shaving water was not ready for him at his door at the precise second when he required it; he had, with the established action of habit, bent down to lift the jug and there had been no jug for him to lift. At this unprecedented and atrocious evidence of neglect, amazement had immediately given way to a sense of personal affront which had added to the bitter temper in which he had arisen from bed. This morning he had awakened to a different perception of the incidents of the previous night, and on turning over the matter in his mind, had slowly become infuriated to think that his son had stumbled on his intrigue with Nancy, had discovered the meeting-place at the house in College Street. Resentment that such a weakling as Matt should have dared to interfere with the manner of his life made him forget the danger which he had survived; the unusual incident of the shooting faded into the realm of the unreal and it was the interference with his pleasure which now aroused his bitter anger. His head felt stuffed from the heaviness of his sleep; the ever-present worry of his failing business, lying perpetually in the background to greet him when he awoke, added to his bitter moody vexation; and now, when he wanted especially to get shaved and freshened up in order to adjust his tangled thoughts, he could not obtain his hot water. It was always the same, he told himself; a man could never get what he wanted in this infernal house, and, with the full force of a legitimate grievance, he bellowed out once more: "Water! Bring it up at once! Damn it all, am I to stand here all day cooling my heels on your pleasure! Water, confound you!"

Nothing happened! To his bewilderment, Mamma did not come panting up the stairs in a paroxysm of abasement and haste, with the familiar steaming jug in her hand and a quivering apology upon her lips. An unusual quiet prevailed below. He sniffed with dilated nostrils like an angry bull scenting the wind, but could discern no appetising smell of cooking ascending from the kitchen. With a snort, he was about to plunge downstairs to make his wants known more forcibly, when suddenly the door of Matt's room opened and, in response to the muffled sound of a parting injunction, Nessie came out and timidly advanced towards her father.

His anger moderated at the sight of her, the frown faded from his forehead, the bitter twist of his lips softened slightly. The inevitable effect of her presence was to soften the harshness of his nature, and it was, indeed, for this reason she had been selected to break the news to him.

"Father," she said diffidently, "Mamma's not up this morning."

"What!" he cried, as though hardly able to believe his ears, "not up yet? Still in her bed at this hour?"

Nessie nodded.

"It's not her fault though, father," she murmured placatingly. "Don't blame her—she's not well. She tried to get up but she couldn't move."

Brodie growled. He knew she was lazy, malingering, that the whole affair was a subterfuge to prevent him from getting his shaving water. Then he thought of his breakfast. Who was to get him that? Abruptly he took a step towards Mamma's room to see if his presence would not make her forget her indisposition, liven her up to a more useful activity.

"Mamma was awful bad through the night," Nessie interposed. "Matt had to run out in the middle of the night and get a doctor."

He stopped dead at this new and startling information, and exclaimed, in amazed displeasure:

"The doctor! What way was I not told? Why was I not consulted about this? Is everything to be done in this house over my head, without telling me about it? Where is Matt?"

Matthew, who had been listening to the conversation through the half-open door, emerged slowly upon the landing. From his streaked, haggard face he looked as if he had not slept and now he regarded his father uncomfortably in the broad light of day. Still, Nessie had done her part in imparting the petrifying news; it would be easier for him to explain.

"Why did ye not tell me about this—this affair, sir?" repeated Brodie fiercely. He refused to refer to it directly as an illness; in his opinion the whole thing was a fabrication against his comfort, a conspiracy to annoy him. "Why did you not come to me first?"

"I didn't want to disturb you, father," mumbled Matt. "I thought you would be asleep."

"You're gey considerate o' me all of a sudden," Brodie sneered. "You're not always so solicitous about my health, are ye?" He paused significantly and added:

"Ye brought Lawrie into the house—well? what did he say about her?"

"It wasn't him," replied Matthew humbly, "I couldn't get him, father. It was Renwick that came."

A thrill of anger ran through Brodie's frame.

"What!" he roared, "Ye brought that snipe to my house. What were ye thinking about, you fool! Do ye not know him and me are sworn enemies. Of course he would put Mamma to her bed. Certainly!" he jeered, "I suppose he wants to keep her there for a week. I suppose we've a' been killin' her here. I've no doubt it'll be chicken and champagne ordered for her now, whilst we've got to scrint to pay his bills."

"Oh! father," entreated Matthew, "I don't think so. He said it was —it was really serious."

"Bah!" snarled Brodie, "there's nothing I wouldna put past a thing like him—and you're as bad for lettin' him in here behind my back. I'll pay ye for that as well. That's something else I owe ye."

"Anyway," faltered Matt, "he said—he said he would come to examine her more thoroughly this morning—that he would be seein' you."

"So!" said Brodie. He stood silent, his lips drawn back in an ugly sneer. Renwick was coming to his house this morning, was he? To start, maybe, a course of daily visits, thinking, no doubt, that with a soft, spineless creature like Mamma, he would have a grand, imaginary invalid to play about with. Brodie's fist clenched involuntarily, as it did always when a powerful resolution moved him, and he gritted his teeth together. "I'll wait on him myself," he said aloud, in a tone of concentrated animosity. "I'll see what he has to say for himself. I'll surprise him. It'll not be her that he'll see, but me."

Then, after a moment during which he gazed ahead of him into space, he turned.

"Nessie," he said, "you go and get your father some hot water. Take care not to scald yourself, pettie! Then get that old mother o' mine up. She maun get some kind o' breakfast made for us. If Mamma can lounge in her bed there's others that have work to do. Off you go now," and, patting her thin shoulders, he went back again into his bedroom.

The hot water arrived quickly and he began to perform the usual routine of his morning toilet. But his thoughts were not upon what he did. Every now and then he would stop short, his eye, glooming into space, would kindle with an angry fire and he would toss his head fiercely, contemptuously.

"He would keep my wife in bed," he muttered angrily, taking it now as a deliberate hit at him by Renwick that his wife should be in bed. "The infernal impudence of him. I'll learn him, though! I'll teach him to interfere with me again!"

Ever since the terrible illness of his daughter, he had borne Renwick a bitter grudge for the aspersions made during that memorable interview when he had refused to visit and assist his daughter in the crisis of her pneumonia. A fulminating antagonism now flared inside him as he considered, in advance, all the cutting insults he would fling at the other. Not for a moment did it occur to him that he should visit his wife; she was an insignificant pawn amongst the movements of this affair, and when he had dealt successfully with Renwick she would unquestionably get up and cook his dinner—an extra good dinner, too, it had better be, to compensate for her defection of the morning.

"Yes! I'll settle him," he muttered, repeatedly, to himself. "I'll chuck his fee in his face and tell him to shift out o' my house."

He could scarcely swallow his breakfast for the surge of his resentment; not that the meal was tempting, in any case. The porridge was singed and watery and, gloomily, he looked at his old mother, with her skirt kirtled round her waist above her striped petticoat, as she made a great commotion of her preparations.

"These porridge are wasted," he flung at her moodily. "They're not fit for pigs to eat."

Everything was wrong. The toast was soft and limp; his tea—he was obliged to accept this instead of his favourite coffee—was weak and made with water which had not reached the boiling point; his egg was like leather and his bacon like cinders.

"She'll need to get up!" he exclaimed aloud. "I can't stand this kind of thing. This meat is enough to poison a man."

The dirty fireplace stared at him, his boots were unbrushed, he had cut himself whilst shaving; flaming, he heaved himself up from the table and sat down in his chair to wait for Renwick. His eye followed with disgust the senile, inept movements of his mother, his ears were jarred by the clatter of a breaking dish which came to him from the scullery. Then, perceiving that Nessie hung about the room, he sent her sharply off to school. She was at least an hour late, and had hoped in the rarity of the occasion to be overlooked, or perhaps excused, but he ordered her to go and, without attempt at protest, she departed. Matthew did not appear but remained invisible upstairs. No sound was heard from Mamma.

Brodie could not settle. He looked at the clock, saw that it was half-past ten, became aware that he was at least an hour late for business, that his shop would be standing open, empty, untended, with only his stupid, careless boy to gape uselessly at any person who might come in; then he reflected bitterly that his absence was of little consequence, that actually it did not matter, so few people did come into his business now.

He got up and restlessly moved about. The kitchen seemed somehow unfamiliar to him in this light; disturbed in his routine, he felt everything strange and unusual about him. The infringement of his daily custom, following so closely upon the unnatural events of the preceding night, gave to him a sensation of monstrous unreality which baffled his mediocre comprehension, and the irritation produced by this puzzled perplexity served like fuel to feed his flaming anger further. Restless as a caged tiger he paced up and down the lobby. The longer he was obliged to wait the more his resentment swelled until, as if in an endeavour to hasten Renwick's arrival, he went into the parlour and gazed fretfully out of the window. Then the thought struck him that the doctor might see his peering face and take it as a sign of weakness upon his part, and at the hateful idea he drew away violently from the window and returned to the kitchen where he forced himself again into his chair, forced himself to a semblance of control. Outwardly impassive, but inwardly seething, he waited, the only sign of his hot impatience the quick action of his foot as it made a ceaseless, tapping movement through the empty air.

At eleven o'clock the door-bell rang. Like a runner who has long awaited the sound of the start, to unleash his restrained store of energy, Brodie leaped out of his chair, strode, himself, to the front door and with a defiant, sweeping gesture threw it wide to the wall. His huge bulk filled the opening, blocking the passage into the house.

"Well! what is it?" he growled. "What do ye want?"

Dr. Renwick stood upon the door-step, dispassionately immaculate in his well-fitting morning coat, and dignified by the background of his man, his well-groomed cob, and smart gig. Secure now in the possession of his large and lucrative practice, he made not the slightest motion towards coming in, but paused appreciably before replying pleasantly:

"Ah! Mr. Brodie, himself, this morning I see!"

"Never mind me," said Brodie loweringly. "What do ye want here?"

"Really," said Renwick tranquilly, "you are the epitome of courtesy. You have not altered since our last meeting—at least not for the better."

"Your purpose, sir?" breathed Brodie heavily. "Don't flash your glib tongue at me. Answer me straight."

"Well! Since you are so blunt I will be equally so. I came last night at the urgent request of your son, and rather against my inclination, to see your wife, and despite your pretence of ignorance I am convinced that you know I was here." He paused and negligently flicked his sleeve with his glove before continuing. "This morning I had proposed to pay a final visit"—he emphasised deeply the word final—"in order to confirm, by a further examination, the melancholy diagnosis which I made last night."

Brodie glowered at him. Renwick's aloof imperturbability infuriated him infinitely more than any display of furious rage would have done. That, he could meet with equal violence. But his clumsy wit was as useless against this quick coolness of mind as a bludgeon against a flashing rapier; he was pricked in a dozen places before he could swing the heavy weapon of his reply.

The other had, indeed, almost disarmed him by the assertion that he proposed to make no further calls, and he had aroused Brodie's attention by the veiled implication of his reference to Mamma's condition.

"What are ye makin' out to be wrong wi' her, then?" he sneered, unconsciously changing his attitude. "She's a graund subject for the bed."

292

Renwick raised his eyebrows delicately, without speaking, a slight gesture which had, nevertheless, the immediate effect of making the other feel the exceeding bad taste of his remark. Raging at this unspoken contempt Brodie rushed on to his inevitable resort when all else failed him—the descent to personalities.

"Don't mock at me like that with your creashy smirk," he cried. "It doesna improve the look of your ugly face, anyway."

Renwick continued to look at him dispassionately. Most men, from their physical stature, were compelled to look upwards to James Brodie and Brodie revelled in this fact; it gave him a sense of superiority and power to stand over a man. Renwick, however, was fully as tall as he, and from the slight eminence of the outer porch, he reversed the usual order of things, and he, instead, looked down upon Brodie.

"I shall not waste my time here further," he said at last, coldly. "If you are not a busy man I am. In your state of mind you are not amenable to reason. You have a delusion of grandeur which makes you wish everyone to be in awe of you. The unfortunate members of your family are, no doubt, afraid of you, but I, happily, am not! Understand that clearly if you can. And now, good morning to you!" He turned on his heel and was about to descend the steps when the other caught hold of his arm. "Wait! Wait!" shouted Brodie. The interview was not proceeding as he had anticipated, for he had visioned himself grudgingly permitting Renwick to have access to the house after he had been scraped and bowed to, after his offended dignity had been suitably appeased. In his heart he felt he must know what the doctor thought of his wife, and though he had desired, first of all, to make Renwick feel like a paid servant who could be discharged contemptuously with his fee, he did not wish to be left completely ignorant of Mamma's condition.

"Don't go like that," he cried. "Ye havena told me what's wrong wi' my wife. What are ye paid for if ye can't tell me what you came here for last night? You'll have to justify yourself in some way."

The other showed him a coldly contemptuous profile.

"The question of fee has not arisen, so far as I am aware. As to the other matter, I have already informed you that I shall give you my definite diagnosis only after a further and internal examination"; and he shook off Brodie's detaining hand and made to resume his exit.

"Damn it all, then," cried Brodie suddenly. "Come in and do what ye want. Since ye are here we may as well make use of ye."

Renwick came back slowly, and with a maddening suavity he said: "Since you beg of me to come back I shall do so, but understand this, it is only for your wife's sake"; then he pushed past the bulky form before him and quickly mounted the stairs.

Brodie, fuming and nonplussed, was left standing in the hall. He bent his brows angrily, rubbed his chin indecisively, stretched out his hand to shut the front door, then refrained from shutting it, as the thought crossed his insulted mind that it would amount almost to subservience for him to close the door for Renwick.

"Let him shut the door for himself," he muttered. "Anyway he'll not be long. He'll soon be out again, and then it'll be for good." He gazed moodily out of the open door at the doctor's spanking turn-out at his gate, his dark envious eye noting the fine legs of the cob, its muscled shoulders, its supple arched neck. He estimated clearly the money which lay in the splendid animal, in the sound coach-built gig, in the man's smart livery, even in the cockaded hat which sat jauntily upon his head, and this tangible vision of the other's prosperity was like gall to him. With a jerk he withdrew his gaze, began to pace up and down the hall. "Will he never come down?" he asked himself. "What does he think he's doin' up there a' this time?"

He reflected impatiently on what must be taking place upstairs, writhed at the thought of what the nature of the examination might be. Although he had finished with his wife in every aspect of his sexual life, and had indeed cast her from him in contumely, the thought of another man interfering, as he mentally worded it, with her made him furious. Although his wife was old, jaded, and worn out, yet she was still his property, his chattel, his possession. He would never need the possession nor use the chattel, yet she must remain wholly and subserviently his. That was his mentality and, had he lived in another age, he would surely have destroyed each mistress when he had tired of her in the perverted fear that she would fall into another's hands. Ridiculous and abominable thoughts now began to torment him.

"By God!" he cried out, "if he doesna come down I'll go up myself."

But he did not go up! Something in Renwick's cold disdain had chilled his animal mind and although, of course, he feared no one, yet the temper of the other's spirit so far surpassed his that it surmounted and even subdued him. Always, a superior, fearless mind aroused in him a faint, lowering distrust, the prelude to hatred, to an unbridled antipathy that weakened, to his undoing such reason as usually controlled his motives. And so he chafed and stamped about in the hall until, when he had been made to wait a full half-hour, he did at last hear Renwick come down. Watching the doctor descend the stairs slowly, he felt, uncontrollably, that he must voice his severe displeasure.

"Did you say you were busy?" he girned. "What a time you were."

"Not too long, surely, for a last visit," said Renwick impassively.

"What's wrong with her then?" shot out Brodie. "I've no doubt you've been puttin' some grand, fancy ideas in her head all this time."

"Which reminds me," continued the doctor tranquilly, ignoring the interjection, "that you must arrange for your own medical man to be called in without fail to-morrow. If you wish, I will communicate with him. Your wife must have constant and unremitting attention."

Brodie stared at him incredulously, then laughed sneeringly.

"Does she need a nurse next?" he exclaimed.

"Your good wife most assuredly does. That is," Renwick added quietly, "if you can afford it."

Brodie drew from the other's words a humiliating imputation.

"Be careful," he breathed. "I asked you what was wrong with her."

"Advanced, incurable cancer of the womb," said Renwick slowly.

Brodie's jaw dropped at the dreadful word. "Cancer," he echoed. "Cancer!" Despite his iron control his cheek blenched slightly; but he fought to recover himself.

"It's a lie!" he exclaimed loudly. "You're trying to get even with me. You're tryin' to frichten me with a demned lie."

"I wish it were a lie, but I have satisfied myself, beyond all shadow of a doubt, that my diagnosis is correct," said Renwick sadly. "There is nothing to be done for the poor soul but to alleviate her pain—and she will never leave the bed she now lies on."

"I don't believe you," snarled Brodie. "I don't give that for your opinion." He snapped his fingers in the other's face like the crack of a whip, caring, not so much for the dreadful affliction which might lie upon his wife, as for the humiliating position into which he imagined the doctor was trying to force him. "I'll have better advice than yours," he cried. "I'll have my own physician. He's head and shoulders above you in skill. If she's ill he'll cure her!"

Renwick inclined his head.

"I hope sincerely that he does, and I must tell you," he added severely, "that in medicine the basis of any treatment is rest and freedom from anxiety."

"Thank ye for nothing," cried Brodie roughly. "Here! what is your fee for a' this tarradiddle?—what do we pay you for tellin' her to lie in bed?" and he plunged his hand into his trousers pocket.

The doctor, on his way to the door, turned and said, with a penetrating look which revealed the fullness of his knowledge of Brodie's unhappy financial position:

"Really, no! not from you, in your present circumstances. I couldn't think of it." He paused and added: "Remember, I shall not call again unless I'm sent for"—then he was gone.

Brodie, his fists clenched, stared impotently at the retreating figure. Only when the gig was out of sight did a suitable retort occur to him.

"Send for him again," he cried. "He'll never come into this house again! The infernal snipe! I don't believe a word of his damned lies. A pack of lies," he repeated, as if to convince himself.

As he stood in the lobby he did not know what to do, but through his indecision, despite his assumed contempt of Renwick's opinion, the word cancer kept beating into his brain with a dire significance. Cancer of the womb! It seemed to him the most horrid manifestation of the dread disease. Although he had violently professed unbelief, now a seeping tide of conviction swept over him; bit by bit he began to piece evidence together which was in itself conclusive. Her ailing look had not, then, been assumed—those secretive ways not an indecency, a reproach to him, but only a piteous necessity.

Suddenly a devastating thought struck him! Had the scourge been passed to him? Knowing nothing of the laws of contagion or infection, still he wondered if he himself might be contaminated, and immediately the recollection of her previous nearness to him, of past contacts, rushed over him, making him feel unclean. Involuntarily he glanced over his muscular body as if it might reveal already some sinister index of the malady. His glance reassured him, but, following the thought, came, inevitably, a small wave of resentment against his wife. "Could she no' have watched herself better?" he muttered, as if she were in measure responsible for her own calamity.

He shook himself and braced out his barrel chest to rid himself of all the oppressive, conflicting ideas within him. Without realising it, he wandered into the cold, unused parlour and sat down in the inhospitable room where he again set himself to decide what he must do. Although he must, of course, justify his threat to Renwick and call in Dr. Lawrie, already he knew it to be useless. This had been merely the spiteful taunt of his inferior mind and, in his inmost heart, he knew Lawrie's skill to be far below the other's. He realised, too, that he must go up to his wife, but he had no heart for this duty, for under the stigma of this awful distemper she had become to him even more unwelcome and repugnant than before. He shrank equally from her and from his onerous duty to visit her. Shifting his mind quickly from her he began to consider the domestic situation. What a mess, he thought; and not unlike the state of his business! A look that was almost piteous in its perplexity slowly invaded the hard, massive face, softening its harshness, driving out the bitterness, lifting the frown from the brow. But that compassionate expression was for himself! He was thinking, not of his wife but of himself, sympathising with himself, pitying James Brodie for the troubles that beset him.

"Ay," he muttered, gently, "it's a good job you're a man amongst a' this injustice. Ye have a wee thing or two to thole." With these words he rose and ascended the stairs as slowly and heavily as if clambering up a ladder; outside Mamma's room he paused, drew himself up, and went in. She had heard him coming up and already was turning to greet him with a pleading, ingratiating smile.

"I'm sorry, father," she immediately murmured. "I tried hard to get up but it was just beyond me. I'm real sorry ye've been so upset. Did ye get a decent breakfast?"

He seemed to be seeing her with new eyes, observing now that her

296

face looked ghastly, with hollowed temples and jaws, that her form appeared to have become suddenly wasted. He did not know what to say. It was so long since he had addressed a kind word to her that his tongue refused to utter one, and in his hesitation he felt uncomfortable, incongruous, absurd. His motive in life was to drive, to demand, to chastise, to flagellate; he could not sympathise. He stared at her desperately.

"You're not angry, I hope, father," she said timidly, misconstruing his look. "I'll be up in a day or two. He says a bit rest is what I need. I'll see that you're not put about more than need be."

"I'm not angry, woman," he said hoarsely. Then after a pause, with an effort, he added: "Ye maun lie still till we see what Dr. Lawrie can do for ye."

Immediately she flinched.

"Oh! no! no! father," she cried, "it's not him I want. I like Dr. Renwick so much I feel he'll make me well. He's so kind and so clever. His medicine made me feel better at once."

He gritted his teeth impotently as her protests rang on endlessly. Previously he would have rammed his intention in her teeth and left her to swallow it as best she liked, but now, in the novelty of her condition, and indeed, of his, he knew not what to say. He resolved that she would have Lawrie, that he would send him in, but modifying his retort with an effort, he exclaimed:

"We'll see then! We'll see how ye get on."

Mrs. Brodie gazed at him doubtfully, feeling that if he took Renwick from her she would surely die. She had loved this doctor's serene assurance, had expanded under his unusual gentleness. Unconsciously she was drawn to him as the one who had attended her daughter, and he had already spoken to her of Mary, in terms that paid tribute to the patience and fortitude of her child under the trials of an almost mortal illness. Now she sensed at once that her husband was antagonistic to her desire, but she knew better than to argue; hastily, she sought to propitiate him.

"What are we goin' to do about you, James?" she ventured. "Ye must be looked after properly. You must have your comforts."

"I'll be all right," he managed to say. "The old lady will do her best."

"No! No!" she urged, "I've been thinkin' out plans all morning. I must get up as soon as I'm able, but in the meantime, could we not get a girl in, someone who would get your meals as ye like them. I could tell her—tell her just what to do—how to make the broth as ye like it, and how to season your porridge, and the airin' o' your flannels and——"

He interrupted her by a definite, intolerant shake of his head. Could she not realise that it cost money to keep a servant? Did she think he was rolling in wealth? He wanted to say something crushing that would shut off her silly twaddle. "Does she think I'm a helpless wean, the way she's going on?" he asked himself. "Does she think the house couldna go on without her?" Yet he knew that if he opened his mouth to speak he would blunder into some blunt rejoinder—the niceties of expression were beyond him—so he closed his lips and maintained a chafing silence.

She looked at him closely, encouraged by his silence, wondering fearfully if she dared to venture the subject nearest her heart. His unaccustomed placidity made her brave and, with a sudden gasp, she exclaimed:

"James! To mind the house now—could we not—could we not have Mary back?"

He recoiled from her. His assumed serenity was not proof against this, and losing control of himself, he shouted:

"No! we will not. I warned ye not even to lift her name. She'll not come back here till she crawls on her bended knees. Me *ask* her to come back! Never! Not even if ye lay on your death-bed."

The last word rang through the room like a trumpet call and, slowly, a frightened look came into Mamma's eyes.

"As you say, James," she trembled. "But please dinna mention that awfu' word. I'm not wantin' to die yet. I'm goin' to get better ye ken. I'll be up soon."

Her optimism exasperated him. He did not realise that the habits of half a lifetime had ingrained in her the feeling that she must always exhibit in his presence this spurious cheerfulness, nor did he understand that the desire to get up arose from an ever-pricking urge to fulfil the innumerable demands that harassed her.

"The doctor didna say much," she continued propitiatingly, "beyond that it was a kind of inflammation. When that goes down I'm sure I'll get my strength up in no time. I canna bear this lyin' in bed. I've got so many things to think of." She was worrying about the payment of her debt. "Just a wee bits o' things that nobody would bother about but me," she added hastily, as if she feared he might read her mind.

He looked at her gloomily. The more she glossed over her illness the more he became convinced that she would not survive it; the more she spoke of the future the more futile she became in his eyes. Would she be as inept when confronted by death as she had been in the face of life? He tried desperately to find something to say; what could he say to this doomed but unconscious woman?

And now his manner began to puzzle her. At first she had assumed gratefully that his quiet had betokened a forbearance in the face of her sickness, a modification of the same feeling which made her move throughout the house on tiptoes when she had nursed him, on such rare occasions as he had been ill. But a curious quality in his regard now perturbed her, and suddenly she queried:

"The doctor didna say anything about me to you, did he? He didna tell you something that he keepit from me? He seemed a long time downstairs before I heard him drive away."

He looked at her stupidly. His mind seemed, from a long distance off, to consider her question slowly, detachedly, without succeeding in arriving at an appropriate answer.

"Tell me if he did, James," she cried apprehensively. "I would far rather know. Tell me." The whole of her appearance had altered, her demeanour, from being calm and sanguine, had become agitated, disturbed.

He had come into the room with no fixed motive as to how he should deal with her. He had no sympathy, no tact, and now no ingenuity to lie to her. He felt confused, trapped, like a blundering animal before the frail, raddled creature on the bed. His temper flared suddenly.

"What do I care what he thinks!" he found himself saying, harshly. "A man like him would say ye were dyin' if ye had a toothache. He knows nothing—less than nothing. Haven't I told ye I'm goin' to get Lawrie to ye." His angry, ill-chosen words struck her like a thunderbolt. Instantly she knew, knew with a fearful conviction that her illness was mortal. She shivered, and a film of fear clouded her eyes like a faint, shadowy harbinger of the last, opaque pellicle of dissolution.

"Did he say I was dying then?" she quavered.

He glared at her, furious at the position into which he had been forced. Angry words now poured from his mouth.

"Can ye not shut up about that runt," he cried. "Ye wad think he was the Almighty to hear you. He doesna ken everything. If he canna cure ye there's other doctors in Levenford! What's the use o' makin' such a fuss about it a'?"

"I see. I see now," she whispered. "I'll no' make any more fuss about it now." Quiescent upon the bed she gazed at him and behind him; her gaze seemed to transcend the limits of the narrow room and focus itself fearfully upon a remoteness beyond. After a long pause she said, as though to herself: "I'll not be muckle loss to you, James! I'm gey and worn out for you." Then she whispered, faintly: "But oh! Matt, my own son, how am I to leave you?"

Silently she turned to the wall and to the mystery of her thoughts, leaving him standing with a sullen, glouting brow, behind her. For a moment he looked lumpishly at her flaccid figure, then, without a word, he went heavily out of the room.

XII

A SUDDEN burst of vivid August sunshine, penetrating the diaphanous veil hung by the last drops of a passing shower, sprayed the High Street with a misty radiance, whilst the brisk breeze which had thrown the fleecy, wool-pack clouds from off the pathway of the sun, now moved the rain slowly onwards in a glow of golden haze.

"Sunny-shower! Sunny-shower!" chanted a group of boys, as they raced along the drying street on their way to bathe in the Leven.

"Look," cried one of them, importantly, "a rainbow!" and he pointed upwards to a perfect arc which, like the thin beribboned handle of a lady's basket, spanned glitteringly the entire length of the street. Everyone paused to look at the rainbow. They lifted their eyes above the drab level of the earth and gazed upwards towards the sky, nodded their heads, smiled cheerfully, exclaimed with delight, shouted to each other across the street.

"It's a braw sight!"

"Look at the bonnie colours!"

"It puts auld Couper's pole in the shade, richt enough." The sudden, unexpected delight of the phenomenon cheered them, elevating their minds unconsciously to a plane that lay above the plodding commonplace of their existence, and, when they looked downwards again, the vision of that splendid, sparkling arch remained, inspiring them for the day before them.

Out of the Winton Arms into this bright sunshine came James Brodie. He saw no rainbow, but walked dourly, with his hat pulled forward, his head down, his hands deeply in his outside pockets, seeing nothing, and, though a dozen glances followed his progress, saluting no one. As he plodded massively, like a stallion, over the crest of the street he felt that "they"—the peering inquisitive swine—were looking at him with prying eyes, knew, though he ignored it, that he was the focus of their attention. For weeks past it had appeared to him that he, and the moribund shop that he tenanted, had been the nidus of a strange and unnatural attention in the Borough, that townspeople, some that he knew and some whom he had never seen before, strolled deliberately outside his business to stare openly, curiously, purposely, into the depths within. From the inner obscurity he imagined that these empty, prying glances mocked him; he had cried out to himself: "Let them look then, the glaikit swine! Let them gape at me for all they're worth. I'll give them something to glower about." Did they guess, he now asked himself bitterly, as he strode along, that he had been celebrating—celebrating the last day in his business? Did they know that, with a ferocious humour, he had just now swallowed a liberal toast to the wreck of his affairs? He smiled grimly to think that to-day he ceased to be a hatter that shortly he would walk out of his office for the last time, and bang the door behind him finally and irrevocably.

Paxton, from across the road, whispered to his neighbour:

"Look, man, quick, there's Brodie," and together they stared at the strong figure on the opposite pavement. "Man! I'm sorry for him somehow," continued Paxton; "his come down doesna fit him weel."

"Na!" agreed the other, "he's the wrang man to be ruined."

"For a' his strength and power," resumed Paxton, "there's something blunderin' and helpless about him. It's been a fearfu' blow to him. Do ye mark how his shoulders have bowed, as if he had a load on his back."

His neighbour shook his head.

"I canna see it like that! He's been workin' for this for a lang, lang time. What I canna stand about the man in his black, veecious pride that grows in spite o' a' things. It's like a disease that gets waur and waur, and the source o't is so downright senseless. If he could but see himself now, as others see him, it micht humble him a wee."

Paxton looked at the other peculiarly.

"I wouldna talk like that about him," he said slowly, "it's a chancy thing even to whisper like that about James Brodie, and at this time more than ordinar'. If he heard ye he would turn on ye and rend ye."

"He's not listenin' to us," replied the other, a trifle uncomfortably; then he added, "He has drink in him again, by the look o' him. Adversity micht bring some men to their senses, but it's drivin' him the other way round."

They both turned again and glanced at the slowly retreating figure. After a pause Paxton said:

"Have ye heard, lately, how his wife goes on?"

"Not a word! From what I can make out not a body sees her. Some leddies from the kirk took up a wheen jellies and the like for her, but Brodie met them at the gate and sent them a' richt about turn. Ay, and waur nor that, he clashed the guid stuff they had brought about their ears."

"Do ye say so! Nobody maun tamper wi' him or his," exclaimed Paxton; then he paused and queried: " 'Tis cancer, is't not, John?"

"Ay! so they say!"

"What a waesome affliction!"

"Man!" replied the other, as he moved away: "it is bad but to my mind 'tis no waur than for that puir woman to be bound body and soul to a man like James Brodie."

By this time Brodie had entered his shop, his footsteps echoing loudly through the almost denuded premises where only a tithe of his stock remained, the rest having been disposed of through the interest and consideration of Soper. The evanescent boy had finally vanished and he was alone in the barren, unhappy, defeated place, where the faint gossamer of a spider's web, spun across the remaining boxes on the shelves, mutely indicated the ebb to which his business had fallen. Now, as he stood in the midst of this dereliction, unconsciously he peopled it with the figures of the past, the past of those lordly days when he had walked with a flourish about the place, disdaining the humbler of his clients but meeting equally and agreeably all persons of importance or consequence. It seemed incomprehensible to him that they should now be merely shadows, entering only in his imagination, that he would no longer laugh and jest and talk with them in these precincts which had enclosed his daily life for twenty years. It was the same shop, he was the same man, yet slowly, mysteriously, these living beings had withdrawn from him, leaving only unhappy, unsubstantial memories. The few old customers, chiefly the country gentlepeople, who had still clung to him had seemed only to prolong the misery of his failure, and now that it was finished a vast surge of anger and sorrow invaded him. With his low forehead contracted he tried, abortively, to realise how it had been accomplished, to analyse how all this strange, unthinkable change had come about. Somehow he had permitted it! A convulsive, involuntary sigh shook his thick chest, then, as if in rage and disgust at such a weakness, he bared his lips over his pale gums, ground his teeth, and went slowly into his office. No letters, no daily paper now cumbered his desk, awaiting his disdainful attention; dust alone lay there, lay thickly upon everything. Yet, as he stood within the neglected office, like the leader of a hopeless cause when he has finally abandoned it, a faint measure of sad relief tinctured his regret, and he became aware that he now faced the worst, that the suspense of this unfair fight was at an end.

The money he had raised by mortgaging his house was finished; though he had eked this out to the last driblet his resources were now entirely exhausted. But, he reflected, he had discharged his obligations to the utmost; he owed no man a penny, and if he were ruined, he had scorned the ignominious refuge of bankruptcy. He sat down upon his chair regardless of dust, scarcely noticing, indeed, the cloud that rose about him, unheeding of the powdery layer that settled on his clothing—he had grown so careless of his person and his dress. He was unshaven, and against the dark, unkempt stubble on his face the white of his eyes glared savagely; his finger nails were ragged and bitten to the quick, his boots were unbrushed, his cravat, lacking the usual pin, was partially undone as though, desiring suddenly more liberty to breathe, he had unloosed it with a single wrench. His clothes, too, were flung untidily upon him as he had dressed that morning regardless of anything but despatch. Now, indeed, his main concern was to leave as quickly as possible a house pervaded with sudden and disturbing cries of pain, filled with disorder and confusion, with unwashed dishes and the fœtor of drugs, a house wherein he was nauseated by ill-cooked and ill-served food, and irritated by a snivelling son and an incompetent old woman. Sitting there, he plunged his hand suddenly into his inside pocket and drew out carefully a flat, black bottle, then, still staring in front of him, without viewing the bottle, he sunk his strong teeth in the cork and with a quick jerk of his thick neck withdrew the cork. The sharp, plucking report filled the silence of the room. Placing the neck of the bottle between his cupped lips he raised his elbow gradually and took a long gurgling drink, then with a sharp intake of breath over his parted teeth, he placed the bottle in front of him on the table and fixed his glance on it. Nancy had filled it for him! His eye lit up, momentarily, as though the bottle mirrored her face. She was a good one, was Nancy, an alleviation of his melancholy, the mitigation of his depression; despite his misfortunes he would never let her go; he would stick to her whatever happened. He tried to penetrate the future, to make plans, to decide what he must do; but it was impossible. The moment he set himself to think deeply his mind wandered off into the remotest and most incongruous digressions. Fleeting visions of his youth revolved before him—the smile of a boy who had been his playmate, the hot sunny wall in the crevices of which, with other boys, he had hunted for bumble bees, the smoke about his gun-barrel when he had shot his first rabbit; he heard the swish of a scythe, the purling of cushat-doves, the sharp skirling laughter of an old woman in the village.

With a shake of his head he banished the visions, took another pull at the bottle, considering deliberately the immense solace that spirits brought to him. His depression lightened, his lip curled sneeringly, and "they," the unheard critics, the antagonists ever present in his mind became more contemptible, more pitiful than ever. Then suddenly, through this new mood, a sparkling idea struck him, which as he considered it more fully, forced from him a short, derisive laugh. With the eyes of the town upon him, peering sneakingly upon his misfortunes, expecting him to slink abjectly from the scene of his ruin, he would nevertheless show them how James Brodie could face disaster. He would provide a fitting climax for his exit with a spectacle that would make their spying eyes blink. Fiercely he drained the last of the whisky, pleased that his brain had at last given him an inspiration to spur him to motion, delighted to loose the confined brooding of his mind in a definite physical activity, no matter how inordinate it might be. He arose and, sending his chair sprawling on the floor, passed into the shop where, surveying with a hostile eye the remaining boxes stacked behind the counter, he advanced upon them and began rapidly to spill their contents upon the floor. Eagerly he tumbled out hats of all descriptions. Disdaining to open the boxes calmly, his huge hands gripped them fiercely and rent the cardboard like tissue paper, furiously ripping and tearing at the boxes as though in frantic avulsion they dismembered the bodies of his dead enemies. He flung the tattered debris from him in every direction with loose, whirling movements, till the fragmentary litter filled the room and lay about his feet like fallen snow. Then, when he had thus roughly shelled each box of its contents, he gathered the pile of hats from the floor into his wide arms and, massing them together in his colossal embrace, marched triumphantly to the door of his shop. A wild exultation seized him. As the hats were useless to him, he would give them away, distribute them freely, spite his enemies next door and spoil their custom, make this noble offering of largess his last remembered action in the street.

"Here," he bawled, "who wants a hat?" The whisky had broken down the restraining barriers of his reserve and the foolish extravagance of his act seemed to him only splendid and magnificent. "It's the chance of a lifetime," he shouted, with a curl of his lip. "Come up, all you braw honest bodies, and see what I've got for ye."

It was nearly noon and the street was at its busiest. Immediately a crowd of urchins surrounded him expectantly, and outside this ring an increasing number of passing townsfolk commenced to gather, silent, incredulous, yet nudging and glancing at each other significantly.

"Hats are cheap to-day," shouted Brodie at the pitch of his lungs. "Cheaper than you can buy them at the waxworks," he cried, with a ghastly facetiousness, hoping that they would hear the jibe next door. "I'm givin' them away! I'll make ye have them whether ye want them or no' "; and immediately he began to thrust hats upon the onlookers. It was as he had said, something for nothing, and dumbly, amazedly, they accepted the gifts that they did not desire and might never use. They were afraid to refuse, and, seeing his dominance over them he gloated, glaring at them the more, beating their eyes to the ground as they met his. A deep-buried, primitive desire in his nature was at last being fed and appeased. He was in his element, the centre of a crowd who hung upon every word, every action, who looked up to him gapingly and, he imagined, admiringly. The fearful quality in his eccentric wildness made them forbear to laugh, but gazing in awed silence, ready to fall back should he run berserk suddenly amongst them, they stood like fascinated sheep before a huge wolf.

But now the mere handing out of the hats began to pall on him and he craved for less restrained, more ungoverned action. He began, therefore, to toss the contents of his arms to the people on the outskirts of the crowd; then, from merely throwing the hats, he commenced to hurl them violently at the onlookers in the ring, hating suddenly every one of the white, vacuous faces; they became his enemies, and the more he despised them the more mercilessly he pelted them, in a growing, turbulent desire to hurt and disperse them.

"Here," he bellowed, "take them a'. I'm finished with them for good. I don't want the blasted things although they're better and cheaper than you'll get next door. Better and cheaper!" he howled over and over again. "If ye didna want them before, I'll make ye take them now."

The mob retreated under the force and accuracy of his fusillade, and as they dispersed, with back-turned, protesting faces, he followed them with long, skimming shots.

"Stop it?" he shouted sneeringly. "I'll be damned if I do. Do you not want them, that you're runnin' awa'? You're missing the chance of a lifetime."

He gloated in the commotion he was causing, and, when they were out of range, he seized a hard hat by its brim and sent it bowling down the hill where, with the full force of the following breeze, it rolled gaily like a ball in a bowling alley and finally skittled against the legs of a man walking far down the street.

"That was a good one!" cried Brodie, laughing with boisterous delight. "I aye had a grand aim. Here's another, and another." As he sent a further volley whizzing after the first shot, hats of all descriptions went madly leaping, whirling, dancing, swerving, bounding, as they pursued each other down the declivity. It was as though a hurricane had suddenly unbared the heads of a multitude; such an unparalleled and monstrous sight had never before been seen in Levenford. But at last his stock was almost exhausted, and with his final missile in his great paw, he paused selectively, weighing the last shot in his locker—a stiff, board-like strawbasher which, by reason of its shape and hardness, he felt dimly to be worthy of a definite and appropriate billet. Suddenly, out of the corner of his eye, he observed the pale, aghast face of Perry, his old assistant, peering from the adjacent doorway. He was there, was he, thought Brodie—the rat that had saved his own skin by leaving the sinking ship; the beautiful manager of the Mungo Panopticon!—In a flash he skimmed the flat projectile like a whirling quoit full at the sallow, horrified face. The hard serrated brim caught Perry full in the mouth, splintering a tooth and, as he saw the blood flow, and the terrified young man bolt back indoors, Brodie yelled with a roar of triumph at the success of his aim.

"That'll fit you to superintend the waxworks, you poor trash. That's something I've been owin' you a long time." It seemed to him the fitting and culminating achievement of a rare and remarkable display. Throwing up his arms into the air he waved them exultantly, then with an elated grin he turned again into the shop. Inside, as he gazed at the emptiness, complete but for the wreckage of the boxes, the smile on his lips stiffened slowly to a fixed, sardonic spasm; but he did not stop to allow himself to think. He walked through the scattered rubbish into his office where, in the continuance of his wild mood of destruction, he dragged out all the drawers in the desk, smashed the empty whisky bottle against the wall, and overturned the heavy desk with a single, powerful heave. Surveying the scene with a moody, wanton satisfaction,

305

he picked up the door key from its hook beside the window, lifted hi
stick and, with his head in the air, went again through and out of th
shop, closing the outer door behind him. This last, single action affected
him, suddenly, with a sense of such absolute finality that the key in hi
grasp became a foolish redundancy; when he withdrew it from the loch
he looked at it senselessly as it lay in his palm, then suddenly drew back
and hurled it far over the top of the building—listening intently unti
he heard the faint splash as it dropped into the river behind. The
could get into the place how they liked, he thought bitterly; he, at any
rate, was finished with it.

On his way home he still could not, or at least refused to think, remain
ing without even a remote idea as to the conduct of his future. He had
a fine stone house, heavily mortgaged, to maintain, an old decrepi
mother, an invalid wife, and a useless son to support, and a youn
daughter who must be educated, but beyond the fact that he was strong
with a physique powerful enough to uproot a fair-sized tree, his asset
towards these responsibilities were negligible. He did not actively con
sider in this fashion but, the abandon of his recent mood subsided, h
felt dimly the uncertainty of his position and it weighed upon him
heavily. He was affected chiefly by the lack of money in his pocket, and
as he neared his house and saw standing outside a familiar, high gi
and bay gelding, his brow darkened. "Damn it all," he muttered
"is he in, again? How does he expect me to pay the blasted long bil
he's runnin' up?" It pricked him with an irritating reminder of hi
circumstances to see Dr. Lawrie's equipage at his gate and, thinkin
to spare himself the necessity of a tedious encounter by entering th
house unobserved, he was more deeply annoyed to meet Lawrie face t
face at the front door.

"Just been having a peep at the good wife, Mr. Brodie," said th
doctor, with an affectation of heartiness. He was a pompous, portly ma
with blown-out cheeks, a small, red mouth, and an insufficient chin
inadequately strengthened by a grey, imperial beard. "Trying to kee
her spirits up, you know; we must do all we can."

Brodie looked at the other silently, his saturnine eyes saying, mor
cuttingly than words: "And much good ye have done her, ye empty
wind bag."

"Not much change for the better, I'm afraid," continued Lawri
hurriedly, becoming a trifle more florid under Brodie's rude stare
"Not much improvement. We're nearing the end of the chapter I fear.'
This was his usual stereotyped banality to indicate the nearness o
death, and now he shook his head profoundly, sighed, and smoothed
the small tuft on his chin with an air of melancholy resignation.

Brodie gazed with aversion at the finicking gestures of this pompou
wiseacre, and though he did not regret having brought him into hi
house to spite Renwick, he was not deceived by his bluff manner, o

by his great display of sympathy.

"Ye've been tellin' me that for a long time," he growled. "You and your chapters! I believe ye know less than onybody what's goin' to happen. I'm gettin' tired of it."

"I know! I know! Mr. Brodie," said Lawrie, making little soothing gestures with his hands, "your distress is very natural—very natural! We cannot say definitely when the unhappy event will occur. It depends so much on the reaction of the blood—that is the crux of the question— the reaction of the blood with regard to the behaviour of the corpuscles! The corpuscles are sometimes stronger than we expect. Yes! the corpuscles are sometimes marvellous in their activities," and, satisfied with his show of erudition he again stroked his moustache and looked learnedly at Brodie.

"You can take your corpuscles to hell," replied Brodie contemptuously. "You've done her as much good as my foot."

"Come now, Mr. Brodie," said Lawrie in a half-expostulating, half-placating tone, "don't be unreasonable. I'm here every day. I'm doing my best."

"Do better then! Finish her and be done wi't," retorted Brodie bitterly, and turning abruptly, he walked away and entered the house, leaving the other standing aghast, his eyes wide, his small mouth pursed into an indignant orb.

Inside his home, a further wave of disgust swept over Brodie as, making no allowance for the fact that he was earlier than usual, he observed that his dinner was not ready, and he cursed the bent figure of his mother amongst the disarray of dishes, dirty water, pots, and potato peelings in the scullery.

"I'm gettin' ower auld for this game, James," she quavered in reply. "I'm not as nimble as I used to be—and forbye the doctor keepit me back."

"Move your auld bones then," he snarled. "I'm hungry." He could not sit down amongst such chaos, and, with a sudden turn of his black mood, he decided that he would fill in the time before his meal by visiting his wife—the good wife, as Lawrie had called her—and give her the grand news of the business.

"She maun hear some time," he muttered, "and the sooner the better. It's news that'll not stand the keepin'." He had lately fallen into the habit of avoiding her room, and as he had not seen her during the last two days, she would no doubt find the unexpectedness of his visit the more delightful.

"Well!" he remarked softly, as he went into the bedroom, "you're still here I see. I met the doctor on my way in and he was gi'en us a great account o' your corpuscles o' the blood—they're uncommon strong by his report."

She did not move at his entry, but lay passive, only the flicker of her eyes showing that she lived. In the six months that had elapsed since she had been forced to take to her bed she had altered terrifyingly, and one who had not marked the imperceptible, day by day decline, the gradual shrinking of her flesh, would not have found her unrecognisable even as the ailing woman she had then appeared. Her form, beneath the light covering of the sheet, was that of a skeleton with hip bones which stuck out in a high, ridiculous protuberance; only a flaccid envelope of sagging skin covered the thin, long bones of her legs and arms, while over the framework of her face a tight, dry parchment was drawn, with cavities for eyes, nose, and mouth. Her lips were pale, dry, cracked, with little brown desiccated flakes clinging to them like scales, and above the sunken features her bony forehead seemed to bulge into unnatural, disproportioned relief. A few strands of grey hair, withered, lifeless as the face itself, straggled over the pillow to frame this ghastly visage. Her weakness was so apparent that it seemed an impossible effort for her to breathe, and from this very weakness she made no reply to his remark, but looked at him with an expression he could not read. It seemed to her that there was nothing more for him to say to wound her.

"Have ye everything ye want?" he continued, in a low tone of assumed solicitude. "Everything that might be necessary for these corpuscles o' yours? Ye've plenty of medicine anyway—plenty of choice, I see. One, two, three, four," he counted, "four different bottles o' pheesic. There's merit in variety apparently. But woman, if ye go on drinkin' it at this rate, we'll have to raise another loan frae your braw friends in Glasgow to pay for it a'."

Deep in her living eyes, which alone of her wasted features indicated her emotions, a faint wound reopened, and they filled with a look of dull pleading. Five months ago she had, in desperation, been forced to confess to him her obligation to the money-lenders and though he had paid the money in full, since then he had not for a moment let her forget the wretched matter, and in a hundred different ways, on the most absurd pretexts, he would introduce it into the conversation. Not even her present look moved him, for he was now entirely without sympathy for her, feeling that she would linger on for ever, a useless encumbrance to him.

"Ay," he continued pleasantly, "ye've proved yoursel' a great hand at drinkin' the medicine. You're as gleg at that as ye are at spendin' other folks' money." Then abruptly he changed the subject, and queried gravely: "Have ye seen your big, braw son the day? Oh! ye have, indeed," he continued, after reading her unspoken reply. "I'm real glad to hear it. I thocht he michtna have been up yet, but I see I'm wrong. He's not downstairs though. I never seem to be fortunate enough to see him these days."

At his words she spoke at last, moulding her stark lips to utter, in a weak whisper:

"Matt's been a good son to me lately."

"Well, that's only a fair return," he exclaimed judiciously. "You've been a graund mother to him. The result o' your upbringing o' him is a positive credit to you both." He paused, recognising her weakness, hardly knowing why he spoke to her thus, yet, unable to discard the habit of years, impelled somehow by his own bitterness, by his own misfortunes, he continued in a low voice: "Ye've brocht up a' your children bonnie, bonnie. There's Mary now—what more could ye wish for than the way she's turned out? I don't know where she is exactly, but I'm sure she'll be doin' ye credit nobly." Then, observing that his wife was attempting to speak, he waited on her words.

"I know where she is," she whispered slowly.

He gazed at her.

"Ay!" he answered, "ye know she's in London, and that's as much as we a' ken—as much as ye'll ever know."

Almost incredibly she moved her withered hand, that looked incapable of movement, and lifting it from the counterpane stopped him with a gesture; then, as her shrunken arm again collapsed, she said weakly, and with many tremors:

"Ye mustna be angry with me, ye mustna be angry with her. I've had a letter from Mary. She's a good girl—she still is. I see more clearly, now, than ever I did that 'twas I that didna do right by her. She wants to see me now, James, and I—I must see her quickly before I die." As she uttered the last words she tried to smile to him pleadingly, placatingly, but her features remained stiff and frigid, only her lips parted slightly in a cracked, pitiful grimace.

The colour mounted slowly to his forehead.

"She dared to write to you," he muttered, "and you dared to read it."

" 'Twas Dr. Renwick, when you stoppit him comin', that wrote to London and told her I was not—not likely to last long. He's aye had a great interest in Mary. He said to me that morning that Mary—my daughter Mary—was brave, ay, and innocent as well."

"He was a brave man himself to raise that name in my house," returned Brodie in a low, concentrated tone. He could not shout and rave at her in her present state, prevented only by some shred of compunction from turning violently upon her, but he added, bitterly: "If I had known he was interferin' like that I would have brained him before he went out the door."

"Don't say that, James," she murmured. "It's beyond me to bear bitterness now. I've had a gey and useless life I think. There's many a thing left undone that should have been done, but I must—oh! I must see Mary, to put things right between her and me."

He gritted his teeth till the muscles of his stubbled jowl stuck out in hard, knotted lumps.

"Ye must see her, must ye," he replied—"that's verra, verra touchin'.

We should a' fall down and greet at the thought o' this wonderful reconciliation." He shook his head slowly from side to side. "Na! Na! my woman ye'll not see her this side o' the grave, and I have strong misgivings if ye'll see her on the other. You're never to see her. Never!"

She did not answer, but, withdrawing into herself, became more impassive, more aloof from him. For a long time her eyes remained fixed on the ceiling. There was silence in the room but for the drowsy drone of an insect as it circled around the few sprays of sweet-scented honeysuckle that had been gathered by Nessie and placed by her in a vase that stood beside the bed. At length a faint tremor ran through Mamma's wasted body.

"Weel, James," she sighed, "if you say it, then it maun be so—that's always been the way; but I wanted, oh! I did want to see her again. There's times though," she went on, slowly, and with great difficulty, "when the pain o' this trouble has been to me like the carryin' of a child—so heavy and draggin' like—and it's turned my mind to that bairn o' hers that never lived for her to see it. If it had been spared I would have liket to have held Mary's bairn in these arms"—she looked downwards, hopelessly, at the withered arms that could scarcely raise a cup to her lips—"but it was the will of God that such things couldna be, and that's all there is about it."

"Woman, you're not squeamish to take such a notion into your head at this time o' day," scowled Brodie. "Have ye not had enough to do with your own children without draggin' out the memory of—of that."

"It was just a fancy," she whispered, "and I've had many o' them since I lay here these six, long months—so long they've been like weary years." She closed her eyes in a tired fashion, forgetting him as the visions that she spoke of rushed over her again. The sweet perfume of the honeysuckle flowers beside her wafted her thoughts backwards, and she was out of the close, sickly room, home again on her father's farm. She saw the stout, whitewashed buildings, the homestead, the dairy, and the long, clean byre forming the three snug sides of the clean yard, saw her father come in from the shooting with a hare and a brace of pheasants in his hand. The smooth, coloured plumage delighted her as she stroked the plump breasts.

"They're as fat as you are," her father cried, with his broad, warm smile, "but not near as bonnie."

She had not been a slut then, nor had her form been the object of derision!

Now she was helping her mother with the churning, watching the rich yellow of the butter as it clotted in the white milk like a clump of early primroses springing from a bank of snow:

"Not so hard, Margaret, my dear," her mother had chided her, for the quickness of her turning. "You'll turn the arm off yourself."

She had not been lazy then, nor had they called her handless!

Her thoughts played happily about the farm and in her imagination she rolled amidst the sweet mown hay, heard the creak of the horses moving in their stalls, laid her cheek against the sleek side of her favourite calf. She even remembered its name—"Rosabelle," she had christened it. "Whatna name for a cow!" Bella, the dairymaid, had teased her. "What way not call it after me and be done wi' it?" An overpowering wave of nostalgia came over her as she remembered long, hot afternoons when she had lain with her head against the bole of the bent apple tree, watching the swallows flirt like winged, blue shadows around the eaves of the white, sun-drenched steadings. When an apple dropped beside her she picked it up and bit deeply into it; even now, she felt the sweetly acid tang refreshing upon her tongue, cooling its parched fever. Then she saw herself in a sprigged muslin frock, beside the mountain ash that grew above the Pownie Burn and, approaching her, a youth whose dark, dour strength her gentleness drew near. She opened her eyes slowly.

"James," she whispered as her eyes sought his with faint, wistful eagerness, "do ye mind that day by the Pownie Burn when ye braided the bonnie, red, rowan berries through my hair? Do ye mind what he said then?"

He stared at her, startled at the transition of her speech, wondering if she raved; here was he on the brink of ruin, and she drivelled about a wheen rowans thirty years ago. His lips twitched as he replied, slowly:

"No! I dinna mind what I said, but tell me, tell me what I said."

She closed her eyes as though to shut out everything but the distant past, then she murmured, slowly:

"Ye only said that the rowan berries were not so braw as my bonnie curly hair."

As, unconsciously, he looked at the scanty, brittle strands of hair that lay about her face, a sudden, fearful rush of emotion swept over him. He did remember that day. He recollected the quiet of the little glen, the ripple of the stream, the sunshine that lay about them, the upward switch of the bough after he had plucked the bunch of berries from it; now he saw the lustre of her curls against the vivid scarlet of the rowans. Numbly, he tried to reject the idea that this—this wasted creature that lay upon the bed had on that day rested in his arms and answered his words of love with her soft, fresh lips. It could not be—yet it must be! His face worked strangely, his mouth twisted as he battled with the urging feeling that drove against the barrier of his resistance like a torrent of water battering against the granite wall of a dam. Some vast, compelling impulse drove at him with an urge which made him want to say blindly, irrationally, in a fashion he had not used for twenty years:

"I do mind that day, Margaret, and ye were bonnie—bonnie and sweet to me as a flower." But he could not say it! Such words as these

could never pass his lips. Had he come to this room to whine som
stupid phrases of endearment? No, he had come to tell her of their rui
and tell her he would, despite this unnatural weakness that had com
upon him.

"Auld wife," he muttered with drawn lips, "ye'll be the death o
me if ye talk like that. When ye're on the parish ye maun give me
crack like this to cheer me up."

At once her eyes opened enquiringly, anxiously, with a look whic
again stabbed him; but he forced himself to continue, nodded at he
with a false assumption of his old, fleering jocosity.

"Ay!" he cried, "that's what it amounts to now. I'll have no mor
fifty pounds to fling away on ye. I've shut my door of the business fo
the last time. We'll all be in the poorhouse soon." As he uttered the la
words he saw her face change, but some devilish impulse, aroused b
his own present weakness, and moving him more fiercely because h
knew that in his heart he did not wish to speak like this, made hin
thrust his head close to her, goaded him to continue: "Do ye hea
The business is gone. I warned ye a year ago—don't you remember tha
wi' your demned rowan berry rot? I tell ye we're ruined! You that
been such a help to me, that's what ye've brought me to. We're finishe
finished, finished!"

The effect of his words upon her was immediate, and terrible. Whe
his meaning burst in upon her a frightful twitching affected the yellov
weazened skin of her features as though a sudden, intense grief attempte
painfully to animate the moribund tissues, as though tears essayed wit
futile effort to well out from the dried-up springs of her body. Her ey
became suddenly full, intense, and glowing and, with a tremendou
shivering effort, she raised herself up in the bed. A stream of word
trembled upon her tongue but she could not utter them, and as a dew c
perspiration broke upon her brow in cold, pricking droplets she stam
mered incoherently, stretched her hand dumbly before her. Then, a
her face grew grey with endeavour, suddenly she spoke:

"Matt," she cried in a full, high tone. "Matt! come to me!" Sh
now stretched out both her quivering arms as though sight failed he
calling out in a weaker, fading tone: "Nessie! Mary! Where are ye?"

He wished to go to her, to start forward instantly, but he remaine
rooted to the floor; yet from his lips broke involuntarily these word
strange as a spray of blossoms upon a barren tree:

"Margaret, woman—Margaret—dinna mind what I said. I didn
mean the hauf o't!"

But she did not hear him, and with a last, faint breath she whispere
slowly:

"Why tarry the wheels of thy chariot, O Lord? I'm ready to g
to ye!"

Then she sank gently backwards upon the pillow. A moment later last, powerful expiration shook the thin, withered body with a convulsive spasm, and she lay still. Limp and flat upon her back, with arms outstretched upon the bed, the fingers slightly flexed upon the upturned palms, she lay, in shape and stillness, as if she had been crucified. She was dead.

XIII

BRODIE looked round the company assembled uncomfortably in the parlour with a brooding eye which passed over Nessie, Matthew, and his mother, lit impatiently upon his wife's cousins—Janet and William Lumsden—and settled with a scowling finality upon Mrs. William Lumsden. They had just buried all that remained of Margaret Brodie, and the guests, clinging even in the face of Brodie's inhospitable frowns, to the privileges endowed to them by old-established precedent, had returned to the house after the funeral to partake of refreshment.

"We'll give them nothing!" Brodie had exclaimed to his mother that morning. His momentary, belated tenderness towards his wife was now forgotten and he resented bitterly the threatened intrusion of her relations. "I don't want them about my house. They can go hame whenever she's ditched." The old woman had herself hoped for a savoury high tea, but in the face of his remark she had modified her demands.

"James," she had pleaded, "ye maun gie them a sip o' wine and a bite o' cake for the honour o' the house."

"None o' our ain folks are left to come," he growled. "What does it matter about hers? I wish I had choked them off when they wrote."

"They're ower scattered for mony o' them to come," she had placated, "but ye canna get ower offerin' them something. It wouldna be decent to do otherwise."

"Give them it, then," he cried, and as a sudden thought struck him, he added: "Ay, give them it, then. Feed the swine. There'll be somebody here to lend ye a hand."

Now it gave him a saturnine pleasure to see Nancy enter briskly with cake, biscuits, and wine and hand them round. He was his own man again, and it appeared a delicious stroke of satire for him to have her enter his house the moment his wife's body had been carried out; the two women—the dead and the quick—had, so to speak, passed each other at the gate; his eyes met hers in a glow of hidden buffoonery.

"Go ahead, Matt," he jeered significantly at his son, as Nancy handed the latter wine, with a pertly conscious air. "Take up a glass. It'll do ye good after all your greetin'. You'll be quite safe. I'm here to see it

313

doesna fly to your head." He watched his son's trembling hand with disgust. Matt had again disgraced him by breaking down abjectly at the graveside, snivelling and whimpering before these relations of Mamma's, and grovelling hysterically on his knees as the first spadeful of earth clumped heavily upon the coffin.

"Nae wonder he's upset," said Janet Lumsden, in a kindly voice. She was a fat, comfortable woman with a high, amiable bosom protruding above the upper edge of her ill-fitting corsets. Now she looked round the assembly and added, agreeably: " 'Twas a merciful release, though, I'm led to believe. She'll be happier where she is now, I'll warrant."

" 'Tis a pity the puir thing wasna allowed a wreath or two," said Mrs. William Lumsden, with a sniff and a toss of her head. Her lips were tight and her mouth downturned beneath her long, sharp, penetrating nose; as she helped herself from the tray she looked intently at Nancy, then looked away again with a slow and upward twist of her head. "A funeral is never the same without flowers," she added, firmly.

"Ay, they're sort o' comfortin' like," said Janet Lumsden placatingly. "They big lilies are bonnie."

"I had never been to a burial before, without flowers," replied Mrs. Lumsden acrimoniously. "The last interment I attended there was a full, open carriage of flowers, forbye what covered the coffin."

Brodie looked at her steadily.

"Weel, ma'am," he said politely, "I hope ye'll have a' the blossoms ye require when ye go to yer ain last repose."

The other looked along her nose at him doubtfully, not knowing exactly whether to accept the remark as a compliment or an insult, then, in her uncertainty, she turned commandingly to her husband for support. He, a small wiry man, uncomfortable in his stiff, shiny black suit, his starched dickey, and tight "made" tie, magnificent, yet none the less still smelling of the stable, interpreted the familiar look, and dutifully began:

"Flowers gang well at a funeral—it's a matter of opinion no doubt, but I would say they were a consolation to the bereaved. But the strangest thing to my mind is that they should gang well with a weddin' too. It's a fair mystery to me how they should suit such opposite ceremonies." He cleared his throat and looked sociably at Brodie. "Ye ken I've been to many a funeral—ay, and to many a weddin' too. Ance I went as far as forty miles away from hame, but would ye believe me, man," he concluded triumphantly, "for thirty-two years I havena slept a nicht out o' ma ain bed."

"Indeed," said Brodie curtly, "I'm not interested."

At this rudeness there was an uncomfortable pause, a silence punctuated only by a small residual sob from the red-eyed Nessie. The two groups looked at each other distrustfully, like strangers on opposite sides of a railway compartment.

314

"It's a gey appropriate day for a funeral, anyway," said Lumsden at last, defiantly, looking out at the drizzling rain; and at his remark a low conversation amongst the three visitors, and confined exclusively to them, again recommenced and slowly gained impetus.

"Ay! it's miserable enough for onything here."

"Did ye mark how heavy the rain cam' on at the graveside whenever the cords were lowered?"

" 'Tis remarkable to me that the meenister wouldna come back to the house to gie us a few words."

"He'll have his reasons, I have nae doubt."

"What he did say at the grave's heid he said unco' weel, onyway. It's a pity she couldna have heard it hersel', puir body."

"What was't he said, 'a loyal wife and a devoted mother,' wasn't to'?"

They looked out of the corners of their eyes at Brodie as though expecting him to confirm decently this last tribute, but he seemed not to have heard them and now gazed broodingly away from them out of the window. And now, seeing Brodie's apparent inattention, they grew bolder.

"I wad like to have seen the puir thing again, but I had the surprise o' my life when I heard she had been screwed down before we arrived."

"She must have altered sadly wi' sicca trouble, ay and a' the worry she cam' through."

"She was a bricht, lively kimmer in her young days. She had a laugh like the song o' a mavis."

"She was a' that," said Janet at last, with a reproachful look at the figure by the window, implying by her words, "She was too good for you."

There was a moment's pause, then, with a guarded look at Nessie that encompassed her blue serge dress, Mrs. Lumsden murmured:

"It fair affronts me to see that puir child without the decent mournin's to her back. It's nothing short of shameful."

" 'Twas the sma' sma' funeral that surprised me," returned Janet. "Only the twa carriages, and not a single body frae the town."

He heard them, actually he had listened to every word—only the heedlessness of his embittered humour had allowed them to proceed—but now he turned to them coarsely:

" 'Twas my express wish that the funeral should be private, and as quiet as might be. Did ye wish the town band out for her, and free whisky and a bonfire?"

They were frankly shocked at such brutality, drew more closely together in their resentment, began to think of leaving.

"Weelum! do ye know onywhere in Levenford we're likely to be able to get our tea before the train goes?" said Mrs. Lumsden, as an indication of departure, in a trembling but rancorous tone. She had

315

expected, instead of this thin, sour wine and bought seed cake a lavish
display of hot and cold cooked meats, baked pastries, scones, tea bread
and other appropriate delicacies; coming from a distant village in
Ayrshire they knew nothing of Brodie's failure, and thought him well
able to provide a more worthy and substantial repast than that of which
they were now partaking.

"Will ye no' have another biscuit then, if ye're hungry?" said old
Grandma Brodie, with a slight titter—"they're Deesides—I can recom-
mend them." The wine was like nectar to her unaccustomed palate
and she had partaken freely of it. so that a faint flush marked the
yellow, wrinkled skin over her high cheek-bones; she was enjoying the
occasion immensely, making high festival of the return to earth of the
poor remains of Margaret Brodie. "Have a wee drap mair wine, will
ye not?"

"Thank ye! No!" said Mrs. Lumsden, compressing her mouth
superciliously into the smallest possible compass, and issuing her words
disdainfully from the diminutive aperture. "I'll not indulge if ye don't
mind. I'm not addicted, and besides I couldna fancy that what you're
drinkin'. Do ye know," she continued, drawing on her black kid glove
"that's a bold-looking quean ye have about the house at a time like
this. Have ye had her long?"

As Grandma Brodie made to answer, a polite hiccough disturbed her.

"I dinna ken her," she replied confusedly, "she's juist come in now.
'Twas James sent her in to gie me a haund."

Mrs. Lumsden exchanged a significant glance with her cousin by
marriage. Each nodded her head with a slight downward gesture of dis-
paragement, as though to say: "Just what we thought," and both
turned ostentatiously compassionate eyes upon Nessie.

"What in the world will ye do without your mother, dearie?" remarked one.

"Ye maun come doun to us, child, for a spell," said the other. "Ye
would like to play about the farm, would ye not?"

"I can look after Nessie," inserted Brodie icily; "she needs neither
your help nor your pity. When ye do hear o' her she'll be shapin' for
something that you and yours could never attain."

As Nancy entered the room to collect the glasses, he continued:

"Here, Nancy! these two ladies have just remarked that you're
brazen—was it quean ye said, leddies—ay, a brazen quean. In return
for this good opinion would mind ye showin' them out o' the house—
and I suppose this bit gentleman they've brocht wi' them better go too.

Nancy tossed her head pertly.

"If it was my house," she said, with a bold look at Brodie, "they
would never have been in it."

The two women, scandalised, stood up.

"The language—and the behaviour! In front of the child too,

sped Janet, on her way to the door, "and at such a time as this."

Mrs. Lumsden, equally shocked, but less intimidated, drew herself
to her tall, angular height and threw her head back defiantly.

"I've been insulted," she shrilled from between thin, compressed lips,
n a house where I came a long and expensive journey to bring comfort.
n goin', oh! indeed yes, I'm goin', nothing would stop me, but," she
ded emphatically, "before I leave I want to know what has been left
our side o' the family by my puir cousin."

Brodie laughed shortly in her face.

"Indeed now! and what had she to leave, pray?"

"I happen to know from Weelum that forbye the china, pictures, and
e ornaments on the best bedroom mantelpiece, and her mother's watch
d locket, Margaret Lumsden took a pickle siller wi' her into the
use," she cried angrily.

"Ay, and she took a pickle out o' it," answered Brodie harshly.
et away wi' ye! the sight o' your sour, graspin', avaricious face fair
nners me!" With whirling movements of his arms he herded them
the door. "Get away with ye a', there's nothing for ye here. I'm sorry
et ye break bread in my house."

Mrs. Lumsden, almost in tears from rage and vexation, turned on
e doorstep.

"We'll have the law on ye about it," she cried. "I'm not surprised
at puir Margaret Lumsden withered out here. She was ower guid for
, wi' your bold besoms. Ye've made a cryin' scandal out of the burial
the puir soul. Come awa' home, Weelum."

"That's right," shouted Brodie tauntingly, "take Weelum away
me to his bed. I'm not surprised he's so fond o' it wi' such a tricksy
nament as yersel' below the blankets." He leered at her, insultingly.
e're richt not to let him out it for a nicht, for if ye did ye might never
t him back."

As she disappeared with the others, her head high, her colour flaming,
cried out after her:

"I'll not forget to send ye your flowers whenever ye require them."

But when he returned to the parlour his hard assumption of indiffer-
ce had dropped from him and, wishing to be alone, in a different,
iet voice he bade them leave him. As they filed out he turned to
atthew and said to him meaningly:

"Away out and find work. I want no more of your useless, watery
r-bag nonsense. Get something to do. Ye'll not live off me much
ger"; but as Nessie passed he patted her head and said, gently:

"Don't greet any more, pettie, your father will take care of ye. Dry
ur eyes, now, and run and take up a book or something. You needna
rry. I'm goin' to look after you in future."

That, he considered, as he sat down again in the empty room, was the
urse towards which his life must immediately shape itself—the

317

vindication of himself through Nessie. She was his asset, clever, yes,
told himself, brilliant! He would nurse her, encourage her, thrust h
forward to triumph after triumph until her name and his own shou
resound in the town. He saw in his colossal failure and in the recent m
fortunes which had beset him only a temporary eclipse from which
time he must necessarily emerge. "Ye cannot keep a good man down
one of his frequently repeated maxims, occurred again to him now co
fortingly. He would be up again presently, more dominant than befo
and in his own mind he considered it an almost masterly strategy to pl
a return to his old, favoured position through Nessie. He heard
anticipation the name of Nessie Brodie upon everyone's lips, beca
aware of himself sharing largely in the universal adulation. "Ther
been no holdin' him since his wife died," he heard them say; "s
must have been a muckle hindrance to the man." How true that w
His main feeling, as he helped to lower the light coffin into its shall
trench, had been one of relief, that he was at last free of a useless encu
brance, a drag upon both his patience and his purse. He remember
nothing in her favour, treasured nothing of her virtues, but dwelt o
upon the weakness, the lack of physical attraction that she had ma
fested in her later years. No gentle sentiment, such as had fain
throbbed within him at her death-bed, no remembrance of the earl
days of their life together now stirred him; his memory was clouded l
an overhung sky that refused to allow one single, relieving gleam
penetrate from the clearer air behind. He imagined that she had fail
him in everything, in her companionship, in the oblation of her physi
being, in the very geniture of her children. No credit was due to her
Nessie, whom he felt to be entirely of his substance, and such obitua
as his consideration gave her was epitomised in the single word
incompetent. As the irrevocable finality of her departure struck h
with a sudden and forceful reality, a feeling of a strange emancipati
came over him. The lightness of her restraint had been—from its ve
feebleness—galling to him. He was a young man yet, and virile,
whom many pleasures lay in store which might be tasted freely now t
she was gone. His lower lip hung thickly forward as his thoughts dalli
appreciatively upon Nancy, then roamed forward in anticipati
amongst the lush, erotic pastures of his mind. Nancy must be alwa
about him—now she could remain in the house for good. There w
nothing to prevent her being beside him, no possible objection to h
serving him, cheering him, and—yes, a man must, after all, have
housekeeper!

Satisfied at this comforting decision, insensibly his meditations turn
again upon his younger daughter. His mind, incapable of embraci
any but one purpose at a time, pursued that purpose, when it had be
adopted, with a relentless obstinacy; and now, he realised that in ord
to continue living in his house, to maintain Nessie and to educate h

as he wished, he must quickly find some means of income. His lips tightened, and he nodded his head profoundly, as he resolved to carry into effect, immediately, a plan which had for the last two days been maturing in his brain. He got up and entered the hall where he put on his hat, took his silk umbrella from the stand, and went slowly out of the house.

Outside it was cool and fresh, with a fine, impalpable rain—soft and subtile as dew—which misted his garments and touched his warm brow like a caress. As he filled his lungs with great draughts of the balmy, misty vapour it felt good to him that he did not lie in a narrow, wooden box beneath four feet of dank earth, but walked in the air, invigorated, alive, and free. Characteristically, in the constrained capacity of his intellect, the memory of his humiliation in business, even the final scene in the High Street when he had given that madly unrestrained exhibition, was now completely obliterated; his failure appeared to him in a different light; he was not crushed and beaten, but a gentlemanly victim of malicious circumstances. The ebullition of temper provoked by the Lumsdens had subsided and, his present mission filling him once more with a conscious dignity, he walked gravely through the streets, addressing no one, but saluting seriously such of those he encountered as he felt to merit his recognition. He responded strongly to his own suggestion that, disencumbered of his wife, and with Nessie as the medium of his expression, a new and more important book of his life was beginning.

At the head of Church Street he turned at right angles and proceeded directly away from the High Street, towards the Newtown. Shops became infrequent; on his left lay a row of workmen's dwellings, mean houses which abutted, without gardens, directly upon the street, and upon his right a high, stone wall ran continuously. Above this wall small, bristling forests of tall, branchless, spars erected themselves, and from over its summit, carried on the salty breeze, a hundred gradations of noise reached his ears. Some few hundred yards along, he drew up opposite a block of buildings which, intersecting the smooth continuity of the lofty wall, fronted the street imposingly; there, opposite the main door, he paused. His appearance was that of one who studied carefully the inconspicuous, brass plate before him—the sign which said neatly, above: Levenford Shipbuilding Yard and, below: Latta & Co.—but actually he was mustering all his forces to enter that doorway which confronted him. Now that he had arrived, an unusual vacillation possessed and weakened his purposeful determination; the sight, even, of the outer confines of the immense yard, the dim realisation of the immense wealth which it represented, impressed him, in his reduced financial situation, with a sensation of inferiority. Angrily he thrust this from him, assuring himself, in his own axiom, that it was the man, not the money that mattered, and, with a quick gesture, he swaggered his way through the imposing portals.

His precipitate entry carried him past the small, sliding window marked "Enquiries" without his observing it, and immediately he became lost in a labyrinth of corridors. For some moments he moved about the corridors, blundering angrily like a trapped minotaur in a maze, until by chance he encountered a young man whom, from the short wooden pen that projected like a spit behind one ear, he correctly adjudged to be a clerk.

"I want to see Sir John Latta," he announced fiercely. He felt a fool in these corridors. "I want to see him at once."

The youth blenched at the august name. For him an impassable regiment of chief clerks, managers, heads of departments, and super-intendents intervened upon his road of access to that supreme head.

"Have you an appointment?" he asked, vaguely.

"No!" said Brodie, "I haven't."

"It's nothing to do with me of course," replied the youth, disclaiming immediately all responsibility, "but you would have more chance if you had an appointment." He spoke the last word as though it were an emblem of high solemnity, like a key that was necessary to open a sacred door.

"Never mind your appointments. I must see him," cried Brodie, so fiercely that the young man felt compelled to offer another suggestion.

"I could see Mr. Sharp for you," he observed, mentioning his own particular demi-god.

"Take me to him then," said Brodie impatiently, "and hurry up about it."

With surprising ease the youth threaded the corridors and, presenting him before Mr. Sharp with a few explanatory words, fled spontaneously as though repudiating all consequences of his act.

Mr. Sharp was not sure, was, in fact, extremely doubtful of Sir John's ability to see anyone to-day. The head of the firm was deeply engaged, had asked not to be disturbed, was shortly going out, and, in fact, unless the business was of the most important nature, Mr. Sharp was exceed-ingly distrustful of himself intruding upon Sir John with Mr. Brodie's name.

Brodie gazed at the other out of his small, angry eyes.

"Tell Sir John that James Brodie asks to see him," he exclaimed hotly. "He knows me well. He'll see me at once."

Mr. Sharp departed in a huff but came back, after some time, to ask Mr. Brodie in a frigid tone to be seated, and to say that Sir John would see him presently.

With a triumphant look at the other which said: "I told ye so, ye fool," Brodie sat down and waited, watching idly, as the moments passed, the hive of busy clerks that hummed around him, their activities controlled, apparently, by the waspish eye of Sharp. As the minutes dragged slowly on, whilst he cooled his heels he reflected, in his suspense, that "presently" must mean a very considerable period, and the longer he waited the more his exultation faded, the more Mr. Sharp's obvious satisfaction increased; it was borne in on him that he could not enter Sir John's office in the easy fashion that Sir John entered his, that it was appreciably more difficult to interview the other here than it had been to accost him casually at the Cattle Show. A heavy depression settled upon him which was scarcely dispelled by the sudden, eventual summons to the office of the head of the firm.

Sir John Latta looked up quickly from his desk as Brodie was shown into the room and, silently indicating a chair, resumed his intent consideration of a plan that lay before him. Brodie lowered his ponderous bulk into the chair and glanced round the sumptuous room, observing the rich, teak panelling and softly tinted colours, the flowing marine paintings on the walls, the exquisite models of ships upon their graceful pedestals; as his feet sank deeply into the many piles of the carpet and he viewed the buhl inlay of the desk and the gold cigar box upon it, his nostrils dilated slightly and his eye glistened with a deep sense of appreciation. "I like these things," his attitude seemed to say; "these are the manner of possessions that should be mine."

"Well, Brodie," said Sir John at last, but without looking up, "what is it?"

The other could scarcely have failed to observe the lack of warmth in the tone, but nevertheless he began, eagerly:

"Sir John! I've come to ask ye for your advice. Ye're the one man in Levenford that I would approach like this. Ye understand me, and all that's to me, Sir John. I've felt that in the past over and over again, and now I've come to ask your help."

Latta looked at him curiously.

"You are talking in riddles, Brodie," he retorted coldly, "and it is a form of speech that does not suit you. You are more suited to direct action than indirect speech"; then he added, slowly: "and action does not apparently always become you."

"What do ye mean, Sir John?" blurted out Brodie. "Who has been speakin' of me behind my back?"

The other picked up a fine ivory ruler and, as he lightly tapped his desk with it, answered slowly:

"You are out of favour with me, Brodie. We cannot help but hear the news and bruit of the town at Levenford House—and you have been making a fool of yourself, or worse."

"Ye don't mean that nonsense about—about skiting away the hats?"

Latta shook his head.

"That certainly was folly, but in you a comprehensible folly. There are other things you must know of. You have lost your wife and I believe you have lost your business. You have had disappointments, so I shall not say too much. Yet I hear bad reports of you. You know I never hit a man when he's down, but," he continued quietly, "I take interest in all our townspeople, and I am sorry to hear ill things spoken even of the meanest labourer in my shipyards."

Brodie hung his head like a whipped schoolboy, wondering vaguely if it were Matthew's failure or the Winton Arms that lay in the background of Sir John's mind.

"You may have observed," continued Latta quietly, "that I have not patronised your establishment since the beginning of last year. That is because I heard then of an action of yours which I consider was both unjust and unmerciful. You behaved like a blackguard and a bully to your unfortunate daughter, Brodie, and though some might condone your act on grounds of outraged propriety, we can have nothing to do with you whilst you are under a stigma of this sort."

Brodie's hands clenched tightly and the frown deepened upon his pendent forehead. Latta, he thought bitterly, was the only person in Levenford who would have dared to address him like this, the only man, indeed, who could have uttered such words with impunity.

"I can do nothing," he said sulkily, restrained in his action only through a glimmering sense of his dependence upon the other's good will. "It's all past and done with now."

"You can forgive her," replied Latta sternly. "You can promise me that she shall have refuge in your house if ever she might require it."

Brodie sat sullenly silent, his mind filled, not by Mary but, strangely, by the picture of Nessie. He must do something for her! It was, after all, easy for him to make an acquiescence of some description, and with his head still lowered and his eyes upon the carpet he blurted out: "Very well, Sir John! It'll be as ye say."

Latta looked for a long time at the huge, lowering figure. He had at one time viewed Brodie, in the limited sphere of their mutual encounter, with the connoisseur's eye for the unusual; regarded him with appreciation as a magnificent mountain of manhood; smiled at his obvious conceit and tolerated, with a puzzled curiosity, his strange, bombastic, and unfathomable allusions. He had observed him with the man of breeding's appreciation of a unique and eccentric specimen, but now he felt the other's presence strangely distasteful to him, thought him altered and debased, considered that some deeper explanation might exist of that bluff, yet pretentious assumption of dignity. Quickly he rejected the thought—after all, the man had conceded his point.

"How can I help you then, Brodie?" he said seriously. "Tell me how you stand."

Brodie at last raised his head, becoming aware that the interview had turned, though he knew not how, into the channel which he desired it to take.

"I've closed my business, Sir John!" he began. "Ye know as well as I do how I've been used by these"—he swallowed and restrained himself—"by that company that sneaked into the town and settled beside me like a thief in the night. They've used every low trick they could, stolen my manager from me; they've undercut me, sold rotten trash instead of honest goods, they've—they've sucked the very blood out o' me."

As memory stirred under his own words, his eye filled with self-sympathy and his chest heaved; he stretched out his arm demonstratively.

But Latta was somehow not impressed and raising his hand, deprecatingly, to stop the other he remarked:

"And what did you do, Brodie, to combat these tactics? Did you branch out into new directions or—or exert yourself more agreeably towards your customers?"

Brodie stared at him with a stupid, mulish obstinacy. "I went my own way," he exclaimed stubbornly, "the way I've always gone."

"I see," said Latta slowly.

"I fought them!" exclaimed Brodie. "I fought them like a gentleman and I fought fair. Ay, I would have riven them to bits with these two hands if they had shown the courage to meet me. But they skulked beneath me—and how could I lower myself down to their level, the dogs?"

"And are you involved now, in your affairs?" asked Sir John. "Are you in debt?"

"No!" replied Brodie proudly, "I'm not. I'm finished—but I owe no man a farthing. I've bonded my house but, if I have nothing, I owe nothing. I can start fair, Sir John, if you've a mind to help me. That wee Nessie of mine must have her chance. She's the cleverest lass in Levenford. She's cut out for the bursary your own father founded if she only gets the opportunity."

"Why don't you sell that ridiculous house of yours?" considered Latta, impressed more favourably by the other's words. "It's too large for you now, anyway. Then you can clear your bond, and start afresh in a smaller house with the balance."

Brodie shook his head slowly.

"It's my house," he said heavily. "I built it, and in it I'll bide. I would drag it down about my head sooner than give it up." Then after a pause he added, sombrely: "If that's all ye have to suggest I'll not take any more o' your time."

"Sit down, man," cried Latta. "You're as touchy as tinder." He toyed absently with his ruler, deep in thought, whilst doubtfully, uncomprehendingly, Brodie watched the quick passage of emotions over the other's face. At last Latta spoke. "You're a strange man, Brodie!" he said, "and your mind puzzles me. I was of opinion, a minute ago, to let you whistle for assistance, but somehow I feel a drag upon me which I can't resist. I will make you an offer. Business is not for you now,

Brodie. You are too big, too slow, too cumbersome. You would never succeed by opening up again in your own line, even if this were possible for you. You ought to be working with these great muscles of yours, and yet I suppose you would consider that beneath you. But you can use a pen, keep books, reckon up figures. We might find a place for you here. As I say, I am making you an offer—it is the most I can do—you may refuse it if you choose."

Brodie's eye gleamed. He had known all along that Sir John would help him, that the strong tie of friendship between them must draw the other to help him, and help him royally; he felt that something large and important was looming near for him.

"Ay, Sir John," he said eagerly, "what do ye suggest? I'm at your disposal if I can assist ye."

"I could offer you," Latta continued, evenly, "a position in the office as a clerk. It so happens that there is a vacancy in the wood department at this moment. You would have something to learn, yet, out of consideration for you, I would increase the salary slightly. You would have two pounds ten shillings a week."

Brodie's jaw dropped, and his face crinkled into striped furrows of bewilderment. Hardly able to believe his ears, his eyes clouded with surprise and chagrin whilst the rosy visions which he had suddenly entertained of sitting in a luxurious room—one such as this perhaps—and of directing a bevy of rushing subordinates, faded slowly from his eyes.

"Think it over a moment," said Latta quietly, as he got up and moved towards an inner room. "You must excuse me just now."

Brodie strove to think. Whilst the other was out of the room he sat crushed, overcome by his humiliation. He—James Brodie—to be a clerk! And yet what other avenue than this could he possibly pursue. For Nessie's sake he must accept; he would take the wretched post—but only—only for the meantime. Later, he would show them all—and this Latta more than any.

"Well," said Latta, coming into the office again, "what is it to be?"

Brodie raised his head dully.

"I accept," he said in a flat voice, and added, in a tone into which he strove to insert an inflection of satire, but which succeeded merely in becoming pathetic, "and thank ye."

Dazedly, he saw Latta pull the bell beside his desk, heard him exclaim to the boy who instantly appeared:

"Send Mr. Blair to me."

Blair came, apparently as quickly and mysteriously as the boy, though Brodie hardly looked at the small, precise figure, or gazed into the eye which outdid Sharp's in formal coldness. He did not hear the conversation between the two others yet, after a period of time which he knew not to be long or short, he felt himself being dismissed by Latta.

He stood up, followed Blair slowly out of the rich room, along the passage, down flights of steps across a courtyard, and finally through the door of a small, detached office.

"Though it is apart from the main department I trust you will take no advantage of this fact. This will be your desk," said Blair coldly. It was clear that he regarded Brodie as an interloper and, as he proceeded to explain the simple nature of the duties to him, he infused as much icy contempt into his tone as he might. The two other clerks in the room, both of them young men, peered curiously from over the edge of their ledgers at the strange sight before them, incredulous that this could be their new colleague.

"You have followed me, I trust?" exclaimed Blair finally. "I've made it clear?"

"When do I begin?" asked Brodie dully, feeling that some acknowledgment was expected of him.

"To-morrow, I suppose," answered the other. "Sir John did not exactly specify. If you wish to get a grasp of the books you can begin now if you choose"; and he added witheringly, as he passed out of the room: "But it's only half an hour till the horn goes. I should imagine it would take you longer than that to master the work."

Mutely, as if he knew not what he did, Brodie sat down upon the high stool before the desk, the open ledger a white blur in front of him. He did not see the figures with which, in the future, he must occupy himself, nor did he feel the staring eyes of the two silent youths bent upon him in a strange constraint. He was a clerk! a clerk working for fifty shillings a week. His mind writhed from the unalterable fact yet could not escape it. But no! he would never stand this—this degradation. The moment he was out of this place he would plunge away somewhere and drink, drink till he forgot his humiliation, steep himself in forgetfulness till the memory of it became a ridiculous nightmare. How long had that other said? Half an hour till the horn went! Yes, he could wait until then! He would remain for that short space of time in this ignoble bondage, then he would be free. A tremor seemed to run through him as, blindly, he reached out for a pen and dipped it into the inkwell.

BOOK III

I

"THEY couldna wear such a thing out there, even if they do have black skins," said Nancy, with a slight titter. "You're just tryin' to take a rise out of me." She cocked her head knowingly at Matt, as she surveyed him from her seat upon the kitchen table, and swung her well-exposed ankles towards him to point her remark more emphatically.

"Sure as anything," he replied in an animated tone, whilst from his reclining position against the dresser he ogled her with his eye, his posture, his air of elegance. "That's what the native ladies—as ye're pleased to call them—wear."

"Get away, you," she cried roguishly, "you know too much. You'll be tellin' me the monkeys in India wear trousers next." They roared together at her joke, feeling that they were having a precious fine time, she, that it was good to break the monotony of her empty forenoon, to have a change from that dour black father of his, he, that the conversation was exhibiting his social graces to the best advantage—almost as if he dazzled her as she sat behind a glittering saloon bar.

"You're a great blether," she resumed, in an admonishing yet encouraging tone. "After tellin' me that they niggers chew red nuts like blood and clean their teeth with a bit of stick you'll be askin' me to believe that they comb their hair wi' the leg o' a chair—like Dan, Dan the funny, wee man." Again they laughed in unison until, drawing herself up with mock modesty she resumed: "But I don't mind these kinds of fairy tales. It's when ye start a' these sly jokes o' yours that ye fair make me blush. You've got a regular advantage over a poor, inno-cent girl like me that's never been abroad—you that's visited such grand, interestin' countries. Now tell me some more!"

"But I thought ye didn't want to hear," he teased her. She pouted her richly red lips at him.

"Ye know fine what I mean, Matt. I love hearin' about a' these strange things out there. Never mind the ladies. If I had been out there I wouldna have let ye even have a glink at them. Tell me about the flowers, and the braw coloured birds and beasts, the parrots, the leopards, the tigers. I want to know about the bazaars, the temples, the gold and ivory images—I just can't get enough about them."

"You're the lass to egg me on to it," he replied. "There's no satisfyin' you. What was I speakin' about before ye asked me about the—about what I'm no allowed to mention?" He grinned. "Oh! I remember now, 'twas about the sacred cows. Ay! Ye mightn't believe it, Nancy, but the cow is a sacred animal to millions of folks out in India. They'll have images of the animal stuck up in all places and in the streets of the native quarters you'll see great big cows slushing about, with flowers on their horns and garlands of marigolds round their necks, poking their noses everywhere like they owned the place, into the houses and into the stalls—that's like the shops you know—and not a body says 'no' to them. I once saw one of the beasts stop at a stall of fruit and vegetables and before you could say 'knife' it had cleared the place from end to end, and the man what owned the shop was obliged to sit helpless and watch it eat up all his stuff, and when it had finished he could do nowt but put up a bit prayer to it or string the remains of his flowers around its big neck."

"Ye don't say, Matt," she gasped, her eyes wide with interest; "that's a strange thing you're tellin' me. To think they would worship the likes of a cow!"

"There's all kinds of cows though, Nancy," replied Matt with a wink; but immediately he resumed, more seriously: "Yes! but what I'm telling you is nothing. I couldn't describe all that I've seen to you, ye've got to travel to appreciate such marvellous sights that you would otherwise never dream of. And there's other places finer than India, mind you, where the climate's better, with less mosquitoes and just as much freedom."

She considered him deliberately as, carried away by his own enthusiasm, he talked; and, viewing the slender figure in the natty brown suit, the engaging neatness of his appearance, the inherent yet not unpleasing weakness of his pale face, she was amazed that she could ever have fled from him as she had done at their first encounter. During the six weeks that had elapsed since Mrs. Brodie's funeral—when she had been formally installed as housekeeper to the Brodie mènage—she had gradually come to regard Matthew with favour, to protect him against his father, to look forward to his lighter conversation after the heavy taciturnity and laboured monosyllables of the elder man.

"You're not listening to me, you little randy," he exclaimed, suddenly. "What's the good of a man using his breath and all his best adjectives if the bonnie lassie pays no heed to him?—and you that asked for it and all."

"Do you think I'm bonnie, then, Matt," she replied, continuing to regard him in a dreamy manner, yet making her eyes more seductive, her whole saucy pose more provocative.

"I do that, Nancy," he cried eagerly, his glance lighting. "You're as bonnie as a picture. It's a treat to have you about the house. I've always thought that since ever I saw you."

"Ay," she continued musingly, "ye were a richt bad boy the first time ye met me, but your manners have improved extraordinar' since then. In fact, when I came here I began to think ye were something feared to talk to me, but I see that's all gone now, and indeed I'm not sorry, though I wonder what your father would say to the change if he but knew."

He had raised himself slightly as though about to move towards her, but, at her last words the kindling gleam in his eye was suddenly quenched, and relaxing his body again upon the dresser, he replied, moodily:

"I don't know what a young thing like you can see in an old man like him, with his sour, crabbed ways. He doesn't seem to fit you like a younger man would."

"There's strength in him though, Matt," she replied reflectively, but still drawing him with her eyes, "and it pleases me to see that strength break down before me. The way things have turned out now I could have him like water in my hands. But don't forget," she added, with a change of manner and a sudden toss of her head, "I'm only the housekeeper here."

"Yes," he exclaimed bitterly, "you've got a grand post! You've settled down pretty well here, Nancy."

"And what about you?" she retorted pertly. "You've settled down no' so badly yoursel', for all your fine talk of finding these grand positions abroad."

He laughed at her admiringly.

"Woman! I can't but admire that gleg tongue o' yours. You could strip a man with it if ye chose."

"I could do all that," she answered meaningly; "quick enough."

How she seemed to fire his blood, this coquettish baggage who belonged entirely to his father, who was so absolutely forbidden to him by the taboo of his father's possessions.

"Ye know as well as I do, Nancy, that it's only a matter of time until I fix it up," he replied earnestly. "I've got my name down with half a dozen firms. The first vacancy is mine. I couldn't stay in this rotten hole of a town for the rest of my life. There's nothing to keep me here now since—since my mother died. But I'm telling you to your face it'll be hard to leave you."

"I'll believe ye better when you've gotten the job, Matt," she remarked tartly. "But ye shouldna let the old fellow down ye so much. Stick up for yourself. Have more faith in your own powers. What I think ye need is a woman, with a good level head on her, that would stiffen ye up and give ye a notion of how to face things out."

"I'll get even with him all right," he asserted sulkily. "My chance will come. I'll make him pay for all that he's done to me——" he paused, and added virtuously, "ay and for all that he made my poor mother

329

suffer. He's drinking himself to death anyway."

She did not reply, but throwing back her head, gazed upwards meditatively at the ceiling, exposing the fine, white arch of her throat and drawing her skirt almost to her knees by the graceful backward inclination of her body.

"You're wastin' yourself on him, I'm tellin' you," he continued eagerly. "He's nothing but a great, surly, big bully. Look what he's doing to Nessie—driving her on at these lessons. Look what he did to Mamma! He's not worth it. Do you not see that yourself?"

A secret merriment shook her as she replied:

"I'm not feared, Matt. I can take care of myself. I'm only thinkin' one or two things all to my wee self. Just a secret between Nancy and me," she whispered captivatingly.

"What is it?" he cried ardently, aroused by her manner.

"I'll tell ye some day, if you're good."

"Tell me now," he urged. But she refused to enlighten him and, with a flirt of her head, looked at the clock, then replied: "Tuts! I was just thinkin' it was time to throw a bit dinner on the stove. I maun remember my official responsibilities and not forget what I'm here for or I'll be gettin' the sack. You'll be out for lunch as usual, I suppose."

He, too, regarded the clock to estimate his margin of safety before he must clear out of the house to avert an encounter with his father; the policy he had followed since Mamma's death was to avoid his father as much as possible.

"Ay, I'll be out! You know it chokes me to eat at the same table as him—not that I'm feared of him, for he's so changed he hasn't got a word in him—but the more we keep out of each other's way the better for everybody concerned. It's just a matter of good sense on my part."

As he moved his position with a great show of indifference and independence, she raised her hands behind her head as though to support its backward tilt and continued to smile at him faintly, enigmatically.

"Come here a minute, Matt," she murmured, at length.

He looked at her doubtingly as he came towards the table on which she sat, advancing so slowly that she urged:

"Closer, man, closer. I'll not bite ye."

He would, he thought, have willingly submitted to such desirable punishment as he caught the glint of her white, even teeth shining under the red, smiling lips, lips that grew more vivid against the pallor of her skin the nearer he approached to her.

"That's more like it," she said at length; "that shows more spunk. Ye know, Matt, your father's an awfu' stupid, senseless man to leave two young folks like us hangin' about this dreich house with time so heavy on our hands. If he had but a grain o' sense to sit down and reflect over the matter he would never have allowed it. I havena been

330

out of the house for days now, except for messages, and he would never think of takin' a lassie out for a bit entertainment. Now listen to me. There's a concert on in the Borough Hall to-morrow, Matt," she whispered, lifting her dark lashes enticingly; "what do you say if you and me take a turn down there? He'll never know a thing about it, and forbye, I'll get the money for our seats out of him somehow."

He gazed at her with a fascinated stare, thinking not of her words, which he hardly heard, but noting how from her posture her firm breasts protruded eloquently towards him, and—as not only he had seen—how the faint, golden freckles dusted her small, straight nose and finally touched the softly rounded curve of her short upper lip. He knew now that he wanted her, although he was afraid to take her, and as he gazed deeply into her dark eyes some half-hidden flicker incited him to a rash, tempestuous action, made him blurt out unconsciously:

"Nancy! Nancy! you're a devil to draw a man!"

For a second her expression lost its enticing look and changed to one of pleased complacency.

"I'm beginning to see that now," she murmured, "and the next man that gets me is not goin' to get me cheap." Then, immediately, her voice altered, and she resumed wheedlingly: "But what about the concert, Matt—it's the McKelvie family—they're grand. I'm just dyin' for a little amusement. You and I could hit it off fine at a concert like that. We've always had such good fun together and this'll brighten us both up. Come on, Matt, will you take me to it?"

He felt her breath fan his cheek with a warm intimacy as he blurted out awkwardly, oddly:

"All right, Nancy! I'll take ye! Anything you like—you've just to say the word."

Her smile rewarded him; she leapt lightly from the table and touched his cheek airily with her finger tips.

"That's settled, then," she cried, gaily. "We'll have a rare time and no mistake. You leave it all to me, tickets and everything. We can arrange to meet at the Hall, but you maun come back that long dark road wi' me," she added slyly. "I would be feared to come home myself. I might need your protection." Then, with a sudden upward glance, she cried: "Sakes alive, will ye look at that clock! I've hardly time to fry up the sausages. Away out with ye, Matt, unless ye want to run slap into that big father o' yours. Away the now, but come back when the coast's clear and we'll have a tasty bite together—just you and me."

She warmed him with a last glance and without a word he went out of the room, the inward struggle of his emotions binding his tongue, making his passage clumsy and his step ungainly.

When he had gone, she commenced her belated preparations for the midday meal, not with any degree of urgency but with an undisturbed and almost deliberate carelessness, flinging a pound of sausages into the frying-pan and leaving them to cook themselves upon the stove whilst she spread a soiled cover upon the table, rattled some plates into their appointed places, and flanked each carelessly by a knife and fork.

The slovenly nature of her housewifery was markedly in contrast to her own trig, fastidious person but was further strongly evidenced by the general appearance of the kitchen. The dust which lay thickly upon the mantelpiece and shelves, the spotted, rusty grate, the unswept floor and hearth, the lax indefinite air of untidiness and neglect that hung upon the room, all became explained in the light of her present actions. The aspect of the interior had changed sadly since the days when Mamma had been unjustly maligned for her sluttishness, when her unappreciated efforts had at least maintained a spotless cleanliness inside the house; now, as the protesting sausages spluttered their grease over the adjacent walls, they seemed to smirch the room with a melancholy degradation.

Suddenly, above the crackle of this cooking, into the fat-drenched vapour that filled the scullery, came the sound of the front door opening and shutting, followed by a heavy but sluggish tread along the hall. This, however, although she recognised it as Brodie's step, did not in the least perturb the unprepared Nancy who still maintained her unconcerned and wary survey of the frying-pan. For her no frantic running with savoury broths, brimming coffee cups, or Britannia metal teapots! As she heard him come ponderously into the kitchen and silently sit down at the table she waited a moment, then called out brightly:

"You're too early the day, Brodie. I'm not nearly ready for ye," then, as he did not reply, she continued to shout out, addressing him—who had never deviated a second from his routine—"You're that uncertain these days I never know when to expect you, or else the clocks in this house o' yours are all wrong. Anyway, hold on and I'll be in the now."

He "held on," waiting without a word. In the short space of time which had elapsed since his entry into the offices of Latta & Co. a change, more striking and profound than that of the room in which he sat, but shaped in a similar direction, had affected him. Now, as he sat, his eyes fixed downwards upon the plate before him, he seemed to have shrunken slightly so that his clothes appeared not to fit him, but to have been made for some larger frame than his, while his upright, firm-chested, and always belligerent bearing had been replaced by a faint yet clearly perceptible stoop. His features, from being rugged, had become morose, his eye, no longer piercing, was fixed, brooding, and shot with faint threads of blood, while his cheeks, too, were veined by a fine, reticulated network of reddish vessels. His lips were dry, compressed; his temples, and indeed his cheeks, gaunt, slightly hollowed, and upon his brow the furrow of his frown had seared itself like a deep-grooved stigma. It was as though the firm outlines of the man had become blurred, his craggy features corroded, the whole solidity of his being eaten and undermined by some strange, dissolving acid in his blood.

When Nancy entered, bearing the platter of sausages, he glanced up quickly, drawn by the magnet of her eyes, but as she placed the plate before him he looked at it and said, in a harsh voice that came like the note of a faintly warped instrument:

"Have ye no soup to-day for me, Nancy?"

"No," she replied shortly, "I have not."

"I would have liked a drop broth to-day," he replied with a shadow of displeasure. "There's a nip in the air already; still, if ye haven't got any that's all about it. Where's the potatoes, then?"

"I hadna time to make any potatoes for ye to-day. I've been fair rushed off my feet. Ye canna expect me to do everything for ye a' days, and dippin' my hands in cold dirty water to peel potatoes is what I've never been used to. Ye were glad enough to get a simpler dinner than that when ye used to come in to see me at the Winton Arms, and things are no better off with ye now. Eat it up and be content, man!"

The pupils of his eyes dilated as he looked at her, his lips shaped themselves to an angry reply, but with an effort he restrained himself, helped himself from the plate before him, and, taking a slice of bread, began his meal. She stood beside him for a moment, her hands upon her hips, flaunting her figure near to him, filled by the conscious sense of her power over him until, as Grandma Brodie entered the room, she flounced back into the scullery.

The old woman came forward to the table with a half-bemused expression upon her sallow, wrinkled visage and as she sat down murmured to herself: "Tch! these things again"; but at her scarcely perceptible words Brodie turned and, showing his teeth at her in his old manner, snarled:

"What harm have the sausages done? If ye don't like plain, honest meat ye can go to the poorhouse, and if ye do like it then shut your auld girnin' mouth!"

At his words, and more especially at the accompanying glance, she at once subsided into herself, and with her tremulous hands began, but without much eagerness, to assist herself to the food she had so indiscreetly condemned. Her ageing, muddled brain, incapable of fully comprehending the significance of the changes around her, accepted only the fact that she was now uncomfortable, presented with scanty, unpalatable meals, and as her weak jaws champed with a dry disrelish she vented her displeasure in quick, darting glances towards the hidden presence in the scullery.

After a few moments during which the two ate in silence, Brodie paused suddenly in his indifferent mastication, raised his head slightly at the light sound of someone entering the house and, fixing his eyes upon the door leading to the hall, waited expectantly for the entry of Nessie. She came in immediately and, although Brodie resumed his eating mechanically, he followed her everywhere about the room with his eyes. She slipped the thin elastic from under her chin and released her plain straw hat, threw this upon the sofa, discarded her blue serge jacket and laid it beside the hat, fluffed out her light flaxen hair and finally subsided in her chair beside him. She sat back in her chair, languidly, surveying the table with a faint childish air of petulance, saying nothing, but feeling in her own mind that the sight of the solidifying grease before her had removed what little appetite she had possessed, that though she might have eaten, and enjoyed, perhaps a little stewed mince or even a small lamb chop, now she turned from the very thought of food. At her present age of fifteen years she had reached that period of her life when her budding and developing body required an additional attention, a more selective dietary, and though she realised nothing of this she felt instinctively, with her slightly throbbing head and the onset of her significant though unmentionable malaise, that it was an injustice to present her with the food she now surveyed. As she rested thus, her father, who had observed her continuously since her entry, spoke; with an unchanged face but in a voice which he tried to render light, persuasive, he said:

"Come on now, Nessie dear, and get your dinner begun. Don't sit and let it get cold. A big lassie like you should be hungry as a hunter and dashin' in for her meals as though she could eat the house up!"

At his words she came out of her meditation and at once began to obey, murmuring in explanation, almost apologetically:

"I've got a headache, father, just right on the front of my brow, like a strap goin' round it," and she pointed listlessly to her forehead.

"Come, come now, Nessie," he replied in a low tone which could not carry to the scullery, "you're aye talkin' about that headache. If you're always crying 'wolf, wolf' we'll not be believing you when it does come to the bit. So long as ye don't have the strap on the palm o' your hand ye shouldna mind it on the front o' your head."

"But it ties my brow so tight sometimes," she murmured mildly; "like a tight band."

"Tut! tut! it's the brain behind that matters, no' the brow, my girl. Ye should be thankful that ye're so well equipped in that respect." Then, as she began negligently to eat, he continued with extravagant approval: "That's better. Ye canna work without food. Take your fill o' whatever is goin'. Hard work should give a young lass like you an appetite, and hunger's guid kitchen." He suddenly shot a rancorous glance at his mother as he added harshly: "I'm pleased ye're not so particular and fasteedious as some folks."

Nessie, gratified that she was pleasing him and unfolding to some extent at his praise, redoubled her flagging efforts to eat but regarded

334

him from time to time with a strained look in her eye as he continued, reminiscently:

"When I was your age, Nessie, I could have eaten an ox when I came rushin' in from the fields for my dinner. I was a hardy chiel—ay —ready for what I could get. I could never get enough though. No! No! Things were different for me than they are for you, Nessie! I didna have your chance. Tell me," he murmured confidentially, "how are things goin' to-day?"

"Quite well," she replied automatically.

"You're still top of the class," he insisted.

"Oh! father," she expostulated, "I'm tired of explaining to you that we don't have that sort of thing now. I've told you half a dozen times in the last three months that it all goes by quarterly examinations." With a faint note of vanity in her voice she added: "Surely you understand that I'm past that stage now."

"Ay! ay!" he hastily replied, "I was forgettin' that a big girl and a fine scholar like you wouldna have to be fashed wi' such childish notions. True enough, it's examinations that you and me are concerned with." He paused, then in a sly tone remarked: "How long have we now till the big one?"

"About six months, I suppose," she answered half-heartedly, as she pallidly continued her meal.

"That's just fine," he retorted. "No' that long to wait and yet plenty of time for ye to prepare. Ye can't say ye havena had warnin' o't." He whispered almost inaudibly: "Ay! I'll keep ye to it, lass—you and me'll win the Latta between us."

At this point old Grandma Brodie, who had been sitting expectantly for a second course to follow and who, regardless of the conversation had been itching, but afraid, to say: "Is there nothin' else comin' " or "Is this a' we're to get," at last abandoned hope; with a resigned but muffled sigh she scraped back her chair from the table, raised her stiff form, and dragged disconsolately from the kitchen. As she passed through the door she was unhappily aware that little comfort was in her, that in the sanctuary of her room two empty tins awaited her like rifled and unreplenished tabernacles mutely proclaiming the prolonged absence of her favourite Deesides and her beloved oddfellows.

Wrapped in the contemplation of his daughter Brodie did not observe his mother's departure, but remarked in a tone that was almost coaxing:

"Have ye no news at all then, Nessie? Surely someone said something to ye. Did nobody tell ye again that ye were a clever lass? I'll warrant that ye got extra good marks for your home work." It was as though he besought her to inform him of some commendation, some pleasing attribute bestowed upon the daughter of James Brodie; then, as she shook her head negatively, his eye darkened to a sudden thought and he burst out savagely: "They havena been talkin' about your father,

335

have they, any o' these young whelps? I daresay they listen to what the backbitin' scum o' their elders might be sayin', but if they come over a thing to ye, just let me know. And dinna believe it. Keep your head up, high up. Remember who ye are—that you're a Brodie—and demand your due. Show them what that means. Ay and ye will show them, my girl, when ye snap awa' wi' the Latta from under their snivellin' nebs." He paused, then, with a twitching cheek, bit out at her: "Has that young brat o' Grierson's been makin' any of his sneakin' remarks to ye?"

She shrank back timidly from him, exclaiming: "No! no, father! Nobody has said anything, father. Everybody is as kind as can be. Mrs. Paxton gave me some chocolate when she met me going down the road."

"Oh! she did, did she?" He hesitated, digesting the information; apparently it disagreed with him, for he sneered: "Well, tell her to keep her braw presents the next time. Say we have all we want here. If ye're wantin' sweeties, like a big saftie, could ye not have asked me for them? Do ye not know that every scandalmonger in the town is just gaspin' for the chance to run us down? 'He canna afford to give his own daughter a bit sweetie next,' that's what we'll be hearin' to-morrow, and by the time it gets to the Cross they'll be makin' out that I'm starvin' ye." His annoyance was progressive and he worked himself up to a climax, crying: "Bah! ye should have had more sense. They're all against us. That's the way o't now. But never mind! Let them fling all the mud they like. Let the hand of every man be turned against me—I'll win through in spite o' them." As he concluded he raised his eye wildly upwards when, suddenly, he observed that Nancy had come into the room, and was watching him from under her raised brows with a critical and faintly amused detachment. At once his inflated bearing subsided and, as though caught in some unwarrantable act, he lowered his head while she spoke.

"What's all the noise about! I thought that somebody had taken a fit when I heard ye skirlin' like that," and as he did not reply she turned to Nessie.

"What was the haverin' about? I hope he wasna flightin' at you, henny?"

With Nancy's advent into the kitchen a vague discomfort had possessed Nessie and now the skin of her face and neck, which had at first paled, flushed vividly. She answered confusedly, in a low voice:

"Oh! no. It was nothing—nothing like that."

"I'm glad to hear it," replied Nancy. "All that loud rantin' was enough to deafen a body. My ears are ringin' with it yet." She glanced round disapprovingly and was about to retire when Brodie spoke, looking sideways at Nessie, and with an effort making his voice unconcerned.

"If you've finished your dinner, Nessie run out to the front and wait for me. I'll not be a minute before I'm ready to go down the road with you." Then, as his daughter arose, picked up her things from the sofa and went silently, uneasily, out of the room he turned his still lowered head; looking upwards from under his brows, he regarded Nancy with a strong, absorbed intensity, and remarked:

"Sit down a minute, woman. I havena seen ye all the dinner hour. Ye're not to be angry at that tantrum. You should know my style by this time. I just forgot myself for a minute."

As she sat down carelessly in the chair Nessie had vacated his look drew her in with a possessive gratification which told more clearly than his words how she had grown upon him. So long without a fresh and vital woman in his house, so painfully encumbered by the old and useless body of his wife, this firm, white, young creature had entered into his blood like an increasing fever, and, by satisfying his fierce and thwarted instincts, had made him almost her slave.

"Ye didna give us any pudding, Nancy," he continued, clumsily taking her hand in his huge grasp; "will ye not give a man something to make up for't—just a kiss, now. That'll not hurt ye, woman, and it's sweeter to me than any dish ye could make."

"Tuts, Brodie! You're always on at the same thing," she answered, with a toss of her head. "Can ye not think o' something else for a change? Ye forget that you're a burly man and I'm but a wee bit lass that canna stand a deal of handlin'." Although the words were admonitory she threw an inflection of seductiveness into them which made him tighten his clasp on her fingers, saying:

"I'm sorry if I've been rough with ye, lass. I didna mean it. Come and sit closer by me, Come on now!"

"What!" she skirled, "in broad daylight. Ye maun be mad, Brodie, an' after last night too, you great lump. Ye'll have me away to shadow —no! no! ye'll not wear me out like ye did the other." She looked little like a shadow with her plump cheeks and solid form that had filled out more maturely from her six months of easy, indolent existence, and, as she regarded him with a substantial appreciation of his dependence upon her, she became aware that he was already losing his hold upon her, that the strange strength which had drawn her was being sapped by drink and her embraces, that he had now insufficient money to gratify her fancies, that he looked old, morose, and unsuited to her. She had almost an inward contempt for him as she resumed slowly, calculatingly: "I might gie ye a kiss, though. Just might, mind ye. If I did, what would ye give me for it?"

"Have I not given ye enough, woman?" he answered gloomily. "Ye're housed and fed like myself and I've sold many a thing out this house to meet your humour. Don't ask for the impossible, Nancy."

"Tuts, ye wad think ye had given me a fortune to hear ye," she cried airily. "As if I wasna worth it, either! I'm not askin' ye to sell any more tiepins or chains or pictures. I'm only wantin' a few shillin's for my purse to go out and see my Aunt Annie in Overtoun to-morrow. Give us five shillin's, and I'll give ye a kiss."

His lower lip hung out sulkily.

"Are ye goin' out again, to-morrow? Ye're aye goin' out and leavin' me. When will ye be back?"

"Man! I believe ye would like to tie me to the leg o' this table. I'm not your slave; I'm only your housekeeper." That was one for him, she thought, as she delivered the pert allusion to the fact that he had never offered to marry her. "I'll not be away all night. I'll be back about ten o'clock or so. Give us the two half-crowns and if ye behave I'll maybe be kinder to ye than ye deserve."

Under her compelling eyes he plunged his hand into his pocket, feeling, not the handful of sovereigns that had once reposed there, but some scanty coins, amongst which he searched for the sum she asked.

"Here ye are, then," he said eventually, handing her the money. "I can ill afford it but ye well know I can deny ye nothing."

She jumped up, holding the money triumphantly, and was about to slip away with it when he, too, got up, and catching her by the arm, cried:

"What about your bargain! You're not forgettin' about that! Do ye not care for me at all?"

Immediately she composed her features, lifted up her face, opened her eyes wide at him with an ingenious simplicity, and murmured:

"I should think I do care for ye. Do ye think I would be here if I didna? Ye shouldna get such strange ideas in your head. That's the way mad folk talk. You'll be sayin' I'm goin' away to leave ye next."

"No, I wouldna let ye do that," he replied, crushing her fiercely against him. As he strained her small unresisting form against his own bulk he felt that here was the anodyne to his wounded pride, forgetfulness of his humiliation, while she, turning her face sideways against his chest, looked away, thinking how ridiculous to her, now, was his infatuated credulity, how she wanted someone younger, less uncouth, less insatiable, someone who would marry her.

"Woman! what is it about ye that makes my heart like to burst when I have ye like this?" he said thickly, as he held her. "I seem to lose count of everything but you. I would wish this to go on for ever."

A faint smile creased her hidden features as she replied:

"And why should it not? Are ye beginnin' to get tired of me?"

"By God! you're fresher to me than ever ye were." Then after a pause he suddenly exclaimed: "It wasna just the money ye wanted, Nancy?"

She turned an indignant face to him, taking the opportunity to release herself.

"How can ye say such a thing? The very idea? I'll fling it back at ye in a minute if ye don't be quiet."

"No! No!" he interposed hurriedly, "I didna mean anything. You're welcome to it, and I'll bring ye something nice on Saturday." This was the day upon which he drew his weekly wage and with the sudden realisation of his subordinate position, of the change in his life, his face darkened again, became older, and looking down he said: "Well, I better go, then. Nessie's waitin' for me." Suddenly a thought struck him. "Where's that Matt, to-day?" he demanded.

"I couldn't say." She stifled a yawn, as though her lack of interest made her positively languid. "He went out straight away after breakfast. He'll not be back now till supper I expect."

He gazed at her for a moment then said, slowly:

"Well I'll away myself, then. I'm off!"

"That's right," she cried gaily. "Off with ye, and mind ye come straight back from the office. If ye have a single drink in ye when ye come in I'll let ye have the teapot at your head."

From under his heavy eyebrows he looked at her with an upward, shamefaced glance that sat ill upon his lined and sombre countenance; nodding his head to reassure her, he gave her arm a final squeeze and went out.

In the front courtyard, now thickly covered by sprouting weeds and denuded of the ridiculous ornament of the brass cannon—which three months ago had been sold for its value as old metal—he found Nessie patiently awaiting him, supporting her unformed drooping figure against the iron post of the front gate. At the sight of him she raised herself and, without a word, they set out together upon their walk to the point where their paths diverged at the end of Railway Road, where he would proceed to his work in the shipyard and she to hers at school. This daily pilgrimage had now become an established custom between Brodie and his daughter, and during its course he had the practice of encouraging and admonishing her, of spurring her onward to achieve the brilliant success he desired; but to-day he did not speak, tapping along with his thick ash stick, his coat sagging upon him, his square hat, faded and unbrushed, thrust back in a painful caricature of his old-time arrogance, marching silently and apart, with an air of inward absorption which made it impossible for her to speak to him. Always, now, in the public gaze he retired into himself, holding his head erect, looking directly in front of him and seeing no one, creating thus, for himself, wide depopulated streets filled, not with curious, staring, sneering faces, but by the solitude of his single presence.

When they reached their place of separation, he stopped—an odd arresting figure—and said to her:

"Away and work hard now, Nessie. Stick into it. Remember what I'm always tellin' you—'what's worth doin' is worth doin' well.' Ye've got to win that Latta—that's a' there is about it. Here!"—he put his hand in his pocket—"Here's a penny for chocolate." He almost smiled. "Ye can pay me back when you've won the Bursary."

She took the coin from him, timidly yet gratefully, and went on her way to face her three hours of work in a stuffy classroom. If she had taken no breakfast and little lunch, she would at least be sustained and fortified against her study by the ample nourishment of a sticky bar of raspberry cream chocolate!

When she had gone the faint show of animation in his face died out completely and, bracing himself up, he turned and continued his progress to the office which he hated. As he drew near to the shipyard he hesitated slightly in his course, wavered, then faded into the doorway of the "Fitter's Bar" where, in the public bar, filled by workmen in moleskins and dungarees, yet to him tenanted by no one but himself, he swallowed a neat whisky, then quickly emerged and, retaining the fumes of the spirit by a compression of his lips, morosely entered the portals of Latta & Co.

II

On the evening of the following day, when Nancy had departed to visit her aunt at Overton, and with Matt, as he always was at this hour, out of the house, a sublime and tranquil domesticity lay upon the kitchen of the Brodie home. So, at least, it seemed to the master of the house as, reclining back in his own chair, head tilted, legs crossed, pipe in mouth, and in his hand a full glass of his favourite beverage, hot whisky toddy, he contemplated Nessie, seated at the table, bent over her lessons, her pale brows knitted in concentration, then surveyed his mother who, in the temporary absence of the hated intruder, had not retired to her room, but sat crouched in her old corner beside the blazing fire. A faint flush marked Brodie's cheeks, his lips, as he sucked at his pipe, were wet and full, the eye, now turned meditatively upon the contents of the steaming tumbler, humid, eloquent; by some strange transformation his troubles were forgotten, his mind filled contentedly by the thought that it was a delightful experience for a man to spend an evening happily in his own home. True, he did not now go out in the evenings, or indeed, at any hours but those of his work, shunning the streets and the club, banned, too, from the small back parlour of the virtuous Phemie, and it should logically have been an event of less moment for him to hug the fire, and one less productive of such unusual gratification. But to-night, recognising that he would not be called upon to account to his housekeeper for his lateness at the tea-table, he had dallied by the wayside on his return from work, and now, mellowed further by a few additional drinks and the thought of more to come, the sadness of his separation from Nancy tempered by the exhilaration of his unwonted liberty and by the consideration of their reunion later in the evening, his induced felicity had enveloped him earlier and more powerfully than on most nights. Viewed from his armchair, through the clear amber of the toddy, his position in the office became a sinecure, his subordinate routine merely an amusing recreation; it was his whim to work like that and he might terminate it at his will; he was glad to be finished with his business, an ignoble trade which had clearly never suited his temper or his breeding; he would, however, shortly abandon the hobby of his present post for a more prominent, more lucrative occupation, startling the town, satisfying himself and delighting Nancy. His Nancy—ah! that was a woman for a man! As her image rose before him he toasted her, hoping enthusiastically that she might now be having a pleasant time with her aunt at Overton. Rosy mists floated through the dirty ill-kept room, tinting the soiled curtains, veiling the darker coloured square which marked the disappearance from the wall of Bell's engraving, sending a glow into Nessie's pale cheeks and softening even the withered, envious face of his mother. He watched the old woman's starting eyes over the edge of his glass as he took a long satisfying drink and, when he had drawn his breath, cried jeeringly:

"Ye're wishin' you were me, ye auld faggot. Ay, I can see from the greedy look about you that you wish this was goin' into your belly and not mine. Well, take it from me, in case ye don't know, it's a great blend o' whisky, the sugar is just to taste and the water is right because there's not too much o't." He laughed uproariously at his own wit, causing Nessie to look up with a scared expression, but catching his glance, she immediately lowered hers as he exclaimed:

"On with the work, ye young limmer! What are ye wastin' your time for? Am I payin' for your education for you to sit gogglin' at folks when you should be at your books." Turning to his mother again, he shook his head solemnly, continuing volubly: "I must keep her at it! That's the only way to correct the touch o' her mother's laziness that's in her. But trust me! I'll make her a scholar in spite of it. The brains are there." He took another pull at his glass and sucked noisily at his pipe.

The old woman returned his glance sourly, dividing her gaze between his flushed face and the whisky in his hand as she remarked:

"Where is that—where is she gane to-night?"

He stared at her for a moment then guffawed loudly. "Ye mean Nancy, ye auld witch. Has she put a spell on you, too, that you're feared even to lift her name?" Then after a pause during which he assumed a leering gravity, he continued: "Well, I hardly like to tell ye, but if ye must know she's awa' to the Band of Hope meetin'."

She followed the vehemence of his mirth, as he shook with laughter, with an unsympathetic eye, and replied as tartly as she dared:

"I don't see much to laugh about. If she had gone to the Band o' Hope when she was younger she might have——" she stopped, feeling his eye upon her, thinking that she had gone too far.

"Go ahead," he gibed; "finish what ye were sayin'. Let us all have our characters when you're about it. There's no pleasin' some folk. Ye werena satisfied with Mamma, and now ye're startin' to pick holes in my Nancy. I suppose ye think you could keep the house yoursel'— that maybe ye might get an odd pingle at the bottle that way. Faugh! the last time ye cooked my dinner for me ye nearly poisoned me." He considered her amusedly from his elevated position, thinking of how he might best take her down a peg. Suddenly a wildly humorous idea struck him, which, in its sardonic richness, made him slap his thigh delightedly. She was grudging him his drink was she, eyeing it like a cat would a saucer of cream, gasping for it, ready to lap it up at the first opportunity. She should have it then, she who was so quick to run down other people! By Gad! she should have it. He would make her fou, yes, fou as a whelk. He realised that he had plenty of whisky in the house, that in any case it would take very little to go to the old woman's head, and as some foretaste of the drollery of his diversion invaded him, he rocked with suppressed hilarity and smote his leg again exuberantly. Losh! but he was a card!

Then all at once he cut off his laughter, composed his features and, narrowing his small eyes slyly, remarked cunningly:

"Ah! it seems hardly fair o' me to have spoken to ye like that, woman, I can see it's put ye right down. You're lookin' quite daunted. Here! would ye like a drop speerits to pull ye together?" Then, as she looked up quickly, suspiciously, he nodded his head largely and continued "Ay, I mean it. I'm quite serious. What way should I have it an' no' you? Away and get yoursel' a glass."

Her dull eye lighted with eagerness, but knowing his ironic tongue too well, she still doubted him, was afraid to move for fear a burst of his derisive laughter should disillusion her, and moistening her lips with her tongue she exclaimed, in a tremulous voice:

"You're not just makin' fun o' me, are ye?"

Again he shook his head, this time negatively, vigorously, and reaching down to the bottle conveniently beside his chair he held it out enticingly before her.

"Look! Teacher's Highland Dew. Quick! Away and get yoursel' a tumbler!"

She started to her feet, eagerly, as though she were beginning a race, and made her way to the scullery, trembling at the thought of her luck, she who had not lipped a drop since the day of the funeral and then only wine, not the real, comforting liquor. She was back, holding out the glass, almost before he had controlled the fresh exacerbation of amusement which her avid, tottering progress had afforded him; but, as he poured her out a generous allowance, he remarked, in a steady, solicitous voice:

"An old body like yersel' needs a drop now and then. See, I'm givin' you plenty, and don't take much water with it."

"Oh no, James," she protested. "Don't give me ower much. You know I'm not fond o' much o't—just a wee drappie to keep out the cold."

At her last words a sudden memory cut across his jocularity like a whip lash, and he snarled at her:

"Don't use these words to me! It minds me too much of somebody I'm not exactly fond of. Why do ye speak like a soft and mealy-mouthed hypocrite?" He glowered at her while she drank her whisky, quickly, for fear he should take it from her, then, urged by a more vindictive spirit he cried out: "Come on. Here's some more. Glass about."

"Na! Na!" she exclaimed mildly. "I've had enough. It's warmed me nicely and gie'n my mouth a bit flavour. Thenk ye all the same, but I'll no' hae any more."

"Ye'll not say no to me," he shouted roughly. "What are ye to refuse good spirits? Ye asked for it and you'll have it, even if I've to pour it down your auld thrapple. Hold out your glass; we'll drink fair."

Wonderingly she submitted, and when he had given her another liberal helping, she drank it more slowly, appreciatively, smacking her lips and rolling it over her tongue, murmuring between her sips: "It's the real stuff richt enough. It's unco' kind o' ye, James, to spare me this. I've never had so much afore. Troth I'm not used to it." She was silent whilst the liquid in her glass dwindled, then all at once she burst out: "It's got a graund tang on your tongue—has it no? 'Deed it almost makes me feel young again." She tittered slightly. "I was just thinkin' ——" she tittered more loudly.

At the sound of her levity he smiled darkly.

"Yes," he drawled, "and what were ye thinkin', auld woman? Tell us so that we can enjoy the joke."

She snickered the more at his words, and covering her wrinkled face with her knotted hands, abandoned herself to a delicious, inward humour until at last she coyly unveiled one senile, maudlin eye and whispered brokenly:

"Soap! I was just thinkin' about soap."

"Indeed now, ye were thinkin' about soap!" he mimicked. "That's very appropriate. Was it a wash that ye were wantin'? For if that's the case I can assure ye that it's high time ye had one."

"Na, na," she giggled, "it's no' that. It just flashed into my heid what the wives used to do in my young days, when they wanted a drop

343

o' speerits without the guid-man knowin' about it. They—they wad go to the village grocer's for their gill and get it marked to the book as soap—Soap!" She was quite overcome by her enjoyment of this delicious subtlety, and again buried her face in her hands; but she looked up after a moment to add: "Not that I ever did a thing like that! No! I was aye respectable and could scrub the house without that kind of cleanser!"

"That's right! Blow your own trumpet," he sneered. "Let us know what a paragon o' virtue you were. I'm listenin'."

"Ay! I did weel in these days," she continued reminiscently, losing, in the present fatuity of her mind, all awe of her son, "and I had muckle to put up wi'. Your father was as like you are now as twa peas in a pod. The same grand way wi' him, and as touchy as gunpowder. Many the night he would come in and let fly at me if things werna to his taste. But I stood up to him in a' his rages! I'm pleased to think on that." She paused, her look becoming distant. "I can see it like it was yesterday. Man, he was proud, proud as Lucifer."

"And had he not reason to be proud?" he exclaimed harshly, becoming aware that the drink was not taking her the way he had expected, that she was ceasing to amuse him. "Do ye not know the stock he came from?"

"Oh, ay, I kenned a' about that lang syne," she tittered spitefully, filled by a heady, rancorous imprudence. "He had the airs o' a duke, wi' his hand me this and reach me that, and his fine clothes, and his talk o' his forebears and what his rights were if he but had them. Oh! he was aye splorin' about his far-back connection wi' the Wintons—But I often wonder if he believed it hissel'. There's a' kinds o' connections," she sniggered, "and 'tis my belief that the lang syne connection was on the wrang side o' the blanket."

He glared at her, unable to believe his ears, then finding his tongue, he shouted:

"Silence! Silence, ye auld bitch! Who are you to talk like that about the Brodies? Ye bear the name yersel' now. How dare ye run it down before me," and he grasped the neck of the bottle as though to hurl it at her.

"Now, now, Jims," she drivelled, quite unperturbed, raising one uncertain, protesting hand, "ye mustna be unreasonable. I'm not the kind o' bird that files its ain nest—this is a' atween the family so to speak—and ye surely know it was a' gone intill and found out that the whole trouble began lang, lang syne wi' an under the sky affair atween Janet Dreghorn, that was the heid gardener's daughter, and young Robert Brodie that cam' to the title many years after. Na! na, they were never bound by ony tie o' wedlock."

"Shut your blatterin' mouth," he roared at her. "If ye don't I'll tear the dirty tongue out o' it. You would sit there and miscall my name like that. What do you think ye are? Ye were lucky my father married you. You—you——" He stammered, his rage choking him, his face twitching as he looked at her senseless, shrunken features. She was now completely intoxicated, and unconscious equally of his rage and of Nessie's frightened stare, continued:

"Lucky!" she babbled, with a drunken smirk, "maybe I was and maybe I wasna, but if ye kenned the ins and outs o' it all ye might think that ye were lucky yoursel'!" She broke into peals of shrill laughter, when suddenly, her false teeth, never at any time secure and how dislodged from her palate by her moist exuberance, protruded from between her lips like the teeth of a neighing horse, and impelled by a last uncontrollable spasm of mirth, shot out of her mouth and shattered themselves upon the floor. It was, in a fashion, a fortunate diversion, for otherwise he must certainly have struck her, but now they both gazed at the detached and scattered dentures that lay between them like blanched and scattered almonds, she staring with collapsed, grotesque cheeks and shrunken, unrecognisable visage, he with a muddled amazement.

"They're lyin' before ye like pearls before swine," he exclaimed at last. "It serves ye right for your blasted impudence."

"My guid false teeth!" she moaned, sobered by her loss yet articulating with difficulty, "that I've had for forty years! They were that strong, too, with the spring atween them. What will I do now? I canna eat. I can hardly speak."

"That'll be a good job, then," he snarled at her, "if it keeps you from gabblin' with your lyin' gongue. It serves you right."

"They'll not mend," she whined. "Ye maun get me a new set." Her forlorn eyes were still fixed upon the floor. "I canna just suck at my meat. Ye don't get the good out o' it that way. Say you'll get me another double set, James."

"Ye can whistle for that," he retorted. "What good would new teeth be to an auld deein' thing like you? You're not goin' to last that much longer. Just look on it as a judgment on ye."

At his words she began to whimper, wringing her bony hands together, and mumbling incoherently: "What a to do! I'll never get ower it. What's to become o' me that's had them so lang. It was a' the fault o' the speerits. I could aye manage them fine. It'll mean the end o' me."

He regarded her ludicrous, whining figure with a scowl, then, moving his glance, he suddenly observed the drawn face of Nessie watching the scene with a frightened yet fixed attention.

"What are you playin' at next?" he growled at her, his mood changed by his mother's recent remarks. "Can ye not get on with your own work? You'll get a braw lot done with that glaikit look about you. What's the matter with ye?"

"I can't get on very well with the noise, father," she replied timidly, lowering her eyes; "it distracts my attention. It's not easy for me to work when there's talking."

"So that's it!" he replied. "Well! there's plenty of room in the house now. If the kitchen isn't good enough for you, we'll put ye in the parlour. You'll not hear a sound there. Then ye'll have no excuse for idlin'." He got up and, before she could reply, advanced with a slight lurch to the table where he swept her books into one disordered heap; clutching this between his two enormous hands, he turned and stalked off, crying: "Come on. Into the parlour with ye. The best room in the house for my Nessie. You'll work in peace there, and work hard too. If ye can't study in the kitchen you'll gang into the parlour every night."

Obediently she arose and followed him into the cold, musty room where, after stumbling about in the darkness, he flung her books upon the table and at length succeeded in lighting the gas. The pale light gleamed from its frosted globe upon the chilly, uncovered mahogany table, the empty, unused fireplace, upon all the cold discomfort of the neglected, dust-shrouded chamber and lit up finally the overbearing figure of Brodie and the shrinking form of the child.

"There you are now," he cried largely, his good humour partially restored. "Everything's ready and to your hand. Draw up your chair and begin. Don't say that I havena helped ye." He put two fingers upon the pile of books and spread them widely over the surface of the table, disarranging them still more and losing all her places. "See! there's plenty o' room for a' your orders. Can ye not say thank ye!"

"Thank you, father," she murmured submissively.

He watched her with a complacent eye whilst she sat down and bent her thin shoulders in a presence of study, then he tiptoed with heavy, exaggerated caution from the room, protruding his head round the door as he went out to say:

"I'll be back in a minute to see how you're gettin' on." As he returned to the kitchen he told himself that he had done the right thing by Nessie, that he was the one to make her get on, and in a mood of self-congratulation he sat down again in his chair and in reward poured himself out another glass of whisky. Only then did he become aware of his mother, still sitting motionless, stupid, like a bereaved woman, with a hollow look, as if some power had sucked her empty.

"Are ye still here?" he shot at her. "You're far too quiet for one that had such a glib tongue in her head a minute ago. When I didna hear ye I thought ye would be away to sleep off your exertions. Go on—get away now, then. Away ye go, I'm sick of the look o' ye." And, as she was slow in moving, he shouted: "Quick! out of my sight."

While he had been in the parlour she had collected the wreckage of her dentures from the floor, and now, clutching these fragments tightly in her hand she faded soberly from the room, her bowed, dejected carriage contrasting sadly with the gay eagerness with which she had

346

rushed for the tumbler towards her own undoing.

Alone and untrammelled in the kitchen, Brodie addressed himself more assiduously to the bottle, washing away the unpleasant memory of her presence and the bitter recollections occasioned by her remarks. He knew, well, that unhappy truth lay in the foundation of her senile yet disconcerting reminiscences, but now, as always he chose to blind himself to their accuracy—a process never difficult to his obtuse and lumbering mind and one now rendered easier than ever by the liberality of his potations. Soon he had forgotten the entire incident except for the ludicrous remembrance of her sudden and embarrassing edentation, and reclining at ease in his chair, and toping steadily, he mounted into the higher altitudes of intoxication. With the gradual elevation of his spirits he began to regret his solitary condition and with an impatient, swinging foot and eager glances at the clock he sought to anticipate the return of Nancy. But it was only nine o'clock, he knew that she would not arrive before ten, and, as the hands moved with a regular and monotonous slowness despite his efforts to expedite their progress, he got up and began to walk about the room. A wild idea of promenading the streets of the town, of bursting in upon the assembly at the club and disconcerting them with a few lurid and well-chosen words presented itself to him, but although he played with the appealing notion, he finally rejected it on the grounds that his Nancy would not approve. He had now lost his morose and gloomy oppression and, striding clumsily within the confines of the kitchen, his hair ruffled, his wrinkled clothes hanging more awkwardly upon him, his hands dangling like inactive flails, he felt he wanted to express the exultation of his mood in some definite and appropriate action. His past was for the moment forgotten and his outlook bounded only by the compass of the next few hours; he was himself again, yet from time to time, when the sound of his steps rang too loudly in his ears, he would pause with a profound concern for his student next door and, admonishing himself with a shake of his head, resume his pacing more silently, with a greater and more exaggerated caution.

At length the limits of the room became inadequate, failed to contain him. Insensibly he passed out of the doorway and began to wander about the house. He ascended the stairs, moved across the top landing, opened the door of his mother's room and flung an objectionable remark at her, chuckled to himself, entered Matt's bedroom, where he viewed with disgust the array of toilet lotions and hair pomades, and, having lit every gas so that the house blazed with light, finally he stood within his own apartment. Here, drawn by a hidden force, he went slowly forward to the chest of drawers where Nancy kept her clothing and, a sly leer mingling with his shamed consciousness, he commenced to pull out and examine the fine embroidered garments which she had bought with the money he had given her. He handled

347

the smooth lace-edged vestments, touched soft lawn, fingered thin cambric, held the long empty stockings in his ponderous grasp, and his mouth curved with an upward slant while he invested the fragrant garments with the person of their owner. His shot eye, fixed upon the whiteness before him, saw actually the alabaster of her body, always to him a source of wonder and delight, and to his mind the texture of the stuff he handled seemed to have absorbed its colour from contact with that milky skin. As he remained there, displaying with stretched arms and for his sole enjoyment these flimsy articles of finery, he looked like some old and uncouth satyr who, stumbling upon the shed raiment of a nymph, had seized upon it and now, by contemplation, whetted his worn fancy capriciously.

At length he closed the drawers by a pressure of his knee and glancing sideways as he walked, moved stealthily from the room, shutting the door silently behind him. Outside, it was as though he had accomplished successfully and without detection some secret enterprise, for his shamed slyness dropped from him, he rubbed his hands noisily together, puffed out his cheeks, and heavily descended the stairs. In the hall he opened the parlour door, and cried, with a facetious assumption of gravity.

"Can I come in, ma'm? or are ye not at home?" Then without waiting for the reply, which indeed she did not utter, he entered the parlour, saying in the same manner: "I've been round my house to see that everything's in order, so there'll be no burglars to trouble ye to-night. Lights in all the windows! A fine splore o' illumination to show a' the rotten swine that we're gay and bricht in the Brodie house." She did not in the least understand what he meant but watched him with her blue, placating eyes that now seemed to be enlarged, to stand out from her cold, stiff face. With arms crossed and shivering, her thin-stockinged legs curled under her for warmth, having lost all sensation but that of numbness in her feet and hands, and her impressionable mind stamped by the scene she had witnessed in the kitchen, having failed completely to make headway with her study, she now regarded him fearfully.

"How are ye gettin' on?" he continued, looking at her closely. "Have ye enough quietness here to suit you? What have ye done since ye came in?"

She started guiltily, knowing that she had done nothing, unable to conceal anything from him.

"I haven't got on very well, father," she replied humbly. "It's so terribly cold in here."

"What! Ye havena got on well—and me that's been keepin' as quiet, as quiet for ye. What are ye thinkin' of?"

"It's the cold room," she repeated again. "I think it must be freezing outside."

"The room!" he cried, raising his brows with a tipsy gravity. "Did ye not beg and beseech me to bring ye in here? Did I not carry in your books in my own hands, and light the gas for ye, and set you down to it? Ye wanted in here and now you turn on me and complain!" Here his flushed face indicated an aggrieved and exaggerated disapproval. "Not got on well, forsooth! Ye better get a bend on and look sharp about it."

"If there had been a fire!" she ventured diffidently, observing now that he was not in his severe vein towards her. "I'm all goose flesh and shivering."

Her words penetrated, struck some responsive chord in his soaked brain, for he started and, with a complete change of manner, cried with profuse pathos:

"My Nessie shiverin'! Here am I as warm as toast and my own, wee lassie freezin' and wantin' a fire! And what for no? It's reasonable. It's more than reasonable. Ye shall have a fire this minute if I've got to get it with my own hands. Sit still now, and wait and see what your father'll do for ye." He held up an admonishing finger to bind her to her seat and, moving unwieldily out of the room and into the cellar that adjoined the scullery, he fumbled in the dark amidst the coal and finally secured what he sought—a long, iron shovel. Then, brandishing this like a trophy, he advanced to the kitchen fire, and knocked down the front bars of the grate; thrusting the shovel under the glowing coals, he secured a flaming heap of red-hot cinders which he bore triumphantly back to the parlour, leaving a smoky trail behind him. Flinging the burning embers into the cold fireplace he cried, in a knowing voice: "Wait a minute! Just wait a minute! Ye havena seen it a' yet," and again disappeared, to return immediately with a huge bundle of sticks in one hand and the shovel, replenished this time with coal, in the other. Kneeling down clumsily he laid the sticks upon the cinders, and lying flat on his stomach, blew them stertorously until they blazed to his satisfaction. With a grunt he now raised himself and sitting within the confines of the hearth like a playful bull within its stall, he fed the flames sedulously with coal so that he achieved, eventually, a high crackling pyramid of fire. With both hands and one full glowing cheek grimed by smoke and coal dust, and his knees somewhat soiled by soot, he nevertheless surveyed his masterpiece with supreme approval, and cried: "Look at that, now! What did I tell ye! There's a fire for ye—fit to roast an ox. Ye couldna be cold at a blaze like that. On wi' the work now that ye've got your fire. There's not many a man would take such a trouble for his daughter, so don't let a' my bother be wasted. On ye go. Stick into the lessons."

Following this exhortation he seemed loath to get up and remained gazing at the leaping flames appreciatively, murmuring from time to time: "A beautiful fire! It's a bonnie blaze!"; but eventually he heaved himself up, and kicking the shovel to one side, muttered: "I'll away and bring my dram in beside ye," and went out of the room. As he departed Nessie—who fully realised from the unnatural manner of his conduct that her father was once again drunk—threw a quick glance, deeply charged with apprehension, at his retreating back. She had not done a stroke of work all evening and was now becoming thoroughly alarmed at her father's extraordinary behaviour. Although his treatment of her had lately been more peculiar—acts of sudden and unaccountable indulgence interpolating his perpetual coercion of her to study—she had never seen him so odd as he appeared to-night. At the sound of his step, when he returned with the remainder of the bottle of whisky, she sat rigid, pretending, with pale moving lips, to be engrossed in her work although she could not see the page which she held so closely before her.

"That's right," he muttered. "I see you're at it. I've done my bit for ye—now you do yours for me. That's another thing doun on my account for ye to settle when ye win the Latta." He subsided in a chair by the fireside and began again to drink. It seemed to him now that the evening had been long, as long even as a year, during which he had experienced a variety of profound and moving sensations, a period which had been a delightful prolongation of accomplishment and anticipation to be capped shortly by his reunion with Nancy. He became more joyful than ever. He wanted to sing! Fragments of tunes ran deliciously through his head, making him nod extravagantly and beat time with his foot and hand to this internal harmony. His small eyes seemed to protrude from his head as they roamed the room seeking some outlet for his culminating beatitude. Suddenly they lit upon the piano. Laud's sake! he told himself, what was the good of that if it wasn't to be used, that fine burr walnut instrument that had come from Murdoch's—bought and paid for these twenty years! It was a scandal to see it lying idle there, when a man had spent money on music lessons for his daughter.

"Nessie," he shouted, making her jump with fright. "You've got a' that book off by heart now. Put it away. You're goin' to have your music lesson now and I'm the teacher." He guffawed, then corrected himself: "No! I'm not the teacher—I'm the vocalist." He threw out his arm with a sweeping gesture. "We'll have some guid Scotch songs. Away—away over and give us 'O' a' the airts the wind can blaw' for a start."

Nessie slipped off her chair and looked at him doubtfully, knowing that he had forbidden the piano to be opened for months, feeling that she must obey, yet fearful of doing so; but as she stood indecisively he cried vehemently:

"Come on! Come on! What are ye waitin' for? 'O' a' the airts the wind can blaw,' I tell ye! I havena felt like this for months. I'm ripe for a sang!"

It was after ten o'clock and, as it was past her bedtime and she was worn by the strain of the long evening, she felt exhausted, but she was too terrified, too much in awe of him, to protest; and going, therefore, to the piano, she opened it, found the Scottish Song Book that had been Mary's, sat down, and began to play. Her small trembling fingers brought out as best they could the air that he demanded whilst from the seat by the fire, waving his pipe in undulating curves, Brodie sang the words boisterously.

> *"O' a' the airts the wind can blow,*
> *I dearly lo'e the west.*
> *It's there the bonnie lassie lives,*
> *The lassie I lo'e best."*

"Louder! Louder!" he shouted. "Hit it harder! I'm singin' about my Nancy. We maun give it pith! 'By day and nicht my fancy's flight is ever with my Jean'!" he roared at the pitch of his voice. "By God! that was good. If we call her Jean—ye're none the wiser. Come on. Give us the second verse again, and sing yoursel'. Sing! Sing! Are ye ready! One, two, three!—

> *"I see her in the dewy flower."*

She had never seen him like this before and in a panic of shame and fear she joined her quavering voice to his bellow so that together they sang the song.

"That was graund!" he cried, when they had finished. "I hope they heard us at the Cross! Now we'll have 'My Love is like a red, red Rose,' although mind ye she's more like a bonnie white rose. Have ye not found it yet? You're awfu' slow and clumsy the nicht. I'm as light as a feather though. I could sing till dawn."

She struck painfully into the song which he made her play and sing twice, and after that she was forced through "The Banks and Braes," "O Rowan Tree," and "Annie Laurie," until with her hands so cramped and her head so giddy that she felt she must fall from the stool, she turned imploringly, and with tears in her eyes, cried:

"Let me go, father. Let me go to my bed. I'm tired." He frowned upon her heavily, her interruption cutting in rudely upon his blissful state. "So ye can't even play for your father," he exclaimed, "and after he's taken all the trouble to go and put on a fire for ye, too. The minute it's on ye want away to your bed. That's gratitude for you. Well, if ye'll not do it for right you'll do it for might. Play! Play till I tell ye to stop, or I'll take the strap to ye. Play my first song over again!"

She turned again to the piano and wearily, with eyes blinded by tears, began again, "O' a' the airts the wind can blaw," whilst he sang, emphasising every discord which her agitation led her to produce by a black look directed towards her bowed and inoffensive back.

They had proceeded half-way through the song when suddenly the parlour door opened and Nancy—her eyes sparkling, the cream of her cheek tinted by a faint colour from the cold, her hair crisping under her attractive toque, the neat fur tippet setting off her firm bust to perfection—Nancy—his Nancy, stood before him. With mouth wide open and pipe poised in mid air he stopped singing, regarding her stupidly, realising that he had failed to hear the opening of the front door, and he continued to stare thus while the unconscious Nessie, as though accompanying his silent astonishment and admiration, played through the song to its end, when silence descended upon the room.

At length Brodie laughed, a trifle uncomfortably. "We were just singin' a wee song to ye, Nancy, and troth ye deserve it for you're lookin' as bonnie as a picture."

Her eyes sparkled more frostily and her lips tightened as she replied:

"The noise comin' up the road was enough to draw a crowd round the house—and lights blazin' out o' every window. And ye've been at your soakin' again and then ye've the impertinence to make me the grounds for it a'! You're a disgrace! Look at your hands and your face. You're like an auld coal-heaver. What a thing for me to come home to, after an elevatin' evenin' like I've had."

He looked at her humbly, yet drinking in, even at its coldness, the freshness of her young beauty, and in an attempt to change the subject, he murmured heavily:

"Did ye have a nice time at your aunt's? I've missed you, Nancy. It's like a year since I saw ye last. Ye were a long time comin' to me."

"And I wish I had made it longer," she exclaimed, with a hard glance at him. "When I want music I know where to get it. Don't bawl at me and don't drink to me—ye blackfaced drunkard."

At these terrible words Nessie, sitting petrified upon the piano stool, shrank back, expecting her father to rise and fling himself upon the mad woman who had uttered them: but to her amazement he remained passive, drooping his lip at Nancy and muttering:

"I tell ye I've been missin' you, Nancy. Don't turn on a man that's so fond o' ye."

Disregarding his daughter's presence entirely, he continued blatantly, with an almost maudlin' sentiment: "You're my white, white rose, Nancy. You're the breath in my body. I had to pass the time somehow! Away up and take off your things and dinna be cross wi' me. I'll—I'll be up mysel' in a minute."

"Oh! you will!" she cried, with a toss of her head. "You're drinkin' like a fish, you rough, big bully. Go up any time ye like for all I care. It makes no odds to me—as you'll soon see," and she flounced up the stairs out of his sight.

With lowered head he sat quite still, filled by the melancholy thought that she was angry with him, that when he went upstairs he would have to appease her, pacify her, before she manifested her kindness towards him. In the midst of his dejected meditations he suddenly realised his daughter's presence and, considering moodily that he had betrayed himself to her, he muttered thickly, without looking up:

"Away up to your bed, you! What are ye sittin' there for?" And when she had slipped like a shadow from the room he continued to sit by the rapidly dying embers of the fire until he adjudged that Nancy might be in bed, and more amenable to his advances. Then, blind to the complete reversal of his position in the house since the days when he had left his wife to brood by the dismal remnants of a dead fire, anxious only to be beside his Nancy, he got up and, having turned out the gas, passed slowly and as lightly as he could, up the stairs. He was consumed by eagerness, eaten by desire, as he entered his lighted bedroom.

It was empty!

With unbelieving eyes he gazed round until it slowly dawned upon him that this night she had kept her word and forsaken him; then, after a moment, he turned and, moving silently across the dark landing, tried the handle of the door of that small room to which his wife had retired —the room, indeed, where she had died. This, as he expected, was locked. For one instant a torrent of resentment surged within him and he gathered himself together to hurl himself against and through the door, to batter it down by the strength of his powerful and desirous body. But immediately came the realisation that such a course would not benefit him, that inside the room he would still find her bitter, more bitter and unyielding than before, more icy, more determined to oppose his wish. She had enslaved him, insidiously yet completely, and for that reason was now stronger than he. His sudden fury died, his hand dropped from the door and slowly he re-entered his own room and shut himself within it. For a long time he remained in sullen silence, then impelled by an irresistible impulse he went to the drawer he had opened earlier in the evening, slowly pulled it out once more, and with a heavy brow stood staring inscrutably at the contents within.

III

MATTHEW BRODIE came out of Levenford Station, leaving the platform, splashed with its pale yellow lamplight, behind him and entered the cold, exhilarating darkness of the frosty February night with a lively feeling of elation. His steps upon the hard ground rang out quick and clear; his face, blurred in the surrounding obscurity, radiated nevertheless a faint excited gleam; the fingers of his inquiet hands twitched continually from the suppression of his pervading exultation. He walked rapidly

M

along Railway Road, through the tenuous low-lying haze above which the tops of trees and houses loomed like darkly smudged shadows against the lighter background of the sky. Towards his expanded nostrils came, from across the open space of the Common, the faint aromatic odour of a distant wood fire and, as he sniffed it, filling his lungs deliciously with the tingling savour of the air, he was permeated by a vivid sense of the zest of living. Despite the forward thrust of his mood, memories rushed across him at that acrid, yet spicy breath, and he became enveloped in a balmy dusk that was filled with strange quiescent sounds, fragrant subtle scents, and the white and liquid shimmer of a tropic moon. His drab and evasive existence of the last six months fell away from his recollection while he considered the glamour of his life abroad, and as if to answer the appeal of such a free and enchanting land, he further accelerated his pace and swung along the road with impetuous eagerness in the direction of his home. This haste, in one who, when approaching the house in the evenings, displayed usually a flagging step, indicative of his disinclination to encounter his father, seemed to betoken an important change in the current of Matt's life. He was indeed, at this moment, bursting with the news of that change, and as he rushed up the steps, opened the front door of the house, and entered the kitchen he trembled, actually, with his excitement.

The room was empty except for Nancy, who, slowly and tardily clearing the tea-table of its dishes, looked up at his sudden appearance with an expression of surprise, mingled also with an unguarded and engaging familiarity which at once indicated to him that his father was not at hand.

"Where is he, Nancy?" he exclaimed, immediately. She rattled a dish contemptuously upon the tray as she replied:

"Out for the usual, I suppose. There's only one thing takes him out at this hour, and that's to get the black bottle filled up again." Then she added slyly: "But if you're wantin' to see him he'll be back soon."

"I'm wantin' to see him, all right," he blustered, looking at her significantly. "I'm not feared to meet him. I've got news for him that'll make him sit up and take notice."

She glanced at him quickly, noting now his slightly hurried breathing, the glitter in his eye, the general concealed importance of his bearing.

"Have ye news, then, Matt?" she said slowly.

"I should think I have!" he declared. "The best that I've had for nine months. I'm just this minute off the train. I've only had word o' the thing an hour ago, and I couldna get back quick enough to tell it— to fling it in that auld devil's face."

She left the dishes entirely and advanced deliberately towards him, saying ingratiatingly:

"Was it only your father ye wanted to tell, Matt? Am I not to know first? I'm gey interested to hear."

354

A broad smile spread over his features.

"Of course you're to know! Ye ought to understand that by this time."

"What is it then, Matt?" she whispered.

As he saw her eagerness, he swelled the more, and, determining to edge her curiosity, he suppressed his own excitement, moved to his favourite spot by the dresser, and reclining in his particular manner, surveyed her with a boasting eye.

"Come, come now. Can ye not guess? Surely a clever wee body like yourself can guess? You haven't got that trig head on your shoulders for nothing."

She knew positively now what the purport of his tidings must be, but, seeing that he was pleased to exhibit his air of consequence, it suited her to pretend ignorance, and with a charming assumption of simplicity, she shook her head and replied:

"No, Matt! I can hardly think. I'm almost afraid to say. Would it be about your father?"

He wagged his head from side to side portentously.

"No! Not this time, Nancy, dear. Leave him out of the question. It's about another man altogether. Somebody younger, that can take a glass without soakin' in it, that can take a lass out to a concert and let her enjoy herself. Think on somebody that's fond of you."

"It's yourself, Matt! Oh!" she gasped, widening her eyes, "ye don't mean to say ye've got that post."

"Did I say I hadn't got it?" he leered at her.

"Have ye, though? Tell us quick, Matt. I'm that excited about I can hardly stand still!"

"Yes!" he cried, unable to restrain himself longer. "I have got it. The job's signed, sealed, and delivered into my hands. It's me for South America—passage paid—free livin'—and plenty of money in my pocket. To hell with this rotten town, and this blasted house and the drunken, auld bully that owns it. It'll be something for him to smoke in his pipe when he hears."

"He'll be pleased enough, Matt," she replied, again advancing to him as he leaned against the dresser.

"Ay, glad to be rid of me, I suppose," he answered sulkily. "But I'm glad enough to go. And I'll be even with him yet. He'll maybe get something he doesn't like before long."

"Never mind about him. He's just an auld fool. I'm as sick o' him as you are. I canna think what I ever saw in him." She paused, then added ingenuously, pathetically; "I'm real pleased too, that ye've got the job, Matt, although—although——"

"Although what," he replied largely, looking down at her soft, appealing eyes. "Surely I've waited long enough for it."

"Ay—it was just nothing," she answered with a sigh, stroking his

355

hand absently, almost unconsciously, with her soft finger tip. "It's a wonderful opportunity for ye. It must be grand for you to gang abroad like that. I can see the big boat drivin' through the blue sea, wi' the sun on it. I can just fancy the lovely place that you're goin' to—Rio—what was it ye called it again?"

"Rio de Janeiro," he replied grandly. "I'll only be a couple of miles out of it. It's a wonderful city and a beautiful climate. There's a chance for a man out there, a hundred times better than in India."

"I'm sure ye'll do well," she murmured, now holding his hand entirely in her soft clasp. "But I'll be that lonely without ye. I don't know whatever I'll do. It's hard for a young lass like me to be tied up here!"

He gazed at her as though his suppressed feeling had not entirely left him, as though, escaping only in part, it had left still an effervescence behind.

"You're not wantin' me to go," he remarked slyly. "I can see that!"

"Of course I am, you wicked man! I wouldn't for the world stop you. It's a grand chance." She gave his hand an admonitory squeeze, and added: "And you said it was such good money too?"

"Yes! it's a handsome salary," he assented impressively, "and they've flung in a bungalow with it as well. I couldn't wish for more. My experience out East has done me a good turn after all."

She was silent, gazing with an appealing candour at his face, but seeing instead, a strange mysterious city, shadowed by exotic trees, with cafés in its streets, a band in the square, with herself there smiling, dashing along gaily in a carriage, veiled in a lace mantilla, drinking red wine, happy, free. Her thoughts were so poignant, so touching, that without difficulty she pressed a tear from her swimming eyes and allowed it to steal slowly, entrancingly down the smooth curve of her cheek as, with a gentle movement, she leant against him and whispered:

"Oh! Matt, dear, it'll be hard to do without ye! You're goin' to leave me just when I'm beginnin' to——"

A strange exultation possessed him as she pressed against him and, seizing her downcast face between his palms, he made her look at him.

"Don't say you're beginning—say you do love me."

She did not speak but, more potently than any words, veiled her soft eyes as though she feared to let him see the intensity of her passion for him.

"Ye do!" he cried. "I can see that ye do!" His lips twitched, his nostrils dilated as a fierce delight filled him, not from the touch of her form alone, but from the understanding that he had ousted his father, that fate had delivered into his hands a powerful weapon of revenge.

"I know I'm a bad girl, Matt," she whispered, "but I mean to do well. I'm goin' to leave him. I went to the front room myself all last night. That—that's finished. I would never look at another man unless

356

I married him, and then I would stick to my man through thick and thin."

He continued to look at her fixedly, whilst she continued, with great feeling:

"I think I could make a man happy if I tried. There's wee things about me that he might like one way and another. I would do my best to give him a' that he wanted!" She sighed and drooped her head against his shoulder.

His thoughts twisted incoherently amongst the conflict of his emotions, but through the warm mists in his brain he saw that this was doubly desirous to him—not only to strike his father but, additionally for his own gratification. Nancy was a woman in a thousand, lovely, entrancing, ardent, not with the strong and clumsy vehemence of Agnes Moir but with a subtler, a more delicate and alluring flame which pervaded her pale white body like an essence and drew him towards its clear heat. Her beauty, too, surpassed by far the merely tolerable comeliness of the unfortunate Agnes; her figure was, not sturdy, but elegant; no umber shadow menaced the exquisite curve of her soft upper lip; not only was she beautiful, but she was, he was convinced, enamoured of him to the point of passionately abandoning his father because of her feeling for him. Filled by these thoughts he was confirmed in his resolution and, in a choked voice, he exclaimed:

"Nancy! There's something I've got to tell you—something else that you don't know. Something that might interest you. Would you like to hear it?"

She looked at him languishingly, throwing her head back so that the inclination of her poise invited his embrace, and was about to murmur "Yes," when suddenly the front door of the house clicked open and was heavily shut, and the sound of footsteps was heard along the hall. Like a flash Nancy recovered herself from the apparent profundity of her feeling and, pushing Matt to the fireplace she cried, in a sharp whisper:

"Bide there, and don't let on. He'll never know," then in the same instant her hands had flown to her hair and, moving as lightly as quick fluttering birds, had adjusted, patted smooth such small disorder as might have existed. She was back at the table immediately, clattering the dishes, when Brodie entered the room.

For a moment Brodie paused in the doorway, an unwrapped bottle swinging in his hand, surveying first his son, whom he so rarely saw, with a black lowering disgust, allowing his glance to travel questioningly to Nancy, then returning it restlessly to the uneasy figure by the fireplace. His dull understanding appreciated nothing of the undercurrent of the events he had disturbed, but his moody eye perceived the faint flush upon Matt's sallow cheek, the downcast look, the nervous agitation of his attitude, and instinctively his memory rushed back to that scene in the house in the Vennel, when he had surprised his son with Nancy struggling in his arms. He knew nothing, suspected nothing, but he was none the less tormented by this vision of his memory, felt instinctively that some secret activity had been in process at his entry; his glance became black and darting, impaling Matt, who moved more uneasily, and hung his head with greater embarrassment, the longer that silent stare continued.

Nancy, at the table, her inveterate hardihood rendering her composed, perfect mistress of her features, inwardly furious at the flustered ineptitude of the hero to whom she had so passionately avowed her devotion, attempted to rescue him by remarking, tartly, to the elder man:

"What are ye standin' there for, Brodie—like a big bear? Come in and sit down, and don't swing that bottle as though ye wanted to brain us. Ye look downright uncanny. Come awa' in." But Brodie did not seem to hear her, and, allowing her remark to pass unheeded, still continued to view his son from the vantage point of the door, still swinging the bottle like a club, until at length he spoke, saying with a snarl:

"What's the honour o' this visit due to? We're not usually so fortunate when we come in at this time—no! your home's not good enough for you in the evenings now. You're one o' these late birds we never seem to see at all."

Matt opened his dry lips to speak, but before he could reply Brodie continued, fiercely:

"Have ye been sayin' anything to Nancy here that ye might like to repeat to me?—If ye have I'm listenin' and waitin'."

Here Nancy broke in, flinging her hands upon her hips, squaring her neat shoulders, and tossing her head indignantly.

"Are ye mad, Brodie, that ye go on like that? What are ye talkin' about at all, at all? If you're goin' to rave in that fashion I'll be muckle obliged if ye'll kindly keep my name out o' it."

He turned slowly and surveyed her. His drawn brows relaxed.

"I know, woman! I know it's all right! I would never doubt ye and I know he's too feared of me to dare it, but somehow the sight o' the glaikit, fushionless loon aye embitters me. He looks as if butter wouldna melt in his mouth and yet I can never forget that he tried to shoot me." He swung round again to Matt who had paled at these last words and exclaimed, bitterly: "I should have given ye over to the police for that —you that tried to shoot your father. Ye got off too easy that night. But I'm no' so good humoured as I used to be, so don't try any more tricks on me or by God! I'll lay your skull open wi' this very bottle. Now will ye tell me what you're doin' here."

"He was tellin' me about some job or other," cried Nancy shrilly, "but I didna ken what it was a' about." Would he never speak? she thought, the stupid fool that was standing there as white and flabby as a soft lump of putty, giving the whole affair away by his lack of gumption.

358

"What job?" said Brodie. "Speak for yourself, sir!"

At last Matthew found his tongue, he who on the homeward journey had visualised his superior attitude during the interview and traced the manner in which he would gradually lead up to it, who had just told Nancy how he would throw his new position in this old devil's teeth.

"I've got a position in America, father," he stammered, Brodie's face did not change but after a pause he sneered:

"So you're goin' to do some work at last. Weel! weel! Wonders will never cease. The heir to the house o' Brodie is goin' to work? It's a good thing too, for though ye've kept out of my way right well, now that I've seen ye again I feel I would soon have flung ye out." He paused. "What is this grand position? Tell us all about the marvels of it."

"It's just my own work," stammered Matt, "storekeeping. I've had my name down for months with two or three firms, but it's not often a chance like this crops up."

"And how did a thing like you get hold o' the chance? Was it a blind man that engaged ye?"

"It was an emergency," replied Matt apologetically. "The man that had the job died suddenly. He was flung off his horse and they wanted somebody in a hurry. I'll have to leave at once—within a week—to fill the place as soon as ever I can. Maybe ye've heard o' the firm. They're ——" Here a cup fell clattering from the tray, and smashed with a sudden, ringing cadence upon the floor.

"Guidsakes," cried Nancy in a great commotion, "that's what comes o' standin' haverin' like auld wives. It's always the way if ye take your mind off what you're doin'—you're sure to go and break something or other." She bent down to pick up the fragments and as she stooped she flashed a glance at Matthew, quick, covert, but full of suppressed and significant warning. "I'm sorry if I interrupted you," she murmured to Brodie as she got up.

Matthew had observed the glance, interpreted its meaning and though his embarrassment grew, swollen from another source, with a feeble attempt at strategy he lowered his eyes and murmured:

"They're—they're in the wool business. It's to do with sheep."

"By God! they've got the right man," cried his father, "for a bigger sheep than yoursel' never went bleatin' about this earth. Take care they don't crop ye, by mistake, at the shearin' time. Look up, ye saft sheep! Can ye not hold your head up like a man and look at me? A' this flash and dash that's come on ye since ye went to India doesna deceive me. I thought it might make a man o' ye to go out there, but I see through the rotten gloss that it's gie'n ye, and you're but the same great, blubberin' sapsy that used to greet and run to your mother whenever I put my een on ye."

He stood looking at his son, filled by a profound and final repugnance which sickened him even of the thought of baiting Matt, who, he considered disgustedly, was not worth even the lash of his tongue. Thank God he was going away, to quit his home, to abandon this sneaking, sponging existence, to be irrevocably out of his sight, out of the country, forgotten.

Suddenly he felt tired, realised dimly that he was not the man he had been and, with a quick rushing desire for the nepenthe of forgetfulness, he wanted to be alone with Nancy, wanted to drink. To his son he said, slowly:

"You and me are finished, Matt. When ye've gone ye'll never come back into this house. I never want to see ye again," then, turning to Nancy, and regarding her with a fond and altered glance he added:

"Bring me a glass, Nancy. He doesna deserve it, but I'm goin' to give him a toast." As she silently departed to obey he followed her with the same glance, feeling that she was warming to him again, that with his son out of the house, they would be more private, more unrestrainedly together than before. "Thank ye, Nancy," he said mildly, as she returned and handed him the glass. "Ye're an obleegin' lass. I don't know how I ever got on without ye." Then he continued, reassuringly: "I'm not goin' to take ower much to-night. No! no! This bottle will do me for a week. I know fine ye don't like me to take too much and I'm not goin' to do it. But we must pledge this big maunderin' sheep before he goes out to join the flock. Will ye have just a wee taste yer'sel', Nancy? It'll do ye no harm. Come along now," he added with a clumsy ingratiating manner, waving his arm at her, "away and get yourself a glass—and I'll give ye just enough to warm ye."

She shook her head, still without speaking, her eyes half-veiled, her lips smoothly parted, her expression neither hostile nor friendly but shaded by a vague reticence which gave to her an air of enigmatic subtlety that encouraged him, drew him towards her by its very mystery. Actually, behind the mask of her face lay a bitter contempt of him, activated the more fiercely as she saw that in choosing thus to humiliate Matt before her he was intimidating his son, making it more difficult for her to achieve the purpose she had set herself.

"No?" he said affably, "well! I winna drive ye, woman. You're a mare that needs gentle guidin'—as I've proved to my cost. Ye maun be humoured—not driven." A short laugh broke from him as he uncorked the bottle, and holding the glass to the level of his eye, which glittered at the first sight of the trickling liquor, slowly poured out a large measure, raised the bottle, paused, moistened his lips with his tongue, then quickly added a further quantity of the spirit. "I may as well take a decent glass to begin with. It saves goin' back and back. And I can stand it onyway," he muttered, keeping his head down and away from her, as he placed the bottle upon the dresser and transferred the glass of whisky to his right hand. Then, stretching out his arm he cried:

"Here's a toast to the heir to the house o' Brodie—the last I'll ever drink to him. May he go to his grand job and may he stay there! Let him get out o' my sight and keep out o' it. Let him go how he likes and where he likes, but let him never come back, and if ever he tries to get on to that horse he was speakin' about, may he fall off and break his useless neck like the man that had the place before him!" He threw back his head and, with a tilt of his wrist, drained the glass at a gulp, then, surveying Matthew with a sardonic grin, he added: "That's my last good-bye to ye. I don't know where ye're goin'—I don't even want to know. Whatever happens to ye makes no odds now, for it'll never reach my ears!" And with these words he ceased to regard his son, ignored him utterly. Now that he had swallowed the whisky he felt more vigorous. Lifting his eye again to the bottle on the dresser, he considered it speculatively for a moment, cleared his throat, straightened himself up and, his head averted from Nancy, remarked solemnly: "But I canna drink a toast to a thing like him and pass over a braw lass like my Nancy." He shook his head at the injustice of the thought as, with the empty tumbler still in his hand, he approached the table. "No! that would not be fair!" he continued, pouring himself out another portion. "I couldna do that in all conscience—we must give the girl her due. There's nothing I wouldna do for her, she means so much to me. Here, Nancy!" he cried, wheedlingly, turning to her: "This is a wee salute to the bonniest lass in Levenford."

She had controlled her temper so long that now it seemed impossible for her to contain herself further, and her veiled eyes sparkled and a faint colour ran into her cheeks as though she might immediately stamp her foot and assail him furiously with her tongue. But instead, she stifled the words she wished to utter behind her tight lips, and, turning on her heel, marched into the scullery where she began noisily to wash the dishes. With a chastened expression Brodie stood, his head slightly on one side, listening to the clatter of china; he heard in it some suggestion of her exasperation, but soon, returning his eyes again to the glass in his hand, he slowly raised it to his lips and slowly drained it; then, advancing to his chair he lowered himself heavily into it.

Matt, who had remained at the place by the fireplace where he had been thrust by Nancy, a silent and dismayed spectator of his father's recent actions, now moved uneasily upon his feet, subdued more abjectly by the closer proximity of the other as he sat brooding in his chair. He moved his eyes restlessly round the room, bit his pale lips, rubbed his soft, damp hands together, wishing fervently to leave the room but, thinking his father's eye to be upon him, was afraid to stir. At length, emboldened by the continued silence in the room, he widened the scope of the sweeping circles of his eye and allowed his flickering glance to touch for a swift second upon the face of the other beside him. Immediately he saw that Brodie was not, as he had feared, contemplating him but instead gazing earnestly towards the open doorway of the scullery and, reassured by the other's abstraction, he ventured one tentative foot in front of him, was not observed, and, continuing his stealthy progress—slid quietly out of the kitchen.

His intention had been to escape from the house as quickly as possible, resigning himself to an interminable wait in the streets outside until his father had gone to bed, but he was arrested, in the dimness of the hall, by a segment of light striking out from the parlour. As he paused, suddenly it occurred to him that since Nessie was within, he might spend a few moments more comfortably with her before departing into the frosty night outside. He felt, too, unconsciously, the pressing need for the opportunity to declaim upon the merit of the attainment of his new post, and the desire for some approving tribute to restore the damage inflicted upon his self-esteem. Consequently he opened the door and looked into the room.

Nessie, seated at the table, surrounded by the inevitable accompaniment of her books, did not look up at his entry but remained with folded arms, hunched shoulders, and bent head. But when he spoke, with a sudden quick start she flinched as though the unexpected waves of speech had struck her across the stillness of the room.

"I'm coming in a minute," was all that he had said.

"Oh! Matt," she cried, pressing her small closed hand into her left side, "what a start you gave me! I didn't hear you come in. I seem to jump at anything these days."

As he observed her present attitude, the inclination of her head, the mild and limpid eyes, filled with a mute apology for her weakness, a striking memory presented itself to him, making him for the moment forget his own concerns.

"My goodness, Nessie," he exclaimed, staring at her. "You're getting as like Mamma as life. I can almost see her looking out of your face the now!"

"Do you think so, Matt," she replied, flattered in some degree to be the object of his interest. "What makes you say that?"

He seemed to consider.

"I think it's your eyes; there's the same look about them as though you thought something was going to happen to you and were looking ahead for it."

At his words she was hurt and immediately lowered these betraying eyes, keeping them fixed upon the table as he continued:

"What's come over you lately?—you don't seem the same to me at all. Is there anything wrong with you that's making you like that?"

"Everything's wrong," she answered slowly. "Since Mamma died I've been as miserable as could be and I haven't had a soul to speak to about it. I can't suffer to be near to—to Nancy. She doesn't like me. She's always at me for something. Everything is different. The house has been so different that it's not like the same place—father's different, too."

362

"You've nothing to be feared of from him. You were always his pet," he retorted. "He's always sucking round you in some way."

"I wish he would leave me alone," she replied dully. "He's just driving me on all the time with this work. I can't stand it. I don't feel well in myself."

"Tuts! Nessie," he exclaimed reprovingly, "that's Mamma all over again. Ye should pull yourself together. What's the matter with you?"

"I've always got a headache! I wake up with it in the morning and it never leaves me all day. It makes me so stupid that I don't know what I'm doing. Besides, I can't eat the food we get now and I'm always tired. I'm tired at this very minute."

"You'll be all right when you've got this exam. over. You'll win the Latta all right."

"I'll win it all right," she exclaimed wildly. "But what's going to become of me then! What is he going to do with me after? Tell me that! Am I to be shoved on like this all the time and never know what's going to come of it? He'll never say when I ask him. He doesn't know himself."

"You'll be a teacher—that's the thing for you."

She shook her head.

"No! that wouldn't be good enough for him. I wanted to do that myself—to put down my name to go on to the Normal, but he wouldn't allow it. Oh! Matt," she cried, "I wish I had somebody to put in a word for me. I'm so downright wretched about it and about everything else—I wish sometimes I had never been born!"

He shifted his gaze uncomfortably from her appealing face which, stamped by a forlorn wistfulness, seemed to implore him to help her.

"You should get out the house and play with the other girls," he advanced, somewhat uncertainly. "That would take your mind off things a bit."

"How can I?" she exclaimed frantically. "Ever since I was a wee thing I've been kept in at these lessons, and now I'm flung in here every night, and will be, too, for the whole of the next six months. And if I dared to go out he would leather me. You wouldn't believe it, Matt, but I sometimes think I'll go out of my mind the way I'm kept grindin' at it."

"I go out," he exclaimed valiantly. "He didn't stop me goin' out."

"You're different," she replied sadly, her puny outburst subsiding and leaving her more dejected than before. "And even if I did go out what good would it do? None of the other girls would play with me. They'll hardly speak to me as it is. One of them said the other day that her father said she was to have nothing to do with anyone that came out of this house. Oh! I do wish you could help me, Matt!"

"How can I help you?" he replied roughly, irritated at her entreaties. "Don't you know I'm goin' away next week?"

She gazed at him with a slight wrinkling of her brow and repeated, without apparently comprehending:

"Going away next week?"

"To South America," he replied grandly; "to a splendid new position I've got out there. Miles and miles away from this sink of a town."

Then she understood, and in the sudden perception that he was leaving immediately for a far-distant land, that she, of all the Brodie children, would be left in a solitary, unprotected state to face the dreadful unhappiness of her present existence in the home, she paled. Matt had never helped her much, and during these latter months had, indeed, comforted her still less, but he was her brother, a companion in her distress, and she had only a moment ago appealed to him for assistance. Her lips quivered, her eyes became blurred, she burst into tears.

"Don't go, Matt," she sobbed. "I'll be left all alone if ye go. I'll have nobody at all in this terrible house."

"What are ye talking about," he retorted savagely. "You can't know what you're saying. Am I going to give up the chance of a lifetime —money and freedom and—and everything for the likes of you? You're mad!"

"I'll be mad if you go," she cried. "What chance will I have here all by myself?—Mary away, and you away, and only me left! What'll become of me?"

"Stop your howling," he shot at her, with a quick glance towards the door. "Do you want everybody to hear you with that bawling? He'll be in at us in a minute if you're not careful. I've got to go and that's all about it."

"Could ye not take me with you then, Matt," she gulped, stifling her sobs with difficulty. "I know I'm young but I could keep the house for ye. That's always the sort of thing I've wanted to do—and not these miserable lessons. I would do everything for you, Matt." Her attitude apprised him that she would serve him like a slave, her eyes implored him not to leave her desolate and forsaken.

"They would never hear of ye going out. The sooner you get it out of your head the better. Can you not look pleased at your brother getting a fine job like this instead of moaning and groaning about it."

"I am pleased for your sake, Matt," she sniffed, wiping her eyes with her saturated handkerchief. "I—I was just thinking about myself."

"That's it," he shot out. "You can't think of anybody else. Try to have some consideration for other people. Don't be so selfish!"

"All right, Matt," she said, with a last convulsive sigh. "I'll try. Anyway, I'm sorry."

"That's better," he replied largely, in a more affable tone; but even as he spoke he shivered, and, changing his tone to one of complaint, he cried: "Gosh! it's cold in here! How do you expect a man to stand talking to you if you haven't got a fire? If your circulation can stand this, mine can't. I'll need to put my coat on and away out to walk up my circulation." He stamped his feet then turned abruptly, calling to her: "I'm away out then, Nessie."

When he had gone she remained rigid, the small, wet ball of the hand-kerchief clutched tightly in her hand, her red-lidded eyes fixed upon the door, which had closed upon her like the door of a prison. The avenue of the future down which she gazed was gloomy, and amidst the dark, forbidding shadows she saw the figure of Nessie Brodie pass fearfully and alone. No one could now come between her and her father, no one interpose between her frailty and the strength of his unknown purpose. Matthew would go as Mary had gone. Mary! She had thought so much of her lately that she longed now for the comfort of her sister's arm around her, for the solace of her quiet smile, the sustaining courage that lay within her steady eyes. She needed someone to whom she might unburden her weary mind, in whom she could confide her sorrows and the thought of her sister's tranquil fortitude drew her. "Mary!" she whispered, like an entreaty, "Mary, dear! I didn't love you as you deserved when you were here, but oh! I wish I had you near me now!"

As the almost incredible words left her lips the expression on her pinched, tear-stained face grew suddenly transfigured, illuminated as from a sudden light within. Hope again shone in the sorrowful eyes mingled by a purpose so rash that only her present despair could have induced her to consider it. Why, she thought, should she not write to her sister?—A terrible consideration, but her only chance of succour! Upstairs, hidden in a secret corner of her bedroom, lay the letter which Mamma had given her some days before she died and which bore the address in London where Mary lived. If she acted carefully her father would never know; she knew, too, that Mary would never betray her, and with the renewed consciousness of her sister's love she got up from her chair, and, as though walking in a dream, went out of the room and tiptoed silently upstairs. After a moment she returned and shutting the door, listened attentively, trembling violently in all her limbs. She had the letter, but she was terrified at what she had done, at what she pro-posed to do. Nevertheless she persisted in her purpose. At the table she tore out a leaf from one of her copy-books and hurriedly composed a short note of pathetic entreaty, telling Mary in a few words how she was situated and imploring her assistance, entreating her to come to her if she could. As she wrote, she looked up from time to time with agitated glances, as though expecting her father to enter, but soon the few scribbled lines, blotted by haste and the fall of an irrepressible tear, were completed. She folded the ragged-edged sheet and thrust it in the en-velope she had brought from upstairs. Then she addressed the envelope, copying each word carefully, and thrust it into the bosom of her dress; finally, with a pale face and palpitating heart she resumed her bent position over her books and made pretence to study. But her precaution was unnecessary. No one entered the room during the whole evening. She was undiscovered and, early next morning, on her way to school, she posted the letter.

IV

JAMES BRODIE was awakening. No sun streamed through his window to stimulate gently his recumbent figure, or set the golden motes swimming through straight rivers of light across his sleep-filled gaze. Instead, a cold fine rain smirred the dripping panes, dulling the interior of the room to one drab monotone and meeting his half-opened, glutinous eye like a melancholy reminder of his altered condition. He marked the unhappy aspect of the weather moodily, then from the window, his visible eye, now more fully opened to reveal the sticky, white coagulum at its corner, turned to the clock, and, observing that the dim hands pointed to ten minutes past eight, ten minutes beyond his appointed but unkept hour of rising, grew more gloomy. To-day he would, he realised, be late at the office once again, would suffer another sharp rebuke from the upstart chief clerk who now attempted to control his working hours, who had threatened even to report him to the under manager should he fail to observe a more constant punctuality.

At this reflection his face, against the lighter background of the pillow, seemed to darken, the lines that marked it deepened like sharp incisions, and the eyes, losing their innate melancholy, were filled instead by a dull, morose obstinacy. Be damned to them all, he thought, they would not order him about; he would have another five minutes in bed in spite of the whole board of directors of the Latta Shipyard! He would, of course, make up the time by omitting to shave which struck him now, as it frequently did, as a cunning way of defeating the powers which sought to move him to their rule and pattern of life. Such a ruse as this suited him, too, in his own inclination, for he was now averse to shaving in the mornings when his unsteady hand so often behaved erratically, trying his temper to control it, and on occasions making him gash his cheek. The early hours of the day never found him at his best, for not only did his hand refuse to obey him, but his head ached, or his tongue felt like dry wood, or his stomach turned within him at the mere consideration of his breakfast. It was, he was well aware, the whisky which was responsible for these unwelcome visitations, and in this grey morning's light he felt, with a gloomy insight, that he must cut down his allowance. When he had made such resolutions in the past he had never, he told himself, been really serious, but now he must definitely make up his mind to take himself in hand, to drink nothing before dinner and thereafter to abstain until the evening, when he would be moderate, when indeed, he must be moderate if he were to please Nancy, whose favour was now of such vital necessity to him. Certainly she had been better disposed towards him during the last two days and he reflected, with a more equable turn of mind that, although she had not come back to his room since their quarrel on the night of her visit to the aunt at Overton, the obvious reason which she had advanced in excuse must surely be correct in view of her recent kindness and more tolerant treatment of him. He could not do without Nancy! She had become as necessary to him and as indispensable as breath to his body, and for this reason alone he must be careful how he addressed himself to the bottle in future. Impossible that he should ever live without her! She would come to him again to-night, the fresher for his enforced abstinence, or he would know the reason why!

Some semblance of his old complacency seemed to flow into him at this last thought and, flinging off the bedclothes, he got out of bed; but as the cold air of the room struck his body he shivered, frowned, and losing his satisfied look, reached hurriedly for his clothes, which lay in a disordered heap upon a near-by chair. He struggled into these garments with the utmost dispatch, giving his face alone some transient attention with water and soap before assuming his soiled linen collar, knotting his stringy tie and throwing on his baggy coat and waistcoat. The economy in time was considerable, for the whole process of dressing had not taken five minutes, and now he was ready, albeit after a fashion, to descend the stairs and consume his morning meal.

"Good mornin' to you, Brodie," cried Nancy agreeably, as he entered the kitchen. "You're on time all right to-day! How did ye sleep?"

"Not so weel as I would have liked," he replied heavily. "I was cold! Still, I've a feeling I'll be cosier to-night."

"You're not blate so early in the mornin'," she answered, with a toss of her head. "Sup up your porridge and be quiet."

He considered the porridge with pursed lips and some show of repugnance as he exclaimed:

"I don't feel like them somehow, Nancy. They're heavy on a man's stomach at breakfast time. They might do for supper but I can't think of them the now. Have ye anything else?"

"I've got a nice, sweet kipper in the pan just done to a turn," she cried complacently. "Don't eat the porridge if ye're not in the mood. I'll get ye the other one this very minute."

He followed her active figure, observing the swirl of her skirts, the fluent movements of her neat feet and ankles as she rushed to carry out her words, and he was filled by a sudden appreciation of the marked improvement in her attitude towards him. She was coming near to him

367

again, no longer looked at him with that sparkle of animosity in her eyes, was even now running after him in a fashion strangely reminiscent of his wife's eagerness to serve him. He felt the comfort of being once more looked after with this devotion, especially as it came from his beloved but independent Nancy, and when she returned with the dish, he looked at her from the corner of his eyes and remarked:

"You're drawin' round to me again, I see. I can mind of mornings when some burnt porridge was good enough to fling at a poor man for his breakfast, but this juicy kipper is more to my taste, and your way o' lookin' at me is more to my likin' still. You're fond of me, Nancy, aren't ye?"

She gazed down at his tired face, lined, hollowed, disfigured by a two days' stubble of beard and split by a forced and unbefitting smile, envisaged his bowed and slovenly figure, his tremulous hands and uncared for finger-nails, and with a shrill little laugh she cried:

"True enough, man! I've such a feelin' for ye now that I hardly like to own it. It fair makes my heart loup when I look at ye sometimes."

His smile was extinguished, his eyes puckered intently, and he answered:

"It's a treat for me to hear ye say that, Nancy! I know it's downright wrong o' me to tell ye, but I can't help it, I've got to depend on ye now something extraordinar'." Then, still disregarding his breakfast, he continued, almost apologetically, as though he defended his conduct: "I never would have believed I could draw to anybody so much. I didna think I was that kind o' man, but ye see, I had to do without for so lang, that when—when we came thegither—weel—ye've fair taken hold of me. That's plain truth. Ye're not angry at me for tellin' ye a' this, are ye now?"

"No! No!" she exclaimed hurriedly. "Not a bit, Brodie. I should understand ye by this time. But come on now, don't waste the good kipper I've taken the trouble to cook ye. I'm wantin' to hear how ye like it. And I'm anxious for ye to make a good breakfast, for you'll have to take your dinner out to-day."

"Take my dinner out! What for?" he exclaimed, in some surprise. "Ye were away at Overton only last week—ye're surely not goin' to see that aunt o' yours again?"

"No, I'm not!" she cried, with a pert toss of her head, "but she's comin' to see me! And I'm not wantin' you runnin' round after me, with her, that's a decent unsuspectin' body—ay and one that's fond o' me—starin' the eyes out of her heid at your palavers. Ye can come home in the evenin'. Then I'll be ready for ye."

He glared at her for a moment with a dark countenance, then, suddenly relaxing, he shook his head slowly: "Damnation, woman! but ye have the cheek on ye. To think that you've got the length o' entertainin' your friends in my house! Gad! it makes me see how far ye can

368

go with me. I should have warmed the backside o' ye for doin' a thing like that without first askin' me—but ye know I canna be angry with ye. It seems there's no end to the liberties you'll take with me."

"What's the harm," she demanded primly. "Can an honest house-keeper body not see her relations if she wants to? It'll do ye good to have a snack outside, then I'll have a surprise all ready for ye when ye come."

He looked at her doubtfully.

"Surprise is the right word, after the way you've been treatin' me." He paused and added, grimly: "I'm damned if I know what makes me so soft wi' ye."

"Don't talk like that, Brodie," she reprimanded mildly. "Your language is like a heathen Chinaman's sometimes."

"What do you know about Chinamen?" he retorted moodily, at last turning his attention towards the kipper, and beginning to consume it in slow, large mouthfuls. After a moment he remarked, in an altered tone: "This has a relish in it, Nancy—it's the sort of thing I can fancy in the mornin's now."

She continued to look at him in an oddly restrained fashion as he conveyed the food to his lowered mouth, then suddenly a thought seemed to strike her, and she cried:

"Guidsakes, what am I dreamin' about! There's a letter came for ye this mornin' that I forgot a' about."

"What!" he retorted, arresting his movements and glancing up in surprise from under his thick, greying eyebrows. "A letter for me!"

"Ay! I clean forgot in the hurry to get your breakfast. Here it is." And she took a letter from the corner of the dresser and handed it to him. He held the letter for a moment in his outstretched hand, drew it near to him with a puzzled look in his eyes, observed that it was stamped by the postmark of London, then, carelessly inserting his thick thumb, ripped the envelope open and drew out the sheet within. Watching him with some slight interest as he read the written words Nancy observed the expressions of bewilderment, amazement, enlightenment, and triumph sweep across his face with the rapidity of clouds traversing a dark and windy sky. Finally his expression assumed a strange satisfaction as he turned the letter, again read it slowly through, and, lifting his eyes, fixed them upon the distance.

"Would ye believe it," he muttered, "and after all this time!"

"What?" she cried. "What is it about?"

"She has climbed down and wants to come crawlin' back!" He paused, absorbed in his own considerations, as though his words had been sufficient to enlighten her fully.

"I don't know what you mean," she exclaimed sharply. "Who are ye talkin' about?"

"My daughter—Mary," he replied slowly; "the one that I kicked out of my house. I swore she would never get back until she had licked my boots, ay, and she said she never would come back, and here she is, in this very letter, cadging to win home and keep house for me. God! it's a rich recompense for me after a' these years!" He held up the letter between his tense fingers as though his eyes would never cease to gloat upon it, sneering as he read: " 'Let the past be forgotten! I want you to forgive me.' If that doesna justify me my name's not Brodie. 'Since Mamma has gone I would like to come home. I am not unhappy here but sometimes lonely,' " he continued with a snarl. "—Lonely! By God, it's what she deserves. Lonely! Long may it continue. If she thinks she'll get back here as easy as that she's far mistaken. I'll not have her. No! Never!" He returned his eyes to Nancy as though to demand her approval and, with twisted lips, resumed, "Don't ye see how this puts me in the right, woman! She was proud, proud as ye make them, but I can see she's broken now. Why else should she want home? God! what a come down for her to have to whine to get taken back like this and—what a triumph for me to refuse her. She wants to be my housekeeper!" He laughed harshly. "That's a good one, is it no', Nancy? She doesna know that I've got you—she's wantin' your job!"

She had picked the letter from his hand and was reading it.

"I don't see much of a whine here," she replied slowly. "It's a decent enough written letter."

"Bah!" he cried, "it's not the way it's written I'm thinkin' of! It's the meanin' of it all that concerns me. There's no other explanation possible, and the very thought of it lifts me like a dram o' rare spirits."

"You're not goin' to let her come back, then?" she queried, tentatively.

"No!" he shouted, "I'm not! I've got you to look after me now. Does she think I want the likes o' her. She can stop in this place in London that she's in, and rot there, for all I care."

"Ye mustna decide in a hurry," she admonished him; "after all she's your own daughter. Think it over well before ye do anything rash."

He looked at her sulkily.

"Rash or not rash, I'll never forgive her," he growled, "and that's all there is to it." Then his eye suddenly lighted as he exclaimed: "I tell ye what might be a bawr though, Nancy—and something that would cut her to the quick. Supposin' ye were to write back and tell her that the post she applied for was filled. That would make her feel pretty small, would it not? Will ye do't, woman?"

"No, I will not," she cried immediately; "the very idea. Ye maun do it yoursel' when you're about it."

"Well, at least ye'll help me to write my answer," he protested. "Suppose you and me do it thegither to-night when I come home. That smart head o' yours is sure to think on something clever for me to put in."

"Wait till to-night, then," she replied after some consideration, "and I'll think about it in the meantime."

"That's grand," he cried, playing in his mind with the idea of collaborating with her in the evening over this delightful task of composing a cutting reply to his daughter. "We'll lay our heads together. I know what you can do when you try."

As he spoke a faint horn sounded in the distance, swelling and falling at times, but always audible, entering the room with gentle though relentless persistency.

"Gracious," cried Nancy quickly, "there's the nine o'clock horn and you not out of the house yet. Ye'll be late as can be if ye don't hurry. Come on now, away with ye!"

"I'm not carin' for their blasted horns," he replied sullenly. "I'll be late if I like. You would think I was the slave of that damned whistle the way it draws me away from ye just when I'm not wantin' to go."

"I don't want ye to get the sack though, man! What would ye do if ye lost your job?"

"I would get a better one. I've just been thinkin' about that lately myself. What I've got is not near good enough for me."

"Wheesht! now, Brodie," she conciliated him, "you're well enough as ye are. Ye might look further and fare worse. Come on and I'll see ye to the door!"

His expression softened as he looked at her and rose obediently, exclaiming:

"Don't you worry anyway, Nancy. I'll always have enough to keep you." At the front door he turned to her and said, in a voice which sounded almost pathetic: "It'll be a' day until I see you again."

She drew back a little and half shut the door as she replied, irrelevantly:

"What a mornin', too. Ye should take an umbrella instead o' that auld stick. Are you minding about gettin' your dinner out, to-day?"

"I'm mindin' about it," he answered submissively. "You know I heed what you tell me. Come on now—give us a kiss before I go."

She was about to shut the door in his face when, at his attitude, something seemed to melt within her and, raising herself on her toes, inclining her head upwards, she touched with her lips the deep furrow that marked the centre of his forehead.

"There," she whispered under her breath, "that's for the man that ye were."

He stared at her uncomprehendingly with eyes that gazed at hers appealingly, inquiringly, like the eyes of a devoted dog.

"What were ye sayin'?" he muttered, stupidly.

"Nothing," she cried lightly, withdrawing herself again. "I was just biddin' ye good-bye."

He hesitated, stammered uncomfortably:

"If it was—if ye were thinkin' about—about the drink, I want to tell ye that I'm going to cut it down to something reasonable. I know ye don't like me to take so much and I want to please ye, woman."

She shook her head slowly, looking at him curiously, intently.

" 'Twasna that at all. If ye feel ye need a dram, I suppose ye maun have it. It's the only—it's a comfort to ye, I suppose. Now away with ye, man."

"Nancy, dear, ye understand a man weel," he murmured in a moved voice. "There's nothing I couldna do for ye when you're like this." He shifted his feet heavily, in some embarrassment at his own outburst, then in a gruff voice full of his suppressed feeling exclaimed: "I'll—I'll away, then, woman. Good-bye just now."

"Good-bye," she replied evenly.

With a last look at her eyes he turned, faced the grey and melancholy morning, and moved off into the rain, a strange figure, coatless, crowned extravagantly by the large, square hat, from under which thick tufts of uncut hair protruded fantastically, his arms behind his back, his heavy ash plant trailing grotesquely behind him in the mud.

He walked down the road, his brain confused by conflicting thoughts amongst which mingled a sense of abashment at the unexpected exhibition of his own emotion; but, as he progressed, there emerged from this confusion a single perception—the worth to him of Nancy. She was human clay like himself, and she understood him, knew the needs of a man, appreciated, as she had just remarked, that he required sometimes the comfort of a glass. He did not feel the rain as it soaked into his clothing, so enwrapped was he in the contemplation of her, and into the dullness of his set face small gleams of light from time to time appeared. As he approached the shipyard, however, his reflections grew less agreeable, evidenced by the unrelieved harshness of his countenance, and he was concerned by his lateness, by the possibility of a reprimand, and affected by a depressing realisation, which time had not eradicated, of the very humiliating nature of his employment. He thought, too, in a different light of the letter that he had just received, which appeared to him as an intolerable presumption on the part of her who had once been his daughter, and which now reminded him bitterly of the past. An acrid taste came into his mouth at his own recollection whilst the salt, smoked fish which he had eaten for breakfast made him feel parched and thirsty; outside the "Fitter's Bar" he deliberately paused and, fortified by Nancy's parting remark, muttered: "Gad, but I'm dry, and I'm half an hour late as it is. I may as weel make a job o' it while I'm about it."

He went in with a half-defiant glance over his shoulder at the block of offices that lay opposite and, when he emerged, a quarter of an hour later, his bearing had regained something of its old challenging assertion. In this manner he entered the main swing doors of the offices and, threading the corridors, now with the facility of habit, entered his own room with his head well in the air, surveying in turn the two young clerks who looked up from their work to greet him.

"Has that auld, nosey pig been round yet?" he demanded; "because if he has I don't give a tinker's curse about it."

"Mr. Blair?" replied one of the pair. "No! he hasn't been round yet!"

"Humph!" cried Brodie, fiercely annoyed at the sudden feeling of relief which had swept involuntarily over him. "I suppose ye think I'm lucky. Well! let me tell ye both that I don't give a damn whether he knows I've been late or not. Tell him if ye like! It's all one to me," and, flinging his hat upon a peg and his stick into a corner, he sat heavily down upon his stool. The other clerks exchanged a glance, and after a slight pause, the spokesman of the two remarked diffidently:

"We wouldn't say a word, Mr. Brodie. You surely know that. But look here, you're wringing wet—will you not take your jacket off and dry it?"

"No! I'll not take it off!" he replied roughly, opening his ledger, lifting his pen, and beginning to work; but after a moment he raised his head and said in a different tone: "But thank ye all the same. You're good lads both, and I know you've lent me a hand in the past. The truth is I've had some news that upset me, so I'm just not quite my usual this mornin'."

They knew something of his affairs from certain bouts of rambling dissertations during the past months, and the one who had not yet spoken remarked:

"Not Nessie I hope, Mr. Brodie?"

"No!" he answered, "not my Nessie! She's as right as the mail, thank God, workin' like a trooper and headin' straight for the Latta! She's never given me a moment's trouble. It was just something else, but I know what to do. I can win through it like I've done with all the rest."

They forbore to question him further, and the three resumed work in a silence broken only by the scratching of pens on paper, the rustle of a turning page, the restless scrape of a stool, and the mutter from Brodie's lips as he strove to concentrate his fogged brain in the effort to contend with the figures before him.

The forenoon had advanced well upon its course when a precise step sounded in the corridor outside, and the door of the room opened to admit the correct figure of Mr. Blair. With a sheaf of papers in his hand he stood for a moment, adjusting his gold-rimmed pince-nez upon his elevated nose, and scrutinising at some length the three clerks now working under his severe eyes. His gaze eventually settled upon the sprawling form of Brodie from whose damp clothing the steam now rose in a warm, vaporous mist, and as he looked his glance became more disapproving; he cleared his throat warningly and strode forward, fluttering the papers in his grasp like feathers of his ruffled plumage. "Brodie," he began sharply, "a moment of your attention, please!"

Without changing his posture Brodie lifted his head from the desk and regarded the other mordantly:

"Well," he replied, "what is it this time?"

"You might get up when you address me," expostulated Blair. "Every other clerk does so but you. It's most irregular and unusual."

"I'm a kind o' unusual man, ye see; that's maybe the reason o' it," retorted Brodie slowly. "I'm just as well where I am! What is't you're wantin'?"

"These accounts," shot out the other angrily. "Do you recognise them? If you don't I may inform you that they represent your work—or so-called work! Every one of them is in error. Your figures are wrong the whole way through and your total is outrageously incorrect. I'm sick of your blundering incompetence, Brodie! Unless you can explain this I shall have to report the whole matter to my superior."

Brodie glowered from the papers to the other's starched and offended face, and, filled by a sense of the insupportable indignity of his position he replied sullenly, in a low voice:

"I did the best I could. I can do no more."

"Your best is not good enough, then," retorted Blair in a high, almost a shrill tone. "Lately your work has become atrociously bad and your behaviour is, if anything, worse. Your very appearance is lowering to the dignity of this office. I'm sure if Sir John knew he would never permit it. Why," he stuttered, choked by indignation, "already your breath is reeking with the smell of drink. It's abominable!"

Brodie sat quite still, his eyes lowered, his mind blurred, wondering if it were he, James Brodie, who remained passive under the insults of this primly insignificant creature. He saw himself leap up, seize the other by the throat, shake him within an inch of his life then hurl him, as he had hurled a man twice his size, ignominiously out of the door. But no, he was still sitting motionless upon his stool, muttering in a dull voice:

"My time is my own outside this place. I can use it how I like."

"You must come to this office in a fit condition to work," insisted Blair coldly. "You're a bad example to these young men here—the look of you is a slur on the whole place!"

"Leave my appearance alone, damn you," ground out Brodie with a sudden fierceness. "I'd rather be as I am than have your smug face on me."

"None of your impertinence, please," cried Blair, a flush rising to his pale countenance. "I'll report you for insolence."

"Well, leave me alone," cried Brodie, looking up from his crouched position on the desk like a wild animal, broken by captivity, but still ferocious. "Don't push me too far or it'll be the worse for ye."

A sense of the latent danger to himself in the other's wild eye restrained Blair from further disparaging comment but, thrusting the file of papers disdainfully upon Brodie's desk, he remarked icily:

"Let me have these corrected at once—faultless if you please—or I'll know the reason of it!" then, turning, he stepped formally out of the office.

With the closing of the door no outburst occurred, but the stillness of the room became more oppressive than any storm. Brodie sat like an effigy in stone turning over within his mind the insults he had just endured, feeling in his humiliation, that the combined glances of the other two were fixed upon him derisively. Out of the corner of his eye he observed a hand appear over the edge of his desk and silently remove the offending accounts and, although he knew that he was again being aided through the good-nature of his colleagues, the hard-hewn moroseness of his features did not relax. He sat thus for an interminable time without lifting his pen, observed, without speaking, the corrected documents slide back again in front of him, maintained his attitude of rigid indifference until the dinner-whistle blew at one o'clock; then he rose immediately from his stool, seized his hat, and walked quickly from the room. Some insults might be washed out in blood, but he now sought urgently, in a different manner, to eradicate the memory of his indignity.

When he returned, punctual to the hour, at two o'clock he was altered, as though some mysterious, benign influence had been at work upon him, potently dispersing his melancholy, smoothing the harsh outlines of his face, injecting into his veins a fluid gaiety which now coursed through him joyously, and emanated radiantly from his being.

"I'm here first, lads, ye see," he cried with a heavy facetiousness, as the two other clerks appeared together shortly after he had arrived, "and on the stroke of the clock too! But what do you mean by comin' in late. It's abominable. If you don't improve your blunderin' irregularity I'll report you to your superior—that pasty pie-face that was in here this mornin'." He laughed boisterously and continued: "Can you not take your example from me that's held up to you as such a paragon o' virtue?"

"You're in fettle now, Mr. Brodie," doubtfully replied one of the youngsters.

"And what for no'," he exclaimed. "I wouldna let a thing like what happened this forenoon put me down. Not on your life, my mannie. It was just the thought of other considerations that forbade me to wring the puir creature's stiff neck for him. You know," he continued confidentially, "he's aye been jealous o' the way I got into this office under his very nose, but I had the influence and he couldna prevent it." He drew his pipe from his pocket, rapped it noisily against the desk, and began to fill it.

"You're not goin' to smoke, Mr. Brodie," cried the first clerk, looking up from his ledger in some concern. "You know it's strictly forbidden."

Brodie glowered at him, swinging a little on his stool, as he answered:

"And who would stop me? I'll do as I like in here. A man like me shouldna have to beg and pray for permission to light his pipe." He effected this action now, defiantly, sucking noisily and flinging the spent match disdainfully upon the floor. Then, with a profound movement of his head, between puffs he resumed: "No! and I'm not agoin' to do it. Gad! if I had my rights I wouldna be sittin' in this rotten office. I'm far above this kind o' work, far above any kind o' work. That's true as death, but it just canna be proved, and I've got to thole things as best I can. But it doesna alter me. No! by God. No! There's many a man in this Borough would be glad to have the blood that runs in my veins." He looked round for approval but, observing that his listeners, tired of the stale recitation of his pretensions, had bowed their heads in a feigned indifference, he was displeased; none the less he turned their defection to account by producing a small, flat bottle from his hip, quickly applying it to his lips, and stealthily returning it to his pocket. Thus refreshed he continued, as though unconscious of their lack of attention: "Blood will tell! There's nothing truer than that. I'll come up again. It's nothing but a lot of rotten jealousy that's put me here; but it'll not be for long. Ye can't keep a good man down. I'll soon be back again where folks'll recognise me again for what I am, back at the Cattle Show rubbin' shoulders with the Lord Lieutenant o' the County and on the best o' terms—equal terms mind ye"—he emphasised this to the air by a jerk of his pipe—"ay, on equal terms with the finest blood in the county, and with my name standin' out brawly in the paper amongst them all." As he viewed the future by regarding the glory of the past his eye moistened, his lower lip drooped childishly, his breast heaved, and he muttered: "God! that's a grand thing to happen to a man."

"Come on now, Mr. Brodie," entreated the other clerk, breaking in upon his meditation, "put away your pipe now you've had a smoke. I don't want to see you getting into trouble."

Brodie glowered at him for an instant then suddenly guffawed:

"Man, you're awfu' feared. True enough, it's as you say. I've had a smoke, but I'm goin' to have another—and more than that—I'm goin' to have a dram as well!" He slyly produced the bottle again and, whilst they watched him with startled eyes, partook of a long pull. Instead of returning the flask to his pocket he stood it before him on top of his desk, remarking: "Ye'll be handier for me there, hinny, and I can look at ye as well, and watch ye goin' down inch by inch." Then, flattered to find himself the focus of their anxious stares, he continued: "Speakin' of trouble—there's one thing that little runt said to me this mornin' that was so ridiculous it's stuck in my head." He frowned prodigiously at the very memory. "I think I mind of him sayin' 'the look o' ye is a slur on the whole place'—ay, that was it—these were his very words. Now tell me, lads—what the devil was he talkin' about? Is there anything wrong with my appearance?" He glared at them with a bellicose mien whilst they shook their heads from side to side, doubtfully. "I'm a fine-lookin' man, am I not!" he shot at them, watching their silent assent with a large and exaggerated approval. "I knew it," he cried. "It was just his measly spite. Ay! I was always a grand upstandin' figure of a man, well set up, with a skin on me as clear as a bairn's. Besides," he continued, looking at them sideways, craftily, as he stroked the coarse stubble on his sallow chin with a rustling sound, "there's another reason why I know he's wrong. Ye're maybe ower young to hear but it's no harm to tell ye that a certain lass—ay, the bonniest in Levenford, puts me first abune everybody else. Odd, I maun have a drink at the very thought of her." He drank a toast with decorous solemnity in honour of the loveliest lady in Levenford, and was for some time silent whilst he considered her happily. He wanted to talk about her, to boast proudly of her attractions, but a shadow of restraint held him back and, searching with contracted brows amongst the recesses of his mind for the reason of his reserve, a sudden illumination shone upon him. He became aware that he could not speak more freely about her because she was not his wife. At this startling realisation of his mused brain he silently reviled himself for his negligence. "Losh," he muttered to himself, "ye havena acted fair, man. Ye should have thought on this before." He shook his head deprecatingly, took another swig of spirits to assist his meditations, and a profound pathos for the plight of Nancy seized him as he whispered in a maudlin tone: "I believe I'll do it. By God! I will do it for her." He almost shook hands with himself at the nobility of the sudden resolution he had formed to make an honest woman of her. True, she was not of much consequence in the social scale, but what of it, his name would cover her, cover them both, and if he married her he would, in one magnificent gesture, keep her more securely in the house, put himself right in the eyes of the town, and still for ever these sad, questioning glances which he had observed from time to time on Nessie's face. He banged his fist on the desk, crying out: "I'll do it! I'll mention it this very night," then, grinning at the strained faces before him he remarked, with an assumption of lofty rectitude: "Don't be alarmed, lads. I've just been planning out things and I've just decided to do something for my wee Nessie. She's well worth it." Then, lowering his elevated tone, he leered at them cunningly and added: "A little matter of domestic policy that you're sure to hear of sooner or later." He was about to enlighten them more lucidly when one of the clerks, perceiving perhaps in advance the drift of the revelations that might follow, hurriedly sought to deflect his attention by exclaiming:

"And how is Nessie getting on, Mr. Brodie?"

He blinked for a moment at the questioner before replying:

"Fine! Ye know she's gettin' on fine. Dinna ask stupid questions, man. She's got the Latta in her pocket already." Then, launching out on this fresh subject that now presented itself to his muddled mind he continued: "She's a great comfort to me is that lass. To see her puttin' a spoke in that young Grierson's wheel time after time is a rich treat to me. She always beats him ye know, and every time she does it, it must be gall and wormwood to that smooth sneakin' father o' his. Ay! Gall and wormwood it must be!" He sniggered at the very reflection of it and, with a more acute tilt of the bottle to his mouth, was emptying it completely of its contents when, failing in the attempt to laugh and drink simultaneously, he choked and burst into a prolonged fit of hoarse coughing. "Pat my back, damn ye," he gasped with congested face and running eyes as he bent forward, heaving like a sick and emaciated elephant. "Harder! Harder!" he cried as one of the others, leaping from his stool, began to thump his bowed back.

"That's a nasty cough," said the young fellow when the paroxysm had finally abated. "That's what comes of sitting in damp clothes."

"Bah! it wasna a hoast at all—that," replied Brodie, wiping his face with his sleeve. "I've never wore a coat yet and I never will. I've lost my umbrella somewhere, but it doesna matter, the rain aye seems to do me good. I'm strong as a Clydesdale stallion," and he extended his gaunt structure to show them the manner of man he was.

"Nessie doesn't take after you, Mr. Brodie," remarked the first speaker. "She doesna look too strong!"

Brodie glowered at him, exclaiming angrily:

"She's as sound as a bell. Are you another o' these safties that are aye trying to make out folks to be ill. She's as right as the mail I tell you. She had a wee bit turn last month, but it was nothing. I had her at Lawrie and he said she had a heid on her in a thousand—ay, in a million, I would say!" He glanced round triumphantly, looked to the bottle to express his elation, but, observing that it was empty, seized it and with a fortunate aim hurled it into the waste-paper basket in the corner—whence it was later retrieved and cast into the Leven through the charity of one of his long-suffering colleagues. "That's an aim for ye," he cried gaily. "I've got an eye in my head! I could bring down a running rabbit at fifty paces without a blink. A rabbit! Damnation! If I was where I should be I would be at the butts bringing down the grouse and the pheasants like droppin' hailstones." He was about to embark once more on the nobility of his estate when suddenly his eyes fell upon the clock. "Gad! would ye believe it. It's nearly five o'clock. I'm the man to pass the hours away." He cocked his eye facetiously, snickered, and resumed: "Time passes quick when you're workin' hard, as that stickit whelp Blair would say. But I'm afraid I must leave ye, lads. Ye're fine fellows and I'm gey an' fond o' ye, but I've something more important to attend to now." He rubbed his hands together in a delightful anticipation and added, with a leer: "If the fancy man comes in before five just tell him his accounts are in order and say I've gone to buy him a rattle." He got off his stool ponderously, slowly assumed his hat, adjusting it twice before the tilt of its dusty brim pleased him, picked up his heavy stick and stood with a gravity now definitely drunken, framing the doorway with his swaying bulk. "Lads!" he cried, apostrophising them with his stick, "if ye knew where I was goin' now, the eyes would drop out your heads for pure jealousy. You couldna come, though. No! No! There's only one man in this Borough could gang this bonnie bonnie gait." Surveying them impressively he added, with great dramatic gusto: "And that's me!"—swept their forbearing but disconcerted faces with a final glare and swung slowly out of the room.

His star was in the ascendant, for as he strode noisily along the passages, bumping from side to side in his erratic career, he met no one and, at five minutes to five, shot through the main swing doors into the open and set his course for home.

The rain had now ceased and the air came fresh and cool in the darkness through which the newly lighted lamps shimmered upon the wet streets, like an endless succession of topaz moons upon the surface of black, still water. The regular repetition of these reflections, each one of which seemed to float insidiously towards him as he walked, amused Brodie monstrously, and he grinned as he told himself he would assuredly inform Nancy of his experience with this strangely inverted celestial phenomenon. Nancy! He chuckled aloud at the consideration of all they had to talk of to-night, from the composition of a real stinger of a letter for that one in London to the delicious proposition which he had determined to put before her. She would of course be perturbed to see him return with perhaps—and he admitted this magnanimously to the darkness—a heavier dram in him than usual, but the sudden delight at his offer of matrimony would dispel all her annoyance. He knew she had always wanted an established position, the randy, such as a fine man like him could give her, and now he heard her overwhelmed voice exclaiming: "Do ye mean it, Brodie! Losh! man, ye've fair sweepit me away. Marry ye? Ye know I would jump at the chance like a cock at a groset. Come till I give ye a grand, big hug." Yes! she would be kinder to him than ever after this sublime concession on his part, and his eyes flickered at the thought of the especial manifestations of her favour which this should elicit from her to-night. As he advanced, warmly conscious that each staggering step took him nearer to her, he could find no comparison strong enough to adequately describe her charm, her possessing hold upon him. "She's—she's bonnie!" he muttered inarticulately; "the flesh o' her is as white and firm as the breist of a fine chicken. I could almost make a meal o' her." His thoughts grew more compelling, served to intensify his longing, to add to his excitement, and with a final rapid struggle he launched himself up the steps of his house, fumbled impatiently at the lock with his key, opened the door, and burst into the obscurity of the hall. "Nancy," he cried loudly, "Nancy! Here I am back for ye!" He stood for a moment in the darkness awaiting her answering cry, but, as she did not reply, he smiled fatuously to think that she should be hiding, waiting for him to go to her, and taking a box of matches from his pocket, he lit the lobby gas, planted his stick firmly in the stand, hung up his hat, and went eagerly into the kitchen. This, too, was in darkness.

"Nancy," he shouted, in astonishment not unmixed with annoyance, "what are ye playin' at? I don't want a game o' blind man's buff. I want none o' these fancy tricks, woman! I want you. Come out from wherever ye be." Still there was no response, and, advancing awkwardly to the gas-bracket above the mantelpiece he lit this gas, turned to survey the room, and to his amazement observed that the table was not laid, that no preparation for tea had been begun. For a moment he remained quite still, fixing the bare table with an astounded gaze, compressing his lips angrily, until suddenly a light seemed to break in upon him and he muttered slowly, with a loosening of his frown: "She's awa' to the station with that aunt of hers. Has not she the nerve though? She's the only body that would dare to do it. Sends me out for my dinner and then keeps me waitin' for my tea." A faint thrill of amusement ran through him, deepening to a roar of laughter as he contemplated, almost proudly, her hardihood. Gad, but she was a fit mate for him! Yet when his mirth had subsided he did not quite know what to do, presumed eventually that he must await the pleasure of her return and, standing with his back to the fireplace, he allowed his gaze to wander idly round the room. To him, the very atmosphere breathed of her presence; he saw her flitting airily about, sitting nonchalantly in his armchair, smiling, talking, even flighting him. Yes! the very hat-pin sticking into the dresser was an indication of her own saucy, impudent, inimitable indifference. But something else lay upon the dresser, held in place by that pin, a letter—that presumptuous communication which he had received at breakfast-time from his daughter—and moving forward he took it up disdainfully in his hands. Suddenly his expression changed, as he observed that it was not the same envelope but another, addressed to him in his son's sloping clerkly hand, a penmanship so like Matt's own smooth plausibility that it had always irritated him. Another letter! and from Matthew! Was the sly, sneaking coward so afraid of him now that he must write his messages instead of delivering them face to face like a man? Filled by a profound contempt he gazed at the neat writing on the envelope which, however, became modified as, tilting his head to one side he considered inconsequently how well his own name looked —almost as well as in print—in these precise characters now before him. James Brodie, Esquire! It was a name to be proud of, that one! Smiling a little, a large and lordly appreciation swept over him, restoring him again to complacency and, in the excess of his own satisfaction, he carelessly tore open the letter and pulled out the single sheet within.

"Dear Father," he read, "You were too high and mighty to hear about my new post or you would have learned that it was a position for a married man. Don't expect Nancy back. She's come to see that I don't fall off my horse! Your loving and obedient son, Matt."

Seized by a vast stupefaction he read over the scanty words twice, looked up, unseeingly, as he muttered incredulously: "What does he mean? What has Nancy got to do with the fool's horse? Your loving and obedient son—the man must be mad!" Then suddenly, blindingly, he felt that he too was mad, as the purport of the note penetrated his dull, fuddled brain, as he observed upon the back of the paper, scrawled in Nancy's childish, illiterate hand these words: "Matt and me are off to be married and have a high old time. You were too fond of your bottle to marry me so you can take it to bed with you the night. You auld fool!"

A great cry burst from his lips. At last he understood that she had left him. The letter faded from his sight, the room swung round and away from him, he was alone in a vast immensity of blackness. Out of his distorted face his wounded eyes gazed dumbly from below his brow, now corroded by the full knowledge of his loss. Matt, his own son, had taken Nancy from him! In the shock of his despair he felt it would have been better far had he been killed outright by that pistol bullet in the house in the Vennel, that this blow his son had delivered was more frightful, more agonising than death! His weakling and despised son had triumphed over him. Complete understanding of the deception to which he had been subjected in the past week flashed upon him—Nancy's indifference, followed by her assumed yet restrained affection, the locking of her door, the fictitious relation at Overton, the complete obliteration of Matthew from the house—he understood all, remembered, too, the scene where he had surprised them in the kitchen, when she had broken the cup at the very moment that he questioned his son about the post. God! what a fool he had been. "An auld fool!"—that was what she called him, and how she must have laughed at him, how they must both be mocking him now. He knew nothing, neither how they had gone nor where they had gone. He was powerless, knowing only that they were together, powerless except to stand and think of them in an inconceivable intimacy which made him writhe with anguish.

He was recalled from his dark oblivion, like an insensible man to whom consciousness momentarily returns, by the voice of Nessie who, entering the kitchen, gazed fearfully at him and murmured, timidly:

"Will I make some tea for you, father? I've not had any tea or any dinner either."

He lifted his tortured face, looked at her stupidly, then cried, thickly:

"Go away! Go to the parlour. Go to your lessons. Go anywhere, but let me alone!"

She fled from him and he sank again into the torment of his thoughts, filled by a profound self-pity as he realised that there was now no one to look after him or Nessie but his dotard and incapable mother. She would have to come back—Mary, his daughter! He would have to allow her to return and keep the house, if only for Nessie's sake. Mary must now come back! The full significance of his discussion of this matter with Nancy struck him like a fresh blow as he recollected how he had coaxed her to write the letter of refusal. And she had known all the time that she was leaving him. He had been too late with his offer of marriage; and now, how would he ever do without her? A piercing anguish took him as he thought of her, even now, in his son's arms, opening her lips to his kisses, offering her firm, white body gladly to his embrace. As though vainly to obliterate the torture of the vision, he raised his hand and pressed it upon his throbbing eyes, whilst his lips twisted painfully and a hard, convulsive sob burst from his swelling breast and echoed through the quiet of the room.

V

THE three-twenty train from Glasgow to Ardfillan, the first half of the journey accomplished successfully, had left Overton behind, and traversing the low, dripping, smoke-filled arches of Kilmaheu Tunnel, emerged into the breezy March afternoon with a short, triumphant whistle, that sent a streamer of steam swirling behind the engine like a pennant, and presently began to coast gently down the slight incline of the track, which marked the approach to Levenford Station. The train was lightly laden, having many of its carriages empty and several with but one passenger in each and, as though conscious of having achieved the sharp ascent of Poindfauld and traversed the dark, grimed caverns of Kilmaheu, it now proceeded at an easier and more leisured pace through the soft, dun countryside across which the railway track advanced like a long, narrowing furrow.

Within the train, alone in a compartment, in a corner facing the engine, and with the small portmanteau that constituted her entire luggage beside her, sat a girl. Dressed in a plain, grey costume of serviceable, inexpensive serge, shaped to a neat yet unfashionable cut, and wearing upon her dark, close-coiled hair a grey velvet hat relieved only by a thin, pink ribbon gathered at one side into a simple bow, she remained upright yet relaxed, directing her gaze out of the window, viewing eagerly, yet wistfully, each feature of the fleeting landscape. Her face was thin, the nose straight and fine, the nostrils delicate, the lips sensitive and mobile, the smooth, pale sweep of the brow accentuated by the dark, appealing beauty of her eyes; and upon the entire countenance lay a melancholy sweetness, a pure and clarified sadness, as though some potent, sorrowful experience had stamped upon every lineament the subtle yet ineradicable mark of suffering. This faint, sombre shadow which lightly touched, accentuating even, the dark beauty of the face, made her seem more mature than her actual age of twenty-two years and gave to her an appearance of arresting delicacy, of refined sincerity which was intensified by the severe simplicity of her apparel. Like the face, but in a different sense, her hands, too, immediately engaged attention, as, denuded of gloves, which lay upon her knee, they rested lightly, palm upwards, passive upon her lap. The face was that of a madonna but the hands, red, conspicuous, coarse-grained, and slightly swollen, were the hands of a servant; and if it was suffering which had sublimated the face to a more exquisite beauty, the hands spoke eloquently of bitter toil that had blemished them into this pathetic, contrasting ugliness.

As she gazed intently out of the window she remained quiescent, passive as her own work-worn hands, yet across her sensitive features a faint excitement quivered which betokened the inner agitation of her turbulently beating heart. There, she thought, was the Mains Farm, its brown, furrowed fields lapped by the wind-beaten, crested waters of the Estuary, its stack-yard a square, yellow patch against the low, white-washed huddle of the homestead; there, too, was the weathered pile of the Linten Lighthouse, and, equally unchanged, the blue, massive outlines of the Rock itself; there, against the sky, the long, skeleton tracery of the Latta Shipyards, and, now, swinging into view, the sharp, stippled steeple of the Borough Hall. Affected by the touching familiarity of all that she saw, she considered how unaltered everything was, how permanent, secure, and solid. It was she, Mary Brodie, who had changed, and she now longed wistfully to be as she had been when she had lived in these surroundings, before the branding iron of circumstance had set its seal upon her. As she meditated thus, with a sudden, wrenching pang like the tearing open of a wound, she observed the Levenford Cottage Hospital where for two months she had lain facing death, where, too, her infant child had died; and, at the sudden poignant reminder, the serenity of her countenance broke and though no tears flowed— they had all been shed before—her lips quivered painfully. She marked the window through which her fixed eyes had ceaselessly sought the sky, the gravel walk flanked by laurel bushes along which she had directed the first, flagging steps of her convalescence, the very gatepost to which she had then clung, fluttering and exhausted from the feebleness of her state. She willed the train to stop that she might linger with her memories, but it bore her quickly away from this sad reminder of the past and, circling the last bend, gave to her spasmodic, transient glimpses of Church Street, a line of shops, the Public Library, the Cross, then swept her into the Station itself.

How small the platform seemed, with its diminutive waiting-rooms and insignificant wooden ticket office, yet when she had once stood in this same station to take the train for Darroch she had, in the agitation of her adventure, trembled at its very magnitude; and, indeed, she trembled now as she realised that she must leave the solitary seclusion of her compartment and venture forth into the public gaze. She stood up firmly, gripping her portmanteau, and although a faint colour tinged her checks, she set her soft lips into the mould of fortitude and stepped bravely out upon the platform. She was back again in Levenford after four years!

To the porter who approached, she surrendered her bag with instructions that it should be delivered to her at the next round of the station van and, having given up her ticket, she descended the short flight of steps to the street and set out with a throbbing bosom for her home. If she had been beset by memories in the train, now they rushed in upon her with an overpowering force, and it seemed to her as if each step she took brought before her some fresh remembrance to further strain her already bursting heart. There was the Common, fringed in the distance by the Leven; here was the school she had attended as a child; and, as she passed the portals of the Public Library, still guarded by the same swing doors, she became aware that it was here, on this very spot, that she had first met Denis. The thought of Denis brought no pang, no bitterness, but now merely a sad regret, as though she felt herself no longer his beloved nor yet the victim of his love, but only the helpless puppet of an irresistible destiny.

While she proceeded along Railway Road she observed coming towards her a woman whom she had known in the days before her banishment, and she settled herself for the wound of a sharp, contemptuous glance; but no glance came, no sharp wound, for the other drew near and passed her with the placid countenance of complete unrecognition. How much I must have changed, thought Mary sadly, as she entered Wellhall Road, and, coming upon Dr. Renwick's house, she wondered with a curious detachment if he, too, might find her changed should she ever encounter him. He had been so good to her, that even to pass this dwelling moved her strangely. While she did not consider the fact that he had saved her life, as though this were of slight importance, she remembered vividly the letters he had written her—first when she had gone to London and later to inform her of her mother's illness and subsequently of her death—all filled with a kind and unmistakable sympathy. She might never have returned to Levenford but for these letters, for, had she not received the second, she would not have written home and Nessie would never have known her address to send her that frantic appeal. Poor, frightened Nessie! Thoughts of her sister and of her father now invaded her, and as she drew near to her home, with the memory of the night on which she had left it stamped like an indelible background upon her mind, she became outwardly agitated; the calm, long-set tranquillity of her appearance was at last melted by the warm, surging currents set racing by the unwonted action of her fast-beating heart.

Again she felt herself tremble at the prospect of meeting her father; she shuddered slightly as, of her own volition, she moved towards the oppressive influence of the dwelling which had once contained her like a prisoner.

When, finally, she reached her home, it was with a shock that she observed the outer aspect of the house, wondering, in her first bewilderment, if it were she who viewed it with different eyes, but in a moment, noting more intently the subtle, individual alterations which gave it an appearance at once slovenly and sordid. The windows were dirty, with such curtains as veiled them soiled and draggled, with blinds hanging unevenly; in the turret one small window was open and uncovered, the other completely shuttered, like a closed eye, so that the face of the tower winked at her with a fixed, perpetual leer. The clean, grey stone of the frontage was stained by a long, irregular, rusty smear, drawn by the rush of water from a broken gutter, and straggling across the house face like a defilement; the gutter sagged, a slate drooped drunkenly from the straight line of the eaves, whilst the courtyard in front was empty, unraked, and green with weeds.

Startled by these slight but revealing variations which so transfigured the exterior of the house, and stirred with a sudden fear of what she might discover within, Mary moved quickly up the steps and rang the bell. Her trepidation increased as she stood for a long time waiting, but at last the door opened slowly and she beheld, against the dimness beyond, the thin, unformed figure of Nessie. The sisters looked at each other, exclaimed together "Nessie!" "Mary!" then, with a mingling cry rushed into each other's arms.

"Mary! Oh, Mary!" Nessie cried brokenly, unable in her emotion to do more than repeat the name, and clinging to her sister in utter abandon. "My own, dear Mary!"

"Nessie! dear Nessie!" whispered Mary, herself overcome by an excess feeling, "I'm so happy to see you again. I've often longed for this when I've been away."

"You'll never leave me any more, will you, Mary?" sobbed Nessie. "I've wanted you so much! Hold me tight and never let me go."

"I'll never leave you, dearie! I've come back just to be with you!"

"I know! I know!" wept Nessie. "It's good of you to do it, but oh! I've needed you sorely since Mamma died. I've had nobody! I've been frightened!"

"Don't cry, dearest," whispered Mary, drawing her sister's head against her breast and gently stroking her brow. "You're all right, now. Don't be frightened any more."

"You don't know what I've come through," cried Nessie frantically. "It's like heaven to see you back; but it's a wonder I'm here at all."

"Hush! dearie, hush! I don't want you to upset yourself and be ending up with a sore, wee head."

"It's my heart that's been sore," said the younger sister, turning up her red-lidded, burning eyes. "I didn't love you enough when I had you, Mary, but I'll make up for it. Everything's so different now. I need you so much I'll do anything, if you'll just bide with me."

"I'll do that, dear," replied Mary consolingly. "Just dry your eyes and you can tell me all about it. Here's my handkerchief for you!"

"It's just like old times for you to give me this," sniffed Nessie, releasing her sister's arm, taking the proffered handkerchief, and applying it to her wet face. "I was aye losing mine." Then as her sobs subsided and she regarded her sister from a slight distance she exclaimed, suddenly: "How bonnie you've got, Mary! There's a look about your face that makes me want never to take my eyes off you."

"It's just the same old face, Nessie."

"No! you were always bonnie, but now there's something seems to shine out of it like a light."

"Never mind about me," replied Mary tenderly. "It's you I'm thinking of, dear. We'll need to see about putting some flesh on these thin arms of yours. You've been needing someone to look after you."

"I have, indeed," answered Nessie pathetically, looking down at her own unsubstantial form. "I can't eat anything. We've had such bad food lately. It was all because of that—that——" She threatened to break down again.

"Hush, pettie, hush—don't cry again," whispered Mary. "Tell me some other time."

"I can't wait to tell you," cried Nessie hysterically, her words coming in a rush. "My letter told you nothing. We've had a terrible woman in the house and she's run away with Matt to America. Father was nearly out of his head and he does nothing but drink from mornin' till night and oh! Mary! he's driving me on to study so much that it's just killing me. Don't let him do it, Mary—will you? You'll save me, won't you, Mary?" and she held her hands out beseechingly towards her sister.

Mary stood quite still; the torrent of the other's speech had overwhelmed her. Then she said, slowly: "Is father changed, Nessie? Is he not good to you now?"

"Changed!" whimpered Nessie. "He's so changed you wouldn't know him. It frightens me to see him sometimes. When he's not had whisky he's like a man walkin' in a dream. You wouldn't believe the change in everything"—she continued with a rising voice, and, seizing her sister's arm, she began to draw her towards the kitchen—"you wouldn't believe it unless you saw it. Look here! Come and see the sight of this room," and she flung open the door widely as though to demonstrate visibly the extent of the alteration in the circumstances of her life.

Mary stood dumbly envisaging the frowsy room, then she looked at Nessie and said, wonderingly:

"Does father put up with this?"

"Put up with it!" cried the other; "he doesn't even notice it, and he looks worse even than this room, with his clothes hanging off him, and his eyes sunk away, down in his head. If I try to lay a finger on the place to clear it up he roars my head off and keeps shouting at me to get on with my work and threatens me in all manner of ways, simply scares me out of my wits."

"Is it as bad as that, then?" murmured Mary, almost to herself.

"It's worse," cried Nessie, mournfully, looking up at her sister with wide eyes. "Grandma does the best she can, but she's near helpless now. Nobody can manage him. You and me better go away somewhere quick before anything happens to us." Her attitude seemed to entreat her sister to fly instantly with her from the ruins of their home. But Mary shook her head, and speaking firmly, cheerfully, said:

"We can't run away, dear. We'll do the best we can together. I'll soon have the place different for you," and, advancing to the window she threw it up and let a gust of the cool, sharp wind come rushing in the room. "There, now; we'll let the breeze in for a little, while we have a walk in the back, then I'll come in and straighten things out." She took off her hat and coat and, laying them on the sofa, turned again to Nessie, put her arm round the other's thin waist, and drew her out of the back door into the outer air.

"Oh, Mary!" cried Nessie ecstatically, pressing her side close against her sister as the two began to walk slowly up and down, "it's wonderful to have you back. You're so strong, I've an awful faith in you. Surely things will go right now." Then she added inconsequently: "What's been happening to you? What have you been doing all this time?"

Mary held out her free hand for a moment.

"Just using these," she said lightly; "and hard work never killed anybody, so here I am."

The younger girl looked with a shocked gaze at the rough calloused palm, seared by a deep white scar; and turning her eyes upwards remarked, wonderingly:

"What gave you that big mark? Was it a cut ye got?"

A quick expression of pain flitted across Mary's face as she replied:

"That was it, Nessie; but it's all better now. I told you never to mind about your stupid old sister. It's wee you we're to think about."

Nessie laughed happily, then stopped short in amazement.

"Would ye believe it!" she exclaimed, in an awestruck tone; "that was me laughin'—a thing I haven't done for months. Goodness! I could be downright happy if it wasn't for the thought of all the work for that old Bursary exam." She shivered exaggeratedly. "That's the worse thing of any."

"Will you not get it?" asked Mary solicitously.

"Of course I will!" exclaimed the other with a toss of her head. "I mean to get it all right, just to show them all—the way some of them have behaved to me at school is a disgrace. But it's father. He goes on about it and worries me to death. I wish he would only leave me alone." She shook her head and added, in an old-fashioned tone that might have been her mother's voice: "My head's like to split the way he raves at me sometimes. He's got me away to a shadow."

Mary looked commiseratingly at the fragile form and thin precocious face beside her and, squeezing her sister's puny arm reassuringly, she said:

"I'll soon get you all right, my girl. I know exactly what to do, and I've a few tricks up my sleeve that might surprise you."

Nessie turned, and using a favourite catchword of their childhood, remarked, with an assumption of great simplicity:

"Is it honky-tonky tricks you've got up there, Mary?"

The sisters gazed at each other, while the years fell away from them, then suddenly they smiled into each other's eyes, and laughed aloud together, with a sound which echoed strangely in that desolate back garden.

"Oh! Mary," sighed Nessie rapturously "this is better than I expected. I could hug you, and hug you. You're lovely. I've got my bonnie, big sister back. Was it not brave of me to write and ask you to come back? If he had found me out he would have taken my head off. You'll not let on it was me though, will you?"

"No, indeed," cried Mary fondly, "I'll not say a word."

"He'll be in soon," said Nessie slowly, her face falling again at the thought of her father's imminent return. "You know all about—about his comin' to work in the Yard I suppose."

A faint colour suffused Mary's cheeks as she answered:

"Yes! I heard about it, just after Mamma's death."

"Such a come down!" said Nessie in a precocious tone. "Poor Mamma was well out of it. It would have finished her if the other hadn't." She paused, and sighed, adding with a sort of sorrowful comfort: "I would like us to go up and put some flowers on her grave some day soon. There's not a thing on it—not even an artificial wreath."

A silence now came between the sisters whilst each followed her own thoughts, then Mary started, and said: "I must go in and see to things, dear. I want to get everything ready. You wait here in the air, for I think it'll do you good. Wait and see how nice I'll have everything for you."

Nessie gazed at her sister doubtfully.

"You're not going to run away and leave me?" she demanded, as though she feared to allow Mary out of her sight. "I'll come in and help you."

"Nonsense! I'm used to this work," replied Mary. "Your business is to stay here and get an appetite for tea."

Nessie loosed her sister's hand, and as she watched her go through the back door cried, warningly:

"I'll keep my eye on you through the window to see you don't go away."

Inside the house, Mary set to work to restore cleanliness and some degree of order to the kitchen and, having assumed an apron which she discovered in the scullery, and directing her activities with the precision of experience, she quickly burnished and blackened the grate, lit the fire and swept the hearth, scrubbed the floor, dusted the furniture, and rubbed the window panes to some degree of brightness. Then, searching for the whitest table cover she could find, she spread this upon the table and commenced to prepare as appetising a tea as the scanty contents of the larder would permit. Standing there by the stove, flushed and a little breathless from the rapidity of her exertions, she seemed to have sloughed off the intervening years and—as though she had never suffered the bitter experiences of her life—to be again a girl engaged in getting ready the evening meal of the household. While she remained thus, she heard a slow shuffling tread in the lobby followed by the creak of the kitchen door as it swung open, and turning, she observed the bowed and decrepit figure of old Grandma Brodie come hobbling into the room, diffidently, uncertainly, like a spectre moving among the ruins of its past glory. Mary left the stove, advanced, and called: "Grandma!"

The old woman looked slowly up, presenting her yellow, cracked visage with its sunken cheeks and puckered lips, and, staring incredulously, as though she too observed a phantom, she muttered at length: "Mary! it canna surely be Mary." Then she shook her head, dismissing the evidence of her aged eyes as unthinkable, removed her gaze from Mary, and with an indeterminate step moved towards the scullery, whispering to herself:

"I maun get some tea thegither for him. James' tea maun be got ready."

"I'm getting the tea, Grandma," exclaimed Mary; "there's no need for you to worry about it. Come and sit in your chair," and taking the other's arm she led her, tottering but unresisting, to her old seat by the fire, into which the crone subsided with a vacant and unheeding stare. As Mary began, however, to journey to and fro from the scullery to the kitchen and the table assumed gradually an appearance such as it had not borne for months, the old woman's eye became more lucid and looking from a plate of hot pancakes, steaming and real, to Mary's face, she passed her blue-lined, transparent hand tremulously over her brows and muttered: "Does he know you're back?"

"Yes, Grandma! I wrote and said I was coming," replied Mary.

"Is he goin' to let you bide here?" croaked the other. "Maybe he'll put ye out again. When was that? Was it before Marg'et deed? I canna think. Your hair looks unco' bonnie that way." Her gaze then faded and she seemed to lose interest, murmuring disconsolately as she turned towards the fire: "I canna eat so weel without my teeth."

"Would you like a hot pancake and butter?" asked Mary in a coaxing tone.

"Would I no'!" replied the other instantly. "Where is't?" Mary gave the old woman her pancake, saw her seize it avidly and, crouching over the fire, begin eagerly to suck it to its destruction. Suddenly she was aroused from her contemplation by a whisper in her ear:

"Please, I would like one too, Mary dear!" Nessie had come in and was now presenting a flatly suppliant palm, waiting to have it covered by the warm solace of a new-made pancake.

"You'll not have one, you'll have two," cried Mary recklessly. "Yes! as many as you like. I've made plenty."

"They're good," exclaimed Nessie appreciatively. "Good as good! You've made them so quick too, and my word what a change you've made in the room! It's like old times again! as light as a feather! That's the way my mother used to make them, and these are just as good, ay, better than we used to get. Yum—yum—they're lovely!"

As Mary listened whilst Nessie talked on in this fashion and watched her quick, nervous gestures as she ate, she began to study her more intently than she had hitherto done, and slowly an impression of vague but deep uneasiness stole in upon her. The facile, running speech of her sister, the jerky and slightly uncontrolled movements perceptible now on her closer observation, seemed to betoken a state of unconscious nervous tension which alarmed her, and as she traced the thin contours of the other's growing body and noted her faintly hollowed cheeks and temples she said, involuntarily:

"Nessie, dear, are you sure you're feeling all right?"

Nessie stuffed the last of the pancake into her mouth before she replied, expressively:

"I'm getting better and better—especially since I've had that. Mary's pancakes are good but Mary herself is better." She chewed for a moment then solemnly added: "I've felt real bad once or twice, but I'm right as the mail now."

Her sudden idea was, of course, mere nonsense, thought Mary, but nevertheless she determined to use every effort in her power to obtain for Nessie some respite from the studies which seemed, at least, to be overtaxing the inadequate strength of her immature frame. A strong feeling, partly from love of her sister, but chiefly from a strong maternal impulse towards the other's weakness, gripped her, and she laid her arm protectingly round Nessie's narrow shoulders, drew her close and murmured, warmly: "I'll do my best for you, dear. I really will. There's nothing I wouldn't do to see you look happy and well."

Whilst the sisters stood together thus the old woman raised her head from the fire and, as she considered them, a sudden, penetrating insight seemed to flash through the obscurity of her senile mind, for she remarked sharply:

"Don't let him see ye like that. Don't hing thegither and show you're so fond o' one another in front of him. Na! Na! he'll have no interference wi' Nessie. Let her be, let her be." The edge in her voice was blunted as she uttered these last words, her gaze again became opaque and, with a slow, unconcealed yawn she turned away, muttering: "I'm wantin' my tea. Is it not tea time yet? Is't not time for James to be in?"

Mary looked interrogatively at her sister and the shadow fell again on Nessie's brow as she remarked, moodily:

"You can infuse the tea. He'll be in any minute now. Then you'll see for yourself—the minute I've finished a cup it'll be the signal for me to be shoved off into the parlour. I'm tired to death of it."

Mary did not reply but went into the scullery to infuse the tea, and filled now by a sudden, private fear at the immediate prospect of meeting her father, the unselfish consideration of her sister slipped for the moment from her mind and she began to anticipate, tremblingly, the manner of his greeting. Her eyes, that were fixed unseeingly upon the steamy clouds issuing from the boiling kettle, flinched as she recollected how he had kicked her brutally as she lay in the hall, how that blow had been in part responsible for the pneumonia which had nearly killed her, and she wondered vaguely if he had ever regretted that single action, if he had, indeed, even thought of it during the four years of her absence. As for herself, the memory of that blow had lived with her for months; the pain of it had lasted during the long delirium of her illness, when she had suffered a thousand savage kicks from him with each stabbing respiration; the indignity had remained until long afterwards, when she would lie awake at night, turning in her mind the outrage upon her body of the inhuman impact of his heavy boot.

She thought again of these thick-soled boots which she had so often brushed for him, which she would, in her voluntary servitude, brush for him again, and as she remembered, too, the heavy tread which had habitually announced his entry, she started, listened, and once again heard his foot in the hall, slower, even sluggish, less firm, almost dragging, but still her father's step. The moment which she had foreseen, had visualised a thousand times, which, though she dreaded it, was of her own seeking, was upon her and, though she shook in all her limbs, she turned and advanced bravely, but with a fluttering heart, to meet him.

They came face to face in the kitchen, where the man who had come in looked at her silently, swept the room, the table, the brightly burning hearth with his dark eye, then returned his glance to her. Only when he spoke did she know actually that it was her father, when his old bitter sneer distorted his furrowed visage and he said:

"You've come back then, have ye?" and walked without further speech to his chair. The devastating change in him, such a change that she had failed almost to recognise him, shocked her so profoundly that she was unable to speak. Could this be her father, this old, shrunken man with his unkempt hair, his stained, untidy clothing, his morose unshaven face, his wild, wretched, malignant eye. Nessie had been right! She could not have believed the magnitude of this change until she had seen it, and even now she could scarcely credit the evidence of her eyes. In a dazed manner she moved herself forward and began to pour out and hand round the tea and, when she had accomplished this, she did not sit down with the others, but remained standing, waiting to serve them, still filled with an incredulous dismay at her father's dreadful appearance. He, on his part, continued to ignore her and to partake of his meal silently, with a careless, almost slovenly manner of eating, apparently regardless of what he consumed or the fashion in which he consumed it. His glance was distrait, oblique, and when it assumed a cognisance of his surroundings, it fell not upon her, but always upon Nessie, as though some rooted conception of his brain was centred upon her, making her the focus of his conscious attention. The others, too, ate without speaking and, although she had not yet had the opportunity to address her father, to break that period of silence now four years long, she passed quietly out of the kitchen into the scullery where she remained intent, listening, and perturbed. When she had determined to sacrifice herself for Nessie's sake and return home she had envisaged herself in combat with an oppression of a different nature, loud, hectoring, even savage, but never with such a strange, inhuman preoccupation as this which she now felt to have possessed her father. His strong and virile character seemed, like his flesh, to have crumbled from him, leaving a warped structure of a man engrossed with something, she knew not what, which had mastered him and now controlled each thought, each action of his body.

She had been in the scullery only a few minutes, considering him thus, when to her straining ears came the harsh, different sound of his voice, saying:

"You've finished, Nessie! You can get into the parlour and begin your work now!" Immediately she steeled herself and re-entered the kitchen, and, observing Nessie rising in a sad, dejected manner with a cowed look in her eyes to obey his command, at the submission of the child she felt a sudden rush of courage within her and in a quiet voice she addressed her father.

"Father, could Nessie not come for a walk with me before she begins her work?"

But he might have been deaf to her words, and utterly oblivious of her presence, for any evidence which he manifested of having heard or seen her, and continuing to look at Nessie, he resumed, in a harder tone:

"Off with you, now. And see you stick into it. I'll be in to see how you're getting on."

As Nessie went humbly out of the door Mary bit her lip and flushed deeply, finding in his silent contempt of her first words to him, the realisation of how he proposed to treat her.—She could be there, but for him she would not exist! She made no comment, but when he had arisen from the table, and the old woman, too, had finished and gone out of the room, she began to clear away the dishes into the scullery, observing as she passed in and out of the kitchen, that he had taken a bottle and glass from the dresser and had settled himself to drink steadily, with an appearance of habitual exactitude as though he proposed to continue imbibing regularly for the course of the entire evening.

She washed and dried the dishes, cleaned and tidied the scullery, then, with the intention of joining Nessie in the parlour, she entered the kitchen and was about to pass through it, when suddenly, and without looking at her. Brodie shouted from his corner in a fierce, arresting tone:

"Where are you going?"

She halted, looking at him appealingly as she replied:

"I was only going in to see Nessie for a moment, father—not to speak —only to watch her."

"Don't go, then," he shot at her, still fixing his eye upon the ceiling and away from her. "I'll do all the watching of Nessie that's required. You'll kindly keep away from her."

"But, father," she faltered, "I'm not going to disturb her. I haven't seen her for so long, I like to be near her."

"And I like that you shouldn't be near her," he replied bitterly.

"You're not the company I want for my daughter. You can cook and work for her and for me too, but keep your hands off her. I'll brook no interference with her or with the work she's set on." This indeed was what she expected, and asking herself why she had come back if it were not to succour Nessie, she stood firmly contemplating him with her quiet gaze, then, mustering all her courage, she said:

"I'm going to Nessie, father," and moved towards the door.

Only then he looked at her, turning the full force of his malignant eyes upon her, and, seizing the bottle by his side he drew himself to his feet and advanced slowly towards her.

"Move another step towards that door," he snarled, "and I'll smash your skull open"; then as though he hoped that she might disobey him he stood confronting her, ready to swing fiercely at her head. She retreated, and as she slipped back from him he watched her sneeringly, crying: "That's better. That's much better! We'll have to teach ye manners again, I can see. But by God! keep away from Nessie and don't think *you* can fool me. No woman living can do that now. Another step and I would have finished ye for good." Then, suddenly his ferocious manner dropped from him and he returned to his chair, sat down and, sinking back into his original air of morose and brooding apathy, he resumed his drinking, not apparently for the achievement of gaiety, but as though in a vain, despairing endeavour to obtain oblivion from some secret and unforgettable misery.

Mary sat down at the table. She was afraid to leave the room. Her fear was not physical, not for herself, but for Nessie, and had she not been concerned solely for her sister, she would a moment ago have advanced straight into the threatening sweep of the weapon with which her father had menaced her. Life was of little value to her now, but nevertheless she realised that if she were to help Nessie from the frightful danger which threatened her in this house, she must be not only brave, but wise. She saw that her presence and, indeed, her purpose in the house would mean a bitter perpetual struggle with her father for the possession of Nessie, and she felt that her own resources were insufficient to cope with this situation to which she had returned. As she sat there watching Brodie soak himself steadily, yet ineffectually, in liquor, she determined to seek assistance without delay, and planned carefully what she would do on the following day. When her conception of what she must do lay clearly defined in her mind, she looked around for something to occupy her, but could find nothing—no book to read—no sewing which she might do, and she was constrained to remain still in the silence of the room, gazing at her father, yet never finding his gaze upon her.

The evening dragged slowly on with lagging hours until she felt that it would never end, that her father would never move, but at last he got up and saying, coldly: "You have your own room. Go to it, but leave Nessie alone in hers," went out and into the parlour, where she heard his voice, questioning, admonishing Nessie. She put out the light and went slowly upstairs to her own, old room where she undressed and sat down to wait, hearing first Nessie come up, then her father, hearing the sounds of their undressing, finally hearing nothing. Silence filled the house. She waited a long time in this small room where she had already known so much waiting and so much bitter anguish. Fleeting visions of the past rushed before her, of her vigils at the window when she gazed so ceaselessly at the silver trees, of Rose—where was she now? —and the throwing of the apple, of the storm, of her discovery, and in the light of her own sad experience she resolved that she would save Nessie from unhappiness, even at the sacrifice of herself, if it lay within her human power. At this thought she arose noiselessly, opened her door, crept across the landing without a sound, passed into Nessie's room, and slipped into bed beside her sister. She folded her arms around the cold, fragile figure of the child, chafing her frigid feet, warming her against her own body, stilling her sobs, comforting her in endearing whispers and at last soothing her into sleep. There, holding in her embrace the sleeping form of her sister, she remained awake long into the night, thinking.

VI

MARY looked at the picture, which hung in solitary distinction against the rich, deep red background of the wall of the room, with a rapt contemplation which removed her momentarily from the anxiety and confusion which beset her. She stood, her clear profile etched against the window beyond, head thrown back, lips faintly parted, her luminous eyes fixed absorbedly upon the painting out of which breathed a cool, grey mist that lay upon still, grey water, shrouding softly the tall, quiet trees—as silvery as her own trees—and sheathing itself around the thin, immobile wands of the rushes which fringed the pool; she was elevated from the confusion of mind in which she had entered this house, by the rare and melancholy beauty of the picture which, exhibiting with such restraint this passive mood of nature, seemed to move from out its frame and touch her like a reverie, like a sad yet serene meditation upon the sorrow of her own life.

So engrossed was she by her consideration of the picture, which had caught her eye as she sat embarrassed, amongst the tasteful furnishings of the room, so moved from her conflicting feelings by the strange, appealing beauty of the painting which had compelled her to rise involuntarily to stand before it, that she failed to observe the smooth movement of the polished mahogany door as it swung open upon its quiet hinges; nor did she observe the man who had entered the room, and who now gazed at her pale, transfigured profile with a sudden intentness, as silent and as entranced as her own contemplation of the picture. He stood as motionless as she did, as though afraid to break the spell which her appearance had laid upon him, but regarding her with pleasure, waiting, too, until she should have filled her eyes enough with the loveliness of the placid pool.

At last she withdrew her glance, sighed, turned unconsciously and, again raising her dark eyes, suddenly perceived him. Immediately all her dispelled confusion rushed back upon her, heightened now to the point of shame, and she flushed, hung her head as he advanced towards her and warmly took her hand.

"It is Mary," he said, "Mary Brodie come back again to see me."

With a great effort she forced her disconcerted gaze upwards, looked at him, and replied, in a low tone:

"You remember me, then. I thought you would have forgotten all about me. I've—I've changed so much."

"Changed!" he cried. "You haven't changed, unless it's that you're bonnier than ever! Tut! Don't look so ashamed of it, Mary. It's not a crime to look as lovely as you do."

She smiled faintly at him as he continued, cheerfully: "As for forgetting you, how could I forget one of my first patients, the one who did me most credit, when I was struggling along with nothing in this very room but the empty packing case that my books had come in."

She looked round the present rich comfort of the room and, still slightly discomposed, she replied, at a tangent to her main thoughts:

"There's more than that here now, Dr. Renwick!"

"You see! That's what you've done for me," he exclaimed. "Made my name by your pluck in pulling through. You did the work and I got the credit!"

"It was only the credit you got," she replied slowly. "Why did you return the fee I sent you?"

"I got your address from the letter—you that ran away without saying good-bye," he cried; "that was all the fee I wanted." He seemed strangely pleased to see her and strangely near to her, as though four years had not elapsed since he had last spoken to her, and he still sat by her bedside compelling her back to life by his vital animation. "Tell me all that you've been doing," he ran on, endeavouring to put her at her ease. "Wag your tongue! Let me see you haven't forgotten your old friends."

"I haven't forgotten you, doctor, or I wouldn't be here now. I'll never forget all that you've done for me."

"Tuts! I don't want you to wag the tongue that way! I want to hear about yourself. I'm sure you've got all London on its knees before you by this time."

She shook her head at his words and, with a faint humour lurking in her eyes, replied:

"No! I've done the kneeling myself—scrubbing floors and washing steps!"

"What!" he cried, in amazed concern. "You haven't been working like that?"

"I don't mind hard work," she said lightly. "It did me good; took my thoughts away from my own wretched troubles."

"You were never made for that sort of thing," he exclaimed reproachfully. "It's scandalous! It was downright wicked of you to run away as you did. We would have found something more suitable for you to do."

"I wanted to escape from everything, then," she answered sadly. "I wished help from no one."

"Well, don't do it again," he retorted with some asperity. "Will you rush away like that again, without saying good-bye to a man?"

"No!" she replied mildly.

He could not forbear to smile at her air of submission as he motioned her to sit down and, drawing a small chair close up beside her, said:

"I have been forgetting such manners as I have to keep you standing like this, but really, Miss Mary, it is such a sudden and unexpected pleasure to see you again! You must be lenient with me." Then after a pause he asked, "You would get my letters? They were dismal reminders of this place were they not?"

She shook her head.

"I want to thank you for them. I would never have known of Mamma's death if you hadn't written. These letters brought me back."

He looked at her steadily and replied:

"I knew you would come back some day. I felt it." Then he added, "But tell me what has actually brought you back?"

"Nessie! my sister Nessie!" she said slowly. "Things have been dreadful at home and she has suffered. She needed me—so I came home. It's because of her I've come to see you. It's a great liberty on my part after you've done so much for me already. Forgive me for coming! I need help!"

"Tell me how you wish me to help you and I'll do it," he exclaimed. "Is Nessie ill?"

"Not exactly ill," said Mary, "although somehow she alarms me; she is so nervous, so easily excited. She laughs and cries by turns and she has got so thin, seems to eat so little. But although it worries me I really did not come about that." She paused for a moment gathering courage to tell him, then continued, bravely: "It is about my father. He treats her so peculiarly, not unkindly, but forcing her so unreasonably to work at her lessons, to study all the time, not only at school, but the whole long evening—and every evening. She is shut up by herself and made to 'stick in' as he calls it, so that she will win the Latta Bursary. He has set his mind on that. She tells me that he throws it at her head every time she sees him, threatening her with all manner of penalties if she fails. If he would leave her alone she would do it in her own way, but he drives and drives at her and she is so fragile I am afraid of what is going to happen. Last night she cried for an hour in my arms before she went to sleep. I am very anxious!"

He looked at her small, sad, earnest face, was filled with a quick vision of her comforting and consoling her sister, thought suddenly of the child which, despite his every effort, had been lost to her, and with a grave face answered:

"I can see you are anxious, but it is a difficult matter to interfere in. We must consider it. Your father is not actually cruel to her?"

"No! but he terrifies her. He used to be fond of her, but he is so changed now, that even his fondness is changed to something strange and terrible."

He had heard, of course, the stories concerning Brodie's altered habits, but forbore to question her more deeply on this particular point and, instead, he exclaimed:

"Why is he so eager for her to win the Latta? It's usually a boy that wins that—is it not—never a girl?"

"That may be the reason," replied Mary sadly; "he's always been mad for some unusual kind of success to bring credit on himself, always wanted Nessie to do well because of his own pride. But now I'm certain he doesn't know what he'll do with her when she's won it. He's shoving her on to no purpose."

"Is young Grierson in the running for the Bursary?" queried Renwick, after a moment's consideration. "Your father and Grierson are not exactly on good terms I believe."

Mary shook her head.

"It's deeper than that I'm sure," she answered. "You would think the winning of it was going to make father the envy of the whole town the way he talks."

He looked at her comprehendingly.

"I know your father, Mary, and I know what you mean. I'm afraid all is not right with him. There was always something—— Well—I've come across him in the past too——" he did not say that it had been chiefly on her behalf, "and we have never agreed. There would be little use in my going to see him if, indeed, it were permissible for me to do so. Any direct action of mine would serve only to aggravate him and make his conduct worse."

As she sat observing him while, with an abstracted gaze, he pondered the question, she thought how wise, how kind and considerate he was towards her, not rushing blindly, but reasoning coherently on her behalf; her eyes moved slowly across his strong dark face, vital yet austere, over his spare, active, and slightly stooping form until they fell at length upon his hands, showing sensitive, strong, and brown against the immaculate, white bands of his starched linen cuffs. These firm, delicate hands had probed the mysteries of her inanimate body, had saved her life, such as it was, and as she contrasted them in her mind with her own blotched and swollen fingers she felt the gulf which separated her from this man whose help she had been bold enough to seek. What exquisite hands! A sudden sense of her own inferiority, of her incongruity amongst the luxury and taste of her present surroundings afflicted her, and she diverted her eyes quickly from him to the ground, as though afraid that he might intercept and interpret her glance.

"Would you care for me to see the Rector of the Academy about Nessie?" he asked at length. "I know Gibson well and might in confidence ask his assistance in the matter. I had thought at first of speaking to Sir John Latta, but your father is engaged at the office of the shipyard now and it might prejudice him there. We doctors have got to be careful of what we are about. It's a precarious existence——" He smiled. "Would you like me to see Gibson, or would you rather send Nessie to me to let me have a look at her?"

"I think if you saw the Rector it would be splendid. He had a great influence with father once," she replied gratefully. "Nessie is so frightened of father she would be afraid to come here."

"And were you not afraid to come?" he asked, with a look which seemed to comfort her with its knowledge of her past fortitude.

"Yes," she answered truthfully. "I was afraid you would refuse to see me. I have no one to ask for help for Nessie but you. She is so young. Nothing must happen to her!" She paused, then added in a low tone: "You might not have wished to see me. You know all about me, what I have been!"

"Don't! Don't say that, Mary! All that I know of you is good. I have remembered you for these years because of your goodness, your gentleness, and your courage." As he looked at her now he would have added: "and your loveliness," but he refrained and said, instead: "In all my life I never met such a sweet, unselfish spirit as yours. It graved itself unforgettably upon my mind. I hate to hear you belittle yourself like that."

She flushed at the warm comfort of his words and replied:

"It's like you to say that, but I don't deserve it. Still, if I can do something for Nessie to make up for my own mistakes I'll be happy."

"Are you an old woman to talk like that! What age are you?" he cried impetuously. "You're not twenty-two yet. Good Lord! you're only a child, with a whole lifetime in front of you. All the pain you've suffered can be wiped out—you've had no real happiness yet worth the name. Begin to think of yourself again, Mary. I saw you looking at that picture of mine when I came in. I saw how it took you out of yourself. Make your life a whole gallery of these pictures—you must amuse yourself—read all the books you can get—take up some interest. I might get you a post as companion where you could travel abroad."

She was, in spite of herself, strangely fascinated by his words and, casting her thoughts back, she recollected how she had been thrilled in like fashion by Denis, when he had opened out entrancing avenues for her with his talk of Paris, Rome, and of travel through wide, mysterious lands. That had been a long time ago, when he had moved horizons for her with a sweep of his gay, audacious hand and whirled her abroad on the carpet of his graphic, laughing speech. He read her thoughts with a faculty of intuition which confounded her and said, slowly:

"You still think of him, I see."

She looked up in some slight dismay, divining that he misjudged the full tendency of her emotion, which was merely a retrospective sadness, but, feeling that she could not be disloyal to the memory of Denis, she did not speak.

"I would like to do something for you, Mary," he resumed quietly, "something which would make you happy. I have some influence. Will you allow me to find some post which is suited to you, and to your worth, before I go away from here."

She started at his words, bereft suddenly of her warm feeling of comfort, and stammered:

"Are you going away, then?"

"Yes," he replied, "I'm off within six months. I'm taking up a special branch of work in Edinburgh. I have the chance to get on the staff there—something bigger than the Cottage Hospital. It's a great opportunity for me."

She saw herself alone, without his strong resolute support, vainly endeavouring to protect Nessie from her father, interposing her own insignificant resolution between Brodie's drunken unreason and her sister's weakness, and in a flash she comprehended how much she had built on the friendship of this man before her, understood how great was her regard for him.

"It's splendid for you to have got on so well," she whispered. "But it's only what you deserve. I know you'll do as well in Edinburgh as you've done here. I don't need to wish you success."

"I don't know," he replied, "but I shall like it. Edinburgh is the city to live in—grey yet beautiful. Take Princes Street in the autumn with the leaves crackling in the gardens, and the Castle russet against the sky, and the blue smoke drifting across Arthur's Seat, and the breeze tingling, as clean and crisp as fine wine. No one could help but love it." He glowed at the thought of it and continued: "It's my native place of course—you must forgive my pride.—Still, everything is bigger there —finer and cleaner, like the air."

She followed his words breathlessly, seeing vividly the picture that he drew for her, but filling it always with his own figure, so that it was not only Princes Street which she saw but Renwick, striding along its grey surface, against the mellow background of the Castle Gardens.

"It sounds beautiful. I have never been there but I can picture it all," she murmured, meaning actually that she could picture him there.

"Let me find something for you to do before I go away " he persisted; "something to take you out of that house."

She could feel that he was anxious for her to accept his offer, but she thrust the enticing prospect away from her, saying:

"I came back of my own choice to look after Nessie! I couldn't leave her now. It's been a terrible life for her for the last few months and if I went away again anything might happen to her."

He perceived then that she was fixed upon remaining and immediately a profound concern for her future disturbed him, as if he saw her already immolated on the altar of her own unselfishness, a sacrifice, despite his intervention, to the outrageous pride of her father. What purpose had it served for him to save her, to have helped her to escape from death, were she to drift back once again into the same environment, the same danger in a more deadly form? He was affected even to the point of marvelling at his own emotion, but quickly masking his feelings he exclaimed, cheerfully:

"I'll do my best for Nessie! I'll see Gibson to-day or to-morrow. Everything that I can do shall be done. Don't worry too much about her. Take more heed of yourself."

She felt when he said these words that the purport of her visit had been achieved and, diffident of occupying his time longer, she at once arose from her chair and prepared to go. He, too, got up but made no movement to the door, remaining silent, watching her face which, as she stood erect, was touched lightly by an errant beam of the pale March sunshine, so pale in the interior of the room, that it gleamed upon her skin like moonlight. Moved as another man had been moved by her in moonlight he caught his breath at the sight of her beauty, luminous in this light, showing against the foil of her indifferent and inelegant garments, and in his imagination he clothed her in satin of a faint lavender, visioned her under the silver radiance of a soft Southern moon in a garden in Florence or upon a terrace in Naples. As she poised her small foot in its rough shoe courageously towards her departure, he wished strangely to detain her, but found no words to utter.

"Good-bye," he heard her say, softly. "Thank you for what you have done for me, now, and before."

"Good-bye," he said mechanically, following her into the hall, realising that she was going. He opened the door for her, saw her move down the steps and with the sudden sense of his deprivation he responded to an appeal within him and called out hurriedly, awkwardly, like a schoolboy: "You'll come and see me again soon, won't you?" Then ashamed of his own clumsiness he came down the steps to her and proffered an explanation of his remark, exclaiming: "When I've seen Gibson I'll want you to know what the outcome is to be."

Again she looked at him gratefully and, exclaiming: "I'll come next week," entered the road and walked rapidly away.

As he turned and slowly re-entered his own house he became gradually amazed at his own recent action, at his sudden outspoken request that she should revisit him shortly; but although, at first, he somewhat ashamedly attributed this to the poignant appeal of her beauty in the light that had encircled her in his room, later he more honestly admitted to himself that this was not the sole reason of his conduct. Mary Brodie had always been for him a strangely beautiful figure, a noble, courageous spirit, who had woven her life through his existence in the town with a short and tragic thread. From the moment when he had first seen her unconscious, in the sad predicament of her condition, and against the gross contamination of her surroundings, like a lily uprooted and thrown on the dung hill, he had been drawn to her in her helplessness and immaturity; later he had been fired by her patience and uncomplaining fortitude during her long period of illness and in the suffering visited upon her by the death of her child; he had seen too, and clearly, that, though she had been possessed by another, she was pure, chaste as that light which had recently encompassed her. His admiration and interest had been aroused and he had promised himself that he would assist her to rebuild her life, but she had run from the town the moment her strength had permitted, fluttering away from the net of opprobrium which she must have felt around her. During the years of her absence he had, from time to time, thought of her; often the memory of her figure, thin, white, fragile, had risen before him with a strange insistent appeal, as if to tell him that the thread of her life would return to weave itself once more into the texture of his existence. He sat down at his desk, considering her deeply, praying that there would be no further tragedy in this return of Mary Brodie to the house of tribulation from which she had been so grievously outcast. After a few moments his thoughts moved into another channel, and from a pigeon-hole in his desk he drew out an old letter, the writing of which, now slightly faded after four years' preservation, sloped in rounded characters across the single page. He read it once more, this, her only letter to him, in which she had sent him some money, the pathetic accumulation, no doubt, of her meagre wages, in an attempt to recompense him in some degree for his service to her. With the letter clasped in the fine tapering fingers of his hand he remained staring in front of him, seeing her working as she had now told him she worked, upon her knees, scrubbing, washing, scouring, performing the menial duties of her occupation—working like a servant.

At length he sighed, shook himself, restored the letter to the desk, and observing that he had a full hour before his afternoon consultations were due to begin, determined to visit the Rector of the Academy at once, to enquire discreetly into the condition of Nessie Brodie. Accordingly, having instructed his housekeeper that he would return before four o'clock he left the house and walked slowly towards the school, wrapped in a strange and sober meditation.

It was but a short way to the Academy, that old foundation of the Borough which lay within the town, backing a little from Church Street to exhibit the better the severe, yet proportioned architecture of its weathered front, and now, in the paved space that lay before it, displaying proudly the two high-wheeled Russian guns captured at Balaclava by Maurice Latta's company of the Winton Yeomanry. But Renwick, when he shortly reached the building, passed inside without seeing its frontage or its guns; mounting the shallow, well-worn stone stairs he advanced along the passage, tapped with a preoccupied manner at the head master's door and, as he was bidden, entered.

Gibson, a youngish-looking man for his position, whose face was not yet completely set into the scholastic mould, was seated at his littered desk in the middle of the small book-lined study, and he did not at once look up, but, an engrossed yet unpedantic figure in his smooth suit of dark brown—a colour he habitually affected—continued to observe a document that lay in front of him. Renwick, a faint smile finally twisting his grave face at the other's preoccupation, remarked whimsically, after a moment:

"Still the same earnest student, Gibson," and as the other looked up with a start, continued, "it takes me back again to the old days to see you grinding at it like that."

Gibson, whose eye had brightened at the sight of Renwick, lay back in his chair and, motioning the other to sit down, remarked easily:

"I had no idea it was you, Renwick. I imagined rather one of my inky brigade trembling in the presence, awaiting a just chastisement. It does the little beggars good to keep them in awe of the imperial dignity."

A smile passed between them that was almost as spontaneous as a grin of their schooldays, and Renwick murmured:

"You're the very pattern of old Bulldog Morrison. I must tell him when I get back to Edinburgh. He'd appreciate the compliment."

"The humour of it, you mean," cried Gibson, surveying the past with a distant eye. "Gad! how I wish I were going back to the old place like you! You're a lucky dog." Then fixing his glance on the other suddenly, he remarked: "You haven't come to say good-bye, already?"

"No! No! man," returned Renwick lightly. "I'm not off for six months. I'm not leaving you in the wilderness yet awhile." Then his face changed and he contemplated the floor for a moment before raising his gaze to Gibson and resuming seriously: "My errand is a peculiar one, I want you to treat it in confidence! You're an old friend, yet it is hard for me to explain what I'm about." He again paused, and continued with some difficulty: "You have a child at school here that I am interested in—even anxious about. It is Nessie Brodie. I'm indirectly concerned about her health and her future. Mind you, Gibson, I haven't the least right to come here like this. I'm well aware of that, but you're not like a board of governors. I want your opinion and, if necessary, your help."

Gibson looked at the other intently, then away again, but he made no enquiry as to Renwick's motive and instead replied, slowly:

"Nessie Brodie! she's a clever child. Yes! very intelligent, but with a curious turn of her mind. Her memory is marvellous, Renwick; you could read her a whole page of Milton, and she would repeat it almost word for word; her perception, too, is acute, but her reasoning, the deeper powers of thought, are not proportionate." He shook his head. "She's what I call a smart pupil, quick as a needle, but with, I'm afraid, some pervading shallowness in her intellect."

"She's going up for the Latta," persisted Renwick. "Is she fit for it—will she win it?"

"She may win it," replied Gibson with a shrug of his shoulders, "but to what purpose! And indeed I can't say if she will do so. The matter is not in our hands. The standards of the University are not school standards. Her vocation is teaching—after a Normal education."

"Can't you keep her back, then?" remarked Renwick, with some slight eagerness. "I have information that her health is suffering from the strain of this preparation."

"It's impossible," returned the other. "As I've just said, the matter is out of our hands. It is a scholarship open to the Borough, set by the University authorities, and everyone may enter who is eligible. To be frank, I did drop a hint to her—her esteemed parent," he frowned here momentarily, "but it was useless. He's set on it grimly. And indeed she has such an excellent chance of winning that it sounds like pure folly to wish her to stand down. And yet——"

"What?" demanded Renwick.

In reply the other took the sheet of paper from his desk and, examining it for a moment, handed it to his friend, saying slowly:

"It is a strange coincidence, but I was studying this when you came in. What do you make of it?"

Renwick took the paper and, perceiving that it was a translation of Latin prose—Cicero, probably, he imagined—written in a smooth yet unformed hand, he began to read the free and ingenuously worded

404

rendering, when suddenly his eye was arrested. Interpolated between two sentences of the interesting and artless interpretation lay the words, written in the doric, and in a cramped and almost distorted hand: "Stick in, Nessie! What's worth doing is worth doing well. Ye maun win the Latta or I'll know the reason why"; then, the easy flow of the translation continued undisturbed. Renwick looked up at the other in astonishment.

"Sent along by her form master this morning," explained Gibson, "from Nessie Brodie's exercise book."

"Was this done at home or in school?" enquired the doctor sharply.

"In school! She must have written these words, unconsciously, of course, but none the less written them with her own hand. What does it mean?—some reversion to these famous Scottish ancestors we used to hear so much about from the old man. Or is it dual personality? —you know more about that sort of thing than I do."

"Dual personality be hanged!" retorted Renwick in some consternation. "This is a pure lapse of mind, a manifestation of nervous overstrain, induced, I'm positive from the nature of these words, by some strong force that has been driven into her. Don't you see, man. She became fatigued in the middle of this exercise, her attention wavered and instantly that something beneath the surface of her mind leaped up—tormenting her—forcing her on, so that, indeed, before she resumed coherently, she had unconsciously written this passage." He shook his head. "It reveals only too clearly, I'm afraid, what she fears!"

"We don't work her too hard here," expostulated Gibson; "she's spared in many ways!"

"I know! I know," replied Renwick. "The mischief is being done outside. It's that madman of a father she has got. What are we to do about it? You say you've spoken to him and I'm like a red rag to a bull where he's concerned. It's difficult," then, as he laid the paper again on Gibson's desk he added: "This really alarms me. It's a symptom that I've seen before to presage a thundering bad breakdown. I don't like it a bit."

"You surprise me," said the head master after a pause, during which he regarded his friend shrewdly. "Are you sure you're not taking an extreme view from—from prejudice perhaps?" then, as the other silently shook his head, he continued tentatively: "Would you like to see the child?—only for a moment of course—otherwise we'll alarm her."

The doctor considered for a moment, then replied, decisively:

"Indeed I would! I would like to see for myself. It's good of you to suggest it."

"I'll fetch her along, then," said Gibson, getting to his feet and adding, as he went to the door, "I know you'll not scare her! I want nothing of this slip in her exercise mentioned on any account."

Renwick agreed silently with a motion of his head, and when the other had gone out of the room remained motionless, his brow slightly bent, his eye clouded and fixed upon the writing across the square of paper, as though the strange, incoherent, intruding words had shaped themselves before his gaze into a vision which startled and distressed him. He was aroused by the return of the head master, now accompanied by Nessie, whom Renwick had never seen before, and now, as he observed her thin, drooping body, her mild placating eye, her white, fragile neck, the irresolution of her mouth and chin, he was not surprised that she desired to lean clingingly on Mary, nor that Mary on her part should desire to protect her.

"This is one of our prize pupils," said Gibson diplomatically, turning towards Renwick as he resumed his chair. "We show her off to all the visitors. She has the best memory in the upper school. Is that not so, Nessie?" he added, touching her lightly with his gaze.

Nessie flushed proudly, filled in her small spirit by a profound gratification and a deep awe, amongst which mingled, also, some confusion as to the obscure purpose which had compelled her suddenly before the combined majesty of Dr. Renwick and the Rector. She was, however, silent, and remained with lowered eyes, her thin legs shaking a little in her long well-worn boots and coarse woollen stockings—not from fear, but from the mere agitation of their imposing presence—knowing that the question had been rhetorical. Not for her to speak unless directly addressed!

"You're fond of your work?" enquired Renwick, kindly.

"Yes, sir," replied Nessie timidly, raising her eyes to his like a young and startled doe.

"Does it never tire you?" he continued mildly, afraid to shape his question in a more definite form.

She looked at the Rector for permission to speak, and reassured by his look, replied:

"No, sir! not much! I get a headache, sometimes." She announced this fact diffidently as though it might be a presumption on her part to have a headache, but she continued with more assurance: "My father took me to Dr. Lawrie about six months ago and he said it was nothing." She even added, naïvely: "He said I had a good head on me."

Renwick was silent, conscious of Gibson's slightly satiric eye upon him, yet although he felt the weak, evasive answers of this timid child to be as unreliable as the opinion of his pompous colleague, just quoted, his impression of Nessie's strained and over-driven nerves was further strengthened by her bearing.

"I hear you're going up for the Latta," he at length remarked. "Would you not like to wait another year?"

"Oh! no, sir! I couldn't do that," she replied quickly. "I must take it this year. My father has said——" a shadow fell and deepened upon her brow; she added more reticently, "He would like me to win it—and it's a great thing for a girl to win the Latta. It's never been done, but I think I can do it!" She again blushed slightly, not at this sudden exhibition of her own small self-complacency, but at her hardihood in making such a long speech before them.

"Don't work too hard, then," replied Renwick finally, turning towards Gibson to indicate that he had concluded his observations.

"That's right then, Nessie," said the head master, dismissing her with a cheerful glance. "Run away back to your form now! And remember what Dr. Renwick here has said. The willing horse never needs the spur. Don't overdo the homework."

"Thank you, sir," replied Nessie humbly, as she slipped out of the room, wondering vaguely in her mind what it had all been about, feeling, despite her uncertainty, that it had been a mark of honour for her to be singled out for attention like this, and—remembering warmly the encouraging look in his omnipotent eye—that she must stand high in the Rector's favour. It would, she considered, as she re-entered her classroom with a conscious air, give that impertinent and inquisitive young Grierson something to think about when he knew she had been hobnobbing with the Rector himself.

"I hope I didn't keep her too long," said Renwick, looking at his friend. "It was enough for me to see her."

"You were the epitome of discretion," replied Gibson lightly; "the governors will not throw me out for allowing my discipline to be tampered with." He paused, then added in the same tone: "She gave you a shrewd one about Lawrie."

"Pshaw!" replied Renwick. "To put it bluntly, 'It doesn't do to cry stinking fish,' but as one old friend to another I don't give a snap of the fingers for Lawrie's opinion. He's a pompous ass! That child is not right by a long way."

"Tuts! Renwick," remarked Gibson soothingly, "don't get a bee in your bonnet. I could see nothing wrong with the girl to-day. She's at a bad age and she's got a beastly old sot of a father, but she'll do, she'll do. You're exaggerating. You were always the incorrigible champion of the oppressed, even if it were an ailing, white mouse."

"That's what she is," replied Renwick stubbornly. "A little white mouse, and it might go hard with her if she's not watched. I don't like that cowed look in her eye."

"I was more struck by the neglected look of her," replied Gibson. "She's getting to be conspicuous in the school by it. Did you mark the poorness of her dress?—there's been a difference there in the last year or so, I can assure you. Brodie can't have a penny now but his wages, and most of that he spends on liquor. Strictly between ourselves too, I hear it rumoured that he's behind with the interest on his mortgaged house—that amazing chateau of nonsense of his. What's going to happen there, I don't know, but the man is rushing towards his ruin."

"Poor Nessie," sighed Renwick; but in his mind it was Mary that he visioned amidst the poverty and degradation of her home. It was impossible to judge from Gibson's expression if some vague glimmering of understanding, regarding his friend's motive in the matter, had dawned upon him; and indeed it might, for in the past he had heard him speak feelingly of the strange case of Mary Brodie; but now he patted him upon the shoulder, and remarked encouragingly:

"Cheer up, you miserable sawbones! It's not going to kill anybody. I'll see to that. I'll keep my eye on Nessie."

"Well," said Renwick at length, "it'll do no good to sit glooming here." He looked at his watch and arose from his chair. "I'm keeping you back and I've got my own work to attend to. It's almost four."

"Rich old ladies queueing up for you, you sly dog!" said Gibson quizzically. "What they see in that ugly face of yours I can't imagine!"

Renwick laughed as he replied:

"It's not beauty they want, or I'd refer them to you." He held out his hand. "You're a good sort, Gibson! I'll miss you more than anyone when I leave here."

"I wonder!" said the other as he pressed his friend's hand affectionately.

Renwick left the room quickly, but as he went down the shallow, stone steps, worn through the years by an endless succession of careless footsteps, and passed between the two grey Russian guns, setting his course along the road for his home, his pace insensibly diminished and his thoughts again grew heavy. "Poor Nessie!" He now saw the shrinking figure before him, enveloped by the soft, protecting arms of her sister who, shielding the child's drooping form by her own soft body, looked at him with brave, enduring eyes. As he passed along the street the vision grew in intensity, oppressing him, rendering somehow unattractive the stimulating prospect which had lately filled his mind, dulling the glamour of his new work in Edinburgh, blotting out the freshness of Castle Gardens and the romantic fortress piled against the sky, blunting the ever keen savour of the wind as he felt it sweep to him from off the Calton Hill. It was with a sombre face that he entered his own house and set himself to work.

VII

THE mild April day had advanced for one hour beyond its noontide and, filled by the fresh odours and soft, stirring sounds of the budding spring, lay upon the town of Levenford like a benison. But to Brodie, as at his dinner hour he walked along the road towards his home, there was no blessing in the sweet burgeoning around him. Filled with bitterness, he did not feel the caress of the gentle air or recognise in each new shoot the running sap within the trees; the yellow clumps of nodding daffodils, the white, elusive snowdrops, the glowing, mingled globes of crocuses, which ornamented the front gardens of the road, were by him unseen; the faint cawing of rooks as they circled around their new-built nest amongst the tall trees at the bend of the road was to him a jangle on his irritated ears. Indeed, as he reached these trees and the sound came to him more loudly he sent a venomous glance at the birds, muttering: "Damn their noise—they ring the lugs off a man. I could take a gun to them," when suddenly, as if in answer to his threat, a low-flying crow swept over him and with a derisive "caw-caw" dropped its excrement upon his shoulder. His brow gathered like thunder as he considered that the very birds had turned against him and defiled him; for a moment he looked as though he could have felled each tree, torn apart the nests, and destroyed every bird in the rookery; but with a wry twist of his lips he cleansed his coat with his handkerchief and, his mood set more bitterly, continued upon his homeward way.

The better conditions of his living since the return of Mary had made little difference in his appearance, for although she sponged and pressed his clothing, washed and starched his linen, and brushed his boots to a fine polish, he had now abandoned himself utterly at nights to the bottle with the result that his face had grown more veined, more sallow and sunken, and his neater dress hung upon his gaunt frame with the incongruity of a new suit upon a scarecrow. He looked, although he knew it not, a broken man, and since he had lost Nancy his disintegration had progressed at a more rapid pace. At first he had told himself fiercely that there were other fish in the sea as good as, and indeed, better than she, that he would quickly fill her place in his affections by another and a finer woman; but gradually, and with a cutting injury to his pride, he had been made to see that he was now too old and unattractive to compel the attention of women and, the lordly days of his overflowing purse being ended, that he had become too poor to buy their favour. He realised, too, after a short and resentful period of self-delusion, that it was his Nancy that he desired, that none other could replace her; she had wrapped herself around his flesh so seductively that in her absence he craved for her only, and knew that no one else would do. He drank to forget her, but could not. The whisky soaked his brain, deadened his vivid appreciation of his loss, but still, and even when he was drunk, tormenting pictures floated before his numbed mind, haunting him with visions of Nancy and Matt as they would be together in their new life. As he saw them, they were always together, and, although he cursed himself for the thought, happy, forgetful of him and of his past bearing on their lives; Nancy's laugh, and it was the laugh of an Aphrodite, echoed in his ears, evoked, not by his but by Matt's caresses, and as, with an agonising lucidity, he saw his son supplanting him in her affections his eyes would close, his look become helpless and livid.

At present, however, he was engrossed by another matter, not, let it be said, the offence of the crow, which had merely thrown another coal upon the fire of his resentment, but a greater and more personal affront; and his air was less apathetic than was usual in the public street, his manner more intent as he moved with an unusual rapidity towards his house.

He had a grievance to air and, as Nessie was the only person whom he now addressed with any freedom, and as the affair in some manner concerned her, it was she whom he now hastened to see. As he opened the front door and entered his home, his morose reticence was for the moment abandoned and he immediately called out:

"Nessie! Nessie!" He was in the kitchen before she could reply, and sternly regarded the startled eye that looked back at him from her half-turned head as she sat at table, a spoonful of her broth arrested in mid air, her whole attitude indicative of sudden apprehension. "Has that young whelp o' Grierson's said anything to you about the Latta?" he shot at her fiercely. She let the spoonful of soup splash back into her plate, as, thinking that mercifully his question was not so bad as she had expected, she shook her head nervously, and replied:

"No, father. At least nothing much."

"Think," he cried. "Think hard. What does nothing much mean?"

"Well, father," she quavered, "he's always saying something or another that's not nice about—about us. He sometimes sneers about me and the Latta."

"Did he ever tell you that you shouldna go in for it?" he demanded. "Answer me!"

"Oh! he would like me not to try for it, father," she replied, compressing her small lips. "I know that as well as anything. I suppose he thinks it would give him some small chance of it—not that he's got any."

His discoloured teeth came together, and he displayed them as his lips parted in a grin of wrath.

"So that's it!" he exclaimed. "I was sure o't. Ay, I was right!" He seated himself at table and, ignoring the steaming bowl which Mary silently placed before him, thrust his face close to Nessie's. "Say that again," he muttered.

"What, father?"

"About that pup o' Grierson's."

"That's he got no chance of the Latta?" she queried timidly; then seeing that she was pleasing him, she harmonised her mood to his and sniffed indignantly: "No! I should think not. He hasn't a ghost of a chance. Even if I didn't go in for it, there's others have as good a chance as he has. But he'll never git it while I'm about."

"You're the stumblin' block to him."

"Yes, indeed, father!"

"That's fine! That's fine!" he muttered, looking at her with dilated eyes. "God! it does me good to hear that." He paused. "Do ye know what happened to me as I was coming home to-day, like any other respectable townsman?" His nostrils quivered at the memory and his voice rose as he cried: "Yes, comin' home quietly and decently, when that blasted swine came up to me—Provost Grierson—our braw new provost—God! what they made a thing like him provost for beats me, he must have sneaked himself into the position—it's—it's a disgrace to the town. I suppose because he's the provost now he thinks he can do anything, for he had the damned insolence to accost me in the open daylight and tell me not to put you in for the Latta." He looked at her as though he expected her to swell visibly with indignation, and, feeling that some response was expected of her she replied, feebly:

"It was just jealousy, father, that was all!"

"Did I not tax him with that?" he cried. "I should think I did. I told him you had always beaten his measly pup and that you would do it again—and again—and again." He repeated the words in an exultant shout. "The damned cheek of the man to try and cadge the thing for his own son by askin' me to keep you back for another year. And when I flung that in his face he had the impudence to turn round and mealy-mouth me with talk of the dignity of his position, and about him bein' the spokesman of the Borough, saying that he had been told ye werena fit to go up—that you were not strong enough—that he was speakin' in your interests and not in his. But I had him." He clenched his fist in something of his old manner, as he exclaimed: "I had him on all points. I threw Lawrie's own words at his sleekit head. I had the whip hand o' him at every turn!" He laughed exultantly, but after a moment his face darkened and he muttered: "By God! I'll make him pay for it —ay, and for the other things he said to me as well. Why I didna level him to the street I canna think! But never mind—you and me will make him pay for't in other ways. Will we not, Nessie?" He gazed at her wheedlingly. "You'll knock that brat o' his into a cocked hat—will ye not, Nessie? and then we'll look at the grand, chawed look on his face. You'll do it—won't ye, woman?"

"Yes, father," she replied obediently, "I'll do it for ye."

"That's fine. That's real fine," he murmured rubbing his veined hands together in suppressed elation. Then suddenly, at some secret thought his expression grew black, and again thrusting his face into hers he exclaimed: "You better do it. By God! you better beat him. If you don't I'll—I'll grip that thin neck o' yours and fair strangle ye. You've got to win that Latta or it'll be the waur o' ye."

"I'll do it father! I'll do it!" she whimpered.

"Yes, you'll do it, or I'll know why," he cried wildly. "I tell you there's a conspiracy in this town against me. Every man's hand is turned against me. They hate me for what I am. They're jealous. They know that I'm away and above them—that if I had my rights I would wipe my dirty boots on the smug faces o' the lot of them. But never mind," he nodded his head to himself in a wild burst of unreason, "I'll show them yet. I'll put the fear o' me into them! The Latta will be the start o' it. That'll put a spoke in the Lord High Provost's wheel —then we'll begin in real earnest."

At this point Mary, who had been standing in the background, observing her father's paroxysm and his manner towards Nessie with an expression of acute anxiety, came forward and said coaxingly:

"Will you not take your broth before it gets cold, father? I took such pains with it. Let Nessie get hers too—she must eat up if she's going to study as hard as she does."

His exaltation was suddenly arrested at her words. His expression changed, as though something withdrew from it, retired quickly from open view into the hidden recesses of his mind, and he exclaimed angrily:

"What do you want to interfere for? Can you not leave us alone? When we want your advice we'll ask for it." He picked up his spoon and sullenly began his soup; then, after a while, as though he had been brooding on her effrontery in speaking, he exclaimed: "Keep your remarks about Nessie to yourself. I'll manage her my own way."

The meal proceeded for some time in silence, but, when they were partaking of the next simple course Brodie again turned to his younger daughter, and staring at her sideways began, in the ingratiating tone which he invariably adopted for this rote of questions and which, from constant repetition and the manner of his address, now excited her almost to the point of hysteria.

"And how did you get on to-day, Nessie?"

"Quite well, father!"

"Did anybody praise my own lass to-day? Come on now; somebody said something about you. It was your French to-day, was it not?"

She answered him mechanically, at random, anyhow—only to be rid of the nerve-racking necessity of formulating new and gratifying replies to his fatuous, yet pressing queries, of appeasing his insatiable demand for tangible evidence of her prowess, of the attention which his daughter was attracting at school. At length, when he had satisfied himself, although she on her part hardly knew what she had said, he lay back in his chair and, regarding her with a bland, proprietary eye, remarked:

"Good enough! Good enough for the Brodies! That was high praise for them to give us. You're doin' not so badly, woman! But ye maun do better. Better and better. Ye've got to make as sure o' that Latta as if it was lying on that plate in front o' ye. Guidsakes! just think on it. Thirty guineas every year for three years—that makes ninety guineas—or near enough to a hundred, golden sovereigns. There's a hundred, golden sovereigns lying there on that plate o' yours waiting to be picked up. Ye havena got to scramble for them, or stoop for them, you've just got to gather them up! God! if ye don't put these wee hands o' yours out to lift them I'll twist the heid off ye!" He looked at the empty plate before her, seeing it piled high with sovereigns, gleaming with the rich lustre of heaped gold, filled with a sum which in his reduced circumstances, seemed to him enormous. "It's a rich, rich prize," he murmured, "and it's yours! I could see it makes the greedy eyes o' that snipe Grierson drop out o' their sockets to think on it comin' into this house. I'll learn him to affront me in the main street of the town!" He was moved by a short, silent laugh that was like a sneer, then, looking again at Nessie, he lifted his eyebrows and, with a resumption of his absurdly arch manner, said in a tone of high confidence: "I'll be home early to-night, Nessie! We'll make a bend the minute we've finished our tea. Not a minute will we waste! We'll be on with our lessons before we've swallowed the last bite." He looked at her slyly, as he remarked: "You can be at it in the parlour, and I'll bide in here to see that not a soul disturbs ye. Quiet! Quiet! That's what ye want, and I'll see that ye have it. Ye'll have the quiet o' the grave!" He seemed pleased with the force of this comparison and repeated the last words impressively and sonorously. Then in a harder tone he added: "Ye maun stick to it! Stick in hard. Put your back into it. What ye do, do well. Remember you're a Brodie and set your teeth to win through with it." His task of exhortation for the moment completed, filled too, by a consciousness of worthy effort accomplished, he removed his eye from Nessie and allowed it to rest oppressively upon the face of his other daughter, daring her to interfere.

"What are you glowerin' at?" he demanded, after a moment. "Have I not told ye to keep out of the way when me and Nessie are speakin' together? When we want you we'll ask for you. I told you when ye entered this house again that you were to keep your paws off her, so see that you do it. I'm not wantin' her spoiled like her namby-pamby mother spoiled the rest o' ye."

She was about to leave the room, knowing this to be the most effectual manner of curtailing his resentment against her, when suddenly the front door bell rang loudly, and she paused at the unexpectedness of the occurrence. Such traffic as came to the house, chiefly from the tradesmen of the Borough, was to the back door, and for the front bell to ring thus was a rare event, so unusual now that Brodie looked sharply up, and exclaimed to her, after a moment:

"See what it is!"

She went to the door and opened it, revealing to her own gaze a messenger, who stood upon the steps of the porch bearing in his hand a medium-sized parcel, and who now touched his cap, saying interrogatively:

"Miss Mary Brodie?"

She nodded, her eyes fixed in some dismay upon the package which he was now apparently delivering into her hands and which, from the smooth brown paper and neat pink cord which enclosed it, she knew to be no ordinary parcel, no clumsily wrapped groceries from a local store, neither provisions nor anything which she had herself ordered, but a paragon of a parcel that she associated immediately in her mind with others bearing the same exclusive air, which had, at intervals, descended mysteriously upon her during the last month. But these other packages had invariably come in the middle of the forenoon, at a fixed hour when she was always alone in the house and now, with a sudden anxiety besetting her, she demanded of the messenger the strange question:

"Are you not late?"

He moved his feet uncomfortably, confirming the suspicion in her mind as he defended himself.

"I've had a lot of deliveries," he said. "This came from Glasgow. I had to wait on it." He was glad apparently to see her accept the package without rebuking him, and clattered off without further speech, leaving her supporting the light weight of the neatly corded box as though it pressed her down into an acute discomfiture. These consignments of delicacies which had regularly arrived for her—enigmatically, yet so safely and opportunely—and which she had lavished upon Nessie with an unquestioning delight—was this another? With a beating heart she slowly closed the door and, her brain moving actively, she slipped into the parlour, secreted the parcel under the sofa, and again re-entered the kitchen, hoping uneasily that her father would make no enquiry into the nature of the visitor. But she saw at once that this faint chance was impossible, that he was impatiently awaiting her return, even now lying back in his chair and fixing her with a large and curious eye.

"Who was that at the door?" Then at her silence he demanded: "Come along! What are ye standing so glaikit for? Who was it?"

"It was only a message boy, father," she replied quietly, essaying to render her voice composed.

"A message boy!" he repeated incredulously. "Coming to the front door of the house! Gad! what have we got to put up with next." Then, his anger rising at a sudden thought, he exclaimed: "I'm not going to sit down under that sort of insult. Who sent him? Tell me and I'll go in about it myself. Who was he from?"

"I don't know!" she faltered.

"Ye don't know!"

"No!" she answered and still using every effort to conciliate him, hastily added, "Never mind, father—it'll not occur again. Don't upset yourself."

He looked at her for a moment with a lowering eye, noting her suppressed air of embarrassment, faint, yet clearly to be perceived against the pervading candour of her expression.

"Show me the messages he brought," he ground out at her at length. "I didna see you bring them in!"

"They're in the parlour," she replied in a low tone, making as though to move into the scullery. "It's only a parcel—nothing you would want to see."

"Get me what he brought," he insisted. "Look sharp about it too. I've a notion to look at this strange, disappearing parcel."

"Oh! father!" she cried, "can you not believe me?"

"Get it!" he roared, "or I'll know that you're a liar as well as the other thing."

She saw that she must obey and, with a halting step, went out of the room and returned with the package in her hands.

He glared at it, surprised to find that there had, indeed, been a parcel but more astonished now at its unwonted appearance.

"Pink ribbon," he muttered. "Gad, that's rich!" Then changing his voice abruptly, he sneered: "Would ye have me believe they send out our oatmeal with these falderals on it. Open that box at once. I'll see with my own eyes what's inside."

She knew that it was useless to protest further, and, with the fatal calmness of inevitable discovery, she took a knife from the table, cut the string and, after a few seconds, drew from their enwrapping packing of wool a large and luscious bunch of black grapes. He stared at them incredulously as they hung suspended from her hand before his startled eyes. It was an exquisite cluster, hanging in the dull room like an exotic blossom, each fruit large, firm, and perfect, and powdered with a bluish bloom as delicate and seductive as the haze upon a distant landfall. They dangled temptingly upon their thick, smooth stalk, fragrant with a rich sun-drenched odour, filled to bursting with their soft, juicy flesh, ready to melt upon the tongue in a subtle mingling of sweet, succulent flavours. Black grapes at this time! An unheard of, expensive, out of season luxury!

"Where did these come from?" he cried in a loud hectoring voice.

"Who sent these?"

"I don't know, father," she answered truthfully, for, indeed, no note had ever accompanied these mysterious delicacies and she had only guessed vaguely, yet happily, that the sender had been Renwick.

"You do know, you slut," he roared at her; "or why should you hide them." As he looked at her in an angry, baffled fashion, the memory rose before him of the deputation of godly self-righteous women from the church who had called upon his wife during her illness to leave her fruit and jellies, and he cried: "Is it some o' these blasted, snivelling women from the kirk that have sent them? Are we getting charity from the town? Is that what we're come to? I suppose they're sorry for you with such a poor mouth as you're aye puttin' on. Good God! they'll be sending us tracts and soup next." He seized the bunch of grapes roughly from her hand, contemplating them contemptuously, but, as he did so, he realised something of the cost of the exquisite fruit before him, knew suddenly that no collection of church workers, however godly, could have sent them. A slow sneer spread over his face as he exclaimed: "No! I think I see what's at the back o' it. We don't know who sent them. It's what they call an anonymous donor. God Almighty! are ye come back to that again, you trollop—back to your presents from your fancy men! Faugh! you sicken me." He looked at her with a snarl on his face, but she returned his gaze with a calm and steady eye, and it was poor Nessie, fortunately unobserved, who manifested some signs of confusion and distress.

"You're not going to eat them, though," he cried roughly. "No! not a single one. Ye may look at them as greedily as ye like, but you'll not lip them. This is what's going to happen." And, as he uttered the words, he dashed the grapes upon the floor with a pulping sound and in a fury stamped his heavy boots upon them, squelching the rich juice in all directions, crushing them into a dark mass that stained the grey linoleum like blood. "There!" he shouted, "that's the bitter winepress that I'm treading. This is my bitter path—but tread it I will. I only wish the swine that sent them was underneath my feet. I would serve him in like fashion whoever he may be. There—that'll be something for ye to clean up—something to keep your mind off the men—you jade. A bit of scrubbin' will take the itch out of ye," and as he spoke he scattered the residue upon the floor with short kicks into every corner of the room. Seizing her by the shoulders he shoved his face into hers and sneered coarsely: "I understand what you're up to, my bonnie tottie, but don't go too far—ye know what happened to ye the last time." As he concluded he flung her from him, sending her reeling against the wall, from where, with a blush of humiliation upon her face, she still looked at him in silence.

After a moment he turned to Nessie and, in a completely opposite voice, soft, fond, wheedling, rendered deliberately contrasting to his tone to Mary in order to wound her the more, remarked:

"Come on, hinny—pay no attention to what you've seen—or to her, either. Ye don't even need to speak to her in future if you don't want to. This sort of thing does not concern you, and besides it's time you and me had our dauner down the road together—we'll have you late for the school if we don't hurry up, and that would never do." He took Nessie's hand and with a great demonstration of affection, led her timid form from the room, but not before she had flashed one frightened, guilty glance at Mary as she turned to go out into the hall.

When the front door closed behind them Mary sighed. She pulled herself up from where Brodie had thrown her against the wall, and although she gazed sorrowfully at the dirty, scattered remnants of the fruit which Nessie would now never eat, she felt with some relief, despite her own humiliation, that her sister had not been prejudiced by the recent, unfortunate incident. The words which her father had hurled at her shamed her almost beyond endurance, whilst the injustice of his attitude made her bury her teeth into her lip to keep back the hot rush of indignant tears. Although she had no evidence but that of her own intuition, she knew that Dr. Renwick in his kindness had sent her these grapes and indeed the other gifts, and now all the fine feelings of gratitude that she had entertained towards him, all her sacrifice for Nessie's sake, had been degraded, thrust down into the mud by her father's gross interpretation of them. She had been made to feel again her position in the eyes of the world, reminded miserably of the smirch that lay upon her name which would cling to her in this town as long as her life endured.

With a faint shiver she bestirred herself and began to clear the table of its dishes, and when she had carried them into the scullery, she set herself slowly to wash and dry them. As she worked she directed her mind deliberately from her own position, considering with some return of comfort that Nessie seemed to be improving slightly in health, that although her long and forced periods of study continued, she was eating better, that her thin cheeks showed some signs of filling out. Nothing was too much for her to endure if she could protect her sister— make her well and strong. It was a supreme satisfaction to have been able to procure some better clothing for Nessie from her savings—the small stock of money that she had brought home to Levenford—and she cheered herself with the thought of the improved appearance of the child from the neglected state in which she had found her upon her return.

When she had dried and put away the last dish she took a bucket of warm water and a cloth into the kitchen, went down upon her knees, and began to wash the floor. While she was thus engaged she was suddenly confronted by a whimsical vision of Renwick's face could he have observed her in her present occupation and perceived thus the

o

grotesque result of his generosity. She did not, however, smile at her thought, but sighed again, considering that she would be obliged to ask him to discontinue these good-hearted offerings towards Nessie and herself. She had seen him on two occasions since her first visit to his house, and on each she had felt more forcibly how compassionate he had been to interest himself so deeply on Nessie's behalf; but somehow, she had begun to shrink from meeting him, to dread the onset of that strange feeling which swept over her whenever she felt his dark, sympathetic eyes upon hers. The remembrance of her father's recent words now came to her suddenly, and even in her solitude within the room she winced, wondering unhappily what indeed was the nature of her regard for this man who had shown her nothing but kindness and friendship. It was a happy circumstance perhaps that he was soon to leave the town, that the uncertain and troubled state of her mind would soon be ended.

Strange, then, that as she considered this happy circumstance her face should cloud so sadly, that as she finished her washing of the floor, and sat down to busy herself on some mending for Nessie, her thoughts should refuse to leave him. He had told her to make her life a gallery of pictures, but her gallery contained now but one picture, and that was the portrait of his face. The kitchen, once so dirty and untidy, now lay about her clean and spotless; the rest of the house was equally immaculate; her main work was finished for the day; and yet, when she should have taken up a book or engaged herself in some diversion, as he had directed, she could only sit and think of him. It was incredible!

True, her opportunities for relaxation were not unlimited for, although her return had caused no apparent ripple upon the surface of the life of the town, she shunned the public gaze, and lately had formed the habit of going out only when the dusk had fallen. Only once had she departed from this custom, when she had made a pilgrimage to Darroch to see the grave that enclosed Denis and her child. The same train had borne her, the same streets echoed to her sad, returning footsteps, but another name now stretched upon the signboard of the Lomond Vaults, and the doctor whom she had consulted on that last, unhappy visit had answered the call of his destiny and vanished, likewise, into some unknown obscurity. No bitter passion of grief had moved her as she stood by the grave that lay on the slope of Darroch Hill, but only a tender melancholy, directed chiefly towards the form of her infant child that lay so near her kneeling body, and was yet so inseparably divided from it. How strange, she had thought, that the throbbing body of the child that had lived so vigorously within her womb, should now lie buried in earth, detached from her for ever. Strange, too, that she, the mother, had never seen, and now could never see, that child. She had been still unconscious in the Cottage Hospital when, from exposure and its too early advent, it had died without her knowing—without her seeing it.

A sense of the injustice of the infant's death had oppressed her as she rose to her feet and made her way out of the graveyard, feeling that she deserved her punishment, and accepting it, but thinking that her child had surely merited some short happiness of life. As she got into the train at the station upon her homeward journey she had felt that this visit was final—she was never return to that grave—and as the train steamed out of the station she had, through the cloud of her depression, faintly visioned upon the platform an illusive figure—the figure of Denis—waving her a brave, encouraging, and a last good-bye.

Now, as she sat at her sewing with a downward, pensive gaze, it was not the memory of this good-bye which filled her mind but the anticipation of another, a less visionary parting, and in the privacy of her own intimate thoughts she admitted to herself at last, abandoning her attempts at self-delusion, that it was hard for her to contemplate the departure of Dr. Renwick from the town. She knew well the gulf that separated them, bridged only by his charity, but, conscious that her desire did not extend even to the presumption of friendship but merely to a longing for his presence near her, she felt it permissible for her to mourn his going. Levenford would be empty for her, then!

She could sew no longer; her eyes refused to see the stitches, the needle to enter the cotton of the garment; she was weeping at the thought of her loss, prompted, alas, by that emotion which presumed not even to friendship. In her agitation she arose, despising herself, wringing her hands at her own miserable weakness, and, as though she felt the need of a freer air than that within the room, made her way blindly out into the back garden where she paced up and down, striving to calm herself. As she walked, filled at last by a returning tranquillity, she suddenly observed that upon the lilac tree, which in her memory had never flowered, there now grew one large and perfect budding blossom. With a quickening interest she advanced and, gently pulling down the bough which bore it, took the green spray within her fingers, touched and caressed it, and perceived to her surprise, from the faint colour that tinged the tips of the unopened buds, that it was white lilac. Delicious white lilac! She had never known that it was a white lilac bush, but now, like some propitious omen for the future, this melancholy tree had burgeoned, and soon would wave a white and scented spray to cheer her during the coming spring. Nessie would love it, she thought, as, gently releasing the branch, she turned and in a happier spirit made her way back to the house.

The afternoon wore on, dusk fell, tea-time came and passed, Nessie was again inevitably established in the parlour with her books, Brodie seated in the kitchen with his bottle and, the dishes once more washed and her house in order, she decided that she would fulfil her purpose to visit Dr. Renwick and explain, with all the delicacy she possessed, her difficulty in accepting these gifts which he had sent for Nessie. It was permissible for her to go out; her movements, indeed, were not restrained in the evening so long as she did not visibly interfere with the progress of the studies within the parlour, and assuming her hat and coat, she slipped out of the back door—by which inferior avenue her father had now ordained that she should always enter and leave the house.

The night was fresh, the air soothing to her cheek, the unseen flowers more fragrant from the dew, and, hidden by the darkness, she moved down the road at a free and rapid pace. Although she did not immediately question the causes of this lightness of her mood, the throb of the coming springtime was stirring her, moving her as she had been moved by the budding lilac tree, and the nature of her present journey was filling her unconsciously with happiness. But, as she drew near to Wellhall Road she seemed to apprehend dimly the reason of her present cheerfulness, and gradually her steps slowed, and she became confronted by a sudden thought. What right had she to inflict herself upon a busy man who had patients waiting at his house? who was doubtless tired from a hard day's work; further, if it were indeed he who had sent the grapes, what impertinence on her part to refuse them! She was stabbed by the thought that her mission was a ruse, a subterfuge invented by her evasive mind to enable her to see him and, while her father's abusive words again rose before her like a judgment, she began to feel how unnecessary it was, now that Nessie appeared to be improving, for her to visit Dr. Renwick as she proposed. By some strange association of season, or was it of her sensations, her mind flew back to another springtime, and she realised that when she had known Denis in the past he had followed her, pursued her ardently; but now, and she blushed painfully in the darkness, it was she who actually wished to thrust her unworthy presence upon a man who had no desire to see her.

By this time she had reached his house and, on the opposite side of the road, she stopped, rather dejectedly, and surveyed it, considering in her mind the tasteful decorations, the exquisite picture which had compelled her rapt attention. No! she would not go in, but merely watch the house for a moment under cover of the darkness and fill it with his presence, just as in the future she would come to this same spot, and vision him again in that rich room when he had left the town for good.

As she stood there she heard the quick crisp chatter of a horse's trot, saw two high yellow lights gleam in the obscurity and, before she could move away, the doctor's gig came whirling to his house. Drawing back into the shadow of the wall she observed the pleasant bustle at the door, heard the pawing of the horse, the jingle of its harness, then Renwick's firm voice, which shook her by its nearness, saying to his man:

"I shan't be out again to-night, Dick; at least I hope not! Good night to you!"

"Good night to you, sir. Hope you won't be disturbed," she heard the groom reply, and clambering back into his seat he drove off to the adjoining stable. With eyes that strained through the blackness she followed Renwick's dim figure to the porch, then, as the door was suddenly flung open and he was silhouetted against the brilliant light within, she saw him vividly. For a moment he turned and surveyed the darkness, looking directly towards her. Although she knew herself to be invisible to him, she trembled as though he had discovered her and would retrace his steps and demand to know the reason of her prying presence at this hour. But he did not return. After a last look at the night he went into his house, closing the door behind him, leaving the darkness unrelieved.

For a moment she remained still, overcome by her thoughts, then she stirred and began to move back towards her home, drooping a little, stealing quietly through the streets, as though some pervading realisation weighed her with a sense of infamy. She knew that she, Mary Brodie, outcast, the despoiled virgin, the mother of a dead and nameless child, loved again, but was herself unloved.

VIII

Sunday afternoon still held for Brodie the indulgence of an afternoon repose, for although he rose late and did not dine until two, custom died hard with him, and the blank hours of three until five found him invariably in his shirt-sleeves and upon his back upon the sofa. It was not, however, the parlour sofa, but the couch within the kitchen upon which he rested; the other room was still hallowed to Nessie's studies, which were pursued on this day of rest with an intensity equal to that of week days, and he considered that it was a sacrifice on his part savouring of the heroic to have suggested, and carried into effect, this transference of his repose to a less dignified settee.

On this Sunday the hot July sun had made him feel drowsy and, having seen his younger daughter begin upon her work, exhorting her the more strongly in the face of the nearness of the great day of examination next week, he now laid himself down with the air of one who must not be disturbed and allowed the drone of a fly upon the window to lull him into sleep.

It was, as he had just impressed upon Nessie, the last lap of the race, and whilst he snored, in the happy consciousness of having done his part towards success by relinquishing the parlour, she addressed herself, with a slightly feverish mind, towards her final perusal of the third book of Euclid. Her face was flushed from the heat inside the parlour, and a buzzing of insects, like that which had sent Brodie so comfortably to sleep, annoyed her and distracted her mind from its intent purpose. She had never been quite sure of her geometry, and now, with the examination coming off in a few days' time, her deficiencies in this subject had intimidated her, and impelled her to rush once more through the entire third book. She knotted her brow and moved her lips as she again began to cram the eighth proposition into her brain but, despite her concentration, the words upon the page wavered, the diagrams became blurred, and the lines ran into strange fantastic shapes, not unlike the eccentric figures which had lately filled her troubled dreams and tormented her at nights in her sleep. The axis of the angle to the vertical was the co-efficient of—no, no, what was she talking about— that was perfect nonsense! She must stick into it better than that, or the Latta would slip out of this pocket of hers where it so safely reposed, and run away like a white mouse that would quickly nibble up all these golden sovereigns like so much cheese. How hot it was! And how her head ached! Her English was excellent, Latin perfect, French quite good, algebra splendid—yes, she was a clever girl, everybody said so, and indeed the examiners for the Bursary would realise it the moment they set eyes upon her. When she had made her way proudly and confidently to school on the day of an examination she had, in the consciousness of her eminence, always felt that people whispered to one another, saying: "That's Nessie Brodie! She's the cleverest scholar in the Academy; she'll come out first in this test as sure as her name's Brodie." Perhaps the professors at the University would put their heads together and talk like that, at least they would do so after they had read her papers. They must do so!—or her father would want to know the reason of it; indeed, if they failed to recognise who she was and to give her the first place he would knock their heads together for them like so many coco-nuts. Coco-nuts! Matt had promised to bring her some when he had left for India and she had wanted a monkey and a parrot, too, but he had somehow forgotten about them, and now that he had gone off with that terrible woman he would never remember about a wee thing like Nessie Brodie. Had he married Nancy? She did not know; but Nancy was wicked, even if Matt had put a ring on her finger, and not like Mary, who was good and kind to her. Yet Mary was not married, although she had somehow had a baby which was dead and never mentioned by anyone. Mary never spoke of it, but had a sadness about her face as though there was something on her mind that she could never forget. Mary was always running after her, giving her soup and eggs and milk, cuddling her and telling her not to work so hard. Mary wanted her to win the Latta, but in a reasonable way, and simply to prevent her from being hurt by their father. Her dear sister would cry if she did not win it—and yet she need not cry. If she failed it would be a wonderful idea never to tell Mary, to let the years run on and never say a single word about it. What was she thinking of? There must be no failing! If she was not sitting high up in that first place—"at the top of the class"—as her father had always called it, she herself would have to take the consequences. "I'll wring that thin neck of yours if you let anybody beat ye—and after the way I've coached ye on for't" —that was what he was always dinning into her ears between his spells of petting and wheedling. He had big hands!

The axis of the angle to the vertical—really it was the height of absurdity that she should be doing this on such a hot day, and on the Sabbath day too, when she might have been at the Bible Class with the white frock and the pink sash that Mamma had made for her. But that was worn out or grown out of now; she was getting a big girl. Yet Mamma had always liked her to go to Sunday School with kid gloves and her face washed after dinner. "Lad and lass, kiss and cas', Nessie's in the Bible Class." She was not in it now though, but working hard, ever so hard at her lessons—"Yes, father, I'm stickin' in hard. What I'm doin', I'm doin' weel." Mamma had liked her to please father, but Mamma was dead. She had no mother and Mary had no baby! Mamma and Mary's baby were together sitting on a cloud, waving to her, and singing: "Nessie Brodie's going to win the Latta." She wanted to join in the chorus with all her might, but something tightened her throat and restrained her. Lately she had not been so sure of herself. No! it was a big thing for a girl, and a Brodie at that, to win the Latta. A big thing and a difficult thing! She had been sure of it at first, so much so that at one time the heap of golden guineas had lain piled upon her plate for everyone to see and admire. But now a dreadful, secret doubt was creeping into her mind as to whether she could do it. No one knew about it—that was a comfort—and no one would ever know. "Yes, father, I'm getting on splendid—couldn't be better. That Grierson hasn't got a chance. I'm the stumbling block. The Latta's mine already." He was pleased at that, rubbing his hands together and smiling at her approvingly—and it was fine for her to feel that she was pleasing him! She would hide everything so cleverly and carefully that he would never see that she was not sure of herself. She had her own ways of doing things, the clever girl that she was! She was inside her own mind, now, creeping about the passages of her brain, admiring, congratulating herself, seeing her very thoughts flow with a marvellous rippling fluency, watching them delightedly as they flashed past her like brilliant, rushing waves of scintillating light.

At last she started suddenly, her eyes lost their vacancy, her face its smooth, unruffled placidity and, as she rubbed her brows with her hand and looked at the clock, she murmured, confusedly: "Good sakes! what have I been thinking about? Have I been asleep or what? There's an hour gone and I can't mind a thing about it!" She shook her head with annoyance at her own weakness, at the loss of this precious hour, and was once more about to apply herself to the Book of Euclid when the door opened quietly and her sister came into the room.

"Here's a glass of milk for you, dear," whispered Mary, tiptoeing up to the table. "Father's asleep now, so I thought I might bring you this. It's cold as can be. I've had the jug in running water for an hour."

Nessie took the glass from her sister and began to sip it in an absent fashion.

"It's cool as cool," she replied, after a moment. "It's as good as ice-cream on a day like this. Did you ever feel it so close?"

Mary pressed her palm lightly against her sister's cheek.

"You're hot!" she murmured. "Will you not take a half an hour off and come out in the air with me?"

"And what would happen to me if he woke up and found I had gone out?" queried Nessie, with a sharp look. "You know you would get it worse than me, too! No! I'll stay where I am. This milk is cooling me fine. Besides, I've got all this book to get through before Friday."

"How is the headache now?" said Mary after a pause, during which she contemplated the other with some anxiety.

"Just the same! It doesn't feel like a headache now. It's more a numbness."

"Would you like me to put on some more cold water and vinegar cloths for you?"

"Never mind, Mary! I don't think they do much good. I'll be better after next Saturday when I've got the exam. over. That's the only thing that'll cure it."

"Is there nothing you can think of that you'd like?"

"No! There's nothing I fancy at all. It's real kind of you though, Mary. You've been wonderful to me, and you've had to put up with so much yourself. But I could never have done without you."

"I've done nothing," replied Mary sadly. "I would like to have done much more. I wish I could have stopped you from going up for the Bursary, but it was impossible! I didn't want you to take it."

"Don't say that!" cried Nessie quickly. "You know I must go up for it. I've thought of nothing else for the last six months, and if I had to draw back now it would fair break my heart. I must take it."

"Do you really want to go on with it?" asked Mary doubtfully.

"Just think how I've worked," replied Nessie with some emotion; "just think how I've been made to work. Am I going to let all that go for nothing? I should hope not. I'm so set on it myself now that I couldn't hold back if I was to try. I feel it now like something that's gripping me and drawing me on."

Mary gazed at the nervous eagerness in her sister's eyes, and, in an attempt to soothe the other, murmured consolingly:

"It'll not be long till it's over now, anyway, Nessie! Don't fret yourself too much about it. Let the work go easy for a day or two."

"How can you talk like that," exclaimed Nessie petulantly. "You know I've got all this ground to get over—and it's most important too. This third book is not right into my head yet. I must get it in. I've—I've got to drive it in like a nail so that it will stay in and never come out. I might get a question on this very thing that you're telling me to leave alone."

"Hush, Nessie, dear! Don't excite yourself," pleaded Mary.

"It's enough to make anybody excited," cried the other wildly. "Here am I working the brains out of myself and you would think that all I had to do was to walk up to that university and ask for the Latta and come home with it in my hand like a stick of toffee. It's not like that at all. I tell you."

"Wheesht, Nessie! Be calm, pettie," soothed Mary. "Don't upset yourself, I didn't mean anything like that."

"You did so!" returned Nessie agitatedly. "Everybody thinks the same thing. They think it's that easy for me because I'm so clever. They don't know the work and the toil that I've been forced to put in. It's been enough to drive me out of my mind."

"I know though, dear," replied Mary softly, stroking the other's brow. "I know all about it and how you've been kept at it! Don't worry yourself though. You're getting tired and anxious. You used to be ever so confident about it. Never mind if you don't win the miserable Bursary. What does it matter!"

Nessie, however, was so strung up that no attitude her sister could have adopted would have pleased her, and now she burst into tears.

"What does it matter," she sobbed hysterically. "That's a good one, that is, for me that's set my very heart on winning it. And to call the good hundred sovereigns that I'll get 'miserable' is enough to discourage anybody. Don't you know what father'll do to me if I don't win it. He'll kill me."

"He'll not do that, Nessie," replied Mary steadily. "I'm here now and I'll protect you from any fear of that. I'll be there when you get the result and if he tries to lay a finger on you it'll be the worse for him."

"What could you do?" cried Nessie. "You talk as if it was better for you to stand up to father than for me to win the Latta."

Mary did not reply to this ungracious speech but stood silent, soothing Nessie by gentle movements of her hands, until at last the other's sobs ceased and, drying her eyes, she remarked with a sudden composure:

"I don't know what we're goin' on about, running round in a circle like that. We've been talkin' nonsense. Of course I'll win the Latta and that's the end of it!"

"That's right, dear," returned Mary, happy to see the other more tranquil. "I know you will. Have you got on well to-day?"

"Splendid!" replied Nessie, in a constrained manner, strangely at variance with her words. "Like a house on fire. I don't know what came over me then. You'll not think any more about what I said will you, Mary!" she continued in a persuasive voice. "Don't say a word about it to anyone! I wouldn't like father to hear I had been so silly. Why, I'm as sure of the Bursary as I am of finishing this milk," and she emptied the remains of the milk at a gulp.

"You know I'll say nothing," answered Mary, looking at her sister perplexedly, considering with some degree of wonder this sudden change in her manner and disposition. Did Nessie really think that she would succeed, or was this attitude assumed to conceal a deeper and more secret fear that she might fail? Thinking anxiously of the immediate future that lay before her sister, Mary said slowly:

"You'll be sure to let me know the result before father, won't you, Nessie? Let me know whenever it comes out."

"Of course I will," replied the other with a continuance of the same manner, but directing her eyes from her sister and looking sideways out of the window. "We'll not know till a fortnight after the examination."

"You're sure now," insisted Mary. "Say that we'll open the letter together."

"Yes! Yes!" cried Nessie fretfully. "Have I not told you that I would long ago. You can open it yourself for all I care. I've promised you and I'll not break my word. You should be letting me get on instead of harping on about that."

Again Mary surveyed her sister with some uneasiness, realising how unlike her usual clinging, artless, mildness was this petulant assumption of assurance, but although she felt troubled in her mind, she decided that this must be the result simply of a natural anxiety at the nearness of the examination and she said, gently:

"I'll go and let you get on then, dear! But please don't tire yourself out too much. I'm anxious for you." Then as she picked up the empty tumbler and retreated to the door she said, tentatively: "You're sure you wouldn't like to come out for a few minutes? I'm going out for my walk now."

"No," cried Nessie with a vehement shake of her head, "I'll not bother about it. I'll get on well and I'll be as right as the mail." She smiled at Mary with a curious complacency—she who a moment ago had been shaken by bitter sobs and whose invariable attitude towards her sister was one of utter dependency. "Away and have your walk, woman!" she added. "I want to have a quiet think to myself."

"About the Euclid?" said Mary doubtfully, from the door.

"Ay! about the Euclid," cried Nessie, with a short laugh. "Away and don't bother me."

Mary shut the parlour door and, as the kitchen was closed to her by its consecration to Brodie's sleep, went slowly up to her room, still bearing in her hand the tumbler which had contained Nessie's milk. She gazed at this empty glass, trying to comfort herself by the recollection of all the care which she had lately bestowed upon her sister, of the additional nourishment which she had obtained for her and induced her to take; but in spite of the reassuring nature of her thoughts she sighed, unable to dismiss from her mind the sudden outburst which had recently occurred, and in which she thought she detected still some evidence of that lack of balance which, since her return, had troubled her in Nessie. While she put on her hat and gloves to take her customary walk, she determined to maintain a closer and more careful observation upon her sister during the climax of Nessie's endeavours, which would be manifested during the coming week.

Outside, the air was warm and still, and the street deserted to that quietude which induced her on Sundays to take her stroll invariably in the afternoon, rather than in the evening, when the same road was crowded by promenading couples. At this time, too, she felt safe in the knowledge that, with Brodie asleep, Nessie would be immune from his hectoring attention for an hour or two, and this assurance gave her a sense of freedom which now she rarely experienced. She proceeded to the head of the road and chose, to-day, the left-hand turn, which led directly towards the distant Winton Hills that stood away from her, rendered more remote by the shimmering haze of heat which almost veiled them. This haze lay also upon the roadway, rising in faint vibrations of the air like a mirage, and giving the illusion of pools of water lying wetly at a distance upon the path in front of her. But there was no wetness, everything was dry with dust which soon covered her shoes with a white, impalpable powder and stirred in little puffs about her skirt with every step she took. The day was delicious, the country lying in a basking warmth, but it was not the hour for walking, and soon the small, front curl which defied always the severity of her brush, lay wisping damply against the whiteness of her brow; her paces dwindled, and she felt tired. With her tiredness came a returning consciousness of Nessie's strange manner to her earlier in the afternoon, the heat all at once became overpowering, and she had made up her mind to turn back towards home when, suddenly, she observed a dogcart coming rapidly in her direction along the road. Immediately, she perceived the nature of the vehicle and the identity of the driver and, in a quick flutter of confusion, she made to turn and retreat, halted, stood indecisively for a moment, looking this way and that as though seeking some place of concealment, then, realising perhaps the futility of flight, she lowered her head and walked rapidly to meet it. As she progressed, she made every effort to compose her features, hoping that she would pass without being observed, but, to her growing agitation, though she observed nothing, she heard the crunching of the advancing wheels gradually subside and come to a halt beside her, heard Renwick's voice saying:

"Good day to you—Miss Brodie!"

She felt it impossible for her to look up to disclose, in her face, the revealing turmoil of her feelings as, thinking unhappily that she was now Miss Brodie to him and not Miss Mary, or even Mary, she stammered out an acknowledgment of his greeting.

"It's a wonderful day," he exclaimed cheerily. "Quite perfect; but it's too hot to be on foot. It must be like crossing the Sahara to walk to-day."

Had he, she asked herself, observed her hot face and the dust upon her boots which must give her the appearance of some dishevelled and disreputable tramp!

"I ought to say, in politeness, that it's a coincidence our meeting here," he continued, "but that's hardly so. I was aware that you took this walk on Sundays when I drove out here to-day. I wanted to know about Nessie."

How wonderful his words would have been without that last explanatory sentence, but, as she stood foolishly with downcast head, she became aware that she must say something in reply or he would consider that she was stupid or uncouth, or both; with a great effort she slowly lifted her eyes to his, thought instantly, despite her embarrassment, how clean cut was his dark, eager face against the background of the sky —and murmured feebly, irrelevantly:

"I haven't been able to tell you about Nessie. I haven't seen you for a long time."

"Far too long," he cried; "and it's been of your own seeking. I haven't seen you about for weeks. I thought you had flown again from Levenford without bidding me good-bye."

"I'm here for good, now," she replied slowly. "It's you that will be saying good-bye to Levenford soon."

His face clouded slightly.

"Yes! it's only another fortnight now. How time flies—like an arrow in its flight." He sighed. "It's curious, but as the day draws near I'm losing interest in the prospect. I was glad to think of going at first, but this old town has its grip on me after all."

"You've so many friends, now, I suppose."

"That's it! I've got friends."

He played idly with his whip, his eyes fixed unseeingly upon the twitching ears of the horse, then he looked at her seriously and said: "Are you free to come for a drive with me, Miss Brodie? I may not see you again and I rather wished to talk to you about one or two matters. Do come if you would care to!"

Of course she would care to come and, thinking of her father resting until five, she realised that no more propitious hour could have been chosen; still, she hesitated, and replied:

"I'm—I'm not dressed for driving, and I should have to be back at five, and——"

"And in that case you're coming," he answered, with a smile, stretching out his hand. "We've got a good hour and a half. As for your dress, it's too good for this old trap of mine."

She was up beside him almost before she knew how, seated close to him on the red velvet cushion, and he had tucked the light, dust cover around her, touched up the horse and she was off with him, gliding forward in an easy yet exhilarating movement. The breeze of their progress through the still air fanned her cheek, the sky lost its glare and became halcyon, the dust was nothing—merely a soft powder to ease the horse's stepping gait—and, after the tedium and fatigue of walking, she was content to sit silent, happy, watching the vivid countryside flit gently past her. But, though she was too conscious of his nearness to look upon him, out of the corner of her gaze she observed the smooth, soft leather of his hand-sewn driving gloves, the silver-plated harness, the monogrammed dust cover, the smart appointments of what he had designated his "old trap," and again, as in his house, she was seized by a feeling of the difference between his life and hers. Now, whatever his early struggles might have been, the manner of his life did not comprise the weighing of every farthing before it was spent, the wearing of clothes until they disintegrated, the stifling of every pleasurable impulse outwith the sphere of a most rigid economy. But she suppressed this rising sense of her inferiority, stifled her thoughts of future sadness and, telling herself that she would not mar her solitary hour of this unusual luxury, abandoned herself to the unfamiliar delight of enjoying herself.

Renwick, on his part, observed her clear profile, the faint colour stirring in her soft cheek, her unwonted animation, with a strange satisfaction, a sense of pleasure more acute than that with which she viewed the countryside. A sudden pressing whim took him to make her turn to him so that he might see into her eyes and he broke the silence, saying:

"You are not sorry you came."

But still she did not look at him, although her lips curved in a faint smile, as she answered:

"I'm glad I came. It's all so wonderful to me. I'm not used to this and I'll be able to look back on it."

"We'll have time to drive up to the Loch shore," he replied pleasantly, "and, if Tim steps out, time for tea there as well."

She was enchanted by the prospect which he proposed and, considering Tim's smoothly groomed back, hoped that he would hasten sufficiently for tea without going so fast as to hurry her home before time.

"Tim," she remarked idly; "what a good name for a horse."

"And a good horse he is too," he replied, calling out in a louder tone, "aren't you, Timmy?"

Tim pricked up his ears at the words and, as though he appreciated them, put a little more mettle into his measured jog-trot.

"You see?" Renwick continued, watching with approval her smile. "He knows that I'm talking about him and is trying not to blush—the wretched hypocrite. He'll be lazier than ever in Edinburgh. Too many oats and not enough exercise!"

"You're taking him with you, then?" she queried.

"Yes. I couldn't sell Timmy. I'm like that somehow." He paused, then continued meditatively: "It's a ridiculous trait in me, but when I've become fond of a thing I can't let it go—pictures, books, a horse—it's the same in every case. When I like a thing I like it. I'm obstinate. I accept no standard of judgment but my own. A critic may tell me a dozen times that such a picture is good, but if I don't like it I won't have it. I take a picture that I do like then, when it's grown upon me, I couldn't bear to part with it."

She looked straight in front of her and remarked:

"That was an exquisite picture in your dining-room."

"Yes," he replied authoritatively, "that is a fine thing—I'm glad you liked it. It's company to me that picture. I bought it at the Institute." Then he added, slyly, "It's not exclusively my taste, though—the critics liked it, too."

The memory of the picture brought before her mind the purpose of her first visit to him and, anticipating his interrogation regarding Nessie, she said:

"I'm grateful for all that you've done about Nessie. You have been more than kind to us both." She had never told him about the tragedy of the grapes, and his favours, these fortunately undiscovered, had continued.

"I wanted to help you," he replied. "How is she getting along, under all the work?"

"She seems better in her health," she answered, with a trace of anxiety in her voice, "but she varies so much. At times she is quite peculiar to me. She's worrying about the nearness of her examination. It's on Saturday. I've done everything I can for her."

"I know you have—everything," he said reassuringly. "Now that she's gone so far without breaking down she ought to be all right! I hope she gets the thing for her own sake." Then, after a considerable silence, he remarked in a serious tone: "I should keep near to her when the results come to hand; and if you want me call on me at once."

She was aware that he would be gone when the result was announced, but, feeling that already he had done enough for her, she made no comment, and remained silent, engrossed by her thoughts. As he had said, Nessie would be all right! She would see to that. She would be with her—watch her, protect her, safeguard her, should she be unsuccessful, from any sudden action of her father.

She was aroused from her meditation, from this strengthening of her resolution, by his voice.

"They've widened the road here. We can get through quite easily, and it's cooler than the other way." Looking up, she was overcome to see that, unconscious of its significance for her, he had branched off the main road and taken that very passage through the fir wood where she had lost herself upon the night of the storm. With a set, startled face she gazed at the wood as it again enclosed her, not now rocking and surging to the passion of the gale, nor crashing with the thunder of uprooting trees, but quiet, appeased, passive with a serene tranquillity. The bright sunbeams stole amongst the sombre foliage of the dark trees, softening them, encrusting their rough branches with gold, and tracing upon their straight, dry trunks a gaily fretted pattern of shimmering light and shadow. As she passed, in her present comfort and security, through the wood, she was stricken by the incredible memory of her own tortured figure, filled then with her living child, rushing blindly through the darkness, staggering, falling, transfixing her hand upon the sharp spear of the branch, beset by mad voices, unseen, unheard.

A tear trembled upon the brink of her humid eye but, clenching her fingers tightly over the long cicatrix upon her palm as though to fortify herself with the remembrance of her endurance then, she refused to let it fall and instead, turned her gaze, as they emerged from the wood, down into the distant valley. Yes! there was the croft where she had lain in her extremity! it stood against the smooth green of the lush meadowland adjoined by the small shed which had contained her anguished body, its white walls rising squarely to its yellow thatched roof, the smoke rising straight from its single chimney like a long, blue ribbon lifting itself tenuously to the sky.

With a wrench she withdrew her eyes and, holding her body tense in the effort to control her emotion, looked straight ahead, whilst Tim's ears blurred and wavered before her swimming gaze. Renwick, perceiving, perhaps instinctively, that some sudden sadness had induced her silence, did not speak for a long time, but as they swept over the crest of Markinch Hill and the placid, smoothly shining sheet of the Loch was revealed stretching below them, he remarked, quietly:

"There's beauty and serenity for you."

It was an exquisite sight. The water, bearing the deep, brilliant blue of the unclouded sky, lay cool and unruffled as a sheet of virgin ice from whose edges the steep and richly wooded slopes of the hills reached back and upwards to the sharp, ridged mountains beyond. Breaking the surface of this still expanse were a series of small islands lying upon the bosom of the Loch like a chain of precious emeralds, green and wooded like the banks, and each mirrored with such perfection that it was impossible for the eyes to distinguish between the islet and its meticulous reflection. Upon the shore nearest to them stood a small hamlet, its aggregation of cottages showing whitely against the vivid background of blue and green, and now Renwick pointed to it significantly.

"There's Markinch—which means tea for you, Mary! Don't let the grandeur of nature spoil your appetite."

Her face, that was serene and beautiful as the surface of the lake, responded to his words, and she smiled with a faint, returning glow of happiness. He had called her Mary!

They descended the winding hill to Markinch where, disdaining the small, somewhat ineffectual inn which stood at the head of the village, Renwick drove on to the last cottage of the row that fringed the shore of the Loch, and with a wise look towards Mary, jumped out and knocked upon the door. The cottage was in perfect harmony with the surrounding beauty, its white walls splashed by the rich yellows of nasturtiums, its green porch embowered by red rambler roses, its garden fragrant with the poignant scent of mignonette—such a cottage, indeed, as she had once visioned for herself in Garshake; and to the door of this small house came a small, bent body of a woman who now lifted her hands and cried, delightedly:

"Doctor! Doctor! It's not yourself? Guidsakes alive! Is it you yourself?"

"Indeed it is, Janet," cried Renwick, in her own tone. "It is I, myself, and a young lady, herself. And the two of us, ourselves, are fair famished from our drive. If we don't get one of your lovely teas, with your own scones, and jam and butter and heaven knows a' what, then we'll just sadly fade awa' and never come back."

"Ye'd no' do that, though," cried Janet vigorously. "Na, na! ye'll have the finest tea in Markinch inside five minutes."

"Can we have it in the garden, Janet?"

"Of course ye can, doctor! Ye can have it on the roof o' my cottage gin ye say the word."

"The garden will do, Janet," replied Renwick with a smile. "And —Janet! let the wee lad look after Tim. And give us a call when you're ready. We'll go along the shore a bit."

"Right! Right, doctor! Ye've only to say the word," answered Janet eagerly, and as she departed to do his bidding, he turned and came back to Mary.

"Shall we go a little way along?" he asked; and at her assent he assisted her from her seat to the ground, saying:

"Janet won't keep us waiting five minutes, but you may well as stretch your legs. You must be cramped from sitting."

How delighted the old woman had been to see him, thought Mary, and like all who were in contact with him, how eager to rush to serve him! Thinking of this, as they proceeded along the fine firm shingle of the shore she remarked:

"Janet's an old friend of yours! Her eye actually leaped when she saw you."

"I did something for a son of hers in Levenford once," he replied lightly. "She's a sweet old soul with a tongue like an energetic magpie," —here he looked at her across his nose, adding—"but better than that, she makes delicious scones. You must eat exactly seven of them."

"Why seven?" she queried.

"It's a lucky number," he answered, "and just the right amount of scone food for a healthy, hungry young lady." He looked at her critically. "I wish I had the dieting of you, Miss Mary. There's a sad loveliness in that faint hollow of your cheek, but it means that you've been neglecting your butter and milk. I'll wager you gave all those things I sent you to that wee Nessie of yours."

She blushed.

"No! I didn't really! It was good of you to send them to us."

He shook his head compassionately.

"Will you ever think of yourself, Mary Brodie? It hurts me to think what will come of you when I'm away. You want someone to keep a severe and stern eye upon you, to make you look after yourself. Will you write to me and tell me how you're behaving?"

"Yes," she said slowly, as though a faint coldness had risen to her from the still water beside them, "I'll write when you've gone!"

"That's right," he cried cheerfully. "I'll regard that as a definite promise on your part."

Now they stood looking out upon the sublime tranquillity of the view before them, that seemed to her so remote from the troubled existence within her home, so exalted above the ordinary level of her life. She was overcome by its appeal and, released by the perception of this beauty, all her suppressed feeling for this man by her side swept over her. She was drawn to him with a deeper and more moving emotion than that which had once stirred her; she wished blindly to show her devotion, visibly to demonstrate her homage to him; but she could not, and was compelled to remain quiet by his side, torn by the beating of her straining heart. The faint murmur of the Loch, as it scarcely lapped its shore, swept across the quietude of the scene, whispering to her who and what she was, that she was Mary Brodie, the mother of an illegitimate child, and echoing in her ears in endless repetition that word with which her father had condemned her when he hurled her from the house upon the night of the storm.

"I hear Janet's cracked cow-bell," he said at length. "Are you ready for the scones?"

433

She nodded her head, her throat too full for speech, and, as he lightly took her arm to assist her across the shingled beach, she was conscious of his touch upon her as more unbearable than any pain which she had ever felt.

"All ready! all ready!" cried Janet, rushing about like a fury. "Table and chairs and everything in the garden for ye, like ye ordered. And the scones are fresh—this mornin's bakin'."

"That's fine!" remarked Renwick, as he seated Mary in her chair and then took his own.

Although his tone had dismissed the old woman, she lingered, and after a full, admiring glance at Mary, moistened her lips, and was about to speak when, suddenly observing the look upon Renwick's face, she arrested, with a prodigious effort, the garrulous speech which trembled upon her tongue, and turned towards the house.

As she departed, shaking her head and muttering to herself a slight constraint settled upon Mary and Renwick; although the tea was excellent and the cool of the garden, spiced by the fragrance of the mignonette, delicious, neither appeared quite at ease.

"Janet's an old footer," he said, with an attempt at lightness. "That's a good Scotch word which just suits her. If I'd given her an opening she'd have deafened us." But after this remark, he fell into an awkward silence which impelled Mary's mind back to that only other occasion in her life when she had sat at table alone with a man, when she had eaten an ice-cream in the gaudy atmosphere of Bertorelli's Saloon, when Denis had pressed her foot with his and charmed her with his gay and sparkling tongue.

How different were her surroundings here, in this cool freshness of the cottage garden filled with the exhaled perfume of a hundred blossoms; how different, too, was her companion, who neither chattered of alluring trips abroad, nor yet, alas, caressed her foot with his. Now, however, he was shaking his head at her.

"You've only eaten two after all," he murmured, looking at her tragically, adding slowly, "and I said seven."

"They're so large," she protested.

"And you're so small—but you would be bigger if you did as you were told."

"I always did as you told me in the hospital!"

"Yes," he replied after a pause, "you did, indeed." A heaviness again seemed to settle upon him while his thoughts flew back to the vision of her as he had first seen her, with her eyes closed, inanimate, blanched, his broken, uprooted lily. At last he looked at his watch, then looked at her with a sombre face. "Time's getting along, I'm afraid. Shall we get back?"

"Yes," she whispered, "if you think it is time."

They arose and went out of the sweet seclusion of the garden—which might have been made for the enclosure of two ardent lovers—without further speech, and when he had helped her into the trap, he returned and paid old Janet.

"I'm not wantin' your siller, doctor," she skirled. "It's a pleasure to do it for you and the bonnie leddie."

"Here, Janet," he cried, "take it now or I'll be cross with you."

She sensed the faint difference in his mood and, as she took the money, whispered in a humble tone:

"Have I put my foot in't? I'm gey and sorry if I've done that. Or was it the scones that werna to your taste?"

"Everything was all right, Janet—splendid," he rejoined, as he mounted into his place. "Good-bye to you."

She waved them a faintly uncomprehending good-bye and, as they disappeared around the bend of the hill, she again shook her head, muttered to herself, and re-entered her cottage.

They spoke little on the way home, and when he had asked her if she were comfortable, or if she wished the covering of a rug—whether she had enjoyed the trip—if he should set Tim to a faster pace—he relapsed into a silence which grew more oppressive the nearer they approached to Levenford.

The tentacles of her home were opening again to receive her, and when they had enclosed her, Brodie, swollen-eyed and with a parched tongue, would awake morosely from his sleep to demand her immediate attention to his tea; Nessie would require her sympathy and consolation; she would be confronted at once by the innumerable tasks which it was her duty to perform. This brief and unexpected departure from the sadness of her life was nearly over and, though she had enjoyed it exquisitely, an exquisitely painful sorrow now filled her heart as she realised, dully, that this was probably—almost certainly—the last time that she would see him.

They were nearly at her gate now, and drawing up a short distance away, he said, in an odd voice:

"Well! here we are back again! It's been very short, hasn't it?"

"Very short," she echoed as she arose from the seat and descended to the ground.

"We should have had longer at Markinch," he said stiffly, then, after a pause: "I may not see you again. I suppose I better say good-bye." They looked at each other a long time and, from beneath him, her eyes shone with a faintly suppliant light; then he drew off his glove and extended his hand to her, saying in a strained tone: "Good-bye."

Mechanically she took his hand and as she felt within her grasp the firm cool strength of his fingers, that she had so often admired, that had once soothed her tortured body but would never again do so, these fingers she loved devotedly, her feelings suddenly overcame her and, with a sob, she pressed her warm lips fervently against his hand

and kissed it, then fled from him down the road and entered her house.

For a moment he looked at his hand incredulously, then raised his head, and, regarding her vanishing figure, made as though to leap out of the trap and follow her; but he did not, and after a long stillness, during which he again gazed at his hand, a strange look entered his eyes, he shook his head sadly, and drawing on his glove he drove slowly down the road.

IX

"BRING in some more porridge for your sister!" cried out Brodie to Mary in a loud voice. "You could put this in your eye what you've given her. How do you expect her to work on an empty stomach, and to-day of all days?"

"But, father," protested Nessie weakly, "I asked Mary not to give me so much. I'm to have a switched egg. The thought of more porridge sickens me this morning."

"Tuts, woman! You don't know what's good for ye," replied Brodie. "It's a good job you've got your father to look after ye and see that ye take what's wholesome. Stick into that porridge, now! That's the stuff to lie against your ribs and fit ye for what's before ye." And he leant back largely in his chair, surveying with a self-satisfied eye the figure of his younger daughter as, with a faintly trembling spoon, she endeavoured to thrust a few further spoonfuls of porridge between her nervous unwilling lips. He did not consider that it nauseated her to eat this morning, or that in her anxiety she might have been happier to be left quietly alone, but, in high fettle at the thought that this was the great day, the day of competition for the Latta, he had not departed for the office at his usual hour but remained to sustain and encourage her with his presence. He would, he thought, be a fine one if he could not see his daughter off to take the Latta. Gad! that was not the style of him, though! He had stuck to his task through all these weary months, ay, and seen that she had stuck to hers, with such perfect thoroughness that now he was not the man to spoil the broth for a halfpennyworth of salt. No! he would not go into the office this morning, would not, indeed, go in all day. He would take a whole holiday for the occasion. It was a festival; he had worked for it, and by God! he would enjoy it. A faint grin marked his features at this consideration and, still surveying her with satisfaction, he cried:

"That's right, woman! Take it steady. There's no need for hurry. Your father's behind ye."

"Has she not taken enough now, father?" ventured Mary, her eyes pleading towards him from out her fine-drawn face. "She's maybe too anxious to eat, this morning. I've a beaten egg for her here."

"Take it up, Ness—take it up," drawled Brodie, ignoring completely the interruption. "We know what puts pith into a body. Ye might be downright starved if it wasna for me. I'm not the one to let ye sit through a three hours examination with nothing inside of ye to stand up to it." He was in his element, reaping the fruits of his labour with her, his vicissitudes forgotten, the stabbing memory of Nancy for the present eased, and, opening his mouth in a broader and more derisive smile, he exclaimed: "Gad! it's just occurred to me that maybe that snipe o' a Grierson is sittin' at the table, watchin' that whelp o' his stap down his breakfast, and wonderin' what'n all the world he's goin' to make o' himself the day. Ay, it's a rich thought for me." His smile dried up, became bitter. "The Provost o' the Borough, forsooth—the fine, easy spokesman o' the town. God! he's lookin' gey small and mean and anxious this mornin', I'll wager." He paused for a moment then, observing that Nessie, who had succeeded in finishing the porridge, was sipping her egg and milk, he cried roughly, as though the bitterness of the thought of Grierson had not quite left him: "Here! take a scone and butter to that slush if ye will drink it." He glowered, too at Mary, adding: "Some folks would make a jaw box o' that stomach of yours!" then, returning his glance to Nessie, he continued, in an admonishing tone: "Don't flicker your een like that, woman; you would think that it was a frichtsome business that you were goin' up for to-day, instead o' an easy osey piece of writin' that you've got to do. It's all in your head waitin' to come out. All that's to do is to take up your pen and write it down. Is that anything to upset ye so that you take a scunner at the good, wholesome porridge?" He reviewed the profound wisdom of his logic blandly, then, as though the absurdity of her nervousness suddenly irritated him, he shot at her questioningly: "What the de'il is it you're feared of? Are ye not my daughter? What is there in this and about it all to make ye grue like that?"

She thought of the lofty examination hall, filled by the scratching of a score of fiercely competitive pens, she saw the silent, black-gowned figure of the examiner upon his rostrum sitting severe and omnipotent like a judge, she saw her own small bowed insignificant figure writing feverishly, but, veiling her gaze, she replied, hurriedly:

"There's nothing I'm afraid of, father! It's maybe the thought of the journey that's upsetting me a bit. I'm not thinkin' of the Latta at all. They might have posted the result already for all the good it'll do the others to go up."

He smiled at her again, broadly, exclaiming:

"That's more like the spirit! That's more like my daughter! We havena put ye through your paces for nothing. Now that I'm showin' you, ye maun step high when you're in the ring." He paused, pleased by his comparison, which, combined with his present elation and the excitement of her departure, reminded him vaguely of those days when he had set out for the Cattle Show, and he cried: "You're on show the day, Nessie, and I'm proud of ye. I know before ye go up who'll come back with the red ticket round her neck. My daughter, Nessie Brodie —that's the name that'll be on everybody's lips. We're goin' to startle the town between us. By God! they'll look the other way along their noses when they meet me now. We'll show them!" He considered her fondly, almost admiringly, remarking, after a moment: "Gad! it fair beats me, when I look at that wee head o' yours and think on all that's in it. Latin and French and mathematics, and heaven knows a' what. And yet it's no bigger than my fist. Ay! it's a true word that good gear gangs in small bulk. It's the quality that counts. It's downright gratifyin' for a man to see his own brains comin' out in his daughter, ay, and to be able to give her the opportunity. When I was your age I never had a chance like you." He sighed, commiseratingly. "No! I would have gone far had I been given the chance, but I had to get out into the world and make my own way. There were no Lattas in those days or I would have lifted the whole jing bang o' them." He lifted his eyes to her and exclaimed in an altered, excited tone: "But it'll be different with you, Nessie. You'll have your chance. I'll see to that. You'll see what I'll do for ye when you've won the Latta. I'll—I'll—I'll push ye on to the highest ye can go." He banged his fist upon the table and considered her triumphantly, adding: "Are ye not pleased with what I'm doin' for ye?"

"Yes, father," she murmured, "I'm—I'm real pleased at it all."

"And I should think so!" he cried. "There's not a man in Levenford would have done what I've done for ye. See that ye don't forget it! When ye come back with that Latta don't let it fly to your head. Remember who has done it for you!"

She glanced at him timidly, as she remarked in a low voice:

"You're not expecting me to bring it home to-night, father? It'll be a good while before the result comes out—a fortnight anyway!"

As though she had suddenly baulked him of the keen zest of his enjoyment, his look took on a sudden displeasure.

"Are ye off again on that tack? What's all this goin' on about results? Do you think I expect ye to bring the money back in a bag? I know it'll come in good time. I know it's for your studies. I'm not just gaspin' for't. But I seem to feel that you're gettin' anxious as to whether you'll get your fingers on it or not."

"Oh! no, father," she said hastily, "I'm not thinking about that at all. I was just afraid ye might think I would know for sure to-night."

"For sure," he repeated slowly; "are ye not 'for sure' already?"

438

"Yes! Yes!" she cried, "I'm sure. I'm dead positive about it. I hardly know what I'm saying I'm so excited at going up to the University."

"Don't let all this grand excitement run awa' with you," he replied, warningly. "Remember you're sixteen years old now, and if that's not old enough for you to have some control then you'll never have it. Don't lose your heid, that's all I say! Have ye got a' things that you need —your pen and your nibs and your rubber and what not?"

"I get everything I want up there," she answered meekly. "Everything like that is supplied to us."

"I see! Well in that case ye canna very well say ye had forgotten your pen." He paused and looked at the clock. "It's gettin' near time for your train. Have ye eaten your fill of everything?"

She felt her stomach turn uneasily as she whispered:

"Yes, father."

He arose and went over to his pipe rack, remarking complacently:

"Well, I've done my bit of the business anyway."

As he turned his back Mary moved nearer to his sister, saying in a low tone, close to Nessie's ear:

"I'll go down to the station with you, Nessie, just to keep you company and see that you get away all right. I'll not worry you by speaking."

"What's that?" cried Brodie, turning like a flash. He had, unfortunately, heard something of her words. "You'll go down to the station will ye?" he sneered. "Indeed now! That is verra considerate of ye. You'll do this and you'll do that with your interferin', the same sleekit way that your mother used to have. Is Nessie not capable of walkin' a few yards by herself that you must tie a bit of string round her neck and lead her along?" His sneer became a snarl. "Have I not told ye to leave my Nessie alone? You'll go to no station. You'll do nothing for her. She'll go down by herself." He turned to Nessie. "You don't want her botherin' you, do you, hinny?"

Her eyes fell as she faltered, in a faint voice: "No, father, not if you say it."

Brodie returned his glance to Mary with a dark insolence.

"You see!" he cried, "she doesna want ye! Keep out of what doesna concern ye. I'll do all that's wanted. I'll get her things for her myself this morning. Here! Nessie! Where's your hat and coat? I'm goin' to see you to the door." He swelled at the thought of the honour he was conferring upon her as she dumbly indicated the sofa where, brushed, sponged, and pressed, lay the worn, blue serge jacket of her everyday wear—the only one she now possessed—and her straw hat which now bravely flaunted a new satin band bought by her sister and stitched in place by her devoted fingers. He lifted the coat and hat, handed them to her, assisted her even in the fullness of his service, to assume the coat so that she now stood, a small, indescribably pathetic figure, clothed and ready for her journey. He patted her upon the shoulder with an extravagant flourish, exclaiming, as though he had dressed her fully with his own hands: "There now! you're all set up for the road. Do ye not think it's a great honour for you that I've taken the day off to see you out like this? Come on and I'll take you to the door."

She was, however, strangely disinclined to move, but remained with her head averted from him, her gaze drawn to Mary's dark and tender eyes, her lower lip drooping slightly, her thin fingers interlocked and twisting nervously. The clear skin of her face, denuded of its one-time colour almost to a pale transparency, seemed stretched tightly over the puny framework of her features, its pallor accentuated by the fine-spun sheen of the flaxen hair which, now unplaited, invested loosely the small, drawn countenance. She stood inert, realising that the climax of her endeavours was at hand and that she was loath to face it; then, suddenly appearing to forget the presence of her father, she advanced close to Mary and murmured in a low, almost inaudible tone: "I'm not wanting to go, Mary. I've got that band round my brow again. I would rather stay at home." Yet almost in the same breath, as though she were unaware that she had uttered these whispered words, she cried:

"I'm ready then, father. I've got everything I want. I'm as right as the mail and ready to stick into it."

He stared at her, then relaxed slowly.

"Come on, then, and look sharp about it. What are you moonin' about her for? No more of your silly dawdlin' or you'll miss your train."

"I'll not miss it, father," she cried eagerly, breaking away from Mary without looking at her—as though she had not heard her sister's last murmur of encouragement, or the promise to meet her at the station on her return. "No! No!" she exclaimed, "that wouldn't be like me to do a thing like that. I haven't worked all these six months for nothing. What an idea!" She drew back her narrow shoulders and, demonstrating her willingness by passing him and hastening into the hall, she went to the front door and opened it wide. "I'm away then, father," she cried loudly and in a fashion something after his own manner, "I'll be back when you see me!"

"Hold on a minute," he exclaimed, with a frown, lumbering after her. "I said I was goin' to see ye to the door, did I not? What's come over ye that you're rushing like this." He surveyed her for a moment from beneath his heavy eyebrows, then, reassured by the brightness now manifested in her eyes, he cried: "You'll do, though—you've got the look on ye as if ye couldna get to that examination quick enough. Away wi' ye, then. I'll warrant ye'll put your back into it. I've got ye just in the right fettle. Ye canna help but win it now." He clapped his hands together as though shooing her off, exclaiming: "Off with ye now and put salt on that Grierson's tail."

"Trust me," she returned lightly. "I'll put so much salt on him that I'll pickle him!"

"Good enough," he cried delightedly, following her fondly with his eyes as she went out of the gate and down the road. She did not once look back. As he stood at his door watching her slight figure dwindling into the distance he was filled momentarily by a powerful return of his old, proud, disdainful complacency. Gad! but she was a smarter, was his Nessie! As clever as you make them, with the sharpness of a needle, a sharpness that would prick that big, swollen bladder of a Grierson until the wind rushed out of him like a burst bagpipe. He had primed her well for the event too, made her as keen as a young greyhound to get out of the leash, and when she had left him just now there had been a gleam in her eye that had fairly warmed him. He had done that by his firm handling of the lass, forcing some of his own fire into her blood, filling her with a determination to succeed. "Stick into it, Nessie!" —that had been his slogan, and one which was more than justified! She would walk away with the Latta, putting a hundred miles, or marks, or whatever it might be, between Grierson and herself. Grierson might even be last! With a grim smile at the relish of his thoughts he slowly turned, sniffed the clear air with an added appreciation from his freedom, mounted the steps and went into the house.

Inside he halted, aimlessly, in the hall, losing something of the first flush of his elation in the realisation that, although it was not yet eleven o'clock and he was to-day a free man, he did not quite know what to do with himself; but after a moment he went into the kitchen and gravitated to his chair, where he sat watching Mary, out of the corner of his eye, as she went about her morning tasks. She made no comment upon his absence from the office and was, as always, quiet and composed, though to-day an added darkness lay in and around the pools of her eyes. In her manner she gave him no indication of the nature of her inward thoughts. He opened his lips to speak to her, to make some scathing comment upon the disparity between Nessie and herself barbed with a bitter innuendo concerning her past history, but he did not utter the words, knowing that whatever he said would be met by the same impenetrable silence. He would not speak yet! She could, he thought, be as dour as she liked and as quiet as she liked, but he knew what was at the back of her mind in spite of all her assumption of indifference. She was after his Nessie, interfering whenever she could, obstructing his intentions, laying herself out slyly at every turn to defeat his purpose. Let her wait though! He, too, was waiting and if ever she directly opposed him with Nessie, it would be a sad day for her!

As, without appearing to observe her, he followed the smooth, graceful movements of his daughter, an association of ideas confronted him suddenly with the memory of another woman whom he had loved as much as he hated this one—Nancy, the ultimate object of his waking, yes, even of his dreaming, mind. Now, however, he clenched his teeth firmly and shook the obsessing vision of her from his head, determined that nothing should mar the triumph of his day. It was Nessie that he wanted to think of—Nessie, his solace—who would now be sitting in the train, revolving in her clever brain some of these lessons which he had kept her at so assiduously, or considering, perhaps, the last exhortation he had given her. He had always felt that this would be a great day for him, and now he was aware that he must not let himself become depressed, that he must sustain his spirits at that high level to which they had risen earlier in the morning. He would have a drink—just to liven him a little.

His eye brightened as he arose from his chair and went to the dresser, where he opened the small cupboard on the left, drew out the familiar black bottle and—now kept always in readiness beside it—his own small tumbler. With the tumbler in one hand and the bottle in the other he sat down again in his chair, poured himself out some whisky and at once savoured it gratefully, appreciatively, holding the liquor for a moment between his palate and his tongue. The first drink of the day always passed over his lips with a richer and more satisfying flavour than any other, and now it trickled so warmly down his gullet that he was impelled to follow it quickly by a second. The first had been to himself —this would be in honour of Nessie! She might now be out of the train if she followed, as she undoubtedly would, his directions to get out at Partick Station, and might at this very moment be ascending the steep slope of Gilmorehill towards the grey pile of the University on its summit. He was conscious that this noble building, breathing of erudition, was well suited for the holding of the Latta examination, well worthy for the making of his daughter's mark within it. The professors might already have heard of her cleverness in some stray manner, for reports of brilliant scholars were circulated in devious but far-reaching ways in the academic world, and, even if this were not so, she had a name which they would recognise at once, which was a passport to her, there and anywhere she might choose to go. He drank to the University, to Nessie, and again to the name of Brodie.

This was better! To-day his mind reacted to the whisky in a different manner from that mere dulling of his morose despondency which had lately been the result of his potations; now, the old-time exhilaration of the early days of his toping was returning to him, and as he became aware of this delicious fact, his spirits rose, and he began to cast about in his mind for some channel into which he might direct his new-found animation. It was unconscionably dull for a cheerful man to sit under the sombre eye of his melancholy daughter, and, perceiving that he would have to seek his amusement out of the house, he considered for a moment the idea of visiting the office, not, of course, to work, but merely, in an informal way, to divert those two young sprigs in his room, and to tweak the offensive nose of the upstart Blair. Being Saturday, however, it was a half-day at the office—which meant that they would soon be stopping work and going home—and he felt, too, that the occasion demanded a more appropriate celebration than merely a return to the scene of his daily labour. He abandoned this idea with only a faint regret, which vanished completely as he drowned it in another glass of Mountain Dew.

Dew! Dew upon the grass—green grass—the bowling green! Ah! he had it at last! Who said that there was not inspiration in that famous blend of Teacher which he always favoured? His face lit up with a lively delight at his aptness in remembering that the summer tournament of the Levenford Bowling Club was to be held at the Wellhall Green this afternoon, and he smiled broadly as he considered that all the worthies would be present—present for a certainty—from wee Johnnie Paxton up to the Lord High Provost Grierson himself.

"Gad!" he muttered, slapping his thigh, in quite his old manner, "that's the ticket, right enough! I'll have them all boxed up in that one place and I'll throw the Latta in their teeth there and then. I'll show them I'm not feared o' them. It's high time I was makin' myself heard again. It strikes me I've been over long about it."

He crowned his satisfaction with a bumper, then, raising his voice, cried:

"Hurry up with my dinner in there. I'm wantin' it quick. I'm goin' out this afternoon and I want something inside of me first. Let it be some decent food too, and none o' that swill ye were foistin' off on Nessie this morning."

"Your dinner's ready, father," Mary replied quietly. "You can have it now, if you wish."

"I do wish, then," he retorted. "Get on with it and don't stand glumphin' at me like that."

She quickly laid the table and served him with his meal, but, though this was to his taste, and, indeed, infinitely better than any which Nancy had ever prepared for him, he gave neither praise nor thanks. He did justice to it however, and with an appetite stimulated by the whisky, for once ate heartily, dividing his thoughts, as he masticated vigorously, between his plans for the afternoon and the further consideration of Nessie. She would have begun, actually, the examination by this time, and would be sitting driving her pen over page after page of paper whilst the others, and particularly young Grierson, chewed the wooden ends of theirs and stared at her enviously. Now he saw her, having entirely finished one exercise book, rise from her place and, her small, self-conscious face glowing, advance to demand another from the examiner. She had used up one book already, the first in the room to do so—Nessie Brodie, his daughter—whilst that young snipe Grierson had not even filled half of his yet! He chuckled slightly at her remarkable prowess and bolted his food with an added gusto from the vision of the other's discomfiture. His thoughts ran chiefly in this strain during the rest of the meal and, when he had finished, he arose and drank again, emptying the bottle to the hope that she would require, not two, but three books to convey to the professors the wide extent of her knowledge.

It was still too early for his descent upon the Wellhall Bowling Green, for he wished to allow a full congregation of the notables to collect, and realising that he was not yet ripe with the careless rapture best suited to such an adventure, confronted, too, by the mere hollow shell which had held the Mountain Dew, he decided to adventure out and rest himself for an hour in the Wellhall Vaults which conveniently adjoined the Green.

Accordingly, he left the house and proceeded down the road not, however, with the set, morose face and unseeing stare which marked him lately in the streets but, fortified by his mood and the knowledge of his daughter's success, with a freer, easier carriage which again invited inspection. Few people were about as yet, but when he had crossed Railway Road he observed on the other side of the street the stately figure of Dr. Lawrie, not driving, but walking, and immediately he crossed over and accosted him.

"Good day to you, Dr. Lawrie," he cried affably. It had been "Lawrie" in the old days and without the affability. "I'm pleased to meet ye."

"Good day," returned the other, thinking of his unpaid bill and speaking with the small store of curtness he possessed.

"It's well met for us just now," retorted Brodie. "Well met! Do ye know what's happening at this very moment?"

Lawrie eyed him warily, as he uttered a cautious: "No."

"My Nessie is up at the University winning the Latta for me while you and me are talkin' here," cried Brodie. "It's a justification of your own words. Don't ye mind what ye told me—that she had a head on her in a thousand?"

"Indeed! Indeed!" returned Lawrie pompously, and with a slight degree of cordiality. "I'm gratified to hear that. Winning the Latta. It all helps. It'll be a little more grist to the mill I suppose." He looked sideways at the other, hoping that he would take the hint, then suddenly he looked directly at Brodie and exclaimed: "Winning?—did ye say she had won the Latta?"

"It's as good as won," replied Brodie comfortably. "She's at it the now—this very minute. I took the day off to see that she got away in the best o' fettle. She went off with a glint in her eye that spoke for victory. She'll fill three books ere she's done!"

"Indeed!" said Lawrie again, and, eyeing the other strangely, he drew insensibly away, remarking: "I'll have to be getting along now— an important consultation—my horse just cast a shoe along the road there —I'm late!"

"Don't go yet, man," remonstrated Brodie, buttonholing the embarrassed Lawrie firmly. "I havena told ye half about my daughter yet. I'm real fond o' that lass, you know. In my own way. Just in my own way. I've wrought hard with her for the last six months."

"Pray let me go, Mr. Brodie," cried Lawrie, struggling to free himself.

"We've burned the midnight oil between us, have Nessie and I," retorted Brodie gravely. "It's been a heap o' work—but by gad, it's been worth it!"

"Really sir," exclaimed Lawrie in a shrill, indignant tone, wrenching himself free and looking round to see if his contact with this ruffianly looking individual had been observed, "you've taken a great liberty! I don't like it! Take care how you address me in future." Then, with a last, outraged look he reinflated his cheeks and bounced off quickly down the road.

Brodie gazed after him in some amazement. He failed to detect anything in his recent conduct which could have aroused indignation, and finally, with a shake of his head, he turned and resumed his way, reaching, without further encounters, the haven of the Wellhall Vaults. Here, he was not known and he remained silent, but drinking steadily, filling himself with liquor and further visions of his daughter's prowess, until three o'clock. Then he got up, set his hat well back upon his head, drew in his lips, and swaggered into the open once more.

The mere step to the Wellhall Green he accomplished with hardly a falter, and soon he was inside the trim enclosure where the smooth square of green lay vivid in the sunshine, marred only by the dark, blurred figures of the players wavering across it before his eye. What a game for grown men, he thought contemptuously; to roll a few balls about like a gang of silly bairns. Could they not take out a gun or a horse, like he had once done, if they wanted their exercise or amusement.

His gaze, however, did not remain long upon the green but, lifting quickly, sought the small group that sat upon the veranda of the pavilion at the further end of the ground, and he smiled with a sardonic gratification as he observed that, even as he had foretold, they were all there—from simple John Paxton to the Lord High Provost of the Borough. He gathered himself together again and advanced deliberately towards him.

For a moment he proceeded unobserved by this small gathering—for they were all concentrating upon the game before them—but suddenly Paxton looked up, observed him and gasped in amazement:

"Guidsakes—just look what's coming!" His tone drew their attention

445

at once, and following his startled gaze, they, too, regarded the strange, uncouth, strutting figure as it bore down upon them, and they exclaimed, variously:

"Good God! it's Brodie. I havena seen him for months!"

"He's as fou as a lord by the looks o' him."

"Losh! it's the drunken earl himsel'."

"Look at the face o' him and the clothes o' him."

"Ay, but look at the swagger o' the thing!"

They were silent as he drew near, directing their eyes away from him towards the green, disowning him, but still failing to perturb him as, oscillating slightly, he stood encompassing them with his sneer.

"Dear, dear," he snickered, "we're very engrossed in watching the wee, troolin' balls. It's a grand, excitin' pastime. We'll be lookin' on at a game o' peever next if we're not careful, like a band o' silly lassies." He paused and queried pertinently: "Who has won, Provost? Will ye tell me—you that's such a grand spokesman for the town?"

"This game's not finished yet," replied Grierson after a moment's hesitation, and still with his eyes averted. The spite which he had once entertained against Brodie now found nothing in the other's wretched condition with which to justify itself and seemed suddenly to have evaporated. Besides, was he not the Provost? "Nobody has won yet," he added more affably.

"This game's not won yet," echoed Brodie sardonically. "Well, well! I'm sorry to hear it. But I can tell ye a game that *is* won!"

He glared round them all and, his anger rising at their indifference, shouted:

"It's the Latta I'm talkin' about. Maybe ye think it's like this rotten game of bowls that you're watchin'—not finished yet. But I tell you it is finished—finished and done wi'—and it's my Nessie that's won it!"

"Hush! man, hush!" exclaimed Gordon, who sat immediately confronted by Brodie. "I can't see the play for ye. Sit down or stand aside and don't blatter the ears off us."

"I'll stand where I like. Shift me if ye can," retorted Brodie dangerously. Then he sneered: "Who are you to talk, anyway? You're only the ex-provost—you're not the king o' the castle any more—it's our dear friend Grierson that's got your shoes on now, and it's him I'm wantin' to speak to." He directed his sneering gaze at Grierson and addressed him: "Did you hear what I said about the Latta, Provost? No! dinna start like that—I havena forgotten about that braw son o' yours. I know well that he's gone up for it. Provost Grierson's son is up for the Latta. God! it must be as good as in his pocket."

"I never said that yet," replied Grierson, provoked in spite of himself. "My boy can take his chance! It's not as if he was needin' the money for his education, onyway."

Brodie ground his teeth at the sharp implication in the other's careless

446

words and tried fiercely to force his brain to contrive some devastating reply, but as always, when opposing Grierson, he could find no suitable expression of his wrath. The thought that he, who had advanced a moment ago in lordly indifference, had been rendered impotent by a word, goaded him, and, sensing also that he was not creating the impression upon them which he had wished, his temper overcame him and he shouted:

"Why did ye ask me to withdraw my daughter if ye didna want your whelp to win it?—Answer me that, you sneakin' swine! You stopped me at the Cross and asked me to keep back my Nessie."

"Tuts! don't shout like that at my ear, man," retorted Grierson coolly. "I don't like the reek o' your breath. I told ye before I was thinkin' of your Nessie. Somebody that's qualified to speak asked me to mention it to ye. I wasna wantin' to do it, and now I'm sorry I did mention it."

"You're a liar!" bawled Brodie. "You're a damned mealy-mouthed liar!"

"If ye've come here to force a quarrel on me, I'll not let ye do it," returned Grierson. "There's no lying about the matter and no secret either. Now that your daughter has gone up, I don't mind tellin' you it was Dr. Renwick asked me to speak to ye."

"Renwick!" exclaimed Brodie incredulously. He paused, then, as a light dawned upon him, he shot out: "I see! I see it plain. You put him up to it. He's hand in glove with you against me. He hates me just as much as do—as much as ye all do." He swept his arm blindly around them. "I know you're all against me, you jealous swine, but I don't care. I'll win through. I'll trample over ye all yet. Have any of ye got a daughter that can win the Latta? Answer me that!"

"If your daughter does win the Latta," cried someone, "what the de'il does it matter to us? Let her get it and good luck to her. I don't give a tinker's curse who wins it."

Brodie gazed at the speaker.

"Ye don't care?" he replied slowly. "Ye do care—you're leein' to me. It'll spite the faces off ye if a Brodie wins the Latta."

"Away home man, for God's sake," said Gordon quietly. "You're not yourself. You're drivellin'. You can't know what you're sayin'."

"I'll go when I like," mumbled Brodie. The stimulation of the drink suddenly left him, his fierceness waned, he no longer desired to rush upon Grierson and tear him apart, and, as he gazed at their varying expressions of unconcern and disgust, he began to feel profoundly sorry for himself, to ask himself if this could be the same company which he had dominated and overawed in the past. They had never liked him but he had controlled them by his power, and now that they had escaped from out his grasp, his sympathy towards himself grew so excessive that it reached the point of an exceeding sorrow which sought almost to express itself in tears. "I see how it is," he muttered gloomily, addressing them at large. "Ye think I'm all over and done wi'. I'm not good enough for ye, now. God! if it didna make me laugh it would make me greet. To think that ye should sit there and look down your noses at me —at me that comes of stock that's so high above ye they wouldna even use ye as doormats." He surveyed them each in turn, looking vainly for some sign of encouragement, some indication that he was impressing them. Then, although no sign came, he still continued, more slowly, and in a dejected, unconvincing tone: "Don't think that I'm finished! I'm comin' up again. Ye can't keep a good man down—and ye'll not keep me down, however much ye may try. Wait and see what my Nessie will do. That'll show ye that stuff that's in us. That's why I came here. I don't want to know ye. I only wanted to tell ye that Nessie Brodie would win the Latta, and now that I've done it I'm satisfied!" His moody eye swept them, then, finding that he had nothing more to say, that they, too, were silent, he moved off; yet after a few paces he arrested himself, turned, opened his mouth to speak; but no speech came, and at length he lowered his head, swung round, and again shambled off. They let him go without a word.

As he left the confines of the Green and proceeded along the road nursing bitterly his wounded pride, he suddenly perceived in the distance the figures of his two daughters approaching him from the station. He stared at them almost stupidly, at Nessie and Mary Brodie, both of them his children, as though the strange sight of them together in the public street confused him, then all at once he realised that Nessie was returning from her examination, that Mary had disobeyed him by meeting the train. No matter! He could deal later with Mary, but now he desired urgently to know how Nessie had fared, to appease his wounded vanity in the knowledge of her success, and, walking forward quickly, he met them, confronted them in the middle of the pavement. There, absorbing eagerly every detail of the younger girl's tired face he cried:

"How did ye get on, Nessie? Quick! tell me—was everything all right?"

"Yes," she murmured. "Everything was all right."

"How many books did ye fill?—was it two or three?"

"Books?" she echoed faintly. "I only wrote in one book, father."

"Only one book!" he exclaimed. "Ye only filled one book for all the time ye've been away." He considered her in astonishment, then, his face slowly hardening, he demanded harshly: "Can ye not speak, woman? Don't ye see I want to know about the Latta. I'm asking you for the last time. Will you tell me once and for all how ye got on?"

With a great effort she controlled herself, looked at him out of her placating eyes and, forcing her pale lips into a smile, cried:

"Splendid, father! I got on splendid. I couldn't have done better."

He stared down at her for a long time, filled by the recollection of the arrogance with which he had proclaimed her success, then he said slowly, in an odd, strained voice:

"I hope ye have done splendid. I hope so! For if ye haven't then, by God! it'll be the pity of ye!"

X

It was the Saturday following that of the examination for the Latta, the time half-past ten in the morning. Nessie Brodie stood looking out of the parlour window with an expression of expectation upon her face mingled, too, by a hidden excitement which made her eyes shine bright and large out of her small face, as though they awaited the appearance of some sudden, thrilling manifestation in the empty roadway that lay before them. The face, despite its ingenuous weakness, wore something of an unguarded look, for the consciousness that she was alone in the room and unobserved allowed a freer and more unrestrained display of these emotions that she had carefully concealed during the course of the past, uneasy week.

During that week her father's attitude to her had been insupportable, alternating between a fond complacency and a manner so disturbing and threatening that it terrified her; yet she had borne it, comforting herself in the knowledge that she possessed a strategy more subtle, more effective than all his bluster and his bullying. She thought she had won the Latta, had experienced, indeed, with the passage of each of the seven days since the examination, a growing certainty that she had won it. It was impossible that all her work, the compulsory toil, all these long, cold hours of endurance in this same parlour could go unrewarded, and, although a feeling of dissatisfaction with her own paper had possessed her when she left the University last week, now her confidence was completely restored; she felt that she must have taken the Bursary —to use her father's phrase—in her stride. Still, there was always the chance, the faint unreasonable chance that she might not have been successful! It was unthinkable, impossible, yet it was against this chance that by some strange, astute working of her mind she had so cleverly formulated her precaution. They thought, both Mary and her father, that the result of the Latta would not be announced for another week —she had told them so and they had believed her—but she knew better than that, knew that the result would reach her this morning. She was expecting it immediately, for the forenoon delivery of letters at eleven o'clock contained the Glasgow mail, and from enquiries which she had made at the University she knew that the results of the examination had been posted to each competitor on the evening of the day before. She smiled slyly, even now, at the consideration of her own cleverness in deluding them all. It had been a brilliant idea, and daring too—not unlike the sudden sending of that letter to Mary—yet she had accomplished it. Her father had so crushed and oppressed her with the preparation for the examination that she had wanted room to breathe, space to think; and now she had contrived it for herself. It was a triumph. She had a whole week to herself before he would demand threateningly to see the evidence of her success, an entire week during which she could think and cleverly contrive some means of escape from him should she have failed. But she had not failed—she had succeeded—and, instead of using every moment of that precious week to prepare herself against her father's anger, she would treat it like a hidden happiness, treasuring her secret until she could no longer contain it, then delivering it unexpectedly, triumphantly, upon their astounded ears. They would not know until she enlightened them; nobody must know, not even Mary, who had been so good, so kind and loving to her. Surely she should have told Mary? No! That would have spoiled the entire plan. When she did speak she would tell her first, but now everything must be kept secret and sealed within her own mind; she wanted no one peering over her shoulders when she opened that letter, she must be alone, secluded from prying glances that might watch the trembling of her fingers or the eagerness of her eyes.

As she stood there, suddenly she started, and a faint tremor passed over her as she observed an indistinct blue figure at the foot of the road —the postman, who would, in the slow regularity of his routine, reach her within the space of half an hour. In half an hour she would be receiving the letter, must, moreover, be alone to receive it undisturbed! With an effort she withdrew her eyes from the distant figure of the postman and involuntarily, almost automatically, turned and advanced to the door, altering her expression, so that her features lost their revealing look, became secretive, blank, then drew slowly into a frown. This troubled frown intensified as she entered the kitchen and went up to Mary when, pressing her hand against her brow, she exclaimed wearily:

"That headache is on me again, Mary! Worse than ever this time."

Mary looked at her sister sympathetically.

"My poor, wee Nessie!" she exclaimed. "I'm sorry about that! I thought you had got rid of them for good."

"No! No!" cried Nessie, "it's come back. It's hurting me—give me one of my powders, quick!"

From under the cover of her hand she watched Mary as she went to the white cardboard box that stood always on the mantelpiece, observed her open the box and discover that it was empty, then heard her exclaim, condolingly:

"They're all finished, I'm afraid! I'm sorry, dear! I was sure you had one or two left."

"Finished?" exclaimed Nessie. "That's terrible. I can't do without them. My head's bursting. I must have one at once."

Mary looked at her sister's lowered face with solicitude, as she remarked:

"What can I do for you, dear? Would you like a cold cloth and vinegar on it?"

"I told you these were no good," cried Nessie urgently. "You'll need to get me a powder. Go out this very minute for me."

Mary's expression grew doubtful and, after a pause, she said:

"I can hardly go out just now, dearie. There's the dinner to make and everything. Lie down a little and I'll rub your head."

"Away and get the powder," the other burst out. "Can ye not do that one, little thing for me—you that's aye sayin' you want to help me? I'll not be right till I get one—ye know that it's the only thing that eases me."

After a moment's hesitation during which she gazed compassionately at Nessie, Mary moved her hands slowly to the strings of her apron, and untied them even more slowly.

"All right, dear! I can't see you suffer like that. I'll go and get them made up for you right away"; then, as she went out of the room, she added sympathetically: "I'll not be a minute. Lie down and rest till I come back."

Nessie lay down obediently, realising with an inward satisfaction that the minute would be a full hour, that she would have ample time to receive her letter and compose herself again before Mary could make the journey to the town, wait tediously at the chemist's for the compounding of the prescription, and return to her. She smiled faintly as she heard the front door close behind her sister; and this smile again unlocked her restraint, for that strangely artful expression returned to her face and she jumped up and ran eagerly into the parlour.

Yes! there was Mary going down the road, hurrying—the poor thing—to secure the powders, as though there were not two still in the house hidden in the dresser drawer, and passing actually, without a sign, the postman as he made his way towards her. He had something in his bag that would bring more relief than all the powders that Lawrie could ever give her. How slow he was, though! It was, she perceived, Dan, the elder of the two postmen who came upon this round, and the very one who used to hand in Matt's letters with such an air of consequential dignity, exclaiming importantly:

"Something worth while in that one by the look o' it." No letter of Matt's had ever been so important as this one! Why did he not hurry?

As she remained there, she felt vaguely that under the same circumstances of excitement and anticipation she had once before stood at this window in the parlour, and she became aware suddenly, without consciously seeking in her mind, that it had been on that day when Mamma had received the wire that had so upset her. She recollected the delicious thrill it had given her to hold the orange slip within her hand and remembered, too, how cleverly she had manœuvred to ascertain the ignorance of Grandma Brodie upon the matter. Now she did not fear that her letter would be discovered by the old woman who, half blind and almost wholly deaf, kept to her room except when the call of mealtimes withdrew her from it.

Dan was getting nearer, leisurely crossing and recrossing the street, hobbling along as though he had corns upon every toe, wearing his heavy bag on his bent back like a packman. Still, how slow he was! Yet now, strangely, she did not wish quite so ardently that he should hurry, but rather that he should take his time, and leave her letter till the last. Everybody in the road seemed to be getting letters to-day, and all, as she desired, before she received hers. Would John Grierson have had his yet? Much good it would do him if he had. She would have liked dearly to see the chawed look upon his face when he opened it. As for herself, she did not now want a letter at all; it was upsetting, and she knew so well she had won the Latta that it was not worth the trouble of opening an envelope to confirm it. Some envelopes were difficult to open!

Yet here was Dan actually advancing to her house, causing her to tremble all over, making her gasp as he passed the gate carelessly—as if aware that there could now be no letters for the Brodies—then, as he stopped suddenly and returned, sending her heart leaping violently into her throat.

An age passed before the door bell rang; but it did ring and she was compelled, whether she now wished it or not, to pull herself away from the window and advance to the door—not with the skipping eagerness that she had displayed when fetching the telegram—but slowly—with a strange detached sense of unreality—as though she still stood by the window and watched her own form move deliberately from the room.

The letter, long, stiff, and important, with a blue shield upon the back, was in Dan's hand and her gaze became fixed upon it as she stood, unconscious of the smile which crinkled his veined, russet cheek and showed his tobacco-stained teeth, almost unconscious of the old postman himself—yet dimly hearing him say, even as she expected: "Something worth while in that one, by the look o' it."

Now it was her hand which was cognisant of the letter, her fingers sensitively perceiving the rich, coarse texture of the paper, her eyes observing the thin, copper-plate inscription of her own name which ran accurately across the centre of its white surface. How long she regarded her name she did not know, but when she looked up Dan had gone, without her having thanked him or even spoken to him, and, as she glanced along the vacant roadway, she felt a vague regret at her lack of courtesy, considered that she must make amends to him in some fashion, perhaps apologise or give him some tobacco for his Christmas box. But first she must open this that he had given her.

She turned, closing the door behind her, and, realising that she need not return to that dismal parlour which she hated so much, traversed the hall without a sound and entered the empty kitchen. There she immediately rid her hand of the letter by placing it upon the table. Then she returned to the door by which she had just entered, satisfied herself that it was firmly shut, advanced to the scullery door, which she inspected in like fashion, and finally, as though at last convinced of her perfect seclusion, came back and seated herself at the table. Everything was as she desired it, everything had befallen as she had so cleverly foreseen, and now, alone, unobserved, concealed, with nothing more to do, nothing for which to wait, she was free to open the letter.

Her eye fell upon it again, not fixedly, as when she had received it, but with a growing, flickering agitation. Her lips suddenly felt stiff, her mouth dried up, and she shook violently from head to foot. She perceived—not the long, white oblong of the letter—but her own form, bent eternally over a book, at school, at home, in the examination hall of the University, and always overcast by the massive figure of her father, which lay above and upon her like a perpetual shadow. The letter seemed to mirror her own face which looked up, movingly, telling her that all she had worked for, all she had been constrained to work for, that the whole object of her life, lay there, upon the table, crystallised in a few written words upon one hidden sheet of paper.

Her name was upon the envelope, and the same name must be upon that hidden sheet within, or else everything that she had done, her very life itself, would be futile. She knew that her name was inside, the single name that was always sent without mention of the failures, the name of the winner of the Latta, and yet she was afraid to view it.

That, clearly, was ridiculous! She need not be afraid of her name which, as her father rightly insisted, was a splendid name, a noble name, and one of which she might justly be proud. She was Nessie Brodie—she was the winner of the Latta! It had all been arranged months beforehand, everything had been settled between her father and herself. My! but she was the clever, wee thing—the smartest lass in Levenford—the first girl to win the Bursary—a credit to the name of Brodie! As in a dream her hand stole towards the letter.

How curious that her fingers should tremble in this strange fashion as, under her own eyes, they opened the stiff envelope. How thin her fingers were! She had not willed them to open the letter and yet they had done so; even now they held the inner sheet in their faintly trembling clasp.

Well! she must see her name—the name of Nessie Brodie. That, surely, was no hardship—to view for one moment her own name. That moment had come!

With a heart that beat suddenly with a frantic, unendurable agitation she unfolded the sheet and looked at it.

The name which met her shrinking gaze was not hers—it was the name of Grierson. John Grierson had won the Latta!

For a second she regarded the paper without comprehension, then her eyes filled with a growing horror, which widened her pupils until the words before her blurred together then faded from her view. She sat motionless, rigid, scarcely breathing, the paper still within her grasp, and into her ears flowed a torrent of words, uttered in her father's snarling voice. She was alone in the room, he at the office a mile away —yet in her tortured imagination she heard him, saw him vividly before her.

"Grierson's won it! You've let that upstart brat beat you. It wouldna have mattered so much if it had been anybody else—but Grierson— the son o' that measly swine. And after all I've talked about ye winnin' it. It's damnable! damnable, I tell ye! You senseless idiot—after the way I've slaved with ye, keepin' ye at it for all I was worth! God! I canna thole it. I'll wring that thin neck o' yours for ye."

She sank deeper into her chair, shrinking from his invisible presence, her eyes still horrified, but cowering too, as though he advanced upon her with his huge open hands. Still she remained motionless, even her lips did not move, but she heard herself cry, feebly:

"I did my best, father. I could do no more. Don't touch me, father."

"Your best," he hissed. "Your best wasna good enough to beat Grierson. You that swore ye had the Latta in your pocket! I've got to sit down under another insult because of ye. I'll pay ye. I told ye it would be the pity of ye if ye failed."

"No! No! father," she whispered. "I didn't mean to fail. I'll not do it again—I promise you! You know I've always been the top of the class. I've always been your own Nessie. You wouldna hurt a wee thing like me. I'll do better next time."

"There'll be no next time for you," he shouted at her. "I'll—I'll throttle ye for what you've done to me."

As he rushed upon her she saw that he was going to kill her and, while she shrieked, closing her eyes in a frantic, unbelievable terror, the encircling band that had bound her brain for the last weary months of her study snapped suddenly and gave to her a calm and perfect peace. The tightness around her head dissolved, she was unloosed from the bonds that had confined her, her fear vanished, and she was free. She opened her eyes, saw that her father was no longer there, and smiled— an easy, amused smile which played over her mobile features like ripples

454

of light and passed insensibly into a high, snickering laugh. Though her laughter was not loud, it moved her like a paroxysm, making the tears roll down her cheeks and shaking her thin body with its utter abandon. She laughed for a long time then, as suddenly as her mirth had begun it ceased, her tears dried instantly, and her face assumed a wise, crafty expression like a gigantic magnification of that slight artfulness which it had worn when she stood thinking in the parlour. Now, however, clearly guided by a force within her, she did not think; she was above the necessity for thought. Pressing her lips into a prim line, she laid the letter, which had all this time remained within her grasp, carefully upon the table like a precious thing, and rising from her chair stood, casting her gaze up and down, moving her head like a nodding doll. When the nodding ceased, a smile, transient this time, flickered across her face and whispering softly, encouragingly to herself: "What ye do, ye maun do well, Nessie dear," she turned and went tiptoeing out of the room. She ascended the stairs with the same silent and extravagant caution, paused in a listening attitude upon the landing, then, reassured, went mincing into her room. There, without hesitation, she advanced to the basin and ewer, poured out some cold water and began carefully to wash her face and hands. When she had washed meticulously, she dried herself, shining her pale features to a high polish by her assiduous application of the towel, then, taking off her old, grey beige dress she took from her drawer the clean cashmere frock which was her best. This, apparently, did not now wholly please her, for she shook her head and murmured:

"That's not pretty enough for ye, Nessie dear. Not near pretty enough for ye, now!" Still, she put it on with the same unhurried precision, and her face lightened again as she lifted her hands to her hair. As she unplaited it and brushed it quickly with long, rapid strokes she whispered, from time to time, softly, approvingly: "My bonnie hair! My bonnie, bonnie hair!" Satisfied at last with the fine, golden sheen which her brushing had produced, she stood before the mirror and regarded herself with a far away, enigmatical smile; then, taking her only adornment, a small string of coral beads, once given her by Mamma to compensate for Matthew's forgetfulness, she made as though to place them round her neck when, suddenly, she withdrew the hand that held them. "They're gey and sharp, these beads," she murmured, and laid them back gently upon her table.

Without further loss of time she marched softly out of her room, descended the stairs, and in the hall put on her serge jacket and her straw hat with the brave, new, satin ribbon that Mary had bought and sewn for her. She was now dressed completely for the street—in her best—dressed, indeed, as she had been on the day of the examination. But she did not go out of the house; instead, she slid stealthily back into the kitchen.

Here her actions quickened. Taking hold of one of the heavy wooden chairs, she moved it accurately into the centre of the room, then turned to her heaped books upon the dresser and transferred these to the chair, making a neat, firm pile which she surveyed with a pleased expression, adjusting some slight deviations from the regular symmetry of the heap with light, fastidious touches of her fingers. "That's a real neat job, my dear," she murmured contentedly. "You're a woman that would have worked well in the house." Even as she spoke she moved backwards from the chair, still admiring her handiwork, but when she reached the door she turned and slipped lightly into the scullery. Here she bent and rummaged in the clothes basket at the window, then, straightening up with an exclamation of triumph, she returned to the kitchen bearing something in her hand. It was a short length of clothes line. Now her movements grew even more rapid. Her nimble fingers worked feverishly with one end of the thin rope, she leaped on the chair and, standing upon the piled books, corded the other end over the iron hook of the pulley on the ceiling. Then, without descending from the chair, she picked up the letter from the table and pinned it upon her bosom, muttering as she did so: "First prize, Nessie! What a pity it's not a red card." Finally, she inserted her neck delicately into the noose which she had fashioned, taking heed that she did not disarrange her hat and, passing the rope carefully under the mane of her hair, tightened it and was ready. She stood gaily poised upon the elevation of the books like a child perched upon a sand castle, her gaze directed eagerly out of the window across the foliage of the lilac tree. As her eyes sought the distant sky beyond, her foot, resting upon the back of the chair, pushed the support from beneath her, and she fell. The hook in the ceiling wrenched violently upon the beam above which still securely held it. The rope strained, but did not break. She hung suspended, twitching like a marionette upon a string, while her body, elongating, seemed to stretch out desperately one dangling foot, straining to reach the floor, yet failing by a single inch to reach it. The hat tilted grotesquely across her brow, her face darkened slowly as the cord bit into her thin, white neck; her eyes that were placating, pleading even, and blue like speedwells, clouded with pain, with a faint wonder, then slowly glazed; her lips purpled, thickened, and fell apart, her small jaw dropped, a thin stream of froth ran silently across her chin. To and fro she oscillated gently, swinging in the room in a silence broken only by the faint flutter of the lilac leaves against the window panes, until, at last, her body quivered faintly and was still.

The house was silent, as with the silence of consummation, but after a long hush the sound was heard of some person stirring above, and slowly, haltingly, descending the stairs. At length the kitchen door opened and Grandma Brodie came into the room. Drawn from her room by the approach of another meal-time and the desire to make herself some especially soft toast, she now tottered forward, her head lowered, totally unobservant, until she blundered against the body.

"Tch! Tch! where am I going?" she mumbled, as she recoiled, mazedly looking upwards out of dim eyes at the hanging figure which the thrust of her arm had once more set in motion, and which now swung lightly against her. Her aged face puckered incredulously as she peered, fell suddenly agape and, as the body of the dead girl again touched her, she staggered back and screamed: "Oh! God in heaven! What—what is't?—She's—she's——" Another scream rent her! Mouthing incoherently, she turned, shambled from the room, and flinging open the front door, stumbled headlong from the house.

Her agitated gait had taken her through the courtyard and into the roadway when, turning to continue her flight, she collided with and almost fell into the arms of Mary, who gazed at her in some distress, and cried:

"What's the matter, Grandma? Are you ill?"

The old woman looked at her, her face working, her sunken lips twitching, her tongue speechless.

"What's wrong with you, Grandma?" repeated Mary in amazement. "Are you not well?"

"There! In there!" stuttered the other, pointing her stark hand wildly to the house. "Nessie! Nessie's in there! She's—she's hangit herself—in the kitchen."

Mary's glance leaped to the house, observed the open door; with a stricken cry she rushed past the old woman, and, still holding the white box of headache powders in her hand, flung herself up the steps, along the lobby, and into the kitchen.

"O God!" she cried, "my Nessie!" She dropped the box she carried, tore out the drawer of the dresser, and, snatching a knife, turned and hacked furiously at the tense rope. In a second this parted, and the warm body of Nessie sagged soundlessly against her and trailed upon the floor. "O God!" she cried again. "Spare her to me. We've only got each other left. Don't let her die!" Flinging her arms around her dead sister, she lowered her to the ground; throwing herself upon her knees, with trembling fingers she plucked at the cord sunk in the swollen neck and finally unloosed it. She beat the hands of the body, stroked the brow, cried inarticulately, in a voice choked by sobs: "Speak to me, Nessie! I love you, dearest sister! Don't leave me." But no reply came from those parted, inanimate lips and in an agony of despair Mary leaped to her feet and rushed again out of the house into the roadway. Looking wildly about, she espied a boy upon a bicycle bearing down on her.

"Stop!" she cried, waving her arms frantically; and as he drew up wonderingly beside her she pressed her hand to her side and gasped, her words tumbling one upon another: "Get a doctor! Get Dr. Renwick!

457

Quick! My sister is ill! Go quickly! Quickly!" She sped him from her with a last cry and, returning to the house, she rushed for water, knelt again, raised Nessie in her arms, moistened the turgid lips, tried to make her drink. Then, laying the flaccid head upon a cushion, she sponged the dark face, murmuring brokenly:

"Speak to me, dearest Nessie! I want you to live! I want you to live! I should never have left you, but oh! why did you send me away?"

When she had sponged the face she knew of nothing more to do and remained upon her knees beside the prostrate form, tears streaming down her cheeks, her hands pressed distractedly together.

She was kneeling thus when hurried footsteps came through the still open door and Renwick entered the room. He failed at first to observe Nessie's body which was masked by her kneeling form, and seeing only her, stood still, crying in a loud voice:

"Mary! what is wrong?"

But, coming forward, he dropped his gaze, saw the figure upon the floor and in a flash knelt down beside her. His hands moved rapidly over the body while she watched him dumbly, agonisingly, then after a moment he raised his eyes to her across the form of her sister and said, slowly:

"Don't kneel any longer, Mary! Let me—let me put her on the sofa."

She knew then from his tone that Nessie was dead, and while he lifted the body on to the sofa she stood up, her lips quivering, her breast torn by the throbbing anguish of her heart.

"I'm to blame," she whispered brokenly. "I went out to get her headache powders."

He turned from the couch and looked at her gently.

"It's not you that is to blame, Mary! You did everything for her."

"Why did she do it?" she sobbed. "I loved her so much. I wanted to protect her."

"I know that well! She must have lost her reason, poor child," he replied sadly. "Poor, frightened child."

"I would have done anything in life for her," she whispered. "I would have died for her."

He looked at her, her pale face ravaged by her grief, thinking of her past, her present sadness, of the grey uncertainty of her future, and as he gazed into her swimming eyes, an overwhelming emotion possessed him also. Like a spring which had lain deeply buried for long years and now welled suddenly to light, his feelings gushed over him in a rushing flow. His heart swelled at her grief and, swept by the certain knowledge that he could never leave her, he advanced to her, saying in a low voice:

"Mary! don't cry, dear. I love you."

She looked at him blindly through her tears as he drew near to her and in an instant she was in his arms.

458

"You'll not stay here, dear," he whispered. "You'll come with me, now. I want you to be my wife." He comforted her as she lay sobbing in his arms, telling her how he must have loved her from that moment when first he saw her, yet never known it till now.

While they remained thus, suddenly a loud voice addressed them, breaking upon them with an incredulous yet ferocious intensity.

"Damnation! what is the meaning of this in my house?" It was Brodie. Framed in the doorway, his view of the sofa blocked by the open door, he stood still, glaring at them, his eyes starting from his head in rage and wonder. "So this is your fancy man," he cried savagely, advancing into the room. "This is who these bonnie black grapes came from. I wondered who it might be, but by God! I didna think it was this —this fine gentleman."

At these words, Mary winced and would have withdrawn from Renwick but he restrained her and, keeping his arm around her, gazed fixedly at Brodie.

"Don't come that high and mighty look over me," sneered Brodie, with a short, hateful laugh. "You can't pull the wool over my eyes. It's me that's got the whip hand o' you this time. You're a bonnie pillar of the town right enough, to come to a man's house and make a brothel o't."

In answer Renwick drew himself up more rigidly, slowly raised his arm, and pointed to the sofa.

"You are in the presence of death," he said.

Despite himself, Brodie's eyes fell under the coldness of the other's gaze.

"Are ye mad? You're all mad here," he muttered. But he turned to follow the direction of the other's finger and as he saw the body of Nessie he started, stumbled forward. "What—what's this?" he cried dazedly. "Nessie! Nessie!"

Renwick led Mary to the door and, as she clung to him, he paused and cried sternly:

"Nessie hanged herself in this kitchen because she lost the Latta and, in the sight of God, you are responsible for her death." Then, taking Mary with him he drew her out of the room and they passed together out of the house.

Brodie did not hear them go, but, stunned by Renwick's last words and by the strange stillness of the figure before him, he muttered:

"They're tryin' to frighten me! Wake up, Nessie! It's your father that's speakin' to ye. Come on, pettie, wake up!" Putting forward his hand haltingly, to shake her, he perceived the paper on her breast and, seizing it, he plucked it from her dress and raised it tremulously to his eyes.

"Grierson!" he whispered, in a stricken voice. "Grierson's got it. She did lose it then!"

459

The paper dropped from his hand and involuntarily his glance fell upon her neck, marked by a livid red weal. Even as he saw it, he touched again her inert, flaccid form and his face grew livid like the weal upon her white skin.

"God!" he muttered. "She has—she has hanged herself." He covered his eyes as though unable to bear the sight longer. "My God," he mumbled again, "she has—she has——" And then, as though he panted for breath, "I was fond of my Nessie." A heavy groan burst from his breast. Staggering like a drunken man he backed blindly from the body, and sank unconsciously into his chair. A rush of dry sobs racked him, rending his breast in anguish. With his head sunk into his hands he remained thus, his tortured mind filled by one obsessing thought, yet traversed by other fleeting thoughts, by an endless stream of images which slipped past the central figure of his dead daughter like a procession of shadows floating round a recumbent body on a cata-falque.

He saw his son and Nancy, together in the sunshine, saw the drooping form and pathetically inclined head of his wife, the sneering face of Grierson mocking at his distress, Renwick holding Mary in his arms, the bold figure of young Foyle bearding him in his office; he saw the obsequious Perry, Blair, Paxton, Gordon, even Dron—they all marched silently before his shuttered eyes, all with heads averted from him, all condemning him, their eyes turned sadly to the body of his Nessie as she reposed upon the bier.

As though unable to bear longer the torment of these inward visions he raised his head from his hands, uncovered his eyes, and looked furtively towards the sofa. At once his eyes fell upon the thin arm of the dead child as it hung over the edge of the couch—limp, pendent, immobile, the pale waxen fingers of the hand drooping from the small palm. With a shudder he raised his eyes and looked blindly out of the window. As he sat thus the door opened slowly and his mother came into the room. Her recent terror had faded from her senile mind—the whole sad event lost in the maunderings of her doting brain—and now, tottering to her chair, she seated herself opposite her son. Her eyes sought him as she sounded his mood with her dim gaze, then, sensing his silence to be propitious, she muttered:

"I think I'll make myself a bit soft toast." At this she rose—oblivious to all but her own needs—hobbled to the scullery and, returning again, sat down and began to toast the slice of bread she had obtained. "I can soak it in my broth," she muttered to herself, sucking in her cheeks. "It suits my stomach brawly that way." Then, as she again looked at her son across the fireplace, she noticed at last the strangeness of his eyes, her head shook agitatedly, and she exclaimed:

"You're not angry wi' me, are ye, James? I'm just makin' myself some nice, soft toast. I was aye fond o't ye ken. I'll make you a bit yoursel', gin ye want it," and she tittered uneasily, propitiatingly, across at him with a senile, senseless sound that broke the heavy silence of the room. But he did not reply, and still gazed stonily out of the window, where the warm summer wind moved gently amongst the thin leaves of the straggling bushes that fringed his garden. The breeze freshened, disporting itself amongst the shoots of the currant bushes then, circling, it touched the leaves of the three, tall, serene, silver trees, flickering them dark and light with a soft caress, when suddenly, striking the house, it chilled, and passed quickly onwards to the beauty of the Winton Hills beyond.

THE END